Springer Proceedings in Business and Economics

More information about this series at http://www.springer.com/series/11960

David Procházka
Editor

The Impact of Globalization on International Finance and Accounting

18th Annual Conference on Finance and Accounting (ACFA)

Springer

Editor
David Procházka
Faculty of Finance and Accounting
University of Economics, Prague
Prague, Czech Republic

ISSN 2198-7246 ISSN 2198-7254 (electronic)
Springer Proceedings in Business and Economics
ISBN 978-3-319-68761-2 ISBN 978-3-319-68762-9 (eBook)
https://doi.org/10.1007/978-3-319-68762-9

Library of Congress Control Number: 2017960836

Printed on acid-free paper

This Springer imprint is published by Springer Nature
The registered company is Springer International Publishing AG
The registered company address is: Gewerbestrasse 11, 6330 Cham, Switzerland

Contents

The Impact of Corporate Income Taxation on Location Choice of Investments: Separate Accounting Versus Formula Apportionment

Hulya Celebi

Abstract This paper investigates the impact of separate accounting (SA) versus that of formula apportionment (FA) on investment decisions in high- and low-corporate income tax countries. As the investment decisions of multinational enterprises are commonly taken by managers and not by owners, the focus is on the impact of SA versus that of FA on the investment location decided by managers. This is done within the framework of the principal-agent setting, where a Monte Carlo simulation is carried out. Considering taxation under SA supports investing in a less risky investment, even if it is located in the country with the highest tax rate. In analysis of FA, allocation of the tax base based on formula and the cross-border loss offset encourages investing in a risky investment. This is in line with the aim of the European Commission regarding making investments more attractive and supporting cross-border investments within the EU. These results also show that the delegation of investment decisions to managers facilitates the investment in the high-tax country, under both systems, SA as well as FA. As a contribution to the literature reviewed, this study demonstrates that taking the differences in expected returns of investments across the countries, as well as the risk-averse behavior of investors, into account, reveals different impacts of taxation on the invested amount under SA and FA.

Keywords Formula apportionment • Corporate income taxation • Principal agent • Cross-border investment

Introduction

The proposal of the common consolidated corporate tax base (CCCTB), published in March 2011 by the European Commission, caused a debate regarding formula apportionment (FA) as an alternative to the existing separate accounting (SA) and

H. Celebi (✉)
School of Management, Department of Accounting, University of Innsbruck, Auditing and Taxation, Austria
e-mail: huelya.celebi@gmail.com

D. Procházka (ed.), *The Impact of Globalization on International Finance and Accounting*, Springer Proceedings in Business and Economics,
https://doi.org/10.1007/978-3-319-68762-9_1

triggered intensive discussions. With the latest proposal, the European Commission stated that FA is still envisaged (European Commission 2016). The object of this proposal is to solve the corporate income taxation dilemma within the EU, which negatively impacts investments within the EU and the growth of the Single Market (caused by, e.g., higher compliance and administrative costs, double taxation, nontransparency regarding tax regulations, etc.). Tax competition across the member states is another reason for this proposal, since the existence of 28 national corporate tax regulations within the EU disadvantages every member state as well as the EU as a whole (see, e.g., Devereux et al. 2002; Genschel et al. 2008; Eggert and Haufler 2006; and Huizinga and Laeven 2008). In a first step, this CCCTB proposal covers the harmonization of tax regulations and in the second step the consolidation of taxable income and FA without the harmonization of tax rates (European Commission 2016). Furthermore, the implementation of CCCTB will lead to a considerable territorial enlargement and to an increased importance of the FA practice, which is currently used in the USA and Canada.

SA means that the tax base of each corporate group member is taxed in its country of registration. However, FA provides for the consolidation of the tax base, which is then taxed in each country where the corporate group member is registered. The determination of the tax base in each country is undertaken according to the FA factors (details of FA will be given in the next part).

In general, the importance of corporate income taxation regarding the location and volume of investments as well as the profits earned by these has been examined by various research studies within the framework of SA (e.g., Becker et al. 2005; Devereux and Maffini 2007; Nicodème 2008; Dharmapala and Riedel 2013).

Studies investigating the relationship between the investment and the tax rate changes under SA and FA show divergent results depending on the factors used for the tax base allocation. For instance, the outcomes of Runkel and Schjelderup (2011) show that changes in tax rates impact the investment of the whole corporate group in the case of FA, whereas SA only impacts the investment in the country in which the tax rate is changed. Moreover, Riedel (2010) considers labor as the sole FA factor. This reveals that FA distorts companies' behavior in the case of tax rate changes that lead to relocation of labor from the country where the tax rate is increased to the country with low tax rates. A further study (Riedel and Runkel 2007) extends its focus by considering a country where FA is not applied. Here, a change in the tax rates leads to profit shifting to a country where FA is not applied. Furthermore, Pethig and Wagener (2007) report in their study that the tax rate changes depend on the elasticity of the FA factors, which can lead, for instance, to excess taxation in the case of payroll apportionment. Another research study on labor and sales as FA factors shows that FA leads to distortions of labor demand and sales. This can result in dislocation of investments by merging with companies in low-tax countries (Gordon and Wilson 1986). Moreover, Nielsen et al. (2010) investigated the impact of tax rates when capital is used as the sole FA factor. Here, they find out that FA enforces the cut in capital stock that depends on the profits, costs of profit shifting, and tax planning behavior of the company.

As shown above, literature investigating the impact of FA on investments does not take into account that the investment decisions, especially in the case of multinational enterprises (MNE), are delegated to managers (also called "investors" or "decision makers") and are not taken directly by the owners of the MNE. This decision delegation requires an investigation of the managers' investment behavior, which is affected by their risk behavior as well as by the riskiness of the investment. On the other hand, this delegation entails an interest conflict between the owners and managers of MNE. As these factors have remained unconsidered so far in the studies analyzing the impact of SA and FA on investments, the aim of this paper is to answer the question: "How does corporate income taxation – under SA and FA – impact the investment location decisions taken by managers?" Here, the principal-agent setting (owners considered "principals" and managers "agents") makes it possible to analyze the investment behavior and this interest conflict.

To investigate the theoretical model, which is designed within the framework of the principal-agent setting, a Monte Carlo simulation is conducted. So the impact of SA and FA is analyzed by using the expected utility of the investments within the framework of an investment location decision of an MNE between a high- and a low-tax country. The reason for using the expected utility is that it takes the riskiness of the returns on the investments and the risk behavior of investor into account. The outcomes of the European Investment Bank (2013) show that there are significant differences in the expected returns and variances across the member states not only in the financial sector but also in the manufacturing sector. Therefore, additionally to tax rates, this difference can provide further information regarding the investment behavior and location.

The outcomes of the study show, when taxation is not considered, in the case of a risk-averse investor, the less risky investment is preferred. This is in line with the behavior of a rational decision maker. However, under SA, the risk aversion of the investor overlaps with the impact of tax rates. Here, the less risky investment in high-tax countries is expected to be more preferable, independent of tax rate differences between the high- and low-tax countries. In contrast to SA, FA encourages cross-border investments by sharing investments between the high- and low-tax countries. This impact corresponds to the aim of the CCCTB regarding making the investments within the EU more attractive by applying FA. This study contributes to the existing literature focusing on tax rates by showing that economic factors (like riskiness of investment returns) as well as the risk behavior of investors also have to be taken into account. From the viewpoint of the impact of delegation of investment decisions to managers, the results show that this delegation favors the less risky investments in a high-tax country under both systems, where the impact of SA is higher than that under FA. Without delegation, the risk-neutral behavior of owners favors the investment with higher expected returns in a low-tax country, where the investment location is chosen independently of the riskiness of the expected returns.

Theoretical Model

The model used in this study focuses on the behavior of the MNE's manager as an investor within the framework of the principal-agent setting. The aim of the risk-averse manager is to maximize the expected utility of the investment by choosing the optimal level of investment concerning its location. Here, the theoretical model of Niemann (2008) is used and extended to the FA, which investigated the impact of differential taxation on the investment.

As it is shown below, the model differentiates between two countries: a high-tax country with a stable economy and a low-tax country with a less stable economy. Because of the lack of stability in the latter case, the expected returns in this country are exposed to higher risk with higher variance in expected returns. The study by the European Investment Bank (2013) supports this assumption, in which it is shown that the returns on investment in the manufacturing sector in low-tax countries (like Bulgaria, Hungary, or Latvia) were higher; however, they were negatively impacted by the financial crisis in 2008 to a larger extent than the high-tax countries were.

Assumptions Without Taxation

In general, this model focuses on a risk-averse manager, the agent (hereinafter referred to as "he"), of an MNE that consists of a parent company in country *P* and a subsidiary in country *S*; the latter is assumed to be a low-tax country with higher expected returns accompanied by higher variances. The manager is considering investing an initial cash of *I* that has been provided to him. He can invest this cash in only one country or split it between both countries, *P* and *S*. The proportion of the investment in *P* is expressed by δ and in *S* by $(1\text{-}\delta)$, where δ is $0 \leq \delta \leq 1$.

The decision-making behavior of the manager of the MNE is based on the Bernoulli Principle, where the expected value of the utility of the investment and the risk-averse behavior of the investors are taken into consideration (Laux et al. 2012). His utility function *U(I)* consists of the risk aversion parameter *(r)* and the utility *(I)* of the invested idle cash *I*, which is formulated as:

$$U(I) = -\exp\left(-rI\right) \tag{1}$$

Furthermore, it is assumed that the investments in both countries generate normally distributed (*N*) returns formulated as in the following:

$$\mathrm{p} = \mu_p + \theta_p \quad resp. \quad \mathrm{s} = \mu_s + \theta_s$$
$$p \sim N\left(\mu_p, \sigma_p\right); s \sim N(\mu_s, \sigma_s) \; with \; \theta_p \sim N(0,1), \;\; resp. \;\; \theta_s \sim N(0,2) \tag{2}$$

where p is the return on investment in country P and s the return in country S and θ_p, θ_s are used for random variables of p and s μ_p and μ_s express the expected values of p and s, whereas σ_p, σ_s stand for the standard deviation of p and s.

Thus, the total return t on the invested initial cash I consists of the sum of the returns of the investments in P and S. Hence, the total expected return (μ_t) of the MNE's invested I with standard deviation σ_t is formulated as:

$$\begin{aligned} \mu_t &= \delta\mu_p + (1-\delta)\mu_s \\ \sigma_t &= \sqrt{\delta^2\sigma_p^2 + (1-\delta)^2\sigma_s^2 + 2\delta(1-\delta)\sigma_{ps}} \end{aligned} \tag{3}$$

The aim of the manager is to maximize the expected utility of the invested initial cash I $(E[U_t])$ by optimally choosing the investment levels in countries P and S. So, his expected utility $E[U_t]$ is formulated as in the following:

$$\begin{aligned} &E[U_t] = -\exp\left(r\mu_t + \frac{1}{2}r^2\sigma_t^2\right) = \\ &-\exp\left[-r(\delta\mu_p + (1-\delta)\mu_s) + \frac{r^2}{2}\left(\delta^2\sigma_p^2 + (1-\delta)^2\sigma_s^2 + 2\delta(1-\delta)\sigma_{ps}\right)\right] \end{aligned} \tag{4}$$

As the manager is risk-averse, the CE (certainty equivalent) derived from the $E[U_t]$ is used, where the risky investment is equal to the risk-free one. Maximizing $CE[U_t]$ in Eq. 5 with respect to δ gives the optimal level of investment in P, as shown in Eq. 6:

$$CE[U_t] = \mu_{ts} - \frac{r}{2}\sigma_t^2 = \delta\mu_p + (1-\delta)\mu_s - \frac{r}{2}\left[\delta^2\sigma_p^2 + (1-\delta)^2\sigma_s^2 + 2\delta(1-\delta)\sigma_{ps}\right] \tag{5}$$

$$\delta^* = \frac{\mu_p - \mu_s + r\sigma_s^2 - r\sigma_{ps}}{r\left(\sigma_p^2 + \sigma_s^2 - 2\sigma_{ps}\right)} \tag{6}$$

Assumptions Regarding Taxation Under SA

When taking corporate income taxation into consideration, it is assumed that the corporate income tax rates of P and S, which are given by τ for the tax rate in P and by γ for S, respectively, vary from each other.

The sum of both investments formulates the expected return μ_{tSA} of invested I with a standard deviation of σ_{tSA} as in the following:

$$\mu_{tSA} = \delta_{SA}(1-\tau)\mu_p + (1-\delta_{SA})(1-\gamma)\mu_s \tag{7}$$

$$\sigma_{tSA} = \sqrt{\delta^2{}_{SA}(1-\tau)^2\sigma_p^2 + (1-\delta_{SA})^2(1-\gamma)^2\sigma_s^2 + 2\delta_{SA}(1-\tau)(1-\delta_{SA})(1-\gamma)\sigma_{ps}}$$

Inserting taxation into the utility function $E[U_{tSA}]$ and deriving the $CE[U_{tSA}]$ from it allow for the formulation of the optimal level of δ_{SA} by maximizing the manager's $CE[U_{tSA}]$ with respect to δ_{SA} as shown in Eqs. 8, 9 and 10:

$$E[U_{tSA}] = -exp\left(r\mu_{tSA} + \frac{1}{2}r^2\sigma_{tSA}^2\right) \tag{8}$$

$$\begin{aligned} CE[U_{tSA}] &= \mu_{tSA} - \frac{r}{2}\sigma_{tSA}^2 \\ &= \left[\delta_{SA}(1-\tau)\mu_p + (1-\delta_{SA})(1-\gamma)\mu_s\right] - \frac{r}{2}\left[\left({\delta_{SA}}^2(1-\tau)^2\sigma_p^2\right.\right. \\ &\quad \left.\left. + (1-\delta_{SA})^2(1-\gamma)^2\sigma_s^2 + 2\delta_{SA}(1-\tau)(1-\delta_{SA})(1-\gamma)\sigma_{ps}\right)\right] \end{aligned} \tag{9}$$

$${\delta_{SA}}^* = \frac{(1-\tau)\mu_p - (1-\gamma)\mu_s - r\left[(1-\tau)(1-\gamma)\sigma_{ps} - (1-\gamma)^2\sigma_s^2\right]}{r\left[\left((1-\tau)^2\sigma_p^2 + (1-\gamma)^2\sigma_s^2 - 2(1-\tau)(1-\gamma)\sigma_{ps}\right)\right]} \tag{10}$$

Assumptions Regarding Taxation Under FA

As mentioned in the introduction above, taxation under FA and SA is based on different tax bases. Therefore, the tax base represented in the previous part by μ_p and μ_s must be expanded to FA. For instance, according to the CCCTB, FA is based on the Massachusetts formula, which uses three equally weighted factors, namely, assets, sales, and labor (split in payroll and number of employees) as in the following (European Commission 2011):

$$fa_P = \left(\frac{1}{3}\frac{sa_P}{sa_G} + \frac{1}{3}\frac{a_P}{a_G} + \frac{1}{6}\frac{e_P}{e_G} + \frac{1}{6}\frac{en_P}{en_G}\right)\delta_{FA}; fa_S = \left(\frac{1}{3}\frac{sa_S}{sa_G} + \frac{1}{3}\frac{a_S}{a_G} + \frac{1}{6}\frac{e_S}{e_G} + \frac{1}{6}\frac{en_S}{en_G}\right)(1-\delta_{FA}) \tag{11}$$

where fa_P/fa_S expresses the tax base allocation in P/S sa_P/sa_S states the sales, a_P/a_S the assets, e_P/e_S the payroll, and en_P/en_S the number of employees in P and S, respectively. Whereas sa_G states the sales, a_G assets, e_G payroll, and en_G the number of employees in sum, which means in P and S. As the MNE only consists of the parent company and the subsidiary, the fa_S can also be written as $(1-fa_P)$.

Taking this into consideration leads to the following expected total value (μ_{tFA}) and standard deviation (σ_{tFA}) under FA:

$$\mu_{FA} = \delta_{FA}\mu_P + (1-\delta_{FA})\mu_s \tag{12}$$

$$\mu_{tFA} = \delta_{FA}(1-\tau)fa_p\mu_{FA} + (1-\delta_{FA})(1-\gamma)(1-fa_p)\mu_{FA}$$

$$\sigma_{tFA} = \sqrt{\sigma_{FA}^2\left[\delta^2{}_{FA}(1-\tau)^2 fa_P^2 + (1-\delta_{FA})^2(1-\gamma)^2(1-fa_P)^2\right] + 2\sigma_{FA}^2\delta_{FA}(1-\tau)fa_p(1-\delta_{FA})(1-fa_P)(1-\gamma)}$$

This changes the expected utility in the case of the FA $E[U_{tFA}]$ as given in Eq. 13. Formulation of the $CE[U_{tFA}]$ and maximizing it with respect to δ_{FA} lead to the optimal level of δ^*_{FA} in country P, as shown in the Eq. 15 below:

$$E[U_{tFA}] = -exp\left(r\mu_{tFA} + \frac{1}{2}r^2\sigma^2_{tFA}\right) \tag{13}$$

$$CE[U_{tSA}] = \mu_{tFA} - \frac{r}{2}\sigma^2_{tFA} = \left[\delta_{FA}(1-\tau)fa_p + (1-\delta_{FA})(1-\gamma)\left(1-fa_p\right)\right]\mu_{FA} - \frac{r}{2}\sigma^2_{tFA} \tag{14}$$

$$\delta^*_{FA} = \frac{(\mu_p\text{-}\mu_s)[(1\text{-}\tau)fa_P + (1\text{-}\gamma)(1\text{-}fa_P)] + r\sigma^2_S\left[fa^2_P(1\text{-}\tau)^2 + (1\text{-}fa_P)^2(1\text{-}\lambda)^2\right]\text{-}r\sigma_{PS}\left[fa_P\left(1\text{-}fa_p\right)(1\text{-}\tau)(1\text{-}\gamma)\right]}{r\left[\sigma^2_P\sigma^2_S fa^2_P(1\text{-}\tau)^2 + (1\text{-}fa_P)^2(1\text{-}\gamma)^2\text{-}2\sigma_{PS}\, fa_P(1\text{-}fa_P)(1\text{-}\tau)(1\text{-}\gamma)\right]} \tag{15}$$

Monte Carlo Simulation

For the purpose of analyzing the theoretical model presented above, a Monte Carlo simulation is carried out. Here, the expectations regarding the returns (p,s) in both countries are estimated by using the BACH database of the manufacturing companies that are registered in ten EU member states.

For further assumptions referring to μ_p, μ_s, as well as θ_p, θ_s, the study outcomes of the European Investment Bank (2013) are also taken into consideration. As these show differences in the expected returns (μ_p, μ_s) in high- and low-tax countries within the EU, the theoretical model is analyzed under three different cases, namely, A, B, and C. This is measured for three levels of expected returns, low, moderate, and high, where Case A assumes low, B moderate, and C the highest differences between both countries. Moreover, based on the assumptions mentioned in the previous part, the standard deviation of S is set higher than the other one. Here, Cases A and B should represent the expectations of the investor under usual stable economic conditions, whereas Case C assumes a higher fluctuation in country S (given by θ_s). The last-mentioned assumption represents the expectations of investors in the case of unstable economic conditions. This and the previous assumptions referring to the expectations of investors are summarized in the following Table 1:

μ_P and μ_S are derived from 20,000 simulations of p and s. In each simulation, 1000 values were generated. These simulations are run for Cases A, B, and C, under the three conditions: without taxation of returns as well as with taxation of returns under SA and FA, respectively. Moreover, it is assumed that the investor compensates any negative outcomes of the investment with the positive outcomes of the

Table 1 Input values for Monte Carlo simulation

Cases	Parameters for simulation in P	Parameters for simulation in S
A	$p = 0.07\,;\theta_P \sim N(0, 0.1)$	$s = 0.1\,;\theta_S \sim N(0, 0.2)$
B	$p = 0.05\,;\theta_P \sim N(0, 0.1)$	$s = 0.1\,;\theta_S \sim N(0, 0.2)$
C	$p = 0.07\,;\theta_P \sim N(0, 0.1)$	$s = 0.2\,;\theta_S \sim N(0, 0.3)$

investment generated in the other country under FA, for instance, CCCTB includes cross-border offset (European Commission 2016).

Furthermore, the risk aversion parameter r is determined between 0.25 and 2. Here, $r = 0.25$ represents the lowest, whereas $r = 2$ is the highest risk aversion level. On the other hand, as the nominal tax rates across the 28 member states vary but only to a small extent in some of them, tax rates are clustered in six groups for γ in S and in three groups for τ in P. Here, the differences across the tax rates are determined in round figures as in the following[1]:

$$r \ldots 0.25, 0.5, 0.75, 1, 2 \quad \tau \ldots 0.125, 0.20, 0.30 \quad \gamma \ldots 0.10, 0.125, 0.15, 0.20, 0.25, 0.30$$

Results and Discussion

Outcomes Without Taxation

As taxation is not considered, here the risk aversion factor r is the sole factor affecting the optimal investment proportion. The parameters of r given above are set in Eq. 6 for Cases A, B, and C. The outcomes show that the optimal investment in country P increases with increasing r in all Cases A–C, which is in line with the fundamental assumptions regarding the risk-averse decision maker. The highest impact is shown when the risk-averse behavior changes from the low level to the moderate one. This means that any condition causing concerns for less risk-averse managers affects the riskier investment to a larger extent than in the case of one with a risk-averse behavior at the moderate level. Furthermore, with increasing risk aversion r, the distribution of the optimal investment levels of the simulation gets narrower. So the range between the minimum and maximum investment levels is wider across the less risk-averse investors and gets tighter with increasing risk aversion. If the investor expects higher fluctuations in S, represented in C, although the risk premium given by the investment in S is very high, it is not able to overlap with the risk factor r. This means, in Case C, that the investment amount for the less risky investment in country P is higher than in Cases A and B. So, if the investor expects the difference between both countries not to be high, the outcomes suggest

[1] As the corporate income tax rates are designed as flat rates in most countries, it is assumed that the marginal tax rate of the investment equals the nominal tax rate.

Table 2 Cases A, B, and C without taxation

	Case A			Case B			Case C		
r	mean δ^*	max δ^*	min δ^*	mean δ^*	max δ^*	min δ^*	mean δ^*	max δ^*	min δ^*
0.25	0.4940	0.7517	0.2211	0.4996	0.7026	0.2787	0.6334	0.8582	0.4073
0.5	0.4996	0.7026	0.2787	0.5014	0.7018	0.2937	0.6380	0.8332	0.4393
0.75	0.5014	0.7018	0.2937	0.5024	0.7062	0.2996	0.6396	0.8261	0.4445
1	0.5024	0.7062	0.2996	0.5033	0.7106	0.2983	0.6403	0.8286	0.4457
2	0.5033	0.7106	0.2983	0.5038	0.7128	0.2976	0.6415	0.8324	0.4474

investing about 50% in both countries. The results show a lower difference for the optimum investment level across the risk aversion levels, i.e., about a 1% difference on average between the lowest and highest risk-averse investors for all three cases as shown in the Table 2.

Outcomes Under SA

As mentioned above, the nominal corporate income tax rates vary to a small extent across some member states. Therefore, they are clustered in six groups, and the differences across them are determined in round figures. The highest tax rate is set at 33%, and the minimum tax rate is determined as 10%, and these represent the highest and lowest tax rates within the EU.

Here, the impact of tax rates and differences is analyzed under three scenarios (S1–S3) – as shown below – and is determined by using Eq. 10 (Table 3).

S1, for instance, assumes that the tax rate of country *P* is 12.5% and that of *S* is 10%, whereas in S3 the tax rate of *P* is assumed to be 33% and that of *S* to be one of the following rates: 10%, 12.5%, 15%, 20%, 25%, or 30%.

In all three scenarios, i.e., S1–S3, the results show that taking taxation into consideration overrides the impact of the risk-related behavior. This means, investment in country *P* is higher in the case of taxation than without taxation for all three scenarios regarding the tax rates (S1–S3) and cases with respect to the expected returns (A–C). For instance, in S2 and S3, the lower γ is, the higher δ^*_{SA} is, i.e., the higher the investment proportion in *P* (see Table 4, rows 2 and 7). This shows that the tax rate differences between the high- and low-tax countries lose their impact when the risk aversion of the investor is taken into consideration. Furthermore, the impact of τ is ambiguous in Cases A and B because increasing τ triggers an increase in the investment proportion in *P*. However, if the variation between *P* and *S* is very high, like in C, an increase in τ from 12.5% to 20% or 33% reveals ambiguous impacts.

However, in S1 to S3, the difference across the different parameters shows that the increasing risk level triggers an increase in the investment in country *P* because of the expected lower deviation. For Case B, this means a 3% increase for *P* on average. Furthermore, as in the case without taxation, higher risk aversion narrows

Table 3 Scenarios

Scenarios	Tax rate in P	Tax rates in alternative S country/countries
S1	$\tau = 0.12.5$	$\gamma = 0.10$
S2	$\tau = 0.20$	$\gamma = 0.10, 0.125, 0.15$
S3	$\tau = 0.33$	$\gamma = 0.10, 0.125, 0.15, 0.20, 0.25, 0.30$

Table 4 Case C and Scenario 3 under SA

	mean δ^*_{SA}					
r	$\gamma = 0.30$	$\gamma = 0.25$	$\gamma = 0.20$	$\gamma = 0.15$	$\gamma = 0.125$	$\gamma = 0.10$
0.25	0.6485	0.6784	0.7051	0.7290	0.7399	0.7502
0.5	0.6555	0.6855	0.7122	0.7360	0.7469	0.7572
0.75	0.6578	0.6878	0.7145	0.7383	0.7492	0.7595
1	0.6590	0.6890	0.7157	0.7395	0.7504	0.7607
2	0.6607	0.6908	0.7175	0.7413	0.7522	0.7624

Table 5 Scenario 1 ($\gamma = 0.10, \tau = 0.125$): Cases A, B, and C under SA

	Case A			Case C		
r	mean δ^*_{SA}	max δ^*_{SA}	min δ^*_{SA}	mean δ^*_{SA}	max δ^*_{SA}	min δ^*_{SA}
0.25	0.5110	0.7875	0.2240	0.6288	0.9594	0.2800
0.5	0.5151	0.7291	0.2890	0.6448	0.8762	0.4139
0.75	0.5165	0.7148	0.3053	0.6501	0.8484	0.4504
1	0.5172	0.7192	0.3134	0.6519	0.8392	0.4568
2	0.5182	0.7259	0.3135	0.6528	0.8369	0.4582

the distribution of the optimal investment levels of the simulation results. So the range between the minimum and maximum investment levels is wider across the less risk-averse investors and gets tighter with increasing risk aversion (see Table 5).

Outcomes Under FA

The impact of FA by means of different FA levels is analyzed in the aforementioned three scenarios, S1–S3 and Cases A–C. In this case, δ^*_{FA} is investigated by using Eq. 15. As shown above in Eq. 11, the calculation of *fa* depends, for instance, within the framework of CCCTB, on the factors assets, sales, and employees (number and payroll) of each corporate group member in relation to the total of these factors. However, in Canada, the allocation of the tax base is based on equally weighted allocation factors of sales and asset, whereas the USA uses different weights for the allocation factors. As the aim of this paper is to analyze the impact of different *fa* levels in relation to risk aversion and tax rate differences, determination of *fa* according to these different weights and factors goes beyond the scope of this paper. Instead, this study investigates how *fa* affects investment *I* in each country, if the FA intensity in each country is taken into consideration, where, for instance, *fa* 0.7 means that the company in *P* occupies 70% of the *fa* allocation factors assets, sales, and employees of the whole corporate group. As FA is based on consolidating the tax base of all corporate group members, the sum of investment returns in both countries represents the tax base of all the corporate group members. *fa* of 0.7 also means that 70% of the total tax base of all the corporate group members is taxed in country *P*, where 30% of the total taxable income is taxed in *S*.[2]

In each scenario, the higher r is, the higher δ^*_{FA} is, which means higher investment proportion in country *P*. This is in line with the principle of a rational decision maker. However, the impact of the risk-averse behavior is lower under FA than under SA, i.e., lower than 1% if r increases from 0.25 to 1.

A further outcome is that the intensity of *fa* has an ambiguous and marginal – nearly no – impact on δ^*_{FA} when it increases between 0.1 and 0.9 (see Tables 6, 7 and 8). Moreover, the outcomes show that FA leads to higher allocation of the investment between the low- and high-tax country. For instance, if τ is 33% and γ is 10% or 30%, the average invested amount in *P* under FA is lower than under SA, which

Table 6 Case C and Scenario 3 ($\gamma = 0.30, \tau = 0.33$) under FA

	mean δ^*_{FA}								
r	fa = 0.1	fa = 0.2	fa = 0.3	fa = 0.4	fa = 0.5	fa = 0.6	fa = 0.7	fa = 0.8	fa = 0.9
0.25	0.6256	0.6224	0.6191	0.6165	0.6153	0.6159	0.6182	0.6214	0.6248
0.5	0.6336	0.6320	0.6305	0.6293	0.6287	0.6290	0.6300	0.6315	0.6332
0.75	0.6363	0.6352	0.6343	0.6335	0.6332	0.6334	0.6340	0.6349	0.6360
1	0.6376	0.6368	0.6361	0.6357	0.6355	0.6356	0.6359	0.6366	0.6374
2	0.6396	0.6392	0.6390	0.6389	0.6388	0.6388	0.6389	0.6391	0.6395

Table 7 Case C and Scenario 3 ($\gamma = 0.10, \tau = 0.33$) under FA

	mean δ^*_{FA}								
r	fa = 0.1	fa = 0.2	fa = 0.3	fa = 0.4	fa = 0.5	fa = 0.6	fa = 0.7	fa = 0.8	fa = 0.9
0.25	0.6294	0.6269	0.6242	0.6215	0.6193	0.6183	0.6189	0.6211	0.6244
0.5	0.6355	0.6343	0.6330	0.6318	0.6308	0.6303	0.6305	0.6315	0.6330
0.75	0.6375	0.6367	0.6359	0.6352	0.6347	0.6343	0.6344	0.6349	0.6359
1	0.6385	0.6379	0.6374	0.6369	0.6366	0.6364	0.6363	0.6366	0.6373
2	0.6400	0.6398	0.6396	0.6395	0.6394	0.6394	0.6392	0.6392	0.6394

[2]The assumption of *fa* being, e.g., 0.1 does not seem to be realistic, because a higher *fa* is expected in the parent company's country *P*. In order to see the impact of all *fa* levels, too, this fact is ignored.

Table 8 Scenario 1 ($\gamma = 0.10, \tau = 0.125$) Case C under FA

	fa = 0.1			fa = 0.2			fa = 0.3		
r	mean δ^*_{FA}	max δ^*_{FA}	min δ^*_{FA}	mean δ^*_{FA}	max δ^*_{FA}	min δ^*_{FA}	mean δ^*_{FA}	max δ^*_{FA}	min δ^*_{FA}
0.25	0.6291	0.8202	0.3999	0.6266	0.8437	0.3837	0.6243	0.8794	0.3661
0.5	0.6353	0.7948	0.4309	0.6342	0.8103	0.4216	0.6331	0.8389	0.4123
0.75	0.6374	0.7961	0.4352	0.6367	0.8036	0.4302	0.6360	0.8254	0.4252
1	0.6385	0.7991	0.4369	0.6379	0.8074	0.4322	0.6375	0.8187	0.4276
2	0.6400	0.8038	0.4394	0.6398	0.8130	0.4353	0.6397	0.8228	0.4311
	fa = 0.4			fa = 0.5			fa = 0.6		
r	mean δ^*_{FA}	max δ^*_{FA}	min δ^*_{FA}	mean δ^*_{FA}	max δ^*_{FA}	min δ^*_{FA}	mean δ^*_{FA}	max δ^*_{FA}	min δ^*_{FA}
0.25	0.6224	0.9100	0.3462	0.6216	0.9237	0.3348	0.6221	0.9136	0.3425
0.5	0.6323	0.8634	0.4048	0.6320	0.8744	0.4015	0.6322	0.8662	0.4038
0.75	0.6356	0.8479	0.4204	0.6355	0.8580	0.4178	0.6356	0.8504	0.4196
1	0.6373	0.8402	0.4238	0.6372	0.8497	0.4223	0.6322	0.8662	0.4038
2	0.6398	0.8308	0.4278	0.6398	0.8379	0.4264	0.6398	0.8316	0.4275
	fa = 0.7			fa = 0.8			fa = 0.9		
r	mean δ^*_{FA}	max δ^*_{FA}	min δ^*_{FA}	mean δ^*_{FA}	max δ^*_{FA}	min δ^*_{FA}	mean δ^*_{FA}	max δ^*_{FA}	min δ^*_{FA}
0.25	0.6238	0.8845	0.3625	0.6262	0.8481	0.3800	0.6287	0.8224	0.3973
0.5	0.6329	0.8427	0.4107	0.6339	0.8134	0.4201	0.6351	0.7947	0.4298
0.75	0.6359	0.8288	0.4245	0.6365	0.8041	0.4296	0.6373	0.7961	0.4348
1	0.6374	0.8218	0.4270	0.6378	0.8080	0.4317	0.6384	0.7993	0.4365
2	0.6397	0.8238	0.4306	0.6397	0.8138	0.4348	0.6400	0.8041	0.4392

varies between 2 and 13% (see Tables 4, 6, and 7). This also means that the tax rate differences between *P* and *S* lose their importance under FA compared to SA. For instance, in Case C Scenario 3 under SA, the investment level for the high-tax country increases by approx. 10% when the tax rate in the low-tax country decreases by 20%. However, under FA, the difference is marginal, i.e., lower than 0.5%, for the same case (see Tables 4, 6, and 7).

Also, the range between the optimal minimum and maximum invested amount in country *P* is narrower in the case of FA than under SA, which means distribution becomes tighter under FA (see Table 5 (Case C) and Table 8).

Conclusion

As mentioned at the beginning, the review of literature shows that increasing tax rate differences across the member states affect the investments in high-tax countries. Despite the tax rate differences, the production costs gap (e.g., in payroll, charges on labor) between the high- and low-tax countries is a further point that makes investment in a low-tax country more advantageous (see, e.g., Schroeder 2012). However, as shown in the study by the European Investment Bank (2013), returns on investments in the manufacturing sector have higher fluctuations in low-tax countries than in high-tax ones. Analyzing the investment locations in the principal-agent setting leads to outcomes that have not been discussed in literature so far. Taking the differences in taxation, the delegation of investment decisions to managers, as well as their risk behavior into consideration, the outcomes show that across the different risk-averse levels, the change from the less to the moderately risk-averse investors has the highest impact on the investment in the high-tax country. Taking taxation into consideration changes this outcome. If risk aversion increases, the investment in the less risky investment (in high-tax country) increases, too, even in the case of higher taxation. However, an interesting outcome is that the lower the tax rate in the low-tax country is, the higher the investment in the high-tax country is, where the risk is lower. Considering the tax rates together with the standard deviation and risk aversion weakens its influence, which becomes ambiguous. In contrast to this outcome under SA, FA shows a more significant impact on the investment location. The impact of tax base allocation factors located in the high-tax country is negatively related to the amount that is invested in this country. Also, here the influence of the tax rate in the low-tax country decreases, which means decreasing tax rates in the low-tax country lead to higher investment in the high-tax one.

And "What if the investment decision was not delegated to managers?" In this case, the rational and risk-neutral owners of the MNE would prefer investing the whole initial cash in the risky investment in the low-tax country, where the expected returns are higher, because the owners' objective is to maximize their returns, which is not impacted by the riskiness of investments (see, e.g., Spremann 1987). This means no investment in the high-tax country at all. So, the difference between the results of the study and investing the whole amount in the low-tax country shows also the impact of decision delegation to managers on the location of investments. Here, this impact is higher under SA than under FA, namely, since SA facilitates investing higher amounts for the less risky investment in the high-tax country.

As discussed above, taking risk-averse behavior of a decision maker into consideration impacts the investment across the high- and low-tax countries. In the case of FA, the allocation of the tax base (*fa*) is measured by means of intensity between 0.1 and 1. Instead of analyzing the impact of *fa* in 0.1 steps, in future research the change of FA factors caused by the investment can be analyzed together with the risk aversion coefficient. Detailed information about the assets, sales, and labor factors in each country can be researched in detail by using data taken from the income statements and balance sheets of companies across the member states.

References

Becker J, Fuest C, Spengel C (2005) Konzernsteuerquote und Invesitionsverhalten. ZEW Discussion Papers

Devereux MP, Griffith R, Klemm A (2002) Corporate income tax reforms and international tax competition. Econ Policy 17:449–495. https://doi.org/10.1111/1468-0327.00094

Devereux MP, Maffini G (2007) The Impact of Taxation on the Location of Capital. Oxford University Center for Business Taxation. WP 07/02

Dharmapala D, Riedel N (2013) Earnings shocks and tax-motivated income-shifting: evidence from European multinationals. J Public Econ 97:95–107. https://doi.org/10.1016/j.jpubeco.2012.08.004

Eggert W, Haufler A (2006) Company-Tax Coordination cum Tax-Rate Competition in the European Union. FinanzArchiv: Public Finance Analysis 62:579–601. https://doi.org/10.1628/001522106X172706

European Commission (2011) Proposal for a council directive on a Common Consolidated Corporate Tax Base (CCCTB). COM 2011, 121/4

European Commission (2016) Proposal for a council directive on a Common Consolidated Corporate Tax Base (CCCTB). COM 2016, 683

European Investment Bank (2013) Investment and Investment Finance in Europe. Economics Department (EIB)

Genschel P, Kemmerling A, Seils E (2008) Speeding up, down the hill : how the EU shapes corporate tax competition in the single market. SFB 597 Staatlichkeit im Wandel

Gordon R, Wilson JD (1986) An examination of multijurisdictional corporate income taxation under formula apportionment. Econometrica 54:1357–1373. https://doi.org/10.2307/1914303

Huizinga H, Laeven L (2008) International profit shifting within multinationals: a multi-country perspective. J Public Econ 92:1164–1182. https://doi.org/10.1016/j.jpubeco.2007.11.002

Laux H, Gillenkirch RM, Schenk-Mathes HY (2012) Entscheidungstheorie. Springer

Nicodème G (2008) Corporate income tax and economic distortions. Social Science Research Network, Rochester

Nielsen SB, Raimondos-Møller P, Schjelderup G (2010) Company taxation and tax spillovers: separate accounting versus formula apportionment. Eur Econ Rev 54:121–132. https://doi.org/10.1016/j.euroecorev.2009.06.005

Niemann R (2008) The effects of differential taxation on managerial effort and risk taking. FinanzArchiv Public Finance Analysis 64:273–310. https://doi.org/10.1628/001522108X374142

Pethig R, Wagener A (2007) Profit tax competition and formula apportionment. Int Tax Public Financ 14:631–655. https://doi.org/10.1007/s10797-006-9017-5

Riedel N (2010) The downside of formula apportionment: evidence on factor demand distortions. Int Tax Public Financ 17:236–258. https://doi.org/10.1007/s10797-009-9116-1

Riedel N, Runkel M (2007) Company tax reform with a water's edge. J Public Econ 91:1533–1554. https://doi.org/10.1016/j.jpubeco.2006.11.001

Runkel M, Schjelderup G (2011) The choice of apportionment factors under formula apportionment*: formula apportionment taxation. Int Econ Rev 52:913–934. https://doi.org/10.1111/j.1468-2354.2011.00654.x

Schroeder C (2012) Industrielle Arbeitskosten im internationalen Vergleich 1980/98. iwtrends 26:35–49

Spremann K (1987) Agent and principal. In: Bamberg G, Spremann K (eds) Agency theory, information, and incentives. Springer, Berlin, Heidelberg, pp 3–37

Environmental Sustainability as a Determinant of Foreign Direct Investments: Empirical Evidence from Sweden

Olga Golubeva

Abstract A regression model which investigates the relationship between locational choice of multinational enterprises (MNE) and environmental sustainability in host countries as the determinant of foreign direct investments (FDI) has been suggested. The following proxies are proposed for analysis of the environmental sustainability: variables measuring environmental damage, efficiency of natural resources' employment, availability of renewable resources and, finally, governmental ability to maintain a fair distribution of resources. Swedish FDIs in 73 countries worldwide have been examined using a dataset provided by Statistics Sweden. According to the study, 83.2% of variation in the dependent variable, FDI, can be explained by the profitability of investments. The empirical evidence also indicates that environmental sustainability has little impact on foreign investors and that most investment location decisions are not made on the basis of environmental sustainability criteria, at least as it represented by proxies chosen in the paper.

Keywords Foreign direct investments (FDI) • Environmental sustainability • Pollution haven hypothesis • Pollution halo hypothesis • Return on invested capital (ROIC)

Introduction: Research Problem and Purpose

Foreign direct investments (FDI) play an increasingly significant role in the modern economy. In 2015, global FDI flows jumped by 38% to USD 1.76 trillion, their highest level since the global financial crisis of 2008–2009. Looking ahead, FDI flows are expected to decline by 10–15% during 2016. This reflects the fragility of the global economy with its persistent weakness of aggregate demand, elevated geopolitical risks and a slump in multinational enterprises' (MNE) profits. Over the

O. Golubeva (✉)
Stockholm Business School, Stockholm University, Stockholm, SE 10691, Sweden
e-mail: olga.golubeva@sbs.su.se

D. Procházka (ed.), *The Impact of Globalization on International Finance and Accounting*, Springer Proceedings in Business and Economics,
https://doi.org/10.1007/978-3-319-68762-9_2

medium term, however, global FDI flows are projected to resume growth in 2017 and to surpass USD 1.8 trillion in 2018 (UNCTAD 2016).

Analysis of the determinants of FDI has already received much attention in the literature. Existing studies suggest that macroeconomic and political issues, institutions, labour costs, human capital, financial and trade openness, country sizes and natural resources, taxes and investment climate in beneficiary countries are all important factors. Empirical evidence, however, in favour of the above suggested determinants often remains ambiguous (Blonigen and Piger 2011; Goswami and Haider 2014). Several factors have been found to have both negative and positive effects; this indicates an eventual lack of robustness and a limited predictive power of regression models (Kok and Ersoy 2009). Many studies emphasise the open-ended character of this research field, and they suggest that more effort needs to be invested in the systematisation and testing of existing hypotheses to reflect the priorities for FDI decision-making in different regions and countries. Furthermore, additional variables that have not yet been properly investigated may also significantly affect the inflow of FDI.

Sustainability as a possible determinant of FDI has started to attract attention of researchers. The concept of sustainable development was launched in 1987 when the World Conference on Environment and Development (WCED) defined the term as a development that meets the needs of the present generation without compromising the ability of future generations to meet their own needs (WCED 1987). The International Union for Conservation of Nature and Natural Resources (IUCN) proposed three main pillars of sustainable development: social, environmental and economic (IUCN 1980). In September 2015, the United Nations Summit adopted the 2030 Agenda for Sustainable Development together with Sustainable Development Goals (SDGs) to be achieved over the next 15 years.

The SDGs carry significant implications for future investments worldwide, including a much larger contribution by MNE through FDI. UNCTAD has estimated that achieving the SDGs by 2030 in developing countries alone will require investment in the range of USD 3.3 trillion to USD 4.5 trillion annually (UNCTAD 2016).

Academic scholars stress the importance of MNE for integrating the SDGs in international investment decision-making and to make FDI to strictly observe the principles of sustainable development (Voica et al. 2015). At the same time, theoretical issues regarding interaction between FDI and the environment of the host countries are far from being settled.

One of the most contentious issues debated today in connection with FDI activities is whether intercountry differences in environmental regulations are turning poor countries into "pollution havens" for foreign investors. The pollution haven hypothesis (PHavenH) predicts that owing to the liberalisation of trade and FDI, firms which are active in pollution-intensive sectors and operate in countries adopting more restrictive environmental policies will transfer production abroad and serve the domestic markets from these new foreign plants (see, e.g. Copeland and Taylor 2003). However, while theoretical studies converge in predicting such a shift, empirical evidence has been mixed.

Studies testing the PHavenH by considering intercountry FDI location choice often do not find robust support for the prediction (Smarzynska Javorcik and Wei 2004). The findings of Dean et al. (2009) regarding the location choice of FDI within China support PHavenH for ethnically Chinese capital in industries that are highly polluting but not for investors from high-income countries.

Mixed evidence is also provided by studies on intra-country FDI location choice, analysing whether differences in environmental stringency across sub-national units affect the spatial allocation of FDI within a country. Eskeland and Harrison (2003) examined the pattern of industrial country FDI across industries within Mexico, Venezuela, Morocco and Cote d'Ivoire but found little evidence to support PHavenH. In contrast, studies focusing on the location of investment in the United States found evidence consistent with the PHavenH (List et al. 2004). These US studies argue that lack of evidence for PHavenH in research articles may be due to a failure to account for endogeneity and measurement error. On the other hand, the behaviour observed in the United States may not characterise FDI flows into developing countries, the focus of concern in the PHavenH (Blonigen and Wang 2005).

A significant part of the research done in this respect has found little evidence for widespread, systematic pollution haven effects; nevertheless, the hypothesis that stricter regulation may, in some given conditions, shift the FDI location still cannot be completely rejected (Golub et al. 2011). Sanna-Randaccio and Sestini (2012) suggested that stricter climate legislation does not lead to relocation of FDI in capital-intensive sectors in the short term. In the long-run, however, total relocation becomes a feasible option, especially for a smaller country with limited market size and when unit transport cost is not high, thus supporting reasonable expenditure for moving the plant to alternative destinations with less strict legislative climates.

The pollution halo hypothesis (PHaloH), by way of contrast, assumes that FDI spreads best environmental management practices and technologies and contributes to the improvement of the environment. According to Gallagher and Zarsky (2007), FDI determines three types of greening effects: transfer of clean technologies, by achieving more efficient and less polluting compared to domestic production; technology leapfrogging, by transferring technologies to control pollution; and spillovers to domestic firms, by transferring best practices in environmental management towards affiliates, domestic competitors and suppliers. Some cross-sectoral econometric studies support the hypothesis that foreign firms are, on average, cleaner than domestic firms after controlling for age, size and productivity of plant (Dardati and Tekin 2010).

Researchers also suggest that FDI, through the adoption of new technologies and the promotion of innovation and efficiency, helps to create a low-carbon economy (Tamazian et al. 2009). MNE, for example, promote environmentally friendly practices in countries with weak regulations by implementing high industrial standards such as ISO 14001 (Zeng and Eastin 2012). Tamazian et al. (2009) found that the increase in FDI inflows is associated with lower levels of CO2 emissions, because FDI inflows encourage research and development investments.

These, in turn, possibly lead to higher technological energy-related efficiency and therefore to lower emissions.

Zheng et al. (2010), testing the hypothesis concerning the relationship between FDI and ambient air pollution across major Chinese cities, found that those cities featuring higher per capita FDI flows have lower pollution levels. Witkowska (2011) examined the potential impact of foreign investors' activities in the Czech Republic, Poland and Slovakia. The research results show that as yet there has been no empirical evidence that FDI has a particularly negative impact on the natural environment in these new EU member states. This study is less conclusive as the absence of such a negative effect does not directly support PHaloH.

A review of the literature suggests that economic theory is ambiguous regarding the question of whether FDI is positive or negative concerning environmental sustainability, as concluded by Yue et al. (2016). The first group of problems in the research field investigating relationships between FDI and environmental issues has been created by weak measures of environmental quality and stringency and by insufficient data for estimating variation in degree of response to different environmental variables (Dean et al. 2009). Another group of problems emerges from the introduction of drastic simplifications in modelling, resulting from attempts to endogenise both location and policy decisions (e.g. Ikefuji et al. 2016). Golub et al. (2011) stressed that the absence of a clear definition of theoretical concepts in the research field constitutes a serious problem and concluded that "the contribution of FDI to the environment is potentially large but largely ignored so far" (p. 33).

This paper attempts to fill some of the gaps in the research field by proposing a theoretical model which investigates the relationship between the locational choice of MNE and environmental sustainability in host countries where environmental sustainability proxies are assessed as determinants of FDI. In our study, we examine Swedish FDI using a dataset provided by Statistics Sweden for the period 2003–2014. The value of Swedish FDI amounted to SEK 2824 billion at the end of 2014, which is approximately 72% of Swedish GDP (Golubeva 2016). A Swedish foreign assets portfolio is relatively diverse, enabling a search to be conducted for general patterns that explain foreign investments made by a particular developed country (Sweden) in the global arena. The study sample covers 73 countries.

Theoretical Model, Method and Definition of Variables

A multiple regression model has been applied to test the ability of suggested independent variables to explain the behaviour of the dependent variable, FDI. We restrict the study of sustainability to an environmental factor. Firstly, economic and social peers in connection with FDI have already been attracted by many researchers, while investigations of environmental sustainability are still rare. Furthermore, there is some evidence that the most important influence comes from the environmental pillar followed by social and economic pillars (Voica et al. 2015).

Several authors suggested that foreign investors are influenced by the profitability of the project (Kok and Ersoy 2009; Kinda 2010; Mottaleb and Kalirajan 2010; Golubeva 2016). In accordance with standard economic textbooks, Nnadozie and Njuguna (2011) defined profit (Π) as the difference between revenues (R) and costs (C). Given that total revenue is a product between quantity of goods (Q) and its corresponding price (P), Π may be expressed as:

$$\Pi = \Pi(P, Q, C), \text{where } \partial\Pi/\partial P > 0; \quad \partial\Pi/\partial Q > 0 \text{ and } \partial\Pi/\partial C < 0 \tag{1}$$

Furthermore, total cost is a combination of the input costs (IN), operational costs (OP) and hidden costs (HD). Input costs are defined as the costs of different factors of production such as land, labour, raw materials and electricity; operational costs include financial and transaction costs, while hidden costs involve, for example, the monetary costs of applying for a licence to start a business.

It is reasonable to assume that profits are maximised in a country where foreign investors can operate their businesses at low cost and produce at full scale with competitive market prices. Therefore, variables which determine profit can also determine the FDI flows into a country. The equation for FDI will be:

$$FDI = f(P, Q, IN, OP, HD) \tag{2}$$

The equations assume that foreign investors prefer to invest in countries where they can produce large amounts of goods at lower costs. We apply return on the invested capital (ROIC) as a measure of profitability of FDI.

Several researchers have argued that the profit-related incentives for investors do not generally work unless they are appropriately combined with other incentives that improve the general investment climate (Athukorala 2009).

The introduction of environmental sustainability variables into the model is handled in a manner similar to the previous studies of Liu (2006), Wang et al. (2011), Voica et al. (2015), Peng et al. (2016) and Yue et al. (2016).

Compared to previous articles, which applied a rather restricted number of variables, this study extends the search to multiple groups of proxies representing the concept of environmental sustainability. These include variables measuring environmental damage (greenhouse gases emission, air pollution), efficiency of natural resources' employment (GDP per energy unit), availability of renewable resources (electricity and freshwater) and a government's ability to maintain a fair distribution of resources (Government Effectiveness Index and Rule of Law). The majority of independent variables chosen for regression analysis are represented by objective data, but two variables are represented by indices (Government Effectiveness Index and Rule of Law). These indices are assigned scores that are used as criteria to rank different countries and are a perception-based data source.

The following equation is proposed for assessing the impact of various environmental sustainability factors on FDI:

FDI (Model 1) = $\alpha + \beta_1$ (ROIC) + β_2 (GDP per energy unit) + β_3 (Greenhouse gases emission) + β_4 (Air pollution) + β_5 (Renewable electricity) + β_6 (Renewable freshwater) + β_7 (Government effectiveness) + β_8 (Rule of law) + ε, where α is a constant, β_1 – β_8 are vectors of parameters to be estimated and ε is the stochastic error term.

The paper goes a step further by removing the profitability factor from the regression model. The revised model (Model 2), with the indicator of ROIC, is as follows:

FDI (Model 2) = $\alpha + \beta_1$ (GDP per energy unit) + β_2 (Greenhouse gases emission) + β_3 (Air pollution) + β_4 (Renewable electricity) + β_5 (Renewable freshwater) + β_6 (Government effectiveness) + β_7 (Rule of law) + ε.

Finally, we investigate whether determinants of FDI and return on these investments, ROIC, can be explained by the same environmental sustainability factors. ROIC becomes the dependent variable, while independent variables previously chosen as determinants remain the same. Model 3 is therefore developed as follows:

ROIC (Model 3) = α + β_1 (GDP per energy unit) + β_2 (Greenhouse gases emission) + β_3 (Air pollution) + β_4 (Renewable electricity) + β_5 (Renewable freshwater) + β_6 (Government effectiveness) + β_7 (Rule of law) + ε.

FDI is defined as an investment involving long-term control by a foreign direct investor of 10% or more of the foreign enterprise resident within a different economy (UNCTAD 2015). The value of Swedish FDI abroad is defined as.

FDI = E + LC + CC – LL – CL + P + IL + OH; where E – total equity; LC – long-term claims; CC – current claims; LL – long-term liabilities; CL – current liabilities; P – directly-owned properties abroad; IL – parent company investment loans; OH – overseas homes.

In the study, as the dependent variable, we use data about FDI stock per country (average for 2003–2014 in million SEK). Direct investment can vary considerably, but for a small country like Sweden, large individual transactions may have a substantial impact on the development of assets going abroad on a year-on-year basis. Averaging allows us to address the long-term implications of foreign stocks mitigating cyclic investment activity.

Income on Swedish direct investment assets abroad, ROIC, is defined as ROIC = R + W + CL – CG – T + I; where R – income after net financial items; W – write-downs (net) included in R; CL – capital losses included in R; CG – capital gains included in R; T – tax in Swedish-owned companies abroad; I – interest on parent company investment loans.

The data for profitability was provided by Statistics Sweden for 2007–2014.[1] Definitions of variables and descriptive statistics are summarised in Table 1.

[1]We performed regression analysis applying FDI stock average as a dependent variable for the periods 2003–2014 and 2007–2014, leaving the other independent variables unchanged. There is no material difference which can lead to disparity in conclusions when results for the two periods 2003–2014 and 2007–2014 are compared.

Table 1 Definition of variables and descriptive statistics

Theoretical concepts	Definition of variables	Time period	Mean	Std. deviation
Swedish FDI	FDI stock per country in MSEK	Average 2003–2014	29679.22	63361.255
Return on capital	Return on capital in MSEK	Average 2007–2014	3049.47	5826.359
GDP per unit of energy used	GDP per unit of energy use is the PPP GDP per kilogramme of oil equivalent of energy use	Average 2007–2013	9.7970	3.80155
Greenhouse gas emission	Total greenhouse gas emissions (kt of CO2 equivalent)	Average 2007–2012	563748.71	1534685.360
Air pollution	Population-weighted exposure to ambient PM2.5 pollution	Average 2010–2014	21.5241	19.02665
Renewable electricity	Renewable electricity output (% of total electricity output)	Average 2007–2012	26.9016	26.35701
Renewable freshwater	Internal renewable resources (billion cubic metres)	Average 2007, 2012, 2014	470.7911	1024.04807
Government effectiveness index	Measures quality of public services; ranges from 0 (lowest) to 100 (highest rank)	Average 2007–2014	69.3771	22.67760
Rule of law	Measures quality of contract enforcement, property rights, police, courts; ranges from 0 (lowest) to 100 (highest rank)	Average 2007–2014	65.4756	25.68195

Source: Author's calculations, Statistics Sweden, World Development Indicators Metadata, The Worldwide Governance Indicators project
N, number of observations = 73

The 73 countries included in the analysis are (in alphabetical order) Algeria, Argentina, Australia, Austria, Bahamas, Belgium, Bosnia and Herzegovina, Botswana, Brazil, Bulgaria, Canada, Chile, China, Colombia, Croatia, Cyprus, Czech Republic, Denmark, Ecuador, Egypt, Estonia, Finland, France, Germany, Greece, Hong Kong, Hungary, Iceland, India, Indonesia, Ireland, Israel, Italy, Japan, Kazakhstan, Kenya, Korea (South), Latvia, Lithuania, Luxembourg, Malaysia, Mexico, Morocco, the Netherlands, New Zealand, Norway, Panama, Peru, the Philippines, Poland, Portugal, Romania, Russia, Saudi Arabia, Serbia, Sierra Leone, Singapore, Slovak Republic, Slovenia, South Africa, Spain, Sri Lanka, Switzerland, Taiwan, Thailand, Turkey, Ukraine, the United Arab Emirates, the United Kingdom, the United States, Uruguay, Venezuela and Vietnam.

A stepwise methodology has been chosen to present the empirical results so that only statistically significant variables are presented in the model. Stepwise regression implies that we add sequentially independent variables that are statistically significant.

Empirical Results

Table 2 summarises the empirical results for Models 1–3. Collinearity statistics are satisfactory. The VIF value being equal to 1 indicates that the independent variables are not strongly correlated with one another. The Durbin-Watson statistic measuring autocorrelation, where successive residuals are correlated, ranges between 1.7 and 2.2, indicating no or very minor autocorrelation.

In our multiple regression, R square for Model 1 as a predictor of FDI is 83.2, which means that 83.2% of variation in the dependent variable, FDI, is explained by the profitability of investments (ROIC). Furthermore, we did not find any evidence that the proxies used for the analysis of environmental sustainability are statistically significant determinants of Swedish FDI. When the profitability factor was removed from the regression model, then the rule of law and greenhouse gases emission appeared to be statistically significant determinants via a stepwise inclusion. R square for Model 2 decreased from 83.2% to 29%. During the next step of analysis, ROIC became the dependent variable, while independent variables previously chosen as determinants remained unchanged. We found that the rule of law and greenhouse gases emission are statistically significant determinants of profitability of investments with R square of 26.2%.

The regression coefficients of greenhouse gases emission are very low in both Model 2 and Model 3. The average amount of increase in FDI (in MSEK) for a 1 unit increase in greenhouse gases emission (kt of CO_2 equivalent) is 0.013 (equal to 13,000 SEK) for Model 2 and 0.001 (equal to 1000 SEK) for Model 3. For these

Table 2 Summary of the empirical results

Model		Unstandardised coefficients B	Std. error	Sig.	VIF collinearity	R square	Durbin-Watson
Model 1							
(Constant)		−572.067	3458.739	0.869			
Profit_MSEK		9.920	0.529	0.000*	1.000	0.832	1.742
Model 2							
1	(Constant)	−41306.017	18481.336	0.029			
	Rule_of_law	1084.148	263.012	0.000*	1.000	0.193	
2	(Constant)	−52466.040	17833.735	0.004			
	Rule_of_law	1143.771	249.272	0.000*	1.006		
	Greenhouse_gas	0.013	0.004	0.003*	1.006	0.290	1.900
Model 3							
1	(Constant)	−2926.636	1732.031	0.095			
	Rule_of_law	91.272	24.649	0.000*	1.000	0.162	
2	(Constant)	−4071.354	1648.692	0.016			
	Rule_of_law	97.388	23.045	0.000*	1.006		
	Greenhouse_gas	0.001	0.000	0.001*	1.006	0.262	2.184

Source: Author's calculations; *Significant at 1%

two models, empirical data supports PHavenH, suggesting that FDI is positively related to higher pollution levels in countries chosen as their investment destinations. More important, however, is the discovery that proxies for environmental sustainability lack statistical significance as soon as ROIC is incorporated into the analysis.

In summary, the empirical results of the regression analysis suggest a decisive role of return on capital in predicting FDI. When the profitability factor is included in the regression, only 16.8% of the variation in FDI stock is due to other sources such as random error or variables outside this analysis. The study therefore provides additional support for the literature highlighting the importance of profitability as a determinant of FDI (Kok and Ersoy 2009; Kinda 2010; Golubeva 2016). The results of this study also suggest that variables associated with environmental sustainability have little impact on the stock of Swedish FDI in 73 countries worldwide.

Only when the profitability factor has been removed from the regression do two variables – the rule of law and greenhouse gases emission – become statistically significant determinants. The predictive power of the model decreases alongside the removal of the profitability factor. It seems that further investigation is required in order to understand how to incorporate the requirements of environmental sustainability into the profitability goals pursued by MNE.

The empirical evidence suggests that the rule of law has a significant impact on foreign investors. Transparency, accountability and predictability in the design and implementation of investment and environmental policies and regulations can be an important step in stimulating FDI. Due to the importance of the rule of law for foreign investors, the possible union of two goals – raising FDI and promoting sustainability – may be achieved through enhancing environmental legislation. This conclusion is consistent with the findings of Golub et al. (2011) who suggested that the lack of predictable and transparent regulations (including environmental regulations) has deterred FDI in a number of countries.

Conclusions

The International Chamber of Commerce (ICC), the world business organisation, believes that investment, broadly, and FDI, specifically, can play a critical role towards realising the SDGs. The Addis Ababa Action Agenda – agreed in July 2015 – places a significant emphasis on mobilising private finance in order to support implementation of the SDGs. Investment, specifically FDI, is a key tool for business involvement in sustainable development (ICC 2016). FDI can potentially play a very important role for two reasons. Firstly, the scale of FDI and its significant growth over recent decades makes it a crucial source of financing. Looking at climate change-related financial flows from developed to developing countries, Buchner et al. (2011) note that FDI is the largest source of financing across all public and private sources. Secondly, whereas trade has largely indirect effects, FDI has the potential to transfer environmentally friendly industries, technology and know-how that directly contribute to environmental progress.

Foreign investors, having multiple options, will seek the best investment opportunities – those with the best prospects for returns on investment and with the lowest perceptions of risk. The empirical evidence of our study shows that most investment location decisions are not made on the basis of environmental sustainability criteria, at least as they are represented by the proxies chosen in this paper. Environmental variables are eventually a small element in these international investment decisions. While the debates regarding the pollution haven or halo hypothesis continue, the current reality might be that businesses, including MNE, are just beginning to take on board the implications of the post-2015 development agenda.

With the SDG targets agreed only in 2015, it is unsurprising that indicators are not yet reflected in the current FDI portfolio of MNE. Neither are policies and processes to encourage further sustainable investment yet in place. It is interesting, however, that one of the policy pillars formulated for investing in sustainable development is related to well-established legal systems (ICC 2016), and the importance of this factor has been supported by our study.

The balance of evidence also suggests that governments must be proactive in capturing the economic, social and environmental benefits of FDI; supportive public policies are required to ensure a reunion between environmental sustainability and the profitability of particular investment projects.

Acknowledgements The author would like to thank Statistics Sweden (SCB) for providing empirical data for research purposes. The author is grateful for helpful comments from the participants of the "18th Annual Conference on Finance and Accounting", Faculty of Finance and Accounting, University of Economics, Prague, Czech Republic, 26th of May, 2017. The author is also indebted to Dr. Alan Wood (UK) for proofreading assistance.

References

Athukorala PC (2009) Trends and patterns of foreign direct investments in Asia: a comparative perspective. J Appl Econ Res 3(4):365–408. https://doi.org/10.1177/097380100900300403

Blonigen BA, Piger J (2011) Determinants of foreign direct investment. NBER working paper series 16704, January 2011. Retrieved from http://www.nber.org/papers/w16704

Blonigen BA, Wang MG (2005) Inappropriate pooling of wealthy and poor countries in empirical FDI studies. In: Moran T, Graham E, Blomstrom M (eds) Does foreign direct investment promote development? Institute for International Economics, Washington, DC, pp 221–243

Buchner B, Brown J, Corfee-Morlot J (2011) Monitoring and tracking long-term finance to support climate action. OECD, Environment Directorate International Energy Agency. Retrieved from http://www.oecd.org/env/cc/48073739.pdf

Copeland BR, Taylor MS (2003) Trade and the environment: theory and evidence. Princeton University Press, Princeton

Dardati E, Tekin M (2010) Multinationals and environmental regulation: are foreign firms harmful or helpful? Retrieved from https://webspace.utexas.edu/ead397/www/index_files/trade_environment.pdf

Dean JM, Lovely ME, Wang H (2009) Are foreign investors attracted to weak environmental regulations? Evaluating the evidence from China. J Dev Econ 90:1–13. https://doi.org/10.1016/j.jdeveco.2008.11.007

Eskeland GS, Harrison AE (2003) Moving to greener pastures? Multinationals and the pollution haven hypothesis. J Dev Econ 70:1–23. https://doi.org/10.1016/S0304-3878(02)00084-6

Gallagher K, Zarsky L (2007) The enclave economy. MIT Press, Cambridge, MA

Golub S, Kauffmann C, Yeres P (2011) Defining and measuring green FDI: an exploratory review of existing work and evidence, OECD working papers on international investment 2011/2, OECD Publishing. https://doi.org/10.1787/5kg58j1cvcvk-en

Golubeva O (2016) Determinants of Swedish foreign direct investments (FDI): how important is profitability? Econ Finance Rev 4(10):1–19. Retrieved from http://www.businessjournalz.org/articlepdf/EFR-41001-June-2016-4(10)-a.pdf

Goswami GG, Haider S (2014) Does political risk deter FDI inflow? J Econ Stud 41(2):233–252. https://doi.org/10.1108/JES-03-2012-0041

ICC (International Chamber of Commerce) Commission on Trade and Investment Policy Foreign Direct Investment – Promoting and Protecting a Key Pillar for Sustainable Development and Growth, 1 March 2016

Ikefuji M, Itaya J, Okamura M (2010) Optimal emission tax with endogenous location choice of duopolistic firms, vol 06. Fondazione Eni Enrico Mattei, Nota di Lavoro, p 2010

Ikefuji M, Itaya J, Okamura M (2016) Optimal emission tax with endogenous location choice of duopolistic firms. Environ Resource Econ 65(2):463–485. https://doi.org/10.1007/s10640-015-9914-0

IUCN (1980) World conservation strategy – living resource conservation for sustainable development: International Union for Conservation of nature and natural resources. United Nations Environment Programme, World Wildlife Fund

Kinda T (2010) Investment climate and FDI in developing countries: firm-level evidence. World Dev 38(4):498–513. https://doi.org/10.1016/j.worlddev.2009.12.001

Kok R, Ersoy BA (2009) Analysis of FDI determinants in developing countries. Int J Soc Econ 36 (1,2):105–123. https://doi.org/10.1108/03068290910921226PO

List JA, McHone WW, Millimet DL (2004) Effects of environmental regulation on foreign and domestic plant births: is there a home field advantage? J Urban Econ 56:303–326. https://doi.org/10.1016/j.jue.2004.03.007

Liu GA (2006) Causality analysis on GDP and air emissions in Norway, Discussion papers 447. Research Department of Statistics Norway, Oslo

Mottaleb KA, Kalirajan K (2010) Determinants of foreign direct investment in developing countries: a comparative analysis. J Appl Econ Res 4(4):369–404. https://doi.org/10.1177/097380101000400401

Nnadozie E, Njuguna AE (2011) Investment climate and foreign direct investment in Africa. Paper presented at the 6th African Economic Conference, Addis Ababa, Ethiopia, 26–28 October 2011

Peng H, Tan X, Li Y, Hu L (2016) Economic growth, foreign direct investment and CO2 emissions in China: a panel granger causality analysis. Sustainability 8(233):1–13. https://doi.org/10.3390/su8030233

Sanna-Randaccio F, Sestini R (2012) The impact of unilateral climate policy with endogenous plant location and market size asymmetry. Rev Int Econ 20(3):580–599. https://doi.org/10.1111/j.1467-9396.2012.01040.x

Smarzynska Javorcik B, Wei SJ (2004) Pollution havens and foreign direct investment: dirty secret or popular myth? Contrib Econ Anal Pol 3:1–32. https://doi.org/10.2202/1538-0645.1244

Tamazian A, Chousa JP, Vadlamannati C (2009) Does higher economic and financial growth lead to environmental degradation: evidence from the BRIC countries. Energy Policy 37:246–253. https://doi.org/10.1016/j.enpol.2008.08.025

UNCTAD (2015) World investment report. Reforming international Investment Governance. United Nations publications, Geneva

UNCTAD (2016) Investor nationality: policy challenges, 2016 United Nations Conference on Trade and Development, United Nations Publication
Voica MC, Panait M, Haralambie GA (2015) The impact of foreign direct investment on sustainable development. Econ Insights Trends Challenges IV(3):89–103
Wang SS, Zhou DQ, Zhou P (2011) CO2 emissions, energy consumption and economic growth in China: a panel data analysis. Energy Policy 39:4870–4875. https://doi.org/10.1016/j.enpol.2011.06.032
WCED (1987) Our common future. World Commision on Environment and Development, Oxford
Witkowska J (2011) Foreign direct investment and sustainable development in the new EU member states: environmental aspects. Comp Econ Res 14(3):5–23. https://doi.org/10.2478/v10103-011-0016-0
Yue S, Yang Y, Hu Y (2016) Does foreign direct investment affect green growth? Evidence from China's experience. Sustainability 8(158):1–14. https://doi.org/10.3390/su8020158
Zeng K, Eastin J (2012) Do developing countries invest up? The environmental effects of foreign direct investment from less-developed countries. World Dev 40(11):2221–2233. https://doi.org/10.1016/j.worlddev.2012.03.008
Zheng SQ, Matthew EK, Liu HY (2010) Towards a system of open cities in China: home prices, FDI flows and air quality in 35 major cities. Reg Sci Urban Econ 40:1–10. https://doi.org/10.1016/j.regsciurbeco.2009.10.003

Are R&D-Active SMEs in the Emerging Markets Financially Constrained? Self-Evaluation Approach

Katarzyna Prędkiewicz and Paweł Prędkiewicz

Abstract The paper aims to examine whether R&D-active companies are financially constrained based on a self-assessment approach. A second aim is to check whether a company's size has any impact on access to capital for R&D-active firms. The study is based on data collected from more than 400 enterprises operating in Poland. The analysis has confirmed that there is a significant difference between R&D-active companies and their peers with no R&D activity; however, the "size effect" was not strongly proven. It seems that both SMEs and large companies are financially constrained, thereby justifying the direct tools (e.g. grants) used for alleviating the problem of access to capital regardless of the company's size.

Keywords Innovation • Financial constraints • R&D

Introduction

Capital market imperfections, such as asymmetry of information between potential capital providers and companies which invest in research and development (R&D), contribute to difficulties in judging the quality of innovative projects and finally lead to financial constraints on R&D-active companies. They may have problems collecting funds for a project, whereas internally generated cash flow is limited and, therefore, insufficient to enable successful completion of the R&D venture. When an innovative project is run by small- and medium-sized companies (SMEs), this problem may become even more severe because this group is also believed to be financially constrained in comparison to larger entities (Stiglitz and Weiss 1981; Chittenden et al. 1996; Beck and Demirguc-Kunt 2006; Agur 2012). Researchers try to identify, understand and explain the occurrence of financing constraints for

K. Prędkiewicz (✉) • P. Prędkiewicz
Wrocław University of Economics, Department of Finance, ul. Komandorska 118-120, 53-345 Wrocław, Poland
e-mail: katarzyna.predkiewicz@ue.wroc.pl; pawel.predkiewicz@ue.wroc.pl

D. Procházka (ed.), *The Impact of Globalization on International Finance and Accounting*, Springer Proceedings in Business and Economics,
https://doi.org/10.1007/978-3-319-68762-9_3

R&D-active companies using a variety of different approaches, and the findings from studies are still mixed, so there is an ongoing need to continue this research. This is also the reason why various tools which aim to reduce this problem are implemented by policymakers (e.g. subsidies and tax relief). Additionally, most of the studies conducted so far were based on data from well-developed markets such as the USA, UK, Germany and Belgium (Harhoff 1998; Bougheas et al. 2003; Cincera and Ravet 2010; Brown et al. 2012; Borisova and Brown 2013; Hottenrott et al. 2016) and only a few from emerging markets (Ayyagari et al. 2011). Therefore, the aim of this paper is to answer the question as to whether R&D-active companies are financially constrained based on a self-assessment approach. We would also like to establish whether there is a significant difference between SMEs and large entities in the overall group of R&D-active firms. The studies are based on surveys of the group of more than 400 enterprises operating in the emerging market – Poland.

Literature Review

When a company is considered to be financially constrained, it is not able to carry out R&D projects at an expected level due to a shortage of funds or very high cost of financing (Hottenrott et al. 2016). On the theoretical level, Stiglitz and Weiss (1981) and Myers and Majluf (1984) comment on possible credit rationing by lenders. One of the first empirical studies but focusing mainly on financing constraints for capital investment was conducted by Fazzari et al. (1988); however, Kaplan and Zingales (1997) have some comments on the methodology and doubt if higher sensitivities of investment to cash flow changes can be interpreted as evidence that firms are more financially constrained. One of the further directions of research has focused on investments in intangible assets, which are a feature of innovative firms, and, potentially, a company with this type of investment is exposed to higher financial constraints. Intangible assets (know-how, patents, R&D) have lower collateral value for lenders than capital goods and raise the asymmetry of information. Some of the research has produced evidence that R&D activities may be sensitive to cash flow changes (Hall 1992; Himmelberg and Petersen 1994; Harhoff 1998; Cincera and Ravet 2010).

The key issue in the described research is still establishing the right measure of financial constraints. Most of the empirical literature uses investment in R&D sensitivity to cash flow changes (Carreira and Silva 2010), but there are also other possible measures like cash holding and financial ratio related to liquidity and debt, e.g. working capital or financial leverage (Czarnitzki et al. 2014; Lööf and Nabavi 2016). In parallel, an approach based on a firm's self-assessment also exists – the company managers indicate how difficult it is to access capital or indicate what the success rate of achieving different forms of capital was (Savignac 2006; van der Zwan 2014). Nevertheless, a better method is based on a combination of self-evaluation with firms' financial information (Carreira and Silva 2010).

Taking into account the above literature review, we formulated the following hypotheses:

H1 R&D-active companies consider access to capital as a more serious problem than their non-R&D-active peers.

The firm's size may play a central role for R&D-active companies because small firms are more likely to be to a higher degree, sensitive to the availability of internal finance (Harhoff 1998; Cenni et al. 2015).

And so, the second hypothesis is as follows:

H2 Smaller R&D-active companies consider access to capital as a more serious problem than their larger R&D-active peers.

Data and Methodology

The research is based on a sample of 409 companies operating in Poland in 5 industries. Most of the sample consists of SMEs (89%) – the rest, large companies, are a control group. The data was collected in a survey in 2015, and respondents in charge of innovation or finance were selected from the upper management levels. The aim of the questionnaire was to collect information on innovative activity from one side and financing decisions from the other side.

In the survey, respondents were asked, inter alia, a simple question: "To what extent is access to capital (funding) an important factor hindering the development of the company". The answers were arranged in five ordinal response categories (Likert scale):

1. No problem
2. Slight problem
3. Moderate problem
4. Significant problem
5. Very serious problem

The respondents also answered questions concerning their innovative activity, inter alia, whether the company has its own research and development department, its own or external R&D expenditure, patents granted, etc.

In the presented study, we used a dummy variable with respect to R&D department. Information on a firm's employment, revenue, assets and independence were also collected, and, based on this information, the company was qualified as belonging either to the group of SMEs or large companies.

The structure of answers was analysed using chi-squared and Welch's t-test which allowed us to check whether differences in answers between groups of companies that declared R&D departments and those with no R&D department were statistically significant. Similar methods were used to check whether there is a difference between SMEs and large companies in this area.

An ordered probit model based on the answers to a question regarding access to capital was also employed in the study. A dummy variable that responds to the presence of an R&D department and the control variable referring to industry, company age, assets structure and profit margin was used in this model.

Results and Discussion

When we consider all the companies in the sample, most of them indicated they have a slight (35% of sample) or moderate (33%) problem with access to capital (Table 1). Every fifth examined company declared that access to capital is not a problem. Only one company declared that fundraising was a very serious problem (relative to the sample as a whole, the share of this one answer is well below 1%, so, in Table 1 in the fifth column, the share is given as 0%). The situation changes when we compare the sample structure separately for companies who have an R&D department and those without. Companies which conduct R&D projects more often than their peers indicated that access to capital may be a problem that hinders company development – it was a significant issue for 15% of innovative companies and 10% of non-innovative companies. Moreover, only 8% of R&D-active companies indicated that raising capital is not a problem, whereas in non-R&D-active companies this share was much higher, reaching 27%. The results initially confirm the first hypothesis – R&D-active companies see access to capital as a more serious problem than their peers, meaning that they may indeed be financially constrained.

When we focus only on R&D-active companies and compare SMEs with large entities, the structure of the sample changes in that access to capital (funding) is a slight (2), moderate (3) and significant (4) factor hindering the development of the company (Table 2). The answers given by SMEs vary especially for 4 (significant problem), with 16% of SMEs indicating this level of difficulty against only 8% of large entities, whereas in 2 (slight problem), 38% of SMEs, as opposed to 50% of large companies, indicated this level of difficulty. These results initially confirm the second hypothesis – small R&D-active companies consider access to capital as a more serious problem than large R&D-active firms.

The difference between R&D and non-R&D firms is statistically significant, with *p*-values of 0.02169% based on the chi-squared test (Table 3). Also, there are significant differences in the structure of answers between R&D-active SMEs and

Table 1 Access to capital as a problem in R&D and no R&D companies

Access to capital as a problem	1	2	3	4	5	Total
No R&D	27%	32%	31%	10%	0%	100%
R&D	8%	40%	37%	15%	0%	100%
Whole sample	20%	35%	33%	12%	0%	100%

Source: authorial computation
Note: Likert scale: 1 – "No problem" to 5 – "Very serious problem"

Table 2 Access to capital as a problem in R&D companies – SME vs. large companies

Access to capital as a problem	1	2	3	4	5	Total
R&D SME	9%	38%	37%	16%	0%	100%
R&D large	8%	50%	35%	8%	0%	100%
R&D all	8%	40%	37%	15%	0%	100%

Source: authorial computation
Note: Likert scale: 1 – "No problem" to 5 – "Very serious problem"

Table 3 Results of chi-squared test – difference is significant?

Category	CHI2	Degree of freedom	*p*-value
No R&D vs. R&D	21.82788	4	0.02169%
R&D large vs. R&D SME	30.52043	3	0.00011%
No R&D large vs. no R&D SME	93.80104	4	0.00000%

Source: authorial computation

Table 4 Average difficulties in capital access and results of Welch's t-test

Access to capital as a problem	No R&D	R&D	*p*-value
SME	2.29	2.61	0.03%
Large	1.86	2.42	1.17%
p-value	3.44%	14.00%	

Source: authorial computation

large companies (*p*-value 0.00011%). Moreover, in non-R&D companies, their size has an impact on reporting of problems with access to capital.

Additionally, we used Welch's t-test (adaptation of student's t-test), a two-sample location test, to check the hypothesis that two populations have equal means. We calculated the average difficulty in accessing capital for each subgroup, assigning values of 1–5 for each answer on the Likert scale (Table 4), and then compared them using Welch's t-test horizontally and vertically. We confirmed that the difference between non-R&D-active companies and R&D-active companies is statistically significant in SMEs (*p*-value 0.03%) and in large companies (*p*-value 1.17%). However, when we compare the groups vertically, the difference between SMEs and large firms in the "non-R&D" and "R&D" group appears only statistically significant in the first set. This could be explained by the fact that innovative activity has a more significant impact on financial constraints than the size of companies and R&D-active firms are financially constrained regardless of their size.

In the next phase of research, an ordered probit model was employed for 403 observations (Table 5) with a 5-point scale response (from 1 – "No problem" to 5 – "Very serious problem"). Different control variables were considered in the model – those reflecting the current financial status of companies, e.g. financial

Table 5 Ordered probit-dependent variable "access to capital"

Variables	Coefficient	Std. error	*z*	*p*-value
LNassets	−0.0482524	0.0461255	−1.0461	0.29551
AGE	0.00653779	0.00309401	2.1130	0.03460**
ASSETS2	−0.0409044	0.298119	−0.1372	0.89087
EBITDAMargin	0.00612711	0.00524906	1.1673	0.24310
RDDEP	0.385776	0.118659	3.2511	0.00115***
Industry dummies	Included			
cut1	−0.948948	0.581377	−1.6322	0.10263
cut2	0.0511244	0.580712	0.0880	0.92985
cut3	1.10983	0.581775	1.9077	0.05643*
cut4	2.76626	0.656119	4.2161	0.00002***
Mean dependent var	2.369727			
Log-likelihood	−524.2792			
Schwarz criterion	1126.545			
S.D. dependent var	0.943570			
Akaike criterion	1074.558			
Hannan–Quinn	1095.140			

Source: authorial computation
Note: Standard errors based on Hessian. **p*-value <0.1; ***p*-value <0.05; ****p*-value <0.01. LNassets, natural logarithm of total assets; AGE, company age; ASSETS2, sum of fixed assets and stocks divided by total assets; EBITDAMargin, earnings before interest, tax, depreciation and amortization (EBITDA) divided by total revenue

liquidity, debt ratios and profit margin; however, none of those variables were statistically important. Nevertheless, the control variable that responds to the R&D department is statistically significant with a positive coefficient. This result could be interpreted as evidence that R&D-active companies with the higher probability indicate that access to capital is a problem slowing down their development compared to companies without R&D department. However, the size of the company (based on a natural logarithm of asset size but also other measures such as number of employees, natural logarithm of revenue size) and the industry have no impact on the answers, whereas age (moderate) and R&D department (significantly) influence the fundraising problem. The last result is in line with Welch's t-tests.

Conclusion

In the paper, we used a self-evaluation approach to assess whether R&D-active companies are financially constrained. We found that entities which have an R&D department more frequently perceive access to capital as a serious problem, hampering the company development, when compared to their non-R&D peers. However, we have not confirmed strongly that there is a significant difference between small and large R&D companies (only the chi-squared test confirmed this). Therefore, R&D activity may give rise to an asymmetry of information for all companies, regardless of their size. Debt and equity providers may have problems with evaluating the worth of a project and future cash flow, both for SMEs and large companies. This means that policymakers should still support both SMEs and large companies in financing R&D (innovative) projects and design tools that mitigate the financial constraints regardless of the company's size.

Acknowledgements The project was funded by the National Science Centre allocated on the basis of the decision number DEC-2013/11/D/HS4/03941.

References

Agur I (2012) Credit rationing when banks are funding constrained. N Am J Econ Finance 23:220–227. https://doi.org/10.1016/j.najef.2012.01.002

Ayyagari M, Demirgüç-Kunt A, Maksimovic V (2011) Firm innovation in emerging markets: the role of finance, governance, and competition. J Financ Quant Anal 46:1545–1580. https://doi.org/10.1017/S0022109011000378

Beck T, Demirguc-Kunt A (2006) Small and medium-size enterprises: access to finance as a growth constraint. J Bank Finance 30:2931–2943. https://doi.org/10.1016/j.jbankfin.2006.05.009

Borisova G, Brown JR (2013) R&D sensitivity to asset sale proceeds: new evidence on financing constraints and intangible investment. J Bank Financ 37:159–173. https://doi.org/10.1016/j.jbankfin.2012.08.024

Bougheas S, Görg H, Strobl E (2003) Is R and D financially constrained? Theory and evidence from Irish manufacturing. Rev Ind Organ 22:159–174. https://doi.org/10.1023/A:1022905102446

Brown JR, Martinsson G, Petersen BC (2012) Do financing constraints matter for R&D? Eur Econ Rev 56:1512–1529. https://doi.org/10.1016/j.euroecorev.2012.07.007

Carreira C, Silva F (2010) No deep pockets: some stylized empirical results on firms' financial constraints. J Econ Surv 24:731–753. https://doi.org/10.1111/j.1467-6419.2009.00619.x

Cenni S, Monferrà S, Salotti V et al (2015) Credit rationing and relationship lending. Does firm size matter? J Bank Financ 53:249–265. https://doi.org/10.1016/j.jbankfin.2014.12.010

Chittenden F, Hall G, Hutchinson P (1996) Small firm growth, access to capital markets and financial structure: review of issues and an empirical investigation. Small Bus Econ 8:59–67. https://doi.org/10.1007/BF00391976

Cincera M, Ravet J (2010) Financing constraints and R&D investments of large corporations in Europe and the US. Sci Public Policy 37:455–466. https://doi.org/10.3152/030234210X508642

Czarnitzki D, Hall BH, Hottenrott H (2014) Patents as quality signals? The implications for financing constraints on R&D. National Bureau of Economic Research, Cambridge, MA

Fazzari SM, Hubbard RG, Petersen BC et al (1988) Financing constraints and corporate investment. Brook Pap Econ Act 1988:141–206. https://doi.org/10.2307/2534426

Hall B (1992) Investment and research and development at the firm level: does the source of financing matter? National Bureau of Economic Research, Inc, Cambridge, MA

Harhoff D (1998) Are there financing constraints for R&D and investment in German manufacturing firms? Annales d'Économie et de Statistique:421–456. https://doi.org/10.2307/20076124

Himmelberg CP, Petersen BC (1994) R & D and internal finance: a panel study of small firms in high-tech industries. Rev Econ Stat 76:38–51. https://doi.org/10.2307/2109824

Hottenrott H, Hall BH, Czarnitzki D (2016) Patents as quality signals? The implications for financing constraints on R&D. Econ Innov New Technol 25:197–217. https://doi.org/10.1080/10438599.2015.1076200

Kaplan SN, Zingales L (1997) Do investment-cash flow sensitivities provide useful measures of financing constraints? Q J Econ 112:169–215. https://doi.org/10.1162/003355397555163

Lööf H, Nabavi P (2016) Innovation and credit constraints: evidence from Swedish exporting firms. Econ Innov New Technol 25:269–282. https://doi.org/10.1080/10438599.2015.1076196

Myers SC, Majluf NS (1984) Corporate financing and investment decisions when firms have information that investors do not have. J Financ Econ 13:187–221

Savignac F (2006) The impact of financial constraints on innovation: evidence from French manufacturing firms

Stiglitz JE, Weiss A (1981) Credit rationing in markets with imperfect information. Am Econ Rev 71:393–410

van der Zwan P (2014) Bank loan application success by SMEs: the role of ownership structure and innovation

Tax Incentives for Innovative Small Business: The Russian Model

Anastasiia Grinkevich, Larisa Grinkevich, and Olga Belomyttseva

Abstract Designing an effective tax regime for small businesses remains a pressing issue. The authors engaged a comparative analysis of types and methods of tax incentives for small business and innovative business in global practice. It is concluded that the stimulating function of the taxation system in the Russian Federation has low efficiency and that innovative tax incentives are to be introduced. The authors propose a model of small business taxation with an embedded automatic regulator of the degree of tax burden on particular small entities with regard to their socio-economic impact and innovativeness.

Keywords Small business • Innovation • Tax incentives

Introduction

The Russian Federation has developed an approach to stimulating innovative small business through tax incentives, which consists in the following: tax reliefs are granted to small business as special tax regimes; innovative tax incentives are implemented within the standard taxation regime; innovative business has the opportunity to use tax incentives, granted to residents of special economic zones of technology and innovation type, in an integrated manner.

The objective of our study is to investigate tax incentives for innovative small business in Russia and other countries and to develop a model for improving this instrument for stimulating innovation.

In fact, mechanisms of tax incentives for small business and evaluation of these mechanisms' effectiveness are attended to in various papers. For example,

A. Grinkevich (✉) • L. Grinkevich
Tomsk State University, Tomsk, Department of Economics, pr. Lenina 36, 634036, Tomsk, Russia
e-mail: tasya-g89@mail.ru; nasty_saturn@mail.ru

O. Belomyttseva
Tomsk State University, Tomsk, Department of Finance and Accounting, pr. Lenina 36, 634036, Tomsk, Russia
e-mail: olbel@f123.ru

D. Procházka (ed.), *The Impact of Globalization on International Finance and Accounting*, Springer Proceedings in Business and Economics,
https://doi.org/10.1007/978-3-319-68762-9_4

contribution of small business to economy as well as types and mechanisms of tax incentives in countries of the Organization for Economic Co-operation and Development (OECD), G20 and EU countries is considered within the *OECD* report (2015) and a study by Blažić (2012). Bergner et al. (2017) suggest a classification of tax incentives and discuss the impact and appropriateness of tax incentives for small- and medium-sized businesses (SMEs) in the European Union. Recommendations for creating an effective tax regime for SMEs are provided by Engelschalk (2007). Logue and Vettori (2010), Yitzhaki (2007) and Engelschalk and Loeprick (2015) state that presumptive taxation systems can enhance small business's tax compliance in developed countries.

Intarakumnerd and Goto (2016) and Gale and Brown (2013) emphasize that stimulation of innovative small business is to be performed by means of tax incentives. A classification of tax incentives for innovation business activity is presented by the European Commission (2014) and Busom (2012).

Approaches to Providing Tax Incentives to Innovative Small Business

Tax Incentives for Small Business in Other Countries

The world's practice has developed two schemes for providing tax incentives to small businesses, which include presumptive tax systems for small business and tax incentives for small business within the standard taxation regime.

Engelschalk (2007) classifies presumptive tax systems for small business into presumptive taxation based on turnover or gross income, presumptive systems based on indicators, combination of turnover and indicator-based systems, patent systems and agreed systems.

According to another approach suggested by Bergner et al. (2017), the following types of tax incentives for SMEs in the European Union are distinguished: expenditure-based tax incentives, which are granted as special depreciation schemes, investment allowances and tax credits (i.e. input-based incentives), and tax incentives that depend on the enterprise's operating results and are granted as special tax rates, tax exemptions and tax holiday (i.e. output-based incentives). Besides, tax incentives are classified into corporate-level incentives and shareholder-level incentives (e.g. general shareholder relief, venture capital incentives). When developing tax incentives for SMEs, additional restrictions can be set on their application with regard to a company's age, location, time period and the area of the taxpayer's activity.

Based on the analysis of tax incentives for micro and small enterprises implemented in the European Union, it can be concluded that only expenditure-based and shareholder-level tax incentives stimulate creation of new jobs and development of new products and technologies (Bergner et al. 2017).

Thus, tax incentives for innovative small business include research and development allowances within the standard taxation regime; however, no additional incentive mechanism for stimulating innovation within presumptive taxation has been developed so far.

Tax Incentives for Small Business in Russia

Presumptive Tax Systems

Tax incentives for small business in Russia are embodied only in the following presumptive tax regimes: simplified tax system (STS), uniform tax on the imputed income (UTII) and patent tax system. These tax regimes substitute for income taxes, property taxes and value-added tax. They have input limitations on the number of employees, turnover and scope of application. STS is based on gross income or gross profit. UTII and patent taxation system use a synthetically estimated amount of income (imputed income, patent fee), which is not related to the actual operating results and is calculated with the following indicators: number of employees, area of the business site, number of vehicles, etc. The size of the final taxable income and the indicators can vary considerably across Russia.

Presumptive tax regimes significantly reduce tax burden on small business in the Russian Federation, which is visualized in Table 1. However, the socio-economic contribution of small business to the development of the nation is insufficient.

For instance, in 2013–2015, the share of revenue from the presumptive tax regimes in the total tax revenues of the consolidated budget of the Russian Federation was only 3%. In 2015, the share of small business employees in the total number of employees was approximately 23%; the share of small enterprises in the total number of enterprises, 42%; and the share of innovative small businesses, 3% of the total number of small businesses (Source: compiled by the authors based on the reported data of the Russian Federation Federal State Statistics Service, http://www.gks.ru).

Incentives for Residents of Special Economic Zones of Technology and Innovation Type

Innovation activity is stimulated by means of special innovation tax incentives within the standard taxation regime (i.e. reduction of the tax base for income tax by deducting research and development expenditure, bonus depreciation, VAT relief on inventions and industrial samples, exemption from property tax on objects with high energy efficiency, investment tax credit, etc.)

Moreover, innovation is stimulated through integrated provision of tax relief to residents of special economic zones of technology and innovation type. These incentives include VAT relief, corporate income tax relief (i.e. the federal part of

Table 1 Tax burden in the Russian economy depending on types of economic activity, %

Type of activity	All businesses			Small businesses		
	2012	2013	2014	2012	2013	2014
Agriculture, hunting and forestry	2.19	2.07	2.69	2.95	2.85	2.56
Fishing, fish farming	9.42	8.12	8.46	5.95	5.71	6.96
Mining	53.86	55.56	59.69	31.44	57.38	158.07
Manufacturing facilities	25.02	24.88	23.95	1.60	1.62	1.58
Production and distribution of electricity, gas and water	15.16	16.78	17.75	2.04	1.85	1.75
Construction	14.92	14.69	15.31	1.18	1.22	1.29
Wholesale and retail trade; repair of motor vehicles, household goods and personal use items	13.37	11.59	12.64	1.25	1.25	1.25
Hotels, restaurants, catering	12.70	12.69	12.36	3.93	4.24	4.15
Transport and communications	16.94	13.85	14.69	2.98	2.62	2.58
Real estate, renting and service provisioning	16.43	16.34	17.05	5.56	5.89	5.87
Education	13.46	13.87	14.91	31.56	32.47	31.04
Health care and social services	8.77	8.80	8.64	4.55	4.80	4.45
Other community, social and personal services	16.61	16.86	16.47	7.16	7.16	7.20
Average tax burden	20.67	19.90	20.64	2.29	2.44	2.87

Source: The table is compiled by the authors based on the reported data of the Russian Federal Tax Service, Form 1-NOM, and the Federal State Statistics Service, GDP section and statistical compilation "Small and Medium Business in Russia", http://www.gks.ru/

the tax rate is 0%; the regional part is reduced), exemption from corporate property tax, transport tax and land tax for a period of 5–10 years and reduced rates of insurance payments to non-budgetary social funds.

A Presumptive Model for Small Business Taxation Targeted at Stimulating Innovation Activity

There is an obvious need to enhance the socio-economic impact of small business and its innovation activity in the Russian Federation. Under these circumstances, presumptive tax regimes remain the primary tax instruments for incentivizing small business in our country. Therefore, we propose a relevant model of implementing tax incentives.

The equation for estimation of patent cost (imputed income) can be presented as follows (Eq. 1):

$$PC = F(\bar{\mathfrak{f}}_1, \bar{\mathfrak{f}}_2) \tag{1}$$

where *PC* is patent cost (imputed input); $\bar{f}_1$ stands for a group of factors that reveal the scale of business; and $\bar{f}_2$ is a group of factors that characterize the social and economic value of business or a particular innovation and investment project.

Assessment of Scale of Business

Assessment of scale of business is based on an analysis of reported data for existing enterprises or on the basis of business plan data for new enterprises.

Patent cost (imputed income) is to be directly proportional to the scale of business and inversely proportional to the socio-economic and innovation impact of the enterprise. The analytical equation used to calculate patent cost can be presented as Eq. 2:

$$PC = \left[\frac{V_c}{50}^* \frac{1}{I_0}\right] \tag{2}$$

where *PC* is patent cost (imputed input); V_c represents the scale of business in ruble; and I_0 stands for an integrated criterion of the socio-economic and innovation impact of business. The range of values of the integral criterion varies from the minimum value, which is close to 0.1, to 1.

The situation, where the value of the integrated criterion of the socio-economic and innovation impact is equal to 1, is best for business. Under this condition, the amount of patent fee will be 1/50 of the sales volume. Conversely, for the least efficient business, the patent cost will be 1/5 of the sales (20%).

Evaluation of the Socio-economic Impact of Business or an Innovation and Investment Project

For the purpose of evaluating the integrated criterion of the socio-economic and innovation impact of an enterprise, or an innovation and investment project, we propose to calculate I_0 as the average of the following components (Eq. 3):

$$I_0 = \frac{(I_1 + I_2 + I_3)}{3} \tag{3}$$

where I_1 is the number of jobs created by a business (project), in relation to the best value of all the proposed projects. I_1 is calculated by means of Eq. 4:

$$I_1 = \frac{I_1(real)}{I_1(best)} \quad (4)$$

where $I_1(real)$ is the number of jobs created within the enterprise, $I_1(best)$ means the best value of the indicator of all the proposed projects and I_2 is used for budget revenues per one job in relation to the best value of all the proposed projects and calculated as (Eq. 5):

$$I_2 = \frac{I_2\left(\frac{BR}{JN}\right)}{I_2\left(\frac{BR}{JN}best\right)} \quad (5)$$

where *BR* is budget revenues, i.e. revenues from an enterprise to budgets of all levels; *JN* stands for job number, i.e. the absolute number of created jobs; and *BR/JN(best)* represents the best of all proposed values of the indicator.

Evaluation of the degree of business (project) innovativeness (I_3) can be performed on the basis of determining a complex (integrated) criterion of innovativeness (Eq. 6). The complex (integrated) criterion of the innovativeness of a small enterprise's development and operation includes expert fractional assessment of the general innovativeness criterion according to its resource intensiveness and ten local indicators that are averaged in a ratio of 2/3 to 1/3. It should be taken into consideration that reduction in significance of the resource intensiveness of the economy should be 2/3:

$$I_3 = CCI_e = \frac{2}{3}^* EID_e + \frac{1}{3}^* \sum_{i=1}^{10} K_i{}^* \frac{1}{10} \quad (6)$$

where CCI_e is the complex (integrated) criterion of innovativeness of business's (enterprise) development and operation, EID_e represents the degree of innovativeness of business (enterprise) according to the resource intensiveness and is obtained by means of Eq. 8 and K_i stands for the indicator of enterprise innovativeness (Eq. 7):

$$K_i = \frac{p_i}{p_{i(best)}} \quad (7)$$

where p_i is the value of the enterprise's local indicator that reveals innovative activity of business. $p_{i(best)}$ represents the best value of the indicator across enterprises or projects proposed for implementation:

$$EID_e = \frac{ri(T-1)}{ri(T)} \quad (8)$$

where $ri(T\text{-}1)$ is resource intensiveness per unit of added value in the base period and $ri(T)$ is resource intensiveness per unit of added value in the analysed period.

The local indicators that are used to evaluate degree of innovativeness comprise the following:

1. Amounts of market-promising innovative products according to the degree of novelty (new products) in the total volume of production
2. Share of promising innovative products according to the degree of novelty (improved products) in the total production volume
3. Preparation of patent applications
4. Obtaining protection documents on applications for inventions
5. Obtaining protection documents on applications for discoveries
6. Total science and innovation costs
7. Internal costs of research and development
8. Personnel engaged in research and development
9. Ratio of the degree of commercialization of research and development to the total amount of research and development
10. Share of products sold on the world market

The presented method can also be used in situations, where enterprises themselves rather than specific innovation and investment projects are selected for comparison analysis. However, in this case, with regard to companies that submit their data for a particular session of expert committee on the cost of patents, it is required to use the best value of enterprises' performance as the base for calculating relative values (denominators to calculate I_1 and I_2).

Thus, the proposed model for determining patent cost is practical and illustrative and makes it possible to ensure greater fairness in taxation of small business as well as efficient and targeted tax regulation in this sector because special feature of this model is that the degree of the tax burden on small business is established depending on its socio-economic contribution to the national economy and its degree of innovativeness.

Conclusion

It is obvious that the modern practice of taxation of small business requires elaboration and introduction of a new mechanism that will establish correlation between the degree of tax burden and business performance of innovative small business entities. This will ensure goal-oriented tax incentives for innovative small business and increase the socio-economic and innovative effect of their operations.

The model we have developed is a contribution to solving the stated problem because implementation of the model can enable us to harmonize the aspects of equity and efficiency in taxation. This model can also be used in European countries.

Acknowledgements This study has been conducted with the financial support of the Global Competitiveness Enhancement Program 2013–2020 of Tomsk State University.

References

Bergner S, Bräutigam R, Evers MT et al (2017) The use of SME tax incentives in the European Union. Discussion paper number 17-006. SSRN Electron J. https://doi.org/10.2139/ssrn.2910339

Blažić H (2012) Preferential corporate income tax treatment for SMEs: an international comparison. Available via SSRN. https://ssrn.com/abstract=2334770. Accessed 1 Jan 2017

Busom I (2012) Tax incentives or subsidies for R&D? Working paper number 2012–056. SSRN Electron J. https://doi.org/10.2139/ssrn.2330222

Engelschalk M (2007) Designing a tax system for micro and small businesses: guide for practitioners. Working paper number 42435. Available via World Bank. http://documents.worldbank.org/curated/en/980291468158071984/Designing-a-tax-system-for-micro-and-small-businesses-guide-for-practitioners. Accessed 12 Jan 2017

Engelschalk M, Loeprick J (2015) MSME taxation in transition economies: country experience on the costs and benefits of introducing special tax regimes. Policy research working paper number 7449. Available via World Bank. https://ssrn.com/abstract=2676418. Accessed 1 Jan 2017

European Commission (2014) A study on R&D tax incentives. Final report working paper number 52–2014. https://doi.org/10.2778/447538

Gale WG, Brown S (2013) Small business, innovation, and tax policy: a review. SSRN Electron J. https://doi.org/10.2139/ssrn.2467620

Intarakumnerd P, Goto A (2016) Technology and innovation policies for small and medium-sized enterprises in East Asia. Working paper number 578. Available via SSRN. https://ssrn.com/abstract=2812432 Accessed 10 Jan 2017

Logue KD, Vettori GG (2010) Narrowing the tax gap through presumptive taxation. Law and economics working papers number 8. Available via University of Michigan Law School. http://repository.law.umich.edu/law_econ_current/art8. Accessed 10 Jan 2017

OECD (2015) Taxation of SMEs in OECD and G20 countries. Organization for Economic Co-operation and Development. OECD Publishing, Paris. https://doi.org/10.1787/9789264243507-en

Yitzhaki S (2007) Cost benefit analysis of presumptive taxation. SSRN Electron J. https://doi.org/10.2139/ssrn.979921

Relationships Between World Stock Market Indices: Evidence from Economic Networks

Vojtěch Fučík

Abstract The main objective of this paper is to analyse the relationships between world stock market indices. Classical minimum spanning tree approach is used, supported by edge stability analysis via bootstrap technique. Centrality measures analysis is applied for finding hubs in the network. Stock market indices are found to cluster according to the geographical continent they belong to. Hang Seng Index and CAC 40 are argued to be the most influential and important indices in the world. Evidence of large intra-continental and lower intercontinental stock market integration is observed.

Keywords Minimum spanning tree • Clustering • Stock market indices

Introduction

The study of topological properties of complex systems such as economic networks has become very popular. This growing interest may be observed not only in economics and finance but also in natural sciences or medicine.

Our main aim in this paper is to investigate the similarities among world stock market indices. Each index is represented as a node in the network. Edge weights in this network are then connected to pairwise cross-correlations. This network, however, contains too much information. For this purpose, we need to apply an algorithm filtering the network. By filtering we mean the removal of the weakest links. As an algorithm for filtering the network, we utilize the minimum spanning tree (MST) approach. After construction of the MST, we determine stability of its links. In the end, our task is to determine which node is central in the MST network, or in other words, we are trying to answer the question which stock market index plays a role of a hub in the network.

V. Fučík (✉)
University of Economics, Prague, Department of Banking and Insurance, Nam. W. Churchilla 4, 130 67 Prague, Czech Republic
e-mail: Fucik.V@seznam.cz

D. Procházka (ed.), *The Impact of Globalization on International Finance and Accounting*, Springer Proceedings in Business and Economics,
https://doi.org/10.1007/978-3-319-68762-9_5

In this paper, we utilize the methodology provided by Mantegna (1999) for the construction of the MST. The MST construction is then accompanied by link stability analysis described in Tumminello et al. (2005) in more detail.

A milestone in the research of topological properties of stock markets is represented by an early work of Mantegna (1999), where he analyses a hierarchical structure of stocks traded on the US stock exchanges. Mantegna analyses portfolios of stocks used to compute S&P 500 and DJIA indices. He finds out that the investigated US stocks cluster according to the industry sector they belong to.

Bonanno et al. (2000) study the links between different world economies through the analysis of time series of the sets of stock market indices. Bonanno et al. (2001) find out that the pairwise cross-correlations between stock returns vary with the changing time horizon.

Although the vast majority of studied stock markets are American or British, there also exist papers focusing on different markets. For instance, Sandoval (2012) studies topological properties of Brazilian stock market, and Situngkir and Surya (2005) researched into the consequences caused by different lengths of the MSTs. Situngkir and Surya (2005) claim that the total length of the MST varies over time. They also find out that a higher length of the MST indicates stock market stabilization after previous monetary crisis.

Tabak et al. (2010) are engaged in the investigation of topological properties of commodities markets. They find out that the commodities form clusters according to the sector they belong to. Methodology similar to the one used in Mantegna (1999) is also often applied to the study of volatility of stock returns, e.g. Micciche et al. (2003).

The paper is structured as follows. In Data and Methodology we present a brief review of methodology utilized in the paper. Data and Methodology also provides data description and subsequent data transformations and statistical tests. We provide the results of our analysis in Results and Discussion. Finally Conclusion concludes the paper.

Data and Methodology

We analyse the price evolutions of 21 most important global stock market indices. Analysed indices named with their tick symbols are presented in Table 1. All data were downloaded from Yahoo Finance.

Our data span the period from January 2007 to February 2017, altogether 2405 daily observations.

Let us denote $P_i(t)$ the adjusted closing price of the i-th index at time t, $t = 1, \ldots, T$, where T corresponds to the last observed time period. We are able to express logarithmic daily returns as follows:

Table 1 Analysed world stock market indices

Europe	USA	Americas	Asia/Pacific
ATX	DJI	MERV	AORD
BFX	IXIC	BVSP	SSEC
FCHI	GSPC	MXX	HSI
GDAXI	GSPTSE		BSESN
SSMI			JKSE
			KLSE
			N225
			KS11
			TWII

Source: Yahoo Finance

$$r_i(t) \equiv \frac{P_i(t) - P_i(t-1)}{P_i(t-1)}, \quad t = 2, 3, \ldots, T. \tag{1}$$

Since for our subsequent analysis we need to work with stationary data, we cannot use highly nonstationary adjusted closing prices but rather logarithmic returns defined in Eq. 1 as is common in scientific literature.

The similarities in a group of stock market indices are standardly expressed using pairwise cross-correlations. The pairwise cross-correlation coefficient ρ_{ij} for a pair of indices i and j with logarithmic returns $r_i(t)$ and $r_j(t)$, respectively, $t = 2, \ldots, T$, can be calculated as follows:

$$\rho_{ij} \equiv \frac{\langle r_i(t) r_j(t)\rangle - \langle r_i(t)\rangle\langle r_j(t)\rangle}{\sqrt{\left\langle r_i^2(t) - \langle r_i(t)\rangle^2\right\rangle\left\langle r_j^2(t) - \langle r_j(t)\rangle^2\right\rangle}} \tag{2}$$

where symbol $\langle\cdot\rangle$ stands for the average over the studied period T. The correlation coefficients range between -1 (perfect anti-correlation) and 1 (perfect correlation). When $\rho_{ij} = 0$, then a pair of indices is uncorrelated. Since we assume n stock market indices, we finally obtain a square correlation matrix $\mathbf{C} = (\rho_{ij})_{i,j=1,\ldots,n}$ of size n.

Using a nonlinear transformation proposed by Mantegna (1999), cross-correlation coefficients are then transformed into the distance coefficients d_{ij} as follows:

$$d_{ij} = \sqrt{2(1 - \rho_{ij})} \tag{3}$$

The distance coefficients range between 0 (perfect correlation) and 2 (perfect anti-correlation). When $d_{ij} = \sqrt{2}$ then a pair of indices (i, j) is uncorrelated. Finally we may arrive at a square symmetric distance matrix $\mathbf{D} = (d_{ij})_{i,j=1,\ldots,n}$ with zeros on diagonal.

Now we are able to construct a graph $\mathrm{G} = (V, E)$, where V is a set of stock market indices and E is a set of edges between these vertices. The weights of the edges are already provided in the distance matrix **D**. The graph G, however, contains too much information for an easy interpretation. There are $\frac{n(n-1)}{2}$ unique edges between pairs of indices in G.

To address this problem, we utilize Kruskal's algorithm for finding the MST of G. The main idea of the MST procedure is that it filters the edges between pairs of indices such that only the most important ones prevail.

The algorithm proceeds as follows. First it finds an edge with a minimum weight and marks it. It then searches for edges with minimum weights among all the unmarked edges that do not produce a loop with the already marked edges. The algorithm stops when it succeeds in finding a spanning tree, i.e. when the set of marked edges contains $n-1$ elements. Kruskal's algorithm produces a MST which is not unique. A number k of different MST produced by the algorithm may exist, but the sum of weights of the edges in the MST is minimized and unique, or

$$\sum_{e \in MST_1} w(e) = \sum_{e \in MST_2} w(e) = \cdots = \sum_{e \in MST_k} w(e) \tag{4}$$

where $w(e): \quad E_i \mapsto [0, 2]$ is a weight function that assigns a weight (distance) to every edge e from the set of edges $E_i \subset E$ corresponding to the $MST_i, i = 1, 2, \ldots,$ k.

After the MST procedure is completed, we arrive at a connected graph that contains only $n-1$ unique edges between pairs of indices and does not contain any loop. Now we can carry out centrality measures analysis. The property of centrality of a particular node coincides with a size of influence this node has in the whole network.

We will assess node's centrality according to the following four criteria: (1) degree, (2) closeness, (3) betweenness and (4) eigenvector centrality. The proper definitions of the above-mentioned measures can be found in Sandoval (2012). For our purposes it, however, suffices to state very informal definitions. *Degree* of a node is the number of neighbours this node has in the network. The higher the degree, the more influence the particular node has in the network. *Closeness* of a node measures the average distance from it to all other nodes in the network. The higher the closeness, the more influence in the network the particular node has. *Betweenness* centrality answers the question whether it is necessary to involve a particular node in communication between any other two nodes, in other words whether the particular node is transitory between other pairs of nodes in the network. If it is, then the particular node is important. *Eigenvector* centrality boosts the strength of degree centrality by taking into account not just the number of neighbours but also their own influence in the network.

The simplicity of the MST methodology is redeemed by its serious drawback. Sometimes we cannot be sure whether a particular edge in the constructed MST is present because of its relevance for the network or only by coincidence. This edge stability problem can be analysed using bootstrap technique described in Tumminello et al. (2007).

In this method we first construct the original MST. Then we resample or bootstrap the original time series such that the length of the series is fixed. Some observations may be repeated, and some may not be present at all in the bootstrapped sample. Then, we construct the MST from the bootstrapped series, and we record the links. Such procedure is repeated up to 1000 times. The stability of a particular link in the original MST is then determined as a proportion of number of occurrences of a particular link in the bootstrapped MSTs and the number of bootstrap samples 1000.

Results and Discussion

In this section we present and comment on the results of the MST for the studied network of stock market indices. In Fig. 1 we illustrate the MST for stock market indices together with stability of the links.

We detected three main clusters of stock market indices:

1. Asia/Pacific
2. Europe
3. USA + Americas

Therefore, we may argue that the stock market indices do cluster according to the geographical location, which is the main finding of this paper. We also detected that a large cluster of Asia/Pacific can be further divided into two smaller subclusters. N225, AORD, TWII and KS11 are Japanese, Australian, Taiwanese and South Korean indices, respectively. We may also argue that this subcluster is composed of indices of more "western-style-oriented" countries, although the definition of "western-style" country is not very rigorous.

Regarding stability of the edges, there are several findings worth noting. First, the stabilities among stock market indices in all three clusters are very high, often as high as 100%. This again proves large interdependence between indices situated in similar geographical locations. Second, the stability of the transitory edges between these three main clusters, i.e. HSI – ATX and GDAXI – GSPC, is very poor. Thus we may argue that relations and similarity between indices from particular geographical areas/cluster are not that high. Based on this and above-mentioned findings, we may argue that the globalization or integration is very high on the local regional level (in terms of continents), but there exist further possibilities for enlarged stock market integration between individual continents (with the exception of USA + Americas). This might suggest a possibility for international diversification while investing in the stocks, i.e. the similarity between stock market indices and different clusters/regions has not reached the levels of similarity that are observable between indices in the particular clusters/regions.

In order to determine the most influential nodes in the network (MST), we utilized centrality measures described in Data and Methodology. The results are depicted in Table 2 in Appendix. Based on degree centrality, there is always one

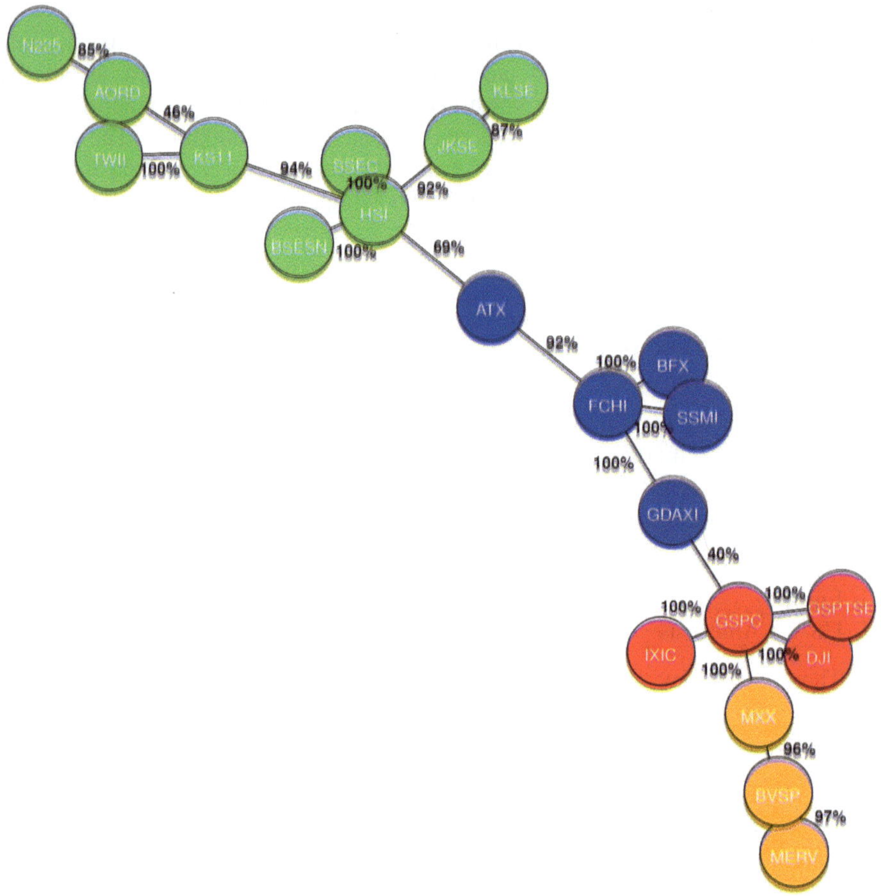

Fig. 1 MST of stock market indices network (Source: Author's computations)

central stock market index for every cluster (geographic area): for Asia/Pacific it is HSI (Hang Seng Index), for Europe it is FCHI (CAC 40), and for USA + Americas it is GSPC (S&P 500). We can also observe the relative importance of KS11 (KOSPI Composite Index) in the Asia/Pacific cluster which again relates to the possible existence of two main subclusters in the overall Asia/Pacific region.

Using betweenness centrality we can draw several conclusions. There are two most transitory indices in the network – FCHI and HSI which further proves the hypothesis about these two indices being the most important in the network. Relative importance of ATX (Austrian Traded Index), GDAXI (DAX 30) and GSPC is also obvious from Table 2. However, importance of KS11 as a means of communication between other indices was not supported by betweenness centrality. Therefore, we can think of KS11 only as a local centroid not the global one.

Finally eigenvector centrality further supports the local dominance of ATX in the Europe cluster (apart from FCHI). HSI can be thought of as an index with the largest number of the most influential neighbours in the network. The results of closeness centrality further indicate most dominant role of FCHI and HSI indices in the network.

To sum up the centrality measures analysis, we found that

1. Every cluster/region has its own hub: FCHI (Europe), HSI (Asia/Pacific) and GSPC (USA + Americas).
2. FCHI and HSI can be thought of as hubs for the entire network, i.e. these are the most influential indices in the network (world).
3. American indices (mainly GSPC) do not play such an overwhelming role as is usually believed (based on our analysis).
4. European indices (ATX, FCHI, GDAXI) are transitory indices, i.e. they are very open and needed in the communication between other global stock market indices.
5. Indices from Americas region are situated in the periphery of the network without much communication and influence of global importance.

Conclusion

We analysed the relationships between world stock market indices in the period of 2007–2017 using the MST approach. We managed to detect three large clusters of indices based on the geographical location of underlying indices. We proved the integration of stock markets on the level of continents but stated that there are possibilities for global stock market integration enlargement still present. This might suggest a possibility for international diversification when investing in stocks. The clustering into three large clusters may not be based solely on geographic location but also on culture and investment style in these locations. For the question of whether this is the case, however, our analysis cannot provide relevant answers.

We managed to detect large interdependence between US and Americas stock market indices, but we argued that the global importance of Americas indices is low.

Using the centrality measures analysis, we argued that every region/cluster has its own hub: HSI for Asia/Pacific, FCHI for Europe and GSPC for the USA. We also argued that based on our analysis the most important stock market indices in the global scale are HSI and FCHI.

The added value of this paper for the investment society is straightforward. Since we are able to describe both visually and quantitatively the hierarchical structure of the stock market indices network, we are also able to detect those indices situated in the periphery of this network. Following the results of Pozzi et al. (2013), we may thus claim that there can be built a well-diversified portfolio that effectively reduces the investment risk.

There exist many possibilities for further research. Mainly we need to mention the MST dynamics. It requires the observation of the changing MSTs with respect to different time windows. This possibility is motivated by our assumption that the MSTs would differ, if we analysed only precrisis period, crisis period or postcrisis period. This kind of research could suggest whether any particular index had set for different trajectory of closing price evolution owing to the postcrisis stock market consolidation.

Acknowledgements This article was supported by IGA of the Faculty of Finance and Accounting, VŠE, (Project No. IG102027, Pokročilé metody risk managementu s použitím umělé inteligence, 59/2017) and by the Czech Science Foundation (Project No. GA 17-02509S).

Appendix

Table 2 Centrality measures

Index	Degree	Closeness	Betweenness	Eigenvector
ATX	2	0.024	99	0.514
BFX	1	0.020	0	0.035
FCHI	4	0.024	117	0.172
GDAXI	2	0.023	91	0.037
SSMI	1	0.019	0	0.046
DJI	1	0.019	0	0.002
IXIC	1	0.018	0	0.002
GSPC	5	0.020	96	0.019
GSPTSE	1	0.016	0	0.006
MERV	1	0.011	0	0.001
BVSP	2	0.014	19	0.003
MXX	2	0.017	36	0.007
AORD	2	0.014	19	0.221
SSEC	1	0.015	0	0.462
HSI	5	0.022	117	1.000
BSESN	1	0.016	0	0.407
JKSE	2	0.017	19	0.490
KLSE	1	0.013	0	0.203
N225	1	0.012	0	0.083
KS11	3	0.018	53	0.505
TWII	1	0.014	0	0.176

Source: Author's computations

References

Bonanno G, Lillo F, Mantegna RN (2001) High-frequency cross-correlation in a set of stocks. Quant Financ 1:96–104. https://doi.org/10.1080/713665554

Bonanno G, Vandewalle N, Mantegna RN (2000) Taxonomy of stock market indices. Phys Rev E 62(6):7615–7618. https://doi.org/10.1103/PhysRevE.62.R7615.

Mantegna RN (1999) Hierarchical structure in financial markets. Eur Phys J B 11:193–197. https://doi.org/10.1007/s100510050929

Micciche S, Bonanno G, Lillo F, Mantegna RN (2003) Degree stability of a minimum spanning tree of price return and volatility. Phys A 324:66–73. https://doi.org/10.1016/S0378-4371(03)00002-5

Pozzi F, Matteo TD, Aste T (2013) Spread of risk across financial markets: better to invest in the peripheries. Sci Rep 3. https://doi.org/10.1038/srep01665

Sandoval LJ (2012) A map of the Brazilian stock market. Adv Complex Syst 15(5). https://doi.org/10.1142/S0219525912500427

Situngkir H, Surya Y (2005) On stock market dynamics through ultrametricity of minimum spanning tree. Tech Rep Surya Res Inter. https://dx.doi.org/10.2139/ssrn.768204.

Tabak B, Serra T, Cajueiro D (2010) Topological properties of commodities networks. Eur Phys J B 74(2):243–249. https://doi.org/10.1140/epjb/e2010-00079-4

Tumminello M, Aste T, Matteo TD, Mantegna RN (2005) A tool for filtering information in complex systems. Proc Natl Acad Sci U S A 102(30):10421–10426. https://doi.org/10.1073/pnas.0500298102

Tumminello M, Coronnello C, Lillo F, Micciche S, Mantegna RN (2007) Spanning trees and bootstrap reliability estimation in correlation based networks. Int J Bifurcation Chaos 17(7):2319–2329. https://doi.org/10.1142/S0218127407018415

The Financial Evaluation of Population Growth in Relation to Development Aid: China Versus India (Two Nation Brands' Stories)

Rostislav Mansfeld and Barbora Růžičková

Abstract For the past 40 years, the most dynamic economies in the world were China and India. From approx. 5% of US GDP level, China grows to 26% and India to 11% of current US levels. The ratio of foreign trade to GDP is similar for both countries as well as capital flows to GDP. So why did China outperform India twice in terms of GDP growth and why is India first now catching up?

This is of extreme relevance in relation to implementation of Sustainable Development Goals (SDGs) of Agenda 2030 in which the objective is to eradicate poverty and to enhance economic growth in developing countries. The reduction of poverty in shortest time was best mastered by China over the last 30 years; hence, to put developing countries on the same track is the beginning of the path of their development. A theoretical comparison analysis, backed by observations of China, India, Uganda, and Chad GDP as well as their population growths, indicates that population growth is the major negative enabler of GDP growth per capita of developing countries. Using our drafted methodology, we can assess if certain levels of development aid will be sufficient to overcome the negative GDP per capita pull driven by overpopulation and calculate how much development aid is needed to get countries on sustainable GDP per capita growth path. We ask ourselves, are current SDGs (especially SDG 1, 2, and 8) in developing countries really financially achievable?

Keywords Growth • Developing countries • Economic development • Development policy • Population

---

R. Mansfeld (✉)
IP100040, University of Economics in Prague, Faculty of Finance and Accounting, Praha 3, Czech Republic
e-mail: rostislav.mansfeld@email.cz

B. Růžičková
University of Economics in Prague, Faculty of International Relations, Praha 3, Czech Republic
e-mail: bruzick@gmail.com

D. Procházka (ed.), *The Impact of Globalization on International Finance and Accounting*, Springer Proceedings in Business and Economics,
https://doi.org/10.1007/978-3-319-68762-9_6

Introduction

The major challenge in implementation of United Nation Agenda 2030 is the fact that there seems to be very little relating to the population growth in developing countries, which clearly influences the financial amounts we need for sustainable development. We even believe it is the second most deciding factor, after macroeconomic and political factors (e.g., North Korea vs. South Korea, which both have no population growth).

On China and India comparison, we will investigate the influence on GDP caused by the reduction of population growth in China caused by one child policy.

The greatest goals of Agenda 2030 are SDG 1 – eradication of poverty - and SDG 2, eliminate hunger (Sachs 2015). Hence the focus is mainly on the least developed countries (LDCs), which is majorly Africa, where population growth ranges between 3% and 4% p.a.

A theoretical comparison analysis, backed by data from the World Bank, International Monetary Fund, UN publications, and OECD statistics about China, India, Uganda, and Chad (especially GDP as well as their population growths), indicate that population growth is the major negative enabler of GDP growth per capita.

India's nominal GDP per capita in 1985 was $313 and China's $295 where India's year-on-year population growth was 2.2% and China's 1.4% and decreasing. Fifteen years later (which is the scope of Agenda 2030), India had GDP per capita of $463 and China of $941. Population growth in India was relatively stable at YoY of 2% throughout the 15 years where China has decreased to 0.8%.

Hence we can summarize that both bordering countries started with similar conditions with less than $1 per day per person but after 15 years of GDP growth over 5% p.a. India GDP per capita almost did not improve; in contrary China on the other hand doubled its GDP per capita per day to $2.

Financial Evaluation of Population Growth

Data and Source

We rely on World Bank database and International Monetary Fund for extracting GDP, GDP per capita, and population growth data as well as on OECD statistics.

Source relating to United Nation Agenda 2030: Sustainable development knowledge platform, custom processing.

Source relating to The Sustainable Development Goals: Global Policy Watch, 7th October 2016 Nr.13.

Population Growth Financial Impact

If an average consumption of one person in India was at, e.g., $400 pear year, then India lost $60 bn p.a. (150 m additional inhabitants on average * $400) on potential investment which is $900 bn wealth creation in 15 years (150 m * $400 * 15 years) in comparison to scenario if India population would not grow at all. Furthermore, if we assume that return on investment in India is at approx. 10% p.a.,[1] then the $60 bn annual investment would generate a return in the 15th year of approx. $191 bn (what would be a net GDP increase in that year), and the India's total wealth would increase by $2.1 tn (of which is $0.9 tn cumulative shift from consumption to return-generating asset creation and $1.2 tn cumulative reinvested returns from undertaken investments). Hence the total cumulated loss for India's wealth was at $2.3 tn or approx. $150 bn p.a. on average.

GDP would be even higher when Indian government and other economic subjects would increase debt levels and foreign direct investments accordingly to GDP grow as India would then consume or invest in the 15th year the additional, e.g., $0.2 tn, hence reaching a GDP of approx. $0.9 tn in the year 2000 (of which 0.5 tn reached GDP, 0.2 tn return on investment, and 0.2 tn higher debt and foreign investment).

The more the country is developed, the higher the debt levels to GDP. In our case we will work conservatively with the assumption that $1 of GDP increase driven by return from investment creates exactly $1 of higher debt or foreign direct investment. Hence in our calculations we very conservatively assume that total debt to GDP of India without population growth will always be below 100%. In comparison China's total debt by mid of 2014 was already at 282% of GDP.

The population annual growth of 2% over 15 years has been equal to approx. 200% loss on potential nominal GDP as shown in Fig. 1.

Two reasons why in the rebased Fig. 1 China (which at that time had 1% population growth p.a.) still outgrows India are:

1. The abovementioned conservative assumption of total debt to GDP never reaching 100%.
2. Wealth destruction by population growth. The additionally net newborn child must obtain the total wealth per capita of the country where it was born to avoid any decrease of wealth per capita or shift from investment into consumption to provide for such a wealth what would then later result into lower GDP per capita driven by lower investment.

[1]The average annualized return of the S&P 500 Index was about 10.8% from 1973 to 2015. 20 Years of Stock Market Returns, by Calendar Year (The balance 2017).

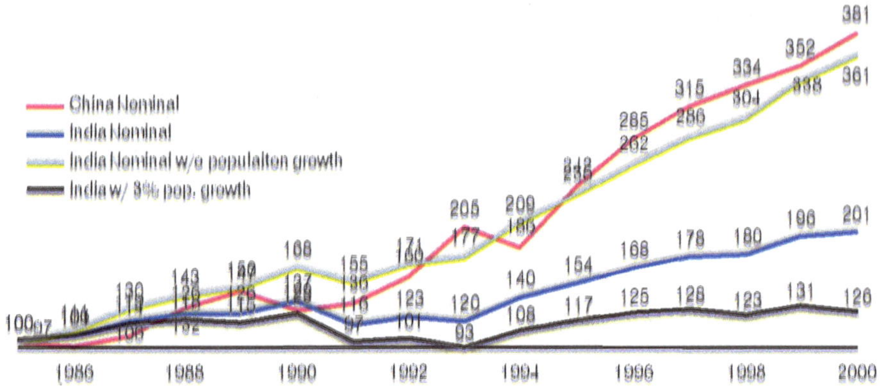

Fig. 1 GDP in percent rebased to 1985 values (Source: World Bank database and authorial computation and Debt and not much deleveraging. McKinsey [online] (2017). Note: Y axes are percentages and X axes are years)

Even when abstracting from the above points 1 and 2 if India would have reduced the annual population growth to pure replacements, then its GDP per capita in 2000 would have been at approx. \$1103 hence well above China's \$941 (China's population during these 15 years was in absolute terms still increasing by more than 1% p.a.).

We can break down the potential GDP per capita of \$1103 to:

- \$463 which is the actual GDP in 2000 per capita in India (India nominal GDP in 2000 was \$476 bn and population was 1 bn)
- \$164 if the population would stay on the level of 1985 (calculated by dividing the nominal GDP in 2000 by population of 1985 which is \$627 minus GDP per capita in 2000 of \$463) and the saved annual consumption of \$60 bn on the new born which would not be reinvested
- \$476 the return on investment and higher debt that was not spent on consumption of the net newborn net Indians instead. In other words, what the consumption could have returned if it was effectively invested (Fig. 2)

If a developing country without effectively used human resources reduces population growth to replacement level and reinvests the consumption, which it would otherwise be forced to spend on the newborn population, it can without any significant international financial aid increase its GDP per capita during 15 years by approx. Four times (to \$1.1 k from \$0.3 k) than with an annual population growth of 2%.

This was shown on the above example of India between the years of 1985 and 2000. This conclusion is realistic as China which was growing annually its population by 0.5% between 2000 and 2015 increased its GDP per capita approx. Three times from \$2939 to \$9328.

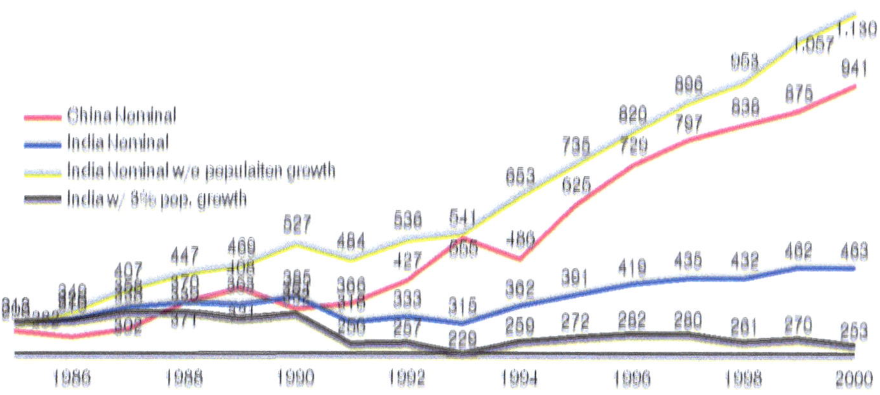

Fig. 2 GDP per Capita in USD between 1985 and 2000 (Source: World Bank database and authorial computation. Note: Y axes are USD and X axes are years)

Population Growth Financial Cost for African Countries in Scope of Agenda 2030

The annual population growth of the developing countries in focus of Agenda 2030 (particularly in Africa, e.g., Nigeria, Congo, DR of Congo, etc.) is at least 2.8% p.a.,[2] (with peaks up to 4% YoY) growth, which is 50% above India's population growth rate. To develop a model for Africa, let us on the example of India simulate a population growth of 3% from 1985 to 2000.

When using the same logic as for the calculation of lower population growth in section "Population Growth Financial Impact", GDP loss in the 15th year would be at $178 bn, the $178 bn is the total approx. Loss on revenue from the not executed investment over 15 years and the loss possibility of debt increase driven by the higher consumption of 70 million additional inhabitants under the assumption of $400 p.a. consumption per capita. Hence, the GDP of India would have to be 40% lower as India had in the year of 2000 GDP of $477 bn when growing its population annually by 2%. This implicates that if a country grows its population annually by 3% or more, it decreases its GDP per capita; hence, the next-generation available nominal consumption is lower than the one of their parents as shown in the charts.

This has adverse effects, e.g., the countries' debt to GDP ratio is increasing; hence, these countries are likely to declare state bankruptcies and have hyperinflation as, e.g., Zimbabwe. As the average GDP decreases hence the average consumption in nominal USD. (This ensures that the GDP mathematically does not turn negative.)

Furthermore as the country is forced to consume more and to invest less, the wealth creation stagnates at best. If we assume amortization of the infrastructure and other assets, the country wealth is accordingly decreasing.

---

[2]Country Comparison (2014).

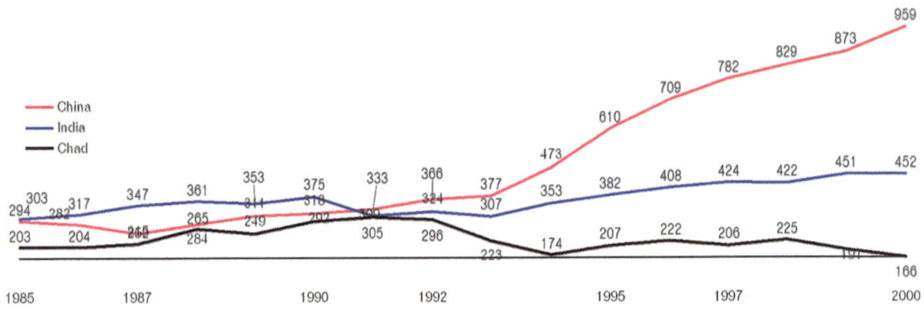

Fig. 3 Chad GDP per capita between the years of 1985 and 2000 (with population growth at 3%) compared with China (1%) and India (2%) (Source: World Bank database and authorial computation. Note: Y axes are USD and X axes are years)

Limited resources on excessive population growth lead to decreasing amount of consumption per capita; hence if the country grows its population over 2% annually, the consumption per capita is decreasing to the level that leads to famine, epidemics (driven by not sufficient funds for health care), migration (due to lack of infrastructure and resources to support the net population additions, this effect is sometimes called an "export of poverty"), and resulting wars (where the countries defend themselves from migrants or fight over the scarce resources). All these effects then accordingly result into lower life expectancy; hence, the excessive population growth rate regulates itself into sustainable levels through higher death rates.

This is visible on most of countries as, e.g., Uganda or Chad that have population growth at approximately 3%, which nominal GDP per capita has not changed during the period in scope (from 1985 to 2000).

The simulated India (with 3% p.a. population growth) as well as in Fig. 3 Chad has per capita nominal GDP decreasing hence the real GDP per capita is significantly worsening (with assumed inflationary USD environment, e.g., just 2% inflation over 15 years decreases real purchasing value from $100 to $63). Growing population must then accordingly decrease its consumption in real terms by approx. 50% in just 15 years.

Evaluation of the Development Aid Needed for African Countries

To durably improve living conditions in Africa we need to compensate for 3% annual population growth that is causing major shift from potential investment to consumption. This consumed amounts we need to invest into the African countries from our own resources as development aid.

In our exercises we have so far ignored the fact that increased population growth effects are not only limited to 15 years but go well beyond as once the additional population turn 16 or 18, they will need on top of their consumption new infrastructure as well as new jobs.

Hence, if we only subsidize the consumption, we improve the living conditions for the parents and their net "replacements" (= core population), but we do not do anything for the net population additions. To durably improve the standing of the whole population, we need to give the new additions the wealth of their parents on top of subsidizing their consumption.

Let us then make an assumption that the wealth per capita in India was at $5000 in the years between 1985 and 2000. To keep the wealth per capita constant, we need to give each of the net new additionally born Indian an infrastructure and housing investment of $5000. The population of India, if assuming 3% annual net population growth, would grow from 757 m to 1182 m hence by 423 m. We need to invest $2115 bn (423 m net additions * $5000) = $2115 bn/15 years = $141 bn per year in our 15-year cycle. As calculated in previous chapters, the annual loss of potential investment was $88 bn, based on assumption that one additional child costs $400 p.a. to feed; hence, on average over 15 years simulated 3% population growth would generate 220 million additional new inhabitants in every single year, (150 m + 70 m) * $400 p.a. = $88 bn p.a.)

To sum it up, if India was growing its population by 3% p.a. to fully compensate for these new population additions, we would need to provide India with a development aid between 1985 and 2000 of $229 bn p.a. (= $141 bn + $88 bn), which is 48% of India GDP in 2000 (= $477 bn when growing a population by just 2%) and 97% of India GDP in 1985 (= 237 bn). Calculated GDP in 2000 when assuming 3% p.a. population growth in India is just $299 bn; hence, the development aid would need to be at approx. 76% of GDP.

The needed development aid ratio to GDP between 76% and 97% in order to elevate 3% p.a. population-growing country to China development path seems precise as growing population by 3% or more keeps the GDP constant as shown in previous charts. Figures are based on the conservative assumption without accounting for the wealth destruction effect as described earlier.

Africa has currently annual population growth at 2.8%; hence, it will increase from current 1.2 bn inhabitants to 2 bn in just next 15 years.

According to our calculations, to bring Africa to a sustainable development path, which it would take without any population growth, we would need to annually transfer in form of development aid somewhere between 48% and 97% of its current GDP of $2.39tn. That is at least $1.14tn p.a. but more realistically approx. $1.82tn p.a. Currently it cannot be achieved only from the governments budgets of which there is only approx. $0.135tn available (Net ODA 2016).

Conclusion

A theoretical comparison analysis indicates that population growth is the major negative enabler of GDP growth per capita.

If a developing country with not effectively used human resources reduces population growth to replacement level and reinvests the consumption, which it would otherwise be forced to spend on the new born population, it can without any significant international help increase its GDP per capita during 15 years by approx. four times.

On the other hand 3% p.a. or more growing population must then accordingly decrease its consumption in real terms by approx. 50% in just 15-year- period.

The financial cost of compensation in terms of transfers needed to offset the 3% p.a. population growth is between 48% and 97% of the respective country GDP. Just for Africa it would be at least $1.14tn p.a. of which only $0.135tn is available.

Hence the current Agenda 2030 of the United Nations should primary concentrate on measures decreasing the population growth, e.g., SDG 5 – gender equality - and SDG 4, education. The consequences of not doing so will be failed states as, e.g., Zimbabwe and resulting famine, migration, and wars.

Currently the UN Agenda 2030 barely mentions the population growth directly in its sustainable development goals. Many of its goals and respective budgets relating to developed world are goals that just increase the already high standard of wellbeing and would be demanded by local populations anyway, e.g., better health in Czech Republic.

In this paper we try to concentrate on countries where achieving SDG goals as gender equality or better education, which should result in lower population growth, will determine borderlines between peace and war hence are decisive for the future survival of the majority of the inhabitants of the developing countries.

Acknowledgments This contribution resulted from the IGA Nation Project Branding and care of the reputation of the state through new forms of diplomacy, C. F2/77/2017.

References

Country Comparison > Population growth rate > TOP 50. Index Mundi [online] (2014) [Cit. 2017-07-28]. Available from: http://www.indexmundi.com/g/r.aspx?t=50&v=24&l=en

Debt and not much deleveraging. McKinsey [online] (2017) [Cit. 2017–07-28]. Available from: www.mckinsey.com/global-themes/employment-and../debt-and-not-much-deleveraging

Global Policy Watch [online] (2016) [Cit. 2017-07-28]. Available from: https://www.globalpolicywatch.org/blog/2016/10/

Net ODA (2016) OECD Data [online]. OECD, Paris [Cit. 2017-07-21]. Available from: https://data.oecd.org/oda/net-oda.htm

Sachs J (2015) The age of sustainable development. Columbia University Press, New York. ISBN 978-0-231-17314-8

The balance [online] (2017) [Cit. 2017-07-28]. Available from: https://www.thebalance.com/stock-market-returns-by-year-2388543

The Relationship Between Government Expenditure on Education and Economic Growth: The Case of France

Nesrin Ozatac, Nigar Taspinar, Oubayda El Rifai, and Baris Eren

Abstract The aim of this study is to investigate the long-run equilibrium relationship between economic growth, capital, labor, and government expenditure on education between the years of 1970 and 2012 for the case of France. Johansen co-integration test results suggest the existence of the long-run equilibrium relationship between variables. Existence of the co-integration relationship indicates that capital, labor, and government expenditure on education are long-run determinants of GDP for the case of France. Granger causality test results suggest that there is a bidirectional long-run causality between GDP and gross capital formation. In addition, there are long-run unidirectional causalities which run from labor and expenditure on education to GDP and from labor and expenditure to capital. Results of the study suggest the existence of education-induced economic growth for the case of France.

Keywords Economic growth • Education • Co-integration

Introduction

Education is one of the most important factors of economic growth, and the relationship between education and economic growth has been an important area of investigation in economics. Education affects the overall economic system at macrolevels such as aggregate production and GDP. Endogenous growth theory and human capital theory suggested that education has a substantial impact on the economic growth at the micro- and macrolevel, respectively. The positive effect of education on economic growth is mostly attached with the production of skillful labor and development of human capital by education, training, and skills.

N. Ozatac • N. Taspinar (✉) • O. El Rifai • B. Eren
Eastern Mediterranean University, Department of Banking and Finance, Famagusta, North Cyprus via Mersin 10, Turkey
e-mail: nesrin.ozatac@emu.edu.tr; nigar.taspinar@emu.edu.tr; oubayda_rifai@yahoo.com; baris.eren@emu.edu.tr

D. Procházka (ed.), *The Impact of Globalization on International Finance and Accounting*, Springer Proceedings in Business and Economics,
https://doi.org/10.1007/978-3-319-68762-9_7

The aim of this paper is to investigate the long-run relationship between economic growth and government expenditure in France. There are various factors that help to put a country's economy at the top for most rapidly growing economy in the world. Government expenditure on education has historically imposed itself as one of these factors in many countries, especially after the period that followed the end of the Second World War, by raising the human development in the countries, which is considered one of the most profitable investments in the long term. This kind of spending can be defined as the amount of money that should be provided for building schools and universities with the supplying of technical and physical tools and laboratories, in addition to teachers' salaries and the support of development of the scientific research, which has allocated the largest amount of education spending in the developed countries. Therefore, the education is a costly project that needs continuous financial resources, and this is because of the increasing demand on education, which is a right for every single individual in the society.

France had the world's 12th highest research and development spending with almost 2.24% of the gross domestic product. In addition, the government spent 3.42% of the gross domestic product on education in 1970, while this number raised to 5.53% in 2012. Therefore, these numbers clarify how much the French government is interested in elevating the quality of education among the last 40 years where they specialized a bigger number for education spending compared with other spending like the military, even though France has witnessed many terrorist attacks during the last years.

There are theoretical framework of the economic growth and its relationship with education (Mankiw et al. 1992; Barro and Sala-i-Martin 1995; Romer 1990; Barro 1991, 2002; Barro and Lee 2013; Krueger and Lindahl 2001; Benhabib and Spiegel 1994). Regarding with the listed literature, the positive relationship between more education and economic growth is indicated that education influences economic growth significantly.

In the last decade, researches have used different methods. In order to examine the impact of education on the economic development, in recent studies Cobb Douglas pattern is used by many researchers (Lin 2004; Aziz et al. 2008; Loening 2002; Odit et al. 2010). Lin (2004) analyzed Taiwan's economic development from the year 1965 through 2000 indicating that higher education left a favorable and important impact on the growth of the economy in Taiwan. The output of higher education on the Pakistani economic development was also examined by Aziz et al. (2008) using the Cobb Douglas pattern in the period between 1972 and 2008, where the findings showed that the higher education's gains affected the development of the Pakistani economy positively. Similar findings were found by Loening (2002) using the same pattern, where his study concluded that a work force that is preferable in proficiency and education is likely to affect the economic development favorably and significantly. Human resources are introduced as the reason behind the progress of the high level of returns by Odit et al. (2010). Moreover, it was proved that work force is able to enhance productivity.

The generality of experimental researches such as Asteriou and Agiomirgianakis (2001), Changzheng and Jin (2009), and Musila and Belassi (2004) used Johansen co-integration test. Asteriou and Agiomirgianakis (2001) examined the connection between the work force and the economic growth in Greece and discovered that co-integrating relationship between education and the GDP per individual. Changzheng and Jin (2010) followed the same analysis for the period between 1978 and 2004 for China, and the findings revealed a favorable connection between the educational equivalence and the fineness of the economic development. The research made by Musila and Belassi (2004) on Uganda between the years of 1965 and 1999 indicates the relation between the country's government education expenditure per laborer and the economic development. By using the error correction model, it was revealed that government spending on education has an essential role in affecting the economic development in the developing countries and predominately in Uganda. On the other hand, Shaari (2014) investigated the connection between the levels of education and economic growth in Malaysia for the period of 1982–2011. He found out that there is no indication that education affected the economic growth. Furthermore, Jaoul (2004) studied the relationship between higher education and gross domestic product in both France and Germany after the Second World War, from 1899 to 1937. He found out that the higher education had an impact on GDP in the case of France, while it did not appear as a reason for Germany. Another study by Babalola (2011) for Nigeria for the period of 1977–2008 indicated a unidirectional causality from economic growth to education. Dănăcică et al. (2010) and Mariana (2015) in which both employed vector autoregression (VAR) model and Granger causality test aimed to examine the occasional connection among the higher education and the economic development in the period between 1980–2008 and 1980–2013, respectively, for the case of Romania. The findings of this researches reached experimental proof of the long-term relation among the GDP per individual and the education through the period, where education has positively affected the economic growth. Hussin et al. (2012) confirmed that in Malaysia, for the period between 1970 and 2010, the education has a long-run relationship on gross domestic product (GDP).

Most of the studies with different regions and different methodology applied showed that there is a positive long-run connection between the education spending and economic growth and in most cases where there is a causal run from education to economic growth.

In this study, we will investigate the long-run equilibrium relationship between economic growth, capital, labor, and government expenditure on education between the years of 1970 and 2012 for the case of France.

Data and Methodology

The data used in this study are annual figures that cover the period 1970–2012. Variables used in this study are real gross domestic product (GDP), gross capital formation (K), labor force (L), and government expenditure on education. The data for GDP, K, and ED are collected from the World Bank (2016), while L is gathered from the OECD database (2016).

This study adopts the endogenous growth model which is suggested by Mankiw et al. (1992), which indicates the relationship between economic growth and education. The functional relationship based on the standard neoclassical growth model can be suggested as follows:

$$\mathrm{GDPt} = \mathrm{f}\ (\mathrm{Kt}, \mathrm{Lt}, \mathrm{ED}) \tag{1}$$

where GDP is a function of capital, labor, and government expenditure on education.

The variables in the model can be transferred into the logarithmic form in order to capture impacts of growth:

$$\ln\ \mathrm{GDP} = \beta_0 + \beta_1 \mathrm{lnK} + \beta_2 \mathrm{lnL} + \beta_3 \mathrm{lnED} + \varepsilon_t \tag{2}$$

where ln GDP, lnK, lnL, and lnED are the natural log of gross domestic product, capital, labor, and education expenditure, respectively. εt stands for the error term.

Unit Root Test

Zivot and Andrews (Z-A) (1992) unit root test under a structural break is employed in the study in order to determine the integration orders of the variables. Z-A (1992) suggests three different specifications in their estimations based on Perron (1990). Model (1) allows an exogenous break in the level form of the series; Model (2) allows an exogenous break in growth rates of the series; and Model (3) combines Models (1) and (2) together. Z-A (1992) unit root test suggests the null hypothesis if there is a unit root in the series.

Johansen Co-Integration Test

The long-run equilibrium relationship between variables is investigated by Johansen co-integration test. Johansen test can be applied when variables are integrated of the same order. Minimum one co-integrating vector is required in order to have long-run equilibrium relationship between variables. Johansen test takes its initial point in the vector autoregression (VAR) of order *p* given by:

$$y_t = \mu + A_1 y_{t-1} + \ldots + A_p y_{t-p} + e_t \text{ for } \mathrm{t} = 1, \ldots, \mathrm{T} \tag{3}$$

where y_t, $y_{t-1}, \ldots, y_{t-p}$ are vectors of level and lagged values of *P* variables, respectively, which are *I(1)* in the model; $A_1, \ldots, A_p$ are coefficient matrices with *(PXP)* dimensions; μ is an intercept vector; and ε_t is a vector of random errors. Johansen (1988) and Johansen and Juselius (1990) suggest that trace statistics are obtained by using the eigenvalues. The trace statistic (λ_{trace}) could be estimated by the formula below:

$$\lambda_{trace} = -T\sum Ln(1-\lambda_i), i = r+1, \ldots, n-1 \quad (4)$$

The null hypotheses are given as follows:

H_0: v = 0 H_1: v ≥ 1
H_0: v ≤ 1 H_1: v ≥ 2
H_0: v ≤ 2 H_1: v ≥ 3

Estimation of Long-Run Coefficients

After revealing a possible co-integration relationship between variables, DOLS methodology can be applied in order to estimate the long-run coefficients of the variables. DOLS method can be applied irrespective of the order of integration of the regressors, but regressand in the conducted model should be integrated of order one, I(1). Esteve and Requena (2006) indicate that the DOLS method provides stronger and more consistent estimations in the presence of internality and auto-correlation problems. The DOLS model can be estimated as follows:

$$\ln GDP_t = \alpha_1 + \alpha_2 \ln K_t + \alpha_3 \ln L_t + \alpha_4 \ln ED_t + \sum_{i=-q}^{q} \beta_i \Delta \ln GDP_{t=i} + \sum_{i=-q}^{q} \gamma_i \Delta \ln K_{t-i} + \sum_{i=-q}^{q} \delta_i \Delta \ln L_{t-i} + \sum_{i=-q}^{q} \mu_i \Delta \ln ED_{t-i} + \varepsilon_t \quad (5)$$

where q stands for lag structure (level) to be determined by Akaike information criterion (AIC) and t is time trend.

Causality Test

In order to test the directionality of the relationships between variables, this study adopts conditional Granger causality tests under the ECM. By doing so, the short-run deviations of series from their long-run equilibrium path are also captured by including an error correction term (Katircioglu 2010). Therefore, conditional error correction models for Granger causality can be estimated as follows:

$$\begin{bmatrix} \Delta \ln GDP_t \\ \Delta \ln K_t \\ \Delta \ln L_t \\ \Delta \ln E_t \end{bmatrix} = \begin{bmatrix} \mu_1 \\ \mu_2 \\ \mu_3 \\ \mu_4 \end{bmatrix} + \begin{bmatrix} \partial_{11,1} & \partial_{12,1} & \partial_{13,1} & \partial_{14,1} & \partial_{15,1} \\ \partial_{21,1} & \partial_{22,1} & \partial_{23,1} & \partial_{24,1} & \partial_{25,1} \\ \partial_{31,1} & \partial_{32,1} & \partial_{33,1} & \partial_{34,1} & \partial_{35,1} \\ \partial_{41,1} & \partial_{42,1} & \partial_{43,1} & \partial_{44,1} & \partial_{45,1} \end{bmatrix} \begin{bmatrix} \Delta \ln GDP_{t-1} \\ \Delta \ln K_{t-1} \\ \Delta \ln L_{t-1} \\ \Delta \ln E_{t-1} \end{bmatrix} + \ldots$$
$$+ \begin{bmatrix} \partial_{11,i} & \partial_{12,i} & \partial_{13,i} & \partial_{14,i} & \partial_{15,i} \\ \partial_{21,i} & \partial_{22,i} & \partial_{23,i} & \partial_{24,i} & \partial_{25,i} \\ \partial_{31,i} & \partial_{32,i} & \partial_{33,i} & \partial_{34,i} & \partial_{35,i} \\ \partial_{41,i} & \partial_{42,i} & \partial_{43,i} & \partial_{44,i} & \partial_{45,i} \end{bmatrix} \begin{bmatrix} \Delta \ln GDP_{t-i} \\ \Delta \ln K_{t-i} \\ \Delta \ln L_{t-i} \\ \Delta \ln E_{t-i} \end{bmatrix}$$
$$+ \begin{bmatrix} \phi_1 \\ \phi_2 \\ \phi_3 \\ \phi_4 \end{bmatrix} ECT_{t-1} + \begin{bmatrix} \varepsilon_{1,t} \\ \varepsilon_{2,t} \\ \varepsilon_{3,t} \\ \varepsilon_{4,t} \end{bmatrix} \tag{6}$$

Empirical Results

Zivot and Andrews (1992) unit root test results under a possible structural break are indicated in Table 1. The null hypothesis if there is a unit root with a structural break cannot be rejected at level forms of the variables which means variables are not stationary at their level forms. They become stationary when their first differences are taken, that is to say, lnGDP, lnK, lnL, and lnED variables are integrated of order one, I(1).

Co-Integration Analysis

According to unit root test results, all variables are integrated of the same order which is I(1). That is why co-integration test should be employed in order to investigate the long-run equilibrium relationship between variables. Table 2 shows Johansen co-integration test results. Trace statistics indicate that there is one co-integrating vector in the conducted model. Co-integration test results suggest that there is a long-run equilibrium relationship between GDP, capital, labor, and government expenditure on education.

Table 1 Zivot and Andrews (1992) unit root test

	Statistics (level)			Statistics (first difference)			
	ZA_B	ZA_T	ZA_I	ZA_B	ZA_T	ZA_I	Result
lnGDP	−3.946	−3.983	−2.964	−5.390[a]	−4.42[a]	−5.301[a]	I(1)
Break year	2005	2005	2006	1986	2005	1997	
Lag length	0	0	0	0	2	0	
lnK	−3.272	−3.119	−3.542	−4.872[a]	−4.466[a]	−4.614[a]	I(1)
Break year	1987	1984	1998	1998	2005	1986	
Lag length	0	0	0	4	4	4	
lnL	−4.959[a]	−3.528	−4.578	−7.117[a]	−6.532[a]	−6.856[a]	I(1)
Break year	1990	2001	2003	2003	1991	1989	
Lag length	0	0	0	0	0	0	
lnED	−3.895	−3.357	−3.455	−6.434[a]	−7.270[a]	−5.472[a]	I (1)
Break year	1993	1997	1997	1981	1980	1991	
Lag length	1	1	1	2	0	3	

Notes: GDP is gross domestic product; K is gross capital formation; L is labor force; ED is government expenditure on education. All of the series are at their natural logarithms. ZAB represents the model with a break in both the trend and intercept; ZAT is the model with a break in the trend; ZAI is the model with a break in the intercept

[a]denotes the rejection of the null hypothesis at the 10% level of significance. Tests for unit roots were carried out in E-VIEWS 9.0

Table 2 Johansen co-integration test

Hypothesized no. of CE(s)	Eigenvalue	Trace statistic	5 percent critical value	1 percent critical value
None [a]	0.535912	58.66315	47.21	54.46
At most 1	0.388883	27.95594	29.68	35.65
At most 2	0.129771	8.257264	15.41	20.04
At most 3	0.065210	2.697316	3.76	6.65

Notes: [a]denotes the rejection of the hypothesis at the 1% level of significance

Estimation of Long-Run Coefficients

After revealing the long-run equilibrium relationship between variables, DOLS regression is applied to estimate the long-run coefficients of independent variables. Estimation results are reported in Table 3.

DOLS estimation results suggest that gross capital formation and government expenditure have statistically significant, inelastic, and positive impacts on GDP which is used as a proxy for economic growth. In addition, the effect of labor force on economic growth is positive and elastic.

Table 3 Estimation of long-run coefficients by DOLS approach

Regressors	Coefficient	Standard error	P-value
lnK	0.247	0.117	0.043
lnL	2.018	0.499	0.000
lnED	0.217	0.122	0.034
C	0.860	2.100	0.086
R-squared 0.995 S.E. of Regr. 0.020			
Long-run variance 0.001			

Notes: Optimum lag length is selected by Akaike information criteria, and long-run covariance is estimated by Bartlett Kernel and Newey-West fixed bandwidth, which is 4

Causality Test

Short-run and long-run causalities between variables are investigated by Granger causality test under block exogeneity approach. According to Table 4, there is a bidirectional long-run causality between GDP and gross capital formation which means any change in gross capital formation causes a change in GDP and vice versa. In addition, there are long-run unidirectional causalities which run from labor and expenditure on education to GDP and from labor and expenditure to capital as the overall $\chi 2$ statistics are significant for both models. Moreover, there are short-run causalities which run from government expenditure on education to GDP and gross capital formation.

Conclusion

The aim of this study is to investigate the long-run equilibrium relationship between economic growth, capital, labor, and government expenditure on education between the years of 1970 and 2012 for the case of France. Johansen co-integration test results suggest the existence of the long-run equilibrium relationship between variables. Existence of the co-integration relationship indicates that capital, labor, and government expenditure n education are long-run determinants of GDP for the case of France. Estimated long-run coefficients suggest that when capital, labor, and government expenditure increase by 1%, GDP of France increases by 0.247%, 2.018%, and 0.217%, respectively. Estimated positive and elastic coefficient of labor suggests that well-educated and qualified labor force may contribute to the manufacturing sector and productivity in France as a developed country.

Granger causality test results suggest that there is a bidirectional long-run causality between GDP and gross capital formation which means any change in gross capital formation causes a change in GDP and vice versa. In addition, there are long-run unidirectional causalities which run from labor and expenditure on

Table 4 Granger causality tests under block exogeneity approach

Dependent variable	ΔlnGDP	ΔlnK	ΔlnL	ΔlnED	Overall χ^2-stat (prob)
ΔlnGDP	–	1.725 [0.189]	2.185 [0.139]	3.338[a] [0.067]	7.048[a] [0.070]
ΔlnK	2.296 [0.129]	–	1.886 [0.169]	3.646[a] [0.056]	8.270[a] [0.040]
ΔlnL	1.878 [0.170]	0.284 [0.593]	–	0.008 [0.927]	4.912 [0.178]
ΔlnED	0.173 [0.677]	0.252 [0.615]	0.728 [0.393]	–	0.905 [0.824]

Notes: [a]denotes the rejection of null hypothesis, respectively, at alpha 0.10% level

education to GDP and from labor and expenditure to capital. Causality which runs from education expenditure to GDP in the long run and in the short run suggests education-induced economic growth. Education expenditures help France to educate its labor force and increase the productivity level and contribute to the economic growth process.

Policy makers should be aware of the positive impact of education expenditures on GDP and allocate their resources more on education expenditures to increase the productivity level of the host country.

References

Asteriou D, Agiomirgianakis GM (2001) Human capital and economic growth: time series evidence from Greece. J Policy Model 23(5):481–489

Aziz B, Khan T, Aziz S (2008) Impact of higher education on economic growth of Pakistan. J Soc Sci Humanit 6(2):15–29

Babalola SJ (2011) Long-run relationship between education and economic growth: evidence from Nigeria. Int J Humanit Soc Sci 1(14):123–128

Barro RJ (1991) Economic growth in a cross section of countries. Q J Econ 106(2):407–443

Barro RJ (2002) Quantity and quality of economic growth. Banco Central de Chile, Santiago de Chile

Barro RJ, Lee JW (2013) A new data set of educational attainment in the world, 1950–2010. J Dev Econ 104:184–198

Barro R-J, Sala-i-Martin X (1995) Economic growth. Advanced series in economics, vol 539. McGraw-Hill, New York/London/Montreal, p xviii

Benhabib J, Spiegel MM (1994) The role of human capital in economic development evidence from aggregate cross-country data. J Monet Econ 34(2):143–173

Changzheng Z, Jin K (2009) An empirical study on the relationship between educational equity and the quality of economic growth in China: 1978-2004. Procedia Soc Behav Sci 1(1):189–194

Changzheng Z, Jin K (2010) Effect of equity in education on the quality of economic growth: evidence from China. J Hum Sci 7(1):47–69

Dănăcică DE, Belaşcu L, Ilie L (2010) The interactive causality between higher education and economic growth in Romania. Int Rev Bus Res Pap 6(4):491–500

Esteve V, Requena F (2006) A cointegration analysis of car advertising and sales data in the presence of structural change. Int J Econ Bus 13(1):111–128
Hussin MYM, Muhammad F, Hussin MFA, Razak AA (2012) Education expenditure and economic growth: a causal analysis for Malaysia. J Econ Sustain Dev 3(7):71–81
Jaoul M (2004) Higher education, causality and growth: a comparison of France and Germany before the Second World War. Compare 34(1):117–133
Johansen S (1988) Statistical analysis of co-integration vectors. J Econ Dyn Control 12:231–254
Johansen S, Juselius K (1990) Maximum likelihood estimation and inference on co-integration with application to the demand for money. Oxf Bull Econ Stat 52:169–209
Katircioğlu ST (2010) International tourism, higher education and economic growth: the case of North Cyprus. World Econ 33(12):1955–1972
Krueger A, Lindahl M (2001) Education for growth: why and for whom? J Econ Lit 39:1101–1136
Lin TC (2004) The role of higher education in economic development: an empirical study of Taiwan case. J Asian Econ 15(2):355–371
Loening JL (2002) The impact of education on economic growth in guatemala: a time-series analysis applying an error-correction methodology. Ibero-America Institute for Economic Research, University of Goettingen
Mankiw NG, Romer D, Weil DN (1992) A contribution to the empirics of economic growth. Q J Econ 107(2):407–437
Mariana DR (2015) Education as a determinant of the economic growth. The case of Romania. Procedia Soc Behav Sci 197:404–412
Musila J, Belassi W (2004) The impact of education expenditures on economic growth in Uganda: evidence from time series data. J Dev Areas 38(1):123–133
Odit MP, Dookhan K, Fauzel S (2010) The impact of education on economic growth: the case of Mauritius. Int Bus Econ Res J (IBER) 9(8):141–152
Perron P (1990) Testing for a unit root in a time series with a changing mean. J Bus Econ Stat 8 (2):153–162
Romer PM (1990) Human capital and growth: theory and evidence. Carn-Roch Conf Ser Public Policy 32:251–286. North-Holland
Shaari MS (2014) Education-led economic growth in Malaysia. SOP Trans Econ Res 1(1):27–32
Zivot E, Andrews DWK (1992) Further evidence on the great crash, the oil price shock and the unit root hypothesis. J Bus Econ Stat 10:251–270
World Bank (2016) World Bank Development indicators. http://databank.worldbank.org. Accessed in Apr 2017

Exchange Rate Exposure and Usage of Foreign Currency Derivatives by Indian Nonfinancial Firms

Krishna Prasad and K.R. Suprabha

Abstract This paper investigates the usage of currency derivatives and its impact on the exchange rate exposure. A sample of 387 nonfinancial Indian firms listed in the National Stock Exchange of India were studied for a period of 5 years from 2011–2012 to 2015–2016. The currency derivatives data was collected from the annual reports of the sample firms, and the stock price data was collected from Ace Equity and Centre for Monitoring Indian Economy (CMIE) database Prowess. The results of the study indicate that the currency forward contract is the most preferred hedging instrument among the sample firms. The Indian firms showed the lower interest in exchange-traded instruments especially currency futures. This is in spite of the growth in the third-generation innovative and low-cost derivative instruments. This study also provided evidence that hedging using currency derivatives decreased the firms' foreign exchange exposure level, while the use of foreign currency borrowing was found insignificant in decreasing the firm's level of currency exposure.

Keywords Currency derivatives • Exchange rate exposure • Currency forward • Exchange-traded derivatives

Introduction

The year 1991 was a major turning point in the liberalization and globalization process in India. In 1991 the foreign exchange reserves had nosedived to $1.2 billion which was barely enough to finance 13 days' worth of imports. The external help of IMF was accompanied by market-oriented conditionalities such as

K. Prasad (✉)
Justice K S Hegde Institute of Management, Nitte, Karkala Taluk, Udupi 574110, India
e-mail: kprasad@nitte.edu.in

K.R. Suprabha
School of Management, National Institute of Technology Karnataka, Srinivas Nagar, Surathkal, Mangalore, India
e-mail: suprabha.kr@gmail.com

D. Procházka (ed.), *The Impact of Globalization on International Finance and Accounting*, Springer Proceedings in Business and Economics,
https://doi.org/10.1007/978-3-319-68762-9_8

liberalization and globalization. At the face of crisis, the Government of India opened up the economy (Gaikwad and Scheve 2016). This important decision of the Indian government opened windows for global business in India; many multinational corporations (MNCs) entered Indian markets; similarly, many Indian companies cashed this opportunity to enter foreign countries. India's total imports were $18,145.2 million and the exports were $24,072.5 million in the fiscal year 1990–1991, and the imports and exports have increased to $262,290.1 million and $ 381,006.6 million in the fiscal year 2015–2016. Besides, there was a spectacular growth in foreign investment to India and Indian firms investing in foreign countries. The foreign direct investment (FDI) inflow to India was $73.5 million in the year 1990–1991 which increased to $44,009.4 million in 2015–2016. These developments led to more volatility in the foreign exchange market (Mondal 2014). The changes in the exchange rate are one of the important risks faced by the firms involved in international business (He and Ng 1998; El-Masry et al. 2007). With the increased international trade coupled with the volatile exchange rates exposed the Indian firms to the exchange rate exposure forcing the Indian MNCs to manage the exposure.

This paper principally answers three questions: First, whether the exchange rate movement influences the stock returns of a firm by using sample Indian nonfinancial firms listed in National Stock Exchange (NSE) for a period of 5 years from 2011–2012 to 2015–2016.[1] Second, we study the currency risk hedging strategies and the usage of derivatives of the sample firms. The information about the usage of derivatives are collected from the published annual reports of the company manually. Third, we examine the relationship between usage of derivatives and exchange rate exposure.

The remainder of the paper is organized as follows. In the second section, we review the existing literature. The third section discusses the methodology along with details about sample and the data. The empirical results and findings will be reported in the fourth section. The paper concludes with the fourth section.

Literature Review

Theoretically, unintuitive movements in the exchange rate should affect the value of the firm and its cash flows. The empirical findings in the past documented the relationship between stock returns and the changes in the exchange rate. The earlier studies measured the exchange rate exposure as the regression coefficients of the value of the firm on the changes in the exchange rates (Hodder 1982; Adler and Dumas 1984). Jorion (1991) developed the two-factor arbitrage pricing model to measure the firm-specific exchange rate exposure after controlling for the market

[1]Some of the sample firms followed calendar year, and the data for those firms were from January 2011 to December 2015.

return. This model reported the weak correlation between the exchange rate changes and stock returns for the sample US firms. However, with the improvements in the measurement techniques, some of the recent studies reported that large number of firms are significantly exposed to the exchange rate exposure (Fraser and Pantzalis 2004; Kang and Lee 2011; Salifu et al. 2007; Agyei-Ampomah et al. 2013; Bartram 2007). As exchange rate exposure affects the firm value and cash flows, it becomes necessary for the firms to hedge the exchange rate exposure.

The hedging of financial risks is a costly activity, and therefore the benefit of hedging should outweigh the cost of hedging in order to increase the firm value. According to Modigliani and Miller (1958), it is useless for a firm to reduce risk by using derivatives under perfect capital market conditions as it would not increase the value of a firm and individual investors can manage hedging strategies themselves by investing in diversified portfolios. The subsequent studies by Stulz (1984) and Smith and Stulz (1985) revealed that, under certain market frictions, corporations having specific operating characteristics, like higher financial distress costs, tax convexity, growth opportunities, managerial holdings and liquidity constraints, have an opportunity to enhance firm value by optimally utilizing hedging techniques. The implications of these findings are that benefits of hedging depend on various firm level factors. In this situation, whether hedging adds value for the firms is an important issue for both shareholders and managers.

The past research findings on the relationship between hedging and exchange rate exposure had given mixed results. Copeland and Joshi (1996) using a sample of 200 US firms found that measuring the outcomes of hedging may be difficult as many other macro-economic factors change along with the changes in exchange rate. Further, they stated that given the scarce resources and substantial amount of capital allocated to hedging, it may diminish the value instead of creating. Therefore, hedging the currency exposure may become wasteful to the shareholders. The hedging may not have yielded the expected results due the behavioural issues also. The survey results of Malindretos and Tsanacas (1995) reported that the managers had the clear understanding about the exchange rate exposures but were unsure about the appropriate techniques to address the exposure. On the other hand, Zhou and Wang (2013) in their study of 500 UK-based firms evidenced that using derivatives to hedge against the risk of unfavourable exchange rate movements was effective in decreasing the exchange rate exposure. This finding was supported by the finding of many other studies (Hagelin and Pramborg 2004; Praveen Bhagawan and Lukose 2014; Al-Shboul and Alison 2009). In the light of contradicting findings, it may be noted that partial or selective hedging could be more effective as it reduces the overall cost of hedging (Cvitanic 1999; Savchenko and Makar 2010).

The use of currency derivatives is one of the important methods to manage the currency risk (McGann and Shade 1997). The survey results indicate the firms extensively use the currency derivatives to manage exchange rate exposure (Bodnár 2009; Loderer and Pichler 2000; Bodnar and Gebhardt 1999). Jesswein et al. (1995) opine that the availability of large variety of foreign exchange risk management products helped the managers to handle the risks effectively. Further, they categorized the development of derivatives market into three generations. The forward contract was considered as first-generation product. In the second generation, exchange-traded instruments such as currency futures, options and warrants along with currency swaps flourished. The third generation witnessed the growth in innovative derivatives such as synthetic derivatives, compound options, foreign exchange agreements, hindsight options and so on. The innovations in the products may be attributed to the demands of corporate and bank users for more sophisticated products at a lower cost over existing products. Marshall (2000) surveyed the large British, American and Asia-Pacific multinational firms and found that the forward contract was the popular method to hedge the transaction exposure, and majority of these firms did not favour the exchange-traded instruments such as currency futures and options. The usage pattern was found similar even in the American context (Jesswein et al. 1995).

Foreign currency borrowings are also viewed as tool to hedge the exchange rate exposure. Based on the sample US and Canadian firms, Graham and Harvey (2001) found that use of foreign currency debt provided a natural hedge against exchange rate devaluation. Similarly, foreign currency debt was found to be an effective tool to reduce the exchange rate exposure (Aabo et al. 2012).

In this paper we first assess the relationship between changes in the exchange rate and stock returns of nonfinancial Indian firms. Subsequently, we analyse the usage of currency derivative instruments by the sample firms and examine whether the currency derivatives reduced the exposure. The usefulness of foreign currency borrowing as a tool to reduce the currency risk is also studied. The size, extent of internationalization and leverage were found to be related to the exposure (Davies et al. 2006; Makar & Huffman 2001). Therefore, the study uses these as control variables.

Methodology

Sample

The sample for this study was drawn from nonfinancial firms listed in NIFTY 500 index of the National Stock Exchange of India. On April 2016, out of 500 firms constituted in the index, 76 were firms from financial services sector. After elimination of 76 nonfinancial firms, the sample was reduced to 424 firms. The data for the companies was collected from Ace Equity database and Centre for Monitoring Indian Economy (CMIE) database Prowess for a period of 5 years starting from April 2011 to March 2016. Some of the sample firms followed calendar year and most were following financial year, and the data was adjusted accordingly. Out of 424 sample firms, data of 37 firms was not available for full 5 years as they were listed during the study period; hence, they were eliminated from the final sample. The final sample consisted of 387 firms. The sample firms represented 17 industry portfolios, namely, automobile, cement and cement products, chemicals, construction, consumer goods, energy, fertilizers and pesticides, healthcare services, industrial manufacturing, IT, media and entertainment, metals, paper, pharma, services, telecom and textiles. The usage of derivatives was manually collected from the annual reports of the sample firms.

Measurement of Exchange Rate Exposure

The two-factor model based on arbitrage pricing model was proposed by Jorion (1991) to estimate the economic exposure sensitivity coefficient of individual firms. A two-factor model, where $R_{it,}$ the return on company *i*'s stock at time *t*. R_{mt} is the market return of the market and e_{it} is the exchange risk factor. This model can be described as below:

$$R_{it} = \beta_0 + \beta_1 e_{it} + \beta_2 R_{mt} + v_{it} \quad (1)$$

From the above regression model, coefficients β_1 and β_2 provide the measure of exchange rate exposure and market risk of the firm *i*; v_{it} is the error term. The similar equation is employed by Adler and Dumas (1984), Bodnar and Gentry (1993) and Jorion (1990). This model is often used to examine the null hypothesis that the exchange rate fluctuations have no effect on stock returns, i.e. H_O: $\beta_1 = 0$. The alternate hypothesis is H_1: $\beta_1 = 0$. The sign of exchange rate coefficient can be positive or negative depending on the foreign currency cash flows of the firm.

This model exhibits potential problem of multicollinearity. That is, while estimating two-factor model, there is a possibility that the market and exchange rate factors are correlated and influenced by similar macro-economic factors. In order to control this problem, we use the component of the market return that is orthogonal to the changes in the exchange rate (Kiymaz 2003; Kanagaraj and Sikarwar 2011). This was done in two steps:

In the first step, the return of market portfolio is regressed on the changes in the exchange rate as shown by Eq. 2:

$$R_{mt} = \theta_0 + \theta_1 e_{it} + e_{it} \quad (2)$$

where R_{mt} is the daily log return of NIFTY 500 index from April 2011 to March 2016 and e_{it} is the corresponding daily log return of the trade-weighted nominal effective exchange rate (NEER) index. The NIFTY 500 index data was collected from the website of National Stock Exchange archives. The data on NEER (39 currency trade-based weights) was collected from the European Central Bank Statistical Warehouse.[2] The error term (ε_{it}), that is, difference between actual and

[2]Available at: http://sdw.ecb.europa.eu/browseSelection.do?df=true&ec=&dc=&oc=&pb=&rc=&DATASET=0&removeItem=&activeTab=&FREQ=D&node=9691301&legendRef=reference&legendNor=

predicted market return, is used as the component of the market portfolio return that is orthogonal to the changes in the exchange rate (F_{mt}).

Finally, exchange rate exposure of firms was estimated by regressing firm's stock returns on adjusted market returns (F_{mt}) and on exchange rate e_{it} as illustrated in Eq. 3:

$$R_{it} = \lambda_0 + \lambda_1 e_{it} + \lambda_2 F_{mt} + u_{it} \quad (3)$$

where R_{it} is the daily log-normal return of i at time t, F_{mt} is estimated orthogonal component of market portfolio and e_{it} is weekly log-normal change in the trade-weighted exchange rate index (NEER) over the same period. Daily closing prices of firm's stock are extracted from CMIE database Prowess and are used to calculate the stock returns of firms.

The time series regression model in Eq. 3 may have the econometric problems of multicollinearity, autocorrelation and heteroskedasticity. The problem of multicollinearity was minimized by using the market portfolio return which is orthogonal to the changes in the exchange rate as explained above. To eliminate the heteroskedasticity, log-normal return of the variables is used in the model. Elton and Gruber (1974) argued that stocks follow log-normal distribution; therefore, log-normal returns should be used in the capital market models. Hence, we use daily log-normal firms' stock returns, market returns and changes in exchange rate index.

Model

The cross-sectional model, summarized in Eq. (4), relates the use of currency derivatives and foreign currency debt to exchange rate exposure while controlling for firm size, extent of internationalization and leverage. Equation (4) is a cross-sectional regression between the coefficients of exchange rate exposure (λ_i) estimated in the capital market model (Eq. 3):

$$\lambda_{it} = \gamma_0 + \gamma_1 FCD_{it} + \gamma_2 FCB_{it} + \gamma_3 SIZE_{it} + \gamma_4 FCI/TI_{it} + \gamma_5 LEV_{it} + z_{it} \quad (4)$$

where λ_i is the exchange rate exposure estimated in the capital market model (Eq. 3), *FCD* is the dummy variable of 1 if currency derivatives are used and 0 otherwise, *FCB* is the dummy variable of 1 if the firm has foreign currency borrowing and 0 otherwise, *SIZE* is the natural log of total assets, *FCI/TI* is foreign currency income divided by total income as measure of the extent of internationalization and *LEV* is the total debt to market capitalization ratio as a measure of leverage.

The model is tested using panel data regression with fixed effects as the Hausman's test statistic was 157.74 ($p < 0.01$) that favoured fixed effect model.

Results and Discussion

The derivatives usage of the sample firms is reported in Table 1. From the table, it can be observed that over 69% of the firms in the 2011–2012 hedged using the currency derivatives and it slightly increased to over 72% for the rest of the years. Clearly, the forward contract was the popular currency derivatives used by sample Indian firms as a hedging tool. All the firms using currency derivatives reported that the currency derivatives were used only for hedging purpose and not for speculation.

The exchange-traded products were not a preferred instrument to hedge in the global context that was found to be true even in the Indian context. The reason could be the flexibility offered by the forward contract. Currency futures were the least preferred instrument, while usage of options contract was ten times more than futures. The options were particularly popular among firms with contingent exposure. Cross-currency interest rate swap was also used by the firms to cover the foreign currency borrowing. Principal-only swaps (POS) were also used in some cases. From the above findings, it can be noted that the second-generation and third-generation currency derivative products were not popular. Especially, the third-generation derivative instruments are still in a nascent stage in India. In spite of the innovations and the cost advantages offered by some of the hybrid products, forward contract still is the most preferred instrument to hedge the exchange rate exposure.

As most of the firms were found using currency derivatives to hedge the currency risk, we now test the model to see the impact of usage of currency derivatives on the foreign exchange exposure. The summary statistics correlation matrix of the variables is presented in Tables 2 and 3. The mean exposure of the sample firms during the study period was 0.912 with the maximum exposure of 4.506 and minimum of −1.364. It was found that 71.7% of the sample firms used foreign currency derivatives and 19.3% of the firms had borrowed in foreign currency. The average total debt to market cap ratio (LEV) was 0.833 with a minimum of 0 indicating zero debt firms and a maximum of 53.419 indicating high leverage.

Table 1 Hedging practices in nonfinancial Indian firms

	2011–2012	2012–2013	2013–2014	2014–2015	2015–2016
Total number of firms	387	387	387	387	387
Firms using currency derivatives	270	280	280	279	279
Hedging using forward contract	268	271	272	273	269
Hedging using futures contract	7	6	6	6	7
Hedging using options contract	73	74	72	70	70
Hedging using forward contract	73	76	76	75	77

Source: Compiled by authors from the respective annual reports

Table 2 Summary statistics

Variable	Obs	Mean	Std. dev.	Min	Max
λ_{it}	1935	0.912	0.747	−1.364	4.506
FCD	1935	0.717	0.450	0.000	1.000
FCB	1935	0.193	0.395	0.000	1.000
SIZE	1935	3.384	0.626	1.621	5.505
LEV	1935	0.833	2.589	0.000	53.419

Source: Compiled by the authors

Table 3 Correlation matrix

	λ_{it}	FCD	FCB	SIZE	LEV
λ_{it}	1				
FCD	0.018	1			
FCB	0.086	0.147	1		
SIZE	0.155	0.119	0.176	1	
LEV	0.113	−0.008	0.190	0.139	1

Source: Compiled by the authors

Table 4 Estimates of the model

	λ_{it}
FCD	−0.626
	(3.48)***
FCB	0.159
	(1.66)*
SIZE	1.837
	(12.84)***
FCITI	−0.003
	(1.60)**
LEV	0.011
	(1.30)
_cons	−4.860
	(9.69)**
R^2	0.11
N	1935

$^{*}p < 0.10$; $^{**}p < 0.05$, $^{***}p < 0.01$

Note: Table 4 reports the cross-sectional regression between exchange rate exposure coefficients (λ) estimated from Eq. (3) and explanatory factors mentioned in Eq. (4). The models include 387 firms studied for a period of 5 years between 2011 and 2012 and 2015–2016. The estimates are obtained by running panel data model with fixed effect. t-statistics for coefficient estimates are reported in parentheses

The results of the relationship between explanatory variables and the exchange rate exposure are presented in Table 4. As argued, the exchange rate exposure (λ_{it}) of the firms using foreign currency derivatives (FCD) was less. In comparison with the firms not hedging, the exposure of firms hedging was 0.626 times lower which was significant at 1% level. The empirical results of this study prove that usage of currency derivatives adds value to the firm.

Foreign currency borrowing (FCB) which was also found to be a method used to hedge exchange rate exposure in the literature was positively related to the exposure. This implies that the exposure of the firms without foreign currency borrowing was lower compared to the firms borrowing in foreign currency. The important finding of this paper is that while usage of FCD reduced the risk, FCB increased the exchange rate exposure. The control variables the log of total assets (SIZE) and debt to market cap ratio (LEV) were positively related to exchange rate exposure. The foreign currency income to total income (FCI/TI) was negatively related to the exposure.

Conclusion

This paper investigates the usage of currency derivatives and its impact on the exchange rate exposure by studying a sample of 387 nonfinancial Indian firms. The results indicate that the currency forward contract is the most preferred hedging instrument among the sample firms. The Indian firms showed the lower interest in exchange-traded instruments especially currency futures. This study also provided evidence for hedging using currency derivatives that decreased the firms' foreign exchange exposure level. Foreign currency borrowing did not reduce the firms' exposure; in fact it increased the level of currency exposure.

Acknowledgements The authors gratefully acknowledges the financial support provided by Nitte Education Trust, Mangalore, India to carry out this research.

References

Aabo T, Hansen MA, Pantzalis C (2012) Corporate foreign exchange speculation and integrated risk management. Manag Financ 38(8):729–751

Adler M, Dumas B (1984) Exposure to currency risk: definition and measurement. Financ Manag (pre-1986) 13(2):41

Agyei-Ampomah S, Mazouz K, Yin S (2013) The foreign exchange exposure of UK non-financial firms: a comparison of market-based methodologies. Int Rev Financ Anal 29(0):251–260

Al-Shboul M, Alison S (2009) The effects of the use of corporate derivatives on the foreign exchange rate exposure. J Account Bus Manag 16(1):72–92

Bartram SM (2007) Corporate cash flow and stock price exposures to foreign exchange rate risk. Finance 13(5):981–994

Bodnár K (2009) Exchange rate exposure of Hungarian enterprises - results of a survey. A magyar vállalatok árfolyamkitettsége - egy kérdőíves felmérés eredményei 80:3–42

Bodnar GM, Gebhardt G (1999) Derivatives usage in risk management by US and German non-financial firms: a comparative survey. J Int Financ Manag Account 10(3):153–187

Bodnar GM, Gentry WM (1993) Exchange rate exposure and industry characteristics: evidence from Canada, Japan, and the USA. J Int Money Financ 12(1):29

Copeland TE, Joshi Y (1996) Why derivatives don't reduce FX risk. Risk Manage 43(7):76

Cvitanic J (1999) Methods of partial hedging. Asia - Pacific Finan Markets 6(1):7–35
Davies D, Eckberg C, Marshall A (2006) The determinants of Norwegian exporters foreign exchange risk management. Eur J Financ 12(3):217–240
El-Masry A, Abdel-Salam O, Alatraby A (2007) The exchange rate exposure of UK non-financial companies. Manag Financ 33(9):620
Elton EJ, Gruber MJ (1974) Note on the maximization of the geometric mean with lognormal return distribution. Manag Sci (pre-1986) 21(4):483
Fraser SP, Pantzalis C (2004) Foreign exchange rate exposure of US multinational corporations: a firm-specific approach. J Multinatl Financ Manag 14(3):261–281
Gaikwad N, Scheve K (2016) India: liberalize in the face of crisis?
Graham JR, Harvey CR (2001) The theory and practice of corporate finance: evidence from the field. J Financ Econ 60(2–3):187–243
Hagelin N, Pramborg B (2004) Hedging foreign exchange exposure: risk reduction from transaction and translation hedging. J Int Financ Manag Account 15(1):1–20
He J, Ng LK (1998) The foreign exchange exposure of Japanese multinational corporations. J Financ 53(2):733–753
Hodder JE (1982) Exposure to exchange-rate movements. J Int Econ 13(3–4):375–386
Jesswein KR, Kwok CCY, Folks WR Jr (1995) Corporate use of innovative foreign exchange risk management products. Columbia J World Bus 30(3):70–82
Jorion P (1990) The exchange-rate exposure of U.S. multinationals. J Bus 63(3):331
Jorion P (1991) The pricing of exchange rate risk in the stock market. J Financ Quant Anal 26 (3):363
Kanagaraj A, Sikarwar E (2011) A firm level analysis of the exchange rate exposure of Indian firms. J Appl Financ Bank 1(4):163–184
Kang S, Lee JW (2011) Estimating Korea's exchange rate exposure. Asian Econ J 25(2):177–196
Kiymaz H (2003) Estimation of foreign exchange exposure: an emerging market application. J Multinatl Financ Manag 13(1):71–84
Loderer C, Pichler K (2000) Firms, do you know your currency risk exposure? Survey results. J Empir Financ 7(3–4):317–344
Makar SD, Huffman SP (2001) Foreign exchange derivatives, exchange rate changes, and the value of the firm: U.S. multinationals' use of short-term financial instruments to manage currency risk. J Econ Bus 53(4):421–437
Malindretos J, Tsanacas D (1995) Hedging preferences and foreign exchange exposure management. Multinatl Bus Rev 3(2):56
Marshall AP (2000) Foreign exchange risk management in UK, USA and Asia Pacific multinational companies. J Multinatl Financ Manag 10(2):185–211
McGann J, Shade D (1997) A strategic approach to foreign exchange. TMA J 17(6):100–102
Modigliani F, Miller MH (1958) The cost of capital, corporation finance and the theory of investment. Am Econ Rev XLVIII(3):261–297
Mondal L (2014) Volatility spillover between the RBI's intervention and exchange rate. Int Econ Econ Policy 11(4):549–560
Praveen Bhagawan M, Lukose PJJ (2014) Currency exposure and hedging practices among Indian non-financial firms: an empirical study. Foreign Trade Rev 49(3):247–262
Salifu Z, Osei KA, Adjasi CKD (2007) Foreign exchange risk exposure of listed companies in Ghana. J Risk Financ 8(4):380
Savchenko O, Makar S (2010) Derivatives use in the partial hedging of currency risk: a firm-specific approach to understanding the exchange rate exposure puzzle. J Appl Bus Res 26 (1):109–120
Smith CW, Stulz RM (1985) The determinants of firms' hedging policies. J Financ Quant Anal 20 (4):391–405
Stulz RM (1984) Optimal hedging policies. J Financ Quant Policies 19(2):127–140
Zhou VY, Wang P (2013) Managing foreign exchange risk with derivatives in UK non-financial firms. Int Rev Financ Anal 29(0):294–302

Are the Central and Eastern European Countries More Vulnerability to the External Shocks?

Vilma Deltuvaitė

Abstract Due to the higher degree of economic openness, the Central and Eastern European countries (CEECs) are more exposed to the external shocks that can be transmitted through international trade channel. The CEECs are one of the most open economies worldwide those have undergone different types of shocks and structural changes during the last two decades. This raise a question: are the CEECs more sensitive to the external shocks compared to most developed countries worldwide? The main findings are that the CEECs with higher share of final domestic consumption and export are more vulnerable to the domestic and global shocks. The CEECs with higher share of gross value added by agriculture, hunting, forestry, fishing, manufacturing, wholesale, retail trade, restaurants and hotels, transport, storage, and communications are more sensitive to different shocks, while these economic activities are focused on domestic market. Higher concentration and diversification of import portfolio of the CEECs affect higher volatility of real GDP. In other words, in the CEECs where import is concentrated on several products and similarity of the import structure between a given CEEC and the rest of the world is lower, volatility of real GDP is higher. In conclusion, the empirical results provide substantial evidence that the CEECs are more vulnerability to the domestic and external shocks.

Keywords Economic openness • Shocks • Vulnerability

Introduction

The Central and Eastern European countries (CEECs) (Bulgaria, Czech Republic, Estonia, Hungary, Latvia, Lithuania, Slovakia, and Slovenia) are one of the most open economies worldwide and vulnerable to the external shocks that can be transmitted through international trade channel. Despite the fact that many economists highlight the importance of trade openness on the vulnerability of countries to

V. Deltuvaitė (✉)
Kaunas University of Technology, Department of Finance, K. Donelaicio g. 73, 44249 Kaunas, Lithuania
e-mail: vilma.deltuvaite@ktu.lt

D. Procházka (ed.), *The Impact of Globalization on International Finance and Accounting*, Springer Proceedings in Business and Economics,
https://doi.org/10.1007/978-3-319-68762-9_9

the external shocks, literature provides very little evidence on factors explaining sensitivity of countries to the external shocks. Jin (2006) found a short-term negative effect of global shocks on economic growth and inflation. Claessens et al. (2012) examined the impact of external shocks on nonfinancial corporations' performance and various shocks transmission channels. They found that in more open economies, the external shocks had a more significant negative impact on nonfinancial corporations. Elekdag et al. (2015) found that increased trade openness in Germany, Czech Republic, Hungary, Poland, and Slovakia resulted a greater exposure of these countries to external shocks. Milani and Park (2015) state that globalization resulted a higher sensitivity of domestic macroeconomic variables, in particular, domestic output and inflation. Vannoorenberghe (2012) states that a higher share of exports in the total sales of a nonfinancial corporation results a higher volatility of its sales. In addition, Vannoorenberghe (2014) shows that international trade induces nonfinancial corporations to make riskier decisions and increases the volatility of sectoral sales. This study investigates factors explaining sensitivity of countries to the external shocks with a special focus on the CEECs.

Data and Methodology

The investigation of countries' sensitivity to the external shocks was examined by applying a panel regression model (1):

$$Y_{i,t} = \alpha + \beta_{i,t} X_{i,t}^{'} + \delta_i + \gamma_t + \varepsilon_{i,t}, \quad \varepsilon_{i,t} \sim WN(0, \Sigma_\varepsilon) \tag{1}$$

where $Y_{i,t}$ is dependent variable characterizing economic vulnerability of country (real GDP volatility (ΔRGDPV)); $X_{i,t}^{'}$ is a k-vector of regressors characterizing the structure of GDP, gross value added by different kind of economic activity, and characteristics of international trade pattern (see Table 1); $\varepsilon_{i,t}$ are the error terms for $i = 1, 2, \ldots, M$ cross-sectional units (countries) observed for dated periods $t = 1, 2, \ldots, T$, α parameter represents the overall constant in the model, while the δ_i and γ_t represent cross section and period fixed effects.

The structure of gross domestic product (GDP) was decomposed by expenditure approach using the following types of expenditure: final consumption expenditure (household consumption expenditure (including nonprofit institutions serving households) and general government final consumption expenditure), gross capital formation, export of goods and services, and import of goods and services. Gross value added (VA) was decomposed by following economic activities: agriculture, hunting, forestry, fishing (ISIC A-B), mining, manufacturing, utilities (ISIC C-E), manufacturing (ISIC D), construction (ISIC F), wholesale, retail trade, restaurants and hotels (ISIC G-H), transport, storage and communication (ISIC I), and other activities (ISIC J-P).

This empirical study focuses on annual data for EU-28 countries, G-8 countries (including Canada, Japan, Russia, the United States), and China with a special focus

Table 1 Definition of variables

Variable	Description	Source
lnGDP	Logarithm of current price GDP expressed in billions of US dollars (GDP in national currency converted to US dollars using market exchange rates (yearly average))	IMF WEO
ΔRGDPV	Real GDP volatility is a rolling standard deviation of real GDP change during the last 5 years	Author's calculation
FCON	Final consumption expenditure as percentage of GDP	UNCTD
HCON	Household consumption expenditure as percentage of GDP	UNCTD
GGCON	General government final consumption expenditure as percentage of GDP	UNCTD
GCFOR	Gross capital formation as percentage of GDP	UNCTD
EXP	Exports of goods and services as percentage of GDP	UNCTD
IMP	Imports of goods and services as percentage of GDP	UNCTD
VAA	VA by agriculture, hunting, forestry, fishing as percentage of GDP	UNCTD
VAI	VA by industry as percentage of GDP	UNCTD
VAMI	VA by mining, manufacturing, utilities as percentage of GDP	UNCTD
VAMA	VA by manufacturing as percentage of GDP	UNCTD
VAC	VA by construction as percentage of GDP	UNCTD
VAS	VA by services as percentage of GDP	UNCTD
VAW	VA by wholesale, retail trade, restaurants, and hotels as percentage of GDP	UNCTD
VAT	VA by transport, storage, and communications as percentage of GDP	UNCTD
VAO	VA by other activities as percentage of GDP	UNCTD
IMPC (EXPC)	Concentration of import (export) index shows how import (export) of individual country is concentrated on several products or otherwise distributed in a more homogeneous manner among a series of products. Index (also named Herfindahl-Hirschman index) is a measure of the degree of import (export) concentration that is calculated for all trading partners. Index has been normalized to obtain values ranking from 0 to 1: a value that is close to 1 indicates a very concentrated market (maximum concentration) and, on the contrary, values closer to 0 reflect a more equal distribution of market shares among importers (exporters)	UNCTD
IMPD (EXPD)	Diversification of import (export) index signals whether the structure of import (export) by product of a given country differs from the world pattern. Diversification index that ranges from 0 to 1 reveals the extent of the differences between the structure of trade of the country and the world average. The index value closer to 1 indicates a higher difference from the world average. Diversification index is computed by measuring absolute deviation of the country share from world structure	UNCTD
TROP	Trade openness indicator is expressed as sum of imports and exports of total trade in goods and services divided by GDP	UNCTD

Source: International Monetary Fund, World Economic Outlook Database, United Nations Conference on Trade and Development

Table 2 The empirical results of fixed-effects panel regression models (Regressors – GDP's components by expenditure approach)

	Model 1		Model 2	
	CEECs countries	All countries	CEECs countries	All countries
C	−35.0314***	5.8193	−30.4326***	4.1359
	(10.9254)	(4.9658)	(10.7745)	(4.7961)
lnGDP	−0.6134***	−0.3768***	−0.5877***	−0.3728***
	(0.0724)	(0.0218)	(0.0712)	(0.0211)
FCON	0.4090***	−0.0202		
	(0.1095)	(0.0496)		
GGCON			0.3112***	−0.0535
			(0.1111)	(0.0480)
HCON			0.3740***	0.0131
			(0.1076)	(0.0480)
GCFOR	0.3761***	0.0047	0.3317***	0.0215
	(0.1094)	(0.0494)	(0.1078)	(0.0477)
EXP	0.4068***	0.0165	0.3668***	0.0456
	(0.1093)	(0.0496)	(0.1076)	(0.0480)
IMP	−0.4142***	−0.0310	−0.3702***	−0.0600
	(0.1096)	(0.0496)	(0.1080)	(0.0480)
Country FE	No	No	No	No
Year FE	Yes	Yes	Yes	Yes
Observations	259	888	259	888
R^2	0.4902	0.3748	0.5145	0.4186
S.E. of regression	0.8957	0.7954	0.8761	0.7675

Source: authorial computation
Note: Standard errors in parentheses. ***$p < 0.01$

on the 11 CEECs': Bulgaria, Czech Republic, Croatia, Estonia, Hungary, Latvia, Lithuania, Poland, Romania, Slovakia, and Slovenia. Annual data for the period from 1980 to 2015 have been obtained from different data sources. The following data sources have been used: International Monetary Fund (World Economic Outlook Database (IMF WEO)) and United Nations Conference on Trade and Development (UNCTD).

Results and Discussion

The empirical results of fixed-effects panel regression models are presented by using two different data samples. The first data sample includes the 11 CEECs while the second one – all 33 countries (EU-28 countries, G-8 countries, and China). The results presented in Table 2 suggest that size of economy is the most significant factor explaining economic vulnerability of country in both data

Table 3 The empirical results of fixed-effects panel regression models (Regressors – VAs by different kinds of economic activity)

	Model 3	
	CEECs countries	All countries
C	0.3553	0.4003
	(0.7935)	(0.3222)
lnGDP	−0.2640***	−0.1261***
	(0.0817)	(0.0180)
VAA	0.1089***	0.0566***
	(0.0190)	(0.0098)
VAMI	−0.1035***	0.0400***
	(0.0387)	(0.0119)
VAMA	0.1176***	−0.0291**
	(0.0363)	(0.0137)
VAC	−0.0377	−0.0093
	(0.0411)	(0.0170)
VAW	0.0753***	−0.0026
	(0.0251)	(0.0096)
VAT	0.1620***	0.1509***
	(0.0247)	(0.0146)
Country FE	No	No
Year FE	Yes	Yes
Observations	259	869
R^2	0.5711	0.4548
S.E. of regression	0.8253	0.7293

Source: authorial computation
Note: Standard errors in parentheses. ***$p < 0.01$, **$p < 0.05$

samples. The results indicate that larger economies are less sensitive to domestic and external shocks. However, the CEECs with higher share of final domestic consumption (both household and general government) and export are more vulnerable to the domestic and global shocks.

The analysis of interrelation between the structure of economy and economic vulnerability revealed that the CEECs with higher share of gross value added by agriculture, hunting, forestry, fishing, manufacturing, wholesale, retail trade, restaurants and hotels, transport, storage, and communications are more sensitive to different shocks. These results confirm the previous empirical results, while economic activities such as agriculture, wholesale, retail trade, restaurants and hotels, transport, storage, and communications are focused on domestic market, in particular in the CEECs. Very similar results are observed for the whole data sample. In addition, the size of economy is more important factor than the structure of economy influencing economic vulnerability of the CEECs (Table 3).

The empirical results suggest that higher concentration and diversification of import portfolio of the CEECs affect higher volatility of real GDP. In other words, in the CEECs where import is concentrated on several products and similarity of the import structure between a given CEEC and the rest of the world is lower, volatility

Table 4 The empirical results of fixed-effects panel regression models (Regressors – different indicators of international trade)

	Model 4		Model 5	
	CEECs countries	All countries	CEECs countries	All countries
C	5.1655***	3.3379***	−1.2501	0.7422**
	(0.4305)	(0.1683)	(0.9103)	(0.3096)
lnGDP	−0.5893***	−0.2631***	−0.1034	−0.1062***
	(0.0697)	(0.0205)	(0.0863)	(0.0237)
TROP	−0.0054**	−0.0017**		
	(0.0021)	(0.0008)		
EXPC			−3.2819	−1.7673**
			(2.2703)	(0.7396)
EXPD			2.2756	2.9651***
			(1.4075)	(0.6603)
IMPC			5.6651*	−1.7871
			(2.5353)	(1.1230)
IMPD			8.9947**	2.4560***
			(2.1660)	(0.8498)
Country FE	No	No	No	No
Year FE	Yes	Yes	Yes	Yes
Observations	270	896	227	682
R^2	0.4595	0.2762	0.5354	0.3511
S.E. of regression	0.9129	0.8821	0.8098	0.8361

Source: authorial computation
Note: Standard errors in parentheses. ***$p < 0.01$, **$p < 0.05$, *$p < 0.1$

of real GDP is higher. In general, higher concentration of export portfolio leads to lower economic vulnerability, while a higher diversification of export and import portfolios results a higher volatility of real GDP. These results contradict economic theory; however, they could be explained by the fact that share of export to GDP is not statistically significant variable explaining volatility of real GDP in the whole data sample (Table 4).

Conclusion

The empirical findings suggest that size of economy is the most significant factor explaining economic vulnerability of country, i.e., larger economies are less sensitive to domestic and external shocks. Higher concentration of export portfolio leads to lower economic vulnerability, while a higher diversification of export and import portfolios results a higher volatility of real GDP. These results contradict economic theory and could be explained by the fact that share of export to GDP is not statistically significant variable explaining volatility of real GDP.

The CEECs with higher share of final domestic consumption and export are more vulnerability to the domestic and global shocks. In addition, the CEECs with higher share of gross value added by agriculture, hunting, forestry, fishing, manufacturing, wholesale, retail trade, restaurants and hotels, transport, storage, and communications are more sensitive to different shocks, while these economic activities are focused on domestic market. Higher concentration and diversification of import portfolio of the CEECs affect higher volatility of real GDP. In other words, in the CEECs where import is concentrated on several products and similarity of the import structure between a given CEEC and the rest of the world is lower, volatility of real GDP is higher.

In conclusion, the empirical results provide substantial evidence that the CEECs are more vulnerable to the domestic and external shocks.

Acknowledgments This research was funded by a grant (No. MIP-016/2015) from the Research Council of Lithuania.

References

Claessens S, Tong H, Wei S (2012) From the financial crisis to the real economy: using firm-level data to identify transmission channels. J Int Econ 88(2):375–387. https://doi.org/10.1016/j.jinteco.2012.02.015

Elekdag S, Muir D, Wu Y (2015) Trade linkages, balance sheets, and spillovers: the Germany-Central European supply chain. J Policy Model 37(2):374–387. https://doi.org/10.1016/j.jpolmod.2015.01.003

Jin JC (2006) Can openness be an engine of sustained high growth rates and inflation? Evidence from Japan and Korea. Int Rev Econ Financ 15(2):228–240. https://doi.org/10.1016/j.iref.2004.03.005

Milani F, Park SH (2015) The effects of globalization on macroeconomic dynamics in a trade-dependent economy: the case of Korea. Econ Model 48:292–305. https://doi.org/10.1016/j.econmod.2014.10.042

Vannoorenberghe G (2012) Firm-level volatility and exports. J Int Econ 86(1):57–67. https://doi.org/10.1016/j.jinteco.2011.08.013

Vannoorenberghe G (2014) International trade, risk taking and welfare. J Int Econ 92(2):363–374. https://doi.org/10.1016/j.jinteco.2013.12.003

Micro-level Evidences of Moral Hazard in the European Financial Institutions

Karel Janda and Oleg Kravtsov

Abstract This article examines the evidences of moral hazard and the determinants of risk-taking among 500 banks in Central Europe, the Baltic, and Balkan region. We analyze moral hazard incentives and investigate which factors impact the risk profile of the banks in empirical relationships between shareholders, bank managers, regulatory restraints, and ownership structure. We find strong link between level of risk-taking and bank manager performance and efficiency, which supports the theoretical argumentation of the moral hazard. The capital requirements and regulatory concerns exhibit significant effect on the risk-taking behavior. A positive relation between government ownership and risk profile is observed in the dataset.

Keywords Moral hazard • Risk-taking • Non-performing loans

Introduction

In this paper, we examine the determinants of bank risk-taking and moral hazard incentives of the financial institutions. We refer to the theoretical framework of Jeitschko and Jeung (2005) to describe the incentives of the agents and to model their risk preferences. An empirical study is conducted to examine these theoretical standings. Based on the dataset of 500 banks located in 21 countries of the Central Europe, Baltic, and Balkan region over the period of 2006–2014, we investigate which factors influence risk profile of the banks and if there are evidences of moral

K. Janda
University of Economics, Prague, Department of Banking and Insurance, Nam. W. Churchilla 4, 13067, Praha 3, Czech Republic

Institute of Economic Studies, Charles University, Opletalova 26,11000, Praha 1, Czech Republic
e-mail: Karel-Janda@seznam.cz

O. Kravtsov (✉)
University of Economics, Prague, Department of Banking and Insurance, Nam. W. Churchilla 4, 13067, Praha 3, Czech Republic
e-mail: krao02@vse.cz

D. Procházka (ed.), *The Impact of Globalization on International Finance and Accounting*, Springer Proceedings in Business and Economics,
https://doi.org/10.1007/978-3-319-68762-9_10

hazard existing in empirical relationships between shareholders, bank managers, from regulatory restraints, and ownership structure. Several regression models have been applied to identify and compare risk-taking patterns and hereby to draw conclusions on the evidences of the moral hazard.

Theoretical literature stresses the key role of asymmetric information in lending markets (Janda 2011; Mejstřík et al. 2015). A majority of studies show that asymmetric information and moral hazard problems can generate market failures such as inefficient provisioning and mispricing of risk and consequently incentivize institutions to take higher risks. The study of the classical principal-agent problem and the conflicts rising from managerial behavior, agency costs, and ownership structure are widely investigated in the theory of the firm, e.g., Furlong and Keeley (1991) Jeitschko and Jeung (2005), Jensen and Meckling (1976), and Laffont and Martimort (2001). However, the empirical evidences are largely divided across various geographies with different banking sector structures. For example, the impacts of domestic, foreign, or state ownership on bank performance are studied by Berger et al. (2005) and Iannotta et al. (2013). They found that the banks with a large share of state ownership are associated with inferior long-term performance and greater risk-taking. Similarly Dong et al. (2014) show that Chinese banks owned by the government tend to exhibit more risk-taking strategies than those owned by private investors. Whereas for the Russian banks (Fungáčová and Solanko 2009) and banks of the Central Eastern Europe (Distinguin et al. 2013), their findings show the opposite effect. The explanation is that state-owned banks may benefit from an implicit government guarantee.

Moral hazard and adverse selection in financial markets could frequently derive from regulations and governmental intervention that result in perverse incentives. Acharya et al. (2015) analyze how the capital requirements can address moral hazard problems in banking associated risk shifting and managerial under-provision of effort in loan monitoring. A number of studies (Antzoulatos and Tsoumas 2014; Cheng et al. 2016; De Caux et al. 2017; Janda 2009; Mariathasan et al. 2014; Raudeliuniene et al. 2016) point to the evidences of moral hazard behavior of financial institutions in case of various forms of government support, i.e., bailout, guarantees, deposit insurance, etc. They suggest that the governmental guarantees reduce the downside risk associated with financing decisions and thus incentivize the banks to assume risks they would not choose to bear without the expected government support. Duran and Lozano-Vivas (2012) and Ngalawa et al. (2016) indicate further that generous deposit insurance schemes seem to incentivize risk shifting to the non-depository creditors. By comparing the different forms of the government support, Janda (2011) concludes that in some situations, the credit guarantees and interest rate subsidies are beneficial for borrowers and lenders, e.g., in the Czech Republic, they positively affect the export finance (Janda et al. 2013).

The moral hazard hypothesis and banking management incentives are empirically studied by Berger and DeYoung (1997). Their results show that decreases in bank capital ratios generally precede increases in non-performing loans for banks. Evidently, poor capitalized banks may respond to moral hazard incentives by taking increased portfolio risks. Moreover, they suggest a positive relation between non-performing loans and cost efficiency. Similar results were found by Podpiera and

Weill (2008) who examine the question of the causality between non-performing loans and cost efficiency whether either of these factors is the determinant of bank failures. Analyzing data of Czech banks between 1994 and 2005, their findings support the evidences of bad management practices as a "bad management" hypothesis, according to which deteriorations in cost efficiency precede increases in non-performing loans. On example of the Chinese banking industry, Zhang et al. (2016) investigated how non-performing loans are related to moral hazard problems. They used a threshold value for the non-performing loans expecting that there is a potential threshold above which risk-taking of banks increases and the non-performing loans worsen. They find the empirical evidences of moral hazard behavior among the banks with higher portion of problematic loans on the book.

Theoretical Framework and Hypotheses

Jeitschko and Jeung (2005) propose a theoretical framework that describes the risk preference of the agents in situation of various risk-return profiles. It is assumed that capital and deposits are given exogenously to the bank, and the choice of risky assets is not influenced by leverage considerations. There are three main incentives that affect bank's asset risk choice. The first is of the bank manager who makes the risk decisions by assets allocation. He has a private interest in maximizing his benefits, and by his choice, the assets risk is impacted. The second is of the shareholders who want to maximize the bank's equity value and influence the asset choice through corporate governance structures. And at last, that of the regulators who are interested in minimizing the cost of bank failures and use regulation provisioning to indirectly affect the asset choice (e.g., deposit insurance or government guarantees). Considering all three above incentives of agents in form of separate objective functions, the bank choice of the risk can be represented by the following maximization equation:

$$\alpha \in \arg\max\{\omega V(\alpha^s) + \beta E(B(\alpha^m)) - \rho OV\ (a^r)\}; \quad \omega, \beta, \rho \geq 0 \tag{1}$$

The risk choice α of the bank in the above function is determined by relative weights (ω, β, ρ) put on the bank's equity value (V), the expected value of private benefit of managers ($E(B)$), and regulatory restraint as option value of deposit insurance (OV). The preferred risk choices of shareholders, managers, and given regulatory restraint are captured in α^s, α^m, and α^r, respectively. The option value (OV) of deposit insurance (or of guaranteeing the promised payment) is considered as a put option on the assets and treated as an expected loss to guarantor. The regulatory constraints obviously are not favored by the banks and are therefore expressed with a negative sign. The weight ω is placed on the value of the bank equity to capture the shareholders' influence. The weight β is put on the managerial private benefit, and ρ is the weight placed on the option value as a regulatory restraint. Thus, the shareholder's agency problems from the underpriced deposit insurance are expressed in ω and ρ, while β refers to the agency problem associated with management. If there were no agency problem with management, then the value of weights would be equal $\omega = \rho$ and $\beta = 0$ .The shareholders will always prefer a risk factor $\alpha^s > 0$ to maximize their profits. The deposit insurance provider preference would be $\alpha^r = 0$, unless the higher risk and higher return profile of the bank will require other optimum level $\alpha^r \in [0, 1]$. The bank manager's risk choice would be $\alpha^m = 0$, when the private benefits are decreasing proportionally ($B \leq 0$) with reducing risk; otherwise, a preference is given to $\alpha^m \in [0, 1]$. In line with theoretical framework, we address the following questions in the empirical analysis: (a) which factors are influencing at most the risk profile of the banks in relationships between shareholders, bank managers, from regulatory restraints point of view, and ownership structure? (b) whether the insufficient monitoring efforts or inefficient allocation of resources by bank managers affects loan-granting behavior and causes the excessive risk practices by banks, thus supporting the evidences of moral hazard or the "bad management" hypothesis (Podpiera and Weill 2008) and rent-seeking behavior (Acharya et al. 2015; Berger and DeYoung 1997).

Data and Methodology

Our dataset consists of 500 financial institutions located in the 21 countries of Central Europe and the Baltic region. The financial data is obtained from the database BankScope and own calculations. The unbalanced data sample is due to the partly not reported financial information for the entire period of 10 years over the period 2006–2014, mostly for the small-sized banks.

Given that the nature of moral hazard problems does not allow direct observation, we will study their indirect impact which is reflected on micro-level in the performance ratios of banking institutions. First of all we examine the factors influencing risk profile of the banks and test whether the explanatory variables reveal moral hazard behavior of the agents from the theoretical model. Several regression models and two types of risk metrics are used with the double motivation to analyze the hypotheses questions on one hand and as a robustness check of the results on the other. By introducing the natural logarithm in the regression models, we extend our analysis to accommodate possible nonlinearity patterns and to investigate the nonlinear dynamics in relations between the observed variables:

Model 1:

$$y_{it} = \beta_0 + \beta_n x_{it-1} + \delta d_{it} + e_{it} \tag{2}$$

Model 2:

$$\log y_{it} = \beta_0 + \beta_n \log x_{it-1} + \delta d_{it} + e_{it} \tag{3}$$

Model 3:

$$y_{it} = a_i + \beta x_{it-1} + \delta d_{it} + \varepsilon_{it} \tag{4}$$

Model 4:

$$\log y_{it} = a_i + \beta log\, x_{it-1} + \delta d_{it} + \varepsilon_{it} \tag{5}$$

Model 1 (Eq. 2) refers to the pooled cross-sectioned ordinary least square (OLS) linear regression. In Model 2 (Eq. 3), we apply similar OLS regression, where both independent and dependent variables are log transformed. Additionally, we consider panel data with fixed effects regression, as indicated by the Hausman test. Model 3 (Eq. 4) is a panel data regression model with fixed effects and in Model 4 (Eq. 5) extended with the log-transformed independent and dependent variables. In all models, x is a vector of bank-specific variables (all of them are listed in Appendix 1), d is assigned dummies in the models, i represents the bank, and t is a time period, respectively. The countries profile effects and the time-invariant individual effect are captured in a_i and the regular unobserved factor in ε_{it}. The bank-specific variables x are lagged with 1-year period (t–1) to mitigate the endogeneity problems and because of the delayed effect of management reaction that is visible next year financial results. The correlation coefficients among all our variables were found not to exceed 0.50 (except between ROE and ROA). The dependent variable y refers to the risk-taking behavior of the financial institutions and is represented by two ratios.

The asset risk is captured in the non-performing loan ratio (NPL), which is a ratio of non-performing loans to total portfolio. The overall riskiness of the bank can be measured by the ratio of risk-weighted assets to total assets (RWATA) that reflects the riskiness of the business model of the banks in regulatory formulating (Janda and Kravtsov 2016). The first ratio is suitable for more traditional banks, where lending constitutes the main source of risk, while RWA includes the exposure of the bank to all types of risks mentioned by the regulations (Tanda 2015; Stádník 2014; Stádník and Miečinskienė 2015). In line with the theoretical framework, our explanatory variables x reflect the incentives of the agents: the shareholders who want to maximize the equity value (return on equity) and managers' efforts in achieving it and the bank manager's efficiency and monitoring efforts (return on equity, return on assets, noninterest income to gross income) and regulatory constraints reflected in the capital adequacy and leverage ratios. Two types of dummies capture the regulatory pressure and the governmental background of the banks in the dataset.

The controllable variable total assets (TA) are taken in the form of natural logarithm to control for potential size effects and gains from diversification of business lines. Efficiency ratios are represented by return on assets (ROA) and ratio of noninterest income to gross income (NITI). As a proxy of bank manager's efficiency, they indicate the efforts in optimizing the resources of the bank. The deteriorations in cost efficiency precede increases in non-performing loans due to the bad management and less monitoring efforts (Berger and DeYoung 1997; Podpiera and Weill 2008). The capital adequacy ratio (CAR) and leverage ratio (LR) address the restraints from regulatory requirements on solvency and capital, i.e., the regulatory pressure considerations (Šútorová and Teplý 2014). For a dummy variable "regulatory pressure," we apply the same approach as Matejašák et al. (2009). The dummy value "*1*" is assigned if the capital ratio of the bank is below the threshold level which is equal to the minimum regulatory requirement CAR (8%) plus one standard deviation of the bank's own capital ratio. Otherwise, the dummy value is *0*. Although the choice of one standard deviation is somehow arbitrary, the rationale for using this measure is that banks build a buffer above the regulatory minimum for precautionary reasons and the amount of this buffer depends on the volatility of capital ratio. Dummy variable "government ownership" takes the value 1 if the share of state ownership is higher than 50% and the opposite value = 0. It addresses the hypothetical incentives for the shareholders to assume higher risks if the potential governmental support is available (Cheng et al. 2016; Mariathasan et al. 2014; Ngalawa et al. 2016).

Results

The estimation results of our Models 1–4 are shown in Appendix 1 together with the coefficients of the explanatory variables, robust p-values, and the t-statistic for individual significance. The models with OLS and fixed effects regression produce in general comparable results and in most instances exhibit similar vector of the regression coefficients. In both linear and log-linear regression models, our estimated coefficients have the signs that we expected and generally compatible with the theoretical arguments in the literature.

The link between risk-taking and banks' performance valuation, as measured by profitability indicator ROE, was found to be statistically significant at level of 5% (p-value <0.05) in all Models 1–4. The negative sign and coefficients of both risk indicators NPL and RWATA in linear and especially in log-linear regressions can be interpreted in a way that deterioration in performance efforts by bank managers or inefficient allocation of resources induce banks to take excessive risks that causes further worsening of the risk profile and thus could indicate the evidences of moral hazard or "rent-seeking" behavior (Acharya et al. 2015). The results are consistent with the theoretical framework which explains the shareholder's motivation on maximizing equity value and manager efforts in achieving it.

The regression estimates for the indicators of the bank manager efficiency, represented by ROA and NITI (noninterest income to gross income), are statistically significant with coefficients from −0.492 to −0.804 in the log-linear models (II, IV) only for the asset risk indicator NPL. This could suggest that the decline in bank managers monitoring efforts and efficiency precedes the deterioration in the assets quality of the banks, described as "bad management" hypothesis by Podpiera and Weill (2008).

The capital adequacy ratio CAR has a strong impact on the level of credit risk taken by the CEE banks contrary to the leverage ratio. The coefficients of CAR are statistically significant (for risk indicator NPL) at a level of 5% (p-value <0.05) in Models 1–3 with the coefficients from −0.356 to −0.157. In general, these estimates imply that the banks adjust capital ratios and risk to desired levels; this is also confirmed in the empirical study by Matejašák et al. (2009). The negative sign of all coefficients are in line with logic of regulatory restraint in the theoretical model. This observation is further reiterated in our empirical evidences by the negative vector of coefficients of regulatory pressure which is represented by the dummy variable (REG). Contrary to the findings of Berger et al. (2005), Dong et al. (2014), and Iannotta et al. (2013), who suggest that the banks with a large share of state ownership are associated with inferior long-term performance and greater risk-taking, our results show a positive relation between government ownership and level of risk-taking. For both risk indicators NPL and RWATA in Models 1–2, the dummy (GOV) has a negative sign and statistically significant coefficients. This fact can be justified by several factors: traditionally less risky business models of the state-owned banks, different bank governance approach, and less pressure from the investor side on the profit maximization. According to our empirical results, the size of the total assets of the bank has no significant impact on the risk profile (NPL) and portfolio risk structure (RWATA), i.e., the diversification and size effects do not play significant role.

Conclusion

This study focuses on the analyses of the moral hazard incentives and the examination of the determinants of risk-taking behavior among the 500 banks in the Central Europe, Baltic, and Balkan region. We analyze moral hazard problems and examine which factors impact the risk profile of the banks in relationships between shareholders, bank managers, regulatory restraints, and ownership structure.

Our empirical findings point to the strong link between level of risk-taking and bank manager performance and efficiency, thus supporting the theoretical argumentation of the moral hazard incentives. The results could indicate that the decline in bank managers monitoring efforts or efficiency could induce excessive risk-taking and generally precedes the deterioration in the assets quality of the banks.

The regression estimates show that the capital requirements and regulatory restraints have the substantial impact on the risk-taking proving the fact that the bank capital requirements play a prominent role in sustaining financial stability. We find positive relation between government ownership and level of risk-taking among the banks in the dataset.

Acknowledgments The article is processed as an output of a research project. This project has received funding from the European Union's Horizon 2020 Research and Innovation Staff Exchange program under the Marie Sklodowska-Curie grant agreement No. 681228. We also acknowledge support from the Czech Science Foundation (grant15-00036S). The views expressed in the paper are those of the authors and not necessarily those of our institutions.

Appendix 1

Table 1 Regression results

NPL					RWA/TA			
	Pooled OLS		Fixed effects		Pooled OLS		Fixed effects	
Variables	Model 1	Model 2	Model 3	Model 4	Model 1	Model 2	Model 3	Model 4
ROE	−13.354*	−1.335*	−10.236*	−1.012*	−0.454*	−0.163*	−0.286*	−0.163*
	(−5.73)	(−2.95)	(−2.69)	(−2.29)	(−5.10)	(−2.71)	(−1.97)	(−2.68)
ROA	0.139	−0.729*	−0.108	−0.654*	0.0252*	0.072	0.017	0.007
	(1.07)	(−2.52)	(−0.43)	(−2.32)	(3.29)	(1.80)	(1.39)	(1.81)
NITI	−0.040*	−0.492*	0.004	−0.804*	0.000	0.042	0.000	0.044
	(−4.58)	(−2.39)	(0.44)	(−3.97)	(0.93)	(0.79)	(−0.2)	(0.84)
CAR	−0.356*	−1.280*	−0.157*	−1.266*	−0.003*	−0.027*	−0.001	−0.027*
	(−12.71)	(−10.30)	(−3.65)	(−10.5)	(−4.66)	(−1.93)	(−0.34)	(−1.91)
LR	0.039*	0.070*	0.024	0.096*	0.007*	−0.039	0.001	−0.040*
	(2.06)	(2.29)	(0.99)	(3.10)	(4.80)	(−2.39)	(0.34)	(−2.36)
TAlog	−0.244	0.048	0.370	−0.013	0.031*	0.078*	0.019	0.078
	(−1.85)	(2.34)	(1.33)	(−0.41)	(6.38)	(4.91)	(1.71)	(4.81)
REG	−2.833	−0.449	7.452*	−0.587*	−0.002	0.027	−0.053	0.019
	(−1.75)	(−1.82)	(4.66)	(−2.45)	(−0.95)	(0.40)	(−1.75)	(0.27)
GOV	−3.239*	−0.078	0.000	0.058	−0.082*	−0.072	0.000	−0.075
	(−3.09)	(−0.49)	(0.00)	(0.37)	(−3.02)	(−1.37)	(0.00)	(−1.43)
Obs	2476	2476	2476	2476	612	612	612	612
Banks	500	500	500	500	500	500	500	500
F test	0.000	0.000	0.000	0.000	0.000	0.000	0.000	0.000
R-sq.	0.1905	0.1299	0.1293	0.1266	0.1716	0.0582	0.1036	0.072

Source: BankScope and own calculations
The 2006–2014 dummy coefficients in Models 1 and 2 are omitted since they are not relevant for our analysis
*Denotes statistical significance p-values below <0.05. In parentheses, we show the t-statistics

References

Acharya VV, Mehran H, Thakor AV (2015) Caught between Scylla and Charybdis? Regulating ank leverage when there is rent seeking and risk shifting. Rev Corp Finance Stud 5 (1):36–75cfv006. https://doi.org/10.1093/rcfs/cfv006

Antzoulatos AA, Tsoumas C (2014) Institutions, moral hazard and expected government support of banks. J Financ Stab 15:161–171. https://doi.org/10.1016/j.jfs.2014.09.006

Berger AN, Clarke GRG, Udell GF, Cull R, Klapper LF (2005) Corporate governance and bank performance: a joint analysis of the static, selection, and dynamic effects of domestic, foreign, and state ownership (SSRN Scholarly Paper No. ID 756948). Social Science Research Network, Rochester, NY

Berger AN, DeYoung R (1997) Problem loans and cost efficiency in commercial banks. Finance Econ Discuss Ser 17:317–347

Cheng J, Dai M, Dufourt F (2016) Banking Crisis, Moral Hazard and Fiscal Policy Responses (Working Papers of BETA No. 2016–06). Bureau d'Economie Théorique et Appliquée, UDS, Strasbourg

De Caux R, McGroarty F, Brede M (2017) The evolution of risk and bailout strategy in banking systems. Phys Stat Mech Appl 468:109–118

Distinguin I, Kouassi T, Tarazi A, Distinguin I, Kouassi T, Tarazi A (2013) Interbank deposits and market discipline: evidence from central and Eastern Europe. J Comp Econ 41:544–560

Dong Y, Meng C, Firth M, Hou W (2014) Ownership structure and risk-taking: comparative evidence from private and state-controlled banks in China. https://doi.org/10.2139/ssrn.2089979

Duran MA, Lozano-Vivas A (2012) Moral hazard, risk shifting and the financial structure of banks. SSRN Electron J. https://doi.org/10.2139/ssrn.2114058

Fungáčová Z, Solanko L (2009) Risk-taking by Russian banks: do location, ownership and size matter? Chapters SUERF Stud 2:129–148

Furlong FT, Keeley MC (1991) Capital regulation and bank risk-taking: a note (reprinted from journal of banking and finance). Econ Rev 13:34–39

Iannotta G, Nocera G, Sironi A (2013) The impact of government ownership on bank risk. J Financ Intermed 22:152–176

Janda K (2011) Inefficient credit rationing and public support of commercial credit provision. J Institutional Theor Econ JITE 167:371–391

Janda K (2009) Bankruptcies with soft budget constraint. Manch Sch 77:430–460

Janda K, Kravtsov O (2016) Interdependencies between leverage and capital ratios in the Banking sector of the Czech Republic. MPRA Paper

Janda K, Michalikova E, Skuhrovec J (2013) Credit support for export: robust evidence from the Czech Republic. World Econ 36:1588–1610. https://doi.org/10.1111/twec.12061

Jeitschko TD, Jeung SD (2005) Incentives for risk-taking in banking – a unified approach. J Bank Financ 29:759–777. https://doi.org/10.1016/j.jbankfin.2004.05.028

Jensen MC, Meckling WH (1976) Theory of the firm: managerial behavior, agency costs and ownership structure. J Financ Econ 3:305–360. https://doi.org/10.1016/0304-405X(76)90026-X

Laffont J-J, Martimort D (2001) The theory of incentives: the Principal-Agent Model. ResearchGate

Mariathasan M, Merrouche O, Werger C (2014) Bailouts and moral hazard: how implicit government guarantees affect financial stability. CEPR Discuss Pap

Matejašák M, Teplý P, Černohorský J (2009) The impact of regulation of banks in the us and the EU-15 countries. E+M Ekonomie a Management

Mejstřík M, Pečená M, Teplý P (2015) Bankovnictví v teorii a praxi/Banking in Theory and Practice – Mejstřík Michal – Pečená Magda – Teplý Petr | Knihkupectví Karolinum. Karolinum

Ngalawa H, Tchana FT, Viegi N (2016) Banking instability and deposit insurance: the role of moral hazard. J Appl Econ 19:323–350

Podpiera J, Weill L (2008) Bad luck or bad management? Emerging banking market experience. J Financ Stab 4:135–148

Raudeliuniene J, Stadnik B, Kindaryte R (2016) Knowledge appliance process: theoretical and practical evaluation aspects. Entrepreneurship Sustainability Issues 3(4):368–379

Stádník B (2014) The volatility puzzle of bonds. Conference: 8th International Scientific Conference on Business and Management Location: Vilnius, Lithuania Date: May 15–16, 2014 8th International Scientific Conference Business and Management 2014 Book Series: Business and Management-Spausdinta Pages: 313–319 Article Number: bm.2014.039 Published: 2014

Stádník B, Miečinskienė A (2015) Complex model of market price development and its simulation. J Bus Econ Manag 16(4):786–807

Tanda A (2015) The effects of bank regulation on the relationship between capital and risk

Šútorová B, Teplý P (2014) The level of capital and the value of EU banks under Basel III. Prague Econ Pap 2014:143–161

Zhang D, Cai J, Dickinson DG, Kutan AM (2016) Non-performing loans, moral hazard and regulation of the Chinese commercial banking system. J Bank Financ 63:48–60

Changes in Mortgage LTV Schemes: Are We Facing New Price Bubble on Residential Market?

David Mazáček

Abstract This paper describes the situation on the current residential real estate market in the Czech Republic, which is driven by Prague residential market. We are facing continuous price increase over the past few years. Recently banks came with a new regulation scheme for mortgages, which limits maximum amount could be lent in percentage of the apartment purchase price. This paper analyses if the residential market in Prague is facing new bubble on the market and if this step taken by banks in mortgage lending is caused by defensive strategy or if the market is not facing any big troubles and the change in LTV is just the regulatory step.

Keywords Real estate • Interest rates • Banking regulation • Price bubbles

Introduction

Apartment prices in Prague are continuously increasing over the few past years – from year 2011 to 2016, prices of new apartment units increased by almost 25% according to the Institute of Strategic Investments (2016). Jones Lang LaSalle (2016) despite that shows the number of available apartments on the market went down from 6200 to 4220 and every year is sold more new apartments. The apartment prices are now slightly higher than were in 2008, when the crisis on Czech real estate market started. The crisis in 2008 and the development on the market before and after showed that the demand is not driven only by the absolute price of an apartment but more is the demand driven by the future expectation of price development when the individuals are speculating if it is better to buy an apartment now or in few years and by the mortgage instalment, which is more important than the absolute price of an apartment. This practical experience from

---

D. Mazáček (✉)
University of Economics, Prague, Institute of Strategic Investments, Nam. W. Churchilla 4, 130 67 Prague, Czech Republic
e-mail: david.mazacek@isti.cz

D. Procházka (ed.), *The Impact of Globalization on International Finance and Accounting*, Springer Proceedings in Business and Economics,
https://doi.org/10.1007/978-3-319-68762-9_11

the market is confirmed also in La Cava (2016). Taking a decision if the prices, which look extremely high now, will cause next collapse or not needs deeper analysis of other fundaments.

The most available papers are concerned on the relation between property prices and one or two explanatory variables. Tsatsaronise and Zhu (2004) demonstrate the characteristic of long cycles of growth and recessions on the real estate market. All of 17 examined countries went through 2 cycles in the past 33 years. Similar situation can be observed in the Czech Republic as well. Englund and Ioannides (1997) proved in their paper that there is not any international real estate market cycle, which does not deny the hypothesis that there can be cycles on national level. Furthermore, Englund and Ioannides (1997) are demonstrating that GDP and interest rates are very good prediction tools of residential price pathway. Bracke (2010) derives that when the price boom is excluded, then the prices are oscillating round stable numbers, while price boom is shifting prices to the next price level. Sunega (2010) derives the presence of price bubble on the Prague market using model consisted among all of residential price level, apartment lease prices, interest rate and disposable income. Girouard and Kennedy (2006) demonstrate the relation between residential price development and fundamental macroeconomic data. Explanatory variables of residential price differ across different studies; Mikhed and Zemcik (2007) allocate the importance to apartment lease prices, consumer price index, disposable income and stock market wealth. Vizek and Posedel (2009) are examining that the common macroeconomic variables like GDP growth, real interest rates, stock market profitability or unemployment can be used for residential price development description also in CEE.

Data and Methodology

This chapter analyses and shows the view on existence of potential real estate bubble on the Prague residential market and benchmarks relations between price of new residential development against the main variables that influence the apartment price and demand.

Introduction demonstrated that the price of new residential development depends on interest rates, income and flat prices. The explanatory variables are selected based on model presented by David Mazacek (2015), where it is demonstrated that the price of new apartments in Prague can be explained by the following variables: real transaction price change, GDP change per household, unemployment rate, change in number of issued mortgages, VAT change, change in rents and the presence of a boom on the market.

The first part is taking into account the empirical data and demonstrates current development and changes in comparison to post-crisis period on the market; the second part then analyses the proximity of real estate bubble on the market.

Development of New Apartment Price Drivers

Figure 1 shows the comparison of individual gross wage burden by mortgage payments over few years. In all years, an average apartment of 60 sq. m. size is compared with market average price.

Nowadays market average price can be taken from Deloitte database[1]; for the past years, the average prices were calculated by complicated model using data from Jones Lang LaSalle reports, from database of Mr. Dolansky and from reports prepared by Trigema, Central Group and Ekospol. Especially the difference between the offering prices, which can be found in developers' price list and the real transaction prices, had to be reflected. The difference is always higher in crisis period. Gross income was gained from Czech Statistical Office.

Figure 2 shows that due to lowering mortgage interest rates and increasing gross wage in Prague, the share of mortgage instalment on the individual gross income is significantly lower than in the real estate market crisis time in 2008, despite the prices per sq. m. of new apartment raised rapidly over the last few years. It also needs to be seen that the increase of average price per sq. m. of new apartment is caused also by the change of the mix on the market. At the end of 2009, there were 60% of very cheap apartments with lower standard, with decreasing interest rates and with better situation on the market; the clients could move to the higher standard of housing; it means that the demand shifted to the more expensive apartments and the share of low standard apartments on the market in year 2016 was below 40%. These shifts between segments played a big role in increasing the average price of sq. m. of a new apartment. The average size of a new apartment is slightly increasing over the past years in Prague. This figure underlines the

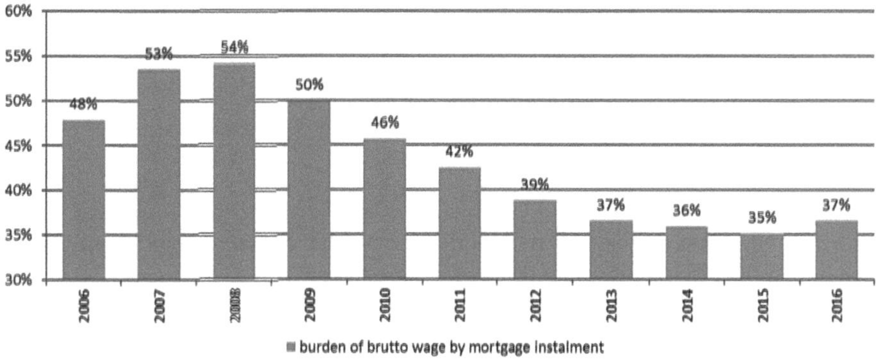

Fig. 1 Burden of average gross wage by average mortgage instalment (Source: Calculation based on data from Czech Statistical Office, Deloitte – Cenova mapa, Jones Lang LaSalle)

[1]Deloitte is running in cooperation with other institutions portal cenovamapa.org where all price indicators for Prague market as well as other cities in the Czech Republic can be found.

Fig. 2 Gross wage vs. 20 years mortgage (Source: Calculation based on data from Czech Statistical Office, Hypoindex data)

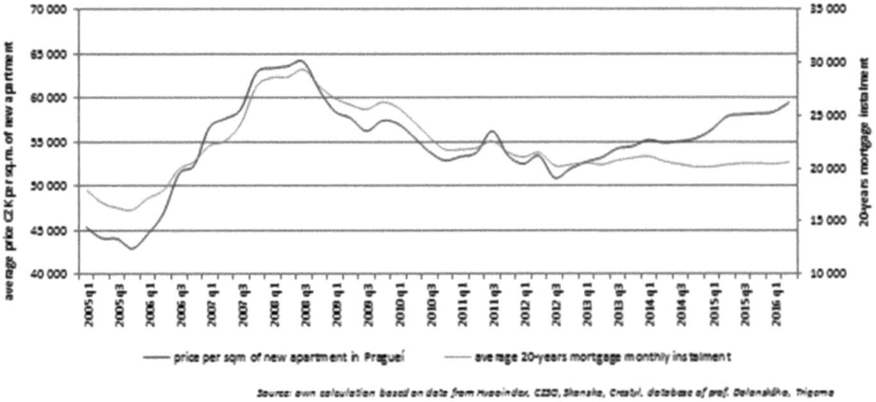

Fig. 3 Interest rates vs. average 20 years mortgage instalment (Source: Own calculation based on data from Hypoindex, CZSO, Crestyl, Skanska)

statement that the demand is more oriented by the current height of mortgage instalment than by the absolute price of an apartment.

Figure 3 shows the development of interest rates and average transaction price of a sq. m. of a new apartment in Prague. It could be awaited that in the period of increasing mortgage, interest rates will be pressured on the prices and demand will be lowering. This figure shows increasing prices before the crises in the same time when the interest rates were increasing as well. In the prior crises, situations were very important in the future expectations on the demand side. This was confirmed by Case and Shiller in their article. In that time was a big discussion about increasing VAT on sale of new apartments and the market was afraid of rapid growth in prices, the feeling necessity of buying apartments before this legislative change caused that the prices were speeding up and clients were able to spend even 54% of their average income to buy the apartment, prices went so high, that after the VAT change was no difference in pricing and the VAT difference were absorbed from the developer profits. Now market profits a lot from expectations of future increase of interest rates, which will make apartments drive the relative expensiveness of new apartments. Increase of interest rates is very probable also in connection with change of Czech National Bank CZK/EUR exchange rate policy – GAPKO (2017).

There is one more player coming on the market and helping to better understand the future situation on the market – the supply. In the model of Mazacek (2015), supply is not an explanatory variable on the Prague market, because in the observed period, it was just too big. In 2016 for the first time in the last 15 years, the number of available apartments on the market is lower than the yearly demand. Supply will start to play significant role on the market in the next years. The gap in supply is caused by low number of new permitted projects and lack of new development sites which corresponds with the absence of a new Prague Metropolitan Plan. The smaller supply in the next years can equal the impact of increasing interest rates, and with the highest probability in the next years, we can expect either slightly growing prices or steady state of the price development. After the new metropolitan plan comes in game (estimated 2022), the supply can then in the next 2 years increase massively, which probably will lead to the fall in apartment prices and recession on the market for some given time, until the overlap of supply will be absorbed.

Bubbles in New Apartment Pricing

There is no one widely accepted definition of a bubble. But we can define it as a difference between real value of the asset and current market value. We talk about bursting bubble when the actors on the market realise that the asset (in our case real estate) is overpriced. By overpriced, it means that high price is not based on fundamental factors but only expectation that prices will go up (Case and Shiller 2003). We can find some evidence about the influence of expectation on real estate market in the work of Case and Shiller. They are stating that bubbles are caused by amateurs on a real estate market who make infrequent transactions. Because they can't estimate the real present value, they are causing unbalance on the market and therefore a bubble. Some academics explain bubble thru mortgage rates. For example, Mints (2006) studied the Russian real estate market and concluded that there is a bubble occurred, because of large disparity between mortgage rates and rate of return risk – equivalent assets. For our purposes, we used adjusted model from Čadil (2009). He chose the following variables to identify if there is any bubble or not – flat prices, households income represented by gross monthly wages and interest rates. The issue of real estate bubbles was described also by EU

Commission in 2016 and real estate bubble index and the Czech Republic reached on of the lowest rankings in Europe, which means low strength of real estate price bubble despite the prices are reaching their maximums.

According to the model of Čadil (2009), we analysed the influence of interest rates, gross income and development on occurrence of bubble this year. As we can see from the data above, the situation on the market now shows just small resemblance to the situation in 2008. The similarity is that the real estate market is going thru a period of great appreciation which can be seen on rising prices per sq. m. Income of households has risen since 2008, and moreover the interest rates went down compared to crises period when the rates were around 6%. This leads to relative decrease in month instalments compared with gross month income. Generally, people have higher income and lower mortgage payments than they have 9 years ago.

For now we are not facing the bubble, but there is danger of rising instalments after end of fixation period of the mortgages provided in the last years.

LTV Regulation on the Market

If the market is not facing the price bubble and the threat of fall in price seems to be not the case of nearly future, why the regulation of LTVs is coming in place? Several reasons can be seen: first of all, risk profile correction, second the awareness of market development in longer term and last client segmentation. The topic of LTV on mortgages is broadly in discussion on EU level as well. The riskiness of mortgages is slightly increasing; especially the risk of increase in interest rates can bring in troubles to those mortgages which fixation period ends. The banks need to lower the number of clients who took mortgage without having savings and are paying instalments up to the last remaining crown. The banks either have to increase the interest rates significantly which will have huge impact on the market or try to lower proportion of such clients on new deals. Individuals having 10% of apartment price in cash will be more resistant to future changes in interest rates. Some banks are offering purposeless loan on the remaining part of purchase price, but this is with higher interest rates, significantly shorter period which makes the instalments in initial period a lot more expensive. As the supply is currently lowering, the potential caused decrease in demand will be not influencing the market.

The regulation regarding buying second and third apartment will clearly segment the clients on those ones who are buying apartment to live there and on those who are buying it as an investment and going to lease them.

Mortgages are very long-term financial instruments; currently common 30 years lending period was not possible few years ago. The banks need to be prepared for situation in the next 8–15 years while giving mortgage to an individual. If the market will collapse in the next 10 years, the LTV limit of 80% will prevent banks from loss and give them space of 20% of purchase price plus already repaid annuity

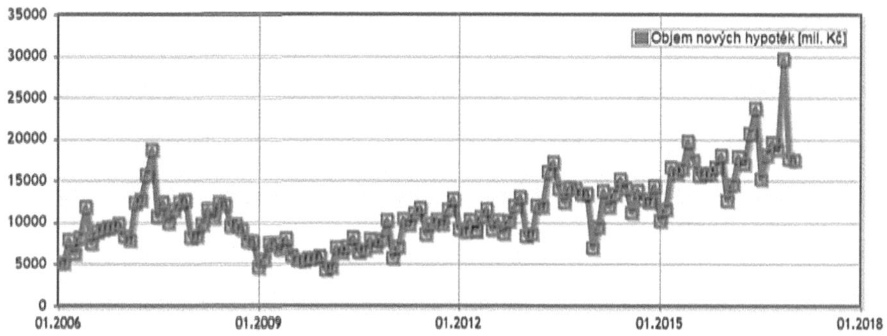

Fig. 4 Volume of new mortgages (Source: Hypoindex.cz)

as the total possible loss of apartment value without losing the value of the mortgage loan.

On the other hand, we need to see as well that the current regulation is not bringing much now and will be doing so in the next few years. Figure 4 shows the percentage of value of new mortgage loans on the total amount lent in mortgages; it shows also the percentage of loans covered under new more protective regulation. Until the percentage will be significant, we have count with few years and would be very beneficiary if the regulation is not changing over next years again and again.

Conclusion

This paper showed that the Prague residential market is not facing price bubble now but will be very probably positioned in the price bubble within the next 6–8 years. The regulatory step in terms of increasing LTV of mortgages is caused very probably by two reasons: one of them is that mortgage is a very long-term financial instrument, so the regulator is reacting now on the situation which might come in the next 6–8 years. The other reason is that the mortgage interest rates were and still are very low. Nowadays we can still obtain the mortgage interest rate under 2% p.a. The pressure on increase of the interest rate is very clear since last year, and this effect can be even multiplied if the Czech National Bank will stop intervening on CZK/EUR exchange rate. Interest rate increase will make the mortgages with elapsed fixation significantly more expensive. Putting limits on LTV brings first kind of filter that only people who are having some savings to pay apartment purchase price not covered by mortgage are of course clients with higher Bonita; secondly it stops some households taking more mortgages just to create their small apartments portfolio and thirdly in case that the client is not able to repay the mortgage, the force sale of an apartment even with some discount repays the outstanding mortgage. The LTV regulation is not the signal of overheated market, but it is a signal of increase of mortgage interest rates, which is coming.

References

Bracke P (2010) How long do housing cycles last? A duration analysis for 19 OECD countries. Working Paper No WP/11/231, International Monetary Fund

Čadil J (2009) Housing price bubble analysis – case of the Czech Republic. Prague Econ Pap 1:38–47

Case KE , Shiller RE (2003) Is there a bubble in the housing market? Cowles Foundation Paper No 1089, Yale University

Englund P, Ionnades Y (1997) House price dynamics: an international empirical perspective. J Hous Econ 6:119–136

Gapko P (2017) Inflation is again over the plan. Actual Macroeconomic Comment, Moneta Bank

Girourard N, Kennedy M, Van Der Noord P, Andre CH (2006) Recent house price developments: the role of fundamentals. Working Paper No ECO/WKP/(2006)3, OECD Economic Department

ISTI (2016) New housing prices vs. households income – is there an opportunity to invest? Institute of Strategic Investments of Faculty of Finance and Accounting University of Economics, Prague

JLL (2016) Prague City report Q3-2016. Jones Lang la Salle, Prague

La Cava G (2016) Housing prices, mortgage interest rates and the rising share of capital income in the United States. Work. Pap. No RDP 2016-04, Reserve Bank of Australia

Lux M, Sunega P (2010) Sustainability of residential price development in the Czech Republic. Polit Econ 2:225–252

Mazacek D (2015) Determinants of residential price development of new apartments in Prague. Diploma Thesis, Institute of Economics Studies, Faculty of Social Sciences, Charles University

Mikhed Y, Zemcik P (2007) Do house prices reflects fundamentals: aggregate and data panel evidence. Working Paper No ISSN 1211-3298, CERGE-EI

Tsatsaronis K, Zhu H (2004) What drives housing price dynamics: cross country evidence. BIS Q Rev

Vizek M, Posedel P (2009) House price determinants in transition and EU-15 countries. Post-Communist Econ 21(3):327–343

Liability Risk Management of Central European Banks Under New Regulatory Requirements

Hana Džmuráňová, Martina Hejdová, and Petr Teplý

Abstract This paper describes liability risk management of Central European banks located in the Czech Republic, Slovakia, Poland, Austria and Hungary. We find that liabilities of the analysed banks have similar features and report similar exposure to both liquidity and interest rate risks. Additionally, we discuss the share of demand and term deposits on bank funding and its implications for liquidity and interest rate risk in relation to new regulatory requirements set by the Basel Committee for Banking Supervision. We conclude that these requirements might be challenging for the analysed banks because of their liabilities' structure.

Keywords Demand deposits • Term deposits • Liquidity risk • Interest rate risk

Introduction

Classical asset and liability management focus on a balance sheet view of the firm and the control of two key balance sheet risks: interest rate risk and liquidity risk (Skoglund and Chen 2015; Resti and Sironi 2007). In this paper, we focus on liquidity and interest rate risk of liability side of banks in the Czech Republic, Slovakia, Poland, Austria and Hungary, further denoted as ACs (analysed countries) in relation to new Interest Rate Risk in the Banking Book (IRRBB) guidelines. The aim of this paper is to assess the banks' readiness for those guidelines by comparative analysis of balance sheet structure.

H. Džmuráňová (✉)
Charles University, Faculty of Social Sciences, Institute of Economic Studies, Prague, Czech Republic
e-mail: hanadzmuranova@gmail.com

M. Hejdová • P. Teplý
University of Economics, Faculty of Finance and Accounting, Department of Banking and Insurance, Prague, Czech Republic
e-mail: mhejdova@gmail.com; petr.teply@vse.cz

D. Procházka (ed.), *The Impact of Globalization on International Finance and Accounting*, Springer Proceedings in Business and Economics,
https://doi.org/10.1007/978-3-319-68762-9_12

The following text continues as follows. First we discuss sound principles of liability management of banks and new regulatory requirements related to this. Second, we investigate structure of liabilities in ACs, and we derive conclusions how this structure will influence interest rate and liquidity risk of liabilities in those banks under the new regulatory requirement. Finally, in conclusion we state final remarks.

Methodology

Bank client liabilities can be divided into two major groups: (i) Non-maturity deposits (NMDs), which are deposits redeemable on notice. Typical examples of NMDs are current accounts and savings deposits without defined maturity. (ii) Maturing deposits (thereby denoted MDs) are deposits with given maturity. Typical examples of MDs are term deposits.

Both NMDs and MDs are in central of regulators attention as both are a source of liquidity and interest rate risk due to their embedded options. The liquidity crisis that started in 2007 clearly showed the importance of stable funding sources for banks (Skoglund and Chen 2015), and henceforth regulators' push in this area is logical consequence of those events.

Regulatory Requirements: Overview of NMDs and MDs

In 2015, the European Bank Authority published final version of an IRRBB guideline (Interest Rate Risk Management of the Banking Book) in which they largely focus on interest rate risk arising from NMDs and set up general rules for their risk management. EBA (2015) is binding for banks from January 1, 2016. In 2016, the Basel Committee for Bank Supervision released their update of the IRRBB guideline as well. BCSB (2016) goes beyond EBA (2015) in a stricter treatment of NMDs. BCBS (2016) goes into action from January 1, 2018. Banks are expected to comply with those guidelines at the discretion of local regulator. For example, the Czech National Bank approved the compliance with EBA (2015) on February 11, 2016 (CNB 2016). Table 1 summarises both guidelines in relation to NMDs and MDs. Last but not least, during 2017, EBA is expected to publish consultation document dedicated to the update of IRRBB guidelines from 2015 (EBA 2017). This consultation document will take into account BCBS (2016).

Table 1 Summary of regulatory requirements linked to modelling of deposits

EBA (2015)	BCBS (2016)	Impact on liability risk management
NMDs must be modelled; special attention must be paid to interest rate sensitivity of volumes	NMDs must be modelled; special attention must be paid to interest rate sensitivity of volumes. NMDs must be segmented according to the client type to retail transactional, retail non-transactional and wholesale. Furthermore, deposits must be divided into stable and non-stable and core and noncore. The aim of division is to separate liabilities that are expected to reprise from those that are not expected to reprise at any condition. Caps are defined on minimum amounts in the given category and their average maturities	Banks need to properly establish models describing relationship between market rates and deposit volumes. This can be for some banks demanding from resources perspective and might imply additional costs into technical resources as well as human resources
Maximum average duration[a] of deposits is 5 years	Maximum average maturity of deposits is 4.5 years for retail transactional, 3.15 years for retail non-transactional and 2.25 years for wholesale. Duration is thus always strictly lower than maturity	In Džmuráňová and Teplý (2016), we show that effective maturity of NMDs in the Czech Republic is far beyond the limit defined by EBA (2015). This limit might hence imply banks to change product structure to ensure compliance with regulation. BCBS (2016) paper is even more restrictive
Disclosure	Disclosure	Banks need to asses models in internal as well as in external validation runs
Data reliability	Minimum requirement of 10-year length of analysed data in internal models and data reliability	To estimate relationship between volumes and interest rates, bank would ideally need at least one full economic business cycle of falling and rising rates. However, for banks this could be a problem as data may not be available in many cases
MDs risk management shall take into account embedded options	MDs risk management shall take into account embedded option. Paper in detail defines how early termination rates shall be modelled under different interest rate shocks	

Source: Authors based on EBA (2015) and BCBS (2016)

[a]By duration, we mean a measure of sensitivity to market rate changes; see Eq. (2)

Non-maturity Deposits

Embedded option of NMDs related to liquidity risk[1] is the fact that client can withdraw balance at wish. Legal maturity of NMD is 1 day, while its effective maturity is much larger however as discussed by Džmuráňová and Teplý (2016). Banks need to employ internal models to estimate effective maturity. EBA (2015), BCBS (2016) and Bohn and Elkenbracht-Huizing (2014) also point out that banks have to have in action proper statistical models that take into account interest rate sensitivity of volumes when assessing liquidity risk of NMDs, mainly in relation to current low-rate environment.

Embedded option of NMDs related to interest rate risk is the fact that client rates are administrated; banks can change them at will. Some types of NMDs exhibit very sticky pricing, for example, transactional accounts. Transactional accounts are used for daily liquidity needs of the client, not for savings. Due to this, client rates on transactional accounts are generally very low and do not respond to changes in market rates; see, for example, Hejdová et al. (2017). In case of insensitive sticky client rates, the interest rate risk arises from nature of liquidity risk as repricing takes place as NMDs mature. On the contrary, in case of NMDs with pricing that is derived from the market, i.e. those banks adjust deposit rate based on market rates development, interest rate risk arises earlier than liquidity risk. A typical example of NMDs with deposit pricing related to market rates is savings deposits. Interest rate risk is also a source of earnings risk as the whole outstanding portfolio's deposit rate of NMDs is adjusted based on changes in market rates, which exposes bank to NII loss under increasing market rates assuming that assets would reprise less quickly than liabilities.

Maturity Deposits

MDs have, in contrast to NMDs, defined maturity and pricing in the contract. Their liquidity risk and interest rate risk are thus straightforward. BCBS (2016) as well as EBA (2015) require banks to take into account two major embedded options of MDs in their internal models. Those options are (i) early termination and (ii) rollover of short-term deposits. Early termination in terms of liquidity risk implies that bank needs to be ready to provide funds to the client early than by maturity, while roll-over option implies that bank should internally estimate maturity of MDs as longer than the defined in the contract. In terms of interest rate risk, it arises under early termination option during increasing market rates, when client might like to get rid of low-interest asset. In case of rollover,

[1]For more details on liquidity risk see, for instance, Resti and Sironi (2007) or Černohorská et al. (2012).

interest rate risk is not present as bank can reprise liability at the moment of maturity and rolled-over MDs are priced at the current market conditions.

Differences in Risk Management of NMDs and MDs

The logical conclusion of description provided above is that NMDs are riskier instruments for bank than MDs given that in case of MDs, an exposure to the risk is defined by the deviance from contractual characteristics of the product, while in case of NMDs, a bank has to fully establish behavioural models of the product.

Empirical Analysis

We define the liquidity development of deposits as follows:

$$AM_i = \frac{\sum_{t=1}^{T} w_t CF_t^i}{T}, \tag{1}$$

where i defines interest rate scenario (flat rates, increasing market rates or decreasing market rates), AM is average maturity, and w_t is weight of each cash flow CF_t in the period t, $t = 1,\ldots,T$. Equation (1) for different scenarios, i gives a measure of liquidity risk.

We define interest rate risk of deposits as in Bohn and Elkenbracht-Huizing (2014), i.e.

$$\Delta V = \frac{V_{i_1} - V_{i=flat}}{V_{i=flat} \Delta r}, \tag{2}$$

where

$$V_i = \sum_{t=1}^{T} \frac{CF_t^i}{(1 + r_t)^t}, \tag{3}$$

i defines interest rate scenario (flat rates, increasing market rates or decreasing market rates) and V_i stands for present value of MDs and NMDs. The measure of sensitivity as presented in Eq. (2) is thus the measure of magnitude of value changes. The further from present day, the bigger the value change. As described in Bohn and Elkenbracht-Huizing (2014), the change in value can be hedged by appropriate selection of hedging instruments under the condition that sensitivity of a hedge is the same as a sensitivity of MDs or NMDs.[2] Under this assumption, the bank could theoretically achieve zero sensitivity on the balance sheet level – i.e. a bank would be fully hedged against movements in interest rates of liability would be fully hedged by assets with same interest rate risk. However, such strategy may not be viable business strategy given that major purpose of the banking system is a maturity transformation of funds from subject with excess of funds to subjects with a lack of them.

Results and Discussion

We analysed yearly structure of deposit liability balance sheet of all banks in ACs using data from the BankScope database from 1990 to 2015. Our aim is to see driving factors of interest rate risk and liquidity risk based on balance sheet structure; our empirical analysis is thus the comparison of balance sheets of banks, which gives us a clear picture regarding the exposure of banks to both liquidity and interest rate risk of deposits. First, we investigate the structure of funding of banks in terms of MDs and NMDs. Figure 1 shows the relative share of demand deposits to total liabilities. The dynamic within the last 10 years is clearly visible – the increase of share of NMDs to total liabilities. This implies that banks in ACs are more exposed to liquidity risk of NMDs than MDs and liability side is riskier due to reasons in differences in the risk management of demand and term deposits discussed above. The BankScope database distinguishes between different levels of consolidation: statement of a mother bank integrating the statements of its controlled subsidiaries or branches with no unconsolidated companion (C1)/with an unconsolidated companion (C2) and statement not integrating the statements of the possible controlled subsidiaries or branches of the concerned bank with no consolidated companion (U1).

Second, we investigate maturity structure of deposits in ACs. As we showed in Eqs. (1) and (2), liquidity risk is directly derived from timing of cash flows, while interest rate risk is related to changes in market values of those cash flows under different interest rate scenarios. In Table 2 we show maturity structure of deposits in ACs. For MDs we apply bucket average contractual maturities as in Table 2, while for NMDs (bucket deposits <3 months), we apply caps from BCBS (2016) to define their maximum average effective maturities assuming equal distribution of types of deposits in all banks. As we can see, NMDs generally drive liability side of assets to larger maturities given their big share and long effective maturities, which given in Eq. (2) implies that the change in

[2]In real situation, first-order derivation like the one presented in Eq. (2) shall be accompanied also by convexity measures and adjustment for basis risk; for details see Bohn and Elkenbracht-Huizing (2014).

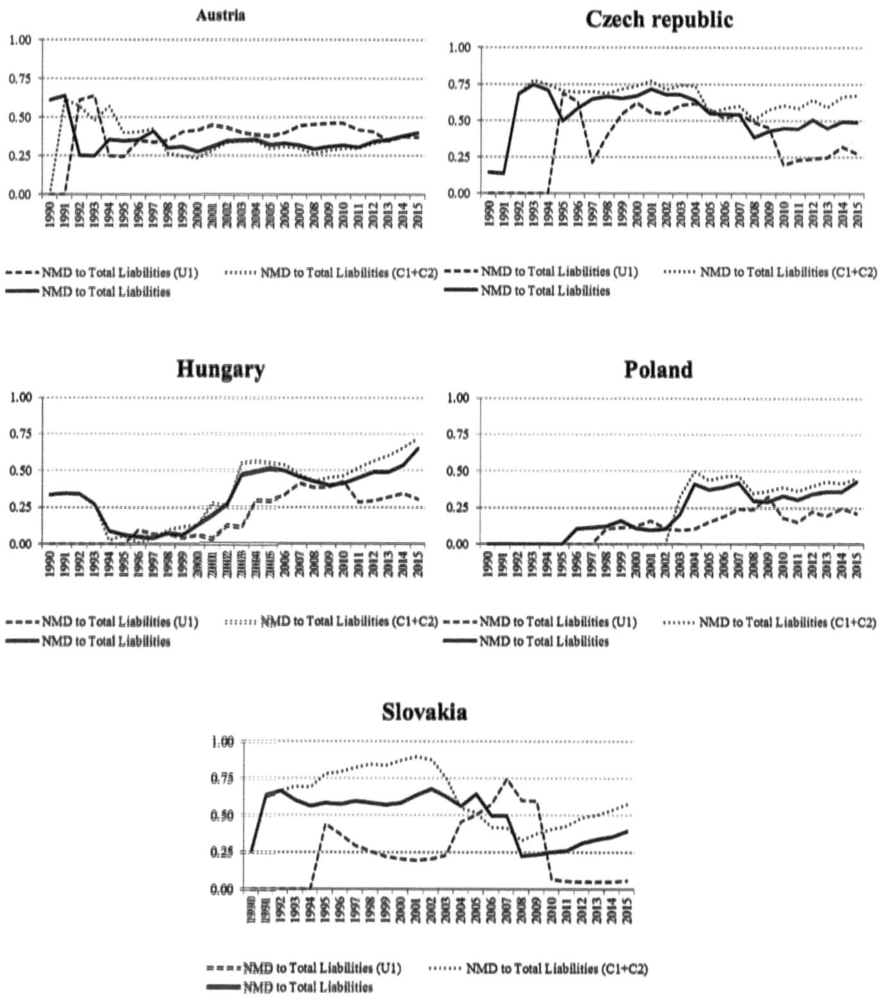

Fig. 1 Share of NMDs to total liabilities (Source: Authors based on data from the BankScope database)

value of liabilities is quite large, implying so high interest rate risk of liabilities of banks in ACs.[3]

Third, in relation to the maturity structure and possibility of hedging of short-term liabilities (on-demand liabilities assuming their legal maturity, not effective one), we look on relative share of short-term deposits and assets on total deposits

[3]Regarding pricing of demand deposits, for simplicity we follow results of Hejdová et al. (2017), and we say that NMD pricing is not sensitive to changes in market rates, which is reasonable assumption for the rest of ACs as well given the large share of transactional funding on total NMDs (BankScope database).

Table 2 Relative distribution of deposits according to its maturity

		Deposits <3 months	Deposits 3–12 months	Deposits 1–5 years	Deposits >5 years	Liquidity risk (approximated in years)
CZ	Share sample	69%	14%	12%	5%	3.04
	Share 2015	85%	4%	9%	2%	3.33
AT	Share sample	55%	16%	24%	6%	2.90
	Share 2015	71%	15%	10%	4%	3.04
SK	Share sample	59%	23%	17%	1%	2.69
	Share 2015	61%	23%	16%	0%	2.68
PL	Share sample	86%	11%	3%	1%	3.17
	Share 2015	74%	18%	5%	3%	2.97
HU	Share sample	49%	41%	7%	3%	2.29
	Share 2015	81%	10%	7%	3%	3.19

Source: Authors. Share sample is the share of deposits <3 months, deposits 3–12 months, deposits 1–5 years and deposits >5 years on sum of all deposits across all observed horizon, while share 2015 shows this number only for 2015

and assets as documented in Fig. 2. We can see that in all analysed ACs, the discrepancy is highly present as banks have more short-term products on a liability side than on the asset side. On the other hand, assuming effective maturities for NMDs under caps required by BCBS (2016), we might in fact receive that banks are naturally hedged against interest rate risk as NMDs will be hedged by long-term assets like mortgages.

Conclusion

In this paper we discussed sources of liquidity and interest rate risk of liability side of banks in Central Europe (the Czech Republic, Slovakia, Poland, Austria and Hungary). We described that non-maturity deposits are due to their embedded options riskier liabilities than maturing deposits. We found that banks in Central Europe share common liability structure of having major share of funding in a form of non-maturity deposits, which translates into high interest rate risk of liabilities of banks given long effective maturities of non-maturing deposits. New regulatory requirements set by the BCBS related to IRRBB may be challenging for Central European banks characterised by large amount of non-maturing funding for two reasons. First, sound models will be required by the regulator. Second, regulated

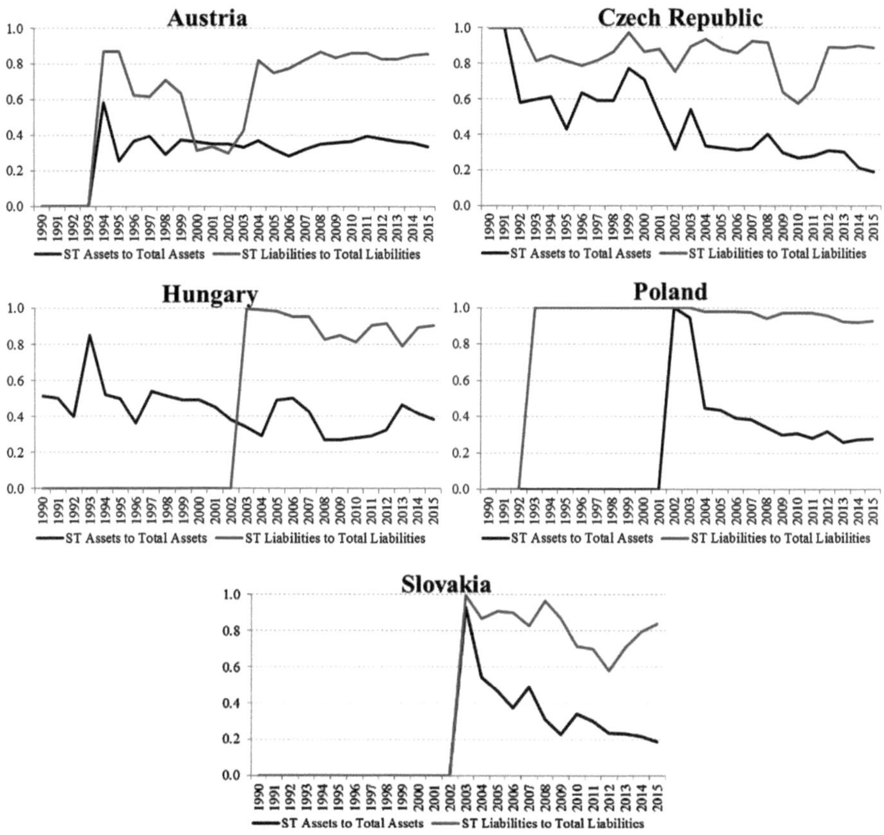

Fig. 2 Share of NMDs to total liabilities (Source: Authors based on data from BankScope database)

banks will need to generate long data history and proceed with model development in case the regulator finds these insufficient.

Acknowledgements This paper has been prepared under financial support of the Grant Agency of Charles University in Prague (Project No. 165215), the Czech Science Foundation (projects No. 16-21506S and No. GA 17-02509S) and University of Economics in Prague (projects No. VŠE IGA F1/21/2016 and VŠE IP100040), which authors gratefully acknowledge.

References

BCBS (2016) Interest rate risk in the banking book. Basel Committee for Banking Supervision, Basel

Bohn A, Elkenbracht-Huizing M (2014) The handbook of ALM in banking: interest rates, liquidity and the balance sheet. Risk Books, London

Černohorská L, Teplý P, Vrábel M (2012) The VT index as an indicator of market liquidity risk in Slovakia. J Econ 60(3):223–238

CNB (2016) Sdělení ČNB o obecných pokynech EBA k řízení úrokového rizika investičního portfolio. CNB, Prague

Džmuráňová H, Teplý P (2016) Why are savings accounts perceived as risky bank products? Prague Econ Pap 25(05):617–633

EBA (2015) Guidelines on the management of interest rate risk arising from non-trading activities. European Banking Authority, London

EBA (2017) EBA outlines roadmap of its plan to update 2017–2018 SREP. European Banking Authority, London

Hejdová M, Džmuráňová H, Teplý P (2017) Interest rate sensitivity of non-maturing bank products. In: Procházka D (ed) New trends in finance and accounting. Springer Proceedings in Business and Economics. Springer, Cham

Resti A, Sironi A (2007) Risk managements and shareholders' value in banking: from risk measurements models to capital allocation policies. Wiley, West Sussex

Skoglund J, Chen W (2015) Financial risk management: applications in market, credit, asset and liability management and firmwide risk. Wiley, Hoboken

Tax Efficiency of Czech Insurance Undertakings

Hana Bártová

Abstract Insurance undertakings belong to a group of highly profitable financial institutions, which is connected with higher level of tax liability. However, representatives of ruling parties in the Czech Republic are considering an implementation of new sector tax focused on commercial insurance undertakings in order to increase tax revenues flowing to public budgets. Tax efficiency is affected by several factors and trends including tax optimization. The implementation of new sector tax is therefore questionable. In order to assess benefits and negatives of additional taxation, tax efficiency has been verified. Insurance undertakings have been distinguished by market positions reflecting financial results of insurers, and different effects have been taken into account. Comparative analysis of tax efficiency respecting market shares of insurers has established a way to assess a level of tax burden on insurance undertakings in conditions of the Czech insurance market. Results of analysis have offered a consideration of tax adequacy concerning the implementation of new sector tax.

Keywords Insurance undertakings • Czech insurance market • Tax efficiency

Introduction

Insurance industry is a subject of taxation. Insurance undertakings are related to corporate tax and withholding tax. Otherwise financial services are exempt from VAT. Nevertheless, considerations about a level of taxation are discussed from time to time. A question of taxation is connected with political and economical cycles (Ducháčková and Daňhel 2010). Former prime minister in 2013 introduced a concept of new sector tax (Tůma 2013). Current prime minister reminded the same idea in 2015 (Kopecký 2015). The last remark was mentioned in 2017 by the same prime minister (Ťopek and Aliapulios 2017). Following analysis concludes main

H. Bártová (✉)
University of Economics, Prague, Department of Banking and Insurance, W. Churchill Sq. 4, 130 67 Prague, Czech Republic
e-mail: hana.bartova@vse.cz

D. Procházka (ed.), *The Impact of Globalization on International Finance and Accounting*, Springer Proceedings in Business and Economics,
https://doi.org/10.1007/978-3-319-68762-9_13

results of an analysis focused on a level of tax burden within insurance undertakings of the Czech insurance market.

Data and Methodology

As of December 31, 2015, the Czech insurance market was formed by 29 insurance undertakings, which were members of the Czech Insurance Association (ČAP). Following analysis is focused on 26 insurers, who provided insurance services also in 2016. Insurers are divided in three categories according to total premiums written (i.e. large, medium and small insurance undertakings). Premiums written of large insurers exceed 5% of overall premiums written of the Czech insurance market. Medium insurers reported premiums written between 1% and 5% of market share. Small insurers reached an amount of premiums written below 1% of market share (Česká asociace pojišťoven 2017).

All data are taken from the ČAP and annual reports of the Czech insurers (Annual reports of insurers 2015). Market shares are deducted from total premiums written reported by individual insurers.

The main aim of the following analysis is to assess tax efficiency of the Czech undertakings. We assume that higher level of tax efficiency is reached by undertakings with better financial efficiency. We also assume that better financial efficiency is achieved by insurance undertakings with bigger market share measured by total premiums written.

Tax efficiency was considered by level of overall tax reported by an individual insurer. Then tax efficiency was assessed through comparative analysis. We assume that an insurer with the highest amount of tax belongs to the most effective insurer in comparison with a sample of 26 selected insurers. Results are summarized within each category of insurers and compared to market share of each insurer. Inferred conclusions are mentioned below.

Taxation in Conditions of the Czech Insurance Market

Tax rate of corporate tax has been set on the level of 19% since 2010. Overall income tax of insurance undertakings was reported on the level of 2.5 bn CZK as of December 31, 2015 (Česká národní banka 2017). The highest amount of income tax was reported by Česká pojišťovna, the largest insurer of the Czech insurance market. Tax reached an amount of 754 mn CZK (Annual reports of insurers 2015), i.e. 30% of total taxes of compared insurers. Česká pojišťovna had market share of 23.3% considered within the insurers of the Czech insurance market. The second place belonged to Kooperativa Insurance Company. As of December 31, 2015, Kooperativa had market share of 20.0%. The total reported tax of Kooperativa exceeded 512 mn CZK (Annual reports of insurers 2015). Both mentioned insurance undertakings are members of category of large insurers. Both companies reported the highest level of overall tax. In this case, our assumption is confirmed. Insurance undertakings with the highest market shares reached the highest level of tax reported. However, medium and small insurance undertakings have different business strategy, specialization, financial resources and other differences, which influence their financial efficiency and market position. Conclusion of main findings within different categories of insurers is described below.

Tax Efficiency of Large Insurers

The most significant differences between tax efficiency and market share within the category of the largest insurers in conditions of the Czech insurance market are reported by Pojišťovna České spořitelny (PČS). According to a comparison in total tax, PČS reported the third highest amount of tax. Nevertheless, market share of PČS amounted to the seventh place. Higher tax than the level of market share means a disadvantage from the perspective of insurer, who is burdened by higher tax liability in comparison with other competitors.

Better result is reached by insurance company Generali. The insurer achieved the seventh place according to a comparison of tax efficiency. A comparison of market share determines the fourth place. This combination of tax efficiency and market share provides an advantage of less level of tax burden. It is probable that Generali is successful in tax optimization. Comparable results are achieved by Česká podnikatelská pojišťovna (ČPP), who is the sixth largest insurer in terms of total premiums written. However, ČPP reached the eighth place within tax efficiency. Results of ČPP could also serve as an example of tax planning with respect to underlying assumptions mentioned in introduction.

Insurance company Allianz, who is the third largest insurer of the Czech insurance market, does not recognize any significant difference. Allianz reached the fourth place in market share, which is not far from a result reflecting tax efficiency. No mismatch between tax efficiency and market share is reported by insurance company ČSOB (ČSOP).

Tax Efficiency of Medium and Small Insurers

Category of medium insurers highlighted several differences between tax efficiency and market share. The highest disparity of results is recognized by insurance company MetLife. The difference equals to five places according to the assumptions of comparative analysis. However, we can assess this difference as advantage from the perspective of insurer. Total amount of taxes does not confirm market position of insurer, who recognized lower level of taxes. Results of insurer are influenced by results of competitors as mentioned in assumptions. Another positive result is reported by Uniqa. This insurer is the 8th largest insurance company with the 11th largest total tax. In cases of MetLife and Uniqa, positions measured by total taxes are not in line with market shares. We can assume that these insurers plan a level of taxes and eventually they optimize their tax liability.

Negative results from the insurers' perspective confirmed insurance companies NN, Komerční pojišťovna (KP) and AXA životní pojišťovna (AXA ŽP). These insurers reported a difference between tax efficiency and market share amounting to three places. In other words tax efficiency is on the higher level than market share. We can assume that it can cause more significant tax burden with negative impact on insurers' financial results. Differences in results of other insurers of medium category are negligible.

Category of small insurance companies recognized several differences between tax efficiency and market share under consideration. The most significant differences are reported by ČKP, who is the insurer with special status collecting contributions flowing from compulsory liability insurance of motor vehicles. Another significant disparity is reported by insurance company Slavia. The difference equals to an amount of eight places. Nevertheless, tax efficiency is worse than position measured by market share, which can cause positive effects on financial results of Slavia. The same examples of possible positive effects are recognized by Hasičská vzájemná pojišťovna (HVP), AXA and HDI. A difference of tax efficiency and market share in case of HVP amounts to five places. It means four places in cases of AXA and HDI.

Negative impacts of monitored differences are also reported within the category of small insurers. The biggest mismatch is reached by insurance company Direct. The 14th place of tax efficiency is not in line with the 18th place of market share. This disparity can cause adverse impacts on financial results of insurer. Minor differences amounting to three places are recognized in case of ČP Zdraví, DAS and ERGO. Negligible differences are reported by remaining members of the category of small insurers, i.e. Evropská pojišťovna (ERV), Pojišťovna VZP (PVZP) and Maxima.

Results of Comparative Analysis

Comparison of tax efficiency of insurers with the largest market share in conditions of the Czech insurance market highlighted differences among insurers. The most significant difference is reported by PČS, who has to deal with higher tax liability in comparison with other insurers in the category of large insurers. Otherwise we assume that examples of tax planning or tax optimization can occur in cases of Generali and Allianz. Satisfactory level of tax efficiency, which is appropriate to the level of market share, is reached by ČSOBP.

Analysis within category of medium insurers highlighted advantages caused by positive effects of less tax burden and higher market share. However, in most cases

Table 1 Main differences between tax efficiency and market share

Insurer	Category	Market share	Tax efficiency
PČS	Large	7	3
Allianz	Large	3	4
NN	Medium	9	6
GP	Large	4	7
ČPP	Large	6	8
KP	Medium	12	9
AXA ŽP	Medium	13	10
Uniqa	Medium	8	11
Direct	Small	18	14
MetLife	Medium	10	15
ČP Zdraví	Small	19	16
ČKP	Small	26	17
AXA	Small	15	19
DAS	Small	23	20
ERGO	Small	24	21
HVP	Small	17	22
Slavia	Small	16	24
HDI	Small	21	25

Source: Česká asociace pojišťoven, Annual reports of insurers, own calculations

higher tax efficiency than a position in the insurance market was analysed. This result could have negative impacts on financial results of insurance undertakings.

Analysis of tax efficiency within the category of small insurers described ambiguous conclusions. Comparable amount of insurers recognized positive effects of lower level of tax liability. Otherwise, similar group of insurers reported higher amount of total taxes, which has negative impacts on financial results. We can assume that the second group is not successful enough in tax planning or tax optimization.

Results of comparative analysis are summarized in the Table 1. The insurers, who recognized only minor or negligible differences between assessment of tax efficiency and market share, are not mentioned in the Table 1.

Conclusion

Analysis of tax efficiency within insurance undertakings in conditions of the Czech insurance market confirmed market positions of the largest insurers. Comparative analysis highlighted deviations especially among the category of medium and small insurers. Results of tax efficiency were in accordance with assumptions in several cases. However, the most of insurers reported a mismatch between assessment of tax efficiency and market share based on total premiums written. Minor group of insurers recognized negligible differences between tax efficiency and market share.

Identified differences between tax efficiency and market share are caused by few factors and their combinations. Due to these reasons, comparative analysis should be extended by an assessment of financial efficiency, which takes into account financial results of insurers. We can assume that it would eliminate some of the mentioned differences. Regarding to assumptions, results of comparative analysis might imply about certain way of insurers' tax planning or tax optimization. Our findings can therefore be used as input information for tax administration. According to results of analysis, we can assess tax burden on several insurers as appropriate in comparison with their market shares. Otherwise, there are identified cases, which confirmed higher level of tax liability inadequate to market shares of insurance undertakings in conditions of the Czech insurance market. The implementation of new sector tax is still questionable.

Acknowledgements The article is processed as an output of a research project Development Trends in Banking and Insurance in Conditions of Changing Financial Markets registered by the Internal Grant Agency under the registration number IG102046.

References

Annual reports of insurers (2015) Members. Česká asociace pojišťoven. Annual reports Available from www.justice.cz or official websites of insurers

ARAD (2017) Základní ukazatele o finančním trhu. Pojišťovny. Česká národní banka. Available from https://www.cnb.cz/docs/ARADY/HTML/index.htm

Česká národní banka (2017) Databáze časových řad ARAD. Základní ukazatele o finančním trhu. Pojišťovny. Výkaz zisku a ztráty tuzemských pojišťoven a poboček zahraničních pojišťoven. Pojišťovny celkem. https://www.cnb.cz/cnb/STAT.ARADY_PKG.STROM_SESTAVY?p_strid=BCDA&p_sestuid=&p_lang=CS

Česká asociace pojišťoven (2017) Statistické údaje. Vývoj pojistného trhu 1-12/2015. Česká asociace pojišťoven. http://cap.cz/images/statisticke-udaje/vyvoj-pojisteno-trhu/STAT-2015Q4-CAP-CZ-2016-01-26-WEB.pdf

Ducháčková E, Daňhel J (2010) Teorie pojistných trhů. Professional Publishing, Prague. ISBN 978-80-7431-015-7

Kopecký J (2015) Sobotka hájil nápad více zdanit banky a pojišťovny. iDnes.cz. http://ekonomika.idnes.cz/zdaneni-financniho-sektoru-je-nizke-rekl-sobotka-hajil-sektorovou-dan-1zd-/ekonomika.aspx?c=A150122_164952_ekonomika_kop

Ťopek M, Aliapulios J (2017) Sobotka chce jít finančním domům po majetku, slibuje zavedení bankovní daně. Hospodářské noviny. http://archiv.ihned.cz/c1-65624560-sobotka-chce-jit-financnim-domum-po-majetku-slibuje-zavedeni-bankovni-dane

Tůma O (2013) Anketa: Kalousek si brousí zuby na pojišťovny. Čeká je zvláštní daň?. Finmag.cz. http://finmag.penize.cz/anketa/268169-anketa-kalousek-si-brousi-zuby-na-pojistovny-ceka-je-zvlastni-dan

Financial Innovations in Equity Issuance: A Prague Stock Exchange Review

Petr Jiránek

Abstract A start of a modern-era financial innovation on capital and financial markets is usually dated around the 1970s. Drawing on two broad assumptions that (i) capital markets are important and (ii) hybrid securities are an important part of capital markets, since hybrid issues exist and continue existing, this article provides a review of all outstanding equity instruments, irrespective of whether listed or private, for all issuers whose shares are traded on the Prague Stock Exchange ("PSE") in order to determine whether the financial innovations as existing on a more developed capital markets have found their seeds on the market or whether the market is largely ignorant of such developments. This paper is divided into three parts: part one provides a brief description of some innovations in capital issuance; the second part provides a review of equity instruments issued by 25 issuers, in which shares are traded on PSE, irrespective whether those are listed or not; and the third part summarizes findings and concludes that a hybrid instrument has been identified at two issuers only, both foreign ones. The most recent annual reports of respective issuers were utilized for the review, accompanied by other public sources if necessary.

Keywords Equity • Stock • Share • Stock exchange • Prague

Introduction

A start of a modern-era financial innovation on capital and financial markets is usually dated[1] around the 1970s – enabled by deregulation of financial markets, high inflation environment, coupled with a high interest volatility, and fueled by increasing computing power of computers.

[1]Many of the features of new hybrid instruments with similar characteristics to recent ones were created during the 1920s (Berle 1928).

P. Jiránek (✉)
University of Economics, Prague, Department of Corporate Finance and Valuations, Nam.W. Churchilla 4, 130 67 Prague, Czech Republic
e-mail: xjirp16@vse.cz

D. Procházka (ed.), *The Impact of Globalization on International Finance and Accounting*, Springer Proceedings in Business and Economics,
https://doi.org/10.1007/978-3-319-68762-9_14

In a broader sense, financial innovations can be viewed as a wide range of improvements, from innovations on sale channels, new financial products on institutional and retail markets (such as derivatives, synthetic exchange-traded funds, collateral swaps, CDOs, etc.), to new functionalities in IT systems enabling a data processing unthought-of only a decade earlier. Some of them have direct or indirect influence on capital issuance, by broadening the investor base, by structuring products to suit particular investors' or issuers' needs, by enabling access to securities traded in geographically distant market with a widespread use of easy-to-open brokerage accounts, which again were absolutely out of the question a decade ago, etc.

In a much narrow sense, this article will focus on financial innovations on capital markets only. Issuers, until the mid-1970s, had fairly limited financing options – equity by issuing common stock or debt by borrowing from a bank or by issuing bonds. A few firms were daring enough to issue convertible bonds (Damodaran 1999).

According to Awrey (2012), financial innovations can be a demand-side response to market imperfections or a supply-side force driven by financial intermediaries. Innovations are usually driven by tax, regulatory, reporting, and rating factors and according to Damodaran (1999) also by flexibility in designing cash flows on borrowings, firms' attempts to keep up with their peer group, securitization of otherwise idle assets, exploitation of information asymmetries, difficulties in valuing complex financial instruments, etc. Resulting securities step outside traditional debt/equity categories with a mix of features for which these are referred to as hybrid securities.

Partnoy (2007) states "Today, most publicly traded corporations do not have only equity and debt. Instead, their capital structures are composed of numerous slices of different hybrid instruments, each with combinations of equity-like and debt-like characteristics." The most elementary securities with hybrid features include preferred shares and convertible bonds; some of more sophisticated instruments are known under acronyms, such as LYONs, TIGRs, DECS, and PERCS; some are known in relation to one of or one main characteristic such as rating sensitive bonds, or more recently buffer capital notes or in a specific setting such as convertible preferred stock, convertible notes, bridge loans, and seed notes in venture capital financing (see Coyle 2014). Characteristics of one specific instrument (such as its structure and financial characteristics) can often be mimicked by one security coupled with a derivative or derivatives. Examples of such issuance are feline PRIDES. According to Hu (2008) equity issues experience relatively strong phenomena of decoupling.

Importance of individual financial innovations changes in time. For example, buffer capital notes in a banking sector are strongly dependent on regulatory treatment, and not only their issuance can cease "immediately" upon shift in a regulatory framework, but they can be immediately converted and as such cease to exist. Other innovations are more permanent, albeit their characteristics evolve over time, for example, $5 billion worth of mandatory convertibles were issued in 1996 (a quarter of the convertible market) compared to $20 billion worth in 2001 (about 18% of the convertible market) (see Chemmanur 2003).

Question of capital market development and its relation to GDP growth has been studied extensively with varying results. For example, Kerr (2014) states there is growing consensus that well-functioning financial markets play a central role in driving economic growth through their ability to spur technological innovation.

Optimal capital structure and related theories have been studied and tested intensively. Hybrid securities bring interesting elements into this discussion. A mere question of advantages of debt over equity, and vice versa, is somehow obscured in the light of securities that do not fit this division.

Review of Equity Issues of Prague Stock Exchange Issuers

As of February 2017, there were 25 individual equity instruments traded on PSE of 25 issuers – 11 were foreign issuers (with a corporate seat outside of the Czech Republic), out of which 4 seated in the UK, 2 in Austria, 2 in the Netherlands, 1 in Slovakia, 1 in Belgium, and 1 in Luxemburg, and 14 domestic issuers, listed on three markets: prime (14 issues), standard (9), and free (2) with distinct admission criteria (see Table 1).

Market listings: 11 issues were traded on PSE only, 11 were dual listings, and three issues were traded on three markets. CETV was traded on NASDAQ; all other issues were traded on markets within EU.

Market capitalization: In terms of market capitalization, the total market cap of all issues was CZK 1104 bln (EUR 40.8 bln), with ERSTE GROUP BANK having the largest market cap of CZK 342 bln (EUR 12.7 bln) and E4U with CZK 237 mln (EUR 9 mln) being the smallest issue traded. Estimated market value[2] of free floats combined was CZK 130 bln (EUR 4.8 bln) or 11.9% of the market capitalization combined. Free float was determined for 22 issues and ranged from 56.24% for CETV to 0%[3] for ENERGOCHEMICA. Average free float was 20.4%, and market cap weighted average free float was 11.9%.

Out of 25 issuers, 5 issuers received ratings, 20 were unrated; 24 issuers prepared annual reports according to IFRS and 1 under US GAAP. Out of the 25 annual reports studied, 3 were for period of 2016, 21 for 2015, and 1 for 2014; 12 were published in the Czech language, 11 in English, 1 in Slovak, and 1 bilingual Czech-English; two annual reports were not searchable (scans of the documents only); three annual reports failed to mention exchange listing completely, and one omitted one of the trading markets (in italics in Table 2).

All issues traded were ordinary (bearer or common) shares, no preferred or with special features. Out of the 25, 17 issuers listed single class, single series equity instruments; the remaining eight issuers issued the following equity instruments (both exchange listed and unlisted):

---

[2]Free float was determined for 22 issuers. Free float market value for 3 undetermined issuers was estimated at 20.4% equal to unweighted average free float of 22 issuers.

[3]Based on data published by the company.

- CETV – the only issuer on PSE, with preferred shares outstanding.[4] Four classes of shares were either issued or authorized: 1 share of Series A convertible preferred stock, 200,000 shares of Series B convertible redeemable preferred shares, and 143,449,913 shares of Class A common stock,[5] with a par value of USD 0.08 each, were issued. Series A share has voting rights of 11,211,449 shares of Class A common stock. The shares of Class A common stock are entitled to one vote per share, and the shares of Class B common stock are entitled to ten votes per share.
- O2 C.R. – two classes of shares: shares with a par value of CZK 10 provide one voting right; these are traded. Shares with a par value of CZK 100 in a quantity of 100 pieces provide ten voting rights and correspondingly higher dividend rights; these are not traded. Both classes are identical otherwise.
- ENERGOAQUA – two classes of shares: shares with a par value of CZK 1000 are admitted to the trading; these provide 125 voting rights per share and corresponding dividend rights. Shares with a par value of CZK 8 are not traded and provide one voting right each and corresponding dividend rights.
- ENERGOCHEMICA – two classes of shares: 1.5 million of shares with a par value of EUR 55 are admitted to trading; 129,091 shares with a par value of EUR 550 were issued in a private placement in 2016. Shares possess voting, dividend,[6] and other rights in 1:10 ratio.
- JÁCHYMOV PM – two classes of shares: one class consisting of one share only of the same par value and otherwise seemingly identical.
- NWR – the company has one of the most complex equity instruments structure among all firms reviewed. Issued were 6,663,538,084 A shares, 10,000 B shares, and 264,477,400,857 D shares. B and D shares were not exchange traded. Par values were approximately 0.04 Eurocent, 0.4 Euro, and 0.04 Eurocent for A, B, and D shares, respectively.
- PHILIP MORRIS ČR – two classes of equal par values: 831,688 unlisted shares are unregistered bearer shares; the remaining shares are registered and traded. Both classes of shares possess the same rights.
- PRAŽSKÉ SLUŽBY – three classes on common shares: 1,556,125 registered common shares with a par value of CZK 1000 each, which is a traded class, 600 common shares with a par value of CZK 1 million, and 1,187,604 shares with a par value of CZK 400; both classes are not traded.[7]
- KOMERČNÍ BANKA – with one class of common shares, the GDRs are traded on LSE.

---

[4]Also, the only issuer traded on a regulated US market.

[5]In addition issuance of shares of Class B common stock with a par value of USD 0.08 was authorized, but not issued. Shares of Class B common stock are convertible into shares of Class A common stock on a one-for-one basis for no additional consideration. Class A common stock and Class B common stock were identical except for voting rights.

[6]Although annual report describes difference in voting rights only, it is relatively safe to assume that other rights are also 1:10.

[7]Although the annual report provides no information on voting, dividend, and other rights, it can be assumed that these are proportionate to par values.

Dilution Effect

Due to a low innovation level in equity instruments, the review has been extended to the existence of equity-dilutive instruments. Convertible or exchangeable debt instruments, warrants and in certain cases options, when exercised for own shares, would have a dilutive effect. Out of 25 issuers, four reported dilution or diluted EPS[8]; these were:

- CETV – dilution due to conversion ratio of preferred shares to common shares and existence of warrants
- ERSTE GROUP BANK – dilution due to the management share option program, employee share option program, and options (convertible bonds were authorized, not issued)
- PEGAS NONWOVENS – dilution due to warrants
- STOCK – dilution due to the options under performance share plan and employee long-term incentive plan

Discussion and Conclusion

The Czech Republic with its 10.5 million inhabitants is a small country. The public equity market is disproportionately small. For example, compared with Poland, there were 486 issues listed on Warsaw Stock Exchange (excluding NewConnect[9]), which is more than 12 listings per million inhabitants (2.4 for the Czech Republic), and one listing is "backed up" by EUR 1 billion of GDP (7.2 for CZ).[10]

Data available for the USA show that private market can be of a higher importance than public markets. According to Bauguess (2015), the importance of private[11] capital markets as a source of financing in the US economy is underscored by the fact that less than 0.03% of the estimated 28 million firms in the USA are currently exchange listed firms. The Czech-based PSE-listed firms

[8]VGP issued subordinated perpetual securities, the debt securities under national regulation, recognized as equity under IFRS, which are not convertible to company shares.

[9]NewConnect is a stock exchange regulated market operated by WSE, similar as free segment of PSE. Unlike the free market of PSE with two listings, there were 406 listings on NewConnect. WSE and NewConnect housed 892 listings combined, i.e., 23 listings per million inhabitants, and one listing is "backed up" by EUR 54 billion of GDP.

[10]One of the possible interpretations would be that the average issue market cap on PSE should be seven times higher than on WSE. Direct comparison based on data provided by respective exchanges is unavailable. WSE reports market cap for domestic companies only, whereas PSE reports market cap based on all shares traded, not accounting for multiple listings for all issuers.

[11]In 2014 amount raised through unregistered securities offerings of USD 2.1 trillion has outpaced the level of capital formation through registered securities offerings USD 1.35 trillion during the recent years and totaled more than $2 trillion during 2014 (Bauguess 2015).

accounted for 0.004% of estimated 357 thousand firms[12] existing in the Czech Republic in 2014. Therefore the private markets could be of even a larger importance. However reliable data on private offerings on the Czech market are unavailable.

This review has been based on data available for the Czech public market represented by the Prague Stock Exchange.[13] Out of the 25 issuers, whose shares are listed on PSE, only one issuer – CETV – issued preferred (two classes). Based on the information available from the latest annual reports, none of the issuers had convertible bonds outstanding (ERSTE GROUP BANK had convertible bonds authorized but not issued). Preferred shares and convertible bonds are the simplest form of innovative instruments with hybrid features. None of the issuers issued any equity security with a more sophisticated innovative feature.

Dilutive effect on the existing equity was found only for four issuers: two due to warrants, two due to management or employees' option programs, and one due to preferred shares. In addition to equity dilutive instruments, one of the issuers – VGP – issued innovative debt instrument, which is recognized as the equity under IFRS, with no diluting effect.

To provide complete picture of the innovative level among all firms listed on PSE, a debt instrument review would need to be completed. However with one exception, none of the issuers reported debt instrument outstanding with dilutive effect, and only one issuer reported debt/equity hybrid instrument. Thereby I would expect that level of innovation in outstanding debt would be also low.

As a conclusion, I believe, the overall picture of innovation in capital rising instruments is rather low, almost non-existent. Taking into account that preferred issues were of foreign issuer, zero-level innovation in equity issuance can be found at Czech issuers (and other foreign issuers).

As the Czech capital market is not a viable financing alternative for vast majority of firms, the activity of PSE in terms of IPOs and new listings is very low, liquidity of several issues is unsatisfying, and the result of this review in terms of innovation level is somehow unsurprising.

Acknowledgement This paper is published as a part of a research project Theoretical Approaches to Capital Structure Optimization registered by the Internal Grant Agency under the registration number IGA VŠE 48/2016.

[12]According to IMPER CZ, available at http://onbusiness.cz/kolik-firem-je-v-cr-v-jednotlivych-krajich-835.

[13]There were no additional Czech issuers traded on RM System (RMS) other than those traded on PSE.

Appendix

Table 1 Issues listed on PSE

#	Issuer	Full name	Market	Number of shares traded	Market cap(CZK mln) (3)	Market cap(EUR mln) (6)	Country ofincorporation
1	BOREALIS	Borealis Exploration Limited	Prime	5,000,000	1323(2)	49	UK (Gibraltar)
2	CETV	Central European Media Enterprises Ltd.	Prime	142,355,060	10,178	377	UK (Bermuda)
3	ČEZ	ČEZ, a.s.	Prime	537,989,759	238,222	8817	CZ
4	ERSTE GROUP BANK	Erste Group Bank AG	Prime	429,800,000	342,121	12,662	AT
5	FORTUNA	Fortuna Entertainment Group N.V.	Prime	52,000,000	4940	183	NL
6	KOFOLA ČS	Kofola ČeskoSlovensko a.s.	Prime	22,295,000	9121	338	CZ
7	KOMERČNÍ BANKA	Komerční banka, a.s.	Prime	190,049,260	182,086	6739	CZ
8	MONETA MONEY BANK	MONETA Money Bank, a.s.	Prime	511,000,000	43,793	1621	CZ
9	O2 C.R.	O2 Czech Republic a.s.	Prime	310,220,057	85,776	3175	CZ
10	PEGAS NONWOVENS	Pegas Nonwovens SA	Prime	9,229,400	7624	282	LUX
11	TMR	Tatry Mountain Resorts, a.s.	Prime	6,707,198	4561	169	SK
12	UNIPETROL	Unipetrol, a.s.	Prime	181,334,764	37,119	1374	CZ
13	VGP	VGP NV	Prime	18,583,050	6560	243	BE
14	VIG	Vienna Insurance Group	Prime	128,000,000	80,768	2989	AT

(continued)

Table 1 (continued)

#	Issuer	Full name	Market	Number of shares traded	Market cap(CZK mln) (3)	Market cap(EUR mln) (6)	Country ofincorporation
15	E4U	E4U a.s.	Standard	2,391,640	237	9	CZ
16	ENERGOAQUA	Energoaqua, a.s.	Standard	701,000	1896	70	CZ
17	ENERGOCHEMICA	Energochemica SE	Standard	1,500,000	3810	141	CZ
18	JÁCHYMOV PM	Jáchymov Property Management, a.s.	Standard	323,867	421	16	CZ
19	NWR	New World Resources Plc	Standard	8,290,496,646	580	21	UK
20	PHILIP MORRIS ČR	Philip Morris ČR a.s.	Standard	1,913,698	25,797	955	CZ
21	PRAŽSKÉ SLUŽBY	Pražské služby, a.s.	Standard	1,556,125	2163	80	CZ
22	RMS MEZZANINE	RMS Mezzanine, a.s.	Standard	1,065,071,134	852	32	CZ
23	TOMA	TOMA, a.s.	Standard	1,477,266	1655	61	CZ
24	PHOTON ENERGY	Photon Energy NV	Free	60,000,000	387	14	NL
25	STOCK	Stock Spirits Group Plc	Free	200,000,000	11,550	427	UK

Source: unless noted otherwise, data published by Prague Stock Exchange (www.pse.cz, retrieved: 21.2.2017, 15:00) and annual reports of respective companies

Notes:

(1) Provided by Quotenet (www.quotenet.com, retrieved 22.2.2017, 23:22)
(2) Reported by NASDAQ OTC (www.quotenet.com, retrieved: 22.2.2017, 23:55)
(3) Intraday data as published by Prague Stock Exchange on 21.2.2017
(4) London Stock Exchange
(5) RMS – A former OTC platform in Prague, transformed to the exchange. Existing parallel to the Prague Stock Exchange
(6) 1 EUR = 27.020 CZK, as reported by the Czech National Bank, 22.2.2017, www.cnb.cz

Table 2 Reporting specifications

#	Issuer	Exchange listings (5)	Equity rating	AR language	Account. standard	Free float	Annual reportfor period	Searchable
1	BOREALIS	Prague		EN	IFRS	n/a	2016	Yes
2	CETV	NASDAQ, Prague		EN	US GAAP	56.24% (1)	2016	Yes
3	ČEZ	Warsaw, Prague, RMS	Yes	CZ	IFRS	8.78%	2015	Yes
4	ERSTE GROUP BANK	Vienna, Prague, Bucharest	Yes	EN	IFRS	6%	2015	Yes
5	FORTUNA	Warsaw, Prague,		EN	IFRS	22.74%	2015	Yes
6	KOFOLA ČS	Warsaw, Prague,		EN	IFRS	6.73%	2015	Yes
7	KOMERČNÍ BANKA	London (4), Prague, RMS	Yes	CZ	IFRS	2.74%	2015	Yes
8	MONETA MONEY BANK	Prague	Yes	EN	IFRS	32%	2015	Yes
9	O2 C.R.	Prague, RMS		CZ	IFRS	18.94%	2016	Yes
10	PEGAS NONWOVENS	Warsaw, Prague		CZ	IFRS	n/a	2015	Yes
11	TMR	Bratislava, Warsaw, Prague		SK	IFRS	14.99%	2015	Yes
12	UNIPETROL	Prague, RMS		CZ	IFRS	13.89% (1)	2015	Yes
13	VGP	Euronext (Brussels), Prague		EN	IFRS	6.04%	2015	Yes

(continued)

Table 2 (continued)

#	Issuer	Exchange listings (5)	Equity rating	AR language	Account. standard	Free float	Annual reportfor period	Searchable
14	VIG	Vienna, Prague	Yes	EN	IFRS	30%	2015	Yes
15	E4U	Prague, RMS, Stuttgart		CZ	IFRS	49%	2015	Yes
16	ENERGOAQUA	Prague		CZ	IFRS	n/a	2015	No
17	ENERGOCHEMICA	Prague		CZ	IFRS	0%	2015	Yes
18	JÁCHYMOV PM	Prague, RMS		CZ	IFRS	7.37%	2015	No
19	NWR	London (4), Warsaw, Prague		EN	IFRS	49.49%	2015	Yes
20	PHILIP MORRIS ČR	Prague, RMS		CZ/EN	IFRS	22.40%	2014	Yes
21	PRAŽSKÉ SLUŽBY	Prague		CZ	IFRS	3.80%	2015	Yes
22	RMS MEZZANINE	Prague, RMS		CZ	IFRS	1.77%	2015	Yes
23	TOMA	Prague, RMS		CZ	IFRS	31.98%	2015	Yes
24	PHOTON ENERGY	Warsaw (NewConnect), Prague		EN	IFRS	10.36%	2015	Yes
25	STOCK	London (4), Prague		EN	IFRS	52.34%	2015	Yes

Source and notes: please see Table 1

Table 3 Equity issue characteristics

#	Issuer	Number of shares traded	Outstanding shares(incl. treasury shares)	Equities issued and authorized	Par value	Currency	EPS dilutionreported
1	BOREALIS	5,000,000	5,000,000	1 common	0.01	USD	No
2	CETV	142,355,060	143,649,914	2 common, 2 preferred	0.08	USD	Yes
3	ČEZ	537,989,759	537,989,759	1 common	100.00	CZK	No
4	ERSTE GROUP BANK	429,800,000	429,800,000	1 common	n/a		Yes
5	FORTUNA	52,000,000	52,000,000	1 common	0.01	EUR	No
6	KOFOLA ČS	22,295,000	22,295,000	1 common	100.00	CZK	No
7	KOMERČNÍ BANKA	190,049,260	190,049,260	1 common	500.00	CZK	No
8	MONETA MONEY BANK	511,000,000	511,000,000	1 common	1.00	CZK	No
9	O2 C.R.	310,220,057	310,220,058	2 common	10.00	CZK	No
10	PEGAS NONWOVENS	9,229,400	9,229,400	1 common	1.24	EUR	Yes
11	TMR	6,707,198	6,707,198	1 common	7.00	EUR	No
12	UNIPETROL	181,334,764	181,334,764	1 common	200.00	CZK	No
13	VGP	18,583,050	18,583,050	1 common	n/a		No
14	VIG	128,000,000	128,000,000	1 common	non-par		No
15	E4U	2,391,640	2,391,640	1 common	100.00	CZK	No

(continued)

Table 3 (continued)

#	Issuer	Number of shares traded	Outstanding shares(incl. treasury shares)	Equities issued and authorized	Par value	Currency	EPS dilutionreported
16	ENERGOAQUA	701,000	960,333	2 common	1000; 8	CZK	No
17	ENERGOCHEMICA	1,500,000	1,629,091	2 common	55; 550	EUR	No
18	JÁCHYMOV PM	323,867	323,868	2 common	1000.00	CZK	No
19	NWR	8,290,496,646	271,139,505,345	3 common	<0.01; 0.04; <0.01.	EUR	No
20	PHILIP MORRIS ČR	1,913,698	2,745,386	2 common	1000.00	CZK	No
21	PRAŽSKÉ SLUŽBY	1,556,125	2,744,329	3 common	1000;1 mln; 400	CZK	No
22	RMS MEZZANINE	1,065,071,134	1,065,071,134	1 common	0.50	CZK	No
23	TOMA	1,477,266	1,477,266	1 common	1000.00	CZK	No
24	PHOTON ENERGY	60,000,000	60,000,000	1 common	0.01	EUR	No
25	STOCK	200,000,000	200,000,000	1 common	0.10	GBP	Yes

Source and notes: please see Table 1

References

Awrey D (2012) Complexity, innovation, and the regulation of modern financial markets. [online]. Harv Bus Law Rev 2(2):236–294. [cited 2nd February, 2017], Retrieved from: papers.ssrn.com/abstract=id1916649

Bauguess S, Gullapalli R, Ivanov V (2015) Capital raising in the U.S.: an analysis of the market for unregistered securities offerings, 2009–2014 [online], Securities and Exchange Commission, White Paper, [cited 2nd February 2017], Retrieved from: https://www.sec.gov/dera/staff-papers/white-papers/unregistered-offering10-2015.pdf

Berle AA (1928) Studies in the law of corporate finance. Callaghan, Chicago

Chemmanur TJ, Nandy DK, Yan A (2003) Why issue mandatory convertibles? theory and evidence, [online], Glasgow, European Finance Association Conference, c2003, [cited 2nd February, 2017], Retrieved from: papers.ssrn.com/abstract=id417601

Coyle JF, Green JM (2014) Contractual Innovation in Venture Capital. [online]. Hastings Law J 66 (1):133–183. [cited 2nd February, 2017], Retrieved from: papers.ssrn.com/abstract=2417431

Damodaran A (1999) Financing innovations and capital structure choices, [online], New York University Stern School of Business Research Paper no. FIN-99-020, [cited 2nd February, 2017], Retrieved from: papers.ssrn.com/abstract=1297066

Hu HTC, Black B (2008) Equity and debt decoupling and empty voting II: importance and extensions. [online], University of Pennsylvania Law Review, 2008, vol. 156, no. 3, pp. 625–739, [cited 2nd February, 2017], Retrieved from: papers.ssrn.com/abstract=1030721

Kerr WR, Nanda R (2014) Financing innovation. [online], Harvard Business School Entrepreneurial Management Working Paper No. 15–034, [cited 2nd February, 2017], Retrieved from: papers.ssrn.com/abstract=519572

Partnoy F (2007) Financial innovation and corporate law. [online], University of San Diego, School of Law, Legal Studies Research Paper Series No. 07–89, [cited 2nd February, 2017], Retrieved from: papers.ssrn.com/abstract=976931

The Reasons Underlying Retail Banking Homogenization in the Second Half of the Nineteenth Century

Vojtěch Müllner

Abstract The paper looks into the process of originating and homogenizing the three credit union streams in the Czech lands territory at the time of the Habsburg Monarchy. The strongest from among the credit union streams was formed of charitable societies. The second stream was created through transforming consumers' cooperatives to district economic credit unions, and the last of the significant streams came to our lands from Germany, in the form of Raiffeisen credit unions. Because of the demand for cheap credits, credit unions soon flourished into a significant group of credit providers, both in terms of the quantity of credits and the volume of provided finances. The main attention is paid to the change in orientation of credit unions after 1873, when Act No. 70, on associations, was passed, significantly influencing the change of originally charitable credit unions to financial institutions providing cheap credits to the general population. This transformation subsequently contributed to unification of the three streams.

Keywords Credit union • Retail banking • Small loans • District credit unions • Raiffeisen credit union • Communal credit union • Farmers' credit union

Introduction

A significant role in the development of the Czech banking system to the form, as it is today, was played by retail financial institutions, booming in the second half of the nineteenth century. We can track their various forms and motives for their establishing which also leave their mark on the credit unions' orientation. One of the roots of our retail banking is associated with consumers' cooperatives, which were continuously transformed to credit unions by state interventions. The

V. Müllner (✉)
Masaryk university Faculty of Economics and Administration, Lipová 41a, 602 00 Brno, Czech Republic
e-mail: vojtech.mullner@econ.muni.cz

D. Procházka (ed.), *The Impact of Globalization on International Finance and Accounting*, Springer Proceedings in Business and Economics,
https://doi.org/10.1007/978-3-319-68762-9_15

second root is associated with the name of Friedrich Wilhelm Raiffeisen, the founding father of credit unions in Germany (Bouček 1894, p. 7). This type of credit unions spread quite fast to the Netherlands, Switzerland, Italy and Austria to subsequently become popular also in the Czech lands, where it existed side by side with district credit unions for economic development and communal credit unions.

The last of the significant roots is the above-mentioned communal credit unions that we can consider to be a Czech anomaly that will be of the utmost interest for us in this paper. The origin of communal credit unions was triggered by multiple significant factors which definitely included inaccessibility of capital to poorer segments of the population. Furthermore, they were the then growing patriotic awareness and the fact that credit unions were allowed to make profit and distribute it with the aim to support charitable activities (Schreyer 1891, p. 32).

These three streams in the credit union development gradually converged at their activities, finally providing nearly the same products. The respective origins of the individual streams differ considerably, and this is the reason why it is interesting to track the main causes underlying the changes. To understand the conversion better, it is necessary to look into the history and point out to individual specificities, especially as regards communal credit unions. It is also necessary to consistently explain the causes that turned the associations and credit unions into nearly homogeneous organizations.

Three Streams of Retail Banking in the Habsburg Monarchy

Credit unions in the Habsburg lands came to existence in several lines that became nearly homogeneous over the period of subsequent 30 years. Before 1873, the legal basis of communal credit unions was the Act on Societies of 1852 (Janák 1987, p. 71). District credit unions for economic development were first governed by Act No. 28 of 1864 and then by Act No. 267 of 1882. The highest rate of occurrence of credit unions of the Raiffeisen type in the Czech lands is detected after the Act on Associations of 1873 had been passed, and the credit unions of this type conformed to the act from its very beginning. The process of converging the activities of all credit unions was triggered by the Act on Associations of 1873. Most influenced by this act were communal credit unions. However, their transformation also left its mark on the remaining credit union streams (Schreyer 1891, p. 226).

Each of the three lines of credit unions is based on a different principle. One of the streams originated due to state regulations, the second was imported from abroad, and the substance of the third of the streams lied in charity. The development of credit unions was also supported by national sentiments. The patriotism was expressed in the form of efforts to achieve emancipation from the foreign capital which was predominantly in the hands of German population. Another significant factor was also general distaste for the usury that was flourishing in the nineteenth century.[1] The providing of credits to poorer citizens followed by investments of surpluses to the industry sector later on is definitely one of the accelerators of the economic growth during the first decades of the twentieth century in the territory of the Czech lands (Jindra et al. 2015, p. 409).

District Credit Unions for Economic Development

The individual streams were triggered off by different impulses. We can consider district credit unions for economic development to be a very specific group as they originated from consumers' cooperatives that were transformed to credit unions through state interventions. Our best-known consumers' cooperatives were called contribution funds and had the form of contribution-based granaries. These funds were established thanks to farmers who deposited their agricultural surpluses to common granaries (Okresní záložny hospodářské 1932, p. 5).

Initially, participation in these funds was voluntary. Due to the restless times and wars of the eighteenth century, the reserves in granaries started to be used to feed armies, and as a result, the reserves declined (Juřík 2011, p. 58). A change occurred after the Imperial Letters Patent No. 358 of 9 June 1788 was issued by Joseph II. This letters patent decreed that the subject serfs who owned arable land should be returning the third portion of the four types of grain – wheat, rye, barley and oats – to the communal granary for the period of 3 years. In this way, reserves were created for the spring and autumn sowing with the aim to prevent famines caused by lacking seed stocks. In the course of time, reserves exceeded consumption, and so a part of the reserves was borrowed to members of a credit fund for a fee. First, an interest in kind amounting to 12.5% p.a. was paid for every borrowed measure; later on, the interest was decreased to 6.25% p.a. Seed corn of no use continued being accumulated in the funds and sold in the following years. The earned money was deposited and lent to fund members (Wenzl 1937, p. 8).

A milestone in the development of consumers' cooperatives was the adoption of Act No. 45 of 9 June 1863, repealing granaries. It was determined that granaries should be transformed to financial capital and the capital should be consolidated with the capital that was earned for sold grain surpluses. Thus, contribution monetary grain funds came to existence. Act No. 28 of 6 August 1864 establishes contribution credit unions from these funds (Doubrava 1924, p. 5–9).

According to the statistics of 1878, there were 894 contribution credit unions in the territory of the Czech lands which however were not equally distributed across the territory. Up to three credit unions would be operating in some municipalities, and completely lacking in others. Another restriction imposed on the contribution credit unions established according to Act No. 28 of 1864 was the prohibition to

[1]Those who charged interest rates higher than 15% were considered to be usurers (Novotný 1911, p. 23).

accept deposits from their own members.[2] With respect to the above-mentioned facts, district credit unions for economic development that consolidated all contribution credit unions in a district were established by Act No. 267 of 22 March 1882. In this way, a district credit union for economic development was established for each district (Doubrava 1924, p. 12). From 1882, credit unions were not obliged to manage only their own assets but were also allowed to accept deposits. A restriction applicable to district credit unions for economic development was the requirement that only land owners should become credit union members (Schreyer 1895, p. 62). From the end of the 19th century to the beginning of the 20th century become interest rate decreasing and converging to 5 % p.a. (50 let okresní záložny hospodářské v Semilech 1882–1932 1933, p. 283).

Credit Unions of the Raiffeisen Type

Credit unions of the Raiffeisen type have been established in Germany since 1849. In the Czech lands, Raiffeisen credit unions, supplementing local citizen community credit unions, had not occurred before the 1880s. The establishing of these credit unions was triggered by the poverty of small farmers in Rhineland and the efforts of countrymen to escape from the clutches of usury. Because of the failing access to capital, usury became so rampant that it had a liquidating impact on many small farmers. Raiffeisen credit unions which operated as associations of groups of farmers who, unlike an individual farmer, were able to meet the requirements for a bank credit grant made efforts to cope with such a situation. Such a bank credit grant would subsequently be divided to smaller credits that were granted to small farmers. In this manner, an access to capital was made possible for small farmers.

By-laws of Raiffeisen credit unions stipulated that no interest could be collected from small farmers that would exceed the interest on the bank credit taken by a credit union itself by 1.5% (Bouček 1894, p. 11). Even after a contribution to operational costs had been added to it, the interest was still considerably lower than the one that small farmers would have obtained from a usurer. Another specificity of Raiffeisen credit unions lied in the form of liability which always was unlimited. In addition to this, small membership shares were collected in the range from 5 to 25 guldens because Raiffeisen credit unions targeted poorer small farmers (Schreyer 1895, p. 69–70).

Applicants for a loan had to have the purpose of the loan approved and subsequently had to keep proving on a continuous basis that finances had really been used for the approved purpose. The last significant specificity was that loans provided in exchange for promissory notes were excluded to protect debtors who, as a result, were sure to be liable solely to a credit union. The reason why Raiffeisen credit unions did not make loans in exchange for promissory notes was that promissory

[2]Contributory credit unions could make loans only from their own funds.

notes were transferable and as such could be resold to other financial institutions or other third persons. In this way, Raiffeisen credit unions protected their debtors (Blažek 1909, p. 10).

Citizen Community, Communal, Sole Traders' and Farmers' Credit Unions

The stream that was unique and also the strongest in the Czech lands consisted of citizen community, sole traders' and farmers' credit unions. All of them were established on the same principle. Their names differed only to refer to their specific target group, which however was not strictly complied with. We can also find the credit union type referred to as *kampelička*, which is the same as the other types of credit unions save for the rule that *kampelička* credit unions are established only with unlimited liability. The other credit unions then could have any liability (Šváb 1935, p. 19). The first credit union in the true sense of the term can be considered to be the credit union in Vlašim, which was established in 1858 (Schreyer 1891, p. 12).

The credit unions established in the territory of the Czech lands had several specificities. The first and the most important was their focus on charity in the form of the cheapest possible credits through which credit unions improved the economic position of sole traders and small farmers. The charitable character also found its expression in direct support provided to various activities, including establishing schools, purchasing aids for schools, providing snacks to poor children, and also contributing to municipal beautification societies, establishing orphanages, charitable housing, asylums and nursing homes and contributing to the construction of water mains, the national theatre, etc. (Schreyer 1891, p. 357). Charity was the essence of the credit unions established in the territory of the Czech lands, and it is also enshrined in the by-laws of credit unions. Credit unions were not allowed to generate profit and pay it out to their members in the form of dividends. Where a profit was made, a credit union was required to transfer it to its reserves or use it for charitable purposes.

The statistics from 1869, this means more than 10 years after the first credit union was established, shows the significant expansion and popularity of credit unions in the Czech lands. At that time, there were 525 credit unions across the whole Austro-Hungarian Empire, out of which 306 accounted for Bohemia, 134 for Moravia, 46 for Lower Austria, and 36 for the rest of Austria (Schreyer 1891, p. 152). Credit unions throve also thanks to the fact that they were exempt from taxes and stamp duty. Ambiguities in law started to surface from 1865, when some credit unions were assessed with taxes, while others continued being exempt from them. The developments came to a head when the Act on Associations of 1873 was passed, stipulating transformation of credit unions to associations that would no longer be considered charitable societies. This act levied the tax and stamp duty on credit unions and also stipulated the methodology according to which credit unions were required to additionally pay up the taxes and duties for the previous 10 years in the amount of at least one tenth and at most two fifths of their assessed taxes (Schreyer 1891, p. 200).

The act passed in 1873 urged the credit unions established in the Czech lands to transform their charitable focus from direct financial support that would be taxed according to the new law to another type of charity, which credit unions used to consider to lie in cheaper credits. The change is apparent in gradually decreasing interest rates and reduced direct support, which however remained partially unchanged despite of that. Before the Act on Associations was passed, credits had been made on an interest ranging from 6% to 8%. After the Act came to force, the interest rate gets lower, amounting to 5.5–6% p.a. In the case of real estate credits, the interest on a credit drops to 4.75% p.a. (Novotný 1911, p. 23).

Results

The original three streams of retail banking started merging towards the end of the nineteenth century, and we can look for the differences in the name of a respective credit union. Because of the popularity of local credit unions, the significance of professional and district credit unions decreased over time too (Vencovský et al. 1999, p. 172–173). Contrary to banks, credit unions focused on loans and retail deposits, and while the volume of received deposits and loans was soaring in the case of credit unions, it was increasing just moderately in the case of banks. Patriotism and certain resentment towards big banks could also play a considerable role in this development. The official language of banks was usually German, which was a thorn in many Czechs' flesh and excluded in particular rural population from access to credits (Schreyer 1891, p. 54).

Act No. 70 of 9 April 1873, on associations, stipulated that the legal form of credit unions be changed from societies to associations. This change was also related to the change in paying duties and taxes. The new act had the biggest impact on communal credit unions that were originally governed by the Act on Societies from 1852. Among other things, the Act on Societies stipulated that charitable societies would be exempt from duties and taxes. This was the key motivation for charitable activities of communal credit unions (Schreyer 1891, p. 60). The amendment to the act levied taxes on surpluses – profits, including in the cases where a surplus would be granted for charitable purposes. For this reason, communal credit unions started first to return their surpluses to reserve funds and then decreased interests to preserve the original charitable purpose at least in the form of cheap credits.

Thanks to the decreasing interest rate on personal credits and the growing number of citizen community and Raiffeisen credit unions, the competition in the retail banking market started increasing. At the very beginning of their development, credit unions faced nearly no competition because banks did not usually make loans to common people and usurers made loans for multiple times higher interests (Rolnická záložna Podřipská v Roudnici N.L. 1874–1934 1934, p. 29). However, the situation significantly changed in the 1870s and 1880s, when always several credit unions emerged in the district at a time. The convergence of interest rates can be seen in the gradually decreasing interest rate on personal credits, which stabilized on 5% p.a. across all credit unions at the end of the nineteenth century (Plicka 1891, p. 48).

Credit unions had been the basis of retail banking in the territory of the Czech lands until the middle of the 1950s when they were transferred under Česká státní spořitelna (The Czech State Savings Bank). Until that time, they had however formed the backbone of retail banking in the territory of the Czech lands. The capital that was accumulated at credit unions can be considered to be one of the accelerators of the economic growth both at the end of the nineteenth century and during the first decades of the twentieth century when small entrepreneurs were still dependent only on financial institutions of the credit union type, thanks to which the entrepreneurs could expand and become medium businesses (Jindra et al. 2015, p. 425).

Conclusion

The convergence of the different credit union streams that originated on the basis of different impulses shows the power of competition that – combined with regulations in the form of laws – influenced the dynamic development of retail banking in the territory of the Czech lands. The development of individual streams suggests that there is a difference between the situation when these banking institutions hold the local monopoly position and the situation when they have to react to their competitors. The originally different streams start showing common features to finally differ only in their origin.

The most essential transformation took place in case of communal credit unions after the Act on Associations was passed in 1873. The Act imposed taxes on credit unions and nearly prevented them from directly supporting charitable purposes which they earlier did in the form of donations, contributions and other forms of support to civic activities. Credit unions thus focused in particular on decreasing interest rates on personal credits. Establishing new credit unions across all the streams and the pressure on decreasing the interest rate then led to the general decreasing of interest rates and standardization of provided products.

Credit unions, which became a synonym for banks also thanks to gradual convergence of credit union streams, are the backbone of the whole retail banking sector. However, the difference lied in particular in the client. Thanks to the products they offered, credit unions made capital accessible to the population that otherwise could not reach to it, hence contributing to the economic growth and growth of the banking sector in the territory of the Czech lands.

References

Blažek A (1909) České spořitelní a záložní spolky dle vzoru Raiffeisenova. 2. doplněné vydání, nákladem "Svépomoci", vydavatelského a tiskařského družstva zemědělců v království Českém. Praha

Bouček J (1894) Záložny raiffeisenovy a hospodářská společenstva. 2. vydání, M. Knappa v Praze-Karlíně. Praha

Doubrava F (1924) Okresní záložny hospodářské, jejich vznik vývoj a působnost. Rolnická tiskárna v Praze. Praha

Janák J (1987) Počátek Moravských záložen a úvěrování průmyslu do roku 1873. Sborník prací Filozofické fakulty Brněnské univerzity

Jindra Z, Jakubec I et. al (2015) Hospodářský vzestup českých zemí poloviny 18.století do konce monarchie.Karolinum. Praha, ISBN 978-80-246-2947-2

Juřík P (2011) Historie bank a spořitelen v Čechách a na Moravě. Libri, Praha, ISBN 978-80-7277-488-3

Novotný A (1911) Paměti padesátiletého trvání záložny občanské v Jičíně 1861–1911. Kabátník a spol. Jičín

Okresní záložny hospodářské 1882–1932: almanach vydaný na paměť padesátiletého jejich trvání (1932) Svaz okresních záložen hospodářských. Praha

Plicka FP (1891) Záložna královského svobodného města Terezína. Tiskem F. Šimáčka. Praha

Rolnická záložna Podřipská v Roudnici N.L. 1874–1934 (1934) 60.výroční zpráva

Schreyer J (1891) Dějiny svépomocných záložen českých. Nákladem jednoty záložen v Čechách, na Moravě a ve Slezsku. Praha

Schreyer (1895) Katechismus záloženský aneb Co věděti má každý člen a každý vkladatel záložny. Jos. R. Vilímek. Praha

Šváb J (1935) Záložna v praxi. Nákladem Svazu hospodářských družstev československých v Praze. Olomouc

Vencovský F, Jindra Z Novotný J (1999) Dějiny bankovnictví v českých zemích. Bankovní institut, a.s. Praha, ISBN 80-7265-030-0

Wenzl F (1937) Dějiny záložen a ostatního družstevního podnikání na Moravě do roku 1885. Kampelíkova knihovna, Praha

50 let okresní záložny hospodářské v Semilech 1882–1932 (1933) Grafický závod Josef Glos v Semilech. Semily

Relationship Between the Company Size and the Value: Empirical Evidence

Přemysl Krch

Abstract The paper provides a research summary on the relation between the levels of valuation multiples and eight criteria of company size. The criteria comprised market capitalization, enterprise value, operating revenues, EBITDA, EBIT, net profit, sum of total assets, and number of employees. Using the linear regressions and correlations, the mutual relationships between the four valuation multiples and the abovementioned criteria were tested. The key conclusions of the research are that there can be observed certain dependence of price to earning valuation multiple on most of the tested size criteria. Low dependence was identified for enterprise value to EBITDA multiple. The results for price to book value and enterprise value to sales multiples proved statistically significant level of neither correlation nor dependence.

Keywords Valuation • Value • Size premium • Germany • Multiples

Introduction

The issue of potential existence of size premium as a factor influencing the value of the business has been subject to discussions on both the intensity of the size factor and even its existence. The author has already provided a review of previous research efforts and published literature relevant to this matter in one of his previous papers (Krch 2017) with inconclusive evidence on existence of size premium. Let us summarize some of them.

According to Pratt and Grabowski (2010 p. 40) the empirical studies showed that the returns reported by the small companies were regularly substantially higher than it would correspond to the original CAPM model. Buus (2008) provided a research of academic studies on existence, origin, and relevance of HML and SMB premiums. His compiled findings showed that the conclusions of individual studies

P. Krch (✉)
University of Economics in Prague, Department of Finance and Business Valuation, Náměstí Winstona Churchilla 4, 130 67 Praha 3, Czech Republic
e-mail: xkrcp03@vse.cz

D. Procházka (ed.), *The Impact of Globalization on International Finance and Accounting*, Springer Proceedings in Business and Economics,
https://doi.org/10.1007/978-3-319-68762-9_16

substantially differed; however, both factors were treated as a certain premium for risk which has to be undergone. Álvarez-Otero et al. (2006) worked out the study analyzing the size effect on the firms entering the Madrid Stock Exchange based on 111 IPO over 1985–1997. The data showed that the undervaluation prior to the IPO compared to the later market valuation using the trading data was 15,34% for the large companies and 8,4% for the small companies. Damodaran (2015) highlighted the fact that over the years (1981–2014), the average annual returns of small-cap company shares were in average lower by 0,18% than the market as a whole. Graham and Harvey (2015) arrived at similar conclusion in their CFO Survey. The authors did not receive any signals from the gathered answers that would prove the existence of the size premium. Ibbotson et al. (2013) arrived at a conclusion that the historical returns of the small companies differed significantly depending on the liquidity. Torchio and Surana (2013) prepared a study based on an analysis of relationship between the size and liquidity. For the first eight size deciles with the high liquidity, no size premium was present. For the ninth and tenth decile, the premium achieved a level around 2–2.5%.

This paper is intended to provide a short empirical test for my further, more comprehensive research of existence of size premium and relevant other issues which may occur during my research. The analysis should provide a preliminary statistic test for eight potential size criteria and their impact on value of companies.

Data and Methodology

The data used in the research were intended to cover one sector of traditional industry in Germany as the country with the largest capital market in Central Europe.

The data set for analyses has been compiled based on the data accessed through the Orbis database (2017). The search criteria were:

1. Quoted publicly traded companies in German capital markets
2. The industry NACE Rev. 2: Division 28 – manufacture of machinery and equipment

The reason for the choice of this sector was that this sector performs in rather steady growth rates, with stabilized capital structure as well as asset structure. Even though the author fully understands that the individual sectors may differ substantially, the scope of this research was limited to the above-described one-industry-specific sample since broader scope would substantially exceed the room dedicated for this paper.

The original data set based on these search steps resulted in total to 47 companies. The data set was further adjusted for the companies which did not have published the data at the end of 2015. This date was chosen as a fixed date for comparison and data collection to prevent any changes in value over time. The narrowed sample used for further research comprised 34 companies, the samples for individual valuation multiples showed different counts based on data availability.

The test assumed that the difference in intrinsic value caused by different size measure of risk should be reflected in the market valuation of the individual entities. Hence, the hypothesis was that there would be a significant observable dependence of company value (stipulated with the market valuation multiples) on the size proxies.

The size factor was based on several criteria. The criteria used as a size measure were inspired by the Duff & Phelps methodology, which is regularly used in the Duff & Phelps Risk Premium Reports. The report (Duff and Phelps 2013) uses the following criteria:

1. Market value of common equity
2. Book value of common equity
3. 5-year average net income
4. Market value of invested capital (MVIC)
5. Total assets
6. 5-year average EBITDA
7. Sales
8. Number of employees

The research was intended to serve as a summarized test of possible relation between the criteria and the equity value; therefore, only 1-year data (last available year) were used. Also, other levels of profit and loss statements were analyzed on their potential impacts on value. Hence, the criteria used in this research were adjusted moderately to the following criteria:

1. Market value of common equity (market capitalization)
2. Market value of invested capital (enterprise value)
3. Operating revenues
4. EBITDA
5. EBIT
6. Net profit
7. Total assets
8. Number of employees

The impact of the individual abovementioned size factors was tested on four market valuation multiples. The multiples comprised both equity and invested capital-based multiples:

- Price to earnings ratio
- Price to book value of equity ratio
- Enterprise value to EBITDA ratio
- Enterprise value to sales ratio

The groups were tested using the single linear regressions based on ordinary least squares calculated in MS Excel. As a result, both coefficients of correlation as a proxy for mutual relationship and coefficients of determination as a tool to verify the dependence of the valuation multiple levels on the individual size criteria on 95% level of certainty were used.

One of the analyzed aspects was also to what extent the impact of size can be observed on equity valuation multiples compared to the invested capital multiples. I assumed that the equity-based multiples would show higher dependence on size factors than the invested capital-based multiples.

Results and Discussion

Price to Earnings Ratio

The price to earnings ratio showed the highest interdependence between the size criteria and the company valuations among all four valuation multiples. In total, 25–26 company observations were available for individual criteria.

The results showed an observable interdependence between company value and five of the eight criteria of size. The linear regressions show that approximately 50–60% of company results could explain the higher valuation of the companies by the size factors. The strongest observable dependence could be observed with the sum of assets and the market capitalization, followed with enterprise value and total revenues with minimum difference of intensity.

On the other hand, the correlation with and dependence on EBIT and net income seemed to be unconfirmable. What is interesting is that even though the revenue and EBITDA criteria showed observable correlation, the EBIT and net income criteria showed no observable correlation or dependence. Also, the nonfinancial criterion based on number of employees showed observable correlation.

The mean error however indicated high levels (Table 1).

Price to Book Value Ratio

The price to book value ratio was available for 26–30 companies. The results indicated that the interdependence between the size criteria and valuation is generally low, and the dependency can be proven up to 22% of the sample in case of net income. The remaining criteria showed determination between 6,6% and 19,1%, which is generally very low. The mean error reached also significant levels.

To sum it up, the dependence of price to book valuation on size criteria cannot be confirmed (Table 2).

Table 1 Results for P/E ratio

	Market cap	Enterprise value	Operating revenue	EBITDA	EBIT	Net income	Total assets	No. of employees
Correlation coefficient	0,763	0,758	0,751	0,621	0,122	0,238	0,764	0,688
Coefficient of determination	0,582	0,575	0,564	0,386	0,015	0,057	0,584	0,474
Mean error	15,049	15,183	15,369	18,612	23,573	22,612	15,015	17,232
No. of observations	26	26	26	25	25	26	26	25

Source: Orbis database + authorial computation

Table 2 Results for P/BV ratio

	Market cap	Enterprise value	Operating revenue	EBITDA	EBIT	Net income	Total assets	No. of employees
Correlation coefficient	0,345	0,344	0,322	0,406	0,437	0,469	0,257	0,286
Coefficient of determination	0,119	0,119	0,104	0,165	0,191	0,220	0,066	0,082
Mean error	0,924	0,925	0,932	0,940	0,928	0,906	0,952	0,959
No. of observations	30	30	30	27	26	26	30	29

Source: Orbis database + authorial computation

Enterprise Value to EBITDA Ratio

The number of observations reached 26–28. The enterprise value to EBITDA showed moderate degree of mutual correlation to the analyzed size criteria for a half of the criteria. The differences among all correlations show similar proportional differences like the correlations for P/E ratio. However, the dependence on individual criteria was significantly lower, reaching at maximum 34,1% of sample explained by the enterprise value (Table 3).

Enterprise Value to Sales Ratio

Total count of observations was the highest of all four groups. The reason is clear – going down through the profit and loss statement, the number of companies with positive results necessary for analysis declined, but the sales are always positive.

Nevertheless, this valuation multiple showed the lowest interdependence of all the observed multiples. Any of the eight criteria did not confirm dependence of the value on size for more than 5% of the sample. Also the mean error calculated reached several times higher proportional levels to the mean values of the sample.

Table 3 Results for EV/EBITDA ratio

	Market cap	Enterprise value	Operating revenue	EBITDA	EBIT	Net income	Total assets	No. of employees
Correlation coefficient	0,576	0,584	0,507	0,385	0,130	0,419	0,531	0,447
Coefficient of determination	0,332	0,341	0,257	0,148	0,017	0,175	0,282	0,199
Mean error	4519	4402	4673	5005	5467	4176	4594	4852
No. of observations	27	28	28	28	27	26	28	28

Source: Orbis database + authorial computation

Table 4 Results for EV/sales ratio

	Market cap	Enterprise value	Operating revenue	EBITDA	EBIT	Net income	Total assets	No. of employees
Correlation coefficient	0,064	0,063	0,083	0,224	0,203	0,152	0,068	0,121
Coefficient of determination	0,004	0,004	0,007	0,050	0,041	0,023	0,005	0,015
Mean error	9853	9687	9236	0,431	0,426	9937	9246	0,432
No. of observations	30	31	34	31	29	29	34	33

Source: Orbis database + authorial computation

In brief, the enterprise value to sales valuation multiple cannot confirm any impact of the observed size criteria (Table 4).

Conclusion

Generally, three groups of criteria were tested. The simple market value of capital size criteria showed practically the same levels of both correlations and determinations, and it makes practically no difference whether the market capitalization or the enterprise value is used. The profit and loss statement items did not show any significant trend common for all four groups. The other criteria comprised sum of assets and number of employees. Even though the very low dependence was indicated, it seems to be significant only for price to earnings ratio.

Overall, the key conclusions of the research are that there can be observed certain dependence of price-to-earning value on most of the tested size criteria. Low dependence was identified for enterprise value to EBITDA multiple. The results for price to book value and enterprise value to sales multiples did not prove any statistically significant level of neither correlation nor dependence. This is also in line with the author's previous experience from valuation practice for similar companies from traditional industries.

Also, it seems that the equity-based multiples show higher dependence on size criteria than the invested capital-based multiples. A possible explanation can be that the providers of loans or bonds are usually more strategically oriented than the financial investors holding their shares through the public markets.

Assuming the price to earnings ratio is generally the most frequently used measure of value in the capital markets among all the four valuation multiples, it seems that market capitalization, enterprise value, operation revenues, and total assets accompanied with number of employees would be a solid proxy for further testing of the size impacts. The results like EBITDA, EBIT, and net profit do not show any significant levels of determination for the valuation multiples, and hence they are probably not the key determinants for a potential size effect.

For further research, it seems that the broader sample would be necessary to confirm this preliminary analysis. There is a question to what extent such sample would show internal dispersion between individual industries and sectors, i.e., machinery compared to IT services, since the individual industries show substantially different structure of creation of value added in terms of both the asset and capital employment and the workforce necessary to be employed.

Acknowledgments This paper has been prepared as a part of and under financial support of the research scope of Faculty of Finance and Accounting of University of Economics in Prague No. IP 100040, which the author gratefully acknowledges.

References

Álvarez-Otero S, González-Mendez VM (2006) The size effect of firms going public on the Spanish Capital Market. In: Gregoriou GN (ed) Initial public pfferings: An international perspective. Elsevier, Oxford, pp 65–79

Buus T (2008) HML a SMB prémie v akademické literatuře - výše a podstata. Český finanční a účetní časopis 2:31–41

Duff & Phelps, LLC (2013) 2013 Duff & Phelps Risk Premium Report. Duff & Phelps, LLC, Chicago

Graham JR, Harvey CR (2015) The Equity Risk Premium in 2015. University of Texas [Online] 05 29, 2015. [Cited: 12 01, 2015.] http://faculty.mccombs.utexas.edu/keith.brown/AFPMaterial/GrahamHarvey-ERP%20Survey-5.15.pdf

Ibbotson RG et al (2013) Liquidity as an investment style. Financ Anal J 69(3):30–44

Krch P (2017) Existence of size premium – a review of literature and room for future research. In: Procházka D (ed) New trends in finance and accounting – proceedings of the 17th annual conference on finance and accounting. Springer International Publishing AG, Cham, pp 771–781

Pratt SP, Grabowski RJ (2010) Cost of capital in litigation: applications and examples, 4th. edn. John Wiley & Sons, p 336. 9780470944912

Torchio F, Surana S (2013) Effect of Liquidity on Size Premium and its Implications for Financial Valuations. The Forensic Economics. [Online] 08 2013. [Cited: 12 24, 2015.] working draft. http://www.forensiceconomics.com/wp-content/uploads/2013/09/Effect-of-Liquidity-on-Size-Premium.pdf

Data Set

Orbis Database (Bureau van Dijk) – accessible online via http://orbis.bvdinfo.com. Data compiled and downloaded on February 15, 2017

A Note on the Gordon Growth Model with Taxes

Olga Belomyttseva, Larisa Grinkevich, and Anastasiia Grinkevich

Abstract This paper analyzes the Gordon Growth Model and its evolution in various studies. A modification of the Gordon Growth Model using corporate income tax and personal income tax is developed. Two equations are presented, one of which is for determining the share price with taxes and the other for determining for the value of growth rate.

Keywords Gordon growth model • Dividend discount model • Corporate income tax • Personal income tax

Introduction

The dividend discount model (DDM) is based on the obvious assumption that dividends are the only expected cash flow received by the investor from the corporation. Accordingly, the DDM assumes that a share is evaluated as the discounted value of expected dividends and is now considered the most widely used fundamental valuation techniques in practice.

The Gordon Growth Model (GGM) was proposed by Gordon in 1962, as opposed to dividend irrelevance theory. It should be noted that many studies rather often refer to this model as the DDM. We agree with the point of view of Damodaran (2012), who considered GGM as one of the variants of DDM. For the purpose of this paper, we will use the acronym GGM and thus emphasize Myron Gordon's personal contribution to the theory. It should also be noted that traditional modifications of DDM and GGM do not involve taxes.

O. Belomyttseva (✉)
Tomsk State University, Tomsk, Department of Finance and Accounting, pr. Lenina 36, 634036 Tomsk, Russia
e-mail: olbel@f123.ru

L. Grinkevich • A. Grinkevich
Tomsk State University, Tomsk, Department of Economics, pr. Lenina 36, 634036 Tomsk, Russia
e-mail: nasty_saturn@mail.ru; tasya-g89@mail.ru

D. Procházka (ed.), *The Impact of Globalization on International Finance and Accounting*, Springer Proceedings in Business and Economics,
https://doi.org/10.1007/978-3-319-68762-9_17

In recent years, based on the analysis of periodical literature, we can recognize a surge of interest in the DDM as a whole and in the GGM, in particular. Studies with reference to DDM and GGM models conducted in various years can be classified into four groups. Authors, who modify and develop various modifications of the DDM, are included in the first group, which is the largest one. For example, Fuller and Hsia (1984) presented a two-phase growth model, "H," wherein the growth rate at the initial stage is not constant but decreases linearly with time until it reaches a stable level in a steady state. Hurley and Johnson (1994, 1997, 1998) introduced a series of dividend models consistent with uncertainty of dividends. Research on GGM modifications was performed in various times by Farrell (1985), Yao (1997), Pages (1999), Gorman (2002), Heinrichs et al. (2013), Hurley (2013), Irons (2014), and Lazzati and Menichini (2015).

The second, small group includes authors who tried to prove validity and applicability of the GGM in other ways, which differed from Gordon's approach. These include Perevozchikov (2009) and Belomyttseva and Grinkevich (2016).

The third group of researchers consists of authors who tested the GGM in different countries and at different time intervals. Most of them came to the conclusion that the GGM is valid and advisable to use. In other words, the results were impressive. This group includes Sorensen and Williamson (1985), Barsky and De Long (1993), and Foerster and Sapp (2005).

The fourth research group is formed by the authors who provided an overview and comparative analysis of the DDM. A good general summary of dividend models in multiple variations was done by Hurley and Fabozzi (1998) and Damodaran (2012).

The objective of our study is to substantiate the after-tax version of the GGM. The structure of the paper is as follows. Section "Involving Taxes in the Gordon Growth Model" reveals the need for taking taxes into account for the purpose of the GGM and opinions of particular authors, including Gordon himself, on this issue. The GGM justification using taxes is introduced in section "Modification of the Gordon Growth Model with Taxes". The results and prospects for further investigation are outlined in section "Results and Conclusion".

Involving Taxes in the Gordon Growth Model

Most authors completely ignore taxes in modification or empirical testing of GGM. However, it should be noted that Gordon (1962) raised the issue of the need for taking taxes into consideration. In particular, in his monograph *The Investment, Financing, and Valuation of the Corporation*, a chapter is devoted to the tax issue.

Gordon (1962) notes that in simple models of valuation, where the company exists exclusively due to the reinvestment of profits or to debt financing, we can also use after-tax variables. It is also advisable to study the involvement of the optimal balance of the loan capital and owner's capital in the payment of corporate taxes and interest on debenture deductible from income as an expense. The inference made by Gordon (1962) is as follows: corporate tax does not represent a serious threat to the GGM, while the personal income tax raises serious questions.

Schurman (2009) used the debt tax shield component in relation to the GGM. He extended this model and used it to calculate enterprise value, which means that fixed costs will not include interest expense on debt or dividends on preferred stock. Damodaran (2012) highlights the need for involving taxes in the model and states that if individual taxes are taken into account, this can significantly reduce the excess return determined in the researches performed before the payment of taxes.

Thus, it is evident that there is a need for involving taxes, both corporate income tax and personal income tax, in the GGM modification, which can ensure that the model will be more realistic. In fact, development of the after-tax version of similar models already occurs in financial science. For example, Litzenberger and Ramaswamy (1979) derived an after-tax version of the capital asset pricing model. This model incorporates a progressive tax scheme and for wealth and income-related constraints on borrowing.

Modification of the Gordon Growth Model with Taxes

In this model, the value of the firm's equity can be represented as a growing perpetuity based on next period's expected dividend (Gordon 1962). According to Gordon, the price of a share is equal to the discounted value of expected future dividends. In this case, dividends are expected to grow at the constant rate g; the discount rate (required rate of return) is k. This principle leads to the familiar valuation Eq. 1, which represents the following classical format of the model:

$$P = \frac{D_1}{k - g} \tag{1}$$

where $g < k$, P is the current share price, and D_1 means the next dividend per share the firm will pay.

Equation 1 is simplified. The original format implies direct discounting of the future dividend payments and is as follows (Eq. 2):

$$P = \sum_{t=1}^{\infty} D \frac{(1 + g)^t}{(1 + k)^t} \tag{2}$$

where $g < k$ and D is used for the current dividend.

There are two basic assumptions underlying the GGM, which are as follows: the required return on the firm's common share and the dividend growth rate are constantly moving forward.

Let us introduce the following notation: EPS stands for earnings per share and k_{+t} is the rate of earnings, involving the corporate income tax rate. In this case, $k_{+t} > k$. The discount rate k is not changed.

Consequently, we obtain Eq. 3:

$$EPS_1 = P^* k_{+t} \tag{3}$$

where EPS_1 represents the earnings of the next year.

Next, when the corporate income tax is taken into account, we obtain Eq. 4:

$$EPS_{1n} = EPS_1{}^* (1 - \beta_1) \tag{4}$$

where EPS_{1n} is after-tax EPS of the next year and β_1 is used for the corporate income tax rate.

Then, we arrive at Eq. 5:

$$D_1 = EPS_{1n}{}^* DPR = EPS_1{}^* (1 - \beta_1)^* DPR \tag{5}$$

where DPR is dividend payout ratio, calculated as the percentage of earnings paid to shareholders in dividends.

Finally, we take into account the personal income tax and obtain Eq. 6:

$$D_{1n} = D_1{}^* (1 - \beta_2) = EPS_1{}^* (1 - \beta_1)^* DPR^* (1 - \beta_2) \tag{6}$$

where D_{1n} is the after-tax dividend of the next year and β_2 is the dividend tax rate.[1]

The change in the share price in this (the first) time period will be ΔP_1 (Eq. 7):

$$\Delta P_1 = EPS_{1n} - D_1 = EPS_{1n}{}^* (1 - DPR) = EPS_1{}^* (1 - \beta_1)^* (1 - DPR) \tag{7}$$

P_1 will be presented as Eq. 8:

$$P_1 = P + \Delta P = P^* \left(1 + k_{+t}{}^* (1 - \beta_1)^* (1 - DPR)\right) = P^* (1 + g) \tag{8}$$

With this in mind, the growth rate value g will be determined in Eq. 9:

$$g = k_{+t}{}^* (1 - \beta_1)^* (1 - DPR) \tag{9}$$

At the next stage, we determine the value of P (Eq. 10):

$$P = \frac{P^* k_{+t}{}^* (1 - \beta_1)^* DPR^* (1 - \beta_2)}{1 + k}^* \sum_{t=0}^{\infty} \frac{(1 + g)^t}{(1 + k)^t} \tag{10}$$

[1]Technically, it is the personal income tax rate, but we use "dividend tax rate" to highlight the fact that we mean dividend income here. We do not consider the case when the investor is a legal entity.

When Eq. 10 has been transformed, we arrive at Eq. 11:

$$P = \frac{D_{1n}}{(1+k)} * \frac{(1+k)}{(k-g)} = \frac{P^* k_{+t}^* (1-\beta_1)^* DPR^* (1-\beta_2)}{k - k_{+t}^* (1-\beta_1)^* (1-DPR)} \tag{11}$$

Equation 11 is, then, modified into Eq. 12:

$$\frac{k_{+t}^* (1-\beta_1)^* DPR^* (1-\beta_2)}{k - k_{+t}^* (1-\beta_1)^* (1-DPR)} = 1 \tag{12}$$

Hence, Eq. 13 is derived:

$$k_{+t} = \frac{k}{(1-\beta_1)^* (1 - DPR^* \beta_2)} \tag{13}$$

It can be inferred from Eq. 13 that k_{+t} is minimum when DPR = 0. Then, we use Eq. 11 to obtain Eq. 14:

$$P = \frac{D_{1n}}{(k-g)} \tag{14}$$

Thus, we come to the basic Gordon equation; however, Eq. 15, which we derive from Eq. 1 and Eq. 13, appears to be more illustrative:

$$P = \frac{EPS_1}{k_{+t}} = \frac{EPS_1^* (1-\beta_1)^* (1 - DPR^* \beta_2)}{k} = \frac{EPS_{1n}^* (1 - DPR^* \beta_2)}{k} \tag{15}$$

Results and Conclusion

In the course of our study, we obtained the following results:

1. We derived an equation for determining the share price P, adjusted for the corporate income tax and the dividend tax Eqs. 11, 14, and 15. The equation complies with the general provisions of the GGM. The equation for determining the share price including taxes Eq. 14 is similar to the tax-free Eq. 1, provided that a net dividend is assumed as the dividend in both the equations.
2. By means of Eq. 15, we demonstrate the fact that the share price is determined by the dividend payout policy of a particular joint stock company and that it reaches the peak at DPR = 0 (i.e., under zero dividend payout). Whether this will increase or decrease an investor's wealth, that depends on the rate of personal income tax on subsequent sale of share.

3. Based on the ratio of D_{1n} and g, we determined the value of growth rate g.

$$\frac{D_{1n}}{g} = P* \frac{DPR^*(1-\beta_2)}{(1-DPR)} \tag{16}$$

4. The introduction of tax variables to the GGM contributes to a more realistic model.
5. We agree with Gordon's assertion that corporate income tax does not pose a serious threat to the GGM. However, unlike Gordon, we hold the position that personal income tax is also no threat to the GGM.
6. As areas for further investigation, we consider development of a model alternative to the GGM, which implies no restrictions on the constant growth, as well as studies on the empirical testing of Eq. 16.

Acknowledgments This study has been conducted with the financial support of the Global Competitiveness Enhancement Program 2013–2020 of Tomsk State University.

References

Barsky RB, De Long JB (1993) Why does the stock market fluctuate? Q J Econ CVIII:291–311. https://doi.org/10.2307/2118333

Belomyttseva O, Grinkevich L (2016) A note on the Gordon growth model with earnings per share. In: Proceedings of the 3d international scientific conference on information technologies in science, management, social sphere and medicine, Tomsk, May 2016. https://doi.org/10.2991/itsmssm-16.2016.34

Damodaran A (2012) Investment valuation: tools and techniques for determining the value of any asset, 2nd edn. Wiley, Hoboken

Farrell JL (1985) The dividend discount model: a primer. Financ Anal J 41(6):16–19+22–25. https://doi.org/10.2469/faj.v41.n6.16

Foerster SR, Sapp SG (2005) The dividend discount model in the long-run: a clinical study. J Appl Financ 15(2):1–21

Fuller RJ, Hsia C (1984) A simplified common stock valuation model. Financ Anal J 40:49–56

Gordon M (1962) The investment, financing, and valuation of the corporation. Irwin, Homewood

Gorman L (2002) An internally consistent approach to common stock valuation. Int Bus Econ Res J 1(3):69–78

Heinrichs N, Hess D, Homburg C et al (2013) Extended dividend, cash flow and residual income valuation models - accounting for deviations from ideal conditions. Contemp Account Res 30 (1):42–79. https://doi.org/10.1111/j.1911-3846.2011.01148.x

Hurley WJ, Johnson LD (1994) A realistic dividend valuation model. Financ Anal J 50(4):50–54. https://doi.org/10.2469/faj.v50.n4.50

Hurley WJ, Johnson LD (1997) Stochastic two-phase dividend discount models. J Portf Manag 23 (4):91–98. https://doi.org/10.3905/jpm.1997.409614

Hurley WJ, Fabozzi F (1998) Dividend discount models. In: Fabozzi FJ (ed) Selected topics in equity portfolio management. New Hope, Pennsylvania

Hurley WJ, Johnson LD (1998) Generalized Markov dividend discount models. J Portf Manag 25 (1):27–31. https://doi.org/10.3905/jpm.1998.409658

Hurley WJ (2013) Calculating first moments and confidence intervals for generalized stochastic dividend discount models. J Math Financ 3:275–279. https://doi.org/10.4236/jmf.2013.32027
Irons R (2014) Enhancing the dividend discount model to account for accelerated share price growth. J Account Financ 14(4):153–159
Lazzati N, Menichini AA (2015) A dynamic approach to the dividend discount model. Rev Pac Basin Finan Mark Pol 18:1–36
Litzenberger RH, Ramaswamy K (1979) The effect of personal taxes and dividends on capital asset prices: theory and empirical evidence. J Financ Econ 7:163–196. https://doi.org/10.1016/0304-405X(79)90012-6
Pages H (1999) A note on the Gordon Growth Model with nonstationary dividend growth. BIS Work Pap No 75. Available via SSRN. http://papers.ssrn.com. Accessed 26 Feb 2017
Perevozchikov AG (2009) On the interrelation of Gordon Model and Fisher Equation. Financ Anal Sci Exp 3:65–67
Schurman G (2009) Schurman XGGM model – extended Gordon growth model in continuous time. Available via Applied Business Economics. http://www.appliedbusinesseconomics.com/files/gvsxggm02.pdf. Accessed 26 Feb 2017
Sorensen EH, Williamson DA (1985) Some evidence on the value of the dividend discount model. Financ Anal J 41:60–69
Yao YL (1997) A Trinomial Dividend Valuation Model. J Portf Manag 23(4):99–103. https://doi.org/10.3905/jpm.1997.409618

Indirect Valuation and Earnings Stability: Within-Company Use of the Earnings Multiple

Michal Kaszas and Karel Janda

Abstract This paper investigates statistical significance of earnings stability in the within-company indirect valuation method. We empirically establish superiority of a within-company earnings multiple valuation technique for the relatively most stable companies. Favorable empirical results are robust against different means of operationalization of the stability construct and valuation multiples. Results of this paper indicate that the indirect within-company price-to-earnings valuation yields the most precise and the most accurate value estimates.

Keywords Investment decision • Company valuation • Earnings properties

Introduction

Practitioners and academics agree that the value of an asset is determined by the present value of future payoffs to the owner. Williams (1938) formalizes this view and expresses company value as a function of dividend payments. Building on his work, Gordon and Shapiro (1956) derive the Gordon Growth Model for capital budgeting that in its later adjusted forms, discounted cash flow model or abnormal earnings valuation model (Ohlson 1995), dominates the valuation theory to date.

While finance practitioners focus on cash flow figures (Van Aswegen and Jedlin 2013), academic literature provides empirical evidence that earnings are superior basis for valuation comparing to cash flows. Contrary to the perception of cash flow

M. Kaszas (✉)
Department of Banking and Insurance, Institute of Strategic Investments, University of Economics Prague, Churchilla 4, 13067 Praha 3, Czech Republic
e-mail: kaszas.michal@isti.cz

K. Janda
Department of Banking and Insurance, Institute of Strategic Investments, University of Economics Prague, Churchilla 4, 13067 Praha 3, Czech Republic

Institute of Economic Studies, Charles University, Opletalova 26, 11000 Praha 1, Czech Republic
e-mail: Karel-Janda@seznam.cz

D. Procházka (ed.), *The Impact of Globalization on International Finance and Accounting*, Springer Proceedings in Business and Economics,
https://doi.org/10.1007/978-3-319-68762-9_18

superiority as a basis for valuation, Dechow (1994) provides empirical evidence that the accrual adjustments made to the cash flow figures remedy their timing and matching problems. In line with the findings of Dechow (1994), Kim and Ritter (1999) and Liu et al. (2007) support the earnings superiority as a basis for valuation with empirical results. Furthermore, Penman and Sougiannis (1998) and Francis et al. (2000) evaluate empirically the consequences of timing and matching insufficiency of cash flows in terms of valuation practice and find the abnormal earnings valuation model, also referred to as the residual income model, to clearly dominate traditional DCF method of valuation.

The indirect, multiple, valuation method is among practitioners the most popular and most often utilized one. Asquith et al. (2005) find a strong preference of indirect to direct valuation techniques by studying 1126 analyst reports. They find that 99% of sell-side analysts use indirect multiple valuation methods.

We argue that stability is an important characteristic for multiple valuations which has the potential to capture many idiosyncrasies and develop this argument from the residual income model.[1] We provide evidence in favor of this argument by demonstrating superior out of sample prediction for the most stable companies. We document that earnings stability positively influences the accuracy and precision of indirect within-company valuation. We operationalize the stability concept as a 5-year rolling standard deviation of the inverse hyperbolic sine of earnings before extraordinary items attributable to common equity. Hence, we diverge from the commonly found definition of stable company.[2]

Hypothesis Development

Exploiting earnings stability of some companies and the superiority of the residual income formula over other direct valuation models (Penman and Sougiannis 1998), we derive an argument of stable price-to-earnings (PE) multiple for stable companies by expressing the market value using the residual income valuation model, Eq. (1), as a sum of the book value of equity at the date of valuation (in practice this is essentially the book value of equity at the year's beginning) and the present value of future residual income:

$$\mathrm{MV_t} = \mathrm{BV_0} + \sum_{t=1}^{\infty} \frac{\mathrm{E_t} - \mathrm{BV_{t-1}}^{*} \mathrm{r_t}}{(1 + \mathrm{r_t})^{t}} \tag{1}$$

[1]We exploit the superiority of the residual income valuation formula, provided by Penman and Sougiannis (1998) and Francis et al. (2000), over other valuation techniques.

[2]Literature refers to a company in a stable state if the company earns return on its equity capital equaling the cost of its equity capital (Stauffer 1971).

Then, we apply assumptions of stable earnings and stable cost of equity capital.[3] This allows us to utilize the perpetuity valuation principle. Consequently, we derive the argument of PE multiple stability. We claim that for stable companies this multiple equals the inverse value of the cost of equity capital. This procedure is depicted by Eqs. (2) and (3):

$$MV_t = BV_0 + \frac{E}{r} - \frac{BV_0{}^{*}r}{r} \tag{2}$$

$$MV_t = \frac{E}{r} \quad \rightarrow \quad \frac{MV_t}{E} = r^{-1} \tag{3}$$

Data

The empirical analysis is conducted on the whole universe of publicly traded companies accessible via Thomson Reuters Worldscope® and Datastream®. In order for the company-year observation to be included in the dataset, the following data must be accessible: (1) EPS or earnings before extraordinary items attributable to common equity, (2) book value of equity, (3) number of shares outstanding, (4) fiscal year end date, and (5) closing share price at the end of the fourth month after the fiscal year end. The dataset contains 68,589 unique companies during the time-frame spanning from 1980 to 2015, which yields overall number of 862,050 unique company-year observations.

Outlier Treatment

To alleviate the effect of distressed and bankrupt companies, we follow the approach adopted by Bhojraj and Lee (2002). We first erase all penny stocks and company-year observations with net revenue figure lower than the 1st percentile of net revenue in the given country year.[4] Next, we sort observations with positive aggregate earnings before extraordinary items by the EPS figure and on an annual

---

[3]Archer and Faerber (1966) show empirically a negative correlation between the cost of equity capital of the company and its size, its leverage, its age, and variation of its earnings. Lev (1983) finds leverage and size of the company as two of a few factors causing earnings stability. Building on the empirical evidence of subsample of stable companies with low cost of equity, we assume that variation of the cost of equity capital of these companies closely approximates stability.

[4]Bhojraj and Lee (2002) follow nominal specification of the criterion (Sales <100 MIO USD); however, with respect to international character of this study and the fact that accounting numbers are in local currencies, we erase companies at year T if they belong to the bottom percentile of sales figure constructed on a country basis at year T-1.

basis erase the observations with values higher than 98th or lower than 2nd EPS percentile to tackle the effect of economically nonsensical pricing multiples. After constructing the actual price-to-earnings ratio, we drop the company-year observations with PE ratios lower than 5th and higher than 95th PE ratio percentile on an annual basis. This approach tackles the negative effect of the ratio's numerator.[5]

We calculate a 5-year rolling standard deviation of closing share price 4 months after the fiscal year end; then, we drop the companies for which this rolling standard deviation equals 0 to mitigate the effect of listed but not actively traded companies.

Methodology

Stability Measure Construction

We define the concept of earnings stability using earnings properties. Our concept of stable earnings aims to embrace company observations with low variation of earnings stream over time.

First, we use the earnings before extraordinary items attributable to common equity in an undeflated form for the base-case operationalization of the construct. Second, we normalize the selected measure for all company years from the dataset by applying the inverse hyperbolic sine transformation method, as shown by Eq. (4) which enables us to transform also company-year observations with losses. Next, we opt for the standard deviation of the inverse hyperbolic sine of earnings before extraordinary items attributable to common equity (4) over a 5 consecutive year window to represent our stability measure:

$$Earn_{\mathrm{IHS}} = \ln\left(Earn + \sqrt{(Earn^2 + 1)}\right) \tag{4}$$

Finally, we create ten stability decile groups based on the stability measure in every year to measure relative stability of companies. For this purpose, we sort the companies at year T based on the value of the 5-year rolling standard deviation of the inverse hyperbolic sine of earnings. Subsequently, we create ten stability decile groups in every year. The decile group number 1 encompasses the most stable companies while the decile group number 10 the least stable companies.

[5]While the mean PE ratio of the top 5 deleted percentile groups across all years equals 7917.2 and median 2087.6, the values for the bottom 5 percentile groups are 2.41 and 2.37, respectively.

Statistical Analysis

We carry out the following regression (5) for company-year observations from *final sample* and *subsample of peer companies*[6] conditional on the stability decile groups.

We test a general linear hypothesis that for the individual stability decile groups, $\beta = 1$. Potentially favorable results of the general linear hypothesis lay ground for alternative expression of Eq. (5). If the earnings coefficient equals 1 for stable companies, one can easily derive an argument for a price-to-earnings ratio stability as presented by Eq. 6:

$$\ln(MarketValue) = \alpha + \beta \times \ln(Earnings) + \varepsilon \tag{5}$$

$$E\left[\ln\left(\frac{MarketValue_{it}}{Earnings_{it}}\right)\right] = \alpha_i \tag{6}$$

By using company-fixed effects regressions, we attempt to capture "time demeaned" within-company information about the time series effect of earnings on market value. In the case of favorable regression results,[7] we can argue that market value changes proportionally to earnings of the valued company.

Valuation Analysis

In this paper, we opt for valuation analysis approach to evaluate the valuation accuracy and precision of multiple-based valuation techniques (Penman and Sougiannis 1998). We calculate the valuation error and its dispersion for the within-company valuation method individually for every stability decile group, using solely the information about the valued company.

We test the hypothesis of a higher valuation accuracy and precision of the within-company multiple valuation for companies based on their relative earnings stability. We estimate the price of a company (i) 4 months after the fiscal year end (t) by multiplying the last reported earnings (earnings for the fiscal year T) by the last year's firm-specific price-to-earnings ratio.[8] This ratio is calculated as a closing share price 4 months after the previous fiscal year end (t–1) divided by the

---

[6]We include a company-year observation into a "subsample of peer companies" if the company year observation is from the same *year*, *country*, *industry*, and *stability decile*.

[7]This approach is focused on the time-series within-company relation between earnings and market value. As favorable we consider the outcome where the general linear hypothesis that earnings coefficient equals one is met.

[8]We impose an assumption that during the 4-month period, all companies manage to report their annual results. At the same time, this treatment assumes that at the date of market value measurement, the price effectively reflects fundaments.

arithmetic average of the earnings reported for the fiscal year T–1 and T–2. We opt for the 2-year average earnings in order to marginalize the effect of net income figure fluctuations, since LeClair (1990) argues that this treatment yields the most reliable and the least volatile results comparing to other methods such as declining weights over a longer period or current earnings. Equation 7 expresses the logic of this within-company approach:

$$\widehat{Price_{i,t}} = Earnings_{i,T} \times \left(\frac{Price_{i,t-1}}{\frac{\left(Earnings_{i,T-1} + Earnings_{i,T-2}\right)}{2}} \right) \quad (7)$$

After obtaining the out-of-sample value prediction, we measure the valuation accuracy of the individual methods. For this purpose, we calculate a valuation error for each value prediction by comparing the predicted value with the realized market value. The magnitude of valuation error represents a measure of valuation accuracy and can be calculated in different forms. We calculate the valuation error as an absolute valuation error expressed as a difference between the predicted and observed market value deflated by the observed market value, absolute logarithmic valuation error as absolute difference between the logarithm of the predicted and observed market value, and squared valuation error as a squared value of the difference between the predicted and observed market value deflated by observed market value. These measures are calculated as stated in the description of Table 2.

After evaluating the valuation accuracy, we describe the distributional characteristics of the valuation error in order to evaluate the valuation precision. We evaluate the distributional characteristics, hence valuation precision, by observing the interdecile and interquartile ranges of the absolute valuation error.[9] We calculate the interdecile range as the difference between the value of the 90th and 10th percentile of the absolute valuation error. The interquartile range represents the difference between the value of the 75th and 25th percentile of the absolute valuation error.

Results

Table 1 presents the results of the company-fixed effects panel regressions with company-clustered standard errors conditional on the earnings stability decile group. Panel A of the Table 1 provides results for the whole sample, while Panel B presents results for the subsample of peer companies.

[9]We use the standard deviation as a complementary statistic, but we argue that it is prone to be sensitive, hence exposed to the effect of extreme values.

Throughout the whole sample, the earnings coefficient decreases gradually as company stability decreases.[10] While a 1% increase in earnings for the average company in the 1st stability decile group results in a 0.8% increase in market value, this increase is only 0.66% in the 5th and 0.19% in the 10th decile group. Moreover, the general linear hypothesis of the earnings coefficient being equal to one is rejected in all cases, since none of the earnings coefficient intervals constructed on the 95% confidence level contain 1.000.

Assessing the results for the subsample of peer companies, presented in the Panel B of the Table 1, we find that the tenor of the results changes slightly. While the decreasing determination of market value by earnings figure resulting from the decreasing stability remains, we cannot reject the general linear hypothesis of the earnings coefficient being equal to one for the most stable decile group. Therefore, we claim that in the case of the most stable decile group, on average, the market value of a company is over time fully proportional to earnings of a company.

Table 2 provides results of the within-company PE valuation for the final sample (Panel A) and the subsample of peer companies (Panel B). Based on these results, we can state the following findings. First, relative earnings stability apparently affects the valuation accuracy and precision of the within-company valuation. This effect is documented by increasing absolute valuation error and interquartile and interdecile range with decreasing company stability. Second, conducting the analysis on the companies belonging to a five-member peer group decreases the absolute and squared valuation errors as well as interquartile and interdecile ranges of these measures even further and in a more systematic manner. Moreover, it stabilizes the trend of the remaining valuation error measures.

Conclusion

We argue that the market value of stable companies moves proportionally to earnings. We tested the argument of market value and earnings proportionality empirically by conducting valuation analysis to find that the PE multiple valuation technique[11] provides the most accurate and the most precise value estimate for the relatively most stable companies. These results are robust against numerous methods of stability construct operationalization.

To synthesize, we find that if one is conducting an indirect valuation, on an exceptionally stable and publicly traded company, one should use its last year's PE ratio and multiply it by current earnings figure in order to obtain the superior value

[10]Except for the 2nd stability decile group for which the coefficient is even slightly higher than for the most stable decile group. We argue that this is possible an effect of insufficient outlier treatment.

[11]Results for price to sales and price to free cash flows techniques are untabulated, but their tenor remains.

estimate. We conclude that in the case of the most stable companies, the accounting earnings approximate Black's (1980) concept of economic earnings exceptionally well.

A naturally appealing extension of this study will be to examine empirically the effect of the earnings stability as a peer selection criterion for the between-company peer selection method. Furthermore, research of an active trading strategy in which one would buy stocks marked by this method as undervalued, sell stocks marked as overvalued might yield interesting results. Finally, empirical analysis of the effect of earnings stability on the outcome of privately held company transactions should be addressed.

Acknowledgments This project has received funding from the European Union's Horizon 2020 Research and Innovation Staff Exchange program under the Marie Sklodowska-Curie grant agreement No. 681228. We also acknowledge support from the Czech Science Foundation (grant15-00036S). The views expressed in this paper are those of the authors and not necessarily those of our institutions.

Appendix

This table shows the results of the panel regression of ln(market value) on ln(earnings) using company-fixed effects and company clustered standard errors. Panel A represents the results of the regression applied on a full sample of 284,390 company-years divided into 10 earnings stability deciles based on a 5-year rolling standard deviation of the inverse hyperbolic sine of earnings. Panel B represents the results for the subsample of peer companies. We define a peer-company as one being drawn from the subsample of companies from the same year, country, industry and earnings stability quantile. In orded to include the company into analysis its peer-group has to constitute of at least 5 companies.

$$\ln\left(\text{Market Value}_{i,t}\right) = \alpha + \beta \times \ln\left(\text{Earning}_{i,T}\right) + \varepsilon$$

We construct the confidence intervals of the regression coefficients using 95% confidence level. If the confidence interval includes 1.000 we cannot reject the general linear hypothesis of Beta coefficient being differenct from 1.000.

This table shows the results for the within-company valuation technique. We estimate the market value (hereby "MV") of a company 4 months after its fiscal year end as a result of multiplying the last year's price to earnings ratio of the given company by its last announced earnings. We calculate the absolute, squared and absolute log valuation error as follows:

$$\varepsilon_{i,t} = \frac{\left|\overline{\text{MV}}_{i,t} - \text{MV}_{i,t}\right|}{\text{MV}_{i,t}} \quad \varepsilon_{i,t} = \left(\frac{\overline{\text{MV}}_{i,t} - \text{MV}_{i,t}}{\text{MV}_{i,t}}\right)^2$$

Table 1 Regression coefficient by earnings stability deciles – company-fixed effects

Panel A. Full Sample										
Stability Decile										
	1	2	3	4	5	6	7	8	9	10
lnEARN	0.801***	0.812***	0.777***	0.720***	0.664***	0.560***	0.470***	0.362***	0.265***	0.199***
	(0.770–0.832)	(0.790–0.834)	(0.758–0.796)	(0.702–0.738)	(0.643–0.684)	(0.541–0.579)	(0.452–0.489)	(0.343–0.381)	(0.252–0.279)	(0.184–0.213)
Constant	5.226***	5.129***	5.562***	6.246***	6.916***	8.107***	9.121***	10.314***	11.326***	11.956***
	(4.873–5.579)	(4.874–5.384)	(5.336–5.787)	(6.035–6.457)	(6.682–7.149)	(7.887–8.326)	(8.913–9.329)	(10.104–10.524)	(11.178–11.474)	(11.798–12.114)
N	28,226	31,903	31,846	31,326	30,404	29,388	27,955	25,910	23,482	18,076
Panel B. Subsample of Peer Companies										
Stability Decile										
	1	2	3	4	5	6	7	8	9	10
lnEARN	1.012***	0.898***	0.856***	0.825***	0.754***	0.644***	0.441***	0.338***	0.359***	0.225***
	(0.947–1.077)	(0.839–0.957)	(0.803–0.909)	(0.766–0.884)	(0.668–0.839)	(0.564–0.723)	(0.371–0.510)	(0.273–0.403)	(0.257–0.461)	(0.153–0.296)
Constant	2.675***	3893***	4.369***	4.700***	5.559***	6.836***	9.060***	10.175***	9.842***	11,405***
	(2.012–3.338)	(3.276–4.511)	(3.804–4.933)	(4.064–5.336)	(4.631–6.487)	(5.975–7.697)	(8.312–9.809)	(9.482–10.868)	(8.779–10.905)	(10.657–12.152)
N	3788	3677	3245	2847	2420	2162	1863	1585	1243	937

*$p < 0.05$; **$p < 0.01$; ***$p < 0.001$ (Source: own analysis of data from the Datastream database)

Table 2 Firm-specific PE valuation error analysis

Panel A. Full Sample

Earnings stability Decile	#Companies	Mean absolute error	Mean squared error	Mean absolute log error	Absolute valuation error		Squared valuation error	
					Interquartile range	Interdecile range	Interquartile range	Interdecile range
1	27,743	0.250	1.082	0.234	0.260	0.524	0.092	0.244
2	30,746	0.298	1.031	0.276	0.314	0.624	0.128	0.328
3	30,532	0.347	0.875	0.319	0.368	0.748	0.176	0.438
4	29,976	0.399	0.805	0.367	0.437	0.916	0.239	0.600
5	29,199	0.474	1.645	0.424	0.490	1.136	0.311	0.849
6	28,361	0.564	2.514	0.497	0.561	1.394	0.418	1.224
7	26,848	0.674	1.514	0.591	0.648	1.800	0.539	1.888
8	25,067	0.857	3.204	0.729	0.795	2.322	0.690	3.205
9	22,752	1.120	5.216	0.916	1.051	3.077	0.881	5.842
10	17,683	1.524	13.124	1.154	1.330	4.284	1.406	10.647
Total	268,907	0.574	2.391	0.495	0.552	1.300	0.383	1.106

Panel B. Subsample of Peer Companies

Earnings stability		Mean absolute	Mean squared	Mean absolute log	Absolute valuation error		Squared valuation error	
Decile	#Companies	error	error	error	Interquartile range	Interdecile range	Interquartile range	Interdecile range
1	3788	0.194	0.076	0.192	0.193	0.385	0.062	0.168
2	3677	0.254	0.137	0.245	0.252	0.479	0.109	0.265
3	3245	0.311	0.188	0.298	0.308	0.579	0.162	0.387
4	2847	0.369	0.294	0.351	0.366	0.704	0.229	0.566
5	2420	0.447	0.481	0.405	0.429	0.855	0.310	0.830
6	2162	0.526	0.618	0.476	0.485	0.973	0.415	1.095
7	1863	0.647	1.027	0.558	0.557	1.286	0.530	1.859
8	1585	0.809	1.700	0.688	0.648	1.705	0.727	3.206
9	1243	1.044	4.942	0.816	0.694	2.157	0.848	5.064
10	937	1.658	18.514	1.038	0.954	3.250	1.471	11.261
Total	23,767	0.472	1.250	0.410	0.422	0.866	0.280	0.831

Source: own analysis of data from the Datastream database

$$e_{i,t} = \left|\log\left(\overline{MV}_{i,t}\right) - \log(MV_{i,t})\right|$$

We construct the interquartile range as value of the 75th percentile less value of the 25th percentile and Interdecile range as a value of the 90th percentile less value of the 90th percentile of absolute and squared valuation error

Panel A contains results of the valuation analysis conducted on the *Final Sample*, panel B contains results for the *Subsample of Peer Companies*.

References

Archer SH, Faerber LRG (1966) Firm size and the cost of externally secured equity capital. J Financ 21:69–83

Asquith P, Mikhail M, Au A (2005) Information content of equity analyst reports. J Financ Econ 75:245–282. https://doi.org/10.3386/w9246

Bhojraj S, Lee C (2002) Who is my peer? A valuation-based approach to the selection of comparable firms. J Account Res 40:407–439

Black F (1980) The magic in earnings: economic earnings versus accounting earnings. Financ Anal J 36:19–24. https://doi.org/10.2469/faj.v36.n6.19

Dechow PM (1994) Accounting earnings and cash flows as measures of firm performance. J Account Econ 18:3–42. https://doi.org/10.1016/0165-4101(94)90016-7

Francis J, Olsson P, Oswald DR (2000) Comparing the accuracy and explainability of divi-dend, free cash flow, and abnormal earnings equity value estimates. J Account Res 38:45–70

Gordon MJ, Shapiro E (1956) Capital equipment analysis: the required rate of profit. Manag Science 3:102–110. https://doi.org/10.1287/mnsc.3.1.102

Kim M, Ritter JR (1999) Valuig IPOs. J Financ Econ 53:409–437

LeClair MS (1990) Valuing the closely-held corporation: the validity and performance of es-tablished valuation procedures. Account Horiz 4:31–42

Lev B (1983) Some economic determinants of time-series properties of earnings. J Account Econ 5:31–48. https://doi.org/10.1016/0165-4101(83)90004-6

Liu J, Nissim D, Thomas J (2007) Is cash flow kin valuations? Financ Anal J 63:56–68. https://doi.org/10.2469/faj.v63.n2.4522

Ohlson JA (1995) Earnings, book values, and dividends in equity valuation. Contemp Account Res 11:661–687. https://doi.org/10.1111/j.1911-3846.1995.tb00461.x

Penman SH, Sougiannis T (1998) A comparison of dividend, cash flow, and earnings ap-proaches to equity valuation. Contemp Account Res 15:343–383. https://doi.org/10.1111/j.1911-3846.1998.tb00564.x

Stauffer TR (1971) The measurement of corporate rates of return: ageneralized formation. Bell J Econ Manag Sci 2:434–469. https://doi.org/10.2307/3003000

Van Aswegen D, Jedlin I (2013) Valuation Practices Survey 2013. In: KPMG. http://www.kpmg.com/au/en/issuesandinsights/articlespublications/valuation-practices-survey/pages/valuation-practices-survey-2013.aspx. Feb 2014

Williams JB (1938) The theory of investment value

Measurement of Profit Losses from Brand Damage: The Case of an Unlisted Company

Tomáš Krabec and Romana Čižinská

Abstract This paper deals with the measurement of profit loss stemming from the unfair competition and its negative impact on the brand value of the company ABC Holding in the Czech Republic. Profit loss is the difference of wealth between the state, what the party suffering the damage (unfair competition) achieved, and what it would achieve if the damage did not occur. It is therefore a foregone gain of property which was prevented by the harmful event. Assets (wealth) of the owner of ABC Holding suffering the damage represent the value of its 100% stake in the company, which includes the value of the brand ABC. Therefore, for the purposes of quantifying lost profits in this paper, we first need to quantify the value of the brand ABC affected by the consequences of a damage event and the hypothetical value of the brand ABC under the ordinary course of things. For appraising the fair value of a brand of an unlisted (private) company in this paper, we apply the Verifiable Interdependent Model (VIM), which has been designed specifically for the conditions of the business environment with the lack of empirical data for intangible assets appraisal or their low quality.

Keywords Profit loss • Intangible assets • VIM

Introduction

This paper deals with the quantification of lost profits suffered by a single owner of an unlisted trading company ABC Holding based in the Czech Republic. Reimbursement of property damage in the form of lost profits by the owner of ABC

T. Krabec (✉)
Department of Finance and Business Valuation, University of Economics, Prague, Nam. W. Churchilla 4, 130 67 Prague, Czech Republic
e-mail: tomas.krabec@vse.cz

R. Čižinská
Department of Finance and Accounting, ŠKODA AUTO University, Na Karmeli 1457, 293 01 Mladá Boleslav, Czech Republic
e-mail: cizinska@is.savs.cz

D. Procházka (ed.), *The Impact of Globalization on International Finance and Accounting*, Springer Proceedings in Business and Economics,
https://doi.org/10.1007/978-3-319-68762-9_19

Holding is claimed as a result of damage to reputation or the reputation of the brand ABC.

Lost profit (loss of earnings) and actual damage are two forms of material damage. Material damage is understood as a damage that had occurred in the victim's property which is objectively expressible in generally accepted measurement equivalent, i.e., in money (Hendrych 2009). Unlike actual damages, a profit loss does not constitute reduction of the current economical state, as is the case with actual damage. Assets of the party suffering the damage did not diminish nor increase. Loss of earnings is thus the difference of wealth between the state, what the party suffering the damage achieved, and what it would achieve if the damage did not occur. It is therefore a foregone gain of property which was prevented by the harmful event (Bejček 2005).

In the event that the harmful event occurred and lost profits are claimed while the subject suffering the damage is the owner (operator) of a business enterprise, in which cash flows were negatively affected as a result of unlawful conduct impeding economic activity. The forgone magnification (multiplication) property damage (i.e., lost profits) can be economically quantified as the difference between the hypothetical value of the shares in this company as a "flawless state of affairs" (after deducting the initial investment of the owner) and the actual value of the shares in this company affected by the insured event (after deducting the initial investment owner). Value of the shares (in terms of a particular subject and the basis of value corresponding to the purpose of valuation) corresponds to the aliquot share in the total value of the equity of the company. If a strong brand accounts for a part of the assets of the business enterprise, then the value of the brand affected by unlawful conduct decreases proportionally to the value of the equity of the company operating the business. Lost profits in this case can be perceived as a decline in brand value due to the unlawful conduct. The question to be solved here is thus determining the value of the brand.

The issue of appraising intangible assets, and specifically brands, is discussed extensively in specialized literature (Čižinská and Krabec 2013a, b; Gerzema and Hubbard 2010; Murphy 1990; Perrier and Stobart 1997; Salinas 2009); among other things, this is because intangible assets are becoming more and more important within intensifying competition in hypercompetitive, more and more saturated, product markets. The valuation of identifiable intangible assets is even more difficult than the valuation of a business as whole, especially in the conditions of the business environment with the lack of empirical data for assets appraisal or their low quality.

The value and appraisal of a trademark is based on its economic benefit to its owner or the business that owns the trademark. Products and services produced by a business with a successful trademark are sold at premium prices. The business owning the trademark receives this bonus because it can sell at higher prices than its rivals who are either without a trademark or with a weaker trademark or because it sells and produces more, and thus it has saved more fixed costs per production unit. Financial value-based techniques derive the brand equity value from the value of the selected company financial indicators, such as costs, other assets, income, or revenues. All methods of appraising the fair value of a brand are based on three approaches (see Čižinská and Krabec 2013a; IFRS 2013; IVS 2017; Krabec 2009; Salinas 2009): comparability approach, cost approach, and income approach.

Data and Methodology

We will assume that a misleading advertising by a competitor causes reputational damage to the ABC brand. Within this misleading advertising, the competitor imitated the logo and design of their products so that those products were like the ABC-branded products. As a result, the likelihood of confusion of its products for ABC products arose and led to a decrease in volume of sales of ABC and the resulting decline in the value of equity (and business share) of ABC Holding.

We assume that the ownership of a strong brand brings to the so-called price or quantity premium (or both premiums simultaneously). Price premium can be seen as the difference between the price charged by owning a valuable brand and the price of its cheapest rival seller's comparable product. Quantitative premium is based on the idea that because of the brand, a greater volume of production is sold. Quantitative premium is determined as the difference between the average volume sold under the acclaimed brand and the amounts of a comparable competitor. The higher the price and quantity premiums realized through the branded production, the higher the brand value. The case study aims to quantify the decline in brand value due to a decrease in ABC quantitative premiums realized production yet achieved thanks branded production of ABC, brand image, and its overall customer perception. Assets of the owner of ABC Holding suffering the damage represent the value of its 100% stake in the company, which includes the value of the brand ABC. Therefore, for the purposes of quantifying lost profits in this paper, we first need to quantify the value of the brand ABC affected by the consequences of a damage event and the hypothetical value of the brand ABC under the ordinary course of things.

In applying the aforesaid basic or somehow modified intangible assets' valuation approaches (and methods within them), appraisers usually obtain results which differ significantly. This is usually caused by the subjectivity of parameterization of relevant valuation models and mainly by the lack and/or high scatter of market data. Therefore, we use for the valuation of ABC brand the Verifiable Interdependent Model (VIM) proposed in Čižinská and Krabec (2013b, c), which is the combined application of competitive/market, cost, and income-based methods, so that the results obtained from independent, mutually confirming calculations can be verified. In this paper, we apply only the first step and third step of the VIM to demonstrate the impact of volume premium on the brand value. See Čižinská and Krabec (2013b, c) for the application of all steps of the VIM in the case study.

Within the calculation of the enterprise value of a whole company in step 1, parameters and assumptions of the income-based value of the business were derived and justified. In the third step, we determine the brand value using "premium method" based on the estimated increase in sales of branded business, compared with sales of "benchmark" and increased operating margin of the branded business compared to "benchmark." We start therefore from the total change in profit that was initiated by the branding of the production, mainly due to volume and price premiums, which the company acquires through the brand that, in comparison with the competition without a brand or a less established brand, can afford to sell at a higher price or simultaneously achieves higher sales volumes (see also Smith 1996; Smith and Parr 2000). A benchmark here means a hypothetical company that achieves results at the level of sector-percentile values. Specific percentile is yet determined depending on the structure and branding of the production in the industry in which the company operates.

Results and Discussion

ABC Holding operates in the area of ergonomic leather schoolbag production. Since prices in the market segment are relatively comparable, the key value driver is the design of the product. In order to evaluate brand impact, brand analysis, which is based on the examination of key brand performance indicators such as stability of the turnover, extent, and growth of the brand sales comparing to the comparative list of competitive or similar brands, was applied. Brand impact of the brand ABC is 40%, resulting in sales volume premium of 12% compared to the benchmark. Brand impact adjustor produces brand value discount rate 9.98% compared to company WACC 12.5%. Valuation date is 31.12.2016.

Valuation of Equity of ABC Holding by Income-Based Methods

The business valuation (step 1 of the VIM) is based on an income-based potential at the valuation date. The appraisable income-based potential contains all chances resulting from measures taken prior to the valuation date or from sufficiently specified measures within the current business concept and generally known market information. A financial plan for valuation purposes is based on the analysis and prognosis of value drivers (see Mařík et al. 2011 and many others).

The valuation of equity of ABC Holding was performed by the economic value-added entity method. The conducted analysis proved that the conditions of a going concern have been met. For such a long period of time, it is usually impossible to plan cash flow for individual years, so we applied the standard two-stage method which is usually applied in practice. The basic parameters of the plan for the period of the first stage of the valuation process (years 2017, 2018, and 2019) were borrowed from the plan provided by the management of ABC Holding. The

Table 1 Calculation of the present value of the first stage of valuation based on the EVA entity method

(CZK thousands)	2016	2017	2018	2019
NOPAT (NOPAT after taxes)		500.00	525.00	551.25
NOA	3000.00	3150.00	3307.50	3472.88
WACC*NOAt-1		375.00	393.75	413.44
EVA		125.00	131.25	137.81
Discounted EVA		111.11	103.70	96.79
First stage present value		CZK 311.6 thousand		

Source: own analysis

Table 2 Calculation of the resulting value of equity of ABC Holding as at 31 December 2016 by the EVA method

Present value of the first stage	CZK 311.60 thousand
Present value of the second stage	CZK 1355.06 thousand
MVA	CZK 1666.67 thousand
NOA as at the valuation date	CZK 3000.00 thousand
Gross operating value	CZK 4666.67 thousand
Interest-bearing loan capital as at the valuation date	CZK 0.00 thousand
Net operating value	CZK 4666.67 thousand
Nonoperating assets as at the valuation date	CZK 80.00 thousand
Resulting value of equity as at the valuation date	CZK 4746.67 thousand

Source: own analysis

calculation of the ongoing value requires the selection of parameters of infinite time series of cash flow. In particular, it is an expected rate of growth of free cash flow during the second stage (g) and return on net investment (rI) calculated as a ratio of the total increment of the operating profit after taxes and increment of the invested capital in the previous year. From the long-term point of view, the g/rI ratio corresponds to the investment rate (mI), which is a share of profits devoted to net investments. Based on the industry analysis and current and planned results of ABC Holding, it was estimated that the rate of growth (g) was 5%, investment rate was 30%, and the corresponding return on investment was 16.67%. The income-based value was calculated by the standard method described in literature (e.g., Mařík et al. 2011). Table 1 shows the calculation of the present value of the first stage of valuation based on the EVA entity method Table 2.

Determination of the XZY Brand Value Using Premium Method for the Case of the Ordinary Course of Things

Based on the brand analysis, we assume that ABC Holding sells and produces 12% more than its rivals who are either without a trademark or with a weaker trademark.

However, considering the industry specifics, we do not suppose that products are sold at premium prices. Therefore, the economic benefits of the ABC trademark result in the increase of sales and in the increase in operating margin (as a result of the saved fixed costs per production unit). As a measure of how revenue growth translates into growth in operating margin is used operating leverage. The change in operating income for a given change in sales (revenue) is the degree of operating leverage (DOL):

$$\mathrm{DOL} = \frac{\text{total contribution}}{\text{operating income}} = \frac{\text{sales} - \text{variable cost}}{\text{sales} - \text{variable cost} - \text{fixed cost}} \tag{1}$$

For the estimation of the change in ABC Holding operating income, we used benchmark values of operating margin and operating leverage producing the level of variator (variable cost to total cost):

$$\text{Variator} = \frac{1 - \text{operating margin}^{*}\text{DOL}}{1 - \text{operating margin}} = \frac{\text{variable cost}}{\text{variable cost} + \text{fixed cost}} \tag{2}$$

Profit differential attributable to the brand comparing to benchmark based on previous formulas is then calculated as follows:

$$\text{Profit differential in CZK thousands} = \mathrm{T}_{\mathrm{ABC}}{}^{*}\left(\mathrm{OM}_{\mathrm{ABC}} - \frac{\mathrm{OM}_{\mathrm{Benchmark}}}{1 + \%\Delta\mathrm{T}}\right) \tag{3}$$

where TABC is the total revenue of ABC Holding, OMABC means operating margin of ABC Holding, OMBenchmark is used for operating margin of benchmark companies, and %ΔT expresses percent change in sales attributable to ABC brand comparing to benchmark companies.

Calculated profit differential after income tax (19%) is net earnings of the ABC Brand. After deduction of incremental investments into brand building, it produces free cash flow attributable to the brand and brand value of CZK 1004,21 thousand (as of 31 December 2016) – see Table 3.

Valuation of the XZY Brand Value Using Premium Method for the Case of Loss Event

We will assume that misleading advertising by a competitor caused reputational damage to the ABC brand resulting in the decrease in volume of sales of ABC. Within this misleading advertising, the competitor imitated the logo and design of their products so that those products were like the ABC-branded products. As a

Table 3 Valuation of the ABC brand (under the ordinary course of things)

Premium method	2017	2018	2019	2020 and following
Operating margin (ABC holding)	32.00%			
Operating margin (benchmark)	29.00%			
Variator (benchmark)	1.298			
Sales of ABC holding in CZK thousand	1562.50	1640.63	1722.66	1808.79
Profit differential in CZK thousand	95.42	100.20	105.21	110.47
Corporate income tax	18.13	19.04	19.99	20.99
"Brand earnings" after taxes	77.29	81.16	85.22	89.48
Investments	2.00	2.00	2.10	2.30
FCFF	75.29	79.16	83.12	87.18
WACC	12.5%	12.5%	12.5%	12.5%
Brand value as of 1.1. (CZK thousand)	1004.21	1054.44	1107.09	1162.36

Source: own analysis

Table 4 Valuation of the ABC brand (after harmful event)

Premium method	2017	2018	2019	2020 and following
Operating margin (ABC holding)	32.00%			
Operating margin (benchmark)	29.00%			
Variator (benchmark)	1.298			
Sales of ABC holding in CZK thousand	1562.5	1640.6	1722.6	1808.9
Profit differential in CZK thousand	76.52	80.34	84.36	88.58
Corporate income tax	14.54	15.27	16.03	16.83
"Brand earnings" after taxes	61.98	65.08	68.33	71.75
Investments	2.00	2.00	2.10	2.30
FCFF	59.98	63.08	66.23	69.45
WACC	12.5%	12.5%	12.5%	12.5%
Brand value as of 1.1. (CZK thousand)	800.03	840.05	881.98	926.00

Source: own analysis

result, the likelihood of confusion of its products for ABC products arose and led to a decrease in volume of sales of ABC. Because of the ABC brand damage, the difference between the average volume sold under the brand ABC and the amounts of a comparable competitor (quantitative premium) decreased from 12% to 7%. Brand impact after harmful event resulting in sales volume premium of 7% (instead of 12%) produces brand value of CZK 800,03 thousand (as at 31 Dec 2016) – see Table 4.

Conclusion

The paper deals with the quantification of lost profits suffered by a single owner of an unlisted trading company ABC Holding based on the Czech Republic. Since lost profits of ABC Holding are stemming from the unfair competition and its negative impact on the brand value, we perceive this material damage as a decline in brand value due to the unlawful conduct. The valuation date is 31 December 2016. For the brand valuation, we apply VIM resulting in the hypothetical value of the brand ABC under the ordinary course of things of CZK 1004.21 thousand and the value of the brand ABC affected by the consequences of a damage event of CZK 800.03 thousand. Profit loss to be claimed is therefore CZK 204.2 thousand. However, it is very difficult to prove the decline in sales of a company in relation to damage of its reputation, since this decline may be caused not only by the infringement but also by other relevant aspects of the market.

Acknowledgments This paper has been prepared within the research project under the registration number IP 100040 and Internal Grant Agency (IGA) 7/2016 of the University of Economics, Prague.

References

Bejček J (2005) Ušlý zisk a tzv. zmařená příležitost. In: Sborník příspěvků z mezinárodní konference studentů doktorského studijního programu "obchodní právo" na téma Odpovědnost za škodu, Brno (Czech Republic). Masarykova univerzita, Právnická fakulta, pp 8–15
Hendrych D (2009) Právnický slovník. C.H.Beck, Praha
Čižinská R, Krabec T (2013a) Metody pro ocenění ochranné známky: doporučení pro použití v České republice. Scientia ét Societas IX(2):160–175
Čižinská R, Krabec T (2013b) VIM model for appraising the trademark of an unlisted company according to IFRS 13. J Account Audit Res Pract
Čižinská, R, Krabec, T (2013c) VIM Model for Appraising the Trademark of an Unlisted Company. In Entrepreneurship Vision 2020: Innovation, Development Sustainability, and Economic Growth. Proceedings of The 20th International Business Information Management Association Conference, pp 908–926
Gerzema J, Lebar E (2008) The brand bubble: the looming crisis in brand value and how to avoid it. Jossey-Bass, San Francisco
Hubbard D (2010) How to measure anything: finding the value of intangibles in business (2. vydání). Wiley, Chichester
International Financial Reporting Standards (2013)
International Valuation Standards (2017) London, IVSC
Krabec T (2009) Oceňování podniku a standardy hodnoty. Grada, Praha
Mařík M et al (2011) Metody oceňování podniku – Proces ocenění základní metody a postupy, 3rd edn. Ekopress, Praha
Murphy J (ed) (1990) Brand Valuation. Random House Business Books, London
Perrier R, Stobart P (eds) (1997) Brand valuation, 3rd edn. Premier Books, London
Salinas G (2009) The international brand valuation manual: a complete overview and analysis of brand valuation techniques, methodologies and applications. Wiley, Chichester
Smith GV (1996) Trademark valuation. Willey, New York
Smith GV, Parr R (2000) Valuation of intellectual property and intangible assets. Wiley, New York

Czech Industrial Real Estate Market: The Quest for Realistic Model

Jaroslav Kaizr

Abstract The study presents reconstruction of the Czech industrial real estate market model by using expert data applied along the Fischer-Di Pasquale-Wheaton model. Research shows that literature focuses on office, retail, and residential markets, while industrial real estate sector is being completely overlooked. Multiple regression analysis is used to determine linear regression functions of supply and demand at the space market and of industrial portfolio value at the capital market. The paper concludes that the analysis provided a realistic model which can be used for predictions of shifts in industrial property values. Analysis of the industrial real estate market shall continue to allow adoption of the ongoing structural changes connected to e-commerce, shared economy, and industry 4.0. Productivity of space and behavior on the space market are identified as key subjects of further examination within the economics of space and time.

Keywords Commercial property • Industrial real estate • Market behavior • Market structure • Price formation

Introduction

Ball et al. (1998) describes the commercial property market as a set of four interrelated markets: the market of users (further referred to as the space market), the capital market, the development market, and the land market. With regard to the Walras' law, the balance of three markets brings balance to the fourth market to allow the equilibrium of the entire commercial property market system. One should consider that processes at the commercial property market are rather sluggish and therefore the adaptation to external shocks takes time.

J. Kaizr (✉)
Department of Corporate Finance, University of Economics, Prague, Nám. W. Churchilla 4, 130 67 Prague, Czech Republic
e-mail: xkaij02@vse.cz

D. Procházka (ed.), *The Impact of Globalization on International Finance and Accounting*, Springer Proceedings in Business and Economics,
https://doi.org/10.1007/978-3-319-68762-9_20

Development and changes of the commercial property market can be monitored by using various indicators and indices. Fisher et al. (1994) presents three concepts of value indices for the commercial real estate portfolios in the United States. The first approach is based on selected sample of real estate properties such as the Russell-NCREIF index. The second approach is to determine the value index by monitoring the values of completed transactions in the market, and the third option is an index based on the value of shares of REITs. Historical time series of different types of indices and their comparison helps investors to better understand the market principles and to identify the current and the expected status of the market (Fischer et al. 1994).

The Czech industrial real estate market has more than 20 years of history. The market has risen from zero to today's more than 6.3 million square meters of A class facilities. Renowned advisors are collecting the market data and provide research papers while there is still no database nor index which would describe movement of the market and which would provide evidence that the market works according to the Fischer-Di Pasquale-Wheaton model. At the same time, there is very limited research done on industrial real estate market in general. This paper presents the results of research which aims to reconstruct the Czech industrial real estate market model by using expert data applied along the Fischer-Di Pasquale-Wheaton (FDW) model.

Literature Review

The Space Market

At the space market, supply of industrial space interacts with demand of manufacturers and logistics providers who seek for industrial space. Ball et al. (1998) states that the space demand of firms is driven not only by the rent level but also by:

- Firms' turnover
- Required space per worker
- Technology (space efficiency)

As firms' turnover grows during the boom times and falls in the periods of recession, the demand for space adjusts much quicker than the supply of space. Di Pasquale and Wheaton (1992) define the supply of commercial space to be fixed at period t (supply curve is fully inelastic), and the increase of space stock may occur only at period $t + 1$ due to the mechanism that connects the space market with development market via the capital market. As a result of the demand and supply interaction, the market rent r is set on the space market. Growing demand for space and inelastic supply will push the market rental level up (Fischer 1999).

Industrial Research Forum (IRF) collects quarterly data about the Czech industrial space market and monitors the development of basic indicators of demand and

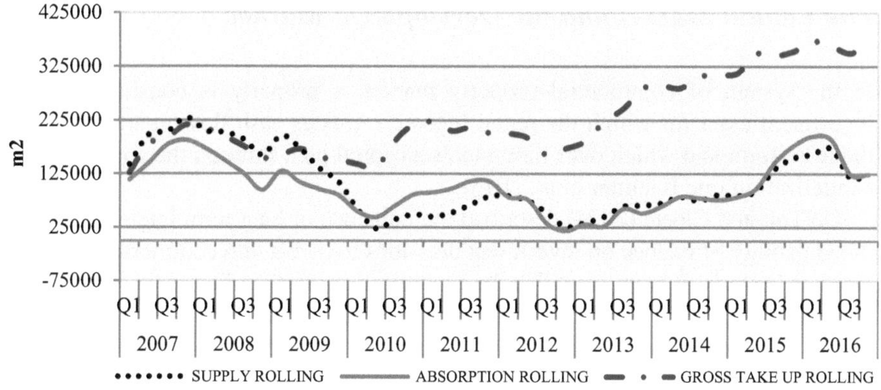

Fig. 1 Rolling averages of gross take-up, supply, and absorption on the Czech industrial real estate market from 2007 to 2016 (in m^2) (Source: author's calculations and data provided by Industrial Research Forum)

supply. On the demand side, IRF watches the gross take-up, which is the sum of newly signed lease contracts and renegotiated lease contracts, and the net take-up, which includes only the newly signed lease contracts. On the supply side, data about supply of new industrial space and about the total stock of space are collected. IRF does not provide data about the absorption which represents the ability of demand to occupy available spaces; however, it is possible to calculate the absorption based on the data provided about the vacancy.

Graphical analysis detected seasonality of the gross take-up, the supply, and the absorption on the Czech industrial property market. In the first quarter, the volumes commonly decrease as the market activity slows down, while the highest activity is traditionally in the second part of the year when firms move into the premises newly constructed by the developers.

Seasonality of the time series was smoothed out by the method of rolling average (Hindls et al. 2007) for four consecutive quarters as shown in Fig. 1. Simple rolling mean of the quarterly absorption for the period from 2007 to the end of 2016 is negative 757 square meters. Hence the ability of demand to fill available spaces has not reached the precrisis levels yet.

It should be noted that the real estate market is fragmented to local submarkets of which characteristics and movements may vary (Witten 1987). The property market has different characteristics in Prague region where approximately 50% of the total industrial stock is located in Brno where supply of land is limited. Mueller and Laposa (1994) stated that the submarkets can move differently from the overall market in the short term; however, in the long term, the submarkets trend with overall market movements. Hence the aggregated data from the Czech submarkets create a compact data set about the overall market.

The Capital Market and the Development Market

In the system of commercial property market, a property is considered as an investment asset for which the rental income r creates cash flow guaranteed over the lease term and which over time yields a capital gain through the application of capitalization rate (Geltner et al. 2013).

Du Toit and Cloete (2004) described the influence of long-term interest rates and of availability of finance on investment decisions to invest into commercial property assets in Pretoria. It is apparent that the capitalization rates applied by investors are in line with the rate of return expected by them. Further Di Pasquale and Wheaton (1992) conclude that ceteris paribus investors are willing to pay higher prices for real estate properties yielding same cash flow during the periods of low interest rates.

In accordance with above conclusions, the capitalization rate gap (CRG) was calculated as a difference between the industrial market capitalization rate (C&W, 2006–2016) and the market interest rate 3 M PRIBOR which is one of the main indicators of the Czech financial market (Fig. 2). The capitalization rate gap can be considered as a risk premium that investors require when investing into real estate assets.

Figure 2 shows that in the precrisis period, the rate of return required from the investments into industrial real estate assets was much lower than at present days. This indicates that there is still room for further compression of industrial real estate yields. The ongoing restructuring of the economy toward the e-commerce and the shared economy provides even better rationale to invest into the industrial real estate assets. Traditional retailers are either replenished or replaced by e-commerce operators who simply need just an efficient warehouse and software to perform the business. Unlike the conventional logistics firms, the e-commerce operators are willing to sign long-term leases as they invest considerable amounts of funds to their warehouse operations. In the context of industry 4.0, this brings further stability to the industrial real estate sector which shall be appreciated by investors.

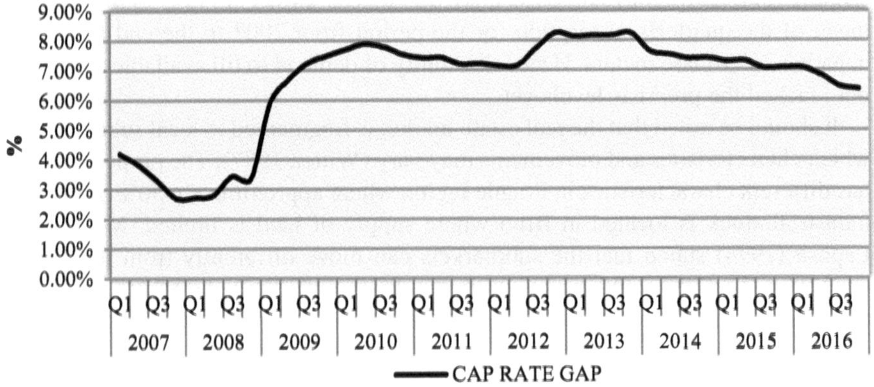

Fig. 2 Capitalization rate gap from 2007 to 2016 (in %) (Source: author's calculations and data provided by Czech National Bank)

In connection to the ongoing restructuring of the economy, specific characteristics of the real estate market cycles shall be considered. According to Wheaton (1999), the commercial real estate market is related to economy cycles but also moves in its own long-term cycles which last between 10 and 12 years. An oscillation around the main cycle occurs due to short-term imbalanced space market conditions when supply tends to lag behind the demand. New development unlike the demand does not reflect state of the economy and rather depends on the difference between the real estate values and construction costs or on availability of funds and permitted land. Furthermore, the space market has different cycle pattern than the capital market which, based on historical data, lags behind the space market (Mueller 1995).

Research Design

A linear regression model was specifically developed for the space market and for the capital market. The IRF provides sufficient and reliable data about the space market. As described in previous paragraphs, the data set was adjusted by the method of rolling average to smooth out the seasonality. In line with the FDW model, a multiple regression analysis was applied to find the most suitable linear functions which explain the development of dependent variables gross take-up (*GTU*) and supply (*SUP*) by independent variables as described in Table 1.

Unlike the space market, the Czech capital market faces lack of reliable data. Neither vendors nor investors have the obligation to disclose any information about capital market transactions for statistical or reporting purposes. There is no institution such as the Investment Property Databank, and a public market with REITs is also missing in the Czechia. The only sources of information about commercial real estate values and capitalization rates are the agents who take part at the transactions as advisors. How shall the capital market be analyzed when no indices are available?

To analyze the capital market, it is necessary to restore the value of industrial real estate portfolio from the data provided by agents about the market rent and the market capitalization rate. For the purposes of this study, an industrial real estate

Table 1 Overview of independent variables of the linear regression model of the space market

Variable	Abbreviation	Description
Value less costs	VLC	The difference between the rolling average of Vp and the construction costs; in CZK/m2
Gross domestic product	GDP	Seasonally adjusted GDP per quarter in CR; in mil. CZK
Average employment	EMP	Average number of employees in production per quarter in CR; in thousands
Capitalization rate gap	CRG	The difference between the market capitalization rate and the interest rate 3 M PRIBOR; in %
Consumer price index	CPI	Consumer price index in CR published by ČSÚ; average year 2005 = 100

Source: author

portfolio was created on the basis of quarterly reports provided by real estate advisors (C&W, 2006–2016) by using the following equation:

$$V_p = \frac{\left(\left(\frac{r_{iP}+r_{iR}}{2}\right)^{*}0.93 + r_{kPR}{}^{*}0,07\right)}{\frac{k_P+k_R}{2}} \tag{1}$$

where

V_p – the value of each square meter of the restored industrial real estate portfolio (CZK/m^2)

r_{iP} – market rent of industrial space in Prague (CZK/m^2/year)

r_{iR} – market rent of industrial space in out of Prague regions (CZK/m^2/year)

r_{kPR} – market rent of office space in industrial properties (CZK/m^2/year)

k_P – market capitalization rate for industrial real estate assets in Prague (%)

k_R – market capitalization rate for industrial real estate assets in out of Prague regions (%).

Based on the equal split of industrial stock between Prague and out of Prague regions, an equal weight is applied to the market rent and to the market capitalization rate for these two locations. Market rents for offices in industrial facilities are the same in both locations, while the share of office space on a total area is at 7%, which is the market average. Because the rent within the restored portfolio is based on the market level, it can be regarded as a certain income into perpetuity. For the same reason, it is not necessary to consider the vacancy because the market rents ensure full occupancy of the portfolio.

Graphical analysis of the quarterly portfolio values detected seasonality with peaks in the first and third quarter of each year and bottoms at the end of each year. Seasonality of the time series was smoothed out by the method of rolling average for four consecutive quarters. Figure 3 presents the rolling average of restored industrial space portfolio value per square meter in CZK.

Figure 3 also provides a comparison of the portfolio value with average construction cost for industrial facilities excluding land prices. From Figs. 2 and 3, it is apparent that the decline of the industrial portfolio value at approximately the same average construction cost between 2008 and 2010 resulted in the lack of space supply in the same period. From 2013 to 2016, the supply is increasing as the difference between the value and the cost is expanding.

Decline in the value of the restored industrial portfolio between 2008 and 2009 reflects the global financial crisis. Industrial property values in the last quarter of 2016 were still 17% lower than at the peak of the market in the third quarter of 2007. Closer examination reveals that the market capitalization rates in 2016 are already at the level of 2007; however, the market rents were considerably higher before the crisis. In the context of expected yield compression, the rental growth may hoist another impulse for further appreciation of Czech industrial portfolio values.

At this point, it is worth mentioning the impact of the currency exchange rate, since rents in modern Czech industrial properties are quoted in euros, while the

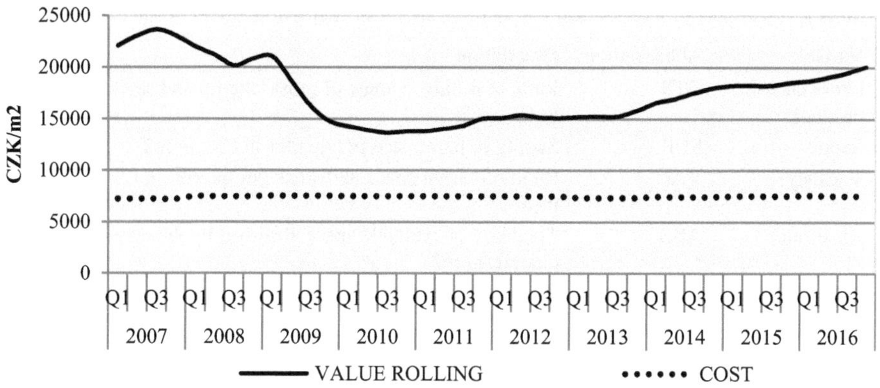

Fig. 3 Rolling averages of restored industrial portfolio value V_p per square meter and average construction costs per square meter from 2007 to 2016 (in CZK/m2) (Source: author's calculations and data provided by Czech Construction Standards)

construction costs are in Czech crowns. For purposes of the analysis, the restored property value was recalculated to Czech crowns by using an average quarterly exchange rate CZK/EUR. Decline of portfolio values measured in Czech crowns was enhanced between 2008 and 2009 by strengthening of the crown in the same period. Expected termination of the currency interventions by the Czech National Bank in the second quarter of 2017 will, on one hand, decrease the property values in CZK but will, on the other hand, create room for rental increase in euros.

In line with the FDW model, a multiple regression analysis was applied to find the most suitable linear functions which explain the development of dependent variable V_p by independent variables as summarized in Table 2.

Di Pasquale and Wheaton (1992) stated that the commercial property market lags behind the economy by several periods. Hence it is appropriate to use the multi regression analysis to find the linear functions for the dependent variables *GTU*, *SUP*, and V_p based on the independent variables at the period *t* so as at the periods $t-1$, $t-2$, and $t-3$.

Results and Discussion

Source data series are disclosed in Appendix to this study. Tables 3 and 4 provide summary statistics of the regression models for variables *GTU* and *SUP*, and Table 5 provides summary statistics of the regression model for variable V_p.

The multiple regression analysis concluded that the dependent variable GTU_t is best described by a single independent variable GDP_t.

Table 2 Overview of independent variables of the linear regression model of the capital market

Variable	Abbreviation	Description
Gross take-up on stock	GTS	Ratio of rolling average of gross take-up and stock per quarter in CR; in %
Supply	SUP	Supply of new space per quarter in CR; in m2
Vacancy	VAC	Ratio of vacant space and stock per quarter in CR divided; in %
Absorption	ABS	Total size of available space absorbed by the take-up during a quarter, in m2
Gross domestic product	GDP	Seasonally adjusted GDP per quarter in CR; in mil. CZK
Average employment	EMP	Average number of employees in production per quarter in CR; in thousands
Capitalization rate gap	CRG	The difference between the market capitalization rate and the interest rate 3 M PRIBOR; in %
Consumer price index	CPI	Consumer price index in CR published by ČSÚ; average year 2005 = 100

Source: author

Table 3 Summary statistics for regression model GTU_t

	Coefficients	Standard error	*t Stat*	*P Value*
Intercept	−823,949.04	181,094.61	−4.55	0.00
GDP_t	1.03	0.17	5.90	0.00

Source: own regression analysis

Table 4 Summary statistics for regression model SUP_t

	Coefficients	Standard error	*t Stat*	*P Value*
Intercept	−88,660.71	29,708.59	−2.98	0.00
VLC_t	19.58	2.83	6.93	0.00

Source: own regression analysis

Table 5 Summary statistics for regression model V_{pt}

	Coefficients	Standard error	*t Stat*	*P Value*
Intercept	5679.89	2927.57	1.94	0.06
GDP_{t-3}	0.01	0.00	3.22	0.00
CRG_{t-3}	−100,842.27	10,853.10	−9.29	0.00
GTS_t	152,403.94	13,329.55	11.43	0.00

Source: own regression analysis

The correlation coefficient r is at 0.69, and the linear regression model explains 48% (R^2) of values of the dependent variable. At the 5% significance level, the hypothesis H_0: $\beta 1 = 0$ can be rejected for the independent variable (t-test), and the existence of linear function between GTU_t and GDP_t can be considered proved and rather relevant. A linear regression model is shown in Eq. 2:

$$GTU_t = -823,949.04 + 1.13GDP_t \tag{2}$$

In accordance with Ball et al. (1998), the correlation between the demand and *GDP* is positive. Increase of *GDP* by 1 billion will result in the demand increase of 1.13 square meters.

As expected, the *CRG* and *CPI* are insignificant for explanation of the shifts in the independent variable *GTU*. Variable *EMP* explains the shifts in demand for industrial space, but the model is not as good as in the case of *GDP*. The model could be improved by adding the labor productivity as a variable. Productivity of industrial space, i.e., the value produced per square meter over a period, could bring further insights into the analysis.

The multiple regression analysis concluded that the dependent variable SUP_t is best described by a single independent variable VLC_t.

The correlation coefficient r is at 0.75, and the linear model explains 56% (R^2) of values of the dependent variable. At the 5% significance level, the hypothesis H_0: $\beta_1 = 0$ can be rejected for the independent variable (t-test), and the existence of linear function between SUP_t and VLC_t can be considered as proven and relevant. A linear regression model is shown in Eq. 3:

$$SUP_t = -88,660.71 + 19.58VLC_t \tag{3}$$

In accordance with the expectations, the correlation between the demand and *VLC* is positive. Increase in the gap between the value and construction cost by 1CZK/m^2 will result in the increase of supply by 19.58 m^2.

As expected the *GDP*, *EMP*, *CRG*, and *CPI* are insignificant for explanation of the shifts in the independent variable. The model could be further enhanced by adding behavioral analysis of the developers' decisions which are often based on expectations of the future demand, availability of land, and finance.

The multiple regression analysis concluded that the dependent variable V_{pt} is best described by independent variables GTS_t, GDP_{t-3}, and CRG_{t-3}.

Multiple correlation coefficient r is at the level of 0.93, and the linear model explains 87% (R^2) of values of the dependent variable. At the 5% significance level, the hypothesis H_0: $\beta i = 0$ can be rejected for all independent variables (individual t-tests), and the existence of linear function between V_{pt} and GDP_{t-3}, CRG_{t-3}, and GTS_t can be considered as proven and very relevant. At the 10% significance level, the hypothesis H_0: $\beta_1 = 0$ can be rejected for the intercept which creates no limit to the relevancy of the model. A linear regression model is shown in Eq. 4:

$$V_{pt} = 5,679.89 + 0.01GDP_{t-3} - 100,842.27CRG_{t-3} + 152,403.94GTS_t \tag{4}$$

At the 5% significance level ($F = 0.081$), the heteroskedasticity test exposed the possibility of heteroscedasticity within the model. However, the abridged White's test rejected the heteroscedasticity at the 5% significance level, and thus the model is realistic.

An increase of *GDP* by 1 billion at the period *t−3* will result in an increase in the value of industrial real estate portfolio V_p at the period *t* by 10CZK/m^2. In contrary, an increase in the risk premium *CRG* by 1% at the period *t−3* will result in a decrease in the value of industrial real estate portfolio V_p at the period *t* by 1,008CZK/m^2. An increase of variable *GTS* by 1% at the period *t* will result in an increase in the value of industrial real estate portfolio V_p at the period *t* by 1,524CZK/m^2.

These results have been expected and are in line with the FDW model. This final model allows to make predictions about the future industrial property values because the dependent variable V_p at the period *t* is described by independent variables *GDP* and *CRG* at period *t−3*, i.e., the values of *GDP* and *CRG* can be available at the time of the prediction.

Conclusion

This study concludes that the restored industrial real estate market model works on the same basis the Fischer-Di Pasquale-Wheaton model of the commercial real estate market.

The analysis further concludes that there is room for further growth of industrial real estate values on the Czech market. Rental levels shall rise as the absorption has still potential to grow, while supply is limited due to lack of permitted land, and yields have potential for further compression as the expected returns are still much higher these days than in the precrisis period. Further compression of capitalization rates to the levels in the Western Europe is possible only by increasing transparency of the market and/or by increasing the share of Czech capital invested in the industrial real estate sector.

Although the lack of market data limits the ability of direct observation of the shifts in the Czech industrial real estate values, it is possible to restore the market model based on data provided by advisors. The study is further limited by relatively short history of the Czech industrial real estate market as the time series fit just into one long property market cycle. As a side effect of this study, it has been proven that expert data provide relevant information about the market for investment decisions.

This paper is the basis for deeper analysis of industrial space productivity and behavioral economics at the industrial development market which is increasingly important due to the ongoing structural changes associated with the shift to e-commerce, shared economy, and industry 4.0. In general, the economics of space and time is still in its infancy. Understanding and correct interpretation of the real estate market behavior and of the value of space in time could be the answer to the imperfections of contemporary economics.

Acknowledgments The paper has been prepared within the research project of the Faculty of Finance and Accounting at the University of Economics in Prague registered by the Grant Agency under the registration number VŠE IP100040.

Appendix

Table 6 Source data of quarterly values of V_p, *GTS*, *SUP*, *VAC*, *ABS*, *GDP*, *EMP*, *CRG*, and *CPI*

Year	Quarter	Vp (CZK/m2)	VLC (CZK/m2)	GTS (%)	GTU (m2)	SUP (m2)	VAC (%)	ABS (m2)	GDP (mil. CZK)	EMP (ths)	CRG (%)	CPI
2007	Q1	22,051	14,853	7,44	175,960	190,686	2,96	93,321	942,051	4848	4,19	103,6
	Q2	23,025	15,827	9,07	256,056	274,113	3,49	250,521	944,126	4870	3,82	105
	Q3	23,619	16,421	8,76	213,438	210,370	4,20	187,862	967,813	4896	3,29	105,9
	Q4	22,991	15,793	8,90	219,518	242,913	4,97	216,186	979,829	4922	2,70	107,2
2008	Q1	21,943	14,486	8,30	147,825	90,006	6,10	31,228	991,805	4945	2,71	111,3
	Q2	21,117	13,660	6,94	192,107	261,955	7,40	161,193	1,005,646	4968	2,79	112,1
	Q3	20,146	12,689	5,97	143,027	158,124	9,16	90,131	1,017,012	4986	3,44	112,9
	Q4	20,819	13,362	5,01	132,218	127,849	10,90	95,085	996,313	5003	3,36	112,2
2009	Q1	21,012	13,495	4,86	174,241	234,211	12,12	172,262	993,972	5004	5,89	113,6
	Q2	18,609	11,092	4,93	233,366	162,212	13,36	75,481	974,788	4989	6,71	113,7
	Q3	16,215	8698	4,47	81,786	13,816	14,42	40,437	971,644	4965	7,25	113
	Q4	14,759	7242	4,29	113,102	30,070	15,01	51,096	983,089	4939	7,49	112,7
2010	Q1	14,247	6768	4,03	141,406	29,435	15,00	52,262	978,222	4905	7,70	114,4
	Q2	13,885	6406	3,86	212,297	17,765	14,33	32,575	988,348	4890	7,89	115,1
	Q3	13,636	6157	5,11	276,218	81,509	13,31	123,668	992,387	4887	7,78	115,2
	Q4	13,768	6289	5,86	238,619	66,606	12,06	136,373	990,361	4885	7,53	115
2011	Q1	13,803	6324	5,96	158,805	13,960	10,80	67,432	998,308	4894	7,42	116,4
	Q2	14,031	6552	5,44	145,160	47,764	9,47	62,197	1,003,298	4901	7,43	117,1
	Q3	14,355	6876	5,39	299,795	141,843	8,01	177,859	1,008,390	4905	7,21	117,2
	Q4	15,033	7554	4,97	198,161	128,450	7,07	135,036	1,019,675	4904	7,22	117,8

(continued)

Table 6 (continued)

Year	Quarter	Vp (CZK/m2)	VLC (CZK/m2)	GTS (%)	GTU (m2)	SUP (m2)	VAC (%)	ABS (m2)	GDP (mil. CZK)	EMP (ths)	CRG (%)	CPI
2012	Q1	15,097	7618	4,92	155,042	16,978	7,09	–49,335	1,017,859	4896	7,15	120,7
	Q2	15,357	7878	4,70	111,741	12,519	7,03	42,824	1,014,883	4888	7,17	121,1
	Q3	15,146	7667	3,87	172,816	51,522	7,42%	2263	1,011,265	4880	7,76	121,1
	Q4	15,099	7620	4,15	247,817	25,038	7,56%	80,049	1,014,942	4872	8,25	121,1
2013	Q1	15,201	7872	4,42	208,600	47,300	7,55	−1293	1,013,154	4873	8,14	122,8
	Q2	15,243	7914	5,23	258,600	55,800	7,86	28,792	1,015,088	4876	8,17	123
	Q3	15,256	7927	5,64	272,000	129,000	7,74	130,578	1,020,879	4882	8,18	122,6
	Q4	15,813	8484	6,46	398,500	32,500	8,01	47,927	1,047,879	4890	8,25	122,5
2014	Q1	16,569	9139	6,47	227,500	63,100	8,05	47,239	1,054,375	4902	7,63	123
	Q2	16,960	9530	6,23	241,000	103,000	7,86	102,320	1,070,196	4919	7,53	123,2
	Q3	17,531	10,101	6,55	357,200	102,100	7,59	121,340	1,086,133	4927	7,40	123,3
	Q4	17,995	10,565	6,52	413,800	75,400	7,67	34,847	1,101,830	4937	7,41	123,1
2015	Q1	18,237	10,731	6,50	238,100	55,000	7,63	67,917	1,119,947	4947	7,31	123,2
	Q2	18,246	10,740	7,05	385,600	139,800	7,33	165,108	1,135,893	4949	7,32	124
	Q3	18,255	10,749	6,63	344,700	268,600	6,71	321,000	1,147,260	4959	7,08	123,8
	Q4	18,533	11,027	6,58	444,700	153,300	6,09	155,722	1,153,639	4974	7,09	123,2
2016	Q1	18,701	11,121	6,83	313,600	84,300	5,39	135,699	1,168,541	4990	7,09	123,7
	Q2	19,048	11,540	6,45	349,300	182,400	4,93	140,400	1,175,475	5011	6,84	124,3
	Q3	19,503	11,995	6,15	291,700	51,800	4,77	66,500	1,183,478	5027	6,46	124,5
	Q4	20,064	12,556	6,31	525,571	178,600	4,63	151,757	1,120,380	5042	6,37	125

Source: Cushman&Wakefield, Industrial Research Forum, Czech Statistical Office, Czech National Bank, Czech Construction Standards

References

Ball M, Lizieri C, MacGregor BD (1998) The economics of commercial property markets. Routledge, Oxon. ISBN-13: 978-0415149938

Di Pasquale D, Wheaton WC (1992) The markets for real estate assets and space:a conceptual framework. J Am Real Estate Urban Econo Assoc 10(1):181–197

du Toit H, Cloete CE (2004) Appraisal of the Fischer-di Pasquale-Whetaon real estate model and development of an integrated property and asset market model. S Afr J Econo Manag Sci 7(2):341–367

Fisher J, Geltner D, Webb RB (1994) Value indices of commercial real estate: a comparison of index construction methods. J Real Estate Financ Econ 9(2):137–164

Fischer D (1999) An integrated property market model. J Real Estate Pract Valuat 2(1):33–43

Hindls R, Hronová S, Seger J, Fischer J (2007) Statistika pro ekonomy, 8th edn. Professional publishing, Praha. ISBN: 978-8086946436

Geltner DM, Miller NG, Clayton J, Einholz P (2013) Commercial real estate: analysis and investments, 3rd edn. OnCourse Learning, Mason. ISBN-13: 978-1133108825

Mueller G, Laposa SP (1994) Submarket Cycle Analysis—A Case Study of Submarkets in Philadelphia, Seattle and Salt Lake, Paper presented at the 1994 American Real Estate Society

Mueller GR (1995) Understanding real estate's physical and financial market cycles. J Real Estate Finance 12:1, 47 –52

Witten RG (1987) Riding the real estate cycle. Real state Today. August 1987, pp 42–48

Wheaton WC (1999) Real Estate "Cycles": some fundamentals. Real Estate Econ 27(2):209–230

Financial Performance of Czech Subsidiaries of the EU-Listed Companies

David Procházka

Abstract The paper examines the development of financial performance of Czech subsidiaries under the control of EU-listed companies during the period 2009–2014. Summary statistics of individual corporate data indicate that both the domicile of the parent and the industry affiliation of the subsidiary have an impact on the subsidiary's performance measured either by return on assets (ROA) or by return on equity (ROE). The association of parents' domiciles and subsidiaries' industries with performance is also confirmed by the analysis of variance (factorial ANOVA). ROE is significantly higher than ROA; the variability in ROE is, although, double compared to the variability in ROA. Finally, the differential between ROA and ROE is not constant over the sample companies.

Keywords Financial performance • EU-listed companies • Czech subsidiaries

Introduction

The Czech Republic is an example of an open small economy with a significant share of foreign investors. A mix of long tradition of high-quality manufacturing, suitable geographic location, and skilled labour force makes the Czech Republic an attractive place for foreign companies to establish the major production plants as well as shared service centres in the country. Companies under foreign control generate, for example, approximately a half of industrial production (Ernest 2014). An intensive presence of multinational enterprises and their positive impact on Czech subsidiaries results in the misbalance in return on investments flows. The net difference between dividends outgoing and incoming dividends was 214 billion CZK in 2014. The amount counts for 5% of GDP, the third largest share among the EU countries after Malta and Ireland (Kučera 2015). The significant proportion of these high-performing subsidiaries is owned by parent companies, which securities

D. Procházka (✉)
Faculty of Finance and Accounting, University of Economics, Prague, Prague, Czech Republic
e-mail: prochazd@vse.c

D. Procházka (ed.), *The Impact of Globalization on International Finance and Accounting*, Springer Proceedings in Business and Economics,
https://doi.org/10.1007/978-3-319-68762-9_21

are traded in capital markets. If only non-financial companies are considered, the Czech subsidiaries under the control of the EU-listed companies own around 12–13% of non-financial sector's assets. Their share on the production of Czech non-financial sector is more than 25% (Procházka 2016).

There are already several studies examining the performance of Czech companies. However, they focus mainly on the outcomes of privatisation process of the 1990s, with emphasis on the differences among various privatisation methods, e.g. Claessens and Djankov (1999), Weiss and Nikitin (1999) and Cull et al. (2002). If the impact of foreign ownership is investigated (Harper 2001) (Švejnar and Kočenda 2003), the difference between domestic and (concentrated) foreign ownership is subject of interest, but without dealing with the heterogeneity across owners' countries. Recent studies, e.g. Konečný and Částek (2016), also search for an association between ownership concentration and performance.

The paper aims at filling in the gap in the literature by examining whether there is any heterogeneity in performance of Czech subsidiaries under foreign control, depending on the domicile of parent company. The paper focuses on those Czech subsidiaries, which belong to the economic groups with the parent company listed in capital markets of any EU member state. The restriction to "EU-listed parents" is made to keep the sample homogenous in terms of institutional settings and enforcement regimes, to which parent companies as public enterprises face.

Data and Methodology

Based on the literature review in the introduction, the paper's goal is refined into two research hypotheses:

- H1: The domicile of parent company (listed at EU capital markets) has effect on the financial performance of the Czech subsidiaries.
- H2: The industry affiliation of the subsidiaries has effect on their financial performance.

Based on the approach of Procházka (2017), Amadeus Bureau van Dijk database is used to obtain EU-listed companies and to identify their subsidiaries. To solve inconsistencies contained in Amadeus, manual procedures suggested by Procházka (2016) are applied. The final sample encompasses 1347 of Czech subsidiaries under control of the EU-listed companies. In the next step, Czech database Albertina was used to generate extracts from the financial statements of sample firms for the period 2009–2014. The Albertina database contains more up-to-date information as well as more detail information compared to Amadeus. The descriptive statistics are presented in Table 1.

Despite many approaches to definition of financial performance are developed, basic metrics of financial analysis – return on assets (ROA) and return on equity

Table 1 Descriptive statistics of the sample

	min	median	max	mean	sd
Assets	6	237,073	176,869,000	1,859,763	8,628,934
Equity	5	88,118	121,549,206	933,938	5,330,610
Sales	1	217,615	304,448,000	2,214,462	11,335,096
CIT	0	1376	2,283,000	22,768	109,572
EBIT	(7,383,528)	12,435	30,197,187	153,171	901,862
EBT	(7,610,198)	10,178	30,187,272	144,763	895,185
EAT	(4,859,433)	8186	24,037,985	122,789	779,686

Source: Own analysis of data from the Albertina database; amounts in thousands CZK

(ROE) – are used as the proxy measures of performance reported in financial statements.

$$ROA_i = \frac{EBIT_i}{Assets_i} \quad (1)$$

$$ROE_i = \frac{EAT_i}{Equity_i} \quad (2)$$

where EBIT is earnings before interest and taxation and EAT is earnings after taxation.

Regarding the methodology applied for inferential analysis, firstly the dataset is decomposed using two criteria – the country origin of the parent company and the industry of the subsidiary. For each subgroup of companies, the median, mean and standard deviations are calculated and compared across all subsets. Finally, the testing of differences in performance rests on the factorial analysis of variance.

Results and Discussion

Adjustments to raw data were made to eliminate non-meaningful or extreme values. Firstly, all instances with negative equity are dropped out of the sample. Secondly, extremely high values of ROA and ROE (over 100% in absolute terms) were adjusted to avoid distortion, when summarizing and interpreting the outcomes. If an indicator is higher than 100%, then 100% is taken as the ceiling. Accordingly, if the measure is below (100%), then (100%) is used as the bottom figure. The aggregate results are outlined in Table 2. The median of ROA is oscillating around 7%; the average fluctuates from 8.6% to 11.2%. Similarly, the median of ROE is 12.2% and the average amounts to 13.4%. ROE is significantly higher than ROA, and the variability in ROE is, although, double compared to the variability in ROA (based on values of the respective standard deviations).

Table 2 Distribution of ROA and ROE

ROA (%)	2009	2010	2011	2012	2013	2014	Total
median	6.78	7.22	7.10	7.25	6.90	7.89	7.15
mean	9.45	9.51	9.54	8.94	8.60	11.20	9.43
sd	17.71	17.35	16.39	16.70	17.37	14.39	16.66
ROE (%)	2009	2010	2011	2012	2013	2014	Total
median	11.37	12.62	11.83	12.90	12.11	14.50	12.20
mean	11.24	14.34	12.50	13.33	12.91	17.47	13.42
sd	37.99	34.95	35.79	34.11	35.14	30.32	34.93

Source: Own analysis of data from the Albertina database

In the next step, the variability of performance across the companies is investigated, using factorial analysis of variance. There are two factors considered – the domicile of parent company and the industry affiliation of its Czech subsidiary. As several combinations of domiciles and industry codes contain just few observations, only subsets with more than 30 instances are included. If countries with 30+ observations are considered, the best performing Czech companies are subordinated to the parents from Spain, Germany and Sweden in case of ROA, respectively, from Spain, France and Sweden in case of ROE. The worst performing subgroups regarding ROA are under the control of the parents from Denmark, Slovakia and Luxembourg, respectively, and Slovakia, Luxembourg and the Netherlands under ROE measure. Regarding the dispersion across industries, the best performing (once again with at least 30 observations) are K (financial services), M (professional and scientific activities), and E (water supply) for ROA. In case of ROE, the top three industries are K (financial services), E (water), and N (administrative and support services). On the other hand, the worst profitability measured by ROA is evidenced for A (agriculture), L (real estates), and F (construction industry). If ROE is assessed, then I (accommodation) is on the tail followed by L (real estates) and A (agriculture). The tables with individual values are presented in the Appendix.

Figures 1 and 2 capture these cross-sectional differences in performance of analysed companies graphically. To simplify the graphics, only six most numerous industries are presented. Comparing the performance (measured by ROA) across the subsets, the most profitable group of Czech subsidiaries is that operating in the sector G (wholesale and retail trade), being controlled by Belgian parent companies. Comparable results are reported by undertakings in M (professional and scientific activities), belonging to the groups under control of companies based in Italy. Both these subsets have average unweighted ROA over 30%. The worst performing are subsidiaries of Swedish parents making business in the industry of J (information and communication) as well as firms from L (real estate industry), having superordinate located in Slovakia or in the Netherlands. These three clusters have negative ROA around 11.5%.

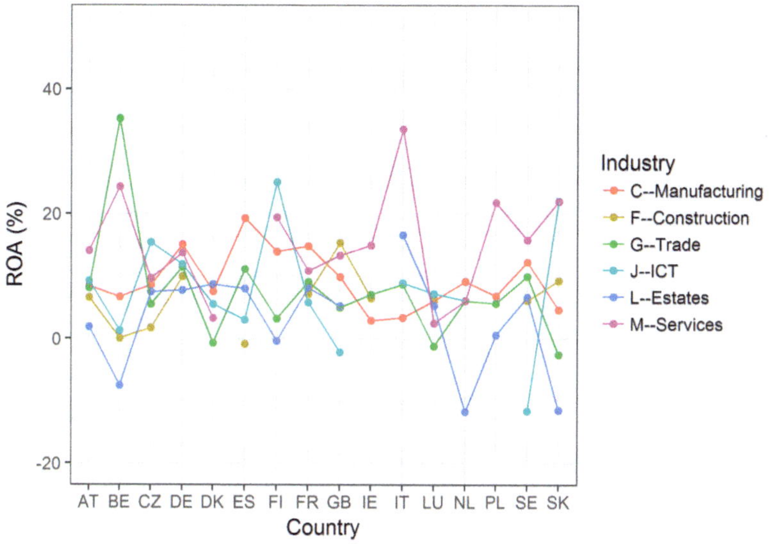

Fig. 1 Average ROA across parent's domicile and subsidiary's industry (Source: Own analysis of data from the Albertina database)

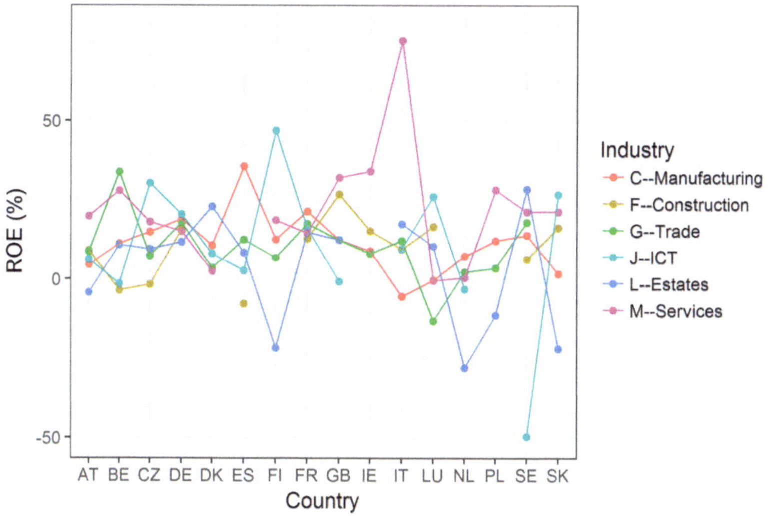

Fig. 2 Average ROE across parent's domicile and subsidiary's industry (Source: Own analysis of data from the Albertina database)

Table 3 Descriptive statistics of the sample

Panel A: ROA	Df	Sum sq	Mean sq	F-statistic	P-value
Parent	15	32,336.04	2155.74	8.607	0.000*
Industry	13	22,741.42	1749.34	6.985	0.000*
Parent: Industry	111	119,125.50	1073.20	4.285	0.000*
Residuals	4777	1,196,432.15	250.46		
Panel B: ROE	Df	Sum sq	Mean sq	F-statistic	P-value
Parent	15	143,447.55	9563.17	8.699	0.000*
Industry	13	59,860.02	4604.62	4.188	0.000*
Parent: Industry	111	530,308.86	4777.56	4.346	0.000*
Residuals	4777	5,251,847.50	1099.40		
Panel C: ROA-ROE	Df	Sum sq	Mean sq	F-statistic	P-value
Parent	15	63,804.31	4253.62	7.390	0.000*
Industry	13	28,682.77	2206.37	3.833	0.000*
Parent: Industry	111	226,272.88	2038.49	3.542	0.000*
Residuals	4777	2,749,426.61	575.56		

Source: Own analysis using R; *1% significance, **5% significance

The dispersion of best and worst results for ROE is more extreme than in case of ROA. However, subsidiaries of Italian parents from M (professional and scientific activities) are still premiant, followed by Finnish-controlled companies in ICT sector (code J). The biggest losses are recorded by firms in the same sector but belonging to Swedish parent companies. Similar values (around −50%) are reported by trading companies (code G), being commanded by Slovak parents. Such extreme negative results suggest either serious economic difficulties of the Czech firms or massive profit shifting within the group.

As far as inferential analysis, a factorial ANOVA test is run to verify whether the above-identified differences across subgroups are statistically significant. The restricted sample consists of 4917 observations for 16 country domiciles and 14 subsidiary industries. The output is presented in Table 3 (Panel A for ROA; Panel B for ROE). The tests' results indicate indeed that the domicile of the parent has a significant impact (at 1% significance level) on both indicators. Similarly, industry variable is significant at 1% significance level for ROA as well as for ROE. Finally, the interaction term between parents' domiciles and industry affiliation of the subsidiaries does matter as well. The hypotheses H1 and H2 are thus confirmed. A significant variability in performance is identified, both across the domicile of parent company and industry membership of the subsidiary, regardless whether performance is measured by ROA or ROE.

The finding of a significantly higher average for ROE than for ROA immediately raises a follow-up question about the (in)variability of this differential between ROA and ROE in the sample. The factorial ANOVA test is therefore run once again; the difference (ROA–ROE) is the dependent variable this time. The results sketched in Table 3 (Panel C) show that the differential between ROA and ROE is not constant over the sample companies. The findings lead to a conjecture that companies attribute a distinct importance to these two metrics of financial performance. However, this preliminary evidence shall be confirmed by further research, considering individual patterns of accounting quality, including earnings management or profit shifting. Massive intercompany loans may be the source of variability and the main channel of the latter case. The interest charges from the parent companies are contained in EAT, and hence, they influence the ROE indicator. However, ROA measure is unaffected, as EBIT excludes the interest expense. However, different explanations, for example, meeting debt covenants and other contacting benchmarks, might be true as well and possible explanation beyond the first case (i.e. earnings management supposition).

Conclusion

The paper examines the development of financial performance of Czech subsidiaries under the control of EU-listed companies during the period 2009–2014. Individual corporate data from financial statements shows that the domicile of the parent influences the subsidiary's performance measured either by return on assets (ROA) or by return on equity (ROE). The heterogeneity is also identified across particular industries, in which respective Czech subsidiaries operate. ROE is significantly higher than ROA; the variability in ROE is, although, double compared to the variability in ROA. Finally, the differential between ROA and ROE is not constant over the sample companies.

Future research shall compare performance of companies covered by the paper with remaining Czech firms, i.e. with subsidiaries of companies listed outside EU capital markets, as well as with domestic family firms. Furthermore, the factors determining heterogeneity in differential between ROA and ROE shall be investigated. Potential explanations of the identified variability can be attributed to earnings management either for tax reasons or for contracting purposes.

Acknowledgments This paper has been prepared within the research project "Economic Impacts of the IFRS Adoption in Selected Transition Countries" (supported by the Czech Science Foundation, No. 15-01280S).

Appendix

Table 4 Matrix for ROA

	A	B	C	D	E	F	G	H	I	J	K	L	M	N	P	Q	R	S	Mean
Austria		16.4	8.4			6.6	8.2		11.3	9.3		1.9	14.1	11.9				(1.4)	7.9
Belgium			6.7	4.1		0.1	35.3		(4.0)	1.3		(7.5)	24.4						11.0
Croatia													4.7						4.7
Cyprus			1.4																1.4
Czech Rep.	(19.7)	9.8	8.6	9.4	9.7	1.7	5.5	9.5		15.5	(0.4)	7.5	9.6	4.9		(9.3)			8.1
Denmark			7.6		7.3		(0.7)	(17.1)		5.6		8.7	3.3						1.5
Finland			14.0				3.2			25.1		(0.3)	19.4	(4.8)	22.7)				9.9
France	17.4	10.6	14.9	21.8	18.8	7.2	9.1	0.6	2.6	5.8	9.7	8.1	10.9	(14.5)	(31.7)		(19.2)		10.7
Germany	(17.4)	4.6	15.1	7.1	(0.2)	9.9	11.5	11.3	22.3	11.9	13.1	7.8	13.8	17.9				(6.8)	11.9
G. Britain			9.9	13.4		15.4	5.0	9.0	22.4	(2.1)		5.3	13.4	8.9			100.0	2.5	8.7
Greece								(1.0)				9.6							5.1
Hungary							1.0												1.0
Ireland			2.9			6.5	7.1						15.0						7.8
Italy			3.4				8.7			8.9		16.7	33.6						8.6
Luxemb.	10.1		6.1	3.0	(0.4)	6.4	(1.2		1.6	7.2	5.6	5.3	2.5	6.1	26.3				4.9
Malta									(2.7)										(2.7)
Netherlands			9.1	1.4			6.1	58.6		6.1		(11.7)	6.0	0.0			10.0		7.3
Poland			6.8	24.3			5.7		4.6			0.6	21.8						8.0
Portugal						0.6						(1.8							(0.4)
Slovakia			4.6			9.3	(2.5)			22.1		(11.4)	22.0						4.5
Slovenia			(0.7)				6.2						17.4						7.6
Spain			19.4	2.4	14.2	(0.8)	11.2			3.0		8.0		34.6					12.5
Sweden			12.3	11.0		6.2	10.0	12.9		(11.6)	52.2	6.7	15.9	11.7					11.6
Mean	4.9	7.3	11.7	8.5	11.9	6.9	8.1	8.0	7.8	10.1	13.2	5.1	12.0	11.2	(3.6)	(9.3)	17.6	(1.0)	9.4

Table 5 Matrix for ROE

	A	B	C	D	E	F	G	H	I	J	K	L	M	N	P	Q	R	S	Mean
Austria		20.6	4.6			9.1	8.8		5.0	6.3		(4.2)	19.9	13.6				(1.5)	6.8
Belgium			11.2	4.5		(3.5)	33.9		(100.0)	(1.4)		(100.0)	27.9						10.9
Croatia													9.0						9.0
Cyprus			1.6																1.6
Czech Rep.	(28.0)	12.8	15.0	13.1	19.0	(1.6)	7.5	10.9		30.4	(0.4)	9.7	18.1	5.9		(11.1)			13.0
Denmark			10.8		77.0		3.6	(26.8)		8.2		23.1	2.7						5.5
Finland			12.7				7.0			47.0		(21.6)	18.7	1.8	17.8				10.7
France	46.2	12.6	21.5	37.4	28.0	12.9	17.7	(4.2)	3.7	16.4	54.0	14.9	14.6	(42.6)	(77.2)		(29.6)		18.0
Germany	(42.0)	11.8	19.1	11.9	(11.9)	15.9	18.0	13.8	25.4	20.6	32.3	11.9	15.2	33.2				(20.2)	17.0
G. Britain			12.6	24.1		26.9	12.6	13.2	50.6	(0.7)		12.6	32.1	10.8			100.0	2.0	16.1
Greece								(28.9)				12.3							(5.3)
Hungary							3.1												3.1
Ireland			9.0			15.3	8.2						34.1						14.9
Italy			(5.4)				12.3			9.7		17.6	75.4						9.6
Luxemb.	16.7		(0.2)	(20.8)	(33.2)	16.7	(13.0)		(13.1)	26.2	8.4	10.6	(0.3)	9.2	41.8				4.9
Malta									(35.7)										(35.7)
Netherlands			7.4	2.0			2.4	95.2		(3.0)		(27.8)	0.6	(1.9)			21.5		5.0
Poland			12.3	68.5			3.6		6.0			(11.3)	28.3						12.2
Portugal						(2.8)						(7.5)							(4.7
Slovakia			1.8			16.4	(51.5)			26.9		(21.9)	21.5						(10.3)
Slovenia			(1.4)				10.1						13.6						8.5
Spain			35.7	18.5	25.5	(7.7)	12.6			2.8		8.5		61.3					20.8
Sweden			14.1	15.9		6.5	18.2	11.6		(49.5)	52.8	28.6	21.4	26.6					17.3
Mean	9.1	13.0	15.1	14.9	20.0	10.6	11.7	8.2	1.8	17.6	36.7	6.6	17.1	18.8	(23.7)	(11.1)	24.9	(3.6)	13.4

References

Claessens S, Djankov S (1999) Ownership concentration and corporate performance in the Czech Republic. J Comp Econ 27:498–513. https://doi.org/10.1006/jcec.1999.1598

Cull R, Matesova J, Shirley M (2002) Ownership and the temptation to loot: evidence from privatized firms in the Czech Republic. J Comp Econ 30:1–24. https://doi.org/10.1006/jcec.2001.1754

Ernest J (2014) Český průmysl je náš jen z poloviny (Only Half of the Czech Industry Is Ours). Statistika&My 4:18–19

Harper JT (2001) Short-Term effects of privatization on operating performance in the Czech Republic. J Financ Res 24:119–131. https://doi.org/10.1111/j.1475-6803.2001.tb00821.x

Konečný L, Částek O (2016) The effect of ownership structure on corporate financial performance in the Czech Republic. Ekonomický časopis 64:477–498

Kučera L (2015) Odliv dividend zesílil (Dividends Outflows Intensified). Statistika&My 5:18

Procházka D (2016) Effective tax rates in the "Foreign Parent – Czech Subsidiary" Links. In: Sedmihradská L (ed) Proceedings of the 21st International Conference: theoretical and practical aspects of public finance 2016. Oeconomica, Prague, pp 70–78

Procházka D (2017) Forced IFRS adoption: direction of the "EU-15 parents—CEE subsidiaries" links. In: Procházka D (ed) New trends in finance and accounting. Springer International Publishing, Cham, pp 361–371

Švejnar J, Kočenda E (2003) Ownership and firm performance after large-scale privatization. William Davidson Institute at the University of Michigan, Ann Arbor

Weiss AM, Nikitin G (1999) Performance of Czech companies by ownership structure. SSRN Electron J. https://doi.org/10.2139/ssrn.148834

Cash Flow Ratios' and Liquidity Ratios' Analysis of Selected Listed Companies in Sri Lanka

Aleksandre Petriashvili

Abstract As it is known, the statement of cash flows is a crucial part of financial reporting. And cash flow ratios have provoked the attention of practitioners and academic researchers to use to evaluate the performance of a company. This study examines, over the 3-year period (2012–2014), the liquidity position of selected 125 companies of the Sri Lankan economy using cash flow statement ratios and classic liquidity ratios suggested by various researchers. The total number of companies listed in the main market of the Colombo Stock Exchange is 313. Classic ratios were obtained from the Osiris database, and cash flow ratios were calculated by using financial statements of selected companies. The ratios, which I examined, are those current ratio, quick assets ratio, total assets to total liabilities ratio, and interest coverage ratio. Similarly, cash flow ratios examined were operating cash flow ratio, critical needs cash coverage ratio, cash flow to total debt ratio, and cash interest coverage ratio. And for investigation to find out how strong is relationship between classic and cash flow ratios correlation analysis were made. Results, which were got after correlation analysis showed positive relationship between classic and cash flow ratios. However additional *t*-tests analysis, showed substantial difference. The main point of the abovementioned results suggests that well-known liquidity ratios should not be used only for calculating liquidity since a company can have serious cash flow problems with positive liquidity ratios and increasing profits. Liquidity ratios developed using the statement of cash flows provide additional information or sometimes better insight on the financial strength or weakness of a company.

Keywords Liquidity ratios • Cash flow • Cash flow ratios • Cash flow statement • Sri Lankan companies

---

A. Petriashvili (✉)
University of Economics, Prague, Department of Corporate Finance, Nam. W. Churchilla 4, 130 67 Prague, Czech Republic
e-mail: xpeta28@vse.cz

D. Procházka (ed.), *The Impact of Globalization on International Finance and Accounting*, Springer Proceedings in Business and Economics,
https://doi.org/10.1007/978-3-319-68762-9_22

Introduction

As we know, the important financial indicator that measures whether the company has the ability to meet its short-term liabilities (or not) without incurring undesirable losses is liquidity. If we are using our assets ineffectively, that can be the reason of increased liquidity risk, which is distinctively the most challenging risk comparing with other financial risks. And nowadays liquidity risk is becoming more complex because of recent developments in financial markets. It must be mentioned too that a liquidity crisis of a single company can affect indirectly or directly all the other companies. Companies should maintain sufficient liquidity to face unexpected conditions. This is a strength for firms, because companies with sufficient liquidity have good financial flexibility, which means that it can negotiate with suppliers and financiers. Everyone remembers what happened with Lehman Brothers company in 2008. This is known as Lehman Brothers collapse. They used their current assets and invested in illiquid long-term assets, and when the stock market started to fall, Lehman's creditors cut credit lines, and clients withdrew their fund, and Lehman didn't have liquid assets to meet short-term obligations (Azadinamin 2012). This was the main reason of the company's bankruptcy. Hence, the company needs to have more current assets than current liabilities. It's more important for smaller firms, because they have fewer potential sources of outside funds than big companies. For evaluation short-term liquidity for current and quick assets ratios are used and long-term solvency for the total assets to total liabilities ratio. But sometimes information of these ratios, which is taken from the balance sheet, isn't always reliable due to different accounting measurement options of the value of assets and accrual accounting. As much, there is the need for a more accurate measure that reflects the actual liquidity position of a firm.

In the past, balance sheet and income statement ratios are widely used by professionals and investors to analyze the liquidity of a company. However, the cash flow statement can be more reliable in assessing the liquidity of a company. Balance sheet, income statement, and retained earnings statement do not provide an overall picture of the financial position of a company which is why the cash flow statement has become an essential component of complete financial reporting by professional accounting bodies. And what is main is that the statement of cash flows can overcome many limitations of accrual accounting procedures used to prepare traditional financial statements. For instance, the balance sheet does not address the financing issues accurately at the end of the period. Even though many types of assets are shown in the statement, no explanation is given on the manner those assets were financed and/or the source of activities that are related to each item. Coprime, the profit mentioned in the income statement does not provide any insight about changes in cash. In contrast, the cash flow statement details the dissimilarity between the operating profits of a firm and any increase or decrease in the cash balance over an accounting period. The statement of cash flows shows how the investing activities were financed, externally or internally. Some authors posit that the cash flow statement helps to assess the capability of a company to generate future positive cash flows.

Gombola et al. (1987) assert that the information provided by the balance sheet and income statement can be misleading. Eyisi and Okpe (2014) provide evidence to support that claim. In their study, several cash flow ratios and classic ratios adapted from previous research for assessing corporate performance were employed.

They discovered that although the classic liquidity and asset management ratios provide evidence that suggest good liquidity position for a company, the cash basis ratios indicate that the liquidity position is indeed negative. Thus, they concluded that cash basis ratios can be better tools for assessing corporate performance as cash basis ratios provide better insight into the viability and liquidity position of a company. Other researchers such as Mills and Yamamura (1998), Armen (2013); Ryu and Jang (2004), as well as Eyisi and Okpe (2014) agree that classic ratios such as current and quick assets ratio are not sufficient to assess the liquidity of a company. Given the importance of liquidity for a company, it is necessary to determine the liquidity position of a company from many different dimensions. On that note, this study aims to examine the level of liquidity for selected Sri Lankan public-listed companies. It employs eight (8) different measures of liquidity for companies that are listed on the Colombo Stock Exchange. Table 1 shows numbers of companies listed in the main market of the Colombo Stock Exchange. The total number of selected companies listed in these sectors (Table 1) represents over 65% of the market value of all listed companies on the Colombo Stock Exchange. In addition to comparing the cash flow ratios with the classic ratios using information from cash flow statement, balance sheet, and income statement, the study seeks to establish the trend of liquidity among companies in these sectors. The empirical results from this study can provide insight into the practice of liquidity management in companies in Sri Lanka. This paper is structured in the following format: the next section will present the literature review. This will be followed by the presentation of the data and the discussion on the methodology employed in this study. The next segment will present the empirical findings in addition to the discussion of the result. Finally, the last part of the paper will present the conclusions.

Data and Methodology

The study involved comparison between classic ratios and newly contrived cash flow ratios of the top 125 companies by market capitalization on the Colombo Stock Exchange Main Market over a 3-year period (2012–2014). In this study, a total of 125 companies were selected based on the following criteria:

- Must be listed in the Colombo Stock Exchange
- Must have complete data for all variables used in this study from 2012 to 2014.

Table 1 Numbers of companies listed in the main market of the Colombo Stock Exchange

Sector	Numbers of Companies
Bank, finance, and insurance (BFI)	74
Beverage, food, and tobacco (BFT)	23
Chemicals and pharmaceuticals (C&P)	12
Construction and engineering (C&E)	4
Diversified holdings (DIV)	19
Footwear and textile (F&T)	3
Health care (HLT)	7
Hotels and travels (H&T)	38
Information technology (IT)	2
Investment trusts (INV)	10
Land and property (L&P)	18
Manufacturing (MFG)	40
Motors (MTR)	6
Oil palms (OIL)	5
Plantations (PLT)	20
Power and energy (P&E)	9
Services (SRV)	8
Stores supplies (S&S)	4
Telecommunications (TLE)	2
Trading (TRD)	9
Total	313

Source: CSE (2017)

Traditional ratios and financial statements for the 3-year period of the selected companies were obtained from the Osiris database. Cash flow ratios were calculated by focusing directly on cash flows from operating activities from the statement of cash flows. Earnings, total assets, total liabilities, current liabilities, and other variables are derived from the income statement and balance sheet.

Exit barriers are high for companies with large market capitalizations. As a result, large companies are supposed to generate sufficient cash from operating activities to meet short- and long-term obligations. This study seeks to find any discrepancies between the two sets of ratios while analyzing classic ratios versus cash flow ratios. Moreover, this study investigates ratios which provide more reliable information about these big companies.

Table 2 presents formulas for classic ratios and cash flow ratios employed in this study. Liquidity was measured by the current ratio and quick assets ratio and cash flow from operations to current liabilities and critical needs cash coverage ratio. Solvency was measured by total assets to total liabilities, time interest earned ratio, cash flow from operations to total liabilities, and cash flow interest coverage.

Quantitative analysis is used in this study to analyze data based on statistical techniques: descriptive statistics and paired sample *t*-tests. Descriptive statistics provide an essential summary of the sample of this study. Pair sample *t*-tests were

Table 2 Comparison of ratios

Classic ratios		Cash flow ratio		
Ratios	Formula	Ratio	Formula	Measure
Current ratio	CA/CL	CFO to CL	CFO/CL	Liquidity
Quick assets ratio	(CA – inventories)/CL	Critical needs cash coverage	(CFO + interest paid)/(total current liabilities + interest	Liquidity
TA to TL ratio	TA/TL	CFO to TL	CFO/TL	Solvency
Interest coverage ratio	EBIT/interest expense	Cash flow-interest coverage	(CFO + interest paid + taxes paid)/interest paid	Solvency

Source: Adapted from Ryu and Jang (2004), Kirkham (2012), and Mills and Yamamura (1998)
Where *CA* current assets, *CL* current liabilities, *TA* total assets, *TL* total liabilities, *EBIT* earnings before interest and income tax, and *CFO* cash flow from operations

used to analyze paired differences between traditional ratios and cash flow ratios for selected companies.

Empirical Results and Discussion

Descriptive Statistics

As I mentioned before, descriptive statistics were used to organize, summarize, and display the research data in this study which include all numerical values that were taken from the Osiris database and financial statements of selected companies. To analyze the characteristics of the variables, means, maximum, minimum, and standard deviations were produced using SAS. Descriptive statistics were analyzed separately for each type of ratios.

Table 3 shows that current ratio ranges from 0,389 to 10,85. If the current ratio is lower than 1, then the company's liquidity position is weak. However, high current ratio is not always good as it shows the excess amount of cash or marketable securities or inventory. Distinctively, the mean of current ratio is 2,2391 which indicates a good liquidity position for most of the selected companies on average. The mean of operating cash flow ratio (0,6418) is smaller than that of current ratio (2,2391) which reflects the fact that the current ratio is calculated at a particular point in time, whereas cash flow from operations is calculated by considering how much cash was generated over a period of time.

Operating cash flow ratio ranges from −0,2069 to 6,0734. The negative figure for operating cash flow ratio indicates that the company did not generate any cash from operation. There might be several good or bad reasons for this negative figure. But without further analysis, a negative operating cash flow ratio indicates that the company is in weak liquidity position with a negative operating cash flow ratio. Standard deviation is higher for current ratio (1,9220) than operating cash flow ratio (0,7515) because ratios are more dispersed for current ratio than operating cash flow

Table 3 Descriptive statistics of current ratio and cash flow ratio

	N	Range	Minimum	Maximum	Mean	Std. deviation	Skewness	
	Statistic	Statistic	Statistic	Statistic	Statistic	Statistic	Statistic	Std. error
Current ratio	125	10,46	0,389	10,85	2,2391	1,9220	2,5139	0,194
Operating CF ratio	125	6,28	−0,2069	6,0734	0,6418	0,7515	3,9241	0,194
Valid N	125							

Source: own analysis

Table 4 Descriptive statistics of quick assets ratio and critical needs cash coverage ratio

	N	Range	Minimum	Maximum	Mean	Std. deviation	Skewness	
	Statistic	Statistic	Statistic	Statistic	Statistic	Statistic	Statistic	Std. error
Quick assets ratio	125	9,9200	0,3643	10,2844	1,7932	1,7545	2582	0,194
Critical needs cash coverage	125	5,8077	−0,1432	5,6644	0,6502	0,7134	3761	0,194
Valid N	125							

Source: own analysis

ratio. Both ratios are positively skewed. As we know inventories are the least liquid assets than receivables and cash. And quick assets ratios are calculated by excluding inventories. Critical needs cash coverage ratio can be compared against quick assets ratio to gauge company's liquidity position. Interestingly, Table 4 shows that maximum and minimum figures for quick assets ratio are quite close to that of current ratio (Table 3) which reflects selected companies did not have much inventory. In Table 4, maximum quick assets ratio (10,2844) indicates that a company with high quick assets ratio has a lot of cash tied up in nonproductive asset presumably. Critical need cash coverage ratio ranges from −0,1432 to 5,6644, which is close to range of operating cash flow ratio (from Table 3), supports the evidence of previously explained liquidity position. The figure of both mean (0,6502) and standard deviation (0,7134) for critical needs cash coverage ratio is much lower than that of quick assets ratio (1,7932 and 1,7545, respectively). These differences again support the argument that cash flow ratios are calculated by directly focusing cash generated from operations.

High liquidity ratio is not preferred by equity investors and owners as high liquidity indicates higher levels of cash or marketable securities or the holding of too much inventory which indicate a reason for losses. But for creditors, high current or quick assets ratio is important, because it shows the company has good capability to pay off short-term obligations. By looking at the descriptive statistics of quick assets ratio, it can be concluded that selected companies had less inventory.

Table 5 Descriptive statistics of total assets to total liabilities ratio and cash flow to total debt ratio

	N	Range	Minimum	Maximum	Mean	Std. deviation	Skewness	
	Statistic	Statistic	Statistic	Statistic	Statistic	Statistic	Statistic	Std. error
TA to TL	125	18,4949	1,1077	19,6026	3,0160	2,9122	3,5074	0,194
CF to total debt ratio	125	1,6592	−0,0956	1,5634	0,3332	0,3098	1,5269	0,194
Valid N	125							

Source: own analysis

That is, companies had the ability to pay short-term obligations without relying on the sale of inventories. But it is important for managers to maintain balance between current assets and current liabilities. For Ryu and Jang, cash flow from operations to current liabilities should be a minimum of 40% for a healthy firm. In this study, the mean of cash flow from operations to current liabilities and critical needs cash coverage was higher than 40% which supports the result of current and quick assets ratios that most of the companies have good position in terms of liquidity.

For calculation of company's solvency, usually, total assets to total liabilities ratio is used. Cash flow to total debt ratio is analogous to traditional ratio (TA to TL). The higher the ratio is, the greater the ability to cover losses during liquidation. Stockholders and creditors have usually contradictory viewpoints in analyzing these two ratios. Particularly, total assets to total liabilities ratio is calculated at a single point in time; in contrast, cash flow to total debt ratio overcomes this problem by covering a period of time.

Table 5 shows that the mean (3,0160) of total assets to total liabilities is much higher than the mean (0,3332) of cash flow to total debt ratio. The standard deviation of total assets to total liabilities ratio (2,9122) is higher than that of cash flow to total debt ratio (0,3098) as well. The significant difference between these two ratios suggests that cash flow to total debt ratio is more reliable in assessing solvency as cash flow operations would be devoted to debt payments. More precisely, even with higher total assets to total liabilities ratio, a company may not have the capability to pay its debt, if the company has scarce cash flow from operation. The mean of selected companies for total assets to total liabilities shows good financial position; however, it needs to be checked whether those companies are generating adequate cash from operations or not. Higher total assets to total liabilities ratio is not desirable from the viewpoint of stockholders as they want companies to have more leverage in order to magnify expected earnings. Finally, creditors and equity investors need to compare these two ratios to have

Table 6 Descriptive statistics of interest cover ratio and cash interest coverage ratio

	N	Range	Minimum	Maximum	Mean	Std. deviation	Skewness	
	Statistic	Statistic	Statistic	Statistic	Statistic	Statistic	Statistic	Std. error
Interest cover	125	1833,35	1,1852	1834,54	73,685	198,109	5682	0,194
Cash interest coverage	125	2452,00	−1,2005	2450,80	97,496	275,378	5429	0,194
Valid N	125							

Source: own analysis

more reliable picture about the solvency of a company. For instance, a company with moderate total assets to total liabilities ratio and higher cash flow to total debt ratio can be more capable of paying debt compared to a company with higher total assets to total liabilities ratio and lower cash flow to total debt ratio.

The interest coverage ratio measures company's ability to make required interest payment obligations. Earnings before interest and tax are used to pay interest expense. On the other hand, cash interest coverage ratio is similar to interest coverage ratio, which looks directly at the cash available to pay interest expense. The later one is more realistic since earnings figure includes all noncash charges (e.g., amortization, depreciation, etc.). A company with low interest coverage ratio may have the ability to make interest expenses, but it may not be understandable by only looking at this traditional ratio due to noncash charges.

Table 6 shows that the mean and standard deviation of cash interest coverage ratio (97,496 and 275,378) are higher than the mean and standard deviation of interest coverage ratio (73,685 and 198,109) which reflects that earning figures were eroded by noncash charges. It is interesting to note that the minimum number for cash interest coverage ratio starts with negative (−1,2005); in contrast to that, the minimum number for interest coverage ratio starts with positive figure (1,1852). The negative figure indicates that the company had negative cash flow from operation; thus, it would have less ability to cover interest obligations which could bring legal action by creditors. However, this realistic picture of true financial condition of a company is hard to get by only considering interest coverage ratio. Maximum figures for both ratios are too high because of insignificant amount of interest paid by the company against earnings before interest and tax or cash flow from operation.

Correlation Analysis

A measure of the correlation is represented by correlation coefficients. The coefficient provides both the direction and strength of the relationship between a pair of variables. In this study, the strength of association between all pairs of variables was statistically measured by Pearson's correlation coefficient. In statistics,

Table 7 Pearson's correlation coefficients of cash flow ratios and traditional ratios

		N	Correlation
Pair 1	Current ratio and cash flow ratio	125	0,5241
Pair 2	Quick assets ratio and critical needs cash coverage ratio	125	0,5630
Pair 3	TA to TL ratio and cash flow to total debt ratio	125	0,3185
Pair 4	Interest coverage ratio and cash interest coverage ratio	125	0,8361

Source: own analysis

Pearson's correlation coefficient measures linear correlation between two variables ranging from −1 to +1, where 1 is the total positive correlation, 0 is no correlation, and −1 is the total negative correlation. The correlations between pairs of cash flow ratios and classic ratios are presented in Table 7. It can be seen that there are significant correlations between cash flow ratios and classic ratios which reflect that if classic ratios increase in value, cash flow ratios will also increase in value. Correlation figure of interest coverage ratio and cash interest coverage ratio demonstrates that there is strong relationship as Pearson's r is 0,8361. This number is very close to 1. However, there is relatively weak relationship between total assets to total liabilities ratio and cash flow to total debt ratio since the figure is 0,3185, which is quite low compared to other pairs. The possible reasons would be capricious of accounting measurement of the values of assets and accrual accounting. Thus, by analyzing the strength of relationship between cash flow ratios and traditional ratios, it can be concluded that these two types of ratios should be considered together to make better conclusion regarding the liquidity of a company.

Test of Hypotheses

Four hypotheses constructed in Chap. 1 are discussed here for statistical test. Pair *t*-tests are used to measure the differences between pair of means for a pair of selected companies. In this study, data are paired data since two measurements (i.e., classic ratios and cash flow ratios) are made on the same company. Classic ratios and cash flow ratios were calculated for the selected of companies, and pair *t*-tests were used to identify significant difference between these two types of ratios.

- Null hypothesis 1: There is no significant difference between current ratio and cash flow ratio.
- Alternate hypothesis 1: There is significant difference between current ratio and cash flow ratio.

From Table 8, it can be seen that probability, *p*-value, is less than 0,05. Therefore, null hypothesis can be rejected, and alternate hypothesis can be accepted. A two-tailed paired sample *t*-test revealed that there is significant difference between current ratio and cash flow ratio, $t\ (124) = 10{,}611, p \leq 0{,}05$. Table 3 shows that the mean of current ratio (2,2391) is higher than that of cash flow ratio (0,6418) which supports alternate hypothesis. Ninety-five percent confidence

Table 8 Paired samples test of current ratio and cash flow ratio

		Paired differences							
		Mean	Std. deviation	Std. error mean	95% confidence interval of the difference Lower	Upper	t	df	Sig. (two-tailed) mean
Pair 1	Current ratio–cash flow ratio	1,597	1,6194	0,1394	1,3217	1,873	10,61	124	0.00

Source: own analysis

Table 9 Paired samples test of quick ratio and critical needs cash coverage ratio

		Paired differences							
		Mean	Std. deviation	Std. error mean	95% confidence interval of the difference Lower	Upper	t	df	Sig. (two-tailed) mean
Pair 2	Quick assets ratio–critical needs cash coverage	1,143	1,437	0,123	0,898	1,388	8,556	124	0.00

Source: own analysis

interval values are given in Table 8, which means true population mean lies between 1,3217 and 1,8735 with a 95% probability.

- Null hypothesis 2: There is no significant difference between quick assets ratio and critical needs cash coverage ratio.
- Alternate hypothesis 2: There is significant difference between quick assets ratio and critical needs cash coverage ratio.

From Table 9, it can be seen that probability, p-value, is less than 0,05. Therefore, null hypothesis can be rejected and alternate hypothesis can be accepted. A two-tailed paired sample t-test revealed that there is significant difference between quick ratio and critical needs cash coverage ratio, $t\ (124) = 8{,}556$, $p \leq 0.05$. Table 4 shows that the mean of quick assets ratio (1,7932) is higher than that of critical needs cash coverage ratio (0,6502) which supports alternate hypothesis. Ninety-five percent confidence interval values are given in Table 9, which means true population mean lies between 0,898 and 1,388 with a 95% probability.

- Null hypothesis 3: There is no significant difference between total assets to total liabilities ratio and cash flow to total liabilities ratio.
- Alternate hypothesis 3: There is significant difference between total assets to total liabilities ratio and cash flow to total liabilities ratio.

Table 10 Paired samples test of total assets to total liabilities ratio and cash flow to total liabilities ratio

		Paired differences							
					95% confidence interval of the difference				
		Mean	Std. deviation	Std. error mean	Lower	Upper	t	df	Sig. (two-tailed) mean
Pair 3	TA to TL – CF to total debt ratio	2,8975	3,0462	0,2622	2,3789	3,4160	11.0510	124	0.000

Source: own analysis

Table 11 Paired samples test of interest coverage ratio and cash interest coverage ratio

		Paired differences							
					95% confidence interval of the difference				
		Mean	Std. deviation	Std. error mean	Lower	Upper	t	df	Sig. (two-tailed) mean
Pair 4	Interest cover–cash interest coverage	−25,71	138,98	11,96	49,37	−2,06	−2,15	124	0.00

Source: own analysis

From Table 10, it can be seen that probability, p-value, is less than 0,05. Therefore, null hypothesis can be rejected, and alternate hypothesis can be accepted. A two-tailed paired sample t-test revealed that there is significant difference between total assets to total liabilities ratio and cash flow to total liabilities ratio, t (124) = 11,0510, $p \leq 0{,}05$. Table 5 shows that the mean of total assets to total liabilities ratio (3,0160) is higher than that of cash flow to total liabilities ratio (0,3332) which supports alternate hypothesis. Ninety-five percent confidence interval values are given in Table 10, which means true population mean lies between 2,3789 and 3,4160 with a 95% probability.

- Null hypothesis 4: There is no significant difference between interest coverage ratio and cash interest coverage ratio.
- Alternate hypothesis 4: There is significant difference between interest coverage ratio and cash interest coverage ratio.

From Table 11, it can be observed that probability, p-value, is less than 0,05. Therefore, null hypothesis can be rejected, and alternate hypothesis can be accepted. A two-tailed paired sample t-test revealed that there is significant difference between interest coverage ratio and cash interest coverage ratio,

$t\ (124) = -2{,}15$, $p \leq 0{,}05$. Ninety-five confidence interval values are given in Table 11, which means true population mean lies between −49,3742 and −2,0577 with a 95% probability.

Conclusion

Cash flow ratios are undeniably important for both internal and external users since these ratios provide more reliable information about a company's ability to meet its payment obligations than do traditional ratios. The major benefit of cash flow ratios is that these ratios test what resources the company has generated to meet its payment commitments over a period of time. In contrast, classic ratios provide misleading information as these ratios indicate how much cash the company had available on single point of time. This study tested the use of cash flow ratios to measure liquidity by comparing with relevant traditional ratios. The empirical result showed statistical significant difference between these two types of ratios. In most cases cash flow ratios supported classic ratios by providing additional insight in this research. Therefore, it is recommended to use these two types of ratios simultaneously in order to make conclusion about a firm's financial strength or weakness.

Acknowledgments The paper has been prepared within the research project "theoretical approaches to optimize the capital structure" (supported by the Internal Grant System of the University of Economics in Prague no. IGA/48/2016).

References

Armen S (2013) Performance assessment of major U.S. airlines via cash flow ratios. Ann Univ Oradea Econ Sci Ser 22(2):398–408

Azadinamin A (2012) The bankruptcy of Lehman brothers: causes of failure & recommendations going forward. (Online). Social Science Research Network, New York, c2012. (Cited 31st January 2017). Retrieved from https://www.researchgate.net/publication/230687440_The_Bankruptcy_of_Lehman_Brothers_Causes_of_Failure_Recommendations_Going_Forward

CSE (2017) Classification of the Colombo stock exchange sectors. (Online). Colombo Stock Exchange, Colombo, c2012. (Cited 31st January 2017). Retrieved from https://www.cse.lk/home/CSESectors

Eyisi AS, Okpe II (2014) The impact of cash flow ratio on corporate performance. Res J Finance Account 5(6):149–158

Gombola MJ, Haskins ME, Ketz JE, Williams DD (1987) Cash flow in bankruptcy prediction. Financ Manag 16(4):55–65

Kirkham R (2012) Liquidity analysis using cash flow ratios and traditional ratios: the telecommunications sector in Australia. J New Bus Ideas Trends 10:1–13

Mills JR, Yamamura JH (1998) The power of cash flow ratios. J Account 186(4):53–61

Ryu K, Jang S (2004) Performance measurement through cash flow ratios and traditional ratios:a comparison of commercial and casino hotel companies. J Hosp Financ Manag 12(1):15–25

Searching for Today's Purpose of Remunerating Employee Inventions Through Grounded Theory

Pavel Svačina and Gabriela Antošová

Abstract Czech Republic and other European countries reward inventive employees by specific reward regulated usually by patent law. There is a controversy how much such a reward should be. The authors used grounded theory approach to discover the purpose of remunerating employee inventions today. Based on interactions of respondents with legal experience, we identify the interests of key stakeholders – employees, employers, and state. We explore and balance these interests and identify solid reasonableness of such a reward especially in enhancing the transfer of knowledge from employees to employers. Thus, we suggest employers, whose business is based on innovations, to implement a level of rewards that would be at least incentive for employees to pass inventive ideas to employers. The analysis is based on Czech and Slovak legal framework; however, the results are general in nature and can have implications in other countries as well.

Keywords Employee inventions • Remuneration • Reward • Intellectual property • Grounded theory

Introduction

In today's economic conditions, innovations are one of the main sources of competitive advantage (Lengnick-Hall 1992; Guan et al. 2006). Within various innovations, intangible assets like patented inventions, know-how, or trademarks are the most discussed (Rivette and Kline 2000; Lev 2001). Underlying ideas of the intangible asset originated mostly from the creativity of particular employees and their inventive activities; however, the owners of such assets are usually employers, because the major part of innovations are conceived as a part of employment duties, and employers claim these ideas through intellectual property law. According to WIPO (2016), 80–90% of patent applicants are organizations (corporations,

P. Svačina (✉) • G. Antošová
Department of Finance and Business Valuation, University of Economics in Prague, Náměstí Winstona Churchilla 4, 130 67 Praha 3, Czech Republic
e-mail: pavel.svacina@vse.cz; gabriela.antosova@vse.cz

D. Procházka (ed.), *The Impact of Globalization on International Finance and Accounting*, Springer Proceedings in Business and Economics,
https://doi.org/10.1007/978-3-319-68762-9_23

universities, research institutions), which is a rough estimate of share of inventions created through employee contract.

Such a large share of employee inventions with potentially high commercial impact on employers' business creates a tension and raises questions how to (or if at all) fairly distribute the contribution from such an invention ("employee invention") between an employee and employer. The patent law of European countries is based on the principle that employee inventions become the property of employers, ruling the obligation to pay employee inventors some reward. Many court proceedings have occurred recently in various countries (Wolk 2011), searching for an answer "How much such a reward should be?" Based on broader research project focused on defining a reasonable reward for employee inventions, in this particular paper, we suggest a complex answer on the main question, which we found important to answer before arguing a level of reasonable remuneration.

This research questions is "What is the purpose of rewarding employee inventions today?" To answer this question, we used grounded theory approach (Strauss and Corbin 1990; Glaser and Strauss 2009). Our results and conclusions are built on the interactions of respondents with legal background. We identified the interests of key stakeholders in the remuneration process – employee inventors, employers, and state/society. We explored and balanced these interests and identified solid reasonableness of such a reward, especially to enhance the transfer of knowledge from employees to employers. The analysis is based on Czech legal framework; however, the results are general in nature and can have implications in other countries as well. This paper is divided into the following chapters: Chap. 2 describes the legal framework for employee inventions and review of literature; Chap. 3 describes objectives, data, and methodology; Chap. 4 brings and discusses the main results; and Chap. 5 concludes the paper and identifies limitations of our research.

Employee Inventions

Employee Inventions in the Czech and Slovak Republic

The Czech legal framework for employee inventions is defined in the Patent Act,[1] par. 9–10, and the Slovak one in the Patent Act,[2] par. 11. Slovak employee invention regulation is basically the same as the Czech one; thus, in the following text, we cite only Czech regulatory framework.

The law says that in case the invention is created within the employee's duties, the invention can be assigned from employee to employer; only a special contract between them can solve it differently. Basically, the employer has an option to acquire such an invention, or give it up within 3 months, after he/she obtains

[1]Law No. 527/1990 on Inventions and Improvement Proposals.

[2]Law No. 435/2001 on Patents and Supplement Patent Certificates.

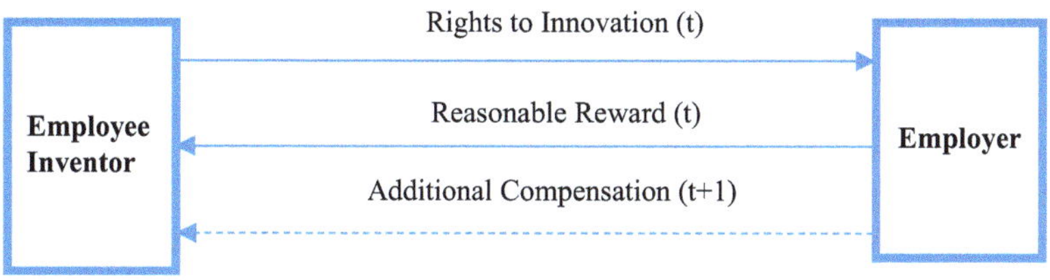

Fig. 1 Process of employee invention assignment and remuneration in the Czech and Slovak Republic (Source: Authorial scheme derived from Czech and Slovak patent law)

relevant materials from the employee. In case the employer uses this option, he/she must pay to the employee a reasonable reward (in time "t"). The Czech patent law also defines the factors which should be considered: technical and economic importance of the invention, income from using the invention, material share of the employer, and scope of work responsibilities of the employee. If the reward paid becomes visibly disproportional to the future income from the invention (in time "t + 1"), the employee should get a reasonable additional compensation. The overall principle of the assignment and remuneration process is described in Fig. 1.

Therefore, the employer in the Czech Republic must pay a specific reward to employee inventors. However, the law is very general about the level of the reward, indicating only general factors should be considered. How much is reasonable? An employer will generally advocate for a minimum amount; an employee inventor can claim a fortune. Several court proceedings in the Czech Republic have already occurred, and many of them end as a hidden conflict between both parties, which is our professional experience with Czech cases. So, should such a special reward exist, at all? Is there any important purpose?

Review of Literature

First, historically and actually, there is no doubt that the assignment process of employee inventions is generally reasonable (Merges 1999), because during the last century, the innovation process has become too complex, costly and risky to be widely driven by individual inventors with limited sources (Fisk 1998). But, secondly, we have no single answer, whether rewarding such employees is appropriate or not. Basically, two opposite legal systems exist: (i) American, which does not grant any specific reward to employee inventors as they should get overall monetary satisfaction in his/her regular salary, and (ii) Continental, which guarantees employees some reward, balancing in this way the transfer of rights from employee to inventor.

As for the continental tradition, even EU countries themselves differ within the compensation rules, on one side with German very employee-solidaristic system and with Great Britain's system on the other side remunerating only outstanding inventions (Peberdy and Strowel 2010). The conception of legal claim of employee inventors on remuneration dates back in the beginning of twentieth century in Germany; however, the specific law was adopted finally after the World War II (Burhop and Lübbers 2010). Some economists identified in this topic the principal-agent problem (Merges 1999; Kirstein and Will 2006; Burhop and Lübbers 2010), watching at employee inventors as agents hired by employers (principals), both with different interests. On this theoretical basics, the recent literature is oriented mostly on quantitative approach, searching for the level of correlation between monetary incentives (rewards) and level of output (number and quality of patents or out-licenses). This research occurs with data from the academic institutions (Friedman and Silberman 2003; Lach and Schankerman 2004, 2008; Link and Siegel 2005), as well as on the corporate data (Leptien 1995; Giummo 2010; Onishi 2013), and generally acknowledges a significant correlation of a reward and output in the US academic sector. The results from the corporate sector have been fragmented and unclear so far. Zirnstein et al. (2010) with their qualitative research paper advocate for a substantial effect of reward systems on spurring innovations.

Data and Methodology

In our underlying research project, we aim at construing a framework for estimating a reasonable reward for employee inventions in the Czech Republic; i.e., we are searching for defining a reasonable level of the reward that would balance the interests of all stakeholders at issue, especially employers and employees. Despite the existence of relevant scholarly papers, we have identified a lack of literature that would be grounded in the evidence from practice and that would offer a solid reason for a corporate, legal, or consultant sector, why the reward should be and what level is appropriate or reasonable. Thus, we approach the problem through the grounded theory searching for solid basis for reward level in the world of those who are stakeholders in this process. The presented paper focuses on a part of our research and explores a fundamental research question within the topic:

What is today's purpose for rewarding employee inventions?

Even if we focus our efforts on the Czech and Slovak regulatory framework, the results can be inspiring also in other countries with legally guaranteed employee invention reward.

We gathered our data through three separate focused groups (Creswell 2013; Eriksson and Kovalainen 2016) with overall 11 respondents during May and June 2016. All respondents were lawyers experienced in intellectual property law; three of them are judges of the Czech supreme court, three Czech and three Slovak legal attorneys with some experience on both employers' and employees' side, and one corporate intellectual property attorney of Czech big industrial corporation. One respondent had combined legal and valuation experience. Three team members were involved in focused groups as inquirers. Their professional roles are an economic sociologist, an academic lawyer, and a valuation consultant/academician. During the focused groups, the team members were offering questions on employee invention remuneration process based on the Czech patent law terms (reasonable reward, additional remuneration, disproportion of reward and income from invention, etc.). The respondents performed brainstorming and offered even various contradictory answers which needed deeper interpretation. Some of the participants recommended other respondents – "snowball sampling" (Biernacki and Waldorf 2016).

We finished with three focused groups as we did not reasonably expect substantially different answers by inquiring more professionals from the legal sphere. The interviews were conducted in the office of the Supreme Court in Prague, at the office of one Slovak law firm in Bratislava, and at the University of Economics in Prague. Semi-structured interviews and discussion were recorded. Average length of one focused group was 120 min. The respondents were free to respond and interact after a question has been raised. The following thematic questions were asked in each focused group:

1. Is it appropriate today to guarantee legally an employee inventor a reward for an employee invention?
2. Are internal organizational guidelines specifying the level of rewards for employee invention always legally binding?
3. How do you understand the term "reward" in this context?
4. How do you understand the term "income realized from using invention or by other means of commercialization?"
5. How do you understand legally defined circumstances at which the additional compensation should be paid to the employee inventor?
6. Could you compare the relationship between employee-inventor and employer to any other legally regulated relationships where a reasonable remuneration is the issue?

Digital recordings were transcribed by transcript F4, and the transcripts were processed in Atlas.ti software. In the first phase, we attributed open codes to individual quotations; in the second phase, we grouped and reformulated the codes into broader categories. As we had presented in this paper, only one is the finished part of the collected data, and we concentrated on identified categories around interim central category "purpose"[3] (see Fig. 2). Consequently, in this paper, we aim at searching for explaining an underlying usefulness of existence of such an employee invention legally enforceable reward, as it has to be logically one of the determinants of the level of such a reward. One of our respondents formulated this:

[3]The other identified main categories are "other countries' experience," "contextual factors," "Czech legal framework," "specific factors of remuneration process," and "economic rationality," all related to the central category "reasonable reward."

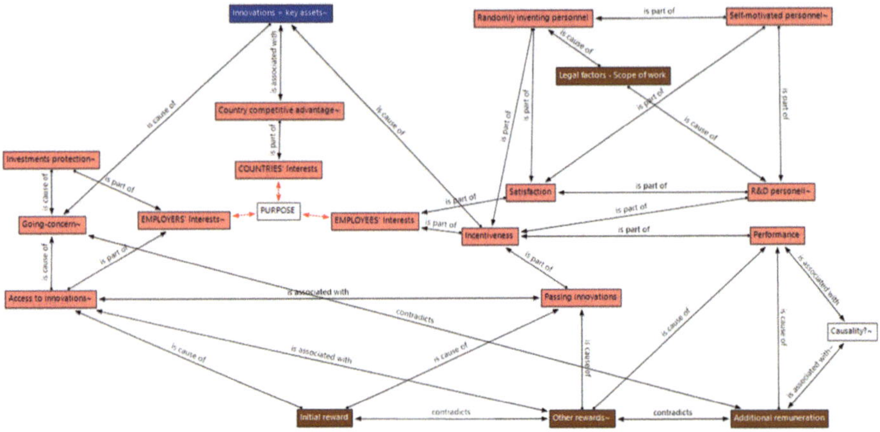

Fig. 2 Visual model: Purpose of remunerating employee inventions (Source: Authors' diagram derived from primary data acquired through focused groups and processed in Atlas.ti. Note: Dark codes are codes attributed primarily to other categories ("contextual factors" and "legal framework")

What is the purpose of the legal regulation? What and who do we want to protect and why?

The Results chapter is accompanied by relevant quotations from our respondents.

Results and Discussion

A structured scheme of our findings is presented in Fig. 2. The (interim) central category is "purpose," representing the possible reasonable objectives of employee inventions' regulatory rewarding in today's world. Around this key category, we identified three categories/subjects to whom the rewarding should serve:

- Employees' interests
- Employers' interests
- Countries' interests

Unlike the majority of papers that focus on motivational aspects of employees, during the discussion, we explored that the rewarding process and the level of reward should in some way reflect the interests of employees, employers, and the relevant country, all called stakeholders. The regulatory framework and reward should be both protective and stimulating for the creation of inventions and other innovations, as these are today one of the key sources of competitive advantage (Lev 2001).

Employees' Interests

For creative employees, today, it sounds logic to have some specific "income premium" in the form of better income or a specific, even regulatory, reward.

> *Today, there is a strong emphasis on experience and knowledge, creativity, individuality of a person; this makes a big difference.*

From the employees' perspective, the reward could be important for two main reasons:

- "Incentiveness" (code) – to motivate or stimulate employees for requested results
- "Satisfaction" (code) – to express appreciation ex post to an employee for achieved results

These are two codes of "employees' interests" in Fig. 2.

Incentiveness

The incentiveness of the reward can occur in two levels:

1. At the moment of passing data about the invention to the employer ("passing innovations" code), according to the Czech patent law, then the employer must decide in 3 months whether he/she assigns the idea or not.
2. For having stronger motivation in creative working ("performance" code), which can lead to higher numbers or higher quality innovations.

The majority of our respondents admitted the strong role of the reward, especially the initial reward paid after rights assignment ("initial reward" code) as a stimulator for passing new ideas from employees to employers:

> *For the employees it will finally worth passing in requested form the information about the invention, if they pay me something... I just fulfilled my work.*

The opinions about the performance effect of the reward were diverse, expressing the need for some solid proof about the causality of rewards and innovative output. Such an effect could be theoretically driven by the additional reward and paid in some circumstances later on ("additional remuneration" code). The review of literature discovered relatively solid proof of the correlation on US university data (Lach and Schankerman 2008); the research performed on the corporate data is more complicated and suggests various results (Leptien 1995) vs. (Onishi 2013). Moreover, the overall incentiveness effect can be theoretically "traded off" by other rewards paid for exceptional performance and regulated by labor law ("other rewards" code).

Satisfaction

The effect of satisfaction can work for creative employees without the strong incentiveness effect. From both focused group and the legal regulation text ("legal factors – scope of work" code), we can identify two main groups of employees according to their working competences:

- "R&D personnel" (code) – those who are paid for being innovative
- "Randomly inventing personnel" (code) – those who are paid for other works

However, both these groups can be mixed in perceiving incentiveness or satisfaction. We can firmly suppose that incentiveness will not work for "self-motivated personnel" (Lam 2011), which can be presented in both groups of employees. For those self-motivated, only satisfactory effect can be considered. As for R&D personnel, we can suppose that for many of them, a major portion of the incentiveness effect can be driven by relatively high salaries, and the reward would be connected with the satisfaction effect. On the other hand, randomly inventing employees will be probably motivated by their salaries to perform common work, feeling satisfaction in case of conceiving an invention as by-product of his/her common duties:

> *When you ask those corporations: Do you think your employee inventor invents that idea five years for getting five thousand Czech crowns at the end? Certainly not.*

Nevertheless, our evidence with respect to incentiveness and satisfactory effect is not strong due to the type of respondents. More research must be done in this context. Some researchers warn of high-performance stimulation, as high reward can motivate employees to seek for rewards through making inventions and neglect other duties that could be actually more valuable for employees (Merges 1999).

Employers' Interests

As mentioned above, to work properly in practice, an employee invention reward should be advantageous for employers as well. One big advantageous aspect is in the patent law already incorporated, i.e., the assignment of invention rights to employers. But, in case of extremely high reward, such an advantage would be traded off. From the responses, we identified one strong argument against commonly high reward, that is, "investment protection" (code). The employer is the main risk-taker in creating innovations and implementing them; thus, the level of reward should reflect the risk roles of both sides:

> *The responsibility of that investor. Shall he commercialize it or not? He puts large investments into it.*

On the other hand, not rewarding employee inventors, employers risk the fact that some valuable innovations will be kept by employees. Thus, "no reward policy" can block the access to internal innovations. "Access to innovations" (code) can threaten future competitiveness of employers. Consequently, both aspects of investment protection and access to innovations can question the going-concern principle of employers ("going-concern" code), especially in sectors based on innovations.

At this point, the need to process the exchange of information from employees to employers and the interests of both employees and employer meet, and a reasonable reward can play a significant role. Such an effect can be attributed especially to the "initial reward" defined by the patent law and paid immediately after the assignment process:

We must have a well-established system how to administer the transfer of knowledge from employees to employers. This is common in all normal countries, paying some reward – not for the expected income from that knowledge, but just for sharing that knowledge. What result occurs from that idea in the future, whether any invention, it shall be solved after...

Countries' Interests

The last stakeholder's (country's) interest is in today's economy in protecting or stimulating, among others, in some way the competitive advantage ("country competitive advantage" code) of the country (Sharif 1997). Such an advantage lies actually in many economic sectors more in intangibles (Lev 2001). So, to these quotations from our respondents, we attributed "innovations = key assets" code. By specific regulation of employee inventions, governments can contribute to the balancing of the interests between employers and employees. An extra benefit for the whole country can be in minimizing the litigation costs.

Conclusions

Based on the grounded theory approach and the focused group interaction of respondents, we identified key codes and categories necessary for suggesting an answer on a fundamental question in employee invention remuneration process:

What is a purpose of remunerating employee inventions today?

Answering this question helps us in our broader research project focused on building a framework for estimating a reasonable reward for employee inventions. We identified three main stakeholders in the remuneration process – employees, employers, and country – whose interests should correspond with the level of rewarding employee inventions. Our main findings suggest that an employee invention reward can have a substantial balancing role in the process of exchanging new ideas from employees to employers, who carry the main portion of risk and responsibility for creation and implementation of innovations in today's economy based on innovations. Consequently, a minimum reasonable reward for an employee invention should be at the level that stimulates employees to pass their new ideas to employers and to fulfill thus their legal duty. The question of the incentive effect on the higher employee performance was left open for our following research, as well as the identification of other key categories except for "purpose," analyzed in this paper. Our research is based primarily on Czech Republic legal framework; however, the results have general nature and are also transferrable to other European countries, especially to Slovak Republic which has basically the same legal framework.

Acknowledgments The article is processed as an output of a research project name of the project registered by the Grant Agency Czech Science Foundation under the registration number GA16-01383S.

References

Biernacki P, Waldorf D (2016) Snowball sampling: problems and techniques of chain referral sampling. Sociol Methods Res. https://doi.org/10.1177/004912418101000205

Burhop C, Lübbers T (2010) Incentives and innovation? R&D management in Germany's chemical and electrical engineering industries around 1900. Explor Econ Hist 47:100–111. https://doi.org/10.1016/j.eeh.2009.06.001

Creswell JW (2013) Qualitative inquiry and research design: choosing among five approaches, 3rd edn. Sage, Los Angeles

Eriksson P, Kovalainen A (2016) Qualitative methods in business research, 2nd edn. Sage, Los Angeles

Fisk C (1998) Removing the "fuel of interest" from the "fire of genius": law and the employee inventor, 1830–1930. Univ Chic Law Rev 65:1127–1198

Friedman J, Silberman J (2003) University technology transfer: do incentives, management, and location matter? J Technol Transf 28:17–30. https://doi.org/10.1023/A:1021674618658

Giummo J (2010) German employee inventors' compensation records: a window into the returns to patented inventions. Res Policy 39:969–984. https://doi.org/10.1016/j.respol.2010.04.004

Glaser BG, Strauss AL (2009) The discovery of grounded theory: strategies for qualitative research, 4. Paperback printing. Aldine, New Brunswick

Guan JC, Yam RCM, Mok CK, Ma N (2006) A study of the relationship between competitiveness and technological innovation capability based on DEA models. Eur J Oper Res 170:971–986. https://doi.org/10.1016/j.ejor.2004.07.054

Kirstein R, Will B (2006) Efficient compensation for employees' inventions. Eur J Law Econ 21:129–148. https://doi.org/10.1007/s10657-006-6646-1

Lach S, Schankerman M (2004) Royalty sharing and technology licensing in universities. J Eur Econ Assoc 2:252–264. https://doi.org/10.1162/154247604323067961

Lach S, Schankerman M (2008) Incentives and invention in universities. Rand J Econ 39:403–433

Lam A (2011) What motivates academic scientists to engage in research commercialization: "gold", "ribbon" or "puzzle"? Res Policy 40:1354–1368. https://doi.org/10.1016/j.respol.2011.09.002

Lengnick-Hall CA (1992) Innovation and competitive advantage: what we know and what we need to learn. J Manag 18:399–429. https://doi.org/10.1177/014920639201800209

Leptien C (1995) Incentives for employed inventors: an empirical analysis with special emphasis on the German law for employee's inventions. RD Manag 25:213–225. https://doi.org/10.1111/j.1467-9310.1995.tb00912.x
Lev B (2001) Intangibles: management, measurement, and reporting. Brookings Institution, Washington, D.C
Link AN, Siegel DS (2005) Generating science-based growth: an econometric analysis of the impact of organizational incentives on university–industry technology transfer. Eur J Finance 11:169–181. https://doi.org/10.1080/1351847042000254211
Merges RP (1999) The law and economics of employee inventions. Harv J Law Technol 13:1
Onishi K (2013) The effects of compensation plans for employee inventions on R&D productivity: new evidence from Japanese panel data. Res Policy 42:367–378. https://doi.org/10.1016/j.respol.2012.09.001
Peberdy M, Strowel A (2010) Employee's rights to compensation for inventions - a European perspective [WWW Document]. EU Life Sci. https://www.insideeulifesciences.com/2010/03/05/employees-rights-to-compensation-for-inventions-a-european-perspective/ (accessed 2.24.17)
Rivette KG, Kline D (2000) Rembrandts in the attic: unlocking the hidden value of patents. Harvard Business School Press, Boston
Sharif MN (1997) Technology strategy in developing countries: evolving from comparative to competitive advantage. Int J Technol Manag 14:309. https://doi.org/10.1504/IJTM.1997.001729
Strauss AL, Corbin JM (1990) Basics of qualitative research: grounded theory procedures and techniques. Sage, Newbury Park
WIPO (2016) Patent cooperation treaty yearly review. In: World intellect. prop. organ. http://www.wipo.int/edocs/pubdocs/en/wipo_pub_901_2016.pdf. Accessed 24 Feb 2017
Wolk S (2011) Employed inventors' remuneration: remuneration for employee inventors – is there a common European ground? Social Science Research Network, Rochester
Zirnstein E, Franca V, Ruzzier M (2010) Legal regulation of innovativeness can spur innovation efforts. In: European conference on innovation and entrepreneurship. Academic Conferences International Limited, Reading, pp 707–XIX

A Fiscal Demography: Toward Demographic Approach to Public Finance

Artur Walasik

Abstract This paper elucidates public finance on the coopetition model of fiscal policy. The mix of competition and cooperation finds the relation between democracy and market. The conjunction of democracy and market is society and its demography. This paper focuses on the field of public economics where a confluence of public finance and demography is investigated. It is coined a fiscal demography, which its primary goal is to discover demographic reason of fiscal processes and structures. This paper announces fiscal demography sensu stricto as the study restricted to nothing but the influence of demography on public finance and fiscal demography sensu *largo* where the impact of public finance on demography is added to the field of art. This paper drafts the scope of fiscal demography which considers four relations, respectively, between demographic structure and fiscal process, demographic structure and fiscal structure, demographic process and fiscal process, and demographic process and fiscal structure.

Keywords Fiscal demography • Society • Demography • Economics

Introduction

Juxtapose two main determinants of fiscal policy are provided by the state operating within the modern society: democracy (being a way to make political decisions by a society) and market (being a way a society produces new value). Both of them could operate less or more efficient. The efficiency of organization and functioning of market determine the level of the wealth distributed, thanks to the efficiency of organization and functioning of democracy. Nevertheless, taken into account that the level of tax revenues and the level of fiscal deficit are determined by market, it is useful to establish that both structure of tax and public expenditures are determined

A. Walasik (✉)
Department of Corporate Finance and Insurance, University of Economics in Katowice, ul. 1 Maja 50, 40-287 Katowice, Poland
e-mail: artur.walasik@ue.katowice.pl

D. Procházka (ed.), *The Impact of Globalization on International Finance and Accounting*, Springer Proceedings in Business and Economics,
https://doi.org/10.1007/978-3-319-68762-9_24

by politics. Hence the product of economy is the level of public finance available for the government, but democracy determines the structure of public finance. The efficiency of market depends on political decisions; it is easy to find that both taxes and public expenditures interfere with business. On the other side, the business cycles influence fiscal policy.

The study of fiscal activity of government forces to take into consideration the crucial relation between economy and policy and between market and democracy, respectively. Market and its failures determine how society is able to organize production by firms and distribution of wealth among households; democracy and its failures determine how the same society organizes allocation and redistribution of wealth provided by the government. Two canonical approaches could be introduced to explain the characteristics of such relations. The first one is based on the assumption that the government is in the opposition to economy and pursues to correct the results of economy. Fiscal policy seems to be the battlefield of the society being the set of citizens represented by democratic elected policymakers, and the same society treated as the set of individuals operated as the members of households and owners of firms. Hence, it is possible to name this relation as the competition model of fiscal policy. The second approach to investigate the conjunction of economy and democracy could be based on the conviction, or even belief, that it is possible to avoid conflict between the goal of individuals when operated on the market, and the goal of the same individuals voted in democratic process. This approach follows the cooperation model of fiscal policy. I suggest to elucidate public finance on the mixture of the canonical approaches and to provide the coopetition model of fiscal policy. The mix of competition and cooperation finds the relation between democracy and market more realistic as well as enhancing effectiveness. Tax structure being the end of political decisions should predict economics of taxation, and changes in public expenditure ought to be the results of fiscal policy interfering business activity. The level of tax revenues and public debt fails to be dependent of nothing but economy; democracy allows for many types of injunctions of policy-driven expectations into market process. The coopetition of economy and democracy creates the public finance. Two-folded investigation of modern fiscal policy (market and democracy) enters demographic approach to public finance, which develops demography as the crucial factor of fiscal activity of the government. Introducing demographic attributes of society frees the models of fiscal policy from being static and allows robustness to grow up of them.

The Essence of Fiscal Demography

A fiscal demography is the field of public economics art that investigates the fiscal consequences of demography. The essence of fiscal demography is to reveal the correlations taken place between demographic processes and fiscal structures as well as demographic structures and fiscal processes. The primary goal of fiscal demography is to discover the demographic reasons of fiscal processes and structures, for very example, Miller (2001). Fiscal demography treats the reverse, where *causa* is the fiscal phenomenon and *effectus* is the demographic one as supplementary field of investigation, for very example, Luci-Greulich and Thévenon (2014). The economics of demographic changes should focus on the demographic *causa* and the fiscal *effectus*. The politics of demographic change could find the influence of fiscal means on demography as the essence of field of political science.

Hence, it is worthy to differentiate fiscal demography sensu stricto as the study restricted to nothing but the influence of demography on public finance and fiscal demography sensu *largo* where the impact of public finance on demography is added to the field of art. Exposed differentiation between *effectus* and *causa* in relation to fiscal and demographic phenomena is well known for demographers, who teach demography as the study of human population which focuses among other fields on socioeconomic determinants and consequences of population change (Swanson and Siegel 2004: 1). It is easy to find that economic phenomenon could be taken into investigation as the determinant (*causa*) as well as the consequence (*effectus*), for a very comprehensive study: Cyrus Chu (1998). Fiscal demography focuses on the study of interrelation between fiscal and demographic phenomena. Hirschman and Tolnay (2005: 419) read multidisciplinary aspects of demography and find it could be both a freestanding field of art and a part of applied statistics as well as an area of specialization within separate discipline of science: economics, geography, anthropology, and sociology. But sociology is the first of them. Hence, if demography could be defined as the science that allows to study and predict social processes (demography as the part of sociology), and its domain is able to take into account the explanation and picture of society structures and their changes (demography as the part of applied statistics), then it is also possible to find demographic relation to economic phenomena, in particular being consequences of fiscal decision of the government. Thus, if we attempt to successfully seek for the answer for a question how society influences economy, it reveals the economics of demographic change, and complementary if we look for the final results of society for policy, it is great for extracting politics of demographic processes and structures.

The idea but not the method of fiscal demography is close to the political arithmetic, one of three reasons for demography as the study of population statistics suggested by Cox (1976: 1). Cox indicates that the first of them is the advancement of knowledge by introducing theories and testing them against demographic events. The second one is to provide information necessary for planning human needs. The last but not the least is the political arithmetic equals to enhance practice of the government, in particular the collection of tax revenues, the provision of public goods which meets social demand, etc. Originally a political arithmetic was coined by W. Petty, as the title of his opus magnum. Brewer (2003) stresses that Petty's concept was founded on introducing Baconian scientific method (the use of number, weight, and measure) to social and political issues.

The Scope of Fiscal Demography

Setting the stage for analysis of fiscal demography subject, it is useful to discuss the scope and method of public finance as well as the scope and method of demography. It could be expected that the fields of art being covered by fiscal demography are fiscal consequences of demography (in narrow sense) and demographic consequences of fiscal activity of the government (in wider sense). Very simply, the scope of the field of public finance is taxing and spending activities of the government; hence, Rosen (2004: 252) primarily locates public finance in economics as its branch that studies the taxing and spending activities of government. If the fundamental issues are related rather to the use of resources than to the use of public funds, it will be correct to name the field of financial activity of the government as public sector economics or public economics. For Tresch (2008: 4–5), a normative approach naturally divides into three main parts of the study of public sector: the public expenditure theory, the theory of taxation, and the theory of fiscal federalism. Consequently, inclusion of public finance in economics brings the methodological basis for study of public finance equals to the methods of mainstream economic theory; the role of welfare economics is principal for normative approach to public finance (Rosen 2005: 33–52). And, if to focus on normative framework of public finance, the methods of welfare economics will play a crucial role in the study of fiscal demography.

Taking into consideration the provided definition of fiscal demography, it would be convenient for further inquiries to state that demographic phenomena could be simply a structure of society (demographic structure) or social process reflecting in changes of demographic structure (demographic process). For demographic structure, the age pyramid of society could be the very best example; for demographic process, the most significant illustration could be the demographic transition process. Respectively, fiscal phenomena could be the structure of taxation, public expenditure, etc. (fiscal structure) or trajectories of taxation, public debt, etc. in time (fiscal process). Consequently, it is convenient to take into consideration the fiscal demography sensu stricto, founded on four canonical relations to discuss, respectively, between:

1. Demographic structure and fiscal process
2. Demographic structure and fiscal structure
3. Demographic process and fiscal process
4. Demographic process and fiscal structure

For each of the four canonical relations, a demographic phenomenon is a reason and a fiscal phenomenon is a consequence. Fiscal phenomena are well known for public economists, but demographic phenomena within *fiscal demography* induce the necessity to study.

Fiscal demography could be a part of a wider economic demography, where the study of the influence of demographic phenomena on business activity and household economics. An example of the macroeconomic demography could be the paper written by Cervellati and Sund (2011) where the consequences of such a phenomenon-like life expectancy increasing in the course of demographic transition for the entire economy are tested. The second perspective, the microeconomic demography, could be the seminal paper of Ando and Modigliani (1963) where life cycle hypothesis of household savings was introduced and its correction by Ando and Modigliani (1964). Further studies by Modigliani (1986) show macroeconomic wider involved into investigation of life cycle hypothesis. It shows the potential of fiscal demography as part of both microeconomics and macroeconomics analyses.

It is necessary to state that fiscal demography would differ far from the study of optimal taxation or welfare distribution in the manner provided by Apps and Rees (2009). They fruitfully attempt to enlarge the analysis of public economics in the universe of a single consumer/worker faces dividing time between market labor supply and leisure. For the sake of more general scholarship, it is made, thanks for bringing together the economics of multi-person households and extracted fields of public economics where generalization of standard model seems to be most relevant and important. But fiscal demography seeks the interaction between changes in demographic attributes of taxpayers, investors, or public spending beneficiaries and political-driven fiscal decision of government reflected in the level and structure of tax revenues, the dynamics and structure of public debt, or the distribution of public expenditures. Hence, fiscal demography could be the composition of public economics (taken from the point of view of public authorities) and household economics (takes into account the demographics of individuals, like their age, gender, etc.). The realm of fiscal demography could be compared to the themes of fiscal sociology, the term proposed by Goldscheid (1917). Fiscal sociology was the way to link sociology and public finance, because of the lack of social context taken into consideration within traditional theory of public finance and deficiency of sociological analysis of the state within sociology and political science (Shionoya 1997: 236). The problem soon was developed by Schumpeter (reproduced in Schwedberg 1991) to explore society from the perspective of public finance. Demographic shocks, like unexperienced earlier in history of population rapid progress in longevity, deserve attention to be Schumpeterian "those turning points," which legitimate the necessity for "fiscal demography." Fiscal demography may plausibly attempt to be the field of art "of which much may be expected," and like fiscal sociology round out economics (Musgrave 1992: 108), it is needed to complete public economics in shade of demographic processes.

Parallel to Schumpeterian study of fiscal sociology as the way to understand milestones in public finance reflected in its crisis, the Italian fiscal sociology started in 1920s, as development of Paretian economics and sociology. McLure (2005) analyzes works of two influential scholars, Benvenuto Griziotti and Guido Sensini, as well as their correspondence with Vilfredo Pareto. The first of them studied *la sociologia finanziara*, and the second investigated *la finanza sociologica*; the difference in name is crucial for the approach to relation between society and fiscal phenomena. For Griziotti the equilibrium within fiscal theory has to take into consideration the influence of fiscal phenomena (implemented, thanks to the work of political institutions) on social equilibrium. Hence fiscal phenomenon is *causa* when social issues are *effectus*. Sensini found two directions of interdependencies between fiscal and non-fiscal phenomena. McLure (2005: 621–622) states five categories of relation between fiscal phenomena and social equilibrium; in particular two of them identify non-fiscal *causa* and fiscal *effectus*. There are impact of circulation of governing elites on public finance and the effect of psychological influences on fiscal phenomena. Consequently, the domain of "fiscal sociology" of Sensini is closer to the scope of fiscal demography as the interpretation of the impact of demography on public finance. Contemporarily, Le Brun (2013: 11) finds fiscal sociology as the field of art which meets several disciplines concerned with the problem of relation between society and fiscal activity of state. Fiscal sociology arose as a fruitful conjunction of such a wide range of scientific disciplines which covers economic sociology, sociology of the state, anthropology, political science, fiscal law, public law, and even, if necessary, regional studies, social geography, and local economics. Very similar approach to the subject of fiscal demography is developed by Campell (1993: 164) who defines fiscal demography as sociological analysis of taxation and public finance, which differs from other approaches because it investigates how these things affect and are affected by a wide range of political, economic, cultural, institutional, and historical factors. Backhaus (2013: 357 *et passim*) reports the evolution of sociological aspects involved in analysis of public finance and manifests refreshment of fiscal sociology as a way to discover crucial for trustful relations between the society and government. He defines fiscal sociology essentially as a separate field which makes sense only once economics and sociology have parted ways, leaving a void between them (Backhaus 2004: 521; Backhaus 2002: 55).

Conclusion

Demographic phenomena implemented in "fiscal demography" induce the necessity to study more than the number of population, but essentially discuss the interdependency between fiscal activity of the government and behavior of different individuals, where the fiscal effects depend on the demographic characteristic of society as the set of these individuals. Hence, fiscal demography should pay attention to either the number of population (and studies per capita indexes) or the structure of population (and investigates structure indexes like dependency ratio). To sum up, in origin "fiscal demography" obliges to discuss how fiscal phenomena change if there are changes not restricted to the number of population, and the structure of population is taken into account. Contemporarily, the fundamental (organic) links between society and both economy and policy are the essence of market and democracy, respectively. In details, taken into account the systematization of fiscal activity of the government provided and introductory discussed in this paper, the structure of complex relations among society, economy, and policy should be provided for comprehensive study of fiscal demography.

References

Ando A, Modigliani F (1963) The "life cycle" hypothesis of savings: aggregate implications and tests. Am Econ Rev 53:55–84

Ando A, Modigliani F (1964) The "life cycle" hypothesis of savings: a correction. Am Econ Rev 54:111–113

Apps P, Rees R (2009) Public economics and the household. Cambridge University Press, Cambridge

Backhaus J (2002) Fiscal sociology: what for? Am J Econ Sociol 61:55–77

Backhaus JG (2004) Fiscal sociology: what for? In: Backhaus JG, Wagner RE (eds) Handbook of public finance. Kluwer, Boston, pp 521–541

Backhaus J (2013) Fiscal sociology and public choice. In: Backhaus J (ed) Essential of fiscal sociology: conception of an encyclopedia [Series: Finanzsoziologie, Bd. 5]. Peter Lang GmBH, Frankfurt am Main, pp 337–349

Brewer A (2003) Pre-classical economics in Britain. In: Samuels WJ, Biddle JE, Davis JB (eds) A companion to the history of economic thought. Blackwell, Malden. https://doi.org/10.1111/b.9780631225737.2003.00007.x

Campbell JL (1993) The state and fiscal sociology. Annu Rev Sociol 19:163–185

Cervellati M, Sund U (2011) Life expectancy and economic growth: the role of the demographic transition. J Econ Growth 16:99–133. https://doi.org/10.1007/s10887-011-9065-2

Cox PR (1976) Demography. Cambridge University Press, Cambridge

Cyrus Chu CY (1998) Population dynamics. A new economic approach. Oxford University Press, New York/Oxford

Goldscheid R (1917) Staatssozialismus oder Staatskapitalismus: ein finanzsoziologischer Beitrag zur Lösung des Staatsschuldenproblem. Anzengruber, Wien

Hirschman C, Tolnay SE (2005) Social demography. In: Poston DL, Micklin M (eds) Handbook of population. Kluwer/Plenum, New York/Boston/Dodrecht/London/Moscow, pp 419–449

Le Brun B (2013) Fiscal sociology: an innovative approach of citizenship and democracy design. In: Backhaus J (ed) Essential of fiscal sociology: conception of an encyclopedia [Series: Finanzsoziologie, Bd. 5]. Peter Lang GmBH, Frankfurt am Main, pp 11–14

Luci-Greulich A, Thévenon O (2014) Does economic advancement 'cause' a re-increase in fertility? An empirical analysis for OECD countries (1960–2007). Eur J Popul 30:187–221. https://doi.org/10.1007/s10680-013-9309-2

McLure M (2005) Equilibrium and Italian fiscal sociology: a reflection on the Pareto-Griziotti and Pareto-Sensini letters on fiscal theory. Eur J Hist Econ Thought 12:609–633

Miller T (2001) Increasing longevity and medicare expenditures. Demography 38:215–226. https://doi.org/10.1353/dem.2001.0018

Modigliani F (1986) Life cycle, individual thrift, and the wealth of nations. Am Econ Rev 76:297–313

Musgrave RA (1992) Schumpeter's crisis of tax state: an essay in fiscal sociology. J Evol Econ 2:89–113

Rosen HR (2004) Public finance. In: Rowley CK, Schneider F (eds) The encyclopedia of public choice, vol I. Kluwer, New York, pp 252–262

Rosen HS (2005) Very similar approach to the subject of fiscal demography is developed by Campell (1993: 164) who defines fiscal demography as sociological analysis Public Finance. McGraw-Hill/Irwin, New York

Schwedberg R (1991) In: Schumpeter JA (ed) The economics and sociology of capitalism. Princeton University Press, Princeton

Shionoya Y (1997) Schumpeter and the idea of social science: a metatheoretical study. Cambridge University Press, Cambridge

Swanson D, Siegel JS (2004) Introduction. In: Swanson D, Siegel JS (eds) The methods and materials of demography. Academic, Amsterdam/Boston, pp 1–8

Tresch RW (2008) Public sector economics. Palgrave Macmillan, New York

Spatial Concentration of Local Government Expenditure in the Czech Republic

Lucie Sedmihradská, Guner Tuncer, and Ersin Nail Sagdic

Abstract The aim of this paper is to analyze the spatial concentration of local government expenditure in the Czech Republic. Expenditure of the regions, municipalities, and voluntary municipal associations in 2003 and 2015 is analyzed using descriptive statistic, cartographic visualization, and Herfindahl–Hirschman index. According to the results, the differences in total local government expenditure per capita among the 14 regions decreased and in no functional area do the current or capital expenditure cluster in a small number of locations. On the other hand, existing differences in the expenditure structure provide arguments in favor of decentralized public investment.

Keywords Spatial concentration • Public expenditure • Herfindahl–Hirschman index

Introduction

There are many reasons for fiscal decentralization; however, the potential welfare gains from a more efficient allocation are the key economic reason. Local governments determine the levels of provided public services in accordance with local preferences, and "such differentiation in local outputs of public services promises gains in economic welfare relative to a centralized outcome involving more uniform levels of public outputs across jurisdictions" (Oates 2008). Therefore, it is to be expected that differences among individual jurisdictions result in differences in the volume and structure of public services provided by the respective local governments.

In the Czech Republic, there are 14 regions, i.e., NUTS 2 territorial units, which show substantial differences in numerous socioeconomic characteristics

L. Sedmihradská (✉)
University of Economics, Prague, Department of Public Finance, Nám. W. Churchilla 4, Praha 3, Czech Republic
e-mail: sedmih@vse.cz

G. Tuncer • E.N. Sagdic
Dumlupınar University, Kutahya, Department of Public Finance, Evliya Celebi Yerleskesi, Maliye Binasi, Kütahya, Turkey
e-mail: guner.tuncer@dpu.edu.tr; ersinnailsagdic@dpu.edu.tr

D. Procházka (ed.), *The Impact of Globalization on International Finance and Accounting*, Springer Proceedings in Business and Economics,
https://doi.org/10.1007/978-3-319-68762-9_25

(see Appendix). Viturka (2010) identifies the regions as the basic spatial unit for dealing with developmental disparities. Existing studies on regional disparities in the Czech Republic show that while they were relatively small at the beginning of the transformation process and are still low comparing to the other three Visegrad countries, they tend to grow (Tvrdoň and Skokan 2011). Maier and Franke (2015) claim the spatial economic disparities of the 1990s turned into spatial social polarization.

The purpose of this paper is to analyze the spatial concentration of local government expenditure in the Czech Republic. Expenditure of the regions, municipalities, and voluntary municipal associations (VMA) in 2003 and 2015 is analyzed using descriptive statistic, cartographic visualization, and Herfindahl–Hirschman index (HH).

The Czech Republic is a unitary state with two levels of local governments: regions (14) and municipalities (about 6250). Municipalities are the basic territorial self-governing communities. They were established in 1990 with the same boundaries as the previous local administrative units. Fourteen regions were established in 1997, the first regional government representatives were elected in November 2000, and the regional governments took office on January 1, 2001. Municipalities can form voluntary municipal associations for joint provision of public services or realization of investment or other activities. Currently there operate about 750 VMA.

Both regions and municipalities are public corporations acting sui juris in legal relations and are responsible for the results of these relations. They care for the general development of its territory and the needs of its citizens. Municipalities and regions operate independently of the central level of the government and of each other. While their revenue autonomy is quite limited, they have substantial autonomy regarding their expenditure. Generally, the autonomy is bigger in case of municipalities than regions.

Data and Methodology

Analyzed expenditure covers expenditure of municipalities, regions, and voluntary municipal associations located at the territory of the individual regions in 2003 and 2015. 2003 is the first year after the existence of 76 districts, i.e., deconcentrated branches of the national government, came to an end as a part of the public administration reform and since when the data are comparable.

The data source is the Ministry of Finance through its portals ARIS and Monitor of the Treasury. Current and capital expenditure are defined according to the economic budget classification: class 5 is current expenditure and class 6 is capital expenditure. All of the expenditure is included regardless its source of financing. Published budget data do not allow to distinguish expenditure financed through the grants from the EU funds. The function of the expenditure is defined according to the first or second level of the functional classification. We use 13 functional categories (Table 1).

The Herfindahl–Hirschman index (HH) which allows to measure concentration statistically has been developed by Albert Otto Hirschman (Hirschman 1945) and Orris

Table 1 Local government expenditure (Bil. CZK 2015)

Expenditures	Total LG expenditure		Share in total LG expenditure		
	CZK	Share	Municipalities	Regions	VMA
Education (31, 32)	111.8	26.1%	6.5%	19.6%	0.0%
Transportation (22)	54.4	12.7%	7.5%	5.2%	0.0%
Public administration (61, 62)	44.6	10.4%	9.3%	1.2%	0.0%
Culture and sport (33, 34)	21.9	5.1%	4.3%	0.8%	0.0%
Social protection (4)	18.6	4.3%	1.9%	2.5%	0.0%
Housing and communal services (36)	17.4	4.1%	3.9%	0.2%	0.0%
Environment (37)	17.2	4.0%	3.9%	0.1%	0.0%
Financial operations (63, 64)	9.2	2.1%	1.7%	0.3%	0.1%
Safety (5)	7.4	1.7%	1.7%	0.1%	0.0%
Health care (35)	6.4	1.5%	0.3%	1.1%	0.0%
Water management (23)	3.2	0.8%	0.7%	0.0%	0.1%
Agriculture (1)	1.7	0.4%	0.3%	0.0%	0.0%
Industry, trade, and services (21, 24, 25)	1.2	0.3%	0.2%	0.1%	0.0%
Capital expenditure	112.5	26.3%	18.2%	6.4%	1.7%
Total	427.4	100.0%	60.3%	37.7%	2.0%

Source: Monitor of the Treasury
Note: Codes of the functional budget classification are in parenthesis

Clemens Herfindahl (Herfindahl 1950) independently. The HH index is calculated by summing the squares of the percentage market shares held by the respective firms:

$$\mathrm{HH}_{1\ldots n} = \sum_{i=1}^{n} S_{i2} \tag{1}$$

where S_i represents the market share of firm i and there are n firms in the market. The maximum value of the index is one, and this value indicates the dominance of a single firm. The minimum value of the index is 1/n, and this value reflects that each firm has the same share (McCann 2007). In this study, we calculate the equation below to determine the concentration of public expenditure:

$$\begin{aligned}\mathrm{HH}_{\mathrm{F}_1} &= \sum_{R=1}^{m}\left(\frac{PE_{FR}}{PE_{FC}} - \frac{PE_R}{PE_C}\right)^2 \\ &= \left(\frac{PE_{FR_1}}{PE_{FC}} - \frac{PE_{R_1}}{PE_C}\right)^2 + \left(\frac{PE_{FR_2}}{PE_{FC}} - \frac{PE_{R_2}}{PE_C}\right)^2 + \ldots \left(\frac{PE_{FR_{14}}}{PE_{FC}} - \frac{PE_{R_{14}}}{PE_C}\right)^2 \end{aligned} \tag{2}$$

In the equation above, $\mathrm{HH_F}$ reflects spatial concentration index on functional basis; $\mathrm{PE_{FR}}$ reflects total public expenditure in R region for function F; $\mathrm{PE_{FC}}$ represents total public expenditure in country C for function F; $\mathrm{PE_R}$ stands for total public expenditure in region R; and $\mathrm{PE_C}$ is for total public expenditure in country C.

The Herfindahl–Hirschman index is used in various types of studies including the public sector. Kalseth and Rattso (1998), Borge (2000), Borge (2005), Borge and Naper (2006), Borge et al. (2008), or Sedmihradská and Bakoš (2016) use HH index for measuring political power – party fragmentation. Gyrogy (2012) uses HH index in order to assess the homogeneity of a social security system of Romania. Ozcan and Tuncer (2015) used HH for public expenditure period of 2004 and 2011 in Turkey.

Results and Discussion

The differences in the local governments in the per capita total expenditure among the individual regions decreased between 2003 and 2015. While in 2003, they ranged from 87 to 135% of the national average, in 2015 it was only 86 to 114%. The difference in the per capita expenditure in Prague comparing to the national average fell from 135 to 114%, and the number of regions above the national average grew from four to six (Fig. 1). The share of capital expenditure grew on average from 23.6 to 26.3. While there was a clear positive relationship between the per capita expenditure and the share of capital expenditure in 2003 (correlation coefficient 0.714), such a relationship did not exist in 2015 anymore (correlation coefficient 0.103).

The major reason for this development was the changes in the tax-sharing law as generally the revenue assignment is the key factor influencing the volume of local government expenditure. The changes in the tax-sharing formula in 2008 and 2013 reduced the revenue advantage of bigger municipalities and led to more equal revenue and hence expenditure in the individual regions. The grants from the EU funds to the local governments may have some impact as well, as the drawings in the individual regions differ substantially.

The spatial distribution of local governments' expenditure for the individual functions in Tables 2 and 3 shows the share of each function in total current or capital expenditure and the HH and the rank for the years 2003 and 2015. In case of

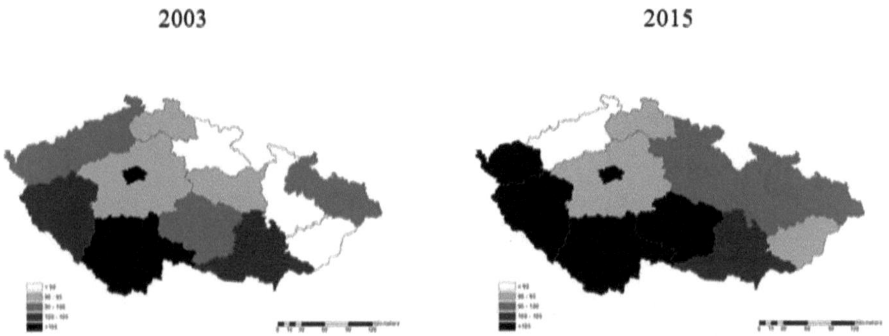

Fig. 1 Per capita local governments' expenditure (2003 and 2015, national average = 100) (Source: Monitor of the Treasury)

Table 2 Current expenditure

Function	Share in current expenditure 2003	2015	HH 2003	2015	Rank 2003	2015
Water management	0.9%	1.0%	0.0260	0.0333	4	1
Agriculture	0.4%	0.5%	0.0285	0.0332	3	2
Transportation	10.6%	17.3%	0.0784	0.0287	1	3
Safety	2.5%	2.4%	0.0327	0.0217	2	4
Industry, trade, and services	0.3%	0.4%	0.0079	0.0175	8	5
Housing and communal services	6.0%	5.5%	0.0027	0.0124	10	6
Financial operations	3.5%	2.9%	0.0134	0.0083	5	7
Health care	2.9%	2.0%	0.0097	0.0068	6	8
Culture and sport	5.0%	6.9%	0.0006	0.0028	13	9
Social protection	9.6%	5.9%	0.0090	0.0023	7	10
Education	42.2%	35.5%	0.0036	0.0014	9	11
Public administration	12.7%	14.2%	0.0008	0.0008	12	12
Environment	3.5%	5.4%	0.0020	0.0008	11	13

Table 3 Capital expenditure

Function	Share in capital expenditure 2003	2015	HH 2003	2015	Rank 2003	2015
Financial operations	1.80%	0.30%	0.2027	0.5411	1	1
Safety	1.30%	2.40%	0.0176	0.1512	9	2
Agriculture	0.30%	0.10%	0.0495	0.0418	5	3
Industry, trade, and services	0.50%	0.90%	0.1388	0.0282	2	4
Water management	14.30%	22.50%	0.0458	0.028	6	5
Social protection	4.30%	2.80%	0.0189	0.0171	8	6
Health care	6.10%	4.30%	0.0634	0.0169	4	7
Environment	2.70%	4.50%	0.0122	0.0132	10	8
Public administration	5.30%	4.00%	0.007	0.007	11	9
Culture and sport	8.00%	8.50%	0.0397	0.0065	7	10
Transportation	23.00%	26.10%	0.097	0.0064	3	11
Education	7.70%	12.30%	0.007	0.0047	12	12
Housing and communal services	24.70%	11.30%	0.0033	0.0032	13	13

current expenditure, the rank of the individual functions remained quite similar: the functions with the lowest HH, i.e., functions which distribution among the regions most closely mirrors the distribution of total current expenditure, are public administration and environment and in 2015 also education. On the other hand, the most diversified in both years are water management, agriculture, transportation, and safety. However, with the exception of transportation, these functions amount only to marginal share of total current expenditure.

Since the index value approaches zero for current expenditure, with the exception of financial operations which do not represent provision of public services or investment but are related to financial management of local governments, none of the functions seem to be systematically clustering.

The spatial concentration of capital expenditure is generally higher than in case of current expenditure. The rank of the functions changed more significantly than in case of the current expenditure. However in case of most functions, the index value is near zero; thus, there is no tendency to cluster in a small number of locations. On the other hand, HH index value of financial operations and safety expenditure in 2015 has increased, so we can imply that these capital expenditures tend to cluster in a small number of locations.

Comparing our results with Ozcan and Tuncer (2015) that used HH index for spatial concentration of public expenditure as well, they found housing and public welfare services expenditure had the highest spatial concentration in Turkey for the period of 2004–2011. In the periods of 2008, 2009, and 2010 affected by the 2008 global crisis, housing and public welfare services expenditure tended to cluster in a small number of locations and did not tend to cluster in a small number of locations in other years.

Conclusion

The distribution of public expenditure may vary in terms of regional and functional classifications. The differences can provide information about the policies favored by the local governments.

Despite regional differences and their tendency to growth local government, expenditures are surprisingly uniform across the country. Thanks to the changes in the tax-sharing formula and grants from the EU funds, the differences among the per capita local government expenditure in the individual regions decreased between 2003 and 2015.

Index results show that especially for current expenditure, since the value of HH indices are near zero for all functions, spatial distribution of current public expenditure nearly mirrors that of the urban hierarchy. A similar conclusion holds for capital expenditure as well. From this viewpoint, we can imply that the HH index of local government expenditure spatial concentration does not capture the degree to which a particular expenditure's spatial distribution reflects that of the national urban hierarchy. In other words, none of local government expenditures do tend to cluster in space or in a small number of locations with the exception of capital expenditure on security in 2015.

Our analysis at the same time showed that especially the functional investment structure differs among the regions reflecting local priorities. Therefore, it provides an argument against more centralized public investment.

Acknowledgments The contribution is processed as an output of the research project "public finance in the Czech Republic and EU" registered by the Internal Grant Agency of the University of Economics, Prague, under the registration number F1/1/2016.

Appendix

Table 4 Characteristics of the regions (2015)

Region	Population	GDP per capita (2014)	Average monthly gross wage	Share of unempl. persons	Incapacity for work	Pension recipients	Number of municipalities
		CZK	CZK	%	%	%	
PHA	1,262,507	829,168	33,852	4.20	3.12	24.40	1
STČ	1,320,721	369,335	26,527	5.41	4.09	25.41	1145
JHČ	637,292	343,817	24,006	5.07	4.77	27.77	623
PLK	575,665	384,101	25,574	4.62	4.57	27.87	501
KVK	298,506	276,941	22,750	7.06	4.38	26.81	132
ULK	823,381	309,564	23,934	8.91	4.34	27.79	354
LBK	439,152	315,209	24,685	6.36	4.45	27.94	215
HKK	551,270	356,040	24,030	4.96	4.05	28.99	448
PAK	516,247	327,545	23,673	5.14	4.26	28.30	451
VYS	509,507	334,994	23,977	6.22	4.54	28.68	704
JHM	1,173,563	397,233	25,718	7.01	4.05	27.74	673
OLK	635,094	314,478	23,483	7.01	4.28	27.66	399
ZLK	584,828	359,354	23,240	5.98	4.89	28.69	307
MSK	1,215,209	337,741	24,208	8.56	4.78	27.99	300
CR	10,542,942	404,843	26,467	6.24	4.06	27.26	6253

Source: Czech Statistical Office, own presentation

References

Borge LE (2000) Charging for public services: the case of utilities in Norwegian local governments. Reg Sci Urban Econ 30:703–718
Borge LE (2005) Strong politicians small deficits: evidence from Norwegian local governments. Eur J Polit Econ 21:325–344
Borge LE, Naper LR (2006) Efficiency potential and efficiency variation in Norwegian lower secondary schools. Public Financ Anal 62(2):221–249
Borge LE, Falch T, Tovmo P (2008) Public sector efficiency: the roles of political and budgetary institutions, fiscal capacity and democratic participation. Public Choice 136:475–795
Gyrogy A (2012) Social contributions in Romania. Rom J Fiscal Policy 3(2):7–26
Herfindahl OC (1950) Concentration in the steel industry. Dissertation Thesis, Columbia University
Hirschman AO (1945) National power and foreign trade. University of California Press, Berkeley
Kalseth J, Rattso J (1998) Political control of administrative spending: the case of local governments in Norway. Econ Polit 10(1):63–83
Maier K, Franke D (2015) Trendy Prostorové Sociálně-Ekonomické Polarizace v Česku 2001–2011. Sociol čas/Czech Sociol Rev 51(01):89–124
McCann P (2007) Urban and regional economics. Oxford University Press, New York
Oates WE (2008) On the evolution of fiscal federalism: theory and institutions. Natl Tax J 61 (2):313–334
Ozcan SE, Tuncer G (2015) Spatial concentration and regional diversification of public expenditure: the case of Turkey. Ömer Halisdemir Üniv İktisadi İdari Bilimler Fak Derg 8(1):185–198
Sedmihradská L, Bakoš E (2016) Municipal tax autonomy and tax mimicking in Czech municipalities. Lex Localis 14(1):75–92
Tvrdoň M, Skokan K (2011) Regional disparities and the ways of their measurement: the case of the visegrad four countries. Technol Econ Dev Econ 17(3):501–518
Viturka M (2010) Regionální Disparity a Jejich Hodnocení v Kontextu Regionální Politiky. Aust Geogr 115(2):131–143

Economic Voting in the 2006 Czech General Election

Ivana Tomankova

Abstract This paper investigates the occurrence and patterns of economic voting in the 2006 election for the Chamber of Deputies of the Parliament of the Czech Republic. I construct multinomial logit models which specify the log odds of electoral support for a given political party as function of the regional economic conditions faced by the voter, controlling for political and socioeconomic factors, and estimate these with opinion-survey data. The results provide evidence of unemployment-based economic voting: other things equal, a 1 percentage point rise in the unemployment rate in the voter's region increases their probability of voting for the leading incumbent socialist party on average by 0.8 percentage points and decreases their probability of voting for the Green party by 0.5 percentage points. Interestingly, these effects are driven by affluent voters. I conclude that the observed pattern of economic voting is most accurately described by the luxury goods voting model and, to some extent, the clientele hypothesis.

Keywords Economic voting • VP-function • Elections

Introduction

Understanding how citizens make their voting decisions is fundamental to our knowledge of how democracies function. The notion that economic outcomes affect the popularity of governments is empirically materialized in the VP-function, a term broadly used to refer to any model attempting to explain support for the government as a function of economic and political variables. Whereas vote functions employ data on electoral outcomes as a measure of government support, popularity functions rely on data from popularity polls.

VP-functions are commonly estimated with aggregate cross-country panel data or aggregate within-country time series. Some aspects of economic voting have

I. Tomankova (✉)
Department of Public Finance, University of Economics, Prague, Czech Republic
e-mail: xtomi00@vse.cz

D. Procházka (ed.), *The Impact of Globalization on International Finance and Accounting*, Springer Proceedings in Business and Economics,
https://doi.org/10.1007/978-3-319-68762-9_26

now been settled with near certainty or at least as much certainty as one may find in economic research anyway, while others – the function's instability in particular – continue to occupy researchers. Lewis-Beck and Paldam (2000) argue that little remains to be gained by refining macroeconomic VP-functions; to provide new insights, studies of economic voting must be brought down to the microlevel. I take their advice.

Exploiting a sociological micro-dataset from the Czech Social Science Data Archive, I analyze voting decisions in the 2006 election for the Deputies Chamber of the Parliament of the Czech Republic, looking for patterns of economic voting and relating them to the existing theories that attempt to explain its underlying workings. I do so by estimating sets of multinomial logit models. On the explanatory variables' side, I focus on objective measures of economic performance rather than individuals' perceptions of the economy.

The paper's value added lies in combining two less common approaches in economic voting research. First, microlevel VP-functions are scarce; one noteworthy exception being the work of Enkelmann (2013), who estimates a microlevel popularity function for Germany, but with voters' economic perceptions as explanatory variables. Second, I use (reported) electoral vote as the dependent variable. Some authors (Paldam and Nannestad 2000; Enkelmann 2013) argue that the common practice of using data from popularity polls as proxy for electoral outcomes due to the limited frequency of the latter may not be appropriate, as voters' motives when responding to popularity polls differ from the incentives and constraints they face during elections.

Theoretical Background

Economic voting refers to the general notion that the economic performance of governments affects their electoral outcomes. For quite some time, the term has essentially been synonymous to the responsibility hypothesis. When researchers estimated vote and popularity functions, they were testing whether voters punish governments for bad economic outcomes and reward them for good ones. The estimates of these VP-functions have turned out to be highly volatile (Lewis-Beck and Paldam 2000), which has led some researchers to pinpoint the institutional conditions under which voters are found to reward and punish governments based on their economic performance. A number of limiting factors have been identified, including insufficient knowledge or inaccurate perceptions of the economy (Nadeau et al. 2011), difficult or incorrect attribution of responsibility (Lewis-Beck and Paldam 2000), lack of credible opposition (Sanders 1999), and low salience of economic issues (Singer 2011). Other researchers have responded to the instability of the VP-function by proposing new theories. Kayser and Grafström (2016) offer a concise overview of the alternative theories of partisan economic voting.

The *clientele hypothesis* pertains to microlevel egotropic voting and postulates that voters support the political party which they see as best advancing their self-interest. The *issue ownership hypothesis* begins by noting that parties "own" certain social and political issues, in the sense that they have long-standing records for focusing on and successfully dealing with those issues, and then goes on to suggest that when the economy weakens, voters turn to the party most associated with general economic competence. The *class interests' hypothesis* has citizens making their voting decisions on the grounds of expected tax policies. It predicts that amidst a faltering economy, wealthier population groups will vote against parties with strong redistribution programs in fear of tax increases. Finally, the *luxury goods model* classifies government policies as material or post-material goods. During economic downturns, voters demand fewer post-material goods (such as environment protection, support for human rights, arts funding) and more material goods (unemployment insurance, tax relief), resulting in weaker electoral support for parties associated with post-material goods.

So far, research on economic voting has established that economic voting concerns few macroeconomic variables, most commonly unemployment or economic growth and inflation and that voters have limited time horizons, taking into consideration only events of the past year or so (Paldam 2004).

Data and Methodology

Models of economic voting are usually estimated with cross-country panel data or single-country time series. If, however, one wishes to analyze this phenomenon specifically for the Czech Republic, one must forgo the benefit of such datasets. Due to the economic transition, which continued until the late 1990s, and the persisting fragmentation and instability of governments, nearly all general elections have had their suitability for the testing of economic voting theories compromised by institutional circumstances. The 2006 general election for the Chamber of Deputies appears to be an exception in this regard.

The dataset I use is an opinion survey from June 2006, available from the Czech Sociological Data Archive. The regional identifiers contained therein enable me to match individual survey responses with measures of objective economic conditions in the respondents' respective regions.[1] The result is a sociological micro-dataset supplemented by economic macro-data from the Czech Statistical Office. It is interesting to note that out of the 2002 survey respondents, 43 percentage believed that governments generally had a lot of influence over the economy and 37 percentage

[1]Models of economic voting may be based on objective economic indicators or subjective perceptions. The former have the advantage of being exogenous and the latter of affecting government popularity without any lags (Kayser and Grafström 2016).

Table 1 Variables' definitions

Variable name	Definition
Age_i	Age of individual i
$Econact_i$	Binary variable equal to one if individual i is economically active
$Educ2_i/educ3_i$	Binary variable equal to one if individual i completed secondary/tertiary education; elementary education is the reference category
GDP_i	Nominal GDP in individual i's region in 2005, in millions CZK
$Goveval_i$	Individual i's evaluation of the work of the government over the past term from 1 (very bad) to 4 (very good)
$Left_i/right_i$	Binary variable equal to one if individual i places himself on the left/right of the political spectrum; the center is the reference category
$Livstd_i$	Self-reported household living standards of individual i from 1 (very bad) to 5 (very good); used as a proxy for household income
$Married_i$	Binary variable equal to one if individual i is married
Sex_i	Binary variable equal to one if individual i is female
U_i	General unemployment rate in individual i's region in 2005, in percent
$Uspells_i$	Binary variable equal to one if individual i experienced at least one spell of involuntary unemployment since 1989; a proxy for whether individual i is threatened by unemployment on a personal level
$Vote_i$	Unordered categorical variable identifying the party individual i reported voting for in the 2006 general election

considered this influence medium, 11 percentage small, and 3 percentage nonexistent. These beliefs facilitate economic voting, since one could hardly expect voters to base their electoral decisions on the economy if they regarded the government as powerless in this domain.

To test for the effects of economic voting, I construct sets of models, which specify the log odds of an individual's vote for a given party as function of the economic conditions in his/her region, controlling for political and socioeconomic factors. Table 1 defines the variables.

The data sample used for estimation is limited to respondents who provide a valid response to the survey question about their recent electoral choice, which is observable only for those who took part in the election. For the purposes of testing voting theories, I deem the investigation of the population of voters adequate; in other words, I do not aim to generalize the results to the general citizenry.

Hypotheses for testing theories of economic voting must acknowledge the partisan background of Czech politics. The two dominant parties on the political scene are the left-wing CSSD and the right-wing ODS. By common knowledge, the CSSD's program is built around social security, while the ODS markets itself as promoting the competitive market environment. According to the 2006 survey, the CSSD was seen as the one party best capable of tackling healthcare and unemployment issues, while the ODS was perceived as apt for dealing with corruption, the budget, taxation, and the economy in general.

I begin by estimating the common version of the VP-function with *GDP* and *U* as the variables of interest[2] and political as well as socioeconomic variables as controls:

$$\ln\frac{P(vote_i = m)}{P(vote_i = ODS)} = \alpha_m + \beta_{m1}GDP_i + \beta_{m2}U_i + \beta_{m3}goveval_i + \beta_{m4}left_i + \beta_{m5}right_i + \beta_{m6}livstd_i + \beta_{m7}educ2_i + \beta_{m8}educ3_i + \beta_{m9}econact_i + \beta_{m10}married_i + \beta_{m11}age_i + \beta_{m12}sex_i \quad (1)$$

In this multinomial logit model, *m* denotes a specific political party with over 5 percentage of the votes cast in 2006, i.e., either the socially democratic CSSD party, which was the leading party in the incumbent coalition government; the civic democratic ODS party, which eventually won the 2006 election; the communist KSCM party; the KDU-CSL, one of the two smaller incumbent coalition partners; or the Green party (SZ). All remaining parties are grouped under "other." The ODS is selected as the base category.[3]

Model 1 is relevant to the responsibility hypothesis (H1), the notion of issue ownership (H2, H3), as well as to luxury goods voting (H4, H5). Table 2 presents the expected partial effects of economic variables under each theory.

The test for the clientele hypothesis (H6) relies on the assumption that the reaction to changes in unemployment should be more pronounced for individuals threatened by it on a personal level. To allow for such differing effects, I add the variable *uspells* and the interaction term $U \times uspells$ to Model 1, thus creating Model 2:

$$\ln\frac{P(vote_i = m)}{P(vote_i = ODS)} = \alpha_m + \beta_{m0}uspells_i + \beta_{m1}GDP_i + \beta_{m2}U_i + \beta_{m3}U_i \times uspells_i + \beta_{m4}goveval_i + \beta_{m5}left_i + \beta_{m6}right_i + \beta_{m7}livstd_i + \beta_{m8}educ2_i + \beta_{m9}educ3_i + \beta_{m10}econact_i + \beta_{m11}married_i + \beta_{m12}age_i + \beta_{m13}sex_i \quad (2)$$

To test for class interests (H7), I introduce interaction terms that allow for different responsiveness of those with high household living standards (relative to those with middle or low ones). For this purpose, I recode *livstd* as a dummy variable *livstd_high*, which equals one for respondents who indicate "very good" or "rather good" living standards. The resulting Model 3 is similar to Model 1, but contains additional terms of interest, namely, *livstd_high*, $GDP \times livstd\_high$, and $U \times livstd\_high$; the variable *uspells* is included to prevent biased estimates:

[2] Inflation, too, is commonly found as an explanatory variable in models of economic voting. Unfortunately, regional inflation indicators are unavailable.

[3] The reader may find a description of the multinomial logit in Stata (2015). Its application to vote choices in a multiparty political system is provided by Doyle and Fidrmuc (2003).

Table 2 Hypotheses and expected partial effects

Hypothesis		Expected partial effects of economic variables
Responsibility hypothesis	H1	If voters reward the incumbent party for good economic outcomes and punish it for bad ones, GDP should be positively and unemployment negatively related to electoral support for the CSSD party
Issue ownership	H2	As the CSSD "owns" unemployment, higher unemployment rate should be positively related to its electoral support
	H3	As the ODS "owns" general economic management – although not as distinctly as the CSSD "owns" unemployment – voters should turn to it under conditions of low GDP
Luxury goods voting	H4	Given that the CSSD is associated with the material good of social protection, its electoral support should grow when the economy falters (as a result of voters' increased demand for social protection)
	H5	Electoral support for the Green party (SZ) should decline with tougher economic conditions as a result of voters' decreased demand for the post-material good of environment protection
Clientele hypothesis	H6	If individuals vote in their self-interest, those personally threatened by unemployment should show greater support for the socialist CSSD party (relative to those not threatened) by greater sensitivity to changes in the unemployment rate
Class interests	H7	If higher classes fear tax increases during economic downturns, individuals with high living standards (i.e. high income) should, under unfavorable economic conditions, vote more strongly against the CSSD, which is associated with greater income redistribution

$$
\begin{aligned}
\ln \frac{P(vote_i = m)}{P(vote_i = ODS)} = {} & \alpha_m + \beta_{m0} livstd\_high_i + \beta_{m1} GDP_i + \beta_{m2} GDP_i \\
& \times livstd\_high_i + \beta_{m3} U_i + \beta_{m4} U_i \times livstd\_high_i \\
& + \beta_{m5} goveval_i + \beta_{m6} left_i + \beta_{m7} right_i + \beta_{m8} educ2_i \\
& + \beta_{m9} educ3_i + \beta_{m10} econact_i + \beta_{m11} married_i \\
& + \beta_{m12} age_i + \beta_{m13} sex_i + \beta_{m14} uspells_i
\end{aligned} \tag{3}
$$

Results

Because multinomial logit coefficients have no direct interpretation, I choose not to report their estimates here. Instead, Table 3 presents the average marginal effects of unemployment and GDP estimated in Model 1.[4]

[4]Standard errors are heteroscedasticity consistent. Diagnostic tests show that the effects of *goveval, left, right,* and *age* are statistically significant at 1 percentage in determining vote choice among different political parties, while the effects of *U* and *livstd* are significant at 5 percentage. The remaining variables (*GDP*, *educ2*/*educ3*, *econact, married,* and *sex*) are insignificant at conventional levels. A Wald test for combining alternatives indicates that the outcomes (political parties) are distinguishable and should not be combined, while tests for the independence of irrelevant alternatives produce mixed results. The model McFadden R2 is 0.381.

Table 3 Average marginal effects of economic variables (Model 1)

Party	Average marginal effect of unemployment	Average marginal effect of GDP
CSSD	0.008***	$3.9 \cdot 10^{-8}$
ODS	$-7 \cdot 10^{-5}$	$8.8 \cdot 10^{-9}$
SZ	−0.005**	$-2.7 \cdot 10^{-8}$
KSCM	0.001	$-1.6 \cdot 10^{-8}$
KDU-CSL	−0.002	$-4.5 \cdot 10^{-8}$
Other	−0.002	$4.0 \cdot 10^{-8}$

Source: Czech Social Science Data Archive, Czech Statistical Office + authorial computation
Note: n = 1164; *p-value <0.1, **p-value < 0.05, ***p-value < 0.01

The average marginal effect of the unemployment rate is statistically significant for two parties, the CSSD and the Green party. On average, voters from regions with higher unemployment are more likely to vote for the CSSD and less likely to vote for the Green party. The magnitude of the effect is negligible: a 1 percentage point increase in the 2005 unemployment rate in the voter's region raises the probability that they vote for the CSSD by 0.8 percentage points, simultaneously lowering the probability that they vote for the Green party by 0.5 percentage points. The average marginal effect of GDP is insignificant for all parties; and this is true in the other models as well. When voting on the economy, voters react first and foremost to unemployment, an observation that is in line with the existing literature.[5] For this reason, in the models that follow, I focus solely on the effects of unemployment.

Figure 1 plots the predicted probabilities for the CSSD, the ODS, and the Green party along with their 95 percentage confidence intervals with respect to the approximate range of unemployment rate values encountered in the sample. The slopes correspond to the marginal effects reported in Table 3.

The positive relationship between unemployment and the probability of voting for the incumbent CSSD party contradicts the prediction of the responsibility hypothesis (H1) but supports the notions of both issue ownership (H2) and luxury goods voting (H4). Hypotheses H3 and H5 offer a further possibility to differentiate between the two. Unfortunately, the insignificant influence of GDP across all parties renders the result for H3 inconclusive. By comparison, the significantly negative influence of unemployment on the probability of voting for the Green party provides evidence in support of luxury goods voting (H5). The weak point of the analysis is that to the extent to which there are voters who give up their vote for the Green party to vote for the CSSD, the marginal effect for the Green party reported in Table 3 would also include voters acting in line with the issue ownership hypothesis. In other words, because the CSSD provides a material good as well as owns unemployment, the extra votes it receives due to higher unemployment may

[5]Paldam and Nannestad (2000) find that unemployment is the one macroeconomic quantity voters are best informed about.

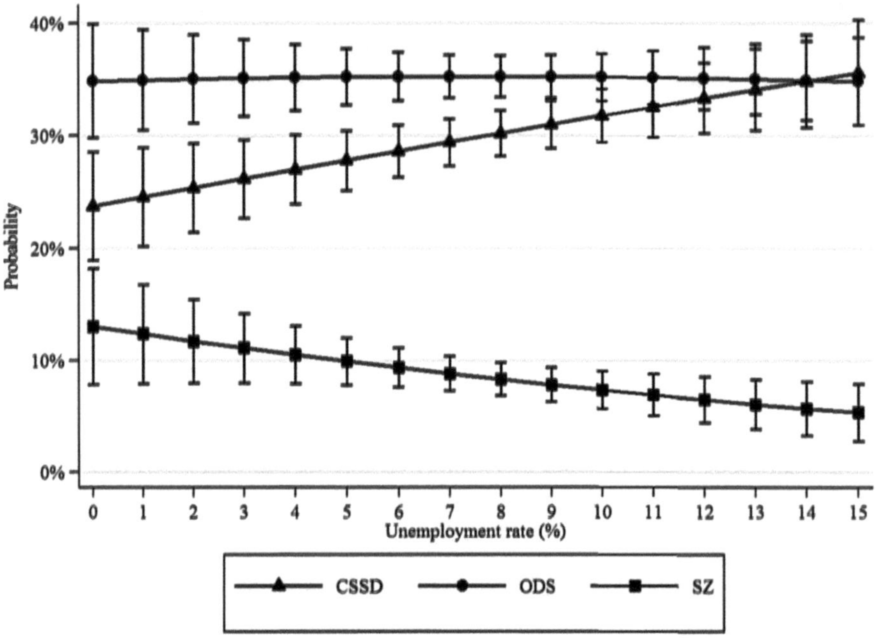

Fig. 1 Predicted probabilities for selected political parties (Model 1)
Source: Czech Social Science Data Archive, Czech Statistical Office + authorial computation

be attributed to either of the two notions. Luckily, some additional insight may be gleaned from looking at vote switchers. A difference of means test indicates that the unemployment rates faced by those remaining loyal to the CSSD between 2002 and 2006 and those abandoning it do not differ significantly: it appears that those who stuck with the CSSD did not do so because they needed it to resolve (higher) unemployment. Zooming in on those who abandoned the incumbent party, one sees that the unemployment rate faced by those turning to the Green party (6.2 percentage) was significantly lower than that faced by those supporting some other party (8.8 percentage). These observations favor luxury goods voting over issue ownership.

Table 4 presents yet another way to look at the results of Model 1. It lists all statistically significant pair-wise comparisons of the coefficient estimate on the unemployment rate. For example, the first row indicates that an increase in the unemployment rate raises the probability of voting for the CSSD relative to the ODS. It follows, logically, that the very same increase lowers the probability of voting for the ODS relative to the CSSD. If the pair of political parties is not shown in Table 4, then unemployment does not significantly alter their relative probabilities.

There is a clear (positive) link between unemployment and electoral support for left-wing parties. Voters from regions with higher unemployment are significantly

Table 4 Comparison of coefficient estimates between parties (Model 1)

Outcome comparison	Coefficient estimate on unemployment	*P*-value
CSSD vs. ODS	0.079	0.022
CSSD vs. SZ	0.132	0.001
CSSD vs. KDU-CSL	0.083	0.031
CSSD vs. other	0.099	0.040
KSCM vs. SZ	0.113	0.016

Source: Czech Social Science Data Archive, Czech Statistical Office + authorial computation

Table 5 Average marginal effects of unemployment (Model 2 and 3)

Average marginal effect of unemployment for				
	Voters w/ personal U threat (n = 186)	Voters w/o personal U threat (n = 885)	Voters w/high living standards (n = 458)	Voters w/o high living standards (n = 613)
CSSD	0.010	0.007*	0.012**	0.004
ODS	−0.011*	0.001	−0.002	−0.001
SZ	0.002	−0.005*	−0.005*	−0.002
KSCM	0.001	0.001	$5 \cdot 10^{-4}$	0.001
KDU-CSL	$-1 \cdot 10^{-5}$	−0.001	−0.004	0.002
Other	−0.002	−0.002	−0.003	−0.004

Source: Czech Social Science Data Archive, Czech Statistical Office + authorial computation
Note: n = 1071; *p-value <0.1, **p-value <0.05, ***p-value <0.01

more likely to vote for the CSSD relative to the ODS, the Green party, the KDU-CSL, or the remaining parties; they are also more likely to vote for the communist party in comparison to the Green party. This resembles the results of Doyle and Fidrmuc (2003) who find that between 1990 and 1998 Czech voters in areas with high unemployment demonstrated greater support for left-wing parties (at that time in opposition). It also brings to mind the article by Kayser and Grafström (2016), which shows that left governments are punished more for economic downturns (relative to right governments) because they provide post-material goods. Here, it is the left parties that gain from unfavorable economic conditions. The cause of this difference is that in Kayser and Grafström (2016), left parties provide post-material goods, while in the Czech context, they offer material goods. However, the mechanism driving the loss/gain of electoral support appears to be luxury goods voting in both papers.

Table 5 shows the marginal effects estimated in Models 2 and 3. Model 2 was intended to test the clientele hypothesis (H6). There is some indication that the probability of voting for the ODS party decreases in response to growing unemployment relatively more for voters who are personally threatened by it (i.e., voters with previous involuntary unemployment experience) than for those not threatened, but it is not clear which party the voters are turning to instead. Nonetheless, judging by the magnitudes of the marginal effects for threatened voters, the CSSD would be a reasonably good guess as the marginal effects would just about compensate. Therefore, I do not reject the clientele hypothesis, although the evidence for it is far from persuasive. Note that the results for non-threatened voters closely resemble those of Model 1. It appears that luxury goods voting is driven by voters with no prior experience of involuntary unemployment.

Model 3 tested the class interests' hypothesis (H7). Its results provide no evidence of affluent voters turning away from the CSSD under conditions of high unemployment. However, once again, the results for voters with high living standards closely resemble those of Model 1, suggesting that economic voting on the unemployment rate is driven by affluent voters.

Overall, the analysis yields consistent support in favor of economic voting occurrence (with respect to the unemployment rate) in the 2006 general election. Its mechanism, best attributed to the luxury goods model, appears to be driven by voters who are better off in terms of living standards as well as experienced unemployment. It could be that these voters are better informed about the state of the economy, and as a result, their voting preferences reflect economic conditions more accurately. Or, due to the relatively generous social security system in place, better-off voters face relatively larger income fluctuations in response to changing economic conditions than the rest, which lead them, in pursuit of their self-interest, to base their voting choices on economic circumstances to a greater extent.

Conclusion

This paper uses opinion survey data matched with regional macroeconomic statistics on gross domestic product and unemployment to determine whether economic voting was present in the 2006 election for the Chamber of Deputies of the Czech Republic, and, if so, which of the theories of economic voting most accurately describe its effects.

Results show that voters from regions with higher unemployment rates are, on average and other things equal, more likely to vote for the CSSD and less likely to vote for the Green party; the average marginal effects are some +0.8 and −0.5 percentage points, respectively. When voting on the economy, voters reflect upon unemployment only. I find no sound evidence that gross domestic product, too, would enter into their electoral decision-making.

Which economic voting theory do these observations favor? The positive effect of unemployment on the probability of voting for the incumbent party runs counter to the responsibility hypothesis. I also reject the class hypothesis since, contrary to its predictions, affluent voters show increased support for the left-wing CSSD party at higher levels of unemployment. Issue ownership is initially in line with the positive effect of unemployment on electoral support for the CSSD; however, its second test is inconclusive and a set of difference of means tests for voters who ceased voting for the CSSD between 2002 and 2006 offers comparatively more credibility to the luxury goods model of economic voting. Thus, it is the luxury goods model that receives the most empirical support: under conditions of high unemployment, voters are more likely to vote for the CSSD (and the political left in general), which offers social protection, a material good, and less likely to vote for the Green party associated with environment protection, a post-material good. The more pronounced responsiveness of affluent voters to the unemployment rate may be rationalized either by different levels of knowledge about the state of the economy or by larger (potential) drops in income under unfavorable economic conditions, the latter being in line with the clientele hypothesis.

The reader is invited to keep in mind that these results stem from one particular election; thus, further investigation is required prior to any generalization. Also, the models estimated employ electoral support and objective economic indicators. If one were to perform the analysis with measures from popularity polls or subjective perceptions, conclusions might differ.

Acknowledgments The article is processed as an output of the research project "Public finance in the Czech Republic and the EU" registered by the Internal Grant Agency of University of Economics, Prague, under the registration number F1/1/2016. The author thanks Jan Zouhar and Jan Pavel for their advice and helpful comments.

References

Doyle O, Fidrmuc J (2003) Anatomy of voting behaviour and attitudes during post-communist transition Czech Republic 1990–98. Disc. Pap. 3801, Centre for Economic Policy Research

Enkelmann S (2013) Government popularity and the economy: first evidence from German micro data. Working Paper No 274, University of Lüneburg

Kayser MA, Grafström C (2016) The luxury goods vote: why left governments are punished more for economic downturns. Working Paper. https://doi.org/10.13140/RG.2.2.24409.31841

Lewis-Beck MS, Paldam M (2000) Economic voting: an introduction. Elect Stud 19:113–121

Nadeau R, Lewis-Beck MS, Bélanger É (2011) Economics and elections revisited. 6th European consortium for political research general conference University of Iceland, Reykjavik, 24–27th August 2011

Paldam M (2004) Are vote and popularity functions economically correct? In: Rawley CK, Schneider F (eds) The encyclopedia of public choice. Kluwer Academic Publishers, New York, pp 49–57

Paldam M, Nannestad P (2000) What do voters know about the economy?: a study of Danish data, 1990–1993. Elect Stud 19(2):363–391. https://doi.org/10.1016/S0261-3794(99)00057-8

Sanders D (1999) The real economy and the perceived economy in popularity functions: How much do voters need to know? A study of British data, 1974–1997. WP No. 170, Institut de Ciències Polítiques i Socials

Singer MM (2011) Who says "it's the economy?" cross-national and cross-individual variation in the salience of economic performance. Comp Pol Stud 44(3):284–312. https://doi.org/10.1177/0010414010384371

Stata (2015) Mlogit – multinomial (polytomous) logistic regression. Base Reference Manual

Social Expenditures and Poverty in Central and Eastern European Union Countries: A Causality Analysis

Yilmaz Bayar and Mahmut Unsal Sasmaz

Abstract Global wealth has increased significantly in recent years. However, poverty and income inequality has stayed at high levels in some countries despite the global economic expansion in the world during the past four decades. In this regard, extensive measures by national governments and international institutions have been taken to combat with poverty and income inequality at national and international levels. Social protection expenditures by governments are one of the prevailing policies to decrease the poverty and inequality in the world. This study examines the causal relationship between social expenditures and poverty in selected Central and Eastern European Union countries during 2005–2014 period employing causality analysis. We found that there was no causal interaction between social expenditures and poverty in our sample.

Keywords Social expenditures • Poverty • Causality analysis

Introduction

Many countries began to follow outward-oriented growth policies, and in this context, they eliminated the constraints on flows of goods, services, and capital gradually and liberalized their economies as of the 1980s with the impact of accelerating globalization. As a result of the policies, global production, trade and capital transfers, and in turn global wealth have raised considerably. However, one of the most discussed parts of this process is that income inequality and poverty has stayed high levels especially in underdeveloped and developing countries. It was estimated that about 767 million people were living below US$1.90 per person per day, in other words 10.7% of the world population were poor in 2013 (World Bank 2016:3). On the other side, Gini coefficient, which reflects the average within-country inequality, was about 39, but income share of the high-income group has been raising (World Bank 2016:10).

Y. Bayar (✉) • M.U. Sasmaz
Usak University Faculty of Economics and Administrative Sciences, Usak, Turkey
e-mail: yilmaz.bayar@usak.edu.tr; mahmut.sasmaz@usak.edu.tr

D. Procházka (ed.), *The Impact of Globalization on International Finance and Accounting*, Springer Proceedings in Business and Economics,
https://doi.org/10.1007/978-3-319-68762-9_27

In this article, we focus on the interaction between poverty and social expenditures. No consensus about the definition of poverty has been realized, although there have been many definitions in the literature. It is resulted from that measurement and specification of poverty line are hard to be determined. However, absolute poverty reflects money income which is necessary to meet basic needs (food, clothing, and shelter), while relative poverty reflects the people who live below prevalent living standards in a society (UNESCO 2016). Poverty has become one of the crucial problems to struggle with for especially underdeveloped, developing, and developed countries. On the other side, poverty has gained a global dimension gradually in recent years, and therefore, poverty alleviation also has gained an international concern. In this regard, governments employ fiscal policy instruments such as government expenditures, government revenues, and public borrowing. Use of social expenditures from public expenditures and more direct tax collection instead of indirect tax from public revenues are the leading public policies in the combat with poverty. For example, the share of public social expenditures (% of GDP) increased to 24.1% in 2012 from 18.6% in 1980 in EU-21 countries (Akçacı and Kocag 2012: 1403). In this study, we researched the causal interaction between social expenditures and poverty in Central and Eastern European Union (CEEU) countries during 2005–2014 period employing Dumitrescu and Hurlin (2012) causality test. In the next part of the paper, empirical literature about the relationship between social expenditures and poverty will be reviewed. Then data and econometric methodology will be described in section "Data and Methodology". Section "Empirical Analysis" presents the major findings of the empirical study. Finally, the study will be over with the Conclusion part.

Literature Review

The empirical literature generally has focused on the impact of social expenditures on income inequality and poverty. Most of the empirical studies on the interaction between social expenditures and income inequality have found that social expenditures decreased the income inequality (e.g., see Niehues (2010); Afonso et al. (2010); Bouvet (2010); Woo et al. (2013)). On the other side, empirical studies on the relationship between social expenditures and poverty generally have found that social expenditures decreased poverty (e.g., see Behrendt (2000); Nolan and Marx (2009); Caminada and Goudswaard (2009); Sarisoy and Koc (2010); Caminada et al. (2012); Celikay and Gumus (2014)).

In one of these studies, Behrendt (2000) researched the impact of social expenditures on poverty in Luxembourg and found that social expenditures contributed to the poverty alleviation. Nolan and Marx (2009) also conducted a similar study for OECD countries and found that social expenditures decreased the poverty. On the other hand, Caminada and Goudswaard (2009) analyzed the impact of social expenditures on poverty alleviation in EU-15 and selected OECD countries and found that interaction between two variables varies from country to country.

In another study, Sarisoy and Koc (2010) examined the impact of public social expenditures on poverty in Turkey during the period 2002–2008 employing regression analysis and revealed that increases in social expenditures reduced poverty. Longford and Nicodemo (2010) also examined the impact of social expenditures on poverty in some selected EU countries and found that social expenditures decreased the poverty in some countries and this finding changed depending on the country. In another study, Caminada and Goudswaard (2012) researched the impact of social expenditures on poverty in OECD countries during 1985–2005 period and revealed that social expenditures contributed to the decreases in poverty.

Lustig et al. (2013) examined the impact of social expenditures on poverty and income inequality in Argentina, Bolivia, Brazil, Mexico, Peru, and Uruguay and found that social expenditures reduced the poverty in Argentina, Brazil, Uruguay, and Mexico. On the other side, Celikay and Gumus (2014) investigated the impact of social expenditures on poverty in 26 regions of Turkey using panel data analysis and found that increasing social expenditures decreased poverty. Finally, Zwiers and Koster (2015) researched the impact of social expenditures on poverty in EU countries in 2008 and revealed that social expenditures decreased poverty.

Data and Methodology

Data

We used yearly values of Gini coefficient proxy for income inequality, social protection expenditures as a percent of GDP, and total trade as a percent of GDP in the study. Data availability was decisive in determination of sample and study period. Our sample consisted of 9 CEEU countries (Bulgaria, Czech Republic, Estonia, Hungary, Latvia, Lithuania, Poland, Slovakia, and Slovenia), and study period was 2005–2014. The summary of data description was given in Table 1.

We benefited from Stata 14.0, E-Views 9.0, and Gauss 11.0 software packages for the econometric analysis of the study. The descriptive statistics and correlation matrix of the variables in the study are presented in Table 2. The correlation matrix showed that there was a negative correlation between both social expenditures and poverty and trade openness and social expenditures.

Table 1 Data description

Variables	Description	Source
POV	People at risk poverty (% total population)	Eurostat (2017)
SOC	Expenditures on social protection (% of GDP)	Eurostat (2016)
TO	Trade (% of GDP)	World Bank (2017)

Source: Authors' own elaboration

Table 2 Descriptive statistics and correlation matrix

Variables	Obs.	Mean	Std. dev.	Min	Max
POV	90	16.28556	4.372477	8.6	26.4
SOC	90	17.95778	3.412271	10.6	24.9
TO	90	130.9377	28.07577	70.27496	183.4055
Correlation matrix					
	POV	SOC		TO	
POV	1	−0.5673		−0.4234	
SOC	−0.5673	1		0.1124	
TO	−0.4234	0.1124		1	

Source: Authors' own elaboration

Table 3 Results of cross-sectional dependence and homogeneity tests

Cross-sectional dependency tests		
Test	Test statistic	*p*-value
LM (Breusch and Pagan (1980))	57.471	0.0130
Homogeneity tests		
Test	Test statistic	*p*-value
Delta_tilde	1.588	0.056
Delta_tilde_adj	1.991	0.023

Source: Authors' own elaboration based on the results of the test

Econometric Methodology

In this study, we will analyze the causal interaction among poverty, social expenditures, and trade openness by causality test of Dumitrescu and Hurlin (2012). In this context, first we will analyze the stationarity of the variables and then implement the causal analysis.

Empirical Analysis

Cross-Sectional Dependency and Homogeneity Tests

We tested cross-sectional independency among the series with LM test of Breusch and Pagan (1980), and the results were introduced in Table 3. The null hypothesis, there is cross-sectional independency, was rejected at 1% significance level, because p value was found to be 0.0070. We revealed a cross-sectional dependence among the series. Furthermore, we analyzed homogeneity with delta tilde test and adjusted delta tilde test of Pesaran and Yamagata (2008), and our findings revealed that null hypothesis, there is homogeneity, was rejected and the cointegrating coefficients were found to be heterogeneous.

Table 4 Results of CIPS panel unit root test

Variables	Constant	Constant + Trend
POV	−0.715 (0.237)	−0.516 (0.303)
d(POV)	−4.402 (0.000)[a]	−3.154 (0.001)[a]
SOC	1.682 (0.954)	1.513 (0.935)
d(SOC)	−5.232 (0.000)[a]	−4.826 (0.000)[a]
TO	0.226 (0.589)	0.919 (0.821)
d(TO)	−5.232 (0.000)[a]	−3.116 (0.001)[a]

Source: Authors' own elaboration based on the results of the unit root test
Note: [a]Significance at 1% level

Table 5 Results of causality test

Null hypothesis	W-Stat.	Zbar-Stat.	Prob.
DSOC does not homogeneously cause DPOV	2.07913	0.26249	0.7929
DPOV does not homogeneously cause DSOC	0.83058	−0.53208	0.5947
DTO does not homogeneously cause DPOV	1.29339	−0.23755	0.8122
DPOV does not homogeneously cause DTO	0.85160	−0.51870	0.6040
DTO does not homogeneously cause DSOC	1.62570	−0.02607	0.9792
DSOC does not homogeneously cause DTO	2.73346	0.67890	0.4972

Source: Authors' own elaboration

Panel Unit Root Test

We analyzed integration levels of the variables by CIPS (cross-sectionally augmented IPS (Im et al. (2003)) unit root test of Pesaran (2007), because we revealed a cross-sectional dependency among the series. We conducted CIPS test, and the results were given in Table 4. The findings indicated that POV, SOC, and TO were I(1).

Causality Test

We analyzed the causal interaction among poverty, social expenditures, and trade openness by causality test of Dumitrescu and Hurlin (2012), and the results were presented in Table 5. The results showed that there was no statistically significant interaction between the variables.

Conclusion

Poverty and income inequality have stayed high levels, although global wealth has increased significantly as of 1980s. In this study, we analyzed the causal interaction among social expenditures, trade openness, and poverty in CEEU countries during 2005–2015 period and revealed that there are no statistically significant interactions among poverty, social expenditures, and trade openness, although the CEEU countries generally increased their social protection expenditures during the same period. This finding can be resulted from malfunctioning of the social protection system, or the ratio of the poor in the EU generally goes below the global poverty ratio. So it becomes harder to make improvements in these poverty levels. However, these countries should check their functioning of social protection systems and take additional measures to increase the efficiency of the social protection system.

References

Afonso A, Schuknecht L, Tanzi V (2010) Income distribution determinants and public spending efficiency. J Econ Inequal 8(3):367–389

Akçacı T, Kocağ E (2012) Türkiye'de sosyal harcamalar ve yoksulluk. Uluslararası Turgut Özal Ekonomi ve Siyaset Kongre Kitabı. İnönü Üniversitesi, Malatya

Behrendt C (2000) Holes in the safety net? Social security and the alleviation of poverty in a comparative perspective. Luxembourg income study working paper, no. 259. Syracuse University, Syracuse

Bouvet F (2010) EMU and the dynamics of regional per capita income inequality in Europe. J Econ Inequal 8(3):323–344

Breusch TS, Pagan AR (1980) The Lagrange multiplier test and its applications to model specification in econometrics. Rev Econ Stud 47(1):239–253

Caminada K, Goudswaard K (2009) Social expenditure and poverty reduction in the EU-15 and other OECD countries. Department of Economics Research Memorandum 2009.02, Leiden University

Caminada K, Goudswaard K, Koster F (2012) Social income transfers and poverty: a cross-country analysis for OECD countries. Int J Soc Welf 21(2):115–126

Celikay F, Gumus E (2014) Sosyal harcamaların yoksulluk üzerine etkileri: Ampirik bir inceleme. Anadolu Üniversitesi Sosyal Bilimler Dergisi 14(4):127–138

Dumitrescu E, Hurlin C (2012) Testing for granger non-causality in heterogeneous panels. Econ Model 29(4):1450–1460

Eurostat (2016) Social protection statistics, http://ec.europa.eu/eurostat/statistics-explained/index.php/Social_protection_statistics (20.12.2016)

Eurostat (2017) At-risk-of-poverty rate by poverty threshold, age and sex - EU-SILC survey [ilc_li02], http://appsso.eurostat.ec.europa.eu/nui/submitViewTableAction.do, (24.01.2017)

Im KS, Pesaran MH, Shin Y (2003) Testing for Unit Roots in Heterogeneous Panels. J Econ 115:53–74

Longford NT, Nicodemo C (2010) The contribution of social transfers to the reduction of poverty. IZA Discussion Paper, No. 5223

Lustig N, Pessino C, Scott J (2013) The impact of Taxes and social spending on inequality and poverty in Argentina, Bolivia, Brazil, Mexico, Peru, and Uruguay: An Overview. CEQ Working Paper No. 13 , http://socialprotectionet.org/sites/default/files/ceqwpno13_lustig_et_al._overview_argbolbramexperury_april_2013.pdf

Niehues J (2010) Social spending generosity and income inequality: a dynamic panel approach. IZA Discussion Paper No. 5178

Nolan B, Marx I (2009) Economic inequality, poverty and social exclusion. In: Salverda W, Nolan B, Smeeding TM (eds) The Oxford handbook of economic inequality. Oxford University Press, New York, pp 315–341

Pesaran MH (2007) A simple panel unit root test in the presence of cross-section dependence. J Appl Econ 22(2):265–312

Pesaran MH, Yamagata T (2008) Testing slope homogeneity in large panels. J Econ 142(1):50–93

Sarisoy İ, Koç S (2010) Türkiye'de kamu sosyal transfer harcamalarının yoksulluğu azaltmadaki etkilerinin ekonometrik analizi. Maliye Dergisi 158:326–348

UNESCO (2016) Poverty, http://www.unesco.org/new/en/social-and-human-sciences/themes/international-migration/glossary/poverty/ (15.11.2016)

Woo J, Bova E, Kinda T, Zhang YS (2013) Distributional consequences of fiscal consolidation and the role of fiscal policy: what do the data say? IMF working paper 13/195. International Monetary Fund, Washington

World Bank (2016) Poverty and shared prosperity 2016: taking on inequality, https://openknowledge.worldbank.org/bitstream/handle/10986/25078/9781464809583.pdf, (25.12.2016)

World Bank (2017) Trade (% of GDP), http://data.worldbank.org/indicator/NE.TRD.GNFS.ZS (03.01.2017)

Zwiers MD, Koster F (2015) The local structure of the welfare state: Uneven effects of social spending on poverty within countries. Urban Stud 52(1):87–102

Are Health-Care Services Luxury Goods?

Paulina Ucieklak-Jeż, Agnieszka Bem, Paweł Prędkiewicz, and Rafał Siedlecki

Abstract In the theory of economy, goods are often split into necessity goods (necessities), which must be purchased for daily life, and luxury goods, which satisfy other needs such as those attributable to social status. Many researches deal with the problem of health-care services – some proved that there are luxury goods, while some proved that health-care benefits are necessity goods. Based on literature review, we have posed the following research hypothesis (H1): income elasticity for health-care spending is lower than 1 in EU countries. We have analyzed the relationship between total health expenditure per capita (THCEPC) and income – represented by gross domestic product per capita (GDPPC). We have also incorporated other variables, characterizing society's structure: Gini coefficient, a percentage of population at risk of poverty, health state self-assessment, and healthy life years (HLY) indicator, separately for male and female population. We have found that (1) decline in the value of the Gini coefficient increased the level of THCEPC; (2) in the case of the female population, shortening of HLY stimulated the growth of THCEPC, while for male population the relationship was reversed; and (3) income elasticity of THCEPC is equal to 1.17, which means that health-care benefits are luxurious goods, with income elasticity higher than 1. Data were obtained from Eurostat Database, covering the years 2004–2014 (26 countries).

Keywords Health-care services • Income elasticity • Demand

P. Ucieklak-Jeż
Jan Dlugosz University in Czestochowa, The Faculty of Philology and History, ul. Waszyngtona 4/8, 42-200 Częstochowa, Poland
e-mail: p.ucieklak-jez@ajd.czest.pl

A. Bem • R. Siedlecki
Wroclaw University of Economics, Wrocław, Department of Corporate Finance and Public Finance, ul. Komandorska 118-120, 53-345 Wrocław, Poland
e-mail: agnieszka.bem@ue.wroc.pl; rafal.siedlecki@ue.wroc.pl

P. Prędkiewicz (✉)
Wroclaw University of Economics, Department of Finance, ul. Komandorska 118-120, 53-345 Wrocław, Poland
e-mail: pawel.predkiewicz@ue.wroc.pl

D. Procházka (ed.), *The Impact of Globalization on International Finance and Accounting*, Springer Proceedings in Business and Economics,
https://doi.org/10.1007/978-3-319-68762-9_28

Introduction

In the theory of economy, goods are often split into necessity goods (necessities), which must be purchased for daily life, and luxury goods, which satisfy other needs such as those attributable to social status. That is way, by defining luxury goods, economists often refer to characteristics such as exclusivity, rarity, or high quality. However, this distinction between necessity goods and luxury ones depends on many factors: individual needs, disposable income, economic development, and sociocultural factors, such as traditions (Bochańczyk-Kupka 2014).

The aim of this paper is to answer whether health-care benefits are luxury goods or not. Intuitively, health-care services can be treated as basic good, which are consumed even forcibly. In the presence of illness or accident, we are forced to buy benefits, if we want to keep the existing state of health – in these situations, financial situation does not play a principal role. Spending on health, however, applies to many other situations – in the case of prevention or esthetic dentistry, we can assume that, since this kind of services does not contribute, in the short term, to save lives, expenditure may be strongly related to financial situation – and along with the increase in income, the share of expenditure in total households' spending increases (Bem et al. 2014).

This problem is important not only from the point of view of academic discussion but also has many practical and political implementations – if health-care services are necessity good, the public sector intervention is strongly justifiable, when market failure occurs (Costa-Font et al. 2011). In the case of uninsured people, it usually leads to medical debt or even bankruptcy, creating important access barriers (Doty et al. 2005; Seifert and Rukavina 2006).

Assuming that the health services are luxury goods, we can expect that those expenses, in accordance with Engel's law, appear only at high income, when basic needs are met (Bochańczyk-Kupka 2014). That implies the analyses of income elasticity, which shows how strong consumption response to changes in income. If income elasticity is higher than 1, consumption increases faster than income – when this elasticity is lower than 1, spending's change is lower than the change in income.

We have posed the following research hypothesis (H1): income elasticity for health-care spending is lower than 1 in EU countries. Our hypothesis assumes that health-care services are necessity goods – they must be purchased regardless patient's financial situation. According to that, the ratio of health-care care expenditure (HCE) to income should decrease along with increasing income – which implies income elasticity lower than 1.

It must be underlined that evidence coming from literature review is not fully consistent. Kujawska and Kordalska (2015), based on data from 39 European countries, found that overall income elasticity is higher than 1, but in countries characterized by lower-than-average income, this elasticity is between 0.6 and 0.8. Research on SAARC countries showed that income elasticity of HCE in lower than 1, both in the short and the long run (Khan et al. 2016), was confirmed in other studies (Abdullah et al. 2017). Dreger and Reimers (2005), using data from 21 OECD countries, confirmed that income elasticity of HCE is below 1. Also

Sen (2005) estimated that income elasticity of per capita expenditures is between 0.21 and 0.51 for 15 OECD countries. Costa-Font et al. (2011) using meta-analysis method found that income of health-care demand is between 0.4 and 0.8 (lower than 1), which suggests that health-care services are necessity goods.

It seems that analysis's horizon and level may influence final results. Okunade and Suraratdecha (2000), using data from 21 OECD countries, found that in a short time, income elasticity of HCE is lower than 1 (0.31), but in the long time, in some countries (Canada, Denmark, Finland, France, Germany, Iceland, Italy, Portugal, Spain, USA), health-care services tend to be a luxury good, while in others (Austria, Belgium, Japan, Luxemburg, the Netherlands, New Zealand, Norway, UK), it seems to be a necessity good. Yavuz, Yilanci, and Ozturk (Yavuz et al. 2013) estimated that, in the case of Turkey, in the short run, income elasticity of HCE is lower than 1 (0.75), while in the long run, they confirmed lack of relationship between income and health-care spending. Getzen (2000) concluded, by analyzing several researches on micro-, regional, and macrolevel, that on individual level (microlevel), income elasticity of HCE is near to 0, while on the macrolevel, it is higher than 1.

Data and Methodology

Our hypothesis requires the analysis on national level. In order to measure the level of health-care expenditure (HCE), we have employed total health expenditure per capita (THCEPC) and for income gross domestic product per capita (GDPPC), due to the fact that most studies confirmed that income per capita was the most important determinant of per capita expenditure on health (Sen 2005). Both variables are in PPP USD.

According to Prieto and Lago-Peñas (Prieto and Lago-Peñas 2012), the analysis should include factors, which influence the volume of health-care spending, because the rise in expenditures may be driven by other factors, like aging society or technological change (see also Dreger and Reimers 2005). They also concluded that income elasticity is very responsive to inclusion of other variables.

According to that, we have incorporated variables, other than income, describing a social structure of European populations, like Gini coefficient (GINI) and a percentage of population at risk of poverty (PRP), as well as variables characterizing population's state of health: health state self-assessment (SPH) and expected life span in good health (healthy life years – HLY), accordingly for female and male populations (Table 1).

We have used a panel analysis method, using data from 26 European Union countries (Austria, Belgium, Czech Republic, Estonia, France, Netherlands, Lithuania, Luxembourg, Germany, Poland, Slovakia, Slovenia, Hungary, Romania, Bulgaria, Switzerland, Denmark, Finland, Greece, Spain, Iceland, Latvia, Norway, Portugal, Sweden, Cyprus), covering the years 2004–2014. Data were obtained from Eurostat Database. We have excluded from our analysis Romania and Croatia, which became EU members after 2004.

Table 1 Potential explanatory variables

Variable	Definition
GDPPC	Gross domestic product per capita
SPH	Health state self-assessment
GINI	Gini coefficient of equivalized disposable income before social transfers
PRP	At-risk-of-poverty rate after social transfers
HLYf, HLYm	The healthy life years (HLY) indicator is the expected remaining number of years, lived from a particular age without long-term activity limitation. HLY is computed as the life expectancy from which the expected number of years lived with long-term activity limitations is subtracted. In this study we used HLY indicator separately for male and female population

Source: own study

Table 2 Estimated model

	Coefficient	Standard error	*t*-Student statistic	*p*-value	
Const	−4.43918	0.448784	−9.8916	<0.0001	***
GDPPC	1.17127	0.0353477	33.1358	<0.0001	***
SPH	0.369246	0.190043	1.9430	0.0535	*
GINI	−0.128853	0.0606137	−2.1258	0.0349	**
HLYf	−0.305251	0.0838498	−3.6405	0.0004	***
HLYm	0.381387	0.0965155	3.9516	0.0001	***

Source: own analysis of data from the Albertina database
* significance level $\alpha = 0.1$, ** significance level $\alpha = 0.05$ *** significance level $\alpha = 0.01$

Results and Discussion

Using the weighted least squares method, we have estimated the model, where the dependent variable is the total health-care expenditure per capita (THCEPC) (Table 2).

Our analysis has shown decline in the value of the Gini coefficient (reduction in income stratification in society) increased the level of expenditure on health (results are statistically significant at the level $\alpha = 0.05$). Because the Gini coefficient measures income stratification before social transfers, we can assume that the smaller the value of this indicator, the greater the part of the population that can afford to buy health benefits. What is important, the variable describing the risk of poverty, after taking into consideration social transfers, has not been incorporated into the model.

Interesting results have been observed in the case of relationship between health expenditure and life expectancies in good health (HLY). In the case of the female population, shortening of HLY stimulated the growth of THCEPC – if the period of healthy life reduces, in particular, along with unchanged or even longer total life span, a period of intense consumption of health benefits increases, resulting in an overall increase in spending. Those relationships have proven to be highly

Table 3 Measures of the model fitting

Residual sum of squares	170.5335	Standard deviation of the dependent variable	0.962711
Coefficient of determination R-squared	0.966718	Adjusted R-squared	0.965813
F(3, 186)	1068.896	*p*-value for test F	7.1e−134
Logarytm wiarygodności	−259.3295	Akaike information criterion	530.6591
Schwarz' Bayes criterion	550.1412	Hannan-Quinn criterion	538.5510

Source: own study

statistically significant (significance level $\alpha = 0.01$). Our observation is consistent with research, showing that although women live longer, their lives in old age is often affected by disability (Bem and Ucieklak-Jeż, 2014a, b; Ucieklak-Jeż and Bem 2015a, b). Conversely, for the male population, it has been shown that increase in HLY was associated with an increase in THCEPC. The source of such dependencies can be increased expenditure on preventive health care, which reduces the risk of men's premature death. This observation also shows different patterns of the use of health benefits for men and women's populations.

We have confirmed that along with the growth of GDPPC (income), health spending also grows and the pace of this growth is faster than the growth rate of GDP. Precisely, GDP growth by 1% results in increased health expenses of 1.17%, which implies that income elasticity of health-care spending per capita (THCEPC) is equal to 1.17 – and, in particular, that is greater than 1. This relationship is statistically significant at the level $\alpha = 0.01$.

This means that the H1 hypothesis, formulated on the basis of literature review, cannot be adopted. Research results have confirmed that health services, in the countries of the European Union, at least in analyzed period, were luxury goods – along with increasing wealth, the share of spending on health increases. Our results are consistent with observations of Getzen (2000), who, using meta-analysis, confirmed that at macro-level health services are luxurious goods, as well as results of Kujawska and Kordalska (2015) who found that that overall income elasticity in UE countries is higher than 1.

The estimated model is characterized by high fitting measures; in particular, the coefficient of determination R-squared is equal to 96.7% (Table 3).

Conclusion

Studies related to the nature of the health benefits are still contemporary. The relationship between the population's state of health and economic growth seems to be undeniable. This suggests the involvement of the State in actions supporting equal access to health services, regardless of level of income. The hypothesis of the necessity character of health-care provision justifies the State's intervention in the process of delivering and financing health-care services. A number of studies confirmed this hypothesis. However, our research indicates that health care is a luxury good in EU countries, at least in the period of analyses, which would suggest that the State should adopt, in this area, the attitude, at least, neutral. This is very questionable, due to social problems, especially in poorer European countries.

In this research, a panel analysis, for all EU countries, has been presented. However, we can assume, based on the evidence from the literature, that, according to a different character of health care, differences in social structure in EU countries, country-by-country analysis, would show other characteristics of health-care demand. This is very important from the perspective of Poland or, broadly speaking, CEE countries, which undeniably generate lower income level than Western European countries. Kujawska and Kordalska (2015) found that income elasticity for poorer European countries is lower than 1, on contrary to richer ones. We surmise that our further research can confirm those findings. We assume that, apart from GDP levels, Gini coefficient values can be an important factor, which split countries into those characterized by low- and high-income elasticity.

Further research will be, so, extended in two directions: EU countries divided on the basis of criterion of wealth (wealthy countries and poorer ones) and on the basis of the criterion of the organization of the health-care provision system (Beveridge system versus systems based on social insurance schemes). We expect that in the richer countries, particularly in those where health care is funded within compulsory or voluntary health insurance, the income elasticity of the demand for health services will be greater than in poorer countries, or those where the financing system is based on taxes. We assume that systems based on, even compulsory, health insurance can create some income barrier, due to mechanisms of demand rationalization, as, for example, cost sharing, or relatively narrow basket of health-care services, offered within insurance plans. On the other hand, system based on national health care can create barriers, which do not have, necessarily, a financial dimension, but through unmet health needs, it forces patient to move toward private sector, which implies service's fees.

References

Abdullah SM, Siddiqua S, Huque R (2017) Is health care a necessary or luxury product for Asian countries? An answer using panel approach. Heal Econ Rev 7(4):1–12. https://doi.org/10.1186/s13561-017-0144-8

Bem A, Prędkiewicz K, Prędkiewicz P, Ucieklak-Jeż P (2014) Health system's financing inequalities in selected European countries. Eur Financ Syst :34–40

Bem A, Ucieklak-Jeż P (2014a) Functional health assessment as the determinant of social care management. Probl Manag 21st Century 9(3):197–205

Bem A, Ucieklak-Jeż P (2014b) Health status of the rural population in Poland. Manag Theory Stud Rural Bus Infrastructure Dev 36(2):235–243

Bochańczyk-Kupka D (2014) Luksus i dobra luksusowe. Studia Ekonomiczne 176:97–108

Costa-Font J, Gemmill M, Rubert G (2011) Biases in the healthcare luxury good hypothesis?: a meta-regression analysis. J R Stat Soc A Stat Soc 1:95–107. https://doi.org/10.1111/j.1467-985X.2010.00653.x

Doty MM, Edwards JN, Holmgren AL (2005) Seeing red: Americans driven into debt by medical bills. Commonwealth Fund 837:1–11

Dreger C, Reimers HE (2005) Health care expenditures in OECD countries: a panel unit root and cointegration analysis. Int J Appl Econ Quant Stud 2:5–20

Getzen TE (2000) Health care is an individual necessity and a national luxury: applying multilevel decision models to the analysis of health care expenditures. J Health Econ 2:259–270

Khan HN, Khan MA, Razli RB, Shehzada G, Krebs KL, Sarvghad N (2016) Health care expenditure and economic growth in SAARC countries (1995–2012): a panel causality analysis. Appl Res Qual Life 3:639–661. https://doi.org/10.1007/s11482-015-9385-z

Kujawska J, Kordalska A (2015) Elastyczność dochodowa wydatków na opiekę zdrowotną w krajach europejskich. Zarządzanie Finanse 2:195–208

Okunade AA, Suraratdecha C (2000) Health care expenditure inertia in the OECD countries: a heterogeneous analysis. Health Care Manag Sci 1:31–42

Prieto DC, Lago-Peñas S (2012) Decomposing the determinants of health care expenditure: the case of Spain. Eur J Health Econ 1:19–27. https://doi.org/10.1007/s10198-010-0276-9

Seifert RW, Rukavina M (2006) Bankruptcy is the tip of a medical-debt iceberg. Health Aff 2:89–92. https://doi.org/10.1377/hlthaff.25.w89

Sen A (2005) Is health care a luxury? New evidence from OECD data. Int J Health Care Finance Econ 2:147–164. https://doi.org/10.1007/s10754-005-1866-4

Ucieklak-Jeż P, Bem A (2015a) Wpływ niefinansowych zasobów systemu ochrony zdrowia na stan zdrowia kobiet i mężczyzn w Polsce. Prace Naukowe Akademii im. Jana Długosza w Częstochowie. Pragmata tes Oikonomias. 9:157–171. https://doi.org/10.16926/pto.2015.09.13

Ucieklak-Jeż P, Bem A (2015b) Zdrowie psychiczne jako element zdrowego starzenia się. In: Andrzejak R (ed) Zdrowie dla regionu, Wydawnictwo Uczelniane Państwowej Wyższej Szkoły Zawodowej im. Angelusa Silesiusa, Wałbrzych, pp 347–355

Ucieklak-Jeż P, Bem A, Prędkiewicz P (2015) Effectiveness of allocation of health system non-financial resources. In: Brătianu C, Zbuchee A, Pînzaru F, Vătămănescu E-M, Leon R-D, (eds) Strategica international academic conference – third edition-local versus global. SNSPA, Faculty of Management, Bucharest, Romania, pp 647–656

Yavuz NC, Yilanci V ‘y, Ozturk ZA (2013) Is health care a luxury or a necessity or both? Evidence from Turkey. Eur J Health Econ 1:5–10. https://doi.org/10.1007/s10198-011-0339-6

The Relationship between Corruption and Tax Burden: The Moderator Effect of Strength of Auditing and Reporting Standards

Gul Yesilcelebi and Nazli Keyifli

Abstract The aim of this study is to examine the moderator effect of strength of auditing and reporting standards on the relationship between corruption and tax burden in the Organisation for Economic Co-operation and Development (OECD) countries. The study was conducted on annual data during the period 2011–2015 about the corruption, tax burden and strength of auditing and reporting standards of OECD member countries. In this context, data of corruption (Corruption Perceptions Index – CPI) were collected from Transparency International – the Global Coalition against Corruption; data of tax burden were collected from International Monetary Fund (IMF) database, and data of strength of auditing and reporting standards were collected from The Global Competitiveness Reports. The study analysed the relationship between corruption and tax burden and the moderator effect of strength of auditing and reporting standards on the relationship between two variables by the panel data analysis. The results of this analysis showed that have significantly and a negative relationship between corruption and tax burden; strength of auditing and reporting standards have significantly and a positive strengthen relationship between corruption and tax burden.

Keywords Auditing and reporting standards • Corruption • Tax burden • Panel data analysis • Moderator

Introduction

Auditing, accounting and reporting standards seek to make financial information transparent and accountable (Malagueño et al. 2010). When the prior studies examined, there are many studies investigating the relationship between corruption

G. Yesilcelebi (✉)
Gumushane University, Department of Business Administration, Gumushane, Turkey
e-mail: gyesilcelebi@hotmail.com

N. Keyifli
Gumushane University, Department of Public Finance, Gumushane, Turkey
e-mail: n.keyifli@hotmail.com

D. Procházka (ed.), *The Impact of Globalization on International Finance and Accounting*, Springer Proceedings in Business and Economics,
https://doi.org/10.1007/978-3-319-68762-9_29

and tax burden (Ghura 1998; Brasoveanu and Brasoveanu 2009) and accounting and corruption (Kimbro 2002; Wu 2005; Malagueño et al. 2010; Houqe and Monem 2013), but there is no study to investigate the relationship between accounting and tax burden.

Ghura (1998) examined the level of economy policies and corruption impact on tax revenue and GDP. This study covered on 39 African countries and the period for 1985–1996. Results of the study showed that there is a negative relationship between corruption and tax burden.

Brasoveanu and Brasoveanu (2009) analysed the evolutions and the correlation between overall tax burden and corruption. The analysis was conducted for European Union (EU) 27 members, for the period 1995–2008. The results showed that there was a negative correlation between tax burden and corruption in EU 12 members, a positive correlation between tax burden and corruption in EU 12 members and no correlation between tax burden and corruption in EU 3 members.

H_1 *There is a negative relationship between the corruption and tax burden.*

Kimbro (2002) investigated the effects of economic, institutional and cultural variables on corruption. The author concluded that the perceptions of corruption are negatively related to accounting quality.

Wu (2005) examined the relationship between corporate accounting practices and corruption. In the study, accounting information standards was used as a corporate governance indicator. Finally, the author found that better accounting practices can help reduce corruption.

Malagueño et al. (2010) examined the relationship between the perceived level of corruption and accounting and auditing quality. The research results showed that accounting and auditing quality are negatively and significantly related to the level of perceived corruption. The authors suggested that countries can reduce the level of perceived corruption by improving accounting and auditing standards to provide the transparency of financial reporting.

Houqe and Monem (2013) investigated the role of accounting information in reducing corruption after controlling for the effects of economic development and political institutions. In the study, data covered from 166 countries over the period 1996–2011. Result of the study showed that countries tend to reduce corruption should enhance in quality of accounting standards.

The prior studies on accounting and corruption showed that there is a negative relationship between the corruption and strength of auditing and reporting standards.

H_2 *Strength and/or direction of the effect of corruption on tax burden will vary according to the strength of auditing and reporting standards (moderator hypothesis).*

As a result of literature review, there are many studies investigating the effects of corruption on public revenues and expenditures, but there is no study to address the relationship between tax burden, corruption and accounting standards. In particular, the study examines empirically the relationship between tax burden, corruption and accounting standards in order to address the gap in the relevant literature. In the study, the relationship between corruption and tax burden is examined by considering the moderator effect of accounting standards and trying to contribute to the related literature.

The paper consists of four sections. In the first section, literature review relates to corruption, tax burden and accounting, auditing and reporting standards and research hypothesis created. Following this, the methodology used in the analysis is identified. Then, in the next section, empirical findings were given. In the final section, it provides a summary of the analysis.

Data and Methodology

In the study, the relationship between corruption and tax burden and the moderator effect of strength of auditing and reporting standards on the relationship between two variables are analysed by the panel data analysis. In the analysis, annual data during the period 2011–2015 was used for OECD countries (total of 34 countries: Australia, Austria, Belgium, Canada, Chile, Czech Republic, Denmark, Estonia, Finland, France, Germany, Greece, Hungary, Iceland, Ireland, Israel, Italy, Japan, South Korea, Luxembourg, Mexico, Netherlands, New Zealand, Norway, Poland, Portugal, Slovak Republic, Slovenia, Spain, Sweden, Switzerland, Turkey, United Kingdom and the United States). The dataset consists of 34 countries over the period 2011–2015 with 170 observations. Variables and sources are described in Table 1.

Dependent Variable

Dependent variable is tax burden (TB) in the analysis. Tax burden of countries was calculated as total tax revenues over the gross domestic product (GDP). On the other hand, tax burden of countries equals tax revenues as a percent of GDP. Data of tax burden were collected from IMF Database.

Independent Variable

Independent variable is corruption (CPI) in the analysis. Corruption level of countries is measured by Corruption Perceptions Index (CPI) that is published by Transparency International Coalition. The index scores countries vary from 0 (highly corrupt) to 10 (lowly corrupt), so it means a higher CPI score reflects less corruption and a lower CPI score reflects high corruption. In this context, data of corruption (Corruption Perceptions Index – CPI) were collected from

Table 1 Variables and sources (2011–2015)

Variable type	Variable name	Variable description	Source
Dependent variable	Tax burden (TB)	Tax burden (TB) of countries was calculated as total tax revenues/gross domestic product (GDP)	The IMF database
Independent variable	Corruption (CPI)	The corruption perceptions index (CPI) ranks countries in terms of the degree to which corruption is perceived. Index units, 10 = least corrupt, 0 = most corrupt. In the study, CPI scores reversed	The transparency international
Moderator variable	Strength of auditing and reporting standards (ARS)	Strength of auditing and reporting standards (ARS) was measured by a question – 'In your country, how strong are financial auditing and reporting standards? [1 = extremely weak; 7 = extremely strong]'	The global competitiveness reports

Source: The Transparency International (2011–2015), The IMF Database (2011–2015) and The Global Competitiveness Reports (2011–2015)

Transparency International – the Global Coalition against Corruption. In the study, CPI scores are reversed and used as formula CPI = 10-CPI.

Moderator Variable

Moderator variable is strength of auditing and reporting standards (ARS) in the analysis. Strength of auditing and reporting standards is measured by The Global Competitiveness Reports published by World Economic Forum. Data of strength of auditing and reporting standards were collected from The Global Competitiveness Reports.

Descriptive statistics have been analysed to obtain information about the dataset. Descriptive statistics are given in Table 2.

As it can be seen in Table 2, during the analysis period (2011–2015), the mean value of tax burden in the countries is 40.38%, minimum value is 20.91%, and maximum value is 57.3%. The mean value for corruption also is 3.08, the minimum value is 0.5, and maximum value is 7.0. So the mean of level of perceived corruption in OECD countries is low.

A simple diagram of the basic panel data regression model is as follows:

$$Y_{it} = \alpha_{it} + \beta_{kit} + X_{kit} + u_{it} \qquad i = 1, 2, \ldots, N \qquad t = 1, 2, \ldots, T \qquad (1)$$

According to the research hypotheses, the research model was constructed as follows:

Table 2 Descriptive statistics

Variable name	Observation	Mean	Std. dev.	Min.	Max.
Tax burden	170	40.38	8.76	20.91	57.43
Corruption	170	3.08	1.63	0.5	7.0
Moderator	170	15.64	7.12	3.05	33.6

Source: own analysis of data from the dataset

Table 3 The trial of unit and time effect: LR test results

	Prob.
Unit effect	0.000
Time effect	1.000

Source: own analysis of using LR

Table 4 The trial of unit effect

Test type	Test statistic	Prob.
F test	375.01	0.000
LM test	326.55	0.000

Source: own analysis of using F and LM

$$TB_{it} = \beta_0 + \beta_1 CPI_{it} + \beta_2 CPI^* ARS_{it} + u_{it} \quad (2)$$
$$i = 1, \ldots \quad N; t = 1, \ldots, T$$

In the equation, symbol of 'TB_{it}' indicates the dependent variable, level of tax burden; the symbol of 'CPI_{it}' indicates the independent variable, corruption perceptions index; the symbol of '$CPI*ARS_{it}$' indicates the moderator variable, multiply corruption perceptions index and strength of auditing and reporting standards; and the symbol of 'u_{it}' indicates the error term.

Results and Discussion

In the model that is planned to be established, firstly it is decided whether unit and/or time effects are present or not. The presence of unit and time effect was tested by LR test. LR test results are presented in Table 3.

According to the LR test result, the hypothesis that the unit effect is $H_0 = 0$ is rejected with a certain result such as 95% (its confidence level is 95%). There is a unit effect in the model, and the result is that the classical model is not suitable. According to the test result with a certain rate (at the 95% confidence level), the hypothesis that the time effect is $H_0 = 0$ could not be rejected. As a result of the tests carried out, it was understood that the unit effect is present in the model but time effect is not. The present of unit effect was tested separately by F test and LM test in the Table 4.

Table 5 2011–2015 period OECD countries panel data results

Dependent variable: tax burden		
Independent variable	Fixed effect	Random effect
Corruption (CPI)	−1.717 (0.007)[a]	−1.828 (0.003)[a]
Moderator (CPI*ARS)	0.296 (0.009)[a]	0.296 (0.008)[a]
Constant	41.03 (0.000)[a]	41.38 (0.000)[a]
Number of observations	170	170
R^2	0.055	0.051
F-Statistic	0.000[a]	0.010[a]
Hausman test		0.390

Source: own analysis of using stata
[a]1% significance

According to both test results, the hypothesis that the unit effect is $H_0 = 0$ is rejected at 95% confidence level. As a result, the model to be installed is the result of unit effect. After determining the presence of unit and/or time effects, the Hausman test was performed to determine whether these effects were fixed or random, and the correct predictor was tried to be reached. Panel data results are given in the Table 5.

In order to choose between the fixed effect model and random effect model, the Hausman (1978) test was conducted. In the Hausman test, the hypothesis $H_0 = 0$ is based on the hypothesis random effects are valid. In the result of the test statistic, if $H_0 \neq 0$, it is assumed that fixed effects estimator is consistent. A probability value in the Hausman test results was greater than 5%, which is the result of the random effect model.

The results of the analysis showed that have significantly ($p = 0.003$) and a negative relationship between corruption and tax burden; strength of auditing and reporting standards have significantly ($p = 0.008$) and a positive strengthen relationship between corruption and tax burden.

Conclusion

The study examined the moderator effect of strength of auditing and reporting standards on the relationship between corruption and tax burden in the OECD countries. The study was conducted on annual data during the period 2011–2015 about the corruption, tax burden and strength of auditing and reporting standards of OECD member countries.

The results of the analysis showed that have significantly and a negative relationship between corruption and tax burden. The empirical results confirm results of prior studies to the relation on corruption and tax burden (Ghura 1998; Brasoveanu and Brasoveanu 2009). The results of the analysis showed that strength of auditing and reporting standards have significantly and a positive strengthen relationship between corruption and tax burden. The analysis results support that strength of auditing and reporting standards moderates the relationship between corruption and tax burden.

References

Brasoveanu IV, Brasoveanu LO (2009) Correlation between corruption and tax revenues in EU 27. Econ Comput Cybern Stud Res 43(4):133–142

Ghura D (1998) Tax revenue in Sub-Saharan Africa: effects of economic policies and corruption. Work. Pap. No 98/135 International Monetary Fund. doi: https://doi.org/10.5089/9781451855685.001

Hausman JA (1978) Specification tests in econometrics. Econometrica 46(6):1251–1271. https://doi.org/10.2307/1913827

Houqe MN, Monem R (2013) Corruption, political institutions, and accounting environment: a cross-country study. SSRN Electron J. https://doi.org/10.2139/ssrn.2263630

International Monetary Fund (IMF) (2011–2015) http://www.imf.org/en/Data

Kimbro MB (2002) A cross-country empirical investigation of corruption and its relation to economic, cultural, and monitoring institutions: an examination of the role of accounting and financial statements quality. J Account Audit Financ 17(4):325–375. https://doi.org/10.1177/0148558X0201700403

Malagueño R, Albrecht C, Ainge C, Stephens N (2010) Accounting and corruption: a cross-country analysis. J Money Laundering Control 13(4):372–393. https://doi.org/10.1108/13685201011083885

The Global Competitiveness Reports (2011–2015) https://www.weforum.org/reports

Transparency International (2011–2015) https://www.transparency.org/

Wu X (2005) Corporate governance and corruption: a cross-country analysis. Gov Int J Policy Adm Inst 18(2):151–170. https://doi.org/10.1111/j.1468-0491.2005.00271.x

Different Approaches in Business Information Disclosures in European Annual Reports

Marcela Žárová

Abstract This paper compares information disclosure in annual reports in British accounting regulatory system with information disclosure requirements for annual reports in Continental European accounting regulatory systems represented by Czech accounting. In spite of the fact that legal framework for information disclosure in annual reports, Directive 2013/34/EU, is identical for companies in both systems, in the UK and in the Continental Europe, this paper brings evidence about fundamental differences in information disclosure between systems. Moreover, results from the comparison confirm hypothesis that in countries with widespread ownership of companies by shareholders who do not have access to internal information, there is a pressure for information disclosure in annual reports.

Keywords Information disclosure • Continental European approach • British approach

Introduction

As European countries operate within two different legal systems, it is evident that there is no unified European approach to financial reporting and disclosing information in annual reports. Disclosure of information in annual reports is based not only on different legal backgrounds but also on different tradition and policies introduced in above-mentioned environments. Despite the fact that Alexander and Archer (2000) suggested that it is a myth that there is a coherent group of countries that was using Anglo-Saxon accounting, this paper uses comparison of simplified British approach against Continental European. Facts that come from the comparison of these approaches do not necessarily bring a clear view on which approach is better (Žárová 2016). Even if we admit that there is no clear answer on which

M. Žárová (✉)
University of Economics, Prague, Department of Financial Accounting and Auditing, Nam. W. Churchilla 4, 130 67 Prague, Czech Republic
e-mail: zarova@vse.cz

D. Procházka (ed.), *The Impact of Globalization on International Finance and Accounting*, Springer Proceedings in Business and Economics,
https://doi.org/10.1007/978-3-319-68762-9_30

approach is better, there is evidence that UK companies have a longer tradition to disclose and publish business information.

For the purpose of this article, the Czech accounting regulatory system, as a representative of Continental European approach, has been chosen. Characteristic features of this accounting regulatory system are that financial reporting is regulated by law, which is too detailed on one hand, and on the other hand most legislators are not well informed about accounting concepts and technicalities of financial reporting. At the second, the stock exchange is less important; companies obtain majority of their funds from banks and other financial institutions McGee (2008). As companies in Britain are more dependent on financial sources from stock exchanges, British companies developed strategies concerning information disclosure in annual reports a long time ago. The approach used in British model could be used for the decision on what kind of information should be disclosed. This paper brings observation of good practice of British companies.

As there is no systematic research in the Czech Republic on information disclosure in annual reports and requirements on business model disclosure in the UK that is rather new, this paper uses research and field study papers provided by Financial Reporting Council (FRC Lab 2016). This paper compares British and Czech accounting systems, highlights experience from both systems and tries to give answer whether British system could bring new aspects into information disclosure attitude in Continental European tradition.

Regulatory Frameworks and Methodology

The development of the Czech Accounting system has been finalized before the Czech Republic joined the European Union (EU) in May 2004. Since January 2004, legislation framework was enhanced into three separate regulatory levels: Accounting Act, Decrees to Accounting Act and Czech Accounting Standards (CAS). Accounting Act is prepared by the Ministry of Finance and approved by the Parliament; Decrees to Accounting Act and CAS are issued by the Ministry of Finance. On the other hand, the Ministry of Finance admits the possibility of existence of a rule-making body since 2004 (Žárová 2011) but not once was any professional body asked to do it. Last amendment of the Act on Accounting is a consequence of the Directive 2013/34/EU. This Directive aims at designing and delivering regulation of the highest quality while respecting that the administrative burdens are proportionate to the benefits they bring. Amended Act on Accounting came into force since 1 January 2016. As a part of the amended Act, requirements concerning published information in annual report have been completed.

In the UK, corporate reporting is regulated by the Government and Financial Reporting Council (FRC). FRC is originally established in 1990 to be responsible for setting and monitoring the UK accounting standards. The number of activities has been increasing since 1990. At present FRC sets standards for corporate reporting, audit and actuarial practice and monitors and enforces accounting and auditing standards. FRC also oversees the regulatory activities of the actuarial profession and the professional accountancy bodies and operates independent enforcement arrangements for public interest cases involving accountants and actuaries. The aim of the FRC is to promote high-quality corporate governance and reporting to foster investment.

The aim of this paper is to compare information disclosure in annual reports in British accounting regulatory system with information disclosure requirements for annual reports in the Czech Republic. As the paper analyses legal requirements on accounting information disclosure in annual reports which is regulated by the Act on Accounting, content analysis was used. Then method of comparison was used to compare disclosure information required by the Act in the Czech Republic with information disclosure in annual reports primarily prepared for shareholders.

Results and Discussion

Due to regulation of accounting in Europe by Directives, there is a space for different transposition of accounting Directives into national legislative system. Even in unified Union accounting legislation, there are differences in financial reporting. Using a widespread opinion that there exists British approach against Continental one (Nobes and Parker 2008; Nobes and Parker 2012; Flower 2002), this paper brings experience of accounting disclosure in annual report from the UK and the Czech Republic as an example of an accounting system with Continental European approach. This paper compares best practice of UK companies with information disclosure requirements for annual reports by representatives of Continental European approach based on disclosure requirements set by Directive 2013/34/EU.

Nobes and Parker (2012) and Flower (2002) see clear distinction between answer on the question, "What is primary objective of financial statements in Europe?" "Primary objective in simplified British approach is to provide information for capital market. Primary objective in simplified Continental European approach is to regulate distributions to stakeholders," while in the preface of the Directive 2013/34/EU is stated that "annual financial statements pursue various objectives and do not merely provide information for investors in capital markets but also give an account of past transactions and enhance corporate governance". Moreover there is a stress on the fact that Union accounting legislation needs to strike an appropriate balance between the interests of the addressees of financial statements and "the interest of undertakings in not being unduly burdened with reporting requirements". It is emphasized that disclosure of accounting policies is one of the key elements of the notes to the financial statements. Such disclosure should include, mainly, the measurement bases applied to various items, a statement on the conformity of those accounting policies with the going concern concept and any significant changes to the accounting policies adopted. Moreover Directive states that "information should not be restricted to the financial aspects of the undertaking's business only, and there should be an analysis of environmental and social aspects of the business necessary for an understanding of the undertaking's development, performance or position".

Czech Experience

In the Czech Republic, accounting information disclosure in annual reports is regulated by the Act on Accounting. The Act determines obligation to prepare annual reports according to categories of undertakings.

Obligation to prepare annual report has audited accounting entities. These entities have obligation to disclose financial and nonfinancial information. Medium-sized, small-sized entities and micro entities are obliged to disclose only financial information in annual report. As medium-sized, small-sized entities and micro entities have exception from obligation to disclose nonfinancial information, this paper will not concern these entities.

The Act on Accounting regulates disclosure of audited accounting entities. All audited accounting entities have obligation to prepare annual report in order to provide overall, well-balanced and comprehensive information on their performance, activity and current economic position. Annual report shall include financial statements.

The Act determines that besides that information in annual report which provides overall, well-balanced and comprehensive information on entity's performance, activity and current economic position including financial statements, there is an obligation to publish other financial and nonfinancial information. Financial and nonfinancial information are to be presented at least on:

- After balance sheet dates events and all material information with regard to compliance with the purpose of an annual report
- The expected development of the accounting entity's activity
- The activities in research and development
- Acquisition of own shares
- The activity in the field of environmental protection and in labour relations
- The fact whether company has an organizational branch abroad
- Including other information required by other statutory provisions

Accounting entity holding financial instruments or other similar financial instruments has obligation to disclose material information in order to assess a certain accounting entity's property and other assets, equity and liabilities, to recognize financial position of entity and profit or loss. Additional information is to be disclosed on:

- Objectives and methods of the company's risk management, including its policies for hedging all types of planned transactions, for which hedging derivatives are used
- The pricing, credit and liquidity risks and also cash-flow risks faced by the accounting entity

The Act on Accounting determines conditions, methods and places, where information shall be published.

British Experience

In August 2013, the UK Government published new Regulations[1] for the strategic report and directors' report. The UK Strategic Report Regulations, applicable for periods ending on or after 30 September 2013, introduced a requirement for quoted companies to disclose their business model. This brought a requirement to disclose the business model into law for the first time, having been required under the UK Corporate Governance Code since 2010 (on a "comply or explain" basis), and is seen as having codified common market practice.

As assistance to public, in June 2014, FRC published non-mandatory Guidance on the Strategic Report which recommends the following information be described in the business model disclosure (FRC 2014):

- How the entity generates or preserves value over the longer term
- How the entity captures that value
- What the entity does and why it does it
- What makes the entity different from, or the basis on which it competes with, its peers
- High-level understanding of how the entity is structured
- High level understanding of the markets in which it operates and how it engages with those markets
- Broad understanding of the nature of the relationships, resources and other inputs that are necessary for the success of the business

The FRC encourages entities to prepare a high-quality strategic report which provides shareholders with a holistic and meaningful picture of an entity's business model, strategy, development, performance, position and future prospects (FRC 2015).

Within FRC structure, several committees provide research and assist public to develop guidance on topics concerned. In order to develop pragmatic solutions to today's reporting needs, the Financial Reporting Lab was launched in 2011 to provide an environment where investors and companies can come together. The Lab works on different project with companies, investment organisations and retail

[1]The Companies Act 2006 (Strategic Report and Directors' Report) Regulations 2013 (the "Regulations").

investors to bring insight and understanding to a number of key areas of financial reporting (FRC 2016). One of project concerning business model reporting includes disclosure. Results from the survey is summarised in text below.

Results from the Survey

Financial Reporting Lab analyzes information and summarizes that investors want more detailed information than most companies are currently providing, although they note that this should not lengthen the disclosure significantly. Instead, investors want companies to better use the space currently taken by the disclosure, to provide relevant factual information.

1. Opinion of investors on disclosed information in annual report (results from the survey are divided on opinion of three groups of investors).
   - Most investors want the company to include information about where it sits in the value chain, key divisions and their contribution and legal structure, key markets and market segments, its competitive advantage, key inputs (assets and liabilities, relationships and resources) and how they are maintained/enhanced, key revenue and profit drivers, value created for other stakeholders that support economic value generation and statistics to indicate relative importance of elements.
   - Many investors also want to know direct threats and market share.
   - Some investors also want culture and values, SWOT analysis, purpose, investment plans, how the business model is likely to evolve, cash flow, capital and assets allocated to business, ROE (return on equity), ROCE (return on capital employed) or ROA (return on assets).
2. Consistency of disclosure
   - Many companies are making significant changes to disclosure each year, in an effort to improve the disclosure. While investors appreciate the improvements, they need to check the disclosure carefully to ascertain whether the underlying structure, or only the disclosure, has changed.
   - Investors would like companies to develop one high-quality disclosure and use it consistently across the different reporting channels, which will give the investment community confidence that the disclosed business model is the real business model. Some investors believe companies could use digital capabilities to better present their business model on the corporate website, in a manner that is easy to access and assimilate.
   - Once the business model disclosure has been clearly defined and meets investor needs, investors expect that companies will only modify the disclosure to reflect changes to the model. Changes in the year, and forthcoming changes, should be clearly identified, including their rationale. Companies should consider how best to communicate significant business model changes – a

small number of investors believe the inclusion of both pre- and post-change business models in the year of change may be helpful in some cases.

3. General observations from survey

   - Investors need more detail than it is currently provided by most companies. Investors ask companies to assume the reader knows nothing about the company and provide disclosure that stands alone in describing the business model – something as fundamental as stating what the company does is often omitted from the disclosure as it is described elsewhere in the annual report or is assumed knowledge.
   - In particular, investors find disclosures are often lacking information that answers questions such as:

     – What are the key revenue and profit drivers and how do profits convert to cash?
     – Are there any key asset and liability items that support the business model?
     – What is the competitive advantage?

   - Many companies express concern that disclosure of their competitive advantage is commercially sensitive and could jeopardize the company's prospects. However, investors believe companies can balance commercial sensitivity with providing sufficient disclosure to enable them to understand what differentiates the company. They are not looking for the "secret recipe" to be published.

4. Linkage between strategic report and business model in annual report

   - Investors refer to key areas in addition to the strategic report linkage mentioned above: segmental reporting, main income statement items, key balance sheet items, accounting policies, cash flow statement, employee numbers and cost disclosure.

Conclusion

This paper compares information disclosure in annual reports in British accounting regulatory system with information disclosure requirements for annual reports in Continental European accounting regulatory systems represented by Czech accounting. In spite of the fact that legal framework for information disclosure in annual reports, Directive 2013/34/EU, is identical for companies in both systems, in the UK and in the Continental Europe, this paper brings evidence about fundamental differences in disclosure regulation between systems.

In the UK, companies are regulated by the Companies Act, approved by the Parliament, and by financial reporting standards issued by professional institution, Financial Reporting Council (FRC). For the purpose of information disclosure in annual report, the UK Government published new Regulations for the strategic report and directors' report in Company Act and FRC published non-mandatory Guidance on the Strategic Report which recommendations. In order to develop pragmatic solutions to today's reporting needs, FRC established the Financial Reporting Lab to provide an environment where investors and companies can come together. Financial Reporting Lab is used by companies as a learning space, where new reporting formats are tested with investors, and investors can indicate areas where management can add greater value through the information they provide. Financial Reporting Lab focuses, as a centre for innovation in reporting, on gathering and sharing evidence from the market and provides the broader corporate community with feedback from shareholders on the value that new reporting formats bring (FRC 2017). While in the Czech Republic information disclosure requirements for companies are regulated by the Act on Accounting where Directive 2013/34/EU was transposed, accountants on the continent must follow the rules. This is also an aspect of difference in the relative importance of the accountancy profession and the state under the both approaches (Žárová 2016). Survey prepared by the UK Financial Reporting Lab confirms hypothesis that in countries with widespread ownership of companies by shareholders who do not have access to internal information, there will be a pressure for disclosure, audit and "fair" information (Nobes and Parker 2012). In most Continental European countries, the comparative lack of "outside" shareholders has meant that external financial reporting has been largely invented for the purpose of protecting creditors and for government, as tax collectors or controllers of economy. It does lead to uniformity.

Acknowledgements This paper has been prepared under financial support of research project IP100040, which author gratefully acknowledges.

References

Alexander D, Archer S (2000) On the myth of "Anglo-Saxon" financial accounting. Int J Account 35:539–557

Directive 2013/34/EU of the European Parliament and of the Council of 26 June 2013

Flower J (2002) Global financial reporting. Palgrave, Basingstoke

FRC (2014) Guidance on the strategic report. Available https://www.frc.org.uk/Our-Work/Publications/Accounting-and-Reporting-Policy/Guidance-on-the-Strategic-Report. Accessed 27 Feb 2017

FRC (2015) FRC's strategy for 2016. Available https://www.frc.org.uk/Our-Work/Publications/FRC-Board/FRC-s-Strategy-for-2016-19. Accessed 27 Feb 2017

FRC (2016) Lab project report: business model reporting. Available https://www.frc.org.uk/Our-Work/Publications/Financial-Reporting-Lab/FRC-Lab-Business-model-disclosure.pdf. Accessed 27 Feb 2017

FRC (2017) Financial reporting lab. Available https://www.frc.org.uk/Our-Work/Corporate-Governance-Reporting/Our-Work-Codes-Standards-Financial-Reporting-Lab.aspx. Accessed 27 Feb 2017

McGee RW (2008) Accounting reform in transition and developing economies. Springer Science, Miami

Nobes C, Parker RH (2008) Comparative international accounting. Pearson Education, London
Nobes C, Parker RH (2012) Comparative international accounting. Pearson Education, London
Žárová M (2011) Impact of international financial reporting standards on development of accounting regulatory system in the Czech Republic. Links. In: Trends in international business. IAE Lyon, Lyon, pp 253–261
Žárová M (2016) Reasons for differences in European financial reporting. Links. In: Procházka D (ed) New trends in finance and accounting – proceedings of the 17th annual conference on finance and accounting (online). Praha, 27.05.2016. Springer International Publishing, Švýcarsko 2017, s. 355–360. ISBN 978-3-319-49558-3. https://doi.org/10.1007/978-3-319-49559-0_33

What Are the Origins of New Leasing Conceptual Models and How These Models Are Coming True in IFRS 16?

Mariana Peprníčková

Abstract The paper examines an origin of newly accepted lease accounting rules under IFRS 16. In historical context, searches for circumstances that had affected certain steps made by IASB in whole developing process of the new standard include also FASB's role and perspectives. The conceptual lease accounting approaches are discussed in general in context with existing rules set out in IAS 17. The originally proposed innovative lease conceptual models are being analysed and compared in perspective of newly accepted IFRS 16. The substantial change of lessee accounting embodied in IFRS 16 has its origin in the proposed single approach by G4+1 in 1996, resp. 2000. The proposal of symmetrical solution for lessor accounting wasn't finally achieved due to its complexity and lack of prospective benefits. Finally, the 10-year joint project of IASB and FASB on improvement of lease accounting did not result into two same standards.

Keywords Lease accounting • Lessee • Lessor • IFRS • IASB • FASB

Introduction

Development of new accounting approach for leases had become a major objective for IASB and FASB for past several years. In fact, the real process which resulted in new IFRS 16 with effective date 1 January 2019 took place for almost 10 years. The almost decade was the necessary time for global standard setters to create through transparent public professional discussion a new standard which finally was able to sufficiently satisfy efficiency of current financial markets in global view. The most interesting fact is that the origin of new rules for lease accounting was founded even the decade before the IASB and FASB started the major project leases. When taking into consideration the historical context and especially the roots from very beginning past, it might be possible to determine and understand the reasons for newly

M. Peprníčková (✉)
University of Economics, Prague, Department of Financial Accounting and Auditing, Nam. W. Churchilla 4, 130 67 Prague, Czech Republic
e-mail: mariana.valaskova@vse.cz

D. Procházka (ed.), *The Impact of Globalization on International Finance and Accounting*, Springer Proceedings in Business and Economics,
https://doi.org/10.1007/978-3-319-68762-9_31

accepted accounting rules in lease area. Also reasons for the ten long period of developing the new lease standard can be multifactorial – a complexity of global professional consensus, politics, development of global economics etc.

The paper's aim is to analyse the accounting conceptual models which were purposed and finally agreed by the Boards in new IFRS 16 with taking into consideration the related historical development of circumstances with effect on the whole developing process. Those circumstances are assumed to be also explanatory for newly accepted lease accounting conceptual models. According to the analysis, the paper has also intention to compare these conceptual models between each other on professional level.

IAS 17 was issued by IASC in September 1982 with effective date 1 January 1984. The basic classification to financial and operating leases was followed from SFAS 13, which was issued in 1976 by FASB. In 1996 the IASC executive committee debated how to proceed the revision of IAS 17, called for by the core standards agreement (Camfferman and Zeff 2007). Although at that time the group G4+1[1] was concluding work on its discussion paper Accounting for Leases: A New Approach written by Warren McGregor, the IASC, in view to fulfil the core standard agreement with IOSCO, had chosen to make just a limited revision of IAS 17. However, the new approach set out in the discussion paper prepared by G4+1 was to abolish the distinction between operating and finance leases, and instead the rights and obligations of all leases that met the definitions of assets and liabilities would be recognised on the balance sheet, and differences between types of leases would be reflected in measurement (McGregor 1996). Another discussion paper was issued by G4+1 in 2000 to explore a conceptual approach to accounting for leases based on the financial reporting principles by the standard-setting bodies represented in the G4+1 (Nailor and Lennard 2000).

The IAS 17 approaches had begun to be criticised officially in 2005 by the US SEC, because of that the standard rules can result in very different accounting for transactions that are economically very similar (IFRS Foundation 2006).

Although there are existing lease accounting standards, these standards are regarded as out of date and unnecessarily complex and result in reporting that does not properly represent leasing transactions (IFRS Foundation 2006).

Lease Conceptual Models

Researchers on financial reporting of lease most often discuss the use and related effects for financial statements from the perspective of operating vs. capital lease accounting, while the distinction is whether method is applied on lessee's or lessor's

[1]The G4+1 was a group consisting of representatives of accounting standard setters from Australia, Canada, New Zealand, the United Kingdom, the United States, and the International Accounting Standards Committee (IASC).

financial statements. In case of lessee, the operating lease accounting means that the lessee recognises rent expense on the income statement and does not recognise lease assets or lease liabilities in the balance sheet. The capital lease accounting means the lessee initially recognises a lease asset and a lease liability in the balance sheet and subsequently records interest expense on the liability and depreciation expense on the asset.

In case of lessor accounting the reporting, a rental agreement as a capital lease instead of an operating lease does not add new liabilities or assets to the lessor's balance sheet. Instead, amounts are reclassified from *property under lease* to *lease receivable* (Lipe 2001). Moreover, these amounts are similar at lease inception. Nevertheless, subsequent recognition for operating leases produces rental revenue and depreciation expense, whereas capital leases generate interest revenue. Generally, capital lease accounting cases the lessor to recognise larger amounts of income in the early years of lease. This fact is caused by the method used for discounting cash flows embodied by lease receivable.

Existing Approach by IAS 17

Existing lease accounting approach embodied in IAS 17 is based on distinguishing capital and operating lease accounting. According to IAS 17 lease is classified as a finance lease if it transfers substantially all the risks and rewards incident to ownership. The IAS 17 specifies 8 situations that might normally lead to a lease being classified as a finance lease. All other leases are classified as operating leases.

When the lease is treated as finance lease, the lessee records the finance lease as an asset and a liability at the lower of the fair value of the asset and the present value of the minimum lease payments. Finance lease payments should be apportioned between the finance charge and the reduction of the outstanding liability (the finance charge to be allocated so as to produce a constant periodic rate of interest on the remaining balance of the liability). The lessor records a finance lease in the balance sheet as a receivable, at an amount equal to the net investment in the lease, and recognises finance income.

If a lease is an operating lease, the asset is not recorded on the lessee's balance sheet, and the lessee records the lease payments as an expense in the income statement over the lease term as it becomes payable. The lessee is not required to record either an asset or a long-term liability on the balance sheet. However, the lessee must disclose, at least in a note to the financial statement certain amounts of future minimum lease payments.

Existing lease accounting concepts were based on that assessment of ownership depends on the economic substance rather than the legal form of the lease contract. That is illustrated by making clear that the quantitative criteria set by the standard are to be used only as guidance, and the determination of whether a particular lease arrangement is to be classified as a finance or operating lease is a matter of professional judgement (made on the substance of the arrangement bases).

Unfortunately, "in practise the quantitative criteria typically have been perceived as precise rules and applied as absolute thresholds" (McGregor 1996).

After financial accounting scandals in early 2000s (including those involving Enron and WorldCom), the Sarbanes-Oxley Act emphasised "to promote high professional standards among, and improve the quality of audit services offered by … in order to protect investors" (USA 2002). The US SEC in its June 2005 Report under the Sarbanes-Oxley Act into off-balance-sheet issues noted: "The "all-or-nothing" nature of the guidance means that economically similar arrangements may receive different accounting – if they are just to one side or the other of the bright line test. … Nonetheless, because of the bright-line nature of the lease classification tests, this small difference in economics can completely change the accounting. Conversely, economically different transactions may be treated similarly" (US SEC 2005). A Comment by the Financial Accounting Standards Committee of the American Accounting Association stated that the "current accounting for leases (based on an ownership model) is probably the clearest example of a dysfunctional accounting standard because the rules-based approach of that standard has led to widespread non compliance with the intent of standard setters to have lease contracts reported on the balance sheet" (Biondi et al. 2011).

"Over the centuries, the form of a lease has been used to mask the substance of a financing arrangement" (Weidner 2016). Relating to all the criticism of lease accounting, it should be added that G4 + 1 initiative has brought to light a first new approach abolishing the distinction between operating and finance leases in 1996. It was maybe too far difficult to make the new approach alive earlier than 2016.

The G4+1 Proposal

In light to develop improved lease accounting standards (particularly in respect of accounting by lessees) and to provide information for making economic decisions in ensuring the reporting of relevant and reliable information, the G4+1 initiative brought into alive an aforementioned new approach for lease accounting. A new approach brought by G4+1 in 1996 proposed only the application of accounting concepts to lease contracts and focused principally on accounting by lessees. Concepts proposed by G4+1 should provide a base for development of standards requiring recognition as assets and liabilities of all material rights and obligations arising under lease contracts. According to definition of asset contained in conceptual framework, an ownership of a right to use a physical asset is embodying future economic benefits. Therefore, the clear implication of applying the conceptual framework is that it can be reasoned that all finance leases and most noncancelable operating leases qualify for recognition as assets and liabilities. Both finance and operating leases those contractual rights give rise to future economic benefits which the enterprise controls and obligations which it must meet. This approach should simplify the application of lease accounting standards in practice because of avoiding any assessment if substantial risks and rewards incident to ownership of the leased asset passed from the lessor to the lessee and nor qualitative guidelines.

Although the new approach did not focus on lessor accounting, it briefly stated that according to new proposed approach for lessee accounting, the symmetry of accounting between lessor and the lessee should be achieved (McGregor 1996). That leads to recognition of two assets in lessors balance sheet, one representing a right to receive lease payments under the lease and second a right to the service potential embodied in the leased property at the end of the lease terms.

The objective of discussion paper issued in 2000 by G4+1 was to specify in more detail the implementation of a new approach. In other words, the discussion paper presented proposals for how that approach might be reflected in accounting standards. Lessees should recognise the fair value of any rights and obligations contained in a lease contract. The fair value of the rights obtained by a lessee would generally be measured as the present value of the minimum payments required by the lease, plus any other liabilities incurred (IASB 2007). Recognition begins when the lessor makes the property available to the lessee. Lessors should capitalise all noncancelable leases and separately identify the present values of the lessee commitments (a receivable in respect of payments required by the lease) and the residual value of the leased asset (an interest in the residual value of the property), since they are subject to different risks (Lipe 2001; Nailor and Lennard 2000). In addition, the proposal sets out limit amounts of gain the lessor could recognise at inception.

The Group also recommended no specific exemption for short leases which would be inconsistent with the fundamental approach.

New Approach by IFRS 16

In June 1996, the IASC Board approved a project to revise IAS 17 to address certain essential issues communicated to IASC by IOSCO (core standards agreement). Completion of core standards in 1998 had leaded into IOSCO recommendation "that its members allow multinational issuers to use 30 IASC standards" (IOSCO 2000). In order to fulfil IOSCO's requirement for core standards completion, the IASC decided that new approaches for lease capitalization should be considered at a later stage. Encouraged by the US SEC (2005) Report and other critics of existing lease accounting, the IASB and FASB in 2006 undertook joint project under the Memorandum of Understanding towards improvement and convergence. As the US SEC Report had predicted, the project was both complicated and controversial (Weidner 2016). The two Boards issued a discussion paper in 2009, which was followed by a first exposure draft in 2010 and second exposure draft in 2013. The response rate (around 800 letters in 2010 and over 600 letters in 2013) to both of the exposure drafts was extensive. The early proposals were established on former G4 +1 discussion papers when according to previous feedback received, second exposure draft has even intention for proposal of a dual concept of accounting (named Type A and Type B).

After long time period of developing proposals, deliberations and redeliberations with all possible stakeholders, on January 2016, the IASB issued IFRS 16 which determines new accounting rules for leases. The IASB "now requires almost all leases, both capital and operating, to be recorded on the lessee's balance sheet" (Weidner 2016).

IFRS 16 defines a lease as a contract, or part of a contract, that conveys to the customer the right to control the use an identified asset for a period of time in exchange for consideration. IFRS 16 does not affect the accounting for services. It is applied only to leases, or lease components of a contract. It has two exemptions for leases: short-term leases (12 months or less) and leases of low-value assets (such as laptops and office furniture).

For a new definition of lease, there are important two elements: control of the use and an identified asset. Control is defined as it is conveyed where the customer has both the right to direct the identified asset's use and to obtain substantially all the economic benefits from that use. Definition of control emphasis on the concept of control, which has been used also in new revenue standard (IFRS 15) as well as in new consolidation standard (IFRS 10). An asset can be identified by being explicitly specified in a contract, but an asset can also be identified by being implicitly specified at the time it is made available for use by the customer.

IFRS 16 introduces a single lessee accounting model based on right-of-use approach. Lessee recognises lease assets and liabilities on the balance sheet, initially measured at the present value of future unavoidable lease payments. Lessee recognises amortisation of lease assets and interest on lease liabilities over the lease terms. It is expected that the amortisation of property, plant and equipment would often be calculated on straight line over the lease terms.

Consequently, the new single lessee model brings separate expense recognition and presentation. Amortisation of lease assets should be recognised within operating profit unlike interest on lease liabilities within finance costs. Regarding lease liabilities it has appropriate consequences for cash flow statement that the principal portion of lease liabilities should be recognised within financing activities and the interest portion of lease liabilities in accordance with the requirements relating to other interest paid.

Lessor lease accounting substantially carries forward the lessor accounting requirements in IAS 17. Thus, lessors continue to classify its leases as operating or finance lease with appropriate existing treatment. Even the symmetrical changes for lessors' accounting were proposed originally by G4+1 and then followed by both of the exposure drafts published by IASB, finally both of the Boards agreed not to change existing approach. There were concerns about that "the costs of changing lessor accounting would outweigh the benefit of doing so at this time" (IASB 2016). Also most of the stakeholders consider existing lessor accounting requirements well understood, as well as most users of financial statements are satisfied with information provided as they do not adjust current lessors' financial statements.

Despite the lease project was convergent and both of the Boards (IASB and FASB) were cooperating on developing new rules all along, they were not able to agree on identical standards. FASB does not allow the exemption for lease contract with low-value assets. The more significant and interesting difference is that FASB continues with distinction of finance and operating lease for income statement purposes. On the base of the distinction is made the expense recognition. If lease is classified as operating, the single lease expense is recognised as part of operating income. And consequently, total cash paid within operating activities in cash flow statement.

Conclusion

At the beginning of their intentions, the G4+1 and IASB were proposing a single model approach for lease accounting preferred for both lessees and lessors. Even if the original proposal of G4+1 focused on lessees' accounting, the G4+1 recommended to develop for lessors a model symmetrical to the lessees' model. According to published exposure drafts, the IASB attempted to develop symmetrical model for lessors, but finally after large public consultations, the original proposal was abandoned due to cost versus benefit reasons, complexity of the proposal and overall lack of information about a lessor's risk exposure. The lessors' financial statements were also found that they provide sufficiently needed information for users and the accounting rules are also clear for preparers of financial statements.

The main objective of developing new improved accounting for leases seems to be succeeded and fundamentally based on G4+1 original proposal. The definition of lease was redesigned and specified also with respect of "control concept" contained in new standards. The G4+1 recommended no exemptions from single right-of-use approach for short-term leases, however, defined. IFRS 16 gives exemptions for 12 months or less leases and low-value assets "in way that is expected to substantively reduce the costs of application without having any significant effect on the information provided" (IASB 2016). The decision about two exemptions is also a result of public discussion and IASB's deliberations, as a proposal how to treat short-term leases was originally proposed in exposure draft 2010.

The IASB and FASB require now almost all leases, both finance and operating, to be recognised on the lessee's balance sheet with the single measurement approach. In this light, the IASB and FASB accomplished the journey for improved lease accounting which meet investors' needs and truly reflect economic reality. However, the project was conducted as convergent by both of the Boards; they were not able to be agreed on one single approach for recognition in lessees' income statement. In FASB's view the finance and operating leases are substantively different, while "the economics of leases can vary for a lessee and that those economics should be reflected in the financial statements" (Weidner 2016). The divergent approach adopted by FASB will have different effect on the statement of

	G4+1	IAS 17		IFRS 16	
Lessee					
Balance Sheet	single right of use model - with no exemption	Finance lease	Operating lease	single right of use model - with exemption for: short-term leases of 12 months or less and leases of low value assets	
	Rights to use the asset	Underlying asset	-	An identified asset	
	Lease liabitity	Lease liability	-	Lease liability	
Income statement	-	Operating costs - depreciation	Operating costs - single expense	Operating costs - depreciation	
		Finance costs - interest		Finance costs - interest	
Lessor					
Balance Sheet	Symmetry model	Finance lease	Operating lease	Finance lease	Operating lease
	Lease receivable	Lease receivable	Underlying asset	Lease receivable	Underlying asset
	Residual value of the lease asset				
Income statement	-	Finance income - interest	Operating costs - depreciation - rent	Finance income - interest	Operating costs - depreciation - rent

Source: own elaboration

Fig. 1 Conceptual lease models by different approaches (Source: own elaboration)

comprehensive income and consequently on the statement of cash flows. The FASB explained that "to maintain the presentation of expenses and cash flows consistent with current GAAP are in direct response to U.S. stakeholder feedback to reduce costs associated with implementing the standard" (FASB 2016) (Fig 1).

Time which has been taken – 20 years since first thoughts about new approach, as well as 10 years of active development of IASB and FASB – for developing a new improved lease accounting can be seen as exaggerative. But when assessing length of developing time, there are several factors which might have influenced it. First decade of existing but postponed new approach, this period appeared to be too early for IASB as organisation which was only starting a career of international standard setter and making its efforts to become accepted accounting standards by the securities regulators. Second decade was the time which was spent by the Boards to develop new rules under extensive discussion with all possible interested and involved parties. During the last 10 years, the role of IASB was strengthened as a standard setter of global accounting standards which should provide transparency, comparability, accountability and efficiency to financial markets on global level. To achieve such a goal obviously must be time consuming. Simultaneously for the last 10 years, the IASB was facing to develop important improvements in several areas, such as financial instruments, consolidation, revenues, etc.

Surprising result of join lease project might be the certain distinctions of finally issued standards by IASB and FASB. The main reason already discussed above was justified as cost versus benefit for US stakeholders. Relating that it might be questioned by "the price that domestic companies and auditors would have to pay for changing their reporting language from GAAP to IFRS" (Katz 2014). In general, the current distinction just illustrates that FASB keeps its sovereign rights in developing new rules as national standard setter. That obviously is what the FASB's solution led to, solution in perspective for national stakeholders.

It appears that a big change in lessee accounting, which has its origin in 1996 proposal of G4+1, has become alive through IASB's IFRS 16. It has taken a pretty long time to bring commonly agreed and accepted solution. It will be again the time that will show, if the new rules will provide the desirable effect so called for by the investors.

Acknowledgments The article is processed as an output of a research project "Impact Analysis of changes on the quality of lease accounting in financial statements under new IFRS rules" registered by the Grant Agency under the registration number F1/91/2017.

References

Biondi Y, Bloomfield RJ, Glover JC et al (2011) A perspective on the joint IASB/FASB exposure draft on accounting for leases. Social Science Research Network, Rochester

Camfferman K, Zeff S (2007) Financial reporting and global capital markets: a history of the International accounting standards committee 1973–2000, 1st pub. Oxford University Press, Oxford

FASB (2016) FASB: understanding costs and benefits. Financial Accounting Foundation, Norwalk

IASB. Information for observers – Leases (2007) History of lease accounting (Agenda paper 12C) [online]. [cit. 30.09.2017]. Available at: http://archive.ifrs.org/Meetings/MeetingDocs/IASB/2007/March/22nd/Leases-0703-AP12C-obs.pdf

IASB (2016) Project summary and feedback statement: IFRS 16 leases. IFRS Foundation, London

IFRS Foundation (2006) Leases (AGENDA PAPER 8B) [online]. [cit. 31.07.2013]. Available at: http://www.ifrs.org/Current-Projects/IASB-Projects/Leases/Documents/0606s08b.pdf

IOSCO (2000) Press Release: IASC Standards [online]. Sydney, 2000. [cit. 30.09.2017]. Available at: http://www.iosco.org/news/pdf/IOSCONEWS26.pdf

Katz DM (2014) The Split Over Convergence. In: CFO. http://ww2.cfo.com/gaap-ifrs/2014/10/split-convergence/. Accessed 4 Mar 2017

Lipe RC (2001) Lease accounting research and the G4+1 proposal. Account Horiz 15:299–310. https://doi.org/10.2308/acch.2001.15.3.299

McGregor (1996) Warren. Accounting for leases: A new approach. In: Financial Accounting Series [online], no. 163-A. [cit. 31.07.2013] ISSN 0885-9051. Available at: http://www.ifrs.org/Current-Projects/IASB-Projects/Leases/Documents/FASBSR-1996-Leases-New-Approach.pdf

Nailor H, Lennard A (2000) Leases: Implementation of a New Approach. In: Financial Accounting Series [online]. no. 206-A. [cit. 30.09.2017] ISSN 0885-9051. Available at: http://archive.ifrs.org/Current-Projects/IASB-Projects/Leases/Documents/FASBSR-1996-Leases-New-Approach.pdf

USA (2002) Sarbanes-Oxeley Act of 2002. In: Public law [online]. 2002, no. 107-204. [cit. 30.09.2017]. Available at: https://www.sec.gov/about/laws/soa2002.pdf

US SEC (2005) Report and Recommendations Pursuant to Section 401(c) of the Sarbanes-Oxley Act of 2002 On Arrangements with Off-Balance Sheet Implications, Special Purpose Entities, and Transparency of Filings by Issuers. [online]. [cit. 30.09.2017]. Available at: https://www.sec.gov/news/studies/soxoffbalancerpt.pdf

Weidner DJ (2016) New FASB rules on accounting for leases: a Sarbanes-Oxley promise delivered. Social Science Research Network, Rochester

Company in a Global Environment and Intangible Assets

Teresa Maszczak

Abstract The article discusses the nature and material scope of intangible assets. The author presented that these are key factors in the process of doing business in the global market. The paper also presents possibilities of their identification in the accounting system. To solve the presented problem, the author used methods of analysis of literature, content of legal regulations, and a method of comparison and inference.

Keywords Company • Intangible assets • Accounting

Introduction

Recently growing importance of intangible assets in the process of building a competitive advantage in the market is observed. Among the intangible resources, a special role plays: the knowledge, the brand of a company, the market access and participation in it, the culture of an organization (standards, values, role models), and the qualitative characteristics of human resources (qualifications, skills, attitudes).

It is worth mentioning that among the specified resources, most of them qualify as the intellectual capital. An interesting view was expressed by G. Urbanek stating that "the intellectual capital is an invisible company's resource that produces visible results. The intellectual capital is both knowledge in itself and the result of its transformation to intangible assets" (Urbanek 2007). It is therefore necessary to determine the impact of intangible assets on the functioning of economic entities in the global environment, in conditions of constant changes, uncertainties, and risks, to formulate appropriate measures of intangible assets, their valuation, and the possibility of presentation of multi-section information about these resources in reporting. However, neither the theory of accounting nor business practice does so

T. Maszczak (✉)
Opole University, ul. Ozimska 46, 45-058, Opole, Poland
e-mail: tmaszczak@uni.opole.pl

D. Procházka (ed.), *The Impact of Globalization on International Finance and Accounting*, Springer Proceedings in Business and Economics,
https://doi.org/10.1007/978-3-319-68762-9_32

far present a clear and precise definition of intangible assets or ways of their classification, measurement, and valuation.

The aim of the article is to present the nature and material scope of the intangible assets which are key factors in the process of doing business in the global market, as well as an indication of the possibility of their identification in the accounting system.

To solve the presented problem, the author used methods of analysis of literature, content of legal regulations, and a method of comparison and inference.

Company in the Process of Social and Economic Changes

In the economic literature, lots of views on the nature of the company can be met. Given the purpose of this paper, the essence of the company was adopted from the perspective of systems theory,[1] which emphasizes the holistic nature of the organization separated from the external environment, and at the same time associated with numerous and multidirectional interactions (Bielski 2002; Griffin 1996).

According to Bielski "the organization is an open social and technological goal-oriented system and having a specific structure (the way of order)" (Bielski 2002). At the same time, it should be added that the goals must assume active participation in the processes of changes in the environment, expose the individual's characteristics of company's development, and optimally utilize its potential (Komorowski 2002). Companies cannot avoid participation in the process of changes and social and economic development, because to a large extent are due to permanent and mutual interactions with the environment (Steinerowska 2009). It is worth quoting the view of T. Listwan who drew attention to the phenomenon being crucial for the functioning of the entity, such as "environment's turbulence, globalization, demographic changes, role of technology, economy based on information and services, intellectualization of work" (Listwan 2005).

Given the variety of factors occurring in the external environment of the entity, one should recall the importance of an attribute of company's flexibility in relation with the environment. It is in fact an essential condition for building a permanent competitive advantage and can even determine the existence of the entity. In the modern world, the flexibility of the organizational structure is no longer a subject of choice for the organization but a kind of compulsion. It may possibly choose whether to the flexibility as means/way of shaping their competitive advantage, it will take a reactive or proactive approach (Herman and Poznanska 2008).

The reactive assumption minimizes ongoing efforts of an organization for its adaptation to the changing matching conditions. It is also associated with the risk that necessary changes will be either too late inappropriately diagnosed or too late

[1]Learning about the systems or complex things by Ludwig von Bertalanffy – creator of the theory of systems.

ineffectively implemented. The proactive way involves deliberate anticipating and preventive actions that will be able to contribute to the control of future developments.

In literature there are many models of organizations, ranging from the classic proposed by H. J. Leavitt (subsystems: goals, people, technology, structure), then extended with management subsystem according to the concept by L. Krzyzanowski (Griffin 1996; Kozminski and Piotrowski 2007; Krzyzanowski 1994), until today the 7S model by Peters, Phillips, and Waterman developed by the consulting firm McKinsey (strategy, structure, systems, skills, staff, management style, shared values) (Waterman et al. 1980).

Analyzing the contemporary model of organization functioning in a global environment (economic, political and legal, social, of science and technology, of ecosystem), essential elements (subsystems) of this model were indicated, such as strategy, structure, systems, skills, staff, management style, and shared values (Fig. 1). The contemporary business model considers the elements (subsystems) of the organization in a different way than the previous (classic) models did. The intellectual intangible assets, defined as organization's specific attributes, take precedence over tangible values. Therefore, intangible assets are a key factor in building a strategy for success.

Analyzing the contemporary model of organization functioning in a global environment (economic, political and legal, social, of science and technology, of ecosystem), essential elements(subsystems) of this model were indicated, such as strategy, structure, systems, skills, staff, management style, and shared values (Fig. 1). The contemporary business model considers the elements (subsystems) of the organization in a different way than the previous (classic) models did. The intellectual intangible assets, defined as organization's specific attributes, take precedence over tangible values. Therefore, intangible assets are a key factor in building a strategy for success.

In the presented business model 7S, among all the components, a special importance is given to the subsystem of values (a set of values, attitudes, beliefs) in relation to the business environment in the process of doing business.[2]

The strategy, structure, and system form material resources, which are associated with the technical side of the company. The other three subsystems (staff, qualifications, management styles) represent the social resources of the company.

The evolution of views on the nature of the company in the era of social and economic changes led to distinguishing the resources as key determinants of achieving a competitive advantage by the company.

---

[2]It should be emphasized that in the later period, R. Pascale and Athos A. proposed a change – the replacement of the subsystem of values by part the element "superordinate goals" (Pascale and Athos 1981). The motivation for the change was based on the conviction of Pascale and Athos that the essence of the goal is the overarching concept and mission for taken action of the company in environments. Then J. Weber introduced a subsystem "leadership" in place of "superordinate goals" instead, to put goals in the structure as a secondary.

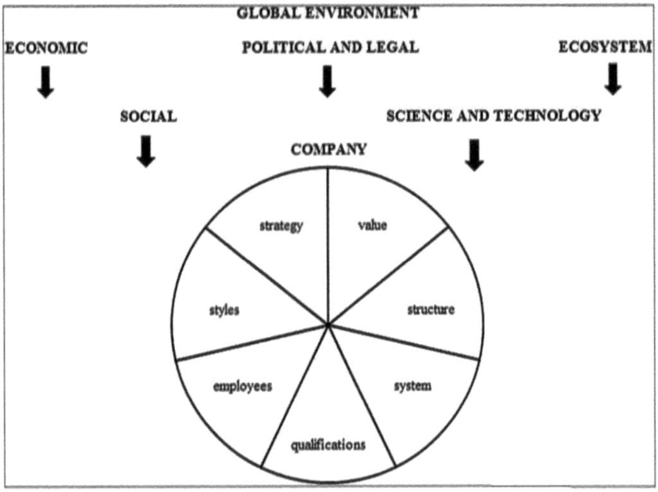

Source: own study based on (Gwiazda 2012)

Fig. 1 Organization as a system in a global environment (Source: own study based on Waterman et al. 1980)

As a result, in contemporary literature and business practice, there is a new look at the essence of the company called "resource approach". Representatives of this concept were B. Wernerfelt, A. Resource, (Prahalad and Hamel 1990; Suszynski 2007). At the same time, it should be noted that a special place in this trend is the knowledge of the intangible assets. They are referred to as "intangible assets without physical form, unique assets elements, which integrated with tangible assets may be the subject of strategic management" (Suszynski 2007).

In conclusion, it must be underlined that the company's environment is the factor influencing the intangible assets. Economic, social, political and legal, ecological, technological changes taking place in the company's surroundings, relations between entities, they all create a range of intangible assets.

Intangible Assets in Accounting

The discussion on the nature of modern company and its potential wealth presented in this article indicates, among others, a broad understanding of the assets of an intangible nature and how large a role they play in the process of building a competitive advantage in today's world. These assets are, among others, knowledge, market access and participation in it, corporate reputation, organization culture, and the qualitative characteristics of human resources. However, neither the theory of accounting nor business practice does so far present a clear and precise definition of intangible assets nor ways of their classification, measurement, and valuation.

Low and Kalafut (2004) rightly expressed the view that "the economists do not know exactly what is happening because the measurements upon which they are based include only a portion of economic activity. The accountants see only a partial picture of the company because they have not developed tools to track and evaluate resources that cannot be touched or spend. The investors are moving in the dark."

Emerging studies of reporting as a final product of accounting focus their attention mainly on intangible assets that meet the statutory requirements of the definition of "fixed assets," regulated by the Accounting Act of 29 September 1994. Meanwhile, there is a need for methodological and tool solutions that can present more opportunities for measurement, valuation, and reporting on business under conditions of uncertainties and changes.

More detailed information on the intangible assets is determined in the International Financial Reporting Standard (IFRS) and in particular IAS 38 Intangible Assets and SIC-32 Intangible Assets: Web Site Costs (Kabalski 2015b). According to the standard, the intangible assets are identifiable as nonmonetary resources without any physical form. Assets are controlled by an entity as a result of past events, and stemming from the asset, it is expected of the entity to generate a future economic benefit.

In accordance with IAS 38, the intangible assets include scientific or technical knowledge, design and implementation of new processes or systems, licenses, intellectual property, market knowledge and trademarks (including brand names and publishing titles), computer software, patents, copyrights, motion picture films, customer lists, mortgage servicing rights, fishing licenses, import quotas, franchises, relations with customers or suppliers, customers loyalty, market share, and marketing rights. At the same time, it should be noted that not all the resources meet the definition of an intangible asset.

In the Polish legal regulations (Art. 3, Section 1, point 14 of the Accounting Act of 29 September 1994), the intangible assets are referred to intangible assets acquired by the entity, included in fixed assets; property rights suitable for business use, with the expected economic life longer than 1 year; intended to use by the entity; and in particular:

- Wealth copyrights, related rights, licenses, concessions
- The rights to inventions, patents, trademarks, utility, and ornamental patterns
- Know-how
- Acquired goodwill and completed development costs

The definition of intangible assets in IAS 38 defines synthetically their essence, does not impose to purchase and use them in the period longer than 1 year, and does not include the goodwill to their scope.

Under the additional requirement of IAS 38 in order to recognize an intangible resource as the intangible asset, they have to be characterized by traceability and controllability. The intangible assets are identifiable not only on the basis of a contract, or in other way, but also when they can be isolated and, for example, sold, transferred, granted rights to its use (a license), leased, and exchanged separately or together with a contract component asset or obligation (Kabalski 2015a). They can also be assets generated on their own if they meet the conditions (Kabalski 2015c):

- It is possible from a technical point of view that the completion of the development works makes them fit for use or sale.
- The entity intends to complete the development works and use or sell their effects.
- The effect of development works in the form of an intangible asset will generate in the future economic benefits.
- There are technological, financial, and other necessary resources to complete the development works and to use or sell their effect.
- It is possible to reliably establish incurred costs of the intangible asset during the development works.

In accordance with IAS 38, the intangible assets are controllable if the entity gains economic benefits from them in a way that prevents simultaneously reaping these benefits by other entities.

Accounting Act of 29 September 1994 defines the intangible assets differently. As opposed to IAS 38, the statutory definition of intangible assets imposes an obligation to purchase (only acquired rights), with the exception of development. This means that this asset class can be classified only by the intangible assets purchased, received through donations or transferred in kind. The class does not include the intangible assets which are not used by the entity, but they are owned by it in order to achieve the economic benefits resulting from the increase in value of these assets, obtaining revenue in the form of interest, dividends (shares in profits), or other benefits, including commercial transactions (Art. 3, Section 1, point 17 of the Accounting Act of 29 September 1994). The differences in material scope between the Act and IAS 38 concerning the intangible assets are presented in Table 1.

In summary of the discussion of the nature and scope of the intangible assets in the accounting, it should be stated that they must meet certain conditions regulated by the provisions of national and international law, so that they can be identified in the accounting system. Their range presented in the financial statements is definitely much narrower than in the management sciences. Attention should be focused in the future on the construction of the model and the improvement of integrated reporting forms, which generates both financial information and nonfinancial (including a wide range of information on intangible assets). The proposed model of integrated reporting generates multi-section information useful in decision-making processes of business operations in the global market.

Table 1 Material scope of the intangible assets

Intangible assets	Accounting Act of 29 September 1994	IAS 38
Goodwill emerging from combined projects	Intangible assets	A separate position not classified as the intangible assets
Costs of unfinished development works	Prepaid expenses	Intangible assets (as long as the conditions are met, otherwise the cost of the reporting period)
Web site costs 1	Unspecified (prepaid expenses or costs of the reporting period)	Intangible assets (as long as the conditions are met, otherwise the cost of the reporting period)
Computer software	Intangible assets	Intangible assets and fixed assets, if they are closely related to a specific fixed asset
Intangible assets maintained in order to achieve the economic benefits resulting from the increase in value of these assets, obtaining revenue in the form of interest, dividends (shares in profits), or other benefits, including commercial transactions	Investments	Intangible assets
Intangible assets held for sale (but nonstock)	Intangible assets	Current fixed assets held for sale (IFRS 5, provided that they are fit for immediate sale in its present condition and the sale is highly probable)

Source: own study based on (Kabalski 2015c)

Conclusion

Presented discussion on the nature and material scope of the intangible assets in the process of building a competitive advantage, as well as an indication of the possibility of their identification in the accounting system, has fulfilled the aim of the paper.

The intangible assets recently occupy a particular place in the structure of business assets of a modern company. They affect the relationship between the entity and the environment in business activity. Among these resources they are, for example, knowledge, market access and participation in it, corporate reputation, organizational culture, and the qualitative characteristics of human resources. Most of intangible assets of the company create the so-called intellectual capital, which determines the strategy to competitively struggle.

The challenges of the modern world determine changes in the sphere of goals choices, and they shape the new way of company's business. The intangible assets which are specific attributes of organizations are seen as superior to material values.

Social and economic transformations also have determined the process of changes in the accounting system, including the reporting subsystem, so that it should be adapted to the current conditions in which the entities operate. However, neither the theory of accounting nor business practice does so far present a clear and precise definition of intangible assets or ways of their classification, measurement, valuation, and the possibility of disclosure in reporting.

Emerging studies on reporting as a final product of accounting focus their attention mainly on the intangible assets that meet the statutory requirements of the definition of "fixed assets" according to the Accounting Act of 29 September 1994. The intangible assets must therefore meet certain conditions regulated by the provisions of national and international law, so that they can be identified in the accounting system. Meanwhile, there is a need for methodological and tool solutions presenting more opportunities for measurement, valuation, and reporting on business under conditions of uncertainties and changes.

The scope of disclosures of intangible assets presented in the financial statement is definitely much narrower than in the management sciences. Attention should be focused in the future on the construction of the model and the improvement of integrated reporting forms, which generates both financial information and nonfinancial (including a wide range of information on intangible assets). The proposed model of integrated reporting generates multi-section information useful in decision-making processes of business operations in the global market.

References

Accounting Act of 29 September 1994. Journal of Laws of 2013, item 330, as amended

Bielski M (2002) Podstawy teorii organizacji i zarzadzania. Beck, Warsaw, pp 38–43 (in Polish)

Griffin RW (1996) Podstawy zarzadzania organizacjami. PWN, Warsaw, pp 86–88 (in Polish)

Herman A, Poznanska K (2008) Przedsiebiorstwo wobec wyzwan globalnych. Oficyna Wydawnicza Szkola Glowna Handlowa w Warszawie, Warsaw, pp 129–130 (in Polish)

Kabalski P (2015a) Miedzynarodowe Standardy Sprawozdawczosci Finansowej a ustawa o rachunkowosci. Rachunkowosc, Warsaw, p 49 (in Polish)

Kabalski P (2015b) Miedzynarodowe Standardy Sprawozdawczosci Finansowej a ustawa o rachunkowosci. Rachunkowosc, Warsaw, p 50 (in Polish)

Kabalski P (2015c) Miedzynarodowe Standardy Sprawozdawczosci Finansowej a ustawa o rachunkowosci. Rachunkowosc, Warsaw, p 51 (in Polish)

Komorowski J (2002) Planowanie finansowe w przedsiębiorstwie. Teoria i praktyka. ODDK Gdańsk In: Komorowski J (ed) Cele i wartosci wspolczesnego przedsiebiorstwa. Oficyna Wydawnicza Szkola Głowna Handlowa w Warszawie, Warsaw, 2011, p 188 (in Polish)

Kozminski AW, Piotrowski W (2007) Zarzadzanie: teoria i praktyka. PWN, Warsaw (in Polish)

Krzyzanowski L (1994) Podstawy nauki o organizacji i zarządzaniu. PWN, Warsaw, p 173 (in Polish)

Listwan T (2005) Zarzadzanie talentami – wyzwanie wspolczesnych organizacji. In: Mlost L (ed) Globalne zarzadzanie talentami w zmiennym otoczeniu gospodarczym In: Szymanski W (ed) Przedsiebiorstwo wobec wymogu elastycznosci. Oficyna Wydawnicza Szkola Głowna Handlowa w Warszawie, Warsaw, 2012, p 114 (in Polish)

Low J, Kalafut PC (2004) Niematerialna wartosc firmy. Ukryte zrodla przewagi konkurencyjnej. In: Grzybek O (ed) Zasoby niematerialne jako przedmiot badan w naukach ekonomicznych. Kierunki harmonizacji polskiej rachunkowosci z miedzynarodowymi standardami sprawozdawczosci finansowej, Studia Ekonomiczne/Uniwersytet Ekonomiczny w Katowicach 190, 2014, pp 71–78 (in Polish)

Pascale R, Athos A (1981) The Art of Japanese Management. Penguin Harmondsworth 81. In: Gwiazda A (ed) Analiza koncepcji czynnikow sprawczych kierowania oraz jej zastosowanie w praktyce. Wspolczesne zarzadzanie 1, 2012 (in Polish)

Prahalad CK, Hamel G (1990) The core competence of the corporation. Harvard Bus Rev, May–June. In: Murawska M (ed) Zasoby niematerialne przedsiebiorstwa w procesie ksztaltowania wartości. In: Suszynski C (ed) Przedsiebiorstwo Wartosc Zarzadzanie. PWE, Warsaw, 2007, p 313 (in Polish)

Steinerowska S (2009) Zarządzanie talentami jako czynnik sukcesu XXI wieku. In: Mlost L (ed) Globalne zarzadzanie talentami w zmiennym otoczeniu gospodarczym, vol 2012. Przedsiebiorstwo wobec wymogu elastycznosci Oficyna Wydawnicza Szkola Głowna Handlowa w Warszawie, Warsaw, p 114. (in Polish)

Urbanek G (2007) Wartość kapitału intelektualnego a koszt kapitału przedsiębiorstwa. Przegl Organ 3:33–36

Waterman R, Peters T, Phillips JR (1980) Structure is not organization. Bus Horiz 23(3). In: Gwiazda A (ed) Analiza koncepcji czynników sprawczych kierowania oraz jej zastosowanie w praktyce. Współczesne zarządzanie 1, 2012 (in Polish)

Wernerfelt B, Resource A (2007) based view of the firm. Strateg Manag J. In: Suszynski C (ed) Przedsiebiorstwo Wartosc Zarzadzanie. PWE, Warsaw, 2007, p 313 (in Polish)

The Concept of Measurement and Reporting of Human Capital

Wojciech Koziol

Abstract For many years, the intangible assets are becoming an increasingly important source of competitive advantage between contemporary enterprises. This limits the relevance of financial measures based on data from traditional financial statements and increases the need for hard data on intangible assets. One such area is human capital (HC). The article is a response to the emerging information gap. The article presents a method for measuring HC, along with the outline of the reporting system, which is illustrated using a practical case. The last part of the article presents the results of a case study of the Polish company. It includes a simplified report on (HC) and examples of basic financial indicators taking into account the data on the (HC).

Keywords Human capital measurement • Human capital reporting

Introduction

Human capital (HC) is one of the most frequently researched areas in economic sciences over the last decades. The dominant research area is the one undertaken by T. Shultz and G.S. Becker, marked by the concept of investing in people (Blaug 1992). This programme has led to researching a number of economic issues including education and household economics. It should be noted, however, that unlike in the alternative research approach presented by the author, traditional research studies do not give much attention to the concept of 'capital'. Many authors offer vague definitions of capital, referring to it as something that is undoubtedly positive and valuable. This simplification has resulted in a great number of traditional research programmes focused on various economic problems. The most commonly discussed subjects of scientific debate in the field of HC include issues of business management, finance and accounting and

W. Koziol (✉)
Cracow University of Economics, Department of Accounting, Rakowicka 27, 31-510 Cracow, Poland
e-mail: koziolw@uek.krakow.pl

D. Procházka (ed.), *The Impact of Globalization on International Finance and Accounting*, Springer Proceedings in Business and Economics,
https://doi.org/10.1007/978-3-319-68762-9_33

macroeconomic analysis. As a result, we can formulate two key functional aspects of human capital – economic and organizational. Organizational aspect emphasizes the role of proper management of human resources, as a way to achieve the business objectives of the organization. In turn, the economic aspect treats the HC as one of the resources used in production processes. In addition, scientific research on the HC can be divided from the HC level perspective into individual, organizational (e.g. company level) and macroeconomic (Harpan and Draghici 2016).

The emergence of the concept of HC initiated extensive research on the possibilities of measuring this value. The result is a lot of definitions of HC and ways of measuring it, but none of the methods have proved to be dominant.

The standard to measure HC stock has been categorized into three types: output-based approach, cost-based approach and income-based approach (Kwon 2009). Moreover, measurement of HC may be expressed in monetary terms or in terms of an index. The benefit of using monetary terms measurement is its comparability, including comparability with financial aspect of an organization's activities. On the other hand, it may be problematic to estimate value of human resources used by an organization. The use of terms of index creates difficulty with comparability with financial aspect of the organization's activities. Still, if there is universally accepted method, it allows for comparisons between companies, geographic regions, etc. The problem which can limit the universalism is the matter of wages used to construct an index (Slaper and Hall 2011).

A report on a chosen field of an organization activity is a formalized way of settling with a group of stakeholders. In some areas (especially the financial ones), reporting is legally normalized and presents the concern of a state about the stakeholders. Nowadays we can see two trends in the field of reporting on the activities of the organization. The first is the growing demand for information on the intangible assets, which are not recognized in the traditional financial statements. This need arises as a result of the growing participation in modern production processes. The second issue is the increase in expectations of the society regarding support of the sustainable development. This generates the need for reporting on socially responsible actions (Koziol 2016).

We can point at the broad application of information on the organization's HC. The most important areas are reporting of corporate social responsibility, systems of evaluation and bonus remuneration of managers (Widener 2006) and systems assessing the effectiveness of the company (Koziol et al. 2014; Lajili and Zeghal 2006). In addition, reporting data related to the HC area can be a tool to create the market value of the company (Gamerschlag 2013).

Still, there are problems with expanding the range of traditional reporting. According to Ijiri (1965), a subject of measurement can only be facts that are possible to identify, and also there should exist a possibility of identification of measures (a precisely defined process of measurement). The resources of an organization are a subject of measurement and reporting. In a narrow depiction, resources are a legal property of a company, however, from the wider point of view, according to International Accounting Standards and International Financial Reporting Standards, the criterion of controllability. A company, on the basis of employment contract, receives HC available and is responsible for its use taking the risk of disposing this capital and is obliged to fair settlement with HC owner.

Alternative Model of Human Capital Measurement

HC as a social and economic category, as well as a subject of the periodic reporting, requires sufficient and theoretically justified definition and rules of measurement. Moreover, if the HC reporting is to become a basis for the organization's performance evaluation, it is necessary to establish criteria for such an evaluation. The model of HC presented in this part of the article allows for the long-reaching implementation of the demand of using theoretical and practical accounting achievements for the evaluation of company performance and income potential.

The starting point for formulating a proper theory of capital (and then HC) is the statement that capital – unlike specific and heterogeneous assets – is abstract, aggregated and homogenous in its character (Dobija and Dobija 2003). This differentiation is reflected in the 5-century-old accounting principle of asset-capital dualism. Capital defined as the ability to perform work is represented by resources, while capital concentration in a given object determines its value.

Capital is a dynamic category, and its understanding requires identifying the factors which have an impact on changes to its value, especially the time factor. A dynamic model of capital changes is presented by formula (Dobija 2011):

$$C_t = C_0 e^{rt} = C_0 e^{(p-s+m)t}. \quad (1)$$

Capital is subject to three key environmental factors: natural capital flow subdued to spontaneous diffusion (s), factors diminishing the impact of destructive forces as a result of work and management (m) and an 8% natural potential growth (p). The level of 8% economic constant of potential growth is confirmed by a number of research studies, especially in the area of rates of return in capital markets where it is reflected in risk premiums in the analysis of rates of return on human capital and agricultural products (Koziol 2011). These factors can increase the initial value of capital (C_0) or lead to its dispersion. Another important implication of the presented model is the fact that capital does not originate from 'nothing' – it originates from initial capital (C_0).

HC is based on capitalized resources necessary to build the economic potential to perform work by humans. In the first place, it includes the costs of professional education increased by the costs of living. It is necessary to incur the costs of living to prepare the physical carrier of HC – the human body. Costs are incurred in time (t), which is necessary to prepare people to perform a given profession – from the time of birth to the moment of starting a professional career. If the human body is well prepared and a young person completes his/her education as planned, it indicates that capital diffusion (s) is compensated for by parents' efforts (parameter m). A formula of capital can be developed for an employee (H_t), where initial outlays are represented by (H_0), constant economic value (p) and capitalization time (t) (Dobija 2011):

$$H_t = H_0 e^{pt} \tag{2}$$

This HC model can be further extended to represent capital as the sum of capitalized costs of living (HC.L) and education expenditures (HC.E). These outlays lead to the ability to perform work, and this ability increases in the course of gaining experience. The supplementary formulas represent the development of HC based on the costs of living (HC.L) and education costs (HC.E):

$$H(T) = (HC.L + HC.E) \cdot (1 + Q(T)) \tag{3}$$

In the case of annual capitalization, the particular human capital components can be presented in the following way:

$$HC.L = k \cdot 12 \frac{e^{pt} - 1}{p}$$
$$HC.E = e \cdot 12 \frac{e^{pt} - 1}{p} \tag{4}$$

where k are the monthly costs of living and e the monthly education costs.

The process of gaining work experience can be graphically presented as a learning curve. This concept assumes a slower pace of an increase in the work potential in the course of subsequent work cycles (repetitions). It can be assumed that an employee performs a given task in the following year with greater efficiency (%), but efficiency increases slower in the course of time. The adjustment of the learning curve to the needs of the HC model facilitates estimation of increased HC in the course of work (gaining experience). This additional value of HC is subject to valuation and is integrated into the HC structure as a capital combined with an experience. Experience factor (Q(T)) is expressed by the function of years:

$$Q(T) = 1 - T^{\frac{\ln(1-w)}{\ln 2}} \tag{5}$$

where w = learning factor and T = years of work experience $T > 1$.

Finally, the formula of HC comprising component of the acquired professional experience (HC.D) can be represented as follows:

$$H(T) = (HC.L + HC.E) \cdot (1 + Q(T)) = HC.L + HC.E + HC.D \tag{6}$$

From the perspective of the goal of incurred costs of living, costs of living incurred after adulthood (e.g. during university education) should be classified as the cost of education, which increases HC.E. HC.L is limited to capitalized costs of living until reaching adulthood. Therefore, it will be the most common and universal component of HC. HC.E and HC.D have a more individualized dimension, which can be described as the intellectual capital of the employee (HC.I). It can be represented as follows:

$$HC.E + HC.D = HC.I \tag{7}$$

An Outline of Human Capital Reporting

The presented model of HC complies with the subject of measurement defined by Ijiri (1965). Both HC and methodology for measuring it are precisely defined. Admittedly, HC is assigned to employees; however, it may be made available to the employer under an agreement with the employee. Properly formulated employment contract makes the HC controllable and at the disposal of the company.

The rest of this paper describes an example of the use of discussed methods for measuring HC in one of the companies employing 625 employees over the research period. Based on personal data, for each of the workers, the HC value and its components were calculated (HC.E, HC.L and HC.D) (Table 1).

On the basis of data on the value of individual HC among staff, a statement of values and structure of the HC at the disposal of the researched enterprise was prepared, with division into organizational units (Table 2). The report shows the production potential of a unit contained in human resources. It informs not only about the number of employees but mainly about their qualifications. The higher value of the HC of employees, the higher are their qualifications. HC division into HC.I and HC.L allows for separation of component qualifications from the total amount of HC, which consists of the acquired knowledge and experience of employees. Depending on the information requirements, we can use a more detailed analysis of HC.

Table 1 Structure of individual human capital, selected employees

Employee personal data	HC.L	HC.E	HC.D	HC	HC.I
Carpenter	280,877	11,687	36,086	328,650	47,773
Accountant I	280,877	83,457	37,688	402,022	121,145
Vice chief accountant	280,877	264,814	73,723	619,414	338,537
Construction worker	280,877	11,687	22,204	314,768	33,891
Marketing specialist	280,877	46,192	0	327,069	46,192
Construction manager	280,877	264,814	91,659	637,350	356,473
Unit Total	174,832,000	38,486,000	23,450,000	236,797,000	61,936,000

Source: authorial computation
Note: All values are in Polish zlotys

Table 2 Report on human capital structure in the researched company

Department	Amount of empl.	HC	HC.L	HC.E	HC.D	HC.I
Administration	57	31,381	16,010	11,483	3888	15,371
Financial administration	7	4187	1966	1635	586	2221
Construction sites administration	30	15,540	8707	5179	1654	6833
Construction department DDB	10	3104	2808	38	257	295
Construction department DPU	72	22,957	20,223	570	2164	2734
Construction department DUR	13	3704	3402	48	255	303
Purchasing department	11	4765	3090	1205	470	1675
Construction department DX	123	37,621	33,830	1029	2762	3791
Procurement department	18	9600	5056	3342	1202	4544
Department of construction equipment exploitation (HTS)	55	19,076	15,448	1710	1918	3628
Accounting	12	6081	3371	2192	519	2711
Construction department TDB	85	30,679	23,845	3916	2888	6804
Technical analysis department	15	8422	4213	3135	1074	4209
Steel structures department (WKS)	117	39,680	32,863	3004	3813	6817
Sum	625	236,797	174,832	38,486	23,450	61,936

Source: authorial computation
Note: All values are in thousands Polish zlotys

The report on the HC can provide information base for financial analysis for internal and external users. The use of financial indicators based on traditional financial statements and reports on HC allows for an analysis of not only traditional resources of the organization but also human resources. These indicators can therefore provide additional support for managerial decision-making by the company and investment decisions by investors. In Table 3 there are some basic indicators on the HC in the studied company.

Conclusion

Outline of the report on HC of a company provides information on the production potential of an organization contained in human resources. It is therefore a proposal to fill the information gap on the key area of intangible assets of organizations, which are not recognized in the traditional financial statements. The inclusion of a report on the HC to the annual financial report on the activities of the company may require the creation of standards in order to achieve comparability of reports on HC. These standards should clarify the detailed guidelines for measuring HC of workers, particularly in specific cases.

Table 3 Basic human capital indicators in the researched company

Department	HC per empl.	HC.I per empl.	HC.I share (HC.I/HC)
Administration	550.5	269.7	49.0%
Financial administration	598.1	317.3	53.0%
Construction sites administration	518.0	227.8	44.0%
Construction department DDB	310.4	29.5	9.5%
Construction department DPU	318.8	38.0	11.9%
Construction department DUR	284.9	23.3	8.2%
Purchasing department	433.2	152.3	35.2%
Construction department DX	305.9	30.8	10.1%
Procurement department HDZ	533.3	252.4	47.3%
Department of construction equipment exploitation (HTS)	346.8	66.0	19.0%
Accounting	506.8	225.9	44.6%
Construction department TDB	360.9	80.0	22.2%
Technical analysis department TDT	561.5	280.6	50.0%
Steel structures department (WKS)	339.1	58.3	17.2%
Average value	378.9	99.1	26.2%

Source: authorial computation
Note: All values are in thousands Polish zlotys

The proposed method of measurement and reporting of HC is based on a traditional accounting methodology, in particular on the basis of historical cost valuation in monetary units. This allows to extend the range of financial analysis with a combination of reporting data on HC with data from traditional financial statements. A supplement of this measurement method can be other methods based on nonmonetary indicators.

Acknowledgments Publication was financed from the funds granted to the Faculty Management at Cracow University of Economics, within the framework of the subsidy for the maintenance of research potential.

References

Blaug M (1992) The methodology of economics or how economists explain. Cambridge University Press, Cambridge

Dobija D, Dobija M (2003) O naturze kapitału. Zesz Teor Rachunkowości 17(73):5–27

Dobija M (2011) Labor productivity vs. minimum wage level. Mod Econ 02:780–787. https://doi.org/10.4236/me.2011.25086

Gamerschlag R (2013) Value relevance of human capital information. J Intellect Cap 14 (2):325–345. https://doi.org/10.1108/14691931311323913

Harpan I, Draghici A (2016) Debate on the multilevel model of the human capital measurement. Procedia Soc Behav Sci 124:170–177. https://doi.org/10.1016/j.sbspro.2014.02.474

Ijiri Y (1965) Axioms and structures of conventional accounting measurement. Account Rev 40 (1):36–53
Koziol L, Koziol W, Wojtowicz A, Pyrek R (2014) An outline of compensation system based on human capital theory. Proc Soc Behav Sci 148:551–558. https://doi.org/10.1016/j.sbspro.2014.07.078
Koziol W (2016) Human capital reporting as a source of reliable information for marketing communication process in a socially responsible company. Int J Strateg Innov Market 3 (2):28–40. https://doi.org/10.15556/IJSIM.03.02.003
Kozioł W (2011) Stała potencjalnego wzrostu w rachunku kapitału ludzkiego. Nierówności społeczne a wzrost gospodarczy 19:252–260. Uniwersytet Rzeszowski
Kwon D-B (2009) Human capital and its measurement. In: The 3rd OECD world forum on "statistics, knowledge and policy" charting progress, building visions, improving life, Busan, Korea 27–30 Oct. 2009
Lajili K, Zeghal D (2006) Market performance impacts of human capital disclosures. J Account Public Policy 25:171–194. https://doi.org/10.1016/j.jaccpubpol.2006.01.006
Slaper TF, Hall TJ (2011) The triple bottom line: what is it and how does it work? Indiana Bus Rev 86(1):4–8. Spring
Widener SK (2006) Human capital, pay structure, and the use of performance measures in bonus compensation. Manag Account Res 17:198–221. https://doi.org/10.1016/j.mar.2005.06.001

Exploratory Analysis of Voluntary Reporting on Human Resources in the Czech Republic

Petr Petera and Jaroslav Wagner

Abstract Our paper strives to analyse quantity and content of voluntary disclosures relating to human resources within annual reports of the largest corporations domiciled in the Czech Republic. In this context, we distinguish disclosures on social responsibility (which are interesting especially for stakeholders like employees and unions) and disclosures related to human capital (which are interesting especially for shareholders). Joined analyses of these two intertwined areas are infrequent because scholars usually aim their attention either on social responsibility reporting or human capital reporting. Our paper uncovers characteristics of reporting on both social and human capital aspects of human resources in the Czech Republic and thus addresses the research gap. Specifically, we quantify the amount of voluntary disclosure on human resources in annual reports of the 50 Czech largest corporations. We found that in analysed annual reports, voluntary disclosure on human resources relates primarily to social information.

Keywords Annual reports • Corporate responsibility • Disclosure on human resources • Content analysis

Introduction

Our paper investigates status quo of voluntary disclosure on human resources (hereinafter abbreviated as "HR") by corporations domiciled in the Czech Republic (hereinafter abbreviated as "CR"). Initiatives towards the improvement of reporting on social responsibility have a long history in the European Union (Pakšiová 2016). Nevertheless, reporting on HR is still mostly voluntary and unstandardized in the CR except for several disclosures, which are obligatory in annual reports (hereinafter abbreviated "AR"), precisely: the average number of employees, total wages

P. Petera (✉) • J. Wagner
University of Economics, Prague, Department of Management Accounting,
W. Churchill Sq. 1938/4, 130 67 Prague 3, Czech Republic
e-mail: petr.petera@vse.cz; wagner@vse.cz

D. Procházka (ed.), *The Impact of Globalization on International Finance and Accounting*, Springer Proceedings in Business and Economics,
https://doi.org/10.1007/978-3-319-68762-9_34

and related expenses and remuneration for managers. These obligatory disclosures were not considered in our analysis.

It is important to mention that we understand the term "disclosure on HR" broadly, i.e. including both topics traditionally addressed by "corporate social reporting" (e.g. staff compensation, internal communication, etc.) and topics traditionally dealt with by "intellectual capital reporting" (e.g. human capital management, profits per employee, etc.). Such approach is useful because it enables us to analyse all disclosures related to HR of a company (Alvarez 2015).

Social reporting is interesting especially for a broader group of stakeholders, in particular for employees and potential employees as well for unions. This kind of reporting informs these stakeholders about activities, which are of critical importance for them (remuneration, employee well-being, etc.). According to legitimation theory, social reporting serves as a tool for responding to public pressures and altering the public's opinion on the legitimacy of the organisation (Hooghiemstra 2000).

Human capital reporting is interesting especially for shareholders because it enables them to evaluate the value of human capital by disclosing, for example, structure of employees by their education, staff performance, etc. This voluntary disclosure, therefore, has potential to increase the market value of the company by providing additional information on employees as an important determinant of company value. For example, Gamerschlag (2013) found that voluntary provision of human capital information (especially on qualification and competence of employees) has a positive association with share prices.

On the one hand, the body of research on the topic of reporting on HR is continuously growing worldwide (Absar 2016; Alvarez 2015; Fontana and Macagnan 2013; Gamerschlag 2013; Jindal and Kumar 2012; Kaur et al. 2016; Menassa and Brodhäcker 2017; Pisano et al. 2017).

On the other hand, detailed and up-to-date research into this topic among corporations domiciled in the Czech Republic is nearly non-existent. This study is, therefore, a significant attempt to initiate systematic, long-term research into this area of reporting.

Content analysis-based research on HR reporting among corporations domiciled in the CR is insufficient. Existing studies aim at environmental reporting or sustainability reporting in general without a focus on HR. Kašparová and Škapa (2007) analysed annual reports (year = 2005) of 52 Czech companies and also addressed strategy in social area, health and safety of employees, remuneration of employees, equal opportunities and anti-corruption policy. Kašparová (2011) analysed annual reports of selected companies and focused on a broad set of topics including disclosure on HR. Petera et al. (2015) addressed disclosure on HR in annual reports for the year 2012, nevertheless did not distinguish between social reporting and human capital reporting.

In comparison with the above-mentioned articles, we adopt coding scheme suggested by Alvarez (2015) specifically for analysis of disclosure on HR. It enables to assess whether the corporation discloses primarily social or human capital information. Moreover, the existing research in the CR always measured the quantity of disclosure with the help of frequency (number) of disclosures of a given topic within analysed report. We measure the amount of disclosure by counting words related to the selected topics, and thus we obtain more comprehensive information about the quantity of voluntary disclosure.

Data and Methodology

In this chapter, we describe the process of sample selection and methodology of data gathering and analysis.

Data

First, using Albertina database, we selected all companies that fulfilled the following conditions: assets over 20 million EUR, turnover more than 40 million EUR and a number of employees exceeding 250. Consequently, we selected the 50 largest for-profit corporations according to their turnover in the year 2014 from the set of corporations obtained in the first step. In case that some company did not make their AR publicly available, we skipped to following company in the ordered list. The decision to aim at the largest corporations was based on the fact that these corporations often serve as role models in voluntary reporting.

Corporations may disclose information on HR in various types of reports, for example, AR, web pages, social media, etc. In this paper, we analyse only annual reports, which are a mainstream approach (see, e.g. Alvarez 2015; Jindal and Kumar 2012 and many others). Annual reports are usually considered to be an appropriate proxy for the overall approach of the corporation to voluntary reporting because of their properties (publicly available, audited, trustworthy, static).

Methodology

As the main tool of data analysis, we decided to use quantitative content analysis (hereinafter abbreviated as "QCA"), which can be defined as "Research technique for making replicable and valid inferences from texts (or other meaningful matter) to the context of their use" (Krippendorff 2013, p. 24). The QCA uses quantitative analytic techniques to analyse data in a reliable, objective and systematic way (Krippendorff 2013).

In our research, we ensured required properties of the QCA (precise definition of categories, objectivity and a reliable coder) by utilisation of standard coding scheme proposed by Alvarez (2015) and by using a clear set of definitions and coding principles. All analysed AR were coded by one of the researchers.

Table 1 Characteristics of corporations

Descriptive statistic	Assets (thousands CZK)	Employees (number of people)	Turnover (thousands CZK)
Mean	43,900,620	5778	41,825,561
Median	22,208,909	2888	23,482,523
Std. deviation	91,094,348	7322	50,745,142
Skewness	5.664	1.988	3.547
Kurtosis	35.911	3.487	14.648

Source: annual reports of selected corporations, year = 2014

After coding all annual reports, the number of words belonging to individual codes was counted and aggregated to the highest level of codes (total disclosure on human resources and its three main sub-indices—human capital, social information and ethical information). We used NVivo 11 Plus to facilitate coding.

Results and Discussion

Basic descriptive statistics regarding corporations can be found in Table 1.

Table 2 contains descriptive statistics for disclosures examined in our research. Items are grouped into three main topics (human capital, social and ethical information).

First, from the viewpoint of quantity of disclosure, the first place belongs to social disclosure (47.70% of the total HR disclosure), which is followed by disclosure on human capital (39.40% of the total HR disclosure) and finally disclosure of ethical information (12.90% of the total HR disclosure).

Second, within the topic of disclosure on human capital, the most reported theme is “training and human capital” (32.43% of the total HR disclosure; disclosed by 34 companies) followed by the description of staff, and the least reported theme is “staff performance”. The theme of training and human capital is broad and especially includes information on professional qualifications (14.85% of the total HR disclosure; disclosed by 10 companies), information on training (11.37%of the total HR disclosure; disclosed by 28 companies) and general information about the approach to human capital management (5.81% of the total HR disclosure; disclosed by 23 companies). The description of staff is especially comprised of information on various classifications (white collars and blue collars, according to a business unit, age, education, profession, location, gender, nationality) and staff turnover.

Third, within the topic of the social disclosure, there are several important themes. The most disclosed theme is health and safety which is followed by compensation and staff recruiting (opportunities for young people and students in particular, but also flexible forms of work, job stability, the reduction of a working

Table 2 Disclosed items

Disclosed item	N of companies disclosing item	Mean of words disclosed per report	% of disclosed item on total voluntary HR disclosure
Human capital	35	325.50	39.40
Description of staff	21	55.24	6.69
Training and human capital	34	267.94	32.43
Staff performance	5	2.32	0.28
Social	31	394.06	47.70
Compensation	28	141.14	17.08
Interaction with staff	10	15.84	1.92
Health and safety	27	185.56	22.46
Staff recruiting	19	51.52	6.24
Ethical	25	106.56	12.90
Workers' rights and industrial relations	23	46.34	5.61
Anti-corruption	7	3.74	0.45
Equal opportunities	5	14.28	1.73
Ethical values	12	42.20	5.11
Total voluntary disclosure on HR	37	826.12	100.00

Source: annual reports of selected corporations, year = 2014

day). The least disclosed theme within social disclosure is interaction with staff (e.g. internal communication, surveys, etc.).

Fourth, the quantity of information disclosed on ethical issues is substantially lower than disclosure on social issues and human capital. Within ethical issues, it is workers' rights and industrial relations, particularly those with unions, which are mostly reported.

The least disclosed themes overall are staff performance (0.28% of the total HR disclosure; disclosed by five companies), anti-corruption policy (0.45% of the total HR disclosure; disclosed by seven companies), declaration of equal opportunities (1.73% of the total HR disclosure; disclosed by five companies) and interaction with staff (1.92% of the total HR disclosure; disclosed by 10 companies).

It is possible to conclude that because companies disclose more information on social issues (including information on ethical issues) than on human capital issues, reporting aims at stakeholders and not at shareholders primarily. Efforts to disclose how human resources adds value to a company is minimal.

Finally, we checked if corporations disclosing a stand-alone corporate responsibility report disclose more information on HR in their AR than corporations which do not prepare such stand-alone report. The sample was therefore split into two groups. Group 0 contains corporations that do not issue stand-alone corporate responsibility report, and group 1 contains corporations that issue standalone corporate responsibility report.

Table 3 Comparison of corporations issuing and not issuing corporate responsibility report

Disclosure quantity	Group	N of comp.	Mean rank	Mean	Standard deviation	Sig (Mann-Whitney)
HRHCapital	0	46	25.40	297.35	506.738	0.870
	1	4	26.63	649.25	872.435	
HRSocial	0	46	25.65	310.20	447.181	0.797
	1	4	23.75	1358.50	2600.339	
HREthical	0	46	25.00	67.78	111.463	0.379
	1	4	31.25	552.50	709.419	
HRTotal	0	46	25.37	675.33	952.541	0.829
	1	4	27.00	2560.25	4092.789	

Source: annual reports of selected corporations, year = 2014

Consequently, we performed Mann-Whitney non-parametric test to find out if corporations issuing stand-alone corporate responsibility report disclose significantly more information on HR than companies that do not issue such special report. Results can be found in Table 3.

Based on obtained results, we can summarise that companies issuing stand-alone corporate responsibility report have a higher mean of all indicators. Nevertheless, a difference between groups according to Mann-Whitney test is not statistically significant.

Conclusion

This paper provides results of an original empirical research, specifically content analysis of voluntary disclosure on human resources in annual reports of the 50 largest companies domiciled in the CR. We counted the total number of words dedicated to voluntary disclosure on HR in each report as well as the number of words related to main sub-topics (human capital, social and ethical information). It is possible to summarise that majority of information relates to social area. These results are in accordance with Alvarez (2015) and support legitimation theory, which states that voluntary social reporting primarily serves as a tool for altering the public's opinion on the legitimacy of the organisation.

We can summarise that while some topics (items) are disclosed by a relatively large number of companies, other issues are nearly ignored by the majority of corporations (e.g. staff performance and anti-corruption policy). There are significant differences in the quantity of voluntary reporting on HR between companies, for example, 26% of companies in our sample do not disclose information on any of the considered items.

Finally, we tested if corporations publishing a stand-alone corporate responsibility report disclose more information on HR in their AR than other corporations. On the one hand, corporations issuing stand-alone corporate responsibility report disclose more information on HR, but according to the Mann-Whitney test, the difference is not statistically significant.

Acknowledgements The article is processed as an output of a research project managing and reporting on sustainable business development—trends and best practices registered by the Internal Grant Agency of the University of Economics, Prague, under the registration number F1/37/2016.

References

Absar MMN (2016) Stakeholders' views on voluntary human capital disclosures in corporate annual reports of top Bangladeshi and Indian listed companies. J Hum Values 22(3):209–220. https://doi.org/10.1177/0971685816650576

Alvarez A (2015) Corporate response to human resource disclosure recommendations. Soc Responsib J 11(2):306–323. https://doi.org/10.1108/SRJ-06-2013-0076

Fontana FB, Macagnan CB (2013) Factors explaining the level of voluntary human capital disclosure in the Brazilian capital market. Intang Cap 9(1):305–321. https://doi.org/10.3926/ic.315

Gamerschlag R (2013) Value relevance of human capital information. J Intellect Cap 14 (2):325–345. https://doi.org/10.1108/14691931311323913

Hooghiemstra R (2000) Corporate communication and impression management – new perspectives why companies engage in corporate social reporting. J Bus Ethics 27(1):55–68

Jindal S, Kumar M (2012) The determinants of HC disclosures of Indian firms. J Intellect Cap 13 (2):221–247. https://doi.org/10.1108/14691931211225049

Kašparová K (2011) Reportování o společenské odpovědnosti podniku [Reporting on corporate social responsibility]. Masarykova univerzita, Brno

Kašparová K, Škapa R (2007) Sociální zodpovědnost ve výročních zprávách českých a slovenských podniků [Social responsibility in annual reports of Czech and Slovak companies]. In: Semafor 2007: Ekonomika firiem 2007, Košice, Czech Republic. http://semafor.euke.sk/zbornik2007/pdf/kasparova_skapa.pdf. Accessed 10 Feb 2017

Kaur S, Raman VA, Singhania M (2016) Impact of corporate characteristics on human resource disclosures. Asian Rev Account 24(4):390–425. https://doi.org/10.1108/ARA-09-2014-0103

Krippendorff K (2013) Content analysis: an introduction to its methodology. SAGE, Los Angeles

Menassa E, Brodhäcker M (2017) The type and quantity of corporate social disclosures of German 'Universal' banks. J Manag Gov 21(1):119–143. https://doi.org/10.1007/s10997-015-9336-y

Pakšiová R (2016) CSR reporting in Slovakia. In: Kovářová E, Melecký L, Staníčková M (eds) International conference on European integration 2016, Ostrava, Czech Republic, May 19–20, 2016. VŠB – Technical University of Ostrava, Ostrava, pp 698–707

Petera P, Wagner J, Knorova K, Siska L (2015) Human resources disclosure by the largest Czech companies. In: Procházka D (ed) 16th annual conference on finance and accounting, Prague, Czech Republic, May 29, 2015. Elsevier, Amsterdam, pp 96–105. https://doi.org/10.1016/S2212-5671(15)00717-0

Pisano S, Lepore L, Lamboglia R (2017) Corporate disclosure of human capital via LinkedIn and ownership structure: an empirical analysis of European companies. J Intellect Cap 18 (1):102–127. https://doi.org/10.1108/JIC-01-2016-0016

The Pricing of Audit Fees: Empirical Evidence from Czech Republic

Michal Šindelář

Abstract The aim of this paper is to analyze the pricing of audit fees in the Czech Republic, and the main emphasis is placed on the relation between audit and non-audit fees. The analysis is based on the annual reports of the listed companies on the Prague Stock Exchange on 31 December 2015. The analysis represents the regression model that is used in the international research. Besides non-audit fees the regression model contains client size and various types of risks that has to be considered during audit. The analysis shows no statistically significant relation between audit and non-audit fees in the Czech Republic, but the audit fees are mostly dependent on client size.

Keywords Audit fees • Non-audit fees • Auditor's independence • Audit fees pricing

Introduction

The Czech Republic is a small country placed in the Central Europe. From 1945 to 1989, the central planned economy was implemented in the Czech Republic, with all its economic impacts. During this period, there was no place for the specific services as audit or verification of the financial statements. In this type of economic system, there are no conditions for the formation of demand for audit services, as separate management of the company from its owners. Since 1989 the Czech economy has begun to transform into a market economy. After the Velvet revolution, which brought quite a wild privatization, the demand for audit services began to appear. The audit profession started to form in 1993, when the Chamber of Auditors of the Czech Republic was founded. It means that in comparison to Western Europe, the audit profession is in the Czech Republic young and emerging. One of the major milestones in the development of the auditing profession in the

M. Šindelář (✉)
University of Economics, Prague, Department of Financial Accounting and Auditing, Nam. W. Churchilla 4, 130 67 Prague, Czech Republic
e-mail: xsinm00@vse.cz

D. Procházka (ed.), *The Impact of Globalization on International Finance and Accounting*, Springer Proceedings in Business and Economics,
https://doi.org/10.1007/978-3-319-68762-9_35

Czech Republic was the adoption of ISAs in 2005 as mandatory standards for statutory audit of financial statements. The audit market exists only 23 years in the Czech Republic, and it means there are only few research papers dealing with the audit market problems. For example, Sindelar and Mullerova (2016) analyzed the concentration on the Czech audit market. Moreover, this "lack of research" is not only in the area of audit market, but also generally in accounting. Seal (1997) analyzed the problems of transformation of the economy in the Czech Republic and tried to explain the reasons of "lack of research" in the Czech Republic. One of the consequences is that research, which was conducted in Western Europe 15 years ago, gets now to the scene in the Czech Republic. One of the topics, the analysis of determination of audit fees, is presented in this paper.

The Czech Republic is a member of the European Union since 2004, so the legislation in the Czech Republic has to be in compliance with the EU regulation. One of problems of the audit market, which began the European regulators to deal with, is the risk of the independence of auditors due to simultaneous providing both auditing and other services. European Commission (2002) in this regard stated that the remuneration for other services may jeopardize the independence of the auditor. To be unified, the audit approach across the European Union the European Commission issued Directive 2006/43/EC that governs the requirements and rules of statutory audit. Moreover, in the year 2014, the European Commission decided to modify the rules for statutory audit significantly and issued the Directive 2014/56/EU, which amends the Directive 2006/43/EC and separately was issued Regulation 537/2014, which contains specific rules for audits of public interest entities. The European law is implemented to the Czech legal system by the act no. 93/2009 Coll., on auditors.

According to the European and Czech law, the audit fees are not allowed to depend on any of the indicator from the audited company, e.g. total assets, total revenues, etc. This is also expressed in the International Standards on Auditing (ISA). Moreover, the audit fees must not depend on non-audit fees, because the independence of auditor should be threatened in this case. The relation between audit fees and any other proxies is very often tested in the international research. For more than 30 years, the audit research has examined whether knowledge spillovers or synergies exist from the joint provision of audit and non-audit services as well as whether the audit client benefits from knowledge spillovers. However, empirical evidence on knowledge spillover remains mixed and elusive.

Simunic (1984) analyzed the influence of management advisory services on audit fees and found that audit fees depend on management advisory services in the way that, if the client has management advisory services from the auditor, the audit fees are higher. This conclusion was explained by the existence of knowledge spillovers which occur from the management advisory services to audit service. This study was extended by Palmrose (1986), who analyzed not only the management advisory services but also all non-audit services divided into tax services, accounting-related services and non-accounting services of 286 public companies. She reached the same results as Simunic – the audit fees are dependent on non-audit fees. Further, Davis and Ricchiute (1993) analyzed the data collected from the audit firms in the United States and found weakly positive correlation between audit and non-audit fees. Firth (1997) analyzed the Norwegian stock market, concretely the companies listed on Oslo Stock Exchange. He tested 157 listed companies in the period of the year 1991. He found the strongly positive correlation between audit and non-audit fees. The statistically significant relation has been also confirmed in the analyses of Bell et al. (2001), Hay et al. (2006) or Parkash et al. (2012).

On the other hand, there exist some studies that do not confirm the relation between audit and non-audit fees. Abdel-Khalik (1990) and Whisenant et al. (2003) found no relation between audit and non-audit fees. Moreover, the Australian research provided by Barkess and Simnett (1992) also provided no statistically significant relation. As there are many studies confirming the strong relation between audit and non-audit fees, some authors analyzed this topic in a more detail and found very interesting results. One way of investigation tends to the assessment of statistical model used for measurement of the relation. Chan et al. (2012) found that by using two-stage least squares (2SLS) estimation instead of ordinary least square (OLS) estimation, the association between audit and non-audit fees is statistically weaker. Other way of explanation of the positive correlation tends to the fact that audit and non-audit fees are determined by the same variables (Whisenant et al. 2003). Moreover, the recent way of continuing audit research in this topic is based on the extension of this topic and tries to engage the measurement of audit quality to the basic audit fees model. This paper analyzes the audit fees model in Czech Republic and according to this fact following hypothesis is formulated:

- H: I supposed the statistically significant positive correlation between audit fees and non-audit fees in the Czech Republic.

Data and Methodology

Data

The analysis is based on the 46 listed companies on the Prague Stock Exchange at the end of the year 2015. For the data mining, the database MagnusWeb was used. Missing data was collected from singly presented annual reports downloaded from Prague Stock Exchange. Prague Stock Exchange is a small exchange, where 76 companies are listed on 31 September 2015. The reduction in the analyzed companies is caused by two aspects. Firstly, from the sample was removed financial institution. The reason is that financial institution has special business model with different risks and structure of financial statements. The audit fees model used for the analysis cannot comprise specifics of this type of business. Removal of financial institution is fully in keeping with the international research. All above-mentioned international research exclude financial institutions from the analysis. Fields et al. (2004) tried to analyze financial institutions by modified audit fees model according to the special risks, which occur at the financial institutions. Secondly, there were some companies excluded, because the necessary data for the analysis were not available.

Methodology

The analysis is based on the audit fees model used in international research (Simunic 1984; Palmrose 1986; Firth 1997; Whisenant et al. 2003; Thinggaard and Kiertzner 2004). This model is based on the linear regression and comprises the specifics (client size and complexity and risks) of the companies important for the audit service (Thinggaard and Kiertzner 2004). Every important specific has at least one variable in the model. The model is stated in the Eq. (1).

$$\begin{aligned}\text{LNAUDIT} = {} & \beta_0 + \beta_1(LNNA) + \beta_2(LNTA) + \beta_3(SQEMPLS) + \beta_4(DA) \\ & + \beta_5(BIG4) + \beta_6(INVREC) + \beta_7(SQSUBS) + \beta_8(ROA) \\ & + \beta_9(LOSS)\end{aligned} \tag{1}$$

where

- LNAUDIT = natural logarithm of the audit fees
- LNNA = natural logarithm of the sum of non-audit fees
- LNTA = natural logarithm of total assets
- SQEMPLS = square root of the number of employees
- DA = total debt divided by total assets
- BIG4 = dummy variable equal to 1 if the audit is performed by a member of Big 4 (PwC, EY, KPMG a Deloitte) (0 otherwise)
- INVREC = inventory plus accounts receivables, divided by total assets
- SQSUBS = square root of the number of subsidiaries
- ROA = return on assets
- LOSS = dummy variable equal to 1 if the firm reports a loss

The client size is represented in the model by total assets (TA) and the number of employees (EMPLS). Complexity of substance that can be characterized as the complexity in relation to the verifiability of financial statements items by an auditor is represented by inventory and accounts receivables (INVREC). Formal complexity means the complexity in relation to the presentation of financial statements, e.g. number of segments, subsidiaries, etc. In the model is this complexity represented by number of subsidiaries (SQSUBS). The last important client specified is its general risk. This risk can be characterized as the whole risk of the client and can be characterized by variables as leverage (DA), rentability (ROA), loss (LOSS), liquidity or solvency. Where the general risk is higher, the more audit work has to be undertaken. Other variable in the model, BIG4, represents the fact that the audit was performed by an auditor from the Big4. In the international research was confirmed (Whisenant et al. 2003; Firth 1997; Chan et al. 2012) that audits performed by Big4 firms are more expensive than audits performed by non-Big4 firms. This could be named as a Big4 premium. The last variable in the model is the non-audit fees (NA).

Results and Discussion

Correlation among the variables could possibly confound the interpretation of the regression model. The simple correlations among variables are shown in the Table 2 – see Appendix. In general correlations are quite low except one with absolute value of 0.75. There are indeed some suggestions that correlation below 0.8 does not signalize the problems with multicollinearity. Table 1 shows the results of the regression analyzes with expected impact on the audit fees.

Table 1 shows some interesting results of the regression analysis especially with international comparison. There is no statistically significant relation between audit and non-audit fees in the Czech Republic. This means according to the analyzed data that I could not confirm the hypothesis H about the existence of relation between audit and non-audit fees. In the Czech Republic, this could be caused by various reasons, e.g. the existence of special audit firm. This leads to the fact that in the annual reports are reported only the audit fees and the non-audit fees are not reported, because they are payed to another firm even though the firm is from the same group. This could be also caused by imperfectly implemented (translated) EU directive.

Table 1 Regression of audit fees

Dependent variable: LNAUDIT					
Method: Least squares					
Sample: 146					
Included observations: 46					
Variables	Expected impact	Coefficient	Std. error	t-Statistic	Prob.
C	?	(2.267990)	1.505404	(1.506566)	0.1406
LNNA	?	0.030150	0.022424	1.344526	0.1872
LNTA	+	0.479220	0.100229	4.781274[a]	0.0000
SQEMPLS	+	0.002210	0.003419	0.646216	0.5222
DA	+	0.700687	0.481042	1.456602	0.1539
BIG4	+	0.551073	0.308334	1.787261[c]	0.0823
INVREC	+	2.029782	0.921351	2.203050[b]	0.0341
SQSUBS	+	0.196775	0.068927	2.854840[a]	0.0071
ROA	–	4.999686	2.050515	2.438259[b]	0.0198
LOSS	+	0.698366	0.362169	1.928286[c]	0.0617
R-squared		0.843147	Mean dependent var		7.047744
Adjusted R-squared		0.803934	S.D. dependent var		1.679287
S.E. of regression		0.743577	Akaike info criterion		2.434970
Sum squared resid		19.90462	Schwarz criterion		2.832501
Log likelihood		(46.00431)	Hannan-Quinn criter.		2.583888
F-statistic		21.50166	Durbin-Watson stat		2.258926
Prob(F-statistic)		0.000000			

Source: Own processing
Note: [a]significant at 0.01; [b]significant at 0.05; [c]significant at 0.10

Other important result is that the most statistically significant is the size of the client represented by total assets and complemented by formal complexity represented by number of subsidiaries. This means that audit fees are very sensitive on the performed work in relation to the group complexity. This result is in compliance with the international research (Firth 1997; Whisenant et al. 2003; Thinggaard and Kiertzner 2004). The Big4 premium was not also confirmed by the analysis. There is only weak correlation between audit fees and the fact that auditor is from Big4.

Conclusion

The paper analyzes the pricing of audit fees on the Prague Stock Exchange at the companies listed there on 31 December 2015. For the analysis, I used the internationally validated audit fees model. As the database is chosen, the annual reports of listed companies, where companies are obliged to disclose the audit fees and non-audit fees paid to the auditors. For data mining, the database MagnusWeb was used. This database contains accounting data of the companies doing business in the Czech Republic and the companies listed on the Prague Stock Exchange. The audit fees model provides a good statistical fit. The most important findings are:

- The audit fees in the Czech Republic are not statistically significantly correlated with non-audit fees.
- There is only weak statistical correlation between audit fees and the fact that the audit firm represents the Big4 firm.
- The audit fees are mostly correlated with the size of the client measured by total assets.

The results show some differences between Czech audit market and other audit markets, especially in the Western Europe. The most important conclusion is that according to performed analysis, there is no significant relation between audit and non-audit fees and I cannot confirm the hypothesis H. At the end, I consider appropriate to mention the fact that the article contains only a part of the analysis of Czech audit market and will be followed by further more complex research.

Acknowledgments This paper is processed as an output of the research project "Empirical rationalization of fundamental changes in the European audit legislation from the perspective of the auditing profession in the Czech Republic (with a focus on training in audit, quality audit and issue the audit market oligopoly)" (IGA VSE F1/33/2015).

Appendix

Table 2 Pearson's correlation matrix of variables

	LNNA	LNTA	SQEMPLS	DA	BIG4	INVREC	SQSUBS	ROA	LOSS
LNAUDIT	0.57	0.75	0.59	0.00	0.51	0.38	0.54	0.33	0.27
LNNA		0.44	0.31	(0.19)	0.13	0.09	0.48	0.33	0.13
LNTA			0.70	(0.21)	0.31	0.20	0.28	0.18	0.10
SQEMPLS				(0.19)	0.32	0.20	0.23	0.07	0.15
DA					0.36	(0.02)	(0.16)	(0.05)	0.14
BIG4						0.09	0.20	0.13	0.30
INVREC							0.22	0.25	(0.12)
SQSUBS								(0.01)	0.30
ROA									(0.38)

Source: Own processing

References

Abdel-Khalik AR (1990) The jointness of audit fees and demand for MAS: a self-selection analysis. Contemp Account Res 6:295–322

Barkess L, Simnett R (1992) An empirical investigation of the relationship between audit fees and the provision of other services by the incumbent auditor – Australian evidence. Work. Pap. University of New South Wales

Bell TB, Landsman WR, Shackelford DA (2001) Auditor's perceived business risk and audit fees: analysis and evidence. J Account Res 39:35–43

Chan L, Chen T-Y, Janakiraman S, Radhakrishnan S (2012) Reexamining the relationship between audit and nonaudit fees: dealing with weak instruments in two-stage least squares estimation. J Acc Audit Finance 27:299–324. https://doi.org/10.1177/0148558X11409154

Davis LR, Ricchiute DN (1993) Audit effort, audit fees, and the provision of nonaudit services to audit clients. Account Rev 68:135–150

European Commission (2002) Recommendation 2002/590/EC statutory auditors' independence in the EU: a set of fundamental principles. Off J L 191:22–57. 19/07/2002. http://eur-lex.europa.eu/legal-content/EN/TXT/HTML/?uri=CELEX:32002H0590&from=EN. Accessed 15 Jul 2017

Fields LP, Fraser DR, Wilkins MS (2004) An investigation of the pricing of audit services for financial institutions. J Account Public Policy 23:53. https://doi.org/10.1016/j.jaccpubpol.2003.11.003

Firth M (1997) The provision of non-audit services and the pricing of audit fees. J Bus Financ Account 24:511–525

Hay DC, Knechel WR, Wong N (2006) Audit fees: a meta-analysis of the effect of supply and demand attributes. Contemp Account Res 23:141–191

Palmrose Z-V (1986) The effect of nonaudit services on the pricing of audit services: further evidence. J Account Res 24:405–411

Parkash M, Singhal R, Zhu Y (2012) Audit and nonaudit fees from different reporting regimes and perceived audit quality. Indian J Econ Bus 11:185–202

Seal W (1997) Accounting and societal transition: the bohemian accountant and the velvet revolution. Communist Econ Econ Transform 9:383–406

Simunic DA (1984) Auditing, consulting, and auditor independence. J Account Res 22:679–702

Sindelar M, Mullerova L (2016) Auditorske sluzby v Ceske republice pohledem analyzy trzni koncentrace. (Market concentration of audit Services in the Czech Republic: empirical evidence [focusing on auditors of public interest entities]. With English summary). Polit Ekon 64:730–746

Thinggaard F, Kiertzner L (2004) The effect of two auditors and non-audit services on audit fees: evidence from a small capital market. Work. Pap. No. 04-02. Aalborg University

Whisenant S, Sankaraguruswamy S, Raghunandan K (2003) Evidence on the joint determination of audit and non-audit fees. J Account Res 41:721–744. https://doi.org/10.1111/1475-679X.00121

The Going Concern Threats and Deferred Tax Assets Recognition: The Gap Between Theory and Practice

Ireneusz Górowski

Abstract The crucial issue, when assessing the going concern and recognizing deferred taxes, is making the correct judgement about the company's foreseeable future. In this paper, we describe an experiment which tests how accounting standards users make their judgements about deferred tax assets recognition for companies facing serious going concern threats. The results revealed that a knowledgeable group of IAS 12 standard users is willing to recognize the deferred tax assets and create profits in the process even when a company faces going concern threats which are clearly communicated by the management. Explaining the nature of such behaviour would require further research.

Keywords Financial distress • Going concern • Deferred tax

Introduction

Going concern is an underlying assumption of the IFRS framework for financial reporting. It constitutes that the financial statements are normally prepared on the assumption that an entity is a going concern and will continue in operation for the foreseeable future (IASB 2010, Conceptual Framework par. 4.1). This assumption means that the entity has neither the intention nor the need to liquidate or curtail materially the scale of its operations. It becomes a crucial issue when the company faces a financial distress (Andrzejewski and Maślanka 2015; Bauer 2014). Thus, the assessment of the going concern assumption is a trial of peering into a foreseeable future of the entity. It involves making a judgement at a particular point of time about uncertain future outcomes of events. The similar activity should be undertaken when recognizing deferred assets. On the principle, the deferred tax assets shall be recognized to the extent that it is probable that taxable profit will be available against which the deductible temporary difference, unused tax loss or

I. Górowski (✉)
Department of Accounting, Cracow University of Economics, Rakowicka 27, 31-510 Cracow, Poland
e-mail: gorowski@uek.krakow.pl

D. Procházka (ed.), *The Impact of Globalization on International Finance and Accounting*, Springer Proceedings in Business and Economics,
https://doi.org/10.1007/978-3-319-68762-9_36

unused tax credit can be utilized (IASB 1996, IAS 12 par.24 & 34). Thus, this procedure also demands some professional judgement about foreseeable future. To recognize deferred tax assets (which mean also increasing profits), the company should expect reversal of tax deductible differences as well as sufficient future taxable profits and should be able to have some tax planning opportunities at all.

The main goal of this paper is to join these two circumstances: judgement about the recognition of deferred tax assets and threats to company's ability to continue operations as a going concern. We are going to check if the accounting standard users tend to recognize tax assets for companies under a strong financial distress.

Both topics, deferred taxation and going concern, have been researched extensively. In this context, we would like to draw attention to the area of research focusing on deferred taxation as an earning management tool. A strong evidence of using deferred taxes for income smoothing can be found at Holland and Jackson (2004) and for avoiding losses at Noor et al. (2007). Schrand and Wong (2003) showed that banks used high valuation allowances for deferred tax assets to manage future earnings. Dhaliwal et al. (2004) proved that when the actual earnings fall, firms decrease their effective tax mainly by creating tax assets to increase profits. Prior research gives a good starting point for the new research. If we already know that deferred taxation can be used as an earnings management tool, we can expect that it will be used willingly when going concern assumption becomes a questionable issue. Some research on the combined topics of the financial distress and deferred taxes also touches the problem of earnings managements. Mills and Newberry (2001) found that firms facing financial distress will report greater book/tax differences – which are commonly perceived as being useful in detecting earnings management to avoid the earnings decline and to avoid a loss (Philips et al. 2003, Wang et al. 2016). The latest study by Eustler et al. (2016) of going concern reports modifications accompanying the last set of fraudulently stated financials and just mentions deferred asset accounting as one of fraudulent deferred schemes devised to conceal financial distress. They refer to the case of Powerlinx which materially inflated deferred tax assets to 38 percent of the company's total assets. The case study (Górowski 2014) of Polish companies listed on Warsaw Stock Exchange shows that the companies facing a high probability of going bankrupt recognize and decrease their tax assets. We designed an experiment to evaluate the possible interaction between the two issues – going concern and deferred tax judgement.

Data and Methodology

The inspiration for this study was a previously mentioned paper by Górowski (2014). It examined links between management's and auditors' assessment of companies' ability to continue as a going concern and deferred tax assets judgements for selected companies listed on the Warsaw Stock Exchange. The analysis was performed on listed companies which declared bankruptcy in year 2013. In the reports for all of the examined companies, the deferred tax assets were recognized, despite a clear declaration of doubts about their ability to continue as a going concern. Therefore, in the management's opinion (regardless if expressed directly or not), the presence of these doubts was not an obstacle to the recognition of the deferred tax assets that improved financial result reported in the statement of profit or loss.

The aim of this research was to verify if, in the experimental conditions, accounting standards users would decide to recognize deferred tax assets in companies under a strong financial distress. We had expected rather clear results that, following the IAS 12 rules, participants would decide not to disclose the deferred tax assets. The research could also uncover some creative accounting practices rather than institutional problems.

Using the cases described by Górowski (2014), we created three scenarios to be used in a pilot experiment on the students at Cracow University of Economics. The students attending tax accounting master class were lectured on the main ideas of inter-period tax allocation in compliance with the IAS 12. We did our best trying to teach in a 'neutral' way, providing students with a sufficient information required to understand the topic. We focused on explaining the essence of the temporary differences between book value and tax value and general algorithms of the deferred tax recognition. The issue of judgement about future company performance in the deferred tax assets valuation and recognition was only mentioned.

Then students were given a short extract from the IAS 12 and three scenarios for sample companies: Budopol Wroclaw SA., Fota SA and Ideon SA. The names of the companies were changed. The scenarios were based on the data from 2013 financial statements and management letters. We only used excerpts from the original documents. We purposely extracted information disclosed in the financial statement which could signal that companies were under financial distress, including all the information about going concern assumptions. The particulars of these three scenarios are presented below.

The students were asked six questions. The first three were control questions designed to verify student's understanding of the accounting for deferred taxes. The remaining questions related to the three scenarios. We also asked supplementary questions about gender and average grade from the last academic year.

The core question was 'In your opinion, should the financial statement recognize the deferred tax assets, considering only the information given in the scenarios Table 1?' The possible answers were 'yes', 'no' and 'I don't know'.

Results and Discussion

We received 98 responses from students of our two tax accounting courses. Some questionnaires were eliminated because they either missed some answers or gave wrong answers to the control questions. That left 73 responses to the core question regarding the recognition of deferred tax assets.

Table 1 Scenarios used in the experiment

	Scenario 1	Scenario 2	Scenario 3
Industry	Real estate rentals and management	Sale of car's spare parts and repairmen tools	Construction.
Information 1	The company has submitted bankruptcy petition with a possibility of a repayment arrangements	The company needs fundamental restructuring	Continuation of the operations rely on acquiring new projects and repayment of existing debts
Information 2	The company lost its liquidity. The bank accounts are frozen	The financial covenants are broken. Banks are entitled to announce default and demand immediate repayment of loans. It would mean loss of important sources of financing and reduction of operational scale	Continuation of the company's business depends on its key debtor's ability to overcome his financial distress and acquiring new customers
Information 3	The company was forced to reduce costs and scale of operations and consequently lost markets	The company assumes that it will be able to earn accounting and taxable profit in the future	–
Going concern assumption as used with financial statement preparation – management's point of view	Assumption sustained when preparing financial statement, although the Management Board see some serious threats (no further comments)	Assumption sustained when preparing the financial statement	Assumption sustained when preparing the financial statement

Source: own analysis

Table 2 The research outcomes

Answer	Scenario 1	Scenario 2	Scenario 3
Yes	8	10.96%	22
No	52	71.23%	43
Don't know	13	17.81%	8
Total	73	100.00%	73

Source: own analysis

Results are summarized in the Table 2.

It should be emphasized that in all three scenarios, serious threats to survivability of the entities as a going concern could be observed. In our opinion, the 'red flags' were clearly communicated by the Management Boards. All three companies actually went bankrupt during the year after issuing their financial reports. Under the given circumstances, a reliable tax planning was impossible, and the probability of gaining taxable income during the following years was negligible.

The recognition of the deferred tax asset is allowed under the IAS 12 standard 'to the extent that it is probable that taxable profit will be available against which the deductible temporary difference can be utilized'. It means that it should be probable (i.e. according to the IFRS 'more likely than not') that the company will gain taxable profits during the following years, which would allow utilization of the tax deductible differences that would reduce future tax payments. For most situations under the Polish tax system, the majority of the temporary differences are tax deductible during the next fiscal year against the future taxable income. The reason for this is that taxable income compared to book income is based to a greater extent on cash flows rather than accruals. Tax losses – which also are reasons for deferred tax recognition – can be carried forward for the next 5 years. So, one can argue that in that time frame the situation of the company can change. But should one create an asset that will generate future profits on a hope that a company will survive despite frozen bank accounts, broken loan covenants – clear signs of a 'terminal illness'? Our effort to teach the prudence principle concept did not stop them making the wrong judgement.

We could observe that respondents used a judgement process to decide if the deferred assets should be recognized. In the first scenario, only 10.96% of students would recognize deferred tax assets compared to 63.01% in the scenario no. 3.

Surprisingly, in scenario 1, almost 29% did not answer 'no' despite the fact that the Management Board submitted a bankruptcy petition, the company was illiquid and bank accounts were frozen. Perhaps the 17.81% of 'don't know' respondents allowed for an additional not available to them information before making their final judgement (the meaning of "don't know" can have various interpretations and maybe the questionnaire could have addressed it more precisely).

On reflection, if this wasn't an experiment, the respondents could be perhaps forgiven for thinking that available data was too limited to make a definite judgement, but in such case, more should have answered 'I don't know'. The question remains what else would convince them to make the negative judgement about the companies' future.

In scenario 3, we had expected a higher degree of 'don't know' answers as the information provided was less specific and inconclusive. Majority (63% 'yes') of our respondents were quite optimistic about the future taxable incomes of the third company which as we know went bankrupt.

Conclusion

Although we are conscious that this was a pilot experiment, it can be clearly visible that accounting master students familiar with the IAS 12 standard tend to recognize deferred tax assets even for companies that are just days away from bankruptcy. The possible explanations could include:

1. The deferred tax allocation is still a non-consistent procedure and should be thought through again by both researchers and the standard authorities.
2. Teaching process and the standard's presentation are not sufficiently clear for students.
3. The prevailing interpretation of the standard reflects an overly optimistic attitude towards the financial statements and their underlying assumptions.
4. It is worth mentioning that all analysed companies in the 'real world' actually recognized the deferred tax assets and companies one and two received an unqualified opinion. In the first scenario, the auditor only mentioned the risk of recognition and increasing the deferred tax assets.

Acknowledgements The publication was financed from the funds granted to the Faculty of Management at Cracow University of Economics, within the framework of the subsidy for the maintenance of research potential.

References

Andrzejewski M, Maślanka T (2015) Procedures of an audit in the prospective verification of the going-concern principle. IFRS: global rules & local use. In: Proceedings of the 3rd international scientific conference Prague, Anglo-American University, Prague – Czech Republic, pp 49–59. Available via www.car.aauni.edu/wp-content/uploads/IFRS-Global-Rules-Local-Use-AAU-Prague-2015.pdf. Accessed 20 Jan 2017

Bauer K (2014) Fixed assets valuation in the condition of bankruptcy risk: the role of estimates. J Mod Account Audit 10(6):652–666

Dhaliwal D, Gleason C, Mills L (2004) Last-chance earnings management: using the tax expense to meet analysts' forecasts. Contemp Account Res 21(2):431–459

Eutsler J, Nickell E, Robb S (2016) Fraud risk awareness and the likelihood of audit enforcement action. Account Horiz 30(3):379–392. https://doi.org/10.2308/acch-51490

Górowski I (2014) Wpływ polityki rachunkowości w zakresie aktywów z tytułu odroczonego podatku dochodowego na wynik finansowy niewypłacalnych spółek giełdowych (The influence of the accounting policy applied to the deferred tax assets on the financial result of insolvent listed companies). Stud Ekon 201:87–95

Holland K, Jackson R (2004) Earnings management and deferred tax. Account Bus Res (Wolters Kluwer UK) 34(2):101–123

IASB (1996) International Accounting Standard Board, International Accounting Standard 12 Income Taxes, Retrived from www.ifrs.com

IASB (2010) International Accounting Standard Board, The Conceptual Framework for Financial Reporting, Retrived from www.ifrs.com

Mills L, Newberry K (2001) The influence of tax and nontax costs on book-tax reporting differences: public and private firms. J Am Tax Assoc 23(1):1–19

Noor M, R Mastuki N, Aziz Z (2007) Earnings management and deferred tax. Malays Account Rev 6(1):1–17

Phillips J, Pincus M, Rego S (2003) Earnings management: new evidence based on deferred tax expense. Account Rev 78(2):491–521

Schrand C, Wong M (2003) Earnings management using the valuation allowance for deferred tax assets under SFAS No. 109. Contemp Account Res 20(3):579–611

Wang Y, Butterfield S, Campbell M (2016) Deferred tax items as earnings management indicators. Int Manag Rev 12(2):37–42

The IFRS Assessment by Publicly Traded Companies

Simona Tuzarová and Ladislav Mejzlík

Abstract Because the Czech Republic adopted the IFRS for the individual reporting publicly traded companies as well as other companies which are a part of the consolidation under the IFRS, this fact offers the adoption of the IFRS also for taxation supported by the existence of the CCCTB and its possible future acceptance in the EU. The main goal of this paper is to show the research results obtained by a survey made between publicly traded companies in the Czech Republic. This research is based on the IFRS adoption by the companies – a way of the IFRS integration into a company information software, advantages and disadvantages of their adoption, problems in using of these standards, and an attitude of companies to the tax base calculation under the Czech accounting principles instead of the IFRS, which are applied in the individual financial reporting.

Keywords IFRS • Czech GAAP • Taxation • CCCTB

Introduction

Adoption of the IFRS across the European Union comes from the regulation No. 1606/2002 where it is written: "On 13rd June 2000, the Commission published its Communication on EU Financial Reporting Strategy: the way forward in which it was proposed that all publicly traded community companies prepare their consolidated financial statements in accordance with one single set of accounting standards, namely International accounting standards (IAS), at the latest by 2005." In the section number 13:

> "In accordance with the same principle, it is necessary, as regards annual accounts, to leave to Member States the option to permit or require publicly traded companies to prepare them in conformity with international accounting standards... Member States may decide as

S. Tuzarová (✉) • L. Mejzlík
Department of Financial Accounting and Auditing, University of Economics, Prague, Nam. W. Churchilla 4, 130 67 Prague, Czech Republic
e-mail: simona.tuzarova@vse.cz; ladislav.mejzlik@vse.cz

D. Procházka (ed.), *The Impact of Globalization on International Finance and Accounting*, Springer Proceedings in Business and Economics,
https://doi.org/10.1007/978-3-319-68762-9_37

well to extend this permission or this requirement to other companies as regards the preparation of their consolidated accounts and/or their annual accounts."

The main goal of these assignations accepted of the European Parliament is likely to harmonize the financial reporting in EU so that all member states use the same rules at least for the publicly traded companies. However, there is also an ambition for other voluntary expansion of IFRS. It is at least interesting to observe different ways of voluntary adoption of IFRS across the EU. The Czech Republic adopted the IFRS much deeper than some EU countries – in short all publicly traded companies must use IFRS for individual reporting as well as for consolidated reporting (if parent company), non-issuers of security parent companies can use the IFRS for individual and also consolidated reporting, and finally companies included in consolidation under the IFRS can also use the IFRS for individual reporting.

One of the reasons why the IFRS was not mandatorily adopted in the IFRS in EU is the fact that individual accounting/reporting more or less influences corporate taxation in all member states of EU. Even when the professional public does not like to hear – the taxation influences the accounting in many EU countries.

There are several reasons why the financial reporting rules and practices might not always be appropriate for determining the final tax liability. These include the purposes of accounting and taxation and difficulties in defining economic concepts and administrative effectiveness (James and Nobes 2002). While the system of taxation is not formed in order to facilitate and assist users in economic decision-making, but is designed to maintain the viability of each national economy through tax collection, accounting regulations are designed to inform users of financial statements about the financial risks that are inevitably associated with economic transactions and to help them to make rational decisions (Weber 2009). While countries like Germany, Spain, and France maintained and still maintain a strong relationship between the accounting and taxation in order to avoid two sets of rules, others like Britain and Denmark are trying to separate these two systems, where the taxable profit will be calculated according to the tax rules, such as in the USA. Between the main problems belongs the question if the accounting profit is really the value to be taxed? The current concept of accounting profit tends to the economic perspective, which measures future benefits and losses, instead of the law perspective. The law perspective to the profit is much more close to the value to be taxed (Macdonald 1995).

The degree of the dependence between accounting and taxation significantly differs across the EU, which was the subject of many researches (Procházka and Molín 2016). The IFRS were mandatory adopted only for consolidated statements, and calculation of the taxable profit from the IFRS has not been introduced in the most of EU countries (moreover this introduction is not intended in many countries). The European Commission published the common consolidated corporate tax base (CCCTB) in 2011. Major benefits of the introduction of the proposed CCCTB can be seen in the elimination of transfer pricing concerns, removal of double taxation because of conflicts arising the tax claims by the Member States, and of course, reduce the administrative burden and costs of tax compliance. For this purpose, the procedure CCCTB rules are divided into three stages:

1. Determination of first individual tax bases according to accounting tax rules
2. Consolidation of these tax bases
3. Allocation of the third joint tax base of the group among members according to the prescribed formula

Even though it is at least questionable whether all or even some of the member states by strengthening cooperation will adopt the CCCTB in its present form, the European Commission should also consider a strategy that would introduce the CCCTB in two consecutive steps (Fuest 2008). The first step would replace 28 national tax legislations under a single set of harmonized tax rules – such as a common tax base (CCTB) would only affect the calculation of the tax base. The second step is the consolidation of revenues of individual members of the group and the subsequent division of the consolidated tax base. This step would not be implemented at present but at a later stage, when that Member States will be better prepared. Although some of the main benefits of the CCCTB would not be immediately reached thanks to this two-step procedure (Spengel and Zollkau 2012), it seems that it has a better chance of success with regard to the political sensitivity of this issue in the EU. The European Commission in 2015 presented a strategy of restoring efforts adapt the CCCTB in the EU. This strategy is based on two key changes, namely, that the CCCTB will be mandatory, because when the optional application is highly unlikely that it will be used by companies that engage in aggressive tax planning. And it proposes to gradually adapt the CCCTB, which should provide better manageability of member states and their mutual agreement.

Although the proposal introduces autonomous rules for calculating and determining the corporate tax base but does not deal with the harmonization of financial accounting, it is true that the debate in the preliminary stages of the project were also focused on the question of whether and to what extent are the accounting principles of the IFRS in accordance with this proposal (Shön 2004). It is important to note that the European Council directive does not provide a formal link or national accounting standards (GAAP) or to the IFRS. Because the formal starting point for determining the tax base is missing, it is especially important to be considered as comprehensive set of guidelines and rules that will apply to all aspects of establishing a common tax base in order to ensure their uniform application in all 28 member EU countries. Utilization of national GAAP or national tax rules in cases, where it is not explicitly defined procedure, is undesirable and could jeopardize the overall objectives of the CCCTB project (Freedman and Macdonald 2008).

Because the Czech Republic adopt the IFRS also for individual reporting publicly traded companies as well as other companies which are part of consolidation under the IFRS, it offers the adoption of the IFRS also for taxation supported by the existence of the CCCTB and its possible future acceptance in EU. The following survey between publicly traded companies in the Czech Republic shows the company view on the IFRS – advantages and disadvantages of their adoptions, problems in using of these standards, and attitude of companies to the tax base calculation under Czech accounting principles instead of the IFRS, which are applied in individual financial reporting.

Results and Discussion

Thirty permanent publicly traded companies on the Prague stock exchange were asked for the participation in the research. Necessary to say – some of these companies yearly belong to the major taxpayers of the Czech Republic. Sixteen companies decided to cooperate on the research, and simultaneously the most of them are significant taxpayers.

The research focused on the following issues: application of the IFRS in the accounting system, costs resulting from the adoption of the IFRS, balancing of benefits and troubles coming from the adoption of IFRS, and companies approach to quantifying the tax base from the Czech GAAP although the company mandatorily uses the IFRS in annual reporting.

Only three companies conserve the Czech GAAP in the information system. They at first compile the financial statements under the Czech GAAP subsequently converting in accordance with the IFRS. Unchanged preservation of the Czech GAAP is caused by the fact that companies either want to exit the issuer group or must plan and report to the state under the Czech GAAP (the state-owned entity). The most often resolution consists of the fully adoption of the IFRS in an accounting software with a difference how the Czech GAAP are maintained. In most cases the Czech GAAP are discharged from an accounting software with identifying the transactions leading to major differences between IFRS and the Czech GAAP – these are recorded twice. Other transactions are always conducted only in IFRS, and if they have a different impact on the accounting treatment, then adjustments are made outside accounting software. Only two entities keep two accounting system (IFRS and Czech GAAP) in their accounting software, and all transactions are recorded twice.

There is no connection between the way of the IFRS adoption in the accounting software and the business activities of the company. But we can say that the larger the company is (turnover, assets), the more deeply integrated IFRS in its economic life.

Adoption of the IFRS induced increased costs in IT, education, and consulting services. None of the companies could retroactively quantify onetime increase in costs during the first changeover to the IFRS.

Increased costs partly persist because of the obligation to identify profit according to the Czech GAAP for the taxation purposes. These are the personnel costs of one to one and a half-time job (average annually 1.300 thousands CZK). Nine respondents managed to quantify the annual IT costs that come from the Czech GAAP conservation at an average annually level of 400 thousand CZK.

However 12 companies pointed to the evident decline in work efficiency when they are forced to identify profit according to the Czech GAAP for taxation.

Application of the IFRS was 15 of 16 companies evaluated very positively. International standards are perceived as a more coherent set of rules showing the economic substance of transactions. The application of the IFRS meets the expectations, and the most of companies became more open to investors and users of financial statements, while it is possible to compare them at national and international level. Accounting is so much more in line with the principles of corporate governance – especially in the company and capital values management. All 16 respondents also confirmed that IFRS are detailed processed unlike the Czech GAAP and their application solved outstanding problems in some areas, which the Czech GAAP do not deal with. The IFRS are adequate size companies which they are required for. They also mentioned benefits of IFRS in evident increasing knowledge of the workers. Thirteen companies would like to remain the IFRS even when they would lose the obligation. At the same time, it was noted that there is a gradual improvement in the level of the IFRS reporting across the companies. Four respondents fight with problems of practical interpretation of the rules used in the IFRS – lack of methodology and specific examples with solutions including trainings for employees. The intensity of the positive rating of the IFRS is higher for banks and insurance companies.

Twelve companies maintain the Czech GAAP only for taxation. Two state-owned companies keep the Czech GAAP because of the financial reporting duty under the Czech GAAP for the state. The need of the Czech GAAP maintenance creates a fear from overlooking some difference between both systems or some accounting issue will be interpreted differently by the company and by the tax authority (mainly thanks to the lack of the complex and consistent accounting rules in the Czech GAAP). Thirteen companies would appreciate the change in the tax legislation toward the adoption of IFRS profit/loss as variable using for tax base calculation. The calculation of the tax base (coming from the Czech GAAP when the company use for individual reporting the IFRS) is very difficult and meaningless by the opinion of companies. A fear of the treats to the tax collection is unfounded because the most significant differences between both systems are temporal (fall into revenues or expenses in a different time) or the tax legislation deals with them separately from the accounting rules.

If there is an intention to adopt IFRS also for taxation, then it is important to incorporate tax legislation changes clearly. There is a risk of the excessive income tax law "swelling." The best way possibly consists of the income tax law partition – separately a part dealing with the taxpayers using and calculating the tax base from the Czech GAAP and a part for the IFRS users for financial reporting as well as for taxation.

Conclusion

Adoption of IFRS is assessed very positively by the publicly traded companies in the Czech Republic. Moreover most of them do not perceive any problem in the IFRS adoption for annual accounts despite the fact that the EU prescribe the using of the IFRS only for the consolidated financial reporting of the issues of securities. However there is disappointment from the tax solution. The calculation of the tax base (coming from the Czech GAAP when a company use for the individual reporting the IFRS) is very difficult and meaningless by the opinion of companies. Tax authorities could already have responded to the change of the accounting legislation (the IFRS were compulsorily adopted since 2005 in the EU). It is evident that the question of using of the IFRS for taxation is necessary to open today also due to the CCCTB proposal. Although the European Council directive does not provide a formal link to any national accounting standards (GAAP) or to the IFRS, the utilization of a national GAAP or national tax rules in cases, where the procedure is not explicitly defined, is undesirable and could jeopardize the objectives of the CCCTB project. It is almost certain that the CCCTB is/will be based on the accounting rules under the IFRS.

Acknowledgments This paper has been prepared within the research project "Institutional Support" (No. IP 100040).

References

Freedman J, Macdonald G (2008) The tax base for CCCTB: the role of principles. Viena. Centre for Business Taxation WP 08/07, pp 219–270

Fuest C (2008) The European Commission's proposal for common consolidated corporate tax base. Oxford Rev Econ Policy 4:720–739

James S, Nobes C (eds) (2002) The economics of taxation: principles, policy and practice, 7th edn. Financial Times/Practice Hall, Harlow. updated.

Macdonald G (1995) Matching accounting and taxable profits: reflections on Gallagher v. Jones. Br Tax Rev 24:484–498

Procházka D, Molín J (2016) Book-tax conformity: the review of recent research and its implication for the IFRS adoption in Europe. J Tax Res 14:96–118

Shön W (2004) International accounting standards – a starting point for a common European tax base? Eur Tax 44:426–440

Spengel C, Zollkau Y (eds) (2012) Common corporate tax base (CC(C)TB) and determination of taxable income – an international comparison. York. Springer, Berlin/Heidelberg

Weber D (2009) Do analysts and investors fully appreciate the implications of book-tax differences for future earnings? Contemp Account Res 26:1175–1206. https://doi.org/10.1506/car.26.4.7

IFRS 5 and Its Reporting in the Czech Republic

Jan Hospodka

Abstract This paper seeks to assess whether the issuers of listed securities report in accordance with IFRS 5 and whether they do it correctly. IFRS 5 is related to the special reporting of assets held for sale and discontinued operations. It requires the entities that follow IFRS accounting rules to use special methods and principles for such items. While bearing in mind the considerable differences between Czech GAAP and IFRS, many Czech entities are unaccustomed to differentiating between normal assets and assets held for sale as well as providing a separate reporting for some of their operations. However, entities that issue listed securities are obliged to prepare and present their financial statements in accordance with IFRS and should therefore apply the IFRS 5 accounting standard.

Keywords IFRS 5 • Discontinued operations • Assets held for sale • Reporting

Introduction

IFRS 5 refers to international accounting reporting standard which relates to assets held for sale and discontinued operations. The standard was issued in March 2004 and applies to annual periods beginning on or after 1 January 2005. It has replaced IAS 35, discontinued operations, updated the reporting requirements for discontinued operations and at the same included also the accounting rules for assets held for sale, which were until then covered by IAS 16 – property, plant and equipment. The reason for replacing IAS 35 with IFRS 5 lied mostly in intentions to unify requirements for long-term assets between IFRS and US GAAP. Before introducing IFRS 5, US GAAP (US SFAS 144 – Accounting for the impairment or disposal of long-lived assets) contained more detailed and advanced rules for accounting for long-term assets held for sale and their valuation.

J. Hospodka (✉)
University of Economics in Prague, Department of Financial Accounting and Auditing, W. Churchill Sq. 4, 130 67 Prague 3, Czech Republic
e-mail: jan.hospodka@vse.cz

D. Procházka (ed.), *The Impact of Globalization on International Finance and Accounting*, Springer Proceedings in Business and Economics,
https://doi.org/10.1007/978-3-319-68762-9_38

This paper comprises of the literature review, brief explanation of IFRS 5, and presents the results of the research related to whether Czech listed companies report their statements in accordance with IFRS 5. Research focuses on all the companies on the prime market of Prague Stock Exchange (PSE) as of November 2016 and their financial statements for 2015.

Literature Review

This standard has already been covered by several research papers focusing mostly on closer explanation of the standard and its reporting requirements, such as in Muthupandian (2008) or Holt (2007). However, they seem to have only a rather descriptive than experimental approach, unlike this paper. Apart from research papers, this topic also covered by private advisory companies such as Grant Thornton or Mazars, which aim to describe the impact of the standard on individual entities and guide those companies through examples for both assets held for sale and discontinued operations. Barua, Lin and Sparaglia (2010) come with a very interesting investigation into deliberate shifting of expenses into discontinued operations and thus improving the core earnings. The paper, based on empirical research, suggests that management very often tends to shift operating expenses into discontinued operations even though such expenses relate to continuing performance of the company, mostly because discontinued operations are usually not disclosed in such detail in the financial statements. By doing so, the management improves the financial performance of the company as a whole and also per share.

There are not many articles devoted to the application of IFRS 5 by Czech companies. An article "Non-current assets according to IFRS – Praxis" by Krupová (2010) shows the impact of reporting according to IFRS 5 on various business cases. She also debates the unclear definition of assets held for sale and discontinued operations and the troubles it causes to the entities. The paper emphasizes primarily the vague separation of discontinued operations, which might leave the companies in the dark when assessing whether to report about it separately or not. This will be also discussed in the following chapters. Dvořáková (2016) covers very thoroughly all the IFRS standards including IFRS 5. It also presents a few examples of adopting the IFRS 5 approach to discontinued operations and assets held for sale.

This paper poses a hypothesis that "the entities, which report about assets held for sale and discontinued operations, are doing it correctly and in accordance with IFRS 5".

It is unfortunate that it is not possible to analyse whether the companies do not report about assets held for sale or discontinued operations because they have nothing to report about or because they didn't disclose the information even though they should. It is therefore only possible to focus on those entities, which reported about it and analyse, whether they reported correctly.

IFRS 5

It is very important to bear in mind while preparing financial statements that it should provide the reader with the information about everything that happened during the reporting period and is subject to accounting. If the management decides to discontinue a business operation or sell an asset, it is quite likely to be a significant commercial decision that the reader should be aware of. These decisions might influence future economic performance of the entity as well as its net asset value.

Assets Held for Sale and Disposal Groups

To classify assets as held for sale is not an accounting policy choice, but it is a mandatory approach once an asset meets certain conditions. In short, these conditions are:

- Sale of the assets is highly probable.
- The assets are available for immediate sale.

The IFRS 5.8 sets out few conditions for the sale to be highly probable:

- An appropriate level of management must be committed to a plan to sell the asset.
- Active programme to locate a buyer and complete the plan to sale must have been initiated.
- Assets are on the market at a price that is reasonable.

Even though it might seem at the first glance that the standard goes into a considerable detail describing which assets should be considered as assets held for sale, particular situations, which occur during the business cycle of many entities, might prove otherwise. For instance, what should the entity do if it fails to sell the asset as planned to a third party, because the third party decided not to buy it in the end, although the asset is still available for purchase? Who decides whether the level of management committed to a plan to sell the asset is appropriate or whether it is not appropriate enough? Bearing in mind that these assets are still being used and they still contribute to the profit of the company, this decision might have a significant impact on the profit of the company as well as its EBIT, as these assets are no longer depreciated. In case of audited companies, the decision should be also a responsibility of the auditor, especially when this has a significant impact on the financial statements. Considering the auditors should be having more experience with this, the increasing frequency of situations that they encounter should provide them with enough ability to assess the case objectively.

IFRS 5.6 states that "*An entity shall classify a non-current asset (or disposal group) as held for sale if its carrying amount will be recovered principally through a sale transaction rather than through continuing use*". This provision and IFRS 5.13–14 suggest that assets which are to be abandoned or scrapped rather than sold shall not be classified as assets held for sale.

Further, for assets to be recognized as held for sale, and the sale should be expected to happen within a year. There are exceptions to this if the period to complete the sale is extended beyond 1 year because of events and circumstances that are beyond the entity's control.

Assets held for sale and disposal groups are, per IFRS 5.15, supposed to be measured at the lower of their carrying amount and fair value less costs to sell. Such assets are obviously not depreciated nor amortized, as per IFRS 5.25.

If the entity classifies some assets as held for sale, it needs to meet criteria set out in IFRS 5.38–42, which contain the main requirements for their presentation in financial statements and in the disclosure. These requirements and the ability of companies to meet them are analysed in the following chapters.

Noncurrent assets classified as held for sale and the assets of a disposable group should be presented separately from other assets in the statement of financial position. The liabilities classified as held for sale should be presented separately from other liabilities. Assets and liabilities should not be offset and should not be presented in a single amount. The entity is not obliged to adjust prior periods for current period decisions related to held for sale classification (unlike in case of discontinued operations).

The entity needs to analyse major asset classes held for sale either in the disclosure or in the statement of financial position. It also needs to describe the noncurrent assets held for sale, the facts and circumstances of the sale and the related gain or loss, either in the disclosure or statement of comprehensive income.

Discontinued Operations

The concept of classifying part of the business as a discontinued operation is linked to the concept of assets held for sale classification; it is however not the same one in the Appendix A to IFRS 5 discontinued operations are defined as following:

A component of an entity that either has been disposed of or is classified as held for sale and:

- Represents a separate major line of business or geographical are of operations
- Is part of a single coordinated plan to dispose of a separate major line of business or a geographical are of operations
- Is a subsidiary acquired exclusively with a view of resale

It is subject for consideration whether an activity of the entity should be reported as a discontinued operation or not, especially whether the activity is "major enough" to be considered as one. As entities report segments of their operations per IFRS 8, it is plain enough that such segments, if being discontinued, should be reported also in accordance with IFRS 5. Furthermore, IFRS 8.5 relates to these segments as entity's components, which are a similar approach as in IFRS 5. Other obvious discontinued operations might be, for instance, separate divisions or business units of the entity. In comparison to assets held for sale, the author considers the requirements for discontinued operations even vaguer. In some cases, it is abundantly clear whether the activity is separate and "major" enough to be considered as discontinued operation. In other cases, however, it might very well be debatable. That might lead to inconsistency between entities in what they consider to be a discontinued entity and what they do not. Even accounting firms might have a different corporate approach and methodology that would lead to inconsistencies on the market. In the opinion of the author of this paper, it would be therefore useful to narrow the focus of the standard down, for instance, through some examples of what is and what is not a discontinued operation.

Discontinued operation could be something yet to be sold or disposed of in a different way; however, it is also something that has already been discontinued during the reporting period, as per IFRS 5.34. A business unit sold in November should therefore be reported as an operation discontinued during the reporting period as of 31 December.

As already mentioned above, unlike assets held for sale, the entity should adjust prior periods and report the discontinued operations separately also for them.

If the entity classifies its operation as a discontinued operation, it needs to meet criteria set out in IFRS 5.33–46, which contain the main requirements for their presentation in financial statements and in the disclosure.

The unit should disclose its profit or loss for the discontinued operation, as well as profit or loss on the measurement to fair value less costs to sell the related assets. It shall also present the revenue, expenses, pre-tax profit and related cash flow of the discontinued operations. Requirements for the entities will be fully described in the following chapters.

Disclosures on discontinued operations require the entities to provide reader with a lot of information about the operation, which might prove too be quite costly to manage both in terms of time and money. Considering the entities show their profit and loss statement for continuing and discontinued operations separately, classification also has a substantial impact on the statements. That needs to be accounted for by auditors as, as previous research has shown, the management might tend to shift undesired items into discontinued operations and by doing so improve financial performance of the continuing operations. Even more so, that discontinued operations are provided with far less detail than continuing operations.

Data and Methodology

The research has been conducted on entities that issue listed securities on any stock market in the EU and are obliged to disclose by CNB the information required by Act No. 256/2004 Coll., on Capital Market Undertakings (CNB 2016a). The issuers of listed securities and other persons submit to the Czech National Bank information defined in Decree No. 234/2009 Coll. of 21 July 2009, on the Protection against Market Abuse and on Transparency (CNB 2016b). Such entities are also subject to §19a of Act No. 563/1991 Coll. On Accounting, according to which they need to apply international accounting standards, including IFRS 5. List of those entities was obtained from the database of the Czech National Bank available on their website as of 15th of December 2016 (CNB 2016c). After excluding investment funds, the research comprises altogether 53 entities, as illustrated by the table below.

Table 1 shows that from the overall number of 101 issuers, 70 were considered as a part of the research. Seventeen issuers did not have available financial statements for 2015 for various reasons, such as that they have become obliged to report to CNB only after 2015. As a result of this, financial statements of only 53 entities were analysed. From those, 15 entities did not mention in their financial statements anything about IFRS 5, assets held for sale or discontinued operations, and it is, therefore, not possible to say whether they do not report about assets held for sale or discontinued operations because those are not present in the company or simply because the company does not follow IFRS 5 requirements.

Overall 38 issuers mention IFRS 5 in their statements or their disclosure; however only 37% of those report about existing assets held for sale or discontinued operations in 2015 or 2014. The rest either mentions that the value of assets held for sale is zero or that everything relates only to continuing operations and in most cases, they also describe the procedures and requirements set by IFRS 5 in case some assets or operations qualify to be reported as assets held for sale or discontinued operations. From the 14 entities, 12 show assets held for sale and 7 discontinued operations. Effectively, this means that some companies show only one of those items and some companies show both.

Results and Discussion

To help to assess this matter, a check list has been created, which mirrors the requirements set by IFRS 5 standard and each company has been checked whether they provide the required information. Following Tables 2 and 3 describe the information required by IFRS 5 and the amount of companies that provided the reader with this information.

Some of the requirements are reported by most of the entities, such as assets held for sale presented separately from other assets, the entity does not reclassify for other periods or that the entity proved the reader with the information about post tax gain or loss of the discontinued operations. These are caused mainly by the fact that if the entity decides to report in accordance with IFRS 5, it's very hard to report about assets held for sale or discontinued operations. Other requirements, however, were followed with considerably less frequency, such as reporting about the segment, to which the assets held for sale fit, or reporting about gain or loss of

Table 1 Overview of available information in the CNB database

Group	No. of entities
Issuers of listed securities as per CNB in total	101
After excluding investments funds	70
Issuers that have available financial statements for 2015	53
Issuers that mention following IFRS 5 in their statements	38
Issuers that report about existing assets held for sale or discontinued operations:	14
Out of those report existing assets held for sale	12
Out of those report existing discontinued operations	7

Source: CNB (2016a)

Table 2 Assets held for sale checklist

Assets held for sale	Reported in	
Presented separately from other assets	11/12	92%
Not reclassified for other periods	11/12	92%
Description of the non-current asset held for sale	9/12	75%
Description of the facts and circumstances of the sale	8/12	67%
Gain or loss of the sale	3/12	25%
If applicable, the reportable segment in which the non-current asset is presented (IFRS 8)	1/12	8%

Source: Author's own creation, based on CNB (2016a)

Table 3 Discontinued operations checklist

Assets held for sale	Reported in	
Post tax gain or loss of discontinued operations	6/7	86%
Revenues, expenses and pre-tax profit or loss of the discontinued operation	5/7	71%
The related income tax expense	5/7	71%
The net cash flows attributable to the operating, investing and financing	5/7	71%
The amount of income from continuing and discontinued operations attributable to parents	5/7	71%
Re-presenting the disclosures for prior periods in the financial statements	3/7	43%

Source: Author's own creation, based on CNB (2016a)

the sale. For discontinued operations, this was mostly the case for re-presenting the disclosure for prior periods regarding the discontinued operations.

Those 14 companies were further analysed for the quality of their reporting. For the purposes of this research, the author created a scale to quantify how well the entities report in accordance with IFRS 5. This scale is shown in Tables 4 and 5.

The assessment of the quality of the reporting has been based on author's experience with financial statements and is mostly based on relative comparison between the entities. Companies have then been graded regarding how well they meet their criteria set by IFRS 5 as well as how detailed information they provide. An average grade for assets held for sale was 2.3 and for discontinued operations

Table 4 Scale of the quality of reporting in accordance with IFRS 5 – assets held for sale

Description	Value
No further explanation	1
Limited explanation of the assets and circumstances of the sale	2
Detailed explanation of the assets and circumstances of the sale	3

Source: Author's illustration

Table 5 Scale of the quality of reporting in accordance with IFRS 5 – discontinued operations

Description	Value
No further explanation	1
Limited explanation of the assets and circumstances of the sale	2
Detailed explanation of the assets and circumstances of the sale	3

Source: Author's illustration

2.6. That implies that in general, companies which report about the assets held for sale or discontinued operations are explaining the circumstances of the sale well and following the requirements set by IFRS.

Conclusion

Focus of this paper has been on companies which are obliged to follow IFRS standards and whether they follow IFRS 5 in particular. The problem of this standard lies primarily in its difference to Czech GAAP, which makes it harder for the entities to adopt it, as they might have no experience which such requirements and rules.

As was already stated in the introduction, it is not possible to measure the number of companies that should report in accordance with IFRS 5, as we do not know whether they fulfil the conditions to have the obligations to do so. The only approach that might help to narrow the companies down is to check whether they state that they follow IFRS 5 specifically. That might suggest that they would report about it, if they met the criteria.

The research has however proven that we cannot reject our hypothesis and that indeed most the companies which report about assets held for sale or discontinued operations do so with considerable detail and quality. In the author's opinion, this is caused mostly by the fact that these companies are assisted with their reporting by large accounting firms which have the resources and capacity to follow IFRS properly.

What might however be a cause for concern is the fact that even though companies tend to disclose the information required by IFRS 5, such information seldom provides enough detail into the character of expenses and income attributed to discontinued operations as this information rely primarily in management accounting. That might lead to management tendencies to shift expenses and income between continuing and discontinued operations and thus alter the financial results of the company. It is therefore important for IFRS to find a balance between providing enough information and at the same time not to be too time- and resource demanding.

Acknowledgements This paper has been prepared within the research project "Economic Impacts of the IFRS Adoption in Selected Transition Countries" (supported by the Czech Science Foundation, No. 15-01280S).

References

Barua A, Lin S, Sbaraglia AM (2010) Earnings management using discontinued operations. Account Rev 85(5):1485–1509

CNB (2016a) The central storage of regulated information. Retrieved from https://oam.cnb.cz/sipresextdad/SIPRESWEB.WEB21.START_INPUT_OAM?p_lang=cz. [27 Nov 2016]

CNB (2016b) Regular reporting of issuers and other persons. Retrieved from https://www.cnb.cz/en/supervision_financial_market/conduct_of_supervision/information_duties/issuers_other_entities/index.html. [27 Nov 2016]

CNB (2016c) Lists and registers published by the Czech National Bank. Retrieved from http://www.cnb.cz/cs/dohled_financni_trh/seznamy/. [27 Nov 2016]

Dvořáková D (2016) Finanční účetnictví a výkaznictví podle mezinárodních standardů IFRS. BizBooks, Albatros Media a.s., 8026501748

Holt G (2007) IFRS 5: non-current assets held-for-sale and discontinued operations. Account Bus 10(8):46–48

Krupová L (2010) Dlouhodobý majetek dle IFRS – Praktikum. Účetnictví v praxi 2010/11

Muthupandian KS (2008) IFRS 5: non-current assets held for sale and discontinued operations – a closer look. Manag Account 43(3):133–137

PSE (2016) Prague stock exchange prime market. Retrieved from https://www.pse.cz/udaje-o-trhu/akcie/prime-market/. [27 Nov 2016]

Explaining Risk Premium on Bank Bonds by Financial Ratios

Ovunc Gursoy

Abstract This paper examines the relationship between the risk premium on bank bonds and banks' financial ratios. It also tries to show that bonds issued by banks with strong fundamentals offer less premium as they are perceived to be less risky by investors. Components of CAMELS rating methodology are used to establish the link between a bank's financial ratios and the risk premium on their bonds. Financial ratios of 11 Turkish banks, which issued bonds between the years 2012 and 2016, are calculated. This study investigates the links between bond premiums and financial ratios with k-means cluster and discriminant analysis. It also shows the importance of fundamentals on the level of risk premium paid to bond investors by banks.

Keywords Bank bonds • Bond risk premium • CAMELS ratings • Financial ratios • Turkish banks

Introduction

Banks are important for the development of a healthy economy in a country. They provide loans for SME productivity, agriculture, manufacturing, and services. Like most enterprises banks are profit-seeking institutions; thus they take risks for maximizing shareholders' wealth. There are many risks which need to be measured, monitored, and managed by banks. Among the different banking risks, interest rate and liquidity risks challenge the banks at most.

The best way for banks to manage these risks is to diversify their funding base to decrease their duration gap. By prolonging the maturity of their liabilities, they minimize interest rate risk and improve liquidity. Long-term bond issuing is an important funding choice to diversify liabilities, deal with both interest rate and liquidity risks at banks. Five percent of interest earning assets of banks in Turkey are funded by bond issuances at the end of 2016. This ratio was as low as 2% at the

O. Gursoy (✉)
Marmara University, Ressam Namik Ismail Sok., No: 1, 34180 Bahcelievler, Istanbul, Turkey
e-mail: ovuncgursoy@marun.edu.tr

D. Procházka (ed.), *The Impact of Globalization on International Finance and Accounting*, Springer Proceedings in Business and Economics,
https://doi.org/10.1007/978-3-319-68762-9_39

end of 2011. In fact, bank bond issuances accelerated after 2011 in Turkey with the release of the Capital Markets Board of Turkey's (CMB 2013) communique regulating the issuance of debt instruments. The volume of issued bank bonds reached to TRY 108bn by almost five folds over the last 5 years (BRSA 2016).

Banks offer risk premium over the two-year benchmark government bond to arouse investors' appetite for each issuance. Fisher (1959) examined the factors determining risk premiums on corporate bonds. He concluded that default risk and liquidity risks are the main determinants of risk premium. Default risk is the probability of a bond issuer being unable to service its due debt, while liquidity risk prevails when the marketability of the bond is low, and its trading volume is not significant. Thus, it could be difficult for investors to sell the bond quickly. As far as interest rate risk is concerned, bonds with long maturities have higher interest rate risk, meaning that they experience larger price changes for any given change in rates. When someone invests in a bond, he obviously wants to earn a higher return than the yield on the benchmark bond to compensate the additional risk assumed. Therefore, bond risk premium is the return in excess of risk-free rate of return an investment is expected to yield.

I use the components of CAMELS rating methodology to establish the link between a bank's financial ratios and the risk premium on their bonds. Sinkey (1975), Martin (1977), and Espahbodi (1991) developed models to distinguish problem banks using CAMELS ratings information. Sinkey and Greenwich (1979) identified internal factors as the most important reasons leading to problems in banks. Kaya (2001) analyzed the relationship between CAMELS rating of Turkish banks and probability to be undertaken by Saving Deposit Insurance Fund (SDIF) using probit regression. Strong relation between the two was proved as a result. Gasbarro et al. (2002) analyzed the changing relationship between CAMELS ratings and bank soundness in Indonesia during crisis. He concluded that different CAMELS factors are important in different economic environments. Mercan et al. (2003) examined the effect of scale and mode of ownership on the financial performance of the Turkish banking sector. In the study, he used financial ratios available in CAMELS as both inputs and outputs to assess the 1989–1999 relative financial performance of Turkish banks. Avci and Cinko (2008) explored the relationship between CAMELS ratings of Turkish banks and banks' failure probability using discriminant analysis and logistic regression. They could not find any significant relationship.

As far as the statistical analysis of financial ratios is concerned, in the late 1960s, discriminant analysis was brought up to construct a composite empirical indicator of financial ratios. Using financial ratios, Beaver (1966) developed an indicator by conducting univariate analysis to differentiate problem firms. Models for financial institutions became popular when Sinkey (1975) used discriminant analysis for differentiating problem banks and Altman (1977) researched the savings and loan industry. K-means clustering was first introduced by MacQueen (1966). Forgy (1965) later analyzed using the same method. K-means clustering aims to partition observations into k clusters in which each observation belongs to the cluster with the nearest mean, serving as a prototype of the cluster.

Data and Methodology

Financial ratios of 11 commercial banks, which issued bonds between the years 2012 and 2016, are the inputs of our study. I try to establish a relationship between year-end financial ratios of a bank and the risk premium of the respective bank's bond issued in the following year. The maturity of bonds ranges between 365 and 720 days. Risk premiums on bank bonds are calculated by deducting the yield on the 2-year benchmark government bond from the yield on the bank bond at the day of initial public offering (IPO). I have gathered the yields of bank bonds at the day of IPO from daily bulletins of Istanbul Stock Exchange. In this study, each observation is treated independently, meaning that if a bank has bonds issued in different years, each bond is considered as an independent observation. Therefore, we obtain a total of 32 observations for our analysis.

I use the components of CAMELS rating methodology to establish the link between a bank's financial ratios and the risk premium on their bonds. CAMELS rating methodology is used a large set of financial ratios to reveal a bank's soundness in terms of capital adequacy, asset quality, management, earnings, liquidity, and sensitivity to market risk.

A total of 13 financial ratios representing each of CAMELS components are selected in the beginning. A list of these ratios is provided in the Appendix. Then, risk premiums are regressed against financial ratios. The explanatory power or significance of each ratio (variable) in determining the risk premium is assessed by t-statistics. The ones, which are found significant in explaining risk premiums, are further investigated with k-means cluster analysis and discriminant analysis. The results are shown in the Appendix. Accordingly, four ratios are filtered for further analysis, namely, nonperforming loans (NPLs) to total loans, opex to total assets, deposits per branch, and securities to total assets.

Results and Discussion

I employ k-means cluster analysis to classify the selected bonds into two convenient groups: "high-risk premium" and "low-risk premium." K-means clustering aims to partition observations into k clusters in which each observation belongs to the cluster with the nearest mean, serving as a prototype of the cluster. Before starting cluster analysis, data are sorted in ascending order according to risk premiums, and then 32 observations are partitioned into two groups. Risk premiums in the data set range between 0.28% and 2.24%. The seventeenth observation (0.88%) is set as the cutoff point to calculate the hit ratio between my clustering of data and computed clusters. Observations below the cutoff point ($n = 17$) are labeled "1," indicating low-risk premium, while observations above it ($n = 15$) are labeled "0," indicating high-risk premium.

Table 1 Groupings of sampled bond classes

Actual situation	Number of cases	Cluster "low-risk prem." group	Cluster "high-risk prem." group
Actual low-risk prem.	17	16 (76.1%)	1 (9.09%)
Actual high-risk prem.	15	5 (23.8%)	10 (90.9%)

Source: Own analysis of data from the Istanbul Stock Exchange and banks' financial statements

After four iterations, full convergence to cluster centers is achieved. Cluster membership information is provided in Table 1, which resulted in a (16 + 10)/(17 + 15) or 81% hit ratio. I consider it good and acceptable for the aim of the study. Hit ratio shows the percentage of correctly classified cases. The higher the hit ratio, the more accurate the group membership prediction becomes.

Table 2 shows that a low ratio of NPLs to total loans and opex to assets, while a high ratio of deposits per branch and securities to total assets are associated with a low-risk premium. In cluster numbering, 2 corresponds to 1 (low-risk premium) and 1 corresponds to 0 (high-risk premium). All of our ratios (variables) have a significant impact on determining the riskiness of a bank bond (Table 3).

Discriminant analysis (DA) is also used to classify the selected bonds into two groups, namely, "high-risk premium" and "low-risk premium." DA is a statistical technique used to classify an observation into one of at least two a priori established groupings dependent upon the observation's individual characteristics (Emel et al. 2003).

In this study, level of risk premium is used as the qualitative (i.e., a priori grouping) variable. The financial ratios are used as explanatory variables in the DA. A discriminant function is then generated. The firms were classified into two groups with respect to their level of risk premiums. The seventeenth observation (0.88%) is set as the cutoff point to calculate the hit ratio between my clustering of data and clusters computed by DA analysis. Observations below the cutoff point ($n = 17$) are labeled "1," indicating low-risk premium, while observations above it ($n = 15$) are labeled "0," indicating high-risk premium. Next, DA is run using the above classification as the category variable and the four ratios used as the independent variables. The DA generated a discriminant function with four ratios included. As seen from Table 4, DA resulted in a (13 + 12)/(17 + 15) or 78.1% hit ratio.

Equation 1 represents the resulting unstandardized canonical discriminant function:

$$Z = -4.3 - 25.1\frac{NPLs}{Total\ Loans} + 26.6\frac{Opex}{Total\ Assets} + 0.03\ Deposit\ per\ branch + 10\frac{Securities}{Total\ Assets} \quad (1)$$

Table 2 Final cluster centers

	Cluster 1	Cluster 2
Nonperforming loans (NPLs)/total loans	0.04	0.02
Opex/total assets	0.04	0.02
Deposits per branch	50.95	97.42
Securities/total assets	0.15	0.23

Source: Own analysis of data from the Istanbul Stock Exchange and banks' financial statements

Table 3 Significance of cluster centers

	Mean square	df	F	Sign.
Nonperforming loans (NPLs)/total loans	0.002	1	11.7	0.002
Opex/total assets	0.002	1	64.3	0
Deposits per branch	15,583	1	71.7	0
Securities/total assets	0.046	1	9.4	0.004

Source: Own analysis of data from the Istanbul Stock Exchange and banks' financial statements

Table 4 Groupings of sampled bond classes

Actual situation	Number of cases	DA "low-risk prem." group	DA "high-risk prem." group
Actual low-risk prem.	17	13 (81.3%)	4 (0.25%)
Actual high-risk prem.	15	3 (18.7%)	12 (0.75%)

Source: Own analysis of data from the Istanbul Stock Exchange and banks' financial statements

The resulted canonical discriminant function is significant in classifying the risk premium with Wilk's lambda (λ) of 0.647 and significance of 0.016. This discriminant model classifies high-risk premium bonds better than that of low-risk premium with a probability of 80%.

Conclusion

This paper presents a new methodology for determining risk premiums on bank bonds. It involves financial ratio, cluster, and discriminant analysis. Financial ratios computed from each bank's financial statements were used for further statistical analysis. I use the components of CAMELS rating methodology to establish the link between a bank's financial ratios and the risk premium on their bonds. Four ratios are filtered based on t-test results for further analysis, namely, NPLs to total loans, opex to total assets, deposits per branch, and securities to total assets.

I show that bonds issued by banks with strong fundamentals offer less premium as they are perceived to be less risky by investors. The initial partitioning of the sample into two classes, namely, low-risk and high-risk premium, lies parallel with the results obtained from cluster and discriminant analysis. Financial ratios used in the analysis have significant explanatory power on the level of risk premium of bank bonds.

In terms of managerial implications, the methodology gives clear insights as to how "risk premium" of banks' bonds can be reduced. Specifically, banks issuing bonds with "low-risk premiums" have certain characteristics in common, namely, lower NPL ratio, lower opex to total assets, higher deposit per branch, and higher securities to total assets. Therefore, banks which have better asset quality, higher operational efficiency, and more liquid assets may borrow less costly than others.

This study shows the importance of fundamentals on the level of risk premium paid to investors by banks. This is particularly important for banks as the output of this study has an influence on decisions at the level of management, investors, and other stakeholders. Our research has some limitations. We do not have a large population set to select a sample for our study as most bank issuances in Turkey are in the form of bills instead of bonds. Due to the volatility in emerging markets, including Turkey, investors do not usually have a long-term investment horizon, and thus issuers opt for bills. For further research, the impact of financial ratios on the risk premiums of Eurobonds and corporate bonds could be analyzed.

Appendix

Table 5 Candidate financial ratios for the analysis

Ratio no.	Ratio name
	Component 1: Capital adequacy
1	Capital/risk-weighted assets
2	Total assets/total equity
	Component 2: Asset quality
3	Nonperforming loans (NPLs)/total loans
4	NPL coverage
	Component 3: Management
5	Opex/total assets
6	Loans per branch
7	Deposits per branch
	Component 4: Earnings
8	Net profit/average assets
9	Net profit/average equity
	Component 5: Liquidity
10	Deposits >TRY 50.000/total liabilities
11	Liquid assets/total assets
	Component 6: Sensitivity to market risk
12	Securities/total assets
13	Balance sheet net FX position/total equity

Table 6 The financial ratio t-test analysis results

Ratio name	t-statistics	Significance
Capital/risk-weighted assets	−1.163	0.254
Total assets/total equity	0.757	0.455
Nonperforming loans (NPLs)/total loans	2.913	0.007
NPL coverage	−0.509	0.615
Opex/total assets	2.328	0.027
Loans per branch	−1.718	0.096
Deposits per branch	−2.394	0.023
Net profit/average assets	−1.291	0.207
Net profit/average equity	−1.399	0.172
Deposits >TRY 50.000/total liabilities	−0.979	0.335
Liquid assets/total assets	1.038	0.308
Securities/total assets	−2.691	0.012
Balance sheet net FX position/total equity	1.006	0.322

References

Altman EI (1977) Predicting performance in the savings and loan association industry. J Monet Econ 3:443–466. https://doi.org/10.1016/0304-3932(77)90015-0

Avci E, Cinko M (2008) CAMELS rating system and forecasting the financial failure in the Turkish commercial banking sector. J BRSA Bank Financ Mark 2:25–48

Beaver WH (1966) Financial ratios as predictors of failure. J Account Res 4:71. https://doi.org/10.2307/2490171

BRSA (2016) Monthly banking statistics. http://ebulten.bddk.org.tr/ABMVC/en. Accessed 20 Dec 2016

CMB (2013) Communique for debt instruments. http://spk.gov.tr/apps/teblig/displayteblig.aspx?id=467&ct=f&action=displayfile. Accessed 24 Jan 2017

Emel AB, Oral M, Reisman A, Yolalan R (2003) A credit scoring approach for the commercial banking sector. Socio Econ Plan Sci 37:103–123. https://doi.org/10.1016/s0038-0121(02)00044-7

Espahbodi P (1991) Identification of problem banks and binary choice models. J Bank Financ 15:53–71. https://doi.org/10.1016/0378-4266(91)90037-m

Fisher L (1959) Determinants of risk premiums on corporate bonds. J Polit Econ 67:217–237. https://doi.org/10.1086/258172

Forgy EW (1965) Cluster analysis of multivariate data: efficiency versus interpretability of classification. In: Biometrics, 3rd edn, International Biometric Society, USA, pp 768–769

Gasbarro D, Sadguna IM, Zumwalt JK (2002) The changing relationship between CAMEL ratings and Bank soundness during the Indonesian banking crisis. Rev Quant Finan Acc 19:247–260

Kaya Y (2001) CAMELS analysis for Turkish banking sector. Banking regulation and supervision agency of Turkey

MacQueen J (1966) 5th Berkeley symposium on mathematical statistics and probability. In: Some methods for classification and analysis of multivariate observations. University of California Press, California, USA, pp 281–297

Martin D (1977) Early warning of bank failures: a logit regression approach. J Bank Financ 1:249–276

Mercan M, Reisman A, Yolalan R, Emel AB (2003) The effect of scale and mode of ownership on the financial performance of the Turkish banking sector: results of a DEA-based analysis. Socio Econ Plan Sci 37:185–202. https://doi.org/10.1016/s0038-0121(02)00045-9

Sinkey JF (1975) A multivariate statistical analysis of the characteristics of problem banks. J Financ 30:21. https://doi.org/10.2307/2978429

Sinkey F, Greenwich (1979) Conn., JAI Press Inc., Bus Hist Rev 54:553–555. https://doi.org/10.2307/3114230

The Use of Tax and Nontax Provisions and Allowances

Irena Honková

Abstract The basic principle of the creation of accounting provisions and allowances is the principle of prudence and a true and fair view of the entity. The allowances are used to express a temporary reduction in the value of assets, while the provisions are a source of increasing costs intended to cover future debts or expenses, of which purpose is likely to incur but the amount or the date on which they arise are uncertain. There was a questionnaire survey, which was attended by 673 enterprises. The goal was to determine whether the size and scope of enterprises are linked to the creation of provisions and allowances. It was not found out that the creation of provisions and allowances depends on the size and industry of enterprises. The different types of provisions and allowances and their representation in enterprises were also examined. It was found out that 39% of businesses have never created any provisions and allowances. Most often nontax provisions (21%) are created. As a result, insufficient creation of provisions and allowances was found out.

Keywords Accounting provisions • Allowances • Czech GAAP

Introduction

The business is naturally connected with a certain degree of uncertainty and potential as well as very real risks. A sensible entrepreneur is aware of this and creates financial and other provisions during relatively better times for overcoming less favorable times. The situation is similar for allowances which also result from rational concern about future results. Provisions and allowances are mostly divided into legal alias tax, pursuant to the law on provisions for determining the income tax base no. 593/2002 Coll. as amended (LoR), and other alias accounting. The basic principle of the creation of accounting provisions and allowances is the prudence

I. Honková (✉)
University of Pardubice, Institute of Business Economics and Management, Studentská 95, 532 10 Pardubice, Czech Republic
e-mail: irena.honkova@upce.cz

D. Procházka (ed.), *The Impact of Globalization on International Finance and Accounting*, Springer Proceedings in Business and Economics,
https://doi.org/10.1007/978-3-319-68762-9_40

principle and a true and fair view of the accounting unit. This paragraph should contain literature review or review of conducted research.

Literature Review

Allowances in Czech Accounting

Allowances (AE) correct the original value of impaired assets to lower current market value. This is a temporary reduction in assets value. The task of allowances is to adjust the valuation of the relevant assets in the event it is proved during inventorying at the latest that there has been a temporary reduction in value (Kovanicová 2008). Allowances are used to express a temporary reduction in the assets value that is proved during inventorying, is sufficiently important from the perspective of the accounting unit, is not permanent, and is not expressed in other way, e.g., by real value of securities (Poradce 6/2016). The creation of allowances to individual asset categories (long-term assets, stock, short-term financial assets, receivables) must be economically justifiable (Ryneš 2013). Reduction in assets value by AE is only an indirect valuation change; the original accounting valuation does not change, and the created AE is monitored on a separate assets account, which is subject to the correction (Poradce 6/2016). Legal allowances can be created only for receivables. Allowances for receivables enable to capture reduction in receivables for a temporary period. Thus they are the tools enabling a temporary solution which precedes a final solution (execution, assignment, receivable write-off) (Hnátek and Zámek 2014). Allowances for receivables are according to Poradce (6/2016) in practice widespread. According to the LoR as amended, it is possible to create six kinds of legal AE, most of which are three (Poradce 6/2016): insolvency AE for receivables of debtors in insolvency proceedings (§ 8 LoR), time AE for receivables due after 31 December 1994 which are not out-of-date (§ 8a LoR), and the prescription period is of 3 years according to § 629 LoR, "small AE" for relatively small receivables up to 30,000 (§ 8c LoR). Once the AE is created, it is possible to write this receivable off in a tax effectively way (Křemen 2010).

As we have already mentioned, the creation (or increase) of legal allowances is a tax-effective expense of the taxpayer pursuant to § 24 para. 2 letter i of the Act no. 586/1992 Coll., the Income Tax Act (ITA), as amended. Also the cancellation (or reduction) is a tax-deductible record under the general provisions of § 23 para. 2 and 10 of the Income Tax Act. Although the AE are only temporary, they have three significant tax benefits: they reduce the tax base by the formation non-collected claims (§ 24 para. 2 letter i) of the ITA, legal AE increases the tax value of receivables when being assigned (§ 24 para. 2 letter s) of the ITA, and the receivable write-off is a tax cost up to the amount of its legal AE (§ 24 para. 2 letter y) of the ITA. General rules for creating legal AE are set out in § 2 and § 4 LoR as amended. Dealing with problematic receivables is usually one of the most difficult tasks in accounting practice. The accounting practice includes the following: to deal with correct accounting and tax context, it is necessary to have the knowledge of numerous legal regulations and as a follow-up to it to create an internal regulation, in which the enterprise provides options and procedures in dealing with problematic and irrecoverable receivables (Poradce 11/2016). The internal regulation should cover not only procedures for provisions having the support of the Income Tax Act but mainly for provisions, which the accounting entity creates on the grounds of correct statement of assets and liabilities value in accordance with the principle of prudence (Koch 2016).

Provisions in Czech Accounting

Pursuant to § 57 of the Accounting Act no. 563/1991 Coll. as amended (AA), provisions are the source increasing costs intended to cover future debts or expenses, of which purpose is known; it is probable that they will occur but the amount or the date on which they arise is uncertain. Provisions are treated as a liability. Their use is related to the accounting and economic effort to evenly spread the higher expected future one-off costs (expenses) at a time. Provisions are accrued expenses by their nature (Poradce 6/2016). Synek (2006) defines provisions as provisions for unforeseen needs arising from timing differences of costs, occurring continuously, and from expenses that will arise in the future. They are reported as a separate liability item. A reserve is a liability of uncertain timing and amount (Jilek and Svobodová 2013). It is often uncertain if the expense, for which the reserve is created, will certainly occur, but its realization is probable (Sramkova and Křivánková 2007). A reserve is reported in accordance with IAS 37, if an enterprise has a present liability, for which settlement resources outflow will be necessary and the liability reliably realizable (Dvořáková 2008). This is why a reserve is considered a liability (Ryneš 2013): it is a potential liability to third parties, e.g., to product purchasers due to repairs under warranty, and expenses are expected in future periods (internal debt of an accounting entity), e.g., repairing tangible fixed written-off assets. A reserve is reported in the balance sheet within liabilities, because it represents recognition of current liability (Kovanicová 2008).

An accounting entity shall provide in its internal rules (Koch 2016): for what expenses it will form a reserve, under what conditions, how it will determine the amount of these provisions, at what point it will draw it, or cancel it.

As with AE, provisions are also mostly divided into legal (tax) and other (nontax). The most common provisions in business practice are legal (tax), of which creation is set by the LoR as amended, bank provisions § 5 LoR, insurance provisions § 6 LoR, a reserve for tangible assets repairs § 7 LoR, a cultivation activity reserve § 9 LoR, a reserve for electrical waste handling § 11a-11c LoR, and other legal provisions, e.g., for pond sludge removal and land remediation, § 10LoR.

The reserve for tangible assets (HM) repairs pursuant to § 26 par. 2 of the ITA is the most widespread legal reserve, of which tax writing-off period is 5 years or more. The reserve must be created in at least two consecutive tax periods. The expected year of repairs launch is not included in the number of years of reserve formation (Vančurová and Láchová 2008). The reserve for tangible assets repairs shall not be created (Koch 2016): if it is a technical evaluation, for tangible assets intended for disposal, for tangible assets if the repair is carried out repeatedly every year, and for tangible assets to which a taxpayer in bankruptcy and settlement proceedings has a right of ownership. The enterprise must be able to prove the amount and the creation method (Koch 2016). Provisions can be generally formed in two ways: depending on time or depending on performance.

The accounting entity should consider related risks associated with estimating the amount of future payments at the creation of provisions. It should be based on an analysis of various options of potential future development, and, in line with the principle of prudence, it should be rather based on higher estimated amounts (Dvořáková 2008). The enterprise is required to keep a book inventory of provisions (Strouhal 2007). A deposit condition was introduced for provisions for TA repairs, of which production began after January 1, 2009. The taxpayer must deposit an amount corresponding to the reserve creation on a special tied account, until the deadline for submitting tax returns for income tax for the corresponding tax period (Poradce 6/2016).

Creating other provisions is in accordance with the accounting principle of prudence, because the creation of other accounting provisions is not a tax expense; thus, logically their use is not relevant for tax purposes. AA defines these kinds of accounting provisions (Koch 2016): provisions for risks and losses (e.g., legal actions, guarantee repairs, environmental damages), provisions for income taxes, provisions for pensions and similar obligations, and provisions for restructuring.

Data and Methodology

Seven hundred two legal entities – accounting entities, which were categorized pursuant to Regulation No. 250/2015 Coll. – were surveyed during February–May 2016 in a questionnaire survey. Twenty-nine questionnaires were excluded from this amount, because they failed to answer all three questions. Six hundred seventy-three questionnaires were therefore included in the questionnaire survey analysis. The questionnaire construction was very simple and contained the aforementioned three questions. It was necessary to categorize the accounting entity pursuant to the new Regulation No. 250/2015 Coll. in the first question. A note was available to respondents with the information of the limit amount of assets, net turnover, and the number of employees for each accounting entity category. The respondents were asked to state the prevailing industry in which they operate by the CZ NACE (section A-U) (CZ NACE 2016) classification, in the second question. The third question concerned the creation of provisions and allowances. The respondents were asked to comment here as to whether their accounting entities created provisions and allowances and what type of provisions/allowances they created.

This question was half-open, and had variants (a–g), while the respondents were to note the type nontax provisions. The questionnaires also contained information about the enterprise registration number, which was used for checking the questionnaires validity. The questionnaires were collected in paper form, and they are at the author's disposal. The questionnaire results were processed by the method of statistical test of independence and descriptive statistics in Statistica software.

Results and Discussion

The area of provisions and allowances is analyzed with the help of hypotheses:

- H1: The accounting entity size does not affect the creation of provisions and allowances.
- H2: The accounting entity field of activity does not affect the creation of provisions and allowances.

The questionnaire results are analyzed by descriptive statistical methods. The last part of result survey dealt with the analysis of two types of nontax provisions.

The Effect of the Entity Size

Hypothesis H1: The accounting entity size that does not depend on the creation of provisions and allowances was proved (Table 1).

Hypothesis H2: The accounting entity field of activity that does not depend on the creation of provisions and allowances was proved as well (Table 2).

Statistical Evaluation of the Creation of Provisions and AE

The fundamental part of the questionnaire survey was the third question, which inquired the creation of provisions and allowances: (a) the enterprise does not make any provisions, (b) it creates legal (tax) provisions for tangible assets repairs (§ 7 of the Act no. 593/1992 Coll., as amended), (c) other legal (tax) provisions, e.g., for pond sludge removal, sanitation and cultivation activities, electrical waste handling, or bank provisions and insurance provisions (§ 5, 6, 9, 10, 11 of the Act no. 563/1992 Coll. amended), (d) tax allowances for receivables of debtors in insolvency proceedings (§ 8 of the Act no. 593/1992 Coll., as amended), (e) tax allowances for receivables which are not out-of-date (§ 8a of the Act no. 593/1992

Table 1 The dependence of accounting entity size on the creation of provisions and AE

Statist.	Statistical summary; ZP: Prom1 (Chart1)
	Value
R	0.249
R2	0.062
Modified R2	0.060
F(1669)	44.437
p	0.000

Source: Own calculations

Table 2 The dependence of accounting entity field of activity on the creation of provisions and AE

Statist.	Statistical summary; ZP: Prom2 (Chart1)
	Value
R	0.080
R2	0.006
Modified R2	0.005
F(1669)	4.382
p	0.036
Sm. Error of estimate	4.689

Source: Own calculations

Coll., as amended), (f) nontax allowances for receivables, and (g) other nontax provisions. The evaluation of this issue is contained in Table 3. Significant frequencies are in bold.

Table 4 was further modified in order to find out the total amount of individual variants.

The Creation of Other Nontax Provisions

As already mentioned, it was possible to state the purpose for which the reserve is formed for the response variant (g) "the creation of other nontax provisions." The results are shown in Table 5.

It was confirmed that the creation of provisions and allowances does not depend on the size and the entity field of activity by the hypotheses H1 and H2 test. The survey revealed no combination of provisions and allowances that would be significant. As a result of this, companies use only one type of these items. Next, it was found out that about 40% of companies do not use provisions and allowances at all. Twenty-one percent of companies account for nontax provisions, and 16% of companies account for tax provisions for tangible assets repairs. On the contrary, the least used tools for the principle of prudence are tax and nontax allowances for receivables. Concerning the creation of other nontax provisions, provisions for

Table 3 Variants of the creation of provisions and allowances

Variant	Abs. frequency	Rel. frequency	Variant	Abs. frequency	Rel. frequency
a	300	44.58%	c,g	12	1.78%
b	101	15.01%	d	14	2.08%
b,c	4	0.59%	d,e	4	0.59%
b,d	1	0.15%	d,e,f	1	0.15%
b,d,e,f	4	0.59%	d,e,f,g	4	0.59%
b,d,g	2	0.30%	d,e,g	2	0.30%
b,e	4	0.59%	d,g	1	0.15%
b, g	9	1.34%	e	20	2.97%
c	35	5.20%	e,f	4	0.59%
c,d	2	0.30%	e,f,g	3	0.45%
c,d,g	3	0.45%	e,g	3	0.45%
c,e	1	0.15%	f	12	1.78%
c,f	2	0.30%	f,g	2	0.30%
c,f,g	3	0.45%	g	120	17.83%

Source: Own calculations

Table 4 The overall representation of the creation of provisions and allowances

Question variants	Absolute frequency	Relative frequency
a	300	38.76%
b	125	16.15%
c	62	8.01%
d	38	4.91%
e	49	6.33%
f	35	4.52%
g	165	21.32%

Source: Own calculations

unexpended leave (23%), income tax (17%), bonuses (11%), and warranty repairs (10%) are mostly created.

Conclusion

Given the above, it is possible to say that companies do not use allowances. This reduces, to some extent, the true accounting presentation, as assets are overvalued and their reporting is not in line with the principle of prudence. As for the provisions, companies use nontax provisions as resources for future liabilities, usually for unexpended leave payments (23%). However, unexpended leave should be paid out only in exceptional cases of employees' leaving, so the creation of this reserve is misleading, to some extent. On the contrary, the creation of provisions for warranty repairs was found out only in 10%, which is totally insufficient and,

Table 5 The creation of other nontax provisions

Reserve purpose	Freq.	Rel. freq.	Reserve purpose	Freq.	Rel. freq.
Unexpended leave	54	22,78%	Waste disposal	3	1,27%
Income tax	40	16,88%	Credit losses	3	1,27%
Bonuses	27	11,39%	Guarantee commitments	3	1,27%
Warranty repairs/ service	24	10,13%	Unprofitable rent	3	1,27%
Business risks	20	8,44%	Exchange rate and price differences	2	0,84%
Pension	10	4,22%	Disposal of assets	2	0,84%
Litigations	9	3,80%	Restoration	2	0,84%
Benefits	6	2,53%	Environmental damages	1	0,42%
Redundancy payment	6	2,53%	Unclaimed gift vouchers	1	0,42%
Work/life anniversaries	6	2,53%	Risk for violation of budg. Discipline	1	0,42%
Future losses	5	2,11%	Returned goods	1	0,42%
Unreturned packaging	4	1,69%	Purchase of vehicles	1	0,42%
Audit	3	1,27%			

Source: Own calculations

e.g., international financial reporting standards, in particular IAS 37, expressly require the creation of this type of reserve. Legal provisions for tangible assets repairs are also uncommon, which is accounted for by only 16% of companies. A possible reason could be the tightening of rules for their creation, so the companies are obliged to deposit the amount of the reserve on a special bank account. It is possible to conclude that the use of provisions and allowances is inadequate, not respecting the principle of prudence and a true and fair view of assets and liabilities.

References

Accounting Act In: 1991, No. 563

CZ NACE (2016) Retrieved from www.cznace.cz

Dvořáková D (2008) Finanční účetnictví a výkaznictví podle mezinárodních standardů IFRS. Computer Press, Brno

Hnátek M, Zámek D (2014) Daňové a nedaňové náklady 2014. Praha: Esap; Grada

Income Tax Act In: 1992, No. 586

Jílek J, Svobodová J (2013) Účetnictví podle mezinárodních standardů účetního výkaznictví 2013. Grada Publishing, Praha

Koch J (2016) Účetní závěrka podnikatelů za rok 2015. Poradce, Český Těšín

Kovanicová D (2008) Abeceda účetních znalostí pro každého. Trizonia, Praha

Křemen B (2010) 100 legálních daňových triků. ESAP, Praha

Poradce, 11 (2016) Český Těšín: Poradce

Poradce, 6 (2016) Český Těšín: Poradce

Ryneš P (2013) Podvojné účetnictví a účetní závěrka: průvodce podvojným účetnictvím k 1.1.2013. Olomouc, Anag

Šrámková A, Křivánková M (2007) IAS/IFRS: mezinárodní standardy účetního výkaznictví : praktické aplikace. Aktualiz. vyd. pro účetní období 2008. Institut Svazu účetních, Praha

Strouhal J (2007) Účetní závěrka 2007. Praha: Aspi, a. s. Wolters Kluwer

Synek M (2006) Podniková ekonomika. C. H. Beck, Praha

Vančurová A, Láchová L (2008) Daňový systém ČR 2008, aneb, Učebnice daňového práva, Praha, Vox

Revenue Recognition in the Public Hospitals

Josef Krupička

Abstract This paper discusses the subject of revenue recognition in the public hospitals arising from provided healthcare. In its first part, the paper examines this issue within the context of the contemporary literature on the introduction of the accrual principle to the public sector accounting and the role of IPSAS in this process; in the following parts, the paper presents a comparison of the national accounting regulation with the international accounting standards approach on an illustrative example. The conclusion then summarizes the findings from the literature review and underlines the role of accrual accounting basis in the process of improving the public hospital management.

Keywords Public hospital • Revenue recognition • Accrual accounting

Introduction

Managing a public hospital is considered as a matter of great responsibility as well as high prestige. To provide healthcare means to take care of public health and since life is considered one of the highest values, the public hospital is expected to provide its care to all who need it. If not considering out-of-pocket payments, the amount of allocated resources from health insurance companies represents the covered amount of healthcare for the insured. Understanding this a production plan for the public hospital, its director needs to manage its capacity and workforce in the way of securing capability of providing at least the amount of ordered care at any time. To achieve this capability, management body requires the use of measures providing actual and correct information about the use of hospital capacity and available resources. Both kinds of provided information, financial and nonfinancial, are considered complementary (Liguori et al. 2014), and the use of management tools, such as pricing, costing, and budgeting (Anessi-Pessina et al.

J. Krupička (✉)
Department of Management Accounting, University of Economics, Prague,
Nám. W. Churchilla 4, 130 67 Praha 3, Czech Republic
e-mail: xkruj27@vse.cz

D. Procházka (ed.), *The Impact of Globalization on International Finance and Accounting*, Springer Proceedings in Business and Economics,
https://doi.org/10.1007/978-3-319-68762-9_41

2016; Pereira et al. 2016), is essential in this decision-making process. However, one of the main differences between these two kinds of information is the level of their transformation to make them comprehensible. While nonfinancial information is usually presented in raw form (e.g., beds occupied, patients cured, diagnoses treated), the financial information captures the reality through measuring of value in the form of comprehensive reports and statements. To achieve comparability between different entities, most of these accounting activities are formalized by legislation and professional standards (e.g., general accounting standards). As for management of the hospital, the amount of revenue which public hospital recognize for providing healthcare is essential information which varies in timing as well as in amount when different accounting bases are applied.

This paper aims to discuss this issue within the context of contemporary literature and Czech legislation approach. To reach this aim, this paper reviews the results of literature examining the contemporary approach to use of accrual accounting basis in the public sector and more specifically in the public hospitals. The following part presents an illustration of contemporary practice of cash-based approach to revenue recognition within the particular healthcare financing scheme which is analyzed in the context of national accounting legislation and international accounting standard approach. Examination of practical impact upon annual reports follows with the discussion of results. Finally, the conclusion summarizes the role of accrual principle for the public hospital management control systems and underlines the role of accounting regulation within this context.

Accrual Basis in Accounting of Public Hospital

Concerning the public sector global development in general over the last two decades, there has been a consistent tendency toward implementation of accrual principle in which adoption of International Public Sector Accounting Standards (IPSASs) played a major role (Brusca and Martinez 2015; Christiaens et al. 2015). As Christiaens et al. (2015) summarize, this tendency followed the process of globalization in economic activity of the private sector, which introduced the need for accounting systems harmonization to enhance international comparability of financial statements. However, many studies (Bellanca and Vandernoot 2014; Legenkova 2016; Brusca et al. 2013; Sousa et al. 2013, among others) on adoption of IPSAS on the national level underline the reasons for its implementation into the public sector as well; the purpose seems to differ from introducing the accounting standards into the private sector. While both processes aim to standardize and harmonize accounting practice, the introduction of accrual accounting to the public sector is additionally considered as an important aspect of the transformation process of improving the management and decision-making activities under the concept of new public management (Groot and Budding 2008). In accordance, there has been an increase in the number of governments using accrual accounting over the past few years (Dvořák 2016; Flynn et al. 2016), but as Oulasvirta (2014) emphasizes, the level of implementation across the different levels of public entities should be considered.

Since the process of introducing the accrual principle into public accounting still goes on, studies monitoring its development are conducted continuously, but not many researchers in this field give their focus to the context of the public hospitals. As Pereira et al. (2016) conclude in their literature review, budgets are major features of management accounting systems used in public hospital, though new budgeting approaches are encouraged by institutional pressure since traditional techniques appear to be insufficiently efficient. As both budgets and reports are the tools based on financial information, the choice of accounting basis influences information quality these tools contain. Assuming the cash basis as a starting point, the motivation for the change into accrual basis is clear as are the benefits from this change. As Abolhallaje et al. (2014) discuss in their comparative study of both accounting bases in the context of reforms in the health sector, many developed countries (e.g., United States of America, New Zealand, Australia, Canada) which adopted accrual basis benefit from the qualitative information improvement in reporting thus improving the capability of making estimates and predictions. Although this capability might be used to earning management to achieve stable financial performance (Dong 2016; Hui-Fang Tan 2011) from which derive managerial incentives (Brickley and Van Horn 2002), its positive contribution to the management accounting systems in public hospital is out of the question. If this is the case, then is there a practical reason for using cash accounting basis in public hospital beside the legislative support or historical consequences? Given the variance of healthcare financing schemes and contemporary practice, there might be, yet it is unclear whether this is technological or accounting issue.

Revenue Recognition in the Public Hospital

In the context of revenue recognition, there is a reason for the use of cash accounting basis for revenues from providing the healthcare services since revenue recognition in this area depends on the healthcare financing scheme. Due to a broad variety of financing schemes by OECD (2011) and payment mechanisms (Boarchie 2014), the main focus of this paper is set on social health insurance scheme in the context of the payment per case approach since this combination is used for inpatient care reimbursement in central Europe. Under such financing scheme the insurance companies pay the healthcare provider ex ante determined fees for different cases categorized by diagnosis-related group system (DRG),[1] and the

[1]In DRG system, each group of cases is given a relative value (case mix index) determining the amount of resources required to treat patients in this group compared to other groups of cases. Each case consists of various characteristics (age of patient, prime and secondary diagnosis, treatment procedures, etc.) determining its inclusion in particular group.

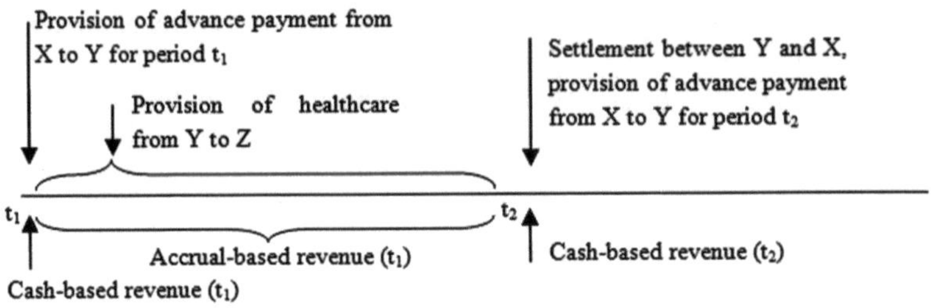

Fig. 1 Discussed approaches to revenue recognition (Source: Own processing)

maximum amount of payment per insurance company is limited on a contractual basis between each healthcare provider and insurance company. For the illustrative purpose of discussed financing scheme, the following simplified example is assumed.

A health insurance company X provides in the form of advance payment one million dollars to a hospital Y for treating patients insured by company X categorized within a particular group of cases Z for one period. After this period the hospital Y presents to insurance company X the record of cases in group Z which is analyzed by insurance company X to verify the amount of treatment provided and coding of cases determining their correct inclusion into group Z. After processing of these records, the settlement between hospital Y and insurance company X takes place, and the final value of healthcare provided by the hospital Y in a group of Z is identified. Possible differences between acknowledged value of treatment provided and advance payment from the beginning of the previous period would be offset against advance payment for the next period (Fig. 1).

In this example, if the cash basis is considered, the hospital would recognize revenue at the level of advance payment in the moment of receiving it. However, with the accrual approach, the revenue recognition process is more complex since the hospital is required to recognize revenues as the healthcare is provided[2] and the entitlement to reimbursement arises. This approach requires from the internal management control system to be sophisticated enough to determine the amount of revenue based on all available information about cases from hospital information system and specifics of contractual relationship with the health insurance companies. Even though the final amount of revenue would be determined after the end of the period, the amount of revenue for provided healthcare estimated in such a way will still be the best information which internal information systems can provide for the decision-making process of the management body. As illustrated above, the difference between information values of each basis is evident, yet the public hospital subjects to accounting standards regulating the public sector in general,

[2]Supposing the moment of recognition as when the case of the particular patient is closed, appropriately coded, and categorized in diagnosis-related group.

which only scarcely solve the specifics of accrual principle application in particular entities. To demonstrate the impact of this issue on the revenue recognition in public hospitals, a comparison of national accounting legislation approach and the international standards approach follows.

Comparison of National Accounting Legislation Approach and International Standards Approach

As an example of national accounting legislation approach, the Czech Republic was chosen since it fulfills all characteristics of the financing scheme mentioned above. Analyzing the Czech Republic accounting legislation relevant to the public hospitals,[3] there is no explicit definition of either cash or accrual basis. Then the moment of recognition is in general accounting practice omitted and replaced with the date of taxable supply (Procházka 2008). The closest definition of revenues for provided healthcare may be found in Article 2 g paragraph 56 of the Regulation No. 312/2014, Coll., which defines revenues for provided healthcare as the amount of payment received from the health insurance system.

This approach clearly corresponds with cash basis, and since the same payment from health insurance system is made periodically, the value of information about the amount of revenue from healthcare provided during the period is questionable. Such information provides the management body with the information about cash flow; but before the settlement with the health insurance companies takes place, the amount of revenue is uncertain. In such environment, the managing activities are limited to budget control with more focus given on the side of costs of production.

With a closer look at the international standards approach, there are two possible options of recognizing the revenues for provided healthcare: first one under the simple approach of IPSAS 9 and the second one under an episodic approach of international reporting standard (IFRS) 15. Under the IPSAS 9 approach, the revenues would be recognized at the moment of providing the healthcare since at this moment both conditions of rendering the service and of its distinguishing are met. On the other hand, Article a paragraph 10 of IPSAS 9 clearly states the standard does not deal with the revenues "arising from insurance contracts of insurance entities," and since social health insurance scheme is considered above, this approach cannot be directly applied. The IFRS 15 approach recognizes revenue gradually as services are provided since the insurer-provider contract would be performance based. Although there might not be a difference between both approaches since both would recognize revenue as the service fulfilling contract specification is rendered, the IFRS 15 presents it in a broader context which takes into account the specifics of the healthcare sector such as estimation of transaction

[3]Explicitly Act No. 563/1991 Coll., Regulation No. 410/2009 Coll. and Regulation No. 312/2014 Coll., and Czech accounting standards.

price or the performance aspect of third-party contract (PricewaterhouseCoopers (PWC) 2016). Furthermore, this approach is consistent with requirements of management body since it stimulates internal management control system to be able to provide actual and correct information about current state of hospital production.

Comparing chosen national legislative accounting approach with international standards approach, the accrual-based approach according to IFRS 15 would provide more useful information for the decision-making process. However, this approach implies the public hospitals have all information about its production, which, if properly combined with contractual arrangements with healthcare funder, allows the hospital to estimate the value of its output. This capability is essential for making the use of more sophisticated management accounting practices such as target costing and capacity management possible, allowing to provide healthcare more efficiently.

Examination of Financial Statements

For illustrative purpose, the practical aspect of compared approaches to revenue recognition for provided healthcare was examined upon annual reports of 40 different healthcare-providing entities[4] from which one-half conduct their financial statement under Czech legislation approach (cash basis), and the other half follows the international standard approach (respectively, national standard approach reflecting IPSAS). Entities of both groups were selected through the means of web search engine (Google Search) using of tags "nemocnice" (hospital) and "výroční zpráva" (annual report) for the first group of entities and tags "public hospital" and "annual report" for the second. From the results of the first search were selected annual reports of hospitals from the Czech Republic, and from the results of the second search were selected annual reports of healthcare providers from the countries which reflected IPSAS principles in their national accounting regulation. No further selection criteria were applied, and from obtained results, annual reports for the year 2015 were examined. With a formal side of the statements put aside, various characteristics of revenue recognition approach have been tracked with results summarized in the Table 1. Numbers represent the number of entities reflecting examined characteristic of revenue recognition approach in their financial statement.

As for identification of the value of revenues arising from healthcare provision, not all entities from each group report in necessary analytical detail to identify revenues arising from healthcare provision. These revenues are simply concluded under operating income. Explanation of revenue recognition approach is omitted in financial statements of all examined entities using cash basis, while all entities

[4]Examined subjects are listed in Appendix section.

Table 1 List of examined characteristics

Examined characteristic	Entities using cash-based approach	Entities using accrual-based approach
Number of examined subjects	20	20
Revenue from healthcare provision reported separately	18	15
Revenue recognition approach stated in annual report	0	20
Revenue recognized as		
Advance payment received	20	0
Deferred income until receiving the lodge of compensation claim	Not stated	3
Estimated net realizable amount from patients and third-party payers for service rendered	Not stated	8
Use of contractual specifics approach	Not stated	5
Combination of above	Not stated	4

Source: Own research of financial statements of healthcare-providing entities

under international standard approach briefly describe used the methodology of revenue recognition.

Though used methodology of revenue recognition within entities using accrual-based approach varies due to specifics of national accounting regulatory framework, a significant number of entities use estimations and fulfillment of contractual specifics while recognizing revenues for provided healthcare. This is already consistent with the IFRS 15 even though it will be effective for annual statements for periods beginning on or after 1 January 2018. The result of this examination is consistent with a theoretical comparison of approaches presented above since accrual-based annual reports and financial statements provide information about revenues for provided healthcare in a way closer to true and fair view compared to cash-based conducted statements. Such statements reflect the activity of the hospital more realistically and provide substantial information value about hospital management activities above the level of simple information about received reimbursement.

Conclusion

As contemporary literature notes, the introduction of the accrual principle into the public sector has been enhancing the quality of information provided to the management body of public institutions. Major role in this process is acknowledged to IPSASs, yet there are some entity-specific areas, such as revenue recognition in the public hospital, which has not yet been covered by it. Since the qualitative improvement of decision-making process under the New Public Management is desired even in the public hospitals, the specifics of possible healthcare financing schemes must not be omitted when introducing accrual principle which, if correctly applied, might provide better information about the entity in comparison to the cash-based accounting information. Although IFRS 15 suggests the solution for this area in the private sector, specific guidelines for the public hospital in the form of IPSAS are yet to be expected.

In the context of the aim of this article, it may be concluded that revenue for provided healthcare recognized on the accrual basis provides management with information about the value of public hospital production which is more timely relevant in comparison to cash-based approach to revenue recognition. Yet to achieve this state, the public hospital management control system must be capable of providing such information. This is an issue of relevant accounting regulation just as it is of technological and procedural improvement of internal management accounting systems, as this is the case of the public hospital in the Czech Republic. In such regulatory context, proper change in revenue recognition approach might just be the stimulus public hospitals need for implementation of more sophisticated management control systems allowing them to be managed more efficiently. Yet to what extent may the possible change in accounting principles actually affect the quality of information provided by public hospital financial statements should be subject of further study as well as research of specifics of the management accounting systems in the public hospital since better understanding of these areas is prerequisite for understanding of financial management of the public hospital under various conditions.

Acknowledgments This paper has been dedicated to the research project "Analysis of strategic management accounting relation to company management and performance" (supported by Internal Grant Agency, No. IG 71/2017).

Appendix: List of Examined Healthcare-Providing Entities

First group – entities using cash-based revenue recognition

1. Nemocnice Na Bulovce, p.s.
2. Nemocnice České Budějovice, a.s.
3. Fakultní nemocnice Brno, p.s.
4. Nemocnice ve Frýdku-Místku, p.s.
5. Nemocnice Havlíčkův Brod, p.s.
6. Nemocnice Na Homolce, p.s.
7. Fakultní nemocnice Hradec Králové, p.s.
8. Nemocnice Jablonec nad Nisou, p.s.
9. Masarykova městská nemocnice v Jilemnici, p.s.
10. Krajskánemocnice Liberec, a.s.
11. Nemocnice Milosrdných sester sv. Karla Boromejského v Praze, c.o.

12. Nemocnice Jihlava, p.s.
13. Fakultní nemocnice Motol, p.s.
14. Fakultní nemocnice Olomous, p.s.
15. Fakultní nemocnice Ostrava, p.s.
16. Nemocnice s poliklinikou v Semilech, p.s.
17. Nemocnice Strakonice, a.s.
18. Nemocnice Tábor, a.s.
19. Nemocnice Třebíč, p.s.
20. Uherskohradišťská nemocnice, a.s.

Second group – entities using accrual-based revenue recognition

1. Anne Arundel Health System, Inc.
2. Frederick Regional Health System, Inc.
3. Saint Agnes Hospital
4. The Edward W. McCready Memorial Hospital
5. The Mid Yorkshire Hospital NHS Trust
6. Royal Free London NHS Foundation Trust
7. The University of North Carolina Health Care System
8. NCH Healthcare System, Inc.
9. Canterbury District Health Board
10. Barnsley Hospital NHS Foundation Trust
11. United Lincolnshire Hospital NHS Foundation Trust
12. North Bristol NHS Trust
13. Frimley Health NHS Foundation Trust
14. St. Jude Children's Research hospital, Inc.
15. Holy Cross Health, Inc.
16. Townsville Hospital and Health Service
17. Monash Health
18. Sheffield Teaching Hospitals NHS Foundation Trust
19. Papsworth NHS Foundation Trust
20. Barwon Health Foundation

References

Abolhallaje M, Jafari M, Seyedin H, Salehi M (2014) Financial management reforms in health sector: a comparative study between cash-based and accrual-based accounting system. Iran Red Crescent Med J. https://doi.org/10.5812/ircmj.15472

Anessi-Pessina E, Barbera C, Silia M, Steccolini I (2016) Public sector budgeting in European accounting and public management journals: missing in action? A review. Account Audit Account J. https://doi.org/10.1108/AAAJ-11-2013-1532

Bellanca S, Vandernoot J (2014) International public sector accounting standards (IPSAS) implementation in European union (EU) member states. J Mod Account Audit 10(3):257–269

Boarchie MK (2014) Healthcare provider payment mechanisms: a review of literature. J Behav Econ Financ Entrep Account Transp. https://doi.org/10.12691/jbe-2-2-2

Brickley JA, Van Horn RL (2002) Managerial incentives in nonprofit organizations: evidence from hospitals. J Law Econ. https://doi.org/10.1086/339493

Brusca I, Martinez JC (2015) Adopting international public sector accounting standards: a challenge for modernizing and harmonizing public sector accounting. Int Rev Adm Sci. https://doi.org/10.1177/0020852315600232

Brusca I, Montesinos V, Chow DSL (2013) Legitimating international public sector accounting standards (IPSAS): the case of Spain. Public Money & Management. https://doi.org/10.1080/09540962.2013.836006

Christiaens J, Vanhee C, Manes-Rossi F, Aversano N, Cauwenberge P (2015) The effect of IPSAS on reforming governmental financial reporting: an international comparison. Int Rev Adm Sci. https://doi.org/10.1177/0020852314546580

Dong GN (2016) Earnings management in U.S. hospitals. J Health Hum Serv Adm 39(1):41–71

Dvořák M (2016) Míra implementace akruálního principu v účetnictví veřejného sektoru statů EU (The rate of implementation of the accrual principle in EU public sector accounting). Český finanční a účetní časopis. 1018267/j.cfuc.478

Flynn S, Moretti D, Cavanagh J (2016) Guide to implementing accrual accounting in the public sector. Int Monetary Fund. https://doi.org/10.5089/9781475521757.005.A001

Groot T, Budding T (2008) New public management's current issues and future prospects. Finan Account Manag. https://doi.org/10.1111/j.1468-0408.2008.00440.x

Legenkova M (2016) International public sector accounting standards implementation in the Russian federation. Int J Econ Finan Issues 6(4):1304–1309

Liguori M, Sicilia M, Steccolini I (2014) Public value as performance: politicians′ and managers′ perspectives on the importance of budgetary, accruals and non-financial information. In: Guthrie J, Marcon G, Russo S, Farneti F (eds) Public value and performance management, measurement and reporting (studies in public and non-profit governance) 3, Emerald Group publishing limited, pp 85–104

OECD, Eurostat, WHO (2011) A system of Health accounts. OECD Publishing. https://doi.org/10.1787/9789264116016-en

Oulasvirta LO (2014) Governmental financial accounting and european harmonization: case study of Finland. Account Econ Law. 101515/ael-2004-0006

Pereira CM, Rodrigues LL, Jorge SMF (2016) The role of management accounting systems in public hospitals and the construction of budgets: a literature review. In: Information resources management association (ed) public health and welfare: concepts, methodologies, tools and applications, pp 289–312

PricewaterhouseCoopers (2016) Revenue from contracts with customers: the standard is final – a comprehensive look at the new revenue model. http://www.pwc.com. Accessed 14 Jan 2017

Procházka D (2008) Základní koncepční znaky české účetní úpravy výnosů (Basic conceptual features of Czech accounting for revenues). In: Účetnictví (Accounting) 9, pp 26–29

Sousa RG, Vasconcelos AF, Caneca RL, Niyama JK (2013) Accrual basis accounting in the Brazilian public sector: empirical research on the usefulness of accounting information. Rev Contabilidade & Finanças. https://doi.org/10.1590/S1519-70772013000300005

Tan HF (2011) Earnings management in non-profit hospitals–evidence from Taiwan. Int J Electron Bus Manag 9(3):243–257

A Literature Review of Financial Performance Measures and Value Relevance

Nattarinee Kopecká

Abstract Performance measurement comprises several metrics and applications used as a benchmark in business sectors for both internal and external users. For managers, it expresses whether company's targets are reached and as a way of evaluating risks and returns for shareholders. A variety of performance measures are utilized to almost every operational process, and the area is rather vast. Therefore, the aim of the study is to find out what kinds of financial tools are better linked to market value. The result of the study shows that financial measures appear to be favorable measures for companies providing relevant and meaningful information to shareholders. Especially, return on investment (ROI) and earnings are significantly relevant to market value, while the superiority of EVA still remains unclear. Above all, companies still prefer traditional financial measures to other financial tools.

Keywords Financial measures • Economic value added • Market measures • Value relevance

Introduction

Company's sustainability is fundamentally derived from internal growth (profits) and external financial expansion (stocks, securities). Along with global trade, technological development and innovation are bringing great opportunities to business sectors at the same time reducing business' barriers for shareholders to access meaningful information. These circumstances are challenging as long as companies still confront risk and uncertainty due to high competition in the marketplace and increasing shareholder demands. In addition, shareholders more require insight a company's operational performance information to perceive a company's strategic orientation, risks, and returns. This information, however,

N. Kopecká (✉)
University of Economic, Prague, Department of Management Accounting,
Nam. W. Churchilla 4, 130 67 Prague 3, Czech Republic
e-mail: Sujira07@live.com

D. Procházka (ed.), *The Impact of Globalization on International Finance and Accounting*, Springer Proceedings in Business and Economics,
https://doi.org/10.1007/978-3-319-68762-9_42

should be measured and presented through efficient tools, and it must be relevant in order that firms will efficiently be able to convince shareholders of their prospects. In this regard companies are required to increase operational performance as well as the quality of measurement tools present results from transparent reports, confidential and transparent approaches and measures.

The establishment of accounting institutions and its regulation requires entities to transparently disclose their accounting numbers and meaningful information on financial reports. Firms' performance measures are therefore one of the important items because they present business's value by referring to the process of measuring firm's operational efficiency and effectiveness (Neely et al. 2005). Since performance measures consist of various tools, there are various ways to which these tools can be applied. It can be applied in the form of nonfinancial indicators such as operational effectiveness, corporate reputation, organization survival, and customer satisfaction (Richard et al. 2009) and/or in the form of financial criteria, which is used to measure accounting profitability such as revenue, operational expenses, earnings before interest and taxes, and/or financial ratio, return on equity, return on asset, etc. (Barney 2002).

A variety of performance measures are applied to almost every operational process, and the literature in this area is vast. The study, therefore, intentionally focuses on the value relevance of accounting information disclosed in financial reports to market values. The paper aims to find out what kinds of financial tools are better linked to the market value and whether it is frequently used by companies. Furthermore, the paper also describes the tendency toward accounting performance measures and value relevance from different sorts. Chapter "The Impact of Corpo rate Income Taxation on Location Choice of Investments: Separate Accounting vs. Formula Apportionment" outlines the structure of the paper. Chapter "Environmental Sustainability as a Determinant of Foreign Direct Invest ments: Empirical Evidence from Sweden" defines theoretical foundations of the performance measures and value relevant definition. Chapter "Are R&D-Active SMEs in the Emerging Markets Financially Constrained? Self-Evaluation Approach" devotes to the methodology of the study, and chapters "Tax Incentives for Innovative Small Business: The Russian Model" and "Relationships Between World Stock Market Indices: Evidence from Economic Networks" present results, discussion, and conclusion; I discussed the significant of performance tools and the potential benefits to future research.

Methodology

- The study is based on the theory background and relevant researches in the areas of performance measures disclosed in financial statements.
- The sample of the case studies and sorts of literature are specifically collected from the well-known and respected accounting journals investigating in performance measures areas from 2010 to 2016, which are available on open access.

- The procedures of the research's considerations are in crucial areas of theories, results, discussions, and suggestions.
- Comparing the important areas of financial performance is provided with accounting measures, economic value added reflecting in company market values in investors' views.
- The results are concluded by analyzing of the strength and weakness of performance measures in the main body of conclusion and discussion.

Literature Review

Corporate Performance Measures

The central growth of firm derives from their performance resulted from efficiency and effectiveness of their operational activities. This performance contributes firms' value to shareholders, who demand meaningful information on efficient measurement metrics. Generally, the definition of business performance and its measurements has been proposed different ways by a number of scholars and intuitions such as it is the process of measuring the actions, efficiency, and effectiveness and the application of measurement metrics to quantify the efficiency and effectiveness of actions (Neely et al. 1994). From this point of view, these measurements and its metrics should be integrated with all financial and nonfinancial dimensions, external and internal factors, as well as monetary and nonmonetary requirements, and the purpose of operational performance measurements highlights on measuring of financial elements reflecting the fulfillment of the economic goals of firms (Venkatraman et al. 1986).

In 1943, the term of performance measurement was introduced to business sectors after the application of the International City Management Association (ICMA) in the municipal activities (Ewoh 2011). Since then, a variety of performance measures are being used. In 1992, the BSC – one of the most popular measurement approach – had been introduced to the Harvard Business Review article as the tools for measuring both financial and nonfinancial of business performance (Kaplan et al. 1992). The measurement aligns firm's mission and strategy into a set of performance measures in four perspectives – operation, customers, financial, and growth perspectives – which believe that they cover all operational aspects and sufficient for shareholders for making better decisions. The approaches are used by top managers to help them formulate organization's strategy and to measure their operational performance (Kaplan et al. 1992).

Along with the application of nonfinancial indicators, financial performance measures are concerned as great issues of creating value to shareholders by associating cash flow and cost of capital. A large number of financial measures are employed; however, the great attention of researchers and firms still draw on traditional financial indicators. This circumstance corresponds with the disclosure of financial statements underlining both monetary and voluntary accounting information. The traditional financial indicators, which firms largely employed such as profit or loss, income statement line items -revenues, operating income, earning before tax and interest (EBITA), return on assets (ROA), return on equity (ROE), return on investment capital (ROIC), earning per share (EPS) and dividend per share (DPS) on which focus firms' performance from past activities. In addition, these financial indicators are critical for users because they reflect how well the strategy was followed, what goals could be reached and also the tendency of a firm strategic orientation. Several critics argue that these traditional measures are no longer adequate for shareholder due to backward-looking financial information and it is still unclear about the relevant between the earning information contained and market capital.

In 1991, the emergence of value-based measurement is called economic value added (EVA) proposed by Stern Stewart company asserting that it is a superiority performance measure (Stewart 1994). He claimed that the economic value added comes closer than other approaches to capturing the true economic profit of an enterprise (Stewart 1994). Steward also believes that EVA is the performance measure which is the most directly linked to the creation of shareholder wealth over time by deducting the cost of capital from its operating profit – adjusted for taxes on a cash basis (Stewart 1994). This approach can also be used as a tool for managers in operating a firm's performance, managing project, and calculating executive compensation. EVA is a useful approach that managers should be aware of the cost of capital before making decisions; however, the weakness can be seen when it is applied for long-term project due to its complication, cost, and benefit of its calculation.

Accounting Information and Its Value Relevance

Firm's ultimate aim is to maximize their value in order to maintain shareholders benefits and satisfaction (Black et al. 1998). To do so, they should provide validity, reliability, transparency, and value relevance of accounting numbers, which directly influence capital market values. Generally, value relevance of accounting information is a capability of making differences in the financial statements that shareholders can make better decisions on evaluating firm's value. It can be assessed its quality by measuring accounting numbers through reliable approaches and enhancing the strength of associations between market returns and earnings. Consistently, Francis and Schipper offer four interpretations of value relevance consisting of financial information influences stock price; financial information is relevant if it contains the variables used for a valuation model of assisting in predicting those variables and the association with financial information and prices or returns (Francis et al. 2003).

Company's value characterizes as amounts of accounting numbers that capture usefulness of information affecting users' discretion; however, the diversity of measurement tools provides different accounting information, and it depends on context and purposes. Accounting value relevance defines as information relating to equity making the discretion to users. Additionally, increasing value relevance associates with lower costs of equity, and then it attributes to investors perceiving value as contributing to lower risks (Francis et al. 2003). For investors, accounting information can be measured by employing valuation theory, and accounting theory reflected the relationship between accounting information and market value such as profit and stock price. Another suggestion, accounting valuation can be evaluated by applying the theory of accounting and standard setting to draw inferences about accounting numbers that purpose is to support standard setters (Holthausen et al. 2001).

Economic value refers to the notion of assets' value equals the future cash flow that can be gained from these assets. In economists' point of view, financial statements should provide information useful in making economic decisions that result from efficient allocations of EVA which is a trademark registered by Stern Stewart & Co. resources (Sortor et al. 2010). In fact, decision-makers are interested in determining how much they must surrender or give up (sacrifice) in order to receive something else that is presumed to be better (benefit) (Sortor et al. 1974). The market value is defined as the value of firms on the stock market which is an indication of investors' perceptions of its business prospects. Market value is the value of a firm on the stock market, and it is based on trade and investors' consensus beliefs about firm value. It is used by a publicly traded company, and it is obtained by multiplying the number of its outstanding shares by the current share price.

Discussion

The performance measures and its value relevance have been studied by many researchers all around the world of different businesses, yet the impact of the issues still affects shareholders, as well as the consensus of the study still has been not met. The paper, therefore, reviewed the performance measures and value relevance in the previous years among various kinds of business which are available on open access journals. The results of the review are the following: the study based on the model of corporate market valuation of nonfinancial indicators (human capital, knowledge, and the reputation of firms) applying among US firms from 2006 to 2009 shows that the model positively affects firms' performance, especially sales growth and net profit margin. They found accounting measures, particularly return on assets (ROA), are positively associated with the market value (stock price) (Alibad et al. 2013).

Going together, the study impact of intellectual capital on financial performance and market valuation of Indian companies shows that intellectual capital (IC) significantly influenced on company profitability. Especially return on equity (ROE) and ROA significantly relates to company profitability, whereas only return on equity (ROE) positively relates to market value (Kamath 2015).

Correspondingly, another researcher whose investigation is about the relevance of earnings and book value revealed that among 129 companies selected from 6 sectors in the Colombo Stock Exchange (CSE), found earnings, book value, and return on equity (ROE) have positive value relevance to the market value of securities (Pathirawasam 2010). The investigation into the application of traditional financial measure in the telecom company revealed that return on investment (ROI) is mainly used as an indicator establishing the link between the center's profitability and capital used (Almasan et al. 2010).

In contrast to the research on the relationship between EVA and market value among Indian companies, the result shows it is not distinct from its relationship. The research also highlighted that EVA is not as a superiority approach as the proponent's assertion, and only minority of Indian companies are applied. In contrast, the traditional measures such as return on investment (ROI), earning, and earning per share positively relate to market value (Bhasin 2016). In the same way, Knápkavá provided an overview of financial analysis tools which are most commonly used by the Czech and Slovak companies and shows that the companies prefer traditional performance measures, such as ROA, ROE, and ROI to value-based measure (EVA) (Knáplová et al. 2011). Similarly, Patel investigated the interaction between EVA and share price in India banks, collecting data from 2004 to 2005 and 2009 to 2010. The study found that EVA has no impact on share price except for Kotak Mahindra bank (Patel et al. 2012).

Other scholars studied the relationship between accounting measures and marketing measures and found that they have a slightly positive relationship. The researcher suggested that accounting measures and marketing measures cannot be equal measurement tools so that a firm should carefully construct the measurement by considering that accounting information represents past performance, while market performance represents strategies and actions influence investors' perception (Gentry and Shen 2010). While Shan suggested that even though accounting information is relevant to the stock prices, it is necessary to connect the impact of market earning per share (EPS), earnings decrease which is related to management value relevance (Shan 2014).

Another suggestion about the value relevance issues, the research explores for the most value relevance of financial measures among the common comprehensive set of financial tools including sales, earnings, comprehensive income, and operating cash flows. They found that there is no pattern of the most value relevant performance measure. The researcher suggested that a measure is more relevant when it captures directly and quickly information about firm's cash flows (Barton et al. 2010).

Conclusion

In the global trade, there are no barriers for investors to access useful information that is an ingredient of successful investments. In fact, not only this information but also a bearish market information reinforced by speculation and rumor have an impact on investors' perception. Generally, accounting information will be relevant if it captures the usefulness of accounting numbers in equity valuation, provided by firms on financial reports fairly measuring and presenting a company's situation. Even though a great attention is given in this research area, it remains the question that there are no absolute financial tools, while some of them assumed to overlap, and investors seem to access sorts of information conveniently; what is really relevant to their equity linking to market values? The paper reviews financial performance measures, namely, financial measures and value-based measure (EVA), reflecting market measures from different sorts which are available on open access.

The research found that the majority of the case studies still rely on traditional financial indicators, namely, ROI, ROE, and earning, although these tools appear a huge number of arguments about its applications. The research analyzed the interaction of financial indicators to market value (share price) especially ROI and earnings, which are extensively utilized by companies and appear to influence share price significantly. The major reasons might be due to its applications facilitating investors, forecasting, and estimating a firm's wealth of an investment. It also provides timely results, whereas long-term operational performance might be neglected that shareholders should carefully make judgments. Considering the advantage of using ROI is to evaluate the efficiency of an investment or to compare the efficiency of a number of different investments. Likewise, earning and ROE focus on return to shareholders of the company; however, shareholders should consider also the company's strategy and other related factors.

In contrast, the application of the value-based measures, namely, EVA, seems not as popular as its assertion. This circumstance might cause the complication from the usage and difficulty in making a comparison; this might reduce the investor's opportunity to analyze firms' potential in other aspects. Therefore, to provide useful and relevant information, firms should improve the disclosure of their EVA to the shareholders as well as disclose multiple performance measurement tools which will efficiently reflect firms' operational performance and effectiveness. Since a variety of performance measures are being used in every sort of business, these financial tools should not only reflect company's operational performance but also should provide transparency and real-time information under the regulation that is reliable for users and investors. What's more, companies should fairly disclose all materiality information in order to encourage better decisions. Otherwise, it might lead to critical problems such as the avoidance of accounting reports in compliance. This might prevent not only investors but also stakeholders of accessing to the perceptive financial information. The author suggests the future research in the areas of financial measures and value relevance that researchers should focus on comparing operational performance on the same sorts of business especially for intellectual capital which becomes the major cost of competition. Furthermore, in the area of performance, measures should be expanded to other related areas such as operational effectiveness, growth and a company's reputation, etc., which will provide other aspects of company performance.

Acknowledgments This paper has been dedicated to the research project "Analysis of strategic management ac-counting relation to company management and performance" (supported by Internal Grant Agency, No. IG 71/2017).

References

Alibad S, Dorestani A, Balsara N (2013) The most value relevant accounting performance measure by industry. J Account Finance. http://www.na-businesspress.com. Accessed 16 Jul 2016

Almasan AC, Grosu C (2010) Financial measures for performance measurements in a regulated environment. Paper presented at the 5th international conference on economy and management transformation, West University of Timisoara, Romania, 24–26 Oct 2010

Barney JB (2002) Gaining and sustaining competitive advantage. Prentice Hall, Upper Saddle River

Black AP, Wright PD, Bachman JE (1998) In search of shareholder value: managing the drivers of performance. Financial Times Prentice Hall, London

Barton J, Hansen B, Pownall G (2010) Which performance measures do investor value the most and why? Account Rev 85:18–19

Bhasin L (2016) Disclosure of EVA in the financial statement: experience of an asian economy. https://www.academia.edu. Accessed 22 Sept 2016

Ewoh AIE (2011) Performance measurement in an era of new public management. http://digitalcommons.kennesaw.edu. Accessed 10 Jul 2016

Francis J, Schipper K, Vincent L (2003) The relative and incremental explanatory power of earnings and alternative (to earnings) performance measures for returns. Contemp Account Res 1:121–164. https://doi.org/10.1506/XVQV-NQ4A-08EX-FC8A

Gentry RJ, Shen W (2010) The relationship between accounting and market measures of firm financial performance : how strong is it? J Manag Issues 22:514–530

Holthausen RW, Watts RL (2001) The relevance of the value-relevance literature for financial accounting standard setting. J Account Econ 31:3–75

Kaplan R, Norton D (1992) The balanced scorecard: measures that drive performance, vol 70. Harvard Business Reviews Press, Boston, pp 71–79

Kamath GB (2015) The impact of intellectual capital on financial performance and market valuation of firm in India. International Letters of Social and Humanistic Sciences. http://wwwscipress.com/ILSHS.48.107. Accessed 18 Sept 2016

Knáplová A, Pavelková D, Chodúr M (2011) Měření a říyení výkonnosti podniku, Praha

Neely A, Mills J, Platts K, Gregory M, Richards H (1994) Realizing strategy through measurement. Int J Oper Prod Manag 14:52–140

Neely A, Gregory M, Platts K (2005) Performance measurement system design. A literature review and research agenda. Int J Oper Prod Manag 15:80–166

Patel RP, Patel M (2012) Impact of EVA on share price. International Journal of Contemporary Business Studies. A Study of Indian Private Sector Banks. https://ssrn.com/abstract=2097467. Accessed 12 Jul 2016

Pathirawasam C (2010) Value relevance of accounting information: evidence from Sri Lanka. Int J Res Commer Manag 8(1):13–20

Richard PJ, Devinney TM, Yip GS, Johnson G (2009) Measuring organizational performance: towards methodological best practice. J Manag. http://jom.sagepub.com/cgi/content/refs/35/3/718. Accessed 20 Sept 2016

Shan YG (2014) Value relevance, earning management and corporate governance in China. http://www.business.adelaide.edu.au. Accessed 25 Jul 2016

Stewart GB (1994) EVA: fact and fantasy. J Appl Corp Financ 7(2):71–87. https://doi.org/10.1111/j.1745-622.1994.tb00406x

Sorter GH, Gans MS, Rosenfield P, Shannon RM, Streit RG (1974) Objectives of financial statements. American Institute of Certified Public Accountants, New York, pp 3–66

Venkatraman N, Ramanujam V (1986) Measurement of business performance in strategy research: a comparison of approaches. Acad Manag Rev 11:801–814

The Relation Between Using Business Intelligence Solutions and Corporate Performance

David Špičák

Abstract This paper deals with the relation between the use of business intelligence (BI) solutions and corporate performance. The content is based on the research, analysis, and synthesis of findings published on this topic in scientific journals. The majority of papers published on this topic begin by introducing the concept of BI, its components, and possible benefits. As could perhaps be expected, two groups of papers can be identified: (a) review papers of existing research and (b) publications of original empirical research findings. Authors of the former group of papers tend to almost unquestioningly support the notion that the introduction of BI solutions is mainly beneficial to companies; authors of the latter group of papers are somewhat divided in their view on this matter. On the one hand, their findings support the notion BI solutions do seem to have positive influence on corporate performance; on the other hand, they warn that there may be more factors coming into play that are to be considered more carefully.

Keywords Corporate Performance • Information and Communication Technology • Business Intelligence • Performance Measurement and Management

Introduction

In the recent years, information and communication technology (ICT) started to play an increasingly more important role in supporting everyday activities in businesses across the whole globe.

Due to the gradually increasing instability and complexity of the business environment, many companies shifted their attention to improving their analytical, forecasting, and decision-making abilities. This led to the development of business intelligence (BI) solutions, which are able to cater to these needs.

D. Špičák (✉)
University of Economics, Prague; Department of Management Accounting, nam. W. Churchilla 4, 130 67 Praha 3, Czech Republic
e-mail: xspid05@vse.cz

D. Procházka (ed.), *The Impact of Globalization on International Finance and Accounting*, Springer Proceedings in Business and Economics,
https://doi.org/10.1007/978-3-319-68762-9_43

This paper is aimed at analyzing scholarly articles dealing with the mutual relation between using BI solutions and corporate performance, attempting to find scientific evidence supporting the notion that there exists a relation between the use of BI and corporate performance, and uncovering what the nature of this relation might be.

Data and Methodology

The research is based on the analysis of existing scholarly papers dealing with the relation between using BI solutions and corporate performance. The analysis focuses on papers that can be obtained using advanced search option across multiple electronic databases accessible to registered users.

The search was conducted following these steps:

- Find records matching the phrase *business intelligence and corporate performance*.
- Order the results by relevance.
- Limit the search results only to: full texts available online; scholarly materials, including materials passing through review process; articles in scientific journals; contributions published in the past 5 years; and contributions published in English.

Materials available on publicly accessible search engines, on the websites of commercial subjects such as consultants, developers, and vendors dealing with ICT and/or BI solutions, were omitted and disregarded for the purposes of this research.

Results and Discussion

The initial search (records matching the phrase *business intelligence and corporate performance*) yielded approximately 500,000 results. The results were sorted by relevance and narrowed down to full texts available online, which did not lead to any reduction in the number of available records. Subsequently narrowing the results down to only scholarly materials, including materials passing through review process, brought the number of available records to approximately 67,000. In the next step, which focused on retrieving only articles published in scientific journals, the total number of available records was brought down to approximately 62,500. Further narrowing of the search results to only those articles that were published in the past 5 years resulted in getting a total number of approximately 19,800 records, of which almost 19,400 were published in English language.

The relevance of the available records was subjected to two stages of further analysis. The first, coarser stage, focused on reviewing the article title, abstract content, and availability of the full paper in electronic version. Due to the fact that the available records were ordered by relevance and the total number of records exceeded 19,000, a sample of the first 250 records was chosen and subjected to this phase of the analysis.

This first stage revealed that, despite matching the search criteria, many of the records were irrelevant and not useful for further analysis. The reasons could be categorized as follows:

- From the article title, it was apparent the article focuses on specific aspects of managing and/or implementing BI-related solutions in general or in particular contexts, conditions, or circumstances, and there was no relation to corporate performance.
- Similarly to the point above, the article abstract revealed the article deals with a different area than desired in the context of the research focus.
- The given particular article was displayed in the search results multiple times.
- The record included a link to the full version of the paper saved at an external location or database; however, clicking on the link resulted in an error message, and the full paper could not be accessed.

This first stage helped to bring down the number of available results further, resulting in approximately 30 records that were subjected to a further, this time more detailed, analysis of the paper content. This subsequent step led to the elimination of other papers as it became apparent their focus lied in a different area than deemed relevant for this research.

The remainder of this chapter summarizes the key findings of papers that were analyzed.

Rajnoha et al. (2016) focus in their article on the relation between using information technology and corporate performance, more specifically on the relation between using BI solutions and strategic corporate performance. In their article, they begin by outlining the benefits BI solutions might bring and listing their possible application and benefits in various contexts. They postulate that strategic performance management systems, which exist for the purpose of ascertaining holistic management of performance in companies, must be supported by BI solutions in order for performance to be achieved on the overall company level.

In order to empirically establish whether or not there exists a correlation between using BI and corporate performance, Rajnoha et al. conducted a research using an online questionnaire, addressing nearly 1500 Slovakian enterprises. In their research, they attempted to prove that companies using transactional type of applications, such as ERP systems, achieve lower levels of business performance than those using transactional applications in combination with BI solutions. They further attempted to prove that companies with higher return of equity (ROE), which was used as a performance indicator, clearly utilize management information systems (MIS) or knowledge-based BI. The responses they collected from enterprises conducting activities in wood processing, engineering, automotive industry, trade, and services indicated that—especially in the case of companies reporting higher performance—the utilization of BI seems to have positive effect on performance. They also noted that companies that already introduced BI solutions or are planning to do so in the near future are overall satisfied with their actual or expected benefits.

Selene Xia and Gong (2012) point out in their article that BI is one of the areas of technology which keeps growing. They continue by outlining the downside of BI, such as the financial strain related to implementing these solutions, especially for smaller- and medium-sized businesses. Xia and Gong mention also the benefits BI may have for businesses, such as supporting decision-making, planning, and forecasting. Paraphrasing the research results of other authors before them, they note that BI allows for better reporting and customer service, higher revenues, and thus better overall corporate performance. In their work, they note data mining (DM), data warehousing (DW or DWH), and data marts, all forming a part of BI, seem to be closely related to numerous other concepts, such as business performance management (BPM), decision support systems (DSS), and management support systems (MSS).

Selene Xia and Gong continue by summarizing the outcomes of a case study they conducted, whose aim was to analyze the role of BI in a data analysis company, proposing the best approach for implementing a BI solution.

Rusaneanu (2013) points out in her paper that the use of BI solutions has been on the rise over the past decade and impacts the way companies manage their operational performance significantly. Rusaneanu states that there is a strong correlation between achieving good performance results and the use of software aimed at improving performance management. The benefits brought by these software solutions include higher sales, lower costs, better decision-making, and improved communication and collaboration. She further stipulates that BI solutions and performance management are so intertwined that they are basically inseparable.

Obeidat et al. (2015) note BI helps to turn diverse data from multiple sources into useful information, enabling more efficient operation of companies and their long-term stability. BI helps to analyze past events, predict future trends, and improve forecasting and enables users to make decisions in real time and gain competitive advantage. According to Obeidat et al., BI has its use in a multitude of areas and scenarios. Despite this, there are areas into which BI hasn't penetrated that deeply yet and which would actually benefit from a stronger BI presence, such as real-time analytics for detecting fraudulent activities, various healthcare-related applications, ad hoc BI supporting better collaboration, etc. Obeidat et al. continue by outlining possible future trends and development, such as better data exploration and visualization, cloud computing, and self-service BI, which in their opinion might help overcome some of the obstacles BI is currently facing.

Zeng et al. (2012) focus in their article on introducing the concept, benefits, and fundamental components of BI in general. They note BI helps gather relevant information and support better decision-making, thus positively impacting business operations, tactics, and strategy. They describe the crucial elements of BI architecture and techniques, together with explaining the fundamentals of their functioning. The benefits of utilizing BI in business practice are implied rather than proven empirically; nonetheless, the added value of this article can be seen in the fact that it provides a very concise overview of BI and may help glean the potential benefits of these technologies in a wider context.

Aruldos et al. (2013), similarly to other authors, point out that BI supports better decision-making, enables the analysis of performance, helps to increase revenues, improves competitiveness, and aids the formulation of strategy, thus satisfying the needs and expectations of various stakeholders. Aruldos et al. list areas where BI solutions found their use, such as higher education, e-learning, crime fighting, finance, stock market, banking, and others. In their paper, Aruldos et al. give an overview of findings various research teams and authors came with, providing a rather exhaustive list of possible positive effects the utilization of BI may have in various scenarios. The research Aruldos et al. conducted is perhaps the most extensive in comparison to other resources that were analyzed.

Visinescu et al. (2017) research the antecedents of perceived quality of decisions made when relying on BI support. Visinescu et al. point out that evidence provided by other researchers suggest the utilization of BI doesn't always bring the desired positive effects. They also point out that there is little research on the quality of decisions made using BI, and therefore, they focus their attention specifically on this matter. Visinescu et al. work with the premise that the use of BI will result in higher quality of decisions. However, they postulate that extensive use of BI solutions might be hindered due to a number of reasons. To test the complex relation between the quality of decisions and the usage of BI, they introduced a research model and conducted an empirical research. The data they gathered and subjected to a detailed analysis brought them to the conclusion that the more users rely on BI during their decision-making, the higher their perceived satisfaction with the decisions they made. They also point out that there seems to be a positive relationship between the complexity of the issue at hand and the satisfaction with the perceived quality of the decisions made with the support of BI. Also, there seems to be a correlation between the information quality and the perceived decision quality, which is further moderated by the complexity of the issue at hand. The overall conclusion they draw is that the whole relationship between information quality, system use, and outcomes may be more complex than previously believed.

Rouhani et al. (2014) focus their attention on the impact of BI on decision support and organizational benefits. They begin their paper by introducing BI in general and continue by listing the various ways BI might be used for the decision-makers' benefit, enabling them better knowledge processing with reduced decision time and reduced decision cost. The benefits include achieving more effective decision-making and gaining competitive advantage and higher stakeholder satisfaction.

In their paper, they introduce a complex research model and a set of 16 hypotheses. The hypotheses were tested using responses from 228 subjects from various segments of economy. With the exception of one hypothesis, all others were confirmed, showing the utilization of BI has numerous positives for the decision-makers and the organizations in general.

Giannakopoulos and Eybers (2015) begin their paper by stating that there is no agreement on whether the use of ICT in general is beneficial to companies, as believed by some, or not. They further focus specifically on the possible benefits the use of BI might have, arguing the topic to be of importance as the implementation of BI solutions requires substantial investments. With reference to the research conducted by other research teams, they point out the ambiguity of findings as to whether or not BI contributes to better corporate performance and under what conditions. To gain a better understanding of this matter, they conducted four case studies amongst business entities in South Africa. Their findings led them to the conclusion that there seems to exist a positive relation between the use of BI and corporate performance.

Popescu (2012) introduces in her article the typical structure of BI solutions and their characteristics. She notes BI can bring companies numerous benefits, such as providing a single version of truth, in-depth analyses, localization of relevant information, making reporting available to the whole company, operational flexibility, alignment of operations with strategic objectives, and others.

Arefin et al. (2014) focus in their research on identifying possible influence of various factors—including the possible mediating role of BI systems—on organizational effectiveness. They begin their paper by introducing what BI means in general and what benefits it might bring to businesses. They continue by noting that in spite of numerous authors mentioning the benefits of BI, organizations in developing countries oftentimes fail to achieve these, potentially due to numerous factors that were not examined in much detail. They continue further by positing that the effectiveness of BI systems mediates the relationship between organizational strategy and effectiveness. Using a research model, together with a related set of hypotheses, they conducted a study, gathering data from 225 business entities in Bangladesh, using this country as an example of rapidly growing developing country. From the results of their research, they conclude that when there is a close alignment between organizational strategy, structure, culture, strategy, and BI systems, BI systems seem to have positive impact on organizational effectiveness. Arefin et al. also note that BI systems seem to have the biggest effect on strategic decision-making. At the same time, they note that the success of BI delivering the expected effects varies strongly from one company to another, based on the industry and company size.

Conclusion

BI solutions can bring enterprises across all sectors of economy numerous advantages, such as providing the decision-makers one version of truth, providing answers to business-critical questions in a timely manner, helping to visualize and make sense of massive amounts of data in a concise way, and thus enabling the users to reach more accurate decisions to more complex questions faster and with more comfort. This, in turn, can contribute to more effective and efficient execution of the activities the companies participate in and subsequently lead to achieving better results and to higher performance.

Nevertheless, it is also important to note that there might be some downsides to utilizing BI. For small- and medium-sized companies, BI solutions might be too costly to implement. For BI to provide accurate information, the data it works with must be of high quality; otherwise, the reliability of answers provided by BI might be compromised, leading to distrust from users and eventually the failure of the whole solution. More advanced and sophisticated usage of the solution also requires users to put a lot of effort into learning how to work with it; failure to do so might lead to the whole solution not reaching its full potential and eventually failing altogether due to the growing skepticism toward its potential from the users. Also, it is virtually impossible to assess the quality of decisions reached as a result of using BI solutions.

Despite the overall optimism and high expectations users might have of BI solutions, it should be noted that BI is not a self-sufficient solution, bringing answers to all issues businesses might face, but it also requires adequate investments of finance, time, and effort from users to bring the desired effects.

Acknowledgments The article is processed as an output of a research project financed by the Grant Agency on the University of Economics, Prague, under the registration number F1/71/2017.

References

Arefin S, Hoque R, Bao Y (2014) The impact of business intelligence on organization's effectiveness: an empirical study. J Sys Inform Technol. https://doi.org/10.1108/JSIT-09-2014-0067

Aruldos M, Lakshmi Travis M, Prasanna Venkatesan V (2013) A survey on recent research in business intelligence. J Enterp Inf Manag. https://doi.org/10.1108/JEIM-06-2013-0029

Giannakopoulos A, Eybers S (2015) An investigation into the effects that business intelligence can have on organisational performance. 9th European Conference on Inf. Mgt. And Evaluation, pp 93–99

Obeidat M, North M, Richardson R et al (2015) Business intelligence technology, applications, and trends. Int Manag Rev 11:47–56

Popescu S (2012) Business intelligence solutions: a way of general improvement of efficiency and effectiveness. Rev Int Comp Manag 13:88–95

Rajnoha R, Stefko R, Merkova M et al (2016) Business intelligence as a key information and knowledge tool for strategic business performance management. Ekonomie a Manag 19:183–203. 10.15240/tul/001/2016-1-013

Rouhani S, Ashrafi A, Zare Ravasan A et al (2014) The impact model of business intelligence on decision support and organizational benefits. J Enterp Inf Manag. https://doi.org/10.1108/JEIM-12-2014-0126

Rusaneanu A (2013) Comparative analysis of the main business intelligence solutions. Informatica Economica. 10.12948/issn14531305/17.2.2013.12

Selene Xia B, Gong P (2012) Review of business intelligence through data analysis. Benchmark Int J. https://doi.org/10.1108/bij-08-2012-0050

Visinescu LL, Jones MC, Sidorova A (2017) Improving decision quality: the role of business intelligence. J Comput Inf Syst. https://doi.org/10.1080/08874417.2016.1181494

Zeng L, Li L, Duan L (2012) Business intelligence in Enterprise computing environment. Inf Technol Manag. https://doi.org/10.1007/s10799-012-0123-z

Economic Security Indicators Forecasting for Management Decisions Based on Integrated Reporting Data

Alsu Ahmetshina, Roza Kaspina, and Linar Molotov

Abstract The growing popularity of integrated reporting is becoming the trend of the best practices among successful companies. Transparent and clear reporting allows attracting additional investment, conducts a better business management, and focuses on sustainable future. Control of the company's sustainable development is a complex and important management task that is possible to handle through ensuring economic security. In order to do this, companies are encouraged to track key performance indicators in the current period and give accurate forecasts. The main idea of the article is driven by the need to improve aspects of forecasting methods of quantitative and qualitative indicators based on integrated reporting in order to ensure economic security and improve the quality of made on their basis management decisions. In this article, a major Russian oil company PJSC "LUKOIL" is being analyzed. The authors conduct their research based on integrated annual reports of the company for the last 5 years. Several forecasting methods were used to estimate future values of several economic security indicators, including simulation, fuzzy sets, and expertise. In combination, they should give more accurate results, therefore suggested by the authors to be used as a possible model in similar calculations to carry out a better decision-making for business management.

Keywords Economic security • Integrated reporting • Fuzzy forecasting • Simulation modeling • Expert forecasting method

A. Ahmetshina (✉)
Kazan Federal University, High School of Business, Podluzhnaya 3a, Kazan, Russia
e-mail: alsoura@yandex.ru

R. Kaspina • L. Molotov
Kazan Federal University, Institute of Management, Economics and Finance, Butlerova 4, Kazan, Russia
e-mail: rosakaspina@yandex.ru; molotov.linar@mail.ru

D. Procházka (ed.), *The Impact of Globalization on International Finance and Accounting*, Springer Proceedings in Business and Economics,
https://doi.org/10.1007/978-3-319-68762-9_44

Introduction

Economic security is the category, which provides not only assessment of the current business affairs but the future changes too, in order to help management find ways to use the opportunities and avoid potential threats. In this context, the concept of integrated reporting is an excellent basis for the implementation of any kind of forecasts, as it primarily aims to disclose companies' strategic plans and their base reinforcement (Busco and Frigo 2013; Brown and Dillard 2014; Carol 2015).

Preparation of an integrated report takes a considerable amount of time. It is necessary to collect heterogeneous material from various departments, branches, and subsidiaries, process it, and associate with the general idea. Therefore, at the time of publication, the information contained in the report may be outdated, which complicates the process of decision-making (Kaspina and Shneydman 2013; Tweedie and Martinov-Bennie 2015).

Therefore, the problem of accurate forecasting is vital to any business and always remains relevant (Petera et al. 2016); this we will discuss further in our paper.

Data and Methodology

Let us consider several economic security indicators of one of the largest Russian oil companies PJSC "LUKOIL" over the past 5 years.

We used the main advantage of the fact that the company publishes annual integrated report and built our own forecast for the end of 2016. In order to do this, we selected two indicators representing economic security from each group of the author's classification: "achieved level of production," "performance per ton," "cost of sales," "EBITDA margin," "net debt/EBITDA ratio for the last 12 months," "capital expenditure on capacity expansion," "average year salary," and "social investment" (Kaspina and Molotov 2016).

The sequence of our actions is defined as follows:

1. Forecast selected indicators using simulation-modeling scenarios.
2. Clarify the experts' forecast values for 2016 using ratings of information disclosure for PJSC "LUKOIL" 2015 integrated report, as there is a clear correlation of reporting transparency and economic security indicators according to the results of our previous study.

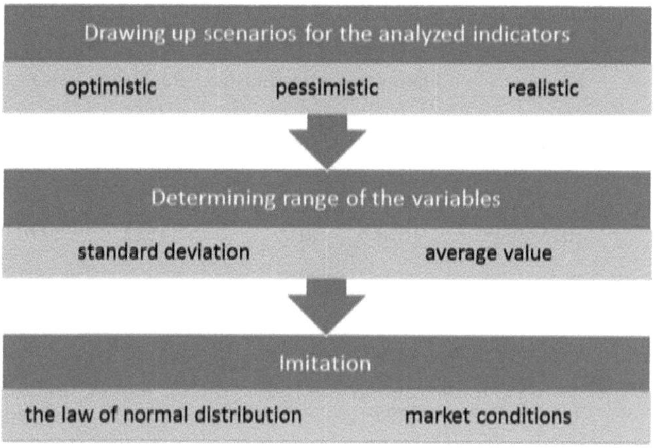

Source: authorial view

Fig. 1 Steps of simulation in scenario modeling (Source: authorial view)

Simulation Modeling

Let us turn to the first stage. Simulation is a powerful tool of economic analysis, which can be used for constructing variants of economic situation development and predicting their values. In this method, real existing model is replaced with a simulator, which becomes a base for future experiments, in our case—to run possible numerical values of chosen indicators in the given range. In such scenarios, simulations allow us to estimate possible options for development as if these processes would occur in reality, taking into account specified limitations. As a result, within a simulation model, it is possible to forecast needed variables with a high probability (Kaspina and Molotov 2015).

Figure 1 presents the general scheme of simulation procedures in scenario modeling.

Let us start with probability, filling it with possible variables, and then start the simulation model. For pessimistic forecast, we take the lowest value of the index over the past 5 years, for optimistic we take the greatest number, and the realistic will be the value of 2015. If the maximum (minimum) value was recorded in 2015, then the optimistic (pessimistic) forecast increases (decreases) this number by 10%. Thus, we get the range of changes as the minimum-maximum values per index.

Now we can build 1000 random experiments for the given range of indicators from Table 1 in "MS Excel," which we use to adjust the final forecast values and prepare our model to launch. Thus, we will have a new column "average value after experiments" and use its results in the next step of our forecasting procedure.

Table 1 The simulation model of the scenario of the forecast indicators for 2016

Index	Range	Optimistic	Pessimistic	Realistic	Average value	Standard deviation
Possibilities		0,2	0,35	0,45		
Achieved level of production, Mt	10,3–13	13	10,3	11,4	11,3	1,0
Performance, ton per unit	1075–1638	1638	1075	1582	1416	251
Cost of sales, $/ton	30–62	30	62	33	43	14
EBITDA margin, %	61–79	79	61	72	70	7
Net debt/EBITDA ratio for the last 12 months	0,95–3,1	0,95	3,1	2,81	2,54	0,81
Capital expenditure on capacity expansion, mln. $	155–223	223	155	160	171	26
Average year salary, $	9402–15,600	15,600	9402	10,447	11,112	2291
Social investment, млн. $	16,8–30,1	30,1	16,8	28	24,5	5,7

Source: author's calculations

Expert and Fuzzy Forecasting Methods

It is necessary to adjust the values obtained by experts in order to make our predictions more realistic. The practice of combining mathematic methods and expertise in forecasting is very popular in the business environment.

Therefore, we use the rating of information aspects disclosed in 2015 integrated reporting of PJSC "LUKOIL," submitted by the Russian Regional Integrated Reporting Network. On the basis of the previously determined correlation between economic security indicators and the level of integrated report transparency, we can adjust the forecast values.

We brought a group of experts from the staff of the Department of Management Accounting of our institute. Obviously, different experts differently estimate the value of an index or sometimes find it difficult to give an accurate estimate. In such situations, the method of fuzzy sets is used; it works with indicators in the form of fuzzy numbers.

This method is based on the use of algorithm for constructing membership functions of fuzzy numbers as follows (Ismagilov and Khasanova 2015):

$$\mu_K(u) = e^{-\alpha(K-u)^2}, u \in U, \tag{1}$$

where U is the universal set (in the general case, the set of real numbers); membership functions are built approximately equal to some number K, where parameterα α depends on the desired degree of fuzziness $\mu_K(u)$. Value α is defined as follows:

$$\alpha = \frac{-4\ln 0,5}{(\beta(K))^2}, \tag{2}$$

where $\beta(K)$ is the distance between transition points for $\mu_K(u)$, in which membership functions equal 0,5 (set these points as a и b, where $\beta(K) = b - a$).

The method is about sequential narrowing of initial interval to corresponding forecast of fuzzy number. First, the current iteration of forecast range is divided into three overlapping subintervals of equal length with further identification of their priorities, same as in Saati hierarchies' analysis method. Taking into account the priorities made, the forecast interval is narrowed again following by the same comparison with the reliability interval of fuzzy number (alpha-slice at 0.5). If the forecast is included in the reliability interval, then the iterations are terminated; otherwise, a new narrowing iteration is carried out. Final forecast value is defined as a fuzzy number obtained in the last iteration.

To simplify the forecasting calculations earlier this year, we created a special Java computer program to support the process of forecasting based on fuzzy group examination procedure and let our experts use it.

In the opening window of the program, user is prompted to create a new project or select from a saved one. The new project starts with administrator's window, who assigns project ID, and description as well as name, log-in, and password for system analyst and experts individually. After each expert adds his forecast range, system analyst reviews and analyzes them. Then experts independently fill the priority matrix, and the system analyst checks the data and conducts the first iteration. Then, following the previously described algorithm, the program checks if the forecast interval fits in the confidence fuzzy number interval to define the fuzzy forecast, or otherwise experts and systems analyst continue their work.

Results and Discussion

Index "capital expenditures for capacity expansion," in our opinion, is most closely associated with the level of quality and transparency of integrated report, which affects the company's investments and, as a consequence, the possibility to spend additional money on expansion of production capacity.

Table 2 The simulation model of the scenario of the forecast indicators for 2016 values and clarification of resulting variables of the simulation model

Variables	Value	Economic meaning	Practical meaning
Average value	191 mln. $	The values of capital expenditures for capacity expansion are grouped around the center (average)	The average value is a guide when determining forecast amount of capital expenditures for capacity expansion
Standard deviation	26 mln. $	The range of values of the capital costs to expand the capacity from central values	Standard deviation creates boundaries where the value of capital expenditures to expand capacity may change
The coefficient of variation	13.6%	The relative indicator which shows how the average value of a share is its average dispersion	It characterizes the homogeneity of the variable and the values of sustainability. The homogeneity is aggregate if the variation is less than 33 percent

Source: author's calculations and explanation

So let us analyze the results obtained for this indicator: the average value of experiments was 191 million dollars a year. In the model, there are only 440 cases out of 1000 where metric value is less than the average; that confirms the reliability of the data. We fill the results of the simulation scenario for this indicator in Table 2, explaining their economic and practical meanings.

Further, while adjusting the results of simulated future values with the involvement of experts using our computer program, we were able to identify the fuzzy forecast of the index already at the third iteration. Capital expenditures for capacity expansion by the end of 2016 turned out to be equal to $ 205 million. Experts noted that the relatively good last year's integrated report's transparency rating made them increase the forecast value of the indicator. In particular, experts have relied on the high rating disclosure for "strategic management, business models, and risk" and "activities in the field of sustainable development."

Conclusion

Thus, based on the analysis of PJSC "LUKOIL" integrated reporting, a two-stage forecasting procedure of selected economic security indicators was carried out. Suggested in the article, approaches and methods of indicators forecasting on the basis of integrated reporting can help the top management in improving the efficiency of economic security.

Proposed model can be used by companies for complex assessment of economic security and forecasting its variables with further publication of such data in integrated reports for both investors and internal users to analyze and assess the stability of business and making management decisions.

Next step in our research will be comparing our forecast results with actual numbers taken from 2016 integrated annual reports of PJSC "LUKOIL" and continue enhancing the methods and forecasting approaches.

References

Brown J, Dillard J (2014) Integrated reporting: on the need for broadening out and opening up. Account Audit Account J 27(7):1120–1156

Busco C, Frigo M (2013) Redefining corporate accountability through integrated reporting. Strateg Finan 8:33–41

Carol A (2015) The international integrated reporting council: a call to action. Crit Perspect Account 27:23–28

Ismagilov I, Khasanova S (2015) Short-term fuzzy forecasting of Brent oil prices. Asian Soc Sci 11:60–67

Ismagilov I, Khasanova S (2016) Algorithms of parametric estimation of polynomial trend models of time series on discrete trans-forms. Acad Strateg Manag J 15:21–28

Kaspina R (2015) Continuing professional development of accounting and auditing: Russian experience and challenges. Procedia – social and behavioral sciences, pp 550–553. ERPA international congress on education, ERPA congress 2015, Istanbul

Kaspina R, Molotov L (2016) Corporate integrated reporting: an efficient tool of economic security management. Acad Strateg Manag J 15(Is.SpecialIssue1):225–232

Kaspina R, Shneydman L (2013) New approach to the oil companies' corporate reporting. Neftyanoe Khozyaistvo. Oil industry. no. 9, pp 14–17

Kaspina R, Khapugina L, Zakirov E (2014a) Interrelation of Company's business model structure and information disclosed in management reporting. Life Sci J 11(12):778–780

Kaspina R, Molotov L, Kaspin L (2014b) Fuzzy forecasting of the cash flow statement based on accounting data. Mediterr J Soc Sci 5(24):237–241

Kaspina R, Molotov L, Kaspin L (2015) Cash flow forecasting as an element of integrated reporting: an empirical study. Asian Soc Sci 11(11):89–94

Petera P, Wagner J, Knorová K (2016) Perception and interpretation of sustainability among the largest corporations established in the Czech Republic. Acta Univ Agric Silvic Mendelianae Brun 64:1053–1065

Tweedie D, Martinov-Bennie N (2015) Entitlements and time: integrated Reporting's double-edged agenda. Soc Environ Account J 35:49–61

Multidimensional Process of Financial Controlling Implementation

Anna Siemionek and Michał Chalastra

Abstract The aim of the article is to present stages of controlling system implementation with some suggestions on who and how should one perform them. This article is based on a case study, and it is based on the data obtained during practical implementation of the controlling system in enterprises. The methodology described in this paper may be implemented in various projects from different areas.

Keywords Financial controlling • Process implementation

Introduction

The process of financial controlling implementation is a very complex project. It requires coordination of many activities from various spheres. Following works should be conducted within different areas such as financial and management accounting, organization management, informatics, and education. During its implementation, one should involve people representing key areas of the company from many departments. Not only employees of the company but also external consultants should be engaged in that process. These consultants may represent various entities. It is a good benchmark to develop the substantive concept by consultant represented by a consulting company specializing in the field of controlling. These efforts should be then implemented in management support systems. ERP and BI systems are mainly used. These tasks to introduce the system are performed by other consultants from the company providing the system. To conclude, this process is carried out by people from different enterprises (Kotapski and

A. Siemionek (✉)
University of Gdansk, Department of Corporate Finance, ul. Armii Krajowej 101, 81-824 Sopot, Poland
e-mail: siemionek.anna@gmail.com

M. Chalastra
University of Gdansk, Department of Accounting, ul. Armii Krajowej 101, 81-824 Sopot, Poland
e-mail: chalastra.m@gmail.com

D. Procházka (ed.), *The Impact of Globalization on International Finance and Accounting*, Springer Proceedings in Business and Economics,
https://doi.org/10.1007/978-3-319-68762-9_45

Hoffmann 2016). Another constraint is the fact that those implementations need long time to be realized. Such projects are usually implemented for longer than a year. This period of time consists of all implementation phases such as organizational works before implementation as well as validation of correctness of the controlling system. That is why it is so important to prepare for this implementation. It is significant to coordinate the implementation of all tasks.

Multidimensional Character of Financial Controlling Implementation

The process of controlling implementation should be analyzed multidimensionally. Following issues should be taken into consideration:

1. Realized tasks
2. People responsible for specific tasks
3. Work schedule and its intensity during different periods
4. Essential time and financial resources devoted to particular tasks

Regarding essential tasks which must be carried out, there is no unique standard that should be applied in each case. The scope of activities depends on needs and the capabilities of this particular company. Some companies share the implementation process into two or more phases. In the first one, there should be introduced only priority tools. Others can be implemented in subsequent phases. For these phases, there are no detailed plans as they regard to the future, and they are going to be realized later on. Limited personal and financial resources might be the reason for such a concept. In Poland, it is a common practice to divide the tasks during implementation of the controlling system into several major categories. According to the situation of each company, there can be observed following tasks in the company:

- Implementation of cost accounting system
- Implementation of budgeting system
- BI system implementation
- Education
- Changes in management methods
- Auditing and controlling development

The order of various stages of controlling system implementation sometimes differs. It depends mainly on needs of a particular company. For example, some companies started the implementation with implementing management accounting system plan. Plan of accounts is modified and cost accounting rules are settled. The tasks in this phase can last even all year long. There are even cases where it is the only system functioning in the framework of controlling. In other entities, controlling implementation starts with budgeting. The reason for that is that the most important task of controlling is to determine responsibility for costs (Kotapski 2014). Another important issue is to implement information systems such as:

- Spreadsheets
- Additional BI system
- Integrated information systems

The usage of controlling spreadsheets for that purpose occurs usually due to low costs of such a solution. However, these are often apparent savings. The major problem is a lot of work and time devoted to prepare those spreadsheets. Controlling IT costs should therefore cover both positions associated with the system itself and its maintenance. The usage of spreadsheets is therefore recommended in smaller companies where controlling systems are not very sophisticated and they do not process too much data. Controlling system can be operated by special BI systems. These systems are operating parallel to the financial accounting systems. Financial accounting systems perform the functions of data registration according to expectations of controlling. These data are later on exported to BI systems. In these IT systems, they are aggregated into management accounting reports in accordance with the requirements of the controlling. The advantage of this solution is negligible interference into functioning of financial accounting. Data recording is usually improved as they are more detailed. The disadvantage of this concept may be the emergence of some differences in the reports created in the framework of financial and management reporting. Another option is to implement the computerization of controlling one integrated IT system. This system performs both controlling and financial accounting tasks. Due to high costs of such a solution, it is rather recommended for large enterprises. To sum up, it should be noted that controlling system must take into account the tasks associated with computerization (Williams 2011; Kotapski and Hoffmann 2016). Another category of tasks to be considered in realizing the implementation of controlling is education. No matter which tools and systems will be implemented, it is necessary to carry out educational activities. This is due to the existence of the education gap in this area. There is a deficit of knowledge between the scope of academic teaching and best practices. Academic knowledge is rather general. Practical needs require detailed and advanced industry knowledge (Chalastra 2015). Educational tasks should be carried out taking into account the individual needs of different groups of workers. They should be carried out for:

- Financial controllers
- Responsibility center managers
- Top executives

Implementation of controlling also requires changes in the management system. They are usually related to the introduction of new job descriptions. Employees receive new tasks arising from the operation of the controlling system. Their responsibility is also very often modified. This is due to the findings made in relation to the responsibilities of the various budget items. It arises from a very important assumption saying that each budget item must be precisely related to the person responsible for it. Summing up the implementation of financial controlling system requires different tasks. Each company can have their own set of tasks. Their selection results from the specific needs of the company. Financial possibilities and the knowledge of professionals in this field are both very important. This freedom is an important obstacle in the analysis of the correctness of the process implementation (Nesterak 2016). It is therefore not possible to develop one standard for every company. It is however worth to develop a catalogue of possible tasks that should be performed. It will be helpful in creating individual implementation plans.

Within good practices, one should implement the following actions:

- Development of business model of the enterprise.
- Identification of cost centers and profit centers.
- Identification of responsibilities for budget positions.
- Structuring a detailed budget for the identified centers of cost and profit.
- Establish principles for settlement of costs of auxiliary activities.
- Establish principles for settlement of costs in the core business.
- Modification of the plan of accounts and accounting policies.
- Preparation of budget procedures in the field of planning, execution, reporting, and correction of the budget.
- Developing a system of budget flexibility—tolerance to deviations.
- The implementation of the substantive concept of controlling system in computer systems.
- Introduction tasks of controlling into the responsibilities of staff requirements.
- Formalize the tasks of controlling department.
- Advanced trainings of controlling department staff.
- Trainings for employees regarding company's solutions.
- Audit of the controlling system.

People Responsible for Implementing Financial Controlling System

Due to multidimensional scope of financial controlling implementation, it is extremely important to determine which people will perform individual tasks. This is extremely important because substantial part of the tasks can be performed simultaneously by many people. Some of the works may also be carried out by employees from different companies. Such a situation will occur when the process of implementation is supported by external services. These are usually consultants in the field of controlling and information systems. They represent quite often two distinct attitudes: business consulting and information technology. Some companies consider implementation without external support. The advantage of this concept is that it is realized by the employees of the company. It is easier to supervise specific tasks by specific individuals, and the costs of the project are lower. On the other side, there are limited competences of employees in the best standards of controlling and information systems. In addition, they do not have practical experience in its implementation, taking into account the specifics of that particular company. In those cases where implementation was carried out by its employees, there have been applied not the best possible solutions. There are mostly implemented tools subordinated to the rules of financial accounting which are also not up-to-date solutions. Forwarding the implementation of this system exclusively to external consultants is also not a good practice. External experts do not know specifics of a particular company. Moreover, it is not recommended to copy solutions from one company to another.

It is therefore extremely important to determine which people will perform particular tasks. It can be carried out by employees from many different companies. Such a situation will occur when the process of implementation will be supported by external services. There are usually hired controlling and information systems consultants. They often represent two distinct businesses: consulting and information technology. Summing up the process of implementation of the controlling system can be performed by the following employees:

- Companies in which controlling system is implemented
- Consulting company specializing in the field of controlling implementation
- IT company providing dedicated system for controlling

One should consider whether it is better to carry out the implementation without external support. The advantage of this concept is the realization of the work by the employees of one company. It is moreover easier to supervise the performance of specific tasks by specific people, and the project costs are lower. A significant drawback of this method is however the limited competence of employees in the best standards of controlling and information systems. Implementation of specific tasks of the identified areas should be therefore performed only by internal controllers. Many tasks will be realized at the same time by several entities. The aim is to conduct consultation within adopted solutions (Rusek 2009). Implementation should be implemented by people from following departments and companies:

- Employees from different departments of the company implementing this controlling system:
  - Controlling
  - Accounting
  - Business divisions
  - The board of directors
- External consultants:
  - Employees from the consulting firm
  - IT systems consultants

Due to the presented factors, it is extremely important to precisely assign specific tasks to the people involved in the implementation. It is also important to coordinate the work carried out by different people. The aim is permanent consultation of all adopted solutions. This will allow to identify quickly and resolve all the difficulties. There is very often the problem of understanding between the sides. Those are however not substantive issues. Due to multiplayer team, it is necessary to choose the project manager. If there is no responsible person for the team, it usually causes a slowdown and then abandoning the entire implementation.

Timetable

The process of financial controlling implementation should never be completed. This system should be developed constantly. This is due to the fact that this system covers a wide range of areas and its implementation requires various and complicated tasks. There is observed dynamic development of the used tools. It is therefore not possible to implement it completely in a specific time. The first phase of its implementation is particularly important because it is a basis for its further development. The solutions adopted in this phase should take into account future requirements of the system. Controlling introduces significant changes in the enterprise, and that is what its implementation must be conducted within an appropriate period of time. Accounting systems and planning ones are fields where important changes are going to be observed. Due to the principle of comparability which is significant in financial accounting, its implementation must be completed before the new financial year starts. It also refers to the planning system. The budget should be determined according to new rules before the period of its duration in accordance with the requirements of the principle of precedence of budgeting. Summing up the above statements, there can be stated the assumption that the implementation of the first phase of the management system would take about a year. During this time, the activities are carried out with a varying intensity, and they are performed by different entities. Some of the works can be done even earlier than during the year of its implementation. There should be conducted trainings referring to advanced tools in controlling department. This knowledge would be especially useful during the adaptation proposed by the external consultants which take into account the specifics of the company. Some tasks such as testing of the system and elimination of detected defects during its functioning would also be conducted after its implementation (Chalastra et al. 2017) (Table 1).

Another aspect of the sustainable implementation is a uniform intensity of the works within the time. There is a good practice to avoid the implementation of the excessive number of tasks and their disappearance (Chalastra et al. 2016). High intensity of works in the first period of implementation appears quite often in the practice. This can be caused by the concentration of operations at the beginning of the project. This commitment to the project may go away, and at the end, it can result in delays during implementing next stages. The intensity of works can be resumed in the last quarter of the year. In this case, it may happen due to a desire to complete the project within the previous deadline. Those mentioned problems are

Table 1 Suggested timetable for financial controlling implementation

Synthetic categories of implementation tasks	Year -1		Year of implementation		Year + 1	
	Q IV	Q I	Q II	Q III	Q IV	Q I
Developing the substantive concept of controlling system						
The implementation of the concept into the specific functioning of the unit						
Information concept preparation						
Implementation of the system						
Education						
Testing the system in practice						

Suggested work intensity	High		Low	

Source: own work

usually caused by bad planning and compliance with the work schedule. Planning the work schedule, one should take into consideration factors such as seasonality functioning of a specific company and holiday leaves. During these periods, there can be expected a decrease in the intensity of activities. That is why all the conceptual works should be completed before the summer break. After the holidays, one should pursue the activities of proposed implementation tools in the enterprise (Table 2).

The costs of implementing the controlling system can be divided into two basic categories. This division is based on the type of resources that perform specific tasks. According to these criteria, there may occur following categories of costs related to the usage of the resources:

- Own
- Foreign

Work of company's own employees is included in the first group such as financial controllers and managers of responsibility centers. The work is determined by settling down the time and hourly wage for people involved in the implementation. The rates should be negotiated individually due to their differentiation. The hourly rate shall include all the ingredients to maintain a particular position such as labor and social insurance costs. This category includes also additional costs of training, job maintenance, etc. The determining of these costs requires the use of management accounting tools. Although these costs directly do not generate financial expenses in determining the full costs of implementation, they should be taken into account. It is a good practice to determine the rules of activity-based costing (ABC) (Bender 2008). The second category is foreign

Table 2 The intensity of the implementation works of controlling system performed by different groups of professionals

Persons implementing implementation	The intensity of work	Year -1		Year 0 – year of implementation		Year + 1	
		Q IV	Q I	Q II	Q III	Q IV	Q I
External consultants in the field of controlling	High		■	■			
	Low	■	■	■	■	■	■
Employees of the company implementing the controlling	High			■	■	■	
	Low	■	■	■	■	■	■
External consultants implementing the IT system	High				■	■	
	Low			■	■	■	■

Source: own work

resources costs such as consulting services, trainings, business travels, and purchase of hardware and software. Data related to those costs are available in financial accounting system.

Conclusion

The process of financial controlling implementation is an extremely complicated process. It is a result of the fact that it is necessary to coordinate various activities from different perspectives. It is not possible to develop a universal pattern as all companies differ from each other. It is however worth to identify the standard range of activities which should be done during such projects. This catalogue of appropriate actions would allow to analyze the individual needs of the enterprise. The aim of this article is to create such a unique pattern.

References

Bender P (2008) Jakie są rzeczywiste koszty controllingu, Controlling nr 5, Infor Warszawa

Chalastra M (2015) Identification of good education practices in the field of management accounting – presentation of results of empirical research conducted in companies in Poland, Knowledge for market use 2015 Department of Applied Economics Palacky University Olomouc Czech Republic

Chalastra M, Siemionek A, Kotapski R, Siemionek-Rukań M (2016) Sustainable process of financial controlling implementation. Societas Scientiarum Olomucensis II, Olomouc

Chalastra M, Siemionek A, Kotapski R (2017) Sustainable controlling: measuring method based on the catalogue of controller tasks, Springer, Proceedings in Business and Economics

Kotapski R (2014) Budżetowanie w zarządzaniu przedsiębiorstwem budowlano-montażowym. Wydawnictwo MARINA, Wrocław
Kotapski R, Hoffmann M (2016) Wdrożenie systemu informatycznego do budżetowania i controllingu, Controlling i Zarządzanie nr 3(11):8–9
Nesterak J (2016) Bariery wdrażania controllingu w przedsiębiorstwach działających w Polsce Controlling i Zarządzanie nr 3(11):66–79
Rusek B (2009) Wdrożenie systemu controllingu w firmie Lumag sp. z o.o., Controlling nr 2, Infor Warszawa
Williams S (2011) 5 barriers to BI success and how to overcome them, Strategic finance, July

Strategic and Operational Perspective of the Principles of Identification of the Scopes of Responsibility for Costs

Michał Chalastra

Abstract One of the key requirements of today's management accounting is the identification of the scopes of responsibility for the costs. There is a theory that to each cost, there should an assigned person who is responsible for it (Leszczyński Z, Wnuk T Controlling, Fundacja Rozwoju Rachunkowości w Polsce, Warszawa, p 12, 1999; Sojak S Rachunkowość zarządcza. Dom Organizatora, Toruń, p. 645, 2003; Drury C Rachunek kosztów. PWN, Warszawa, pp 416–417, 1998; Nowak E Zaawansowana rachunkowość zarządcza. PWE, Warszawa, p 12, 2009). The responsibility should be borne both from the operational and from the strategic perspective (Świderska G Rachunkowość zarządcza i rachunek kosztów. Diffin, Warszawa, p 12, 2003; Szydełko Ł Rachunek odpowiedzialności w strategicznych jednostkach biznesowych, Zeszyty Naukowe politechniki Rzeszowskiej, Nr 248, Rzeszów, p 2002, 2002). In practice, however, the fulfilment of those requirements is not that easy. To satisfy them, various types of responsibility for costs need to be defined. Then, specific tasks that need to be performed by particular persons must be detailed. This article aims to determine the issues.

Keywords Responsibility for costs • Responsibility centres

Introduction

This paper is a result of the interviews with the staff responsible for the operation of the systems used for cost management (financial controllers). Moreover, it includes the findings of the analysis conducted in the studied companies of the documents that describe the operating principles of their accounting system. The study was conducted in five companies operating in Poland. The choice of the companies was made taking into account the following criteria:

M. Chalastra (✉)
University of Gdansk, Department of Accounting, ul. Armii Krajowej 101, 81-824 Sopot, Poland
e-mail: chalastra.m@gmail.com

D. Procházka (ed.), *The Impact of Globalization on International Finance and Accounting*, Springer Proceedings in Business and Economics,
https://doi.org/10.1007/978-3-319-68762-9_46

- Active participation in the promotion of the development of modern management methods (congresses, the press)
- Dynamic development and achievement of satisfactory financial results

The objective of the study is to examine the practices relating to the financial and management accounting systems and the scopes of responsibility of the staff.

Types of Responsibility for Costs

The identification of the types of responsibility for costs should be conducted at the level of a single cost centre. This results from the fact that a cost centre is the smallest unit in which the persons responsible for particular costs are identified. To make correct calculations or to determine the financial viability of a cost centre, it is vital to identify all the costs that are charged to it. At this point, it needs to be said that in majority of cases, the manager of a cost centre is not directly responsible for the total of the costs of his centre. Numerous costs that a particular centre is burdened with are generated following the decisions taken by employees of other units. This results from the centralisation of the specific functions within one company. The situation is a consequence of the following factors:

- The management of a given field requires specialist knowledge.
- It allows for the implementation of a comprehensive operational strategy within the field throughout the company.

For example, the responsibility for the overall IT costs may be borne by the IT department, while the estate management department may be responsible for the costs related to buildings. The situation, known as tasks centralisation, results in the manager of the cost centre that uses the IT and the buildings not being entirely responsible for the costs, even though those costs are charged to his centre. Hence, a problem arises of who is responsible for the costs incurred by particular cost centres and to what extent. In order to determine correctly the persons responsible for the costs, first types of the responsibility should be identified. The following types of responsibility can be distinguished here:

Substantive:

- Direct
- Indirect
- Technical

Substantive responsibility is related to the value of the generated costs. There are two forms of this responsibility – direct and indirect. The direst substantive responsibility involves the cost-generating decisions being taken by the manager of the unit himself. Those costs may be either external or internal. The costs may be related either to his own cost centre or to other units. The indirect responsibility of the manager of cost centre relates to the costs that are charged to his centre but are created as a consequence of the initiatives of other departments. In such a case, the manager does not plan the costs in his budget nor does he take any decisions to incur them. Hence, those are the costs that burden one centre as a result of decisions taken by persons other than the manager of the centre. The situation results from the previously mentioned centralisation of tasks within a company. The person who is directly responsible for the costs of that category is the manager of the unit at whose initiative the task was performed and not the manager of the unit for the sake of which it was done.

The technical responsibility for the costs involves correct determination of their value and exerting ongoing control over them. In such a case, the manager who bears technical responsibility is not responsible for the level of the costs. This type of responsibility for the costs results from:

- Having specialist knowledge with regard to the field the costs relate to
- Having access to the databases in which the costs are registered

Technical responsibility involves provision of assistance to the managers of the substantive responsibility centres. This type of responsibility may be applied in relation to the costs such as remuneration, depreciation, insurance, taxes and fees or financial costs. The managers of direct responsibility centres take decision with regard to the substantive aspect of particular costs. The decision may concern, for example, the number of employees, the level of their remuneration or the rules of depreciation. As there are departments where the employees possess specialist knowledge in a given area, they are entrusted with technical tasks such as budget planning. However, they perform the tasks relying only on the information obtained from the managers of direct substantive responsibility centres. Thus, they are responsible for the correct technical planning and financial accounting of the items. It is also their task to supervise relevant costs. The activities aim at controlling the value of the specific costs both in particular cost centres and within the company as a whole. Consequently, they bear indirect technical responsibility for them. This stems from the fact that the employees do not generate those costs; they only supervise them.

Cost Centres and Cost Responsibility Centres

It needs to be considered why a cost centre is burdened with the costs that are created following a decision taken by a person other than the manager of the centre and whether it would not be better to include those costs in the lists of costs of the centres that actually generate them. This would solve the problem of identification of the scope of responsibility for the costs. However, then they would be incorrectly assigned in relation to the units for the benefit of which they had been incurred. Consequently, the information that is used in order to conduct calculations, to draw up financial reports and to determine the return on resources would be misleading.

If the responsibility for the costs that are created by one unit but are charged to the cost centre of another unit is to be moved to the manager of the other unit, the latter needs to accept the cost-related documents. The method relies on the acceptance by the managers of cost centres of all the source documents under which their respective units are charged with the costs. This includes the costs created by the managers of units other than the burdened cost centre. The method is based on the assumption that the costs of a cost centre may only comprise such items that have been accepted by the manager of the centre. This solution, however, is not correct as:

- The manager of the cost centre who accepts such costs does not possess specialist competence to assess their substantive value.
- The process requires additional administrative work, which prolongs the information access time and debilitates the functional effectiveness of the accounting system.
- The information about who actually generates the cost may be lost.
- It becomes more difficult for the manager of a cost centre to have ongoing control over the implementation of his budget.
- Information on the total value of the costs of particular types of activity in the entire company is lost.

Another solution is to assign the costs first to the units that actually create. This makes it possible to determine the scope of direct responsibility of specific persons. At the next stage, the costs are allocated as the indirect costs to the cost centres they relate to. However, this method has the following disadvantages:

- Occurrence of cross subsidisation of costs resulting from the drawbacks of the cost allocation methods (Chalastra 2012, p. 159–183)
- Breach of one of the accounting principles – the principle of particularity
- Partial loss of information on the type of costs that burden the cost centres

In view of the reasons presented above, cost identification should be developed simultaneously in compliance with the two criteria of data presentation discussed above, i.e. responsibility centre and cost centre. At this point, an attempt could be made to give a definition of the discussed units. A cost responsibility centre is a unit that makes the cost-generating decisions; however, it does not need to be a unit for the benefit of which the costs are incurred. A cost centre, on the other hand, to which the costs are charged and which at the same time does not have to be a unit that creates such costs (see: definition at www.oxforddictionaries.com; Kaplan 2006; Walther 2017) (Janik and Paździor 2012, p.143; Jaruga et al. 2001, p. 608; Nowak 2011, p. 248; Piosik 2006, p. 2; Sobańska 2003, p. 111; Wilkinson 2013). This leads to a situation where costs in one cost centre may be divided into two categories. The first comprises the costs that are created by the manager of the given cost centre. The other group comprises costs generated by the managers of other units (Table 1).

Analysing the relations between the two types of centres discussed above it should be noted that the financial accounting system is focused on the identification of cost centres only. The task is performed in order to calculate and prepare a financial report (Gierusz 2010; Sobańska 2009). The system is not, however, interested in determining the scopes of responsibility. That is why responsibility centres are established only for the sake of management accounting.

Table 1 Differences between a cost centre and a responsibility centre

Type of the centre	Cost centre	Cost responsibility centre
Direction of cost flow	The unit to which the costs are charged	The unit that generates the costs
The tasks of costs analysis	Calculation and analysis of return on resources	Budget planning, implementation and accounting

Source: own research

The Tasks Performed While Exercising Responsibility for Costs

When the manager of a cost centre is directly responsible for a given cost, he should not be free to manage it arbitrarily. The level of the cost should be supervised by a central unit. On the other hand, when it is the manager of the central unit who is directly responsible for the cost in a given cost centre, he should be indirectly supervised by the manager of the cost centre. In a case when it is the manager of the cost centre who exercises direct responsibility, the main tasks of the manager include planning of the budget, disbursing the funds, conducting real value analysis and filing applications for the initiation of optimisation measures. Nevertheless, the manager should not be authorised to manage that the group of costs fully and independently as such a situation could result in the costs reaching an uncontrolled level, both within a single cost centre and the entire company. Following the good practice of budget funds spending, numerous costs have the maximum tolerance for the variance between the level of costs planned in the budget and the level of the actually incurred costs set for them. The mechanism allows the managers to adjust the budgets to the current needs of their departments since the current needs may differ from the historic conditions on the basis of which the budget was set. Such a solution is consistent with the rules of the budget variance tolerance system and follows the current standards in this area. In a cost centre, a situation may occur where the actual level of a certain cost is characterised by a variance that falls within the tolerance limits. The source of its financing will be the savings in other costs that are covered by the budget tolerance system. The analysis of the budget performance at the level of a single cost centre will not show then any irregularities. However, the value of this particular cost in this specific cost centre may be incommensurable with the implemented task. A different situation occurs when in numerous cost centres the budget is exceeded in relation to the same cost. A single variance is not considered worrying as it falls within the assumed tolerance limits. However, their sum in the entire company may turn out to be significant.

Different problems occur when optimisation measures are introduced. In such a case, when the manager of a cost centre finds that the value of some cost that falls within his direct responsibility is incorrect, he should apply for the initiation of an optimisation process. It is not recommended that he take the decision independently. The reason for that is the fact that though the value of such a cost may be incorrect from the point of view of the manager of one cost centre, it is justified from the point of view of the strategic activities implemented throughout the company. Therefore, proper optimisation measures should be taken only after they have received approval of the manager supervising the cost at the company level. In view of the above, the costs that fall within the area of direct responsibility of the managers of cost centres should be supervised at the central level, and the supervision should have indirect responsibility character. The situation creates the need for establishing organisational units (departments or individuals) that would have central control over the costs generated by the managers of cost centres. They could be called central units for cost supervision. The role may be assigned to the departments designated to hold technical responsibility for them. Such a solution is justified by the fact that the employees of such departments have competence to render such control. Nevertheless, not all costs fall under technical supervision. Thus, in the case of the rest of them, the units that are responsible to take control over the way the costs are incurred at the level of the entire company must be identified. The main selection criteria should be the competence of the employees of a given department and its business profile. Application of such a solution will result in a situation where each cost will be covered by two types of responsibility; the first will relate to the way it is disbursed (direct responsibility) while the other to the supervision of the process (indirect responsibility) (Fig. 1).

The main tasks of a centre for central supervision of the costs should include the following:

- Development of the strategy with regard to a given cost
- Establishment of central rules for budget planning
- Technical assistance in budget planning
- Supervision over the planning and spending of the funds by the manager of the cost centre
- Analysis of the real values at the company level
- Informing managers of cost centres and the company executives about the trends that raise concern
- Initiation and reviewing of optimisation measures

An important task of the manager of a centre for central supervision of the costs is to supervise the values of specific costs incurred by particular cost centres. When situations that raise concern are identified, the manager should be obligated to introduce optimisation measures. In view of the fact that the manager of a cost centre bears direct responsibility for those costs, he should be the first to be informed about the occurrence of any worrying situation. When some incorrect value of a given cost occurs, the responsibility for the resulting situation is borne simultaneously by two persons:

- The manager of a cost centre
- The manager of a centre for central supervision of the costs

The responsibility of the manager of a cost centre covers the level of the costs and is of direct character, while the other may be held accountable for his insufficient supervision, and his responsibility is of indirect character.

Costs that lie within the indirect responsibility of central cost supervision centres	Supervises costs	Central cost supervision centre 1	Cost 1	Generates costs	Costs that lie within the direct responsibility of the manager of the cost centre
		Central cost supervision centre 2	Cost 2		
		Central cost supervision centre 3	Cost 3		
Costs that lie within direct responsibility of the managers of responsibility centres	Generates costs	Responsibility centre A	Cost A	Supervises costs	Costs that lie within the indirect responsibility of the manage of the cost centre
		Responsibility centre B	Cost B		
		Responsibility centre C	Cost C		

Note: Total 100% of the costs of a cost centre
Source: own research

Fig. 1 The principle of double responsibility for costs in a cost centre (Note: Total 100% of the costs of a cost centre. Source: own research)

Similar double responsibility relationship occurs in the case of costs generated by responsibility centres which are charged to cost centres. This time, the manager of the cost centre should have control over the costs that are charged to his centre. He fulfils the task by rendering indirect supervision of them. The aim of the supervision is to detect any irregularities. Lack of such control may lead to his unit being unreasonably charged with costs generated by other departments. Their managers care only about the development of their own units or the settling of all the costs they generate. Such activities aim at improving the assessment indexes of those centres at the expense of other entities. In a situation where the manager of a cost centre finds that the costs created by other units and charged to his centre are incorrect (too high or too low), he should officially intervene. The intervention should be addressed to the controlling department as the one responsible for the operation of the cost management system. The aim of the intervention is to trigger the process of cost analysis to check the correctness of charging. The findings of the analysis may be as follows:

- The current solutions applied by the cost accounting are correct.
- There is a mistake in the rules of the operation of the cost accounting system.
- The cost recording and cost accounting have been conducted in an unreliable way.

The first situation implies that information on any irregularities is groundless. A given cost centre does consume costs of the value ascribed to it by the accounting system. In this case, intervention is required with regard to the quantity of the consumed services and not with regard to their accounting. The analysis may also find a mistake in the rules of charging costs to a specific cost centre. The mistake may be so insignificant from the point of view of the company as a whole that it has been overlooked by the central authorities responsible for cost accounting, such as the controlling department. However, for a single cost centre, the value may be significant and may affect the results that are achieved by it and on the basis of which the centre receives bonuses or is subjected to optimisation measures. The third case is the unreliability of cost recording or cost accounting. The situation takes place when the rules of the operation of the cost accounting system are correct but their application is wrong. Most often, the number of units of the provided internal services, on the basis of which the costs are accounted, is overstated. When summarising this part of the considerations, it should be concluded that the manager of a cost centre should be responsible for exercising control over the costs that are borne by other direct responsibility centres for the benefit of his unit. This should even be true for the items that he is not directly responsible for. The supervision should be executed both at the budget planning stage and in the course of its implementation. It is advisable that the supervision be exercised also from the strategic perspective.

Summing up, a conclusion may be drawn that each cost should be supervised at the global company level, that is, from the strategic perspective, by one specifically designated organisational unit. If this refers to the costs that are created by the managers of cost centres under the direct responsibility assigned to them, the supervision should be indirect. In such a case, it is exercised by the centres for central supervision of costs. On the other hand, when this refers to the costs generated by the responsibility centres, direct supervision occurs. It is important that to each cost, there should be assigned one organisational unit responsible for comprehensive management of the cost at company level. Such a solution would make it possible to create consistent strategies for particular costs. That is why the solution fulfils the requirements set for modern management accounting, where the strategic aspect is clearly emphasised (Wnuk-Pel 2011) (Fig. 2).

Given the double responsibility for the costs, as described above, a question arises of who should be responsible for the total costs of a cost centre. It is not correct when the total costs of the centre are not the responsibility of one person. Hence, a conclusion should be reached that the manager of a cost centre should be responsible for the total costs of that centre. This should be the case even if he is directly responsible for part of the costs only. This results from the fact that he is obliged to render control of the costs that are generated by other persons and charge his cost centre. Lack of such supervision could result in the deterioration of the results achieved by his cost centre.

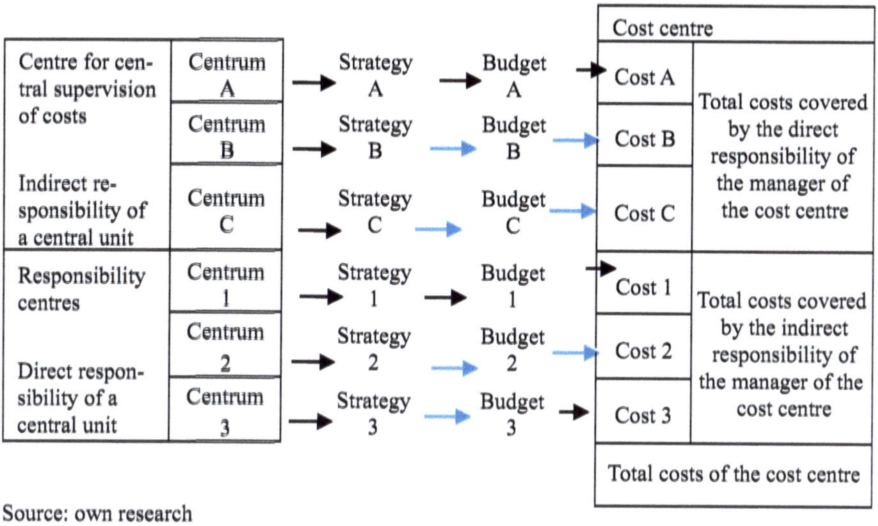

Source: own research

Fig. 2 The principles of central supervision of the costs from the strategic and operational point of view (Source: own research)

The Costs Dependent on and Independent of the Manager of a Cost Centre and a Suggestion on How to Classify Them

The suggested division of costs into those that lie within the scope of direct or indirect responsibility is consistent with their classification into the ones that are dependent on and independent of the manager of a cost centre. The classification is correct; however, the scopes of responsibility of the particular employees should be specified in detail in consistence with the suggested rules. When there are no proper arrangements, the following problems may arise:

- No central supervision over the costs that are dependent on the manager of a cost centre
- No control at the single cost centre of the costs independent of the manager of the centre

In the first case, the problem is that an assumption may be made that when the cost is dependent on the manager of a cost centre, the manager is free to incur it. This, however, is undesired as it would lead to a situation where the company would slowly give up on a complex and strategic policy in the field. The solution follows the thesis that each cost should be managed both strategically and operationally. Lack of such supervision is sometimes justified by the low value of a specific cost. Though it may be true that at the level of a single centre, the cost is of little significance, at the global scale of the entire company and over a longer period of time, the cost may be perceived quite differently. It is worth mentioning that nowadays, with cost optimisation, there are not many examples when a single action could bring significant results. Today, it is the sum of the values of numerous small improvements that results in noticeable benefits.

As regards the second case, according to good management practice, each cost should have a person responsible for it assigned to it. In the case of items that are independent of the manager of a cost centre, a question arises of who is responsible for a given cost. In economic practice, the situation where numerous such items have no person responsible for them occurs quite often. The situation manifests itself by the lack of ongoing and strategic supervision. The budgets for such items are often based on historical data at the level of single cost centres. Still, the ongoing management of such a cost involves payment handling and document registration. When a problem arises, occasional remedial actions are implemented. There is no regular analysis of such costs that would make it possible to exercise their regular and comprehensive control. No actions are taken to develop a long-term strategic policy for the area the costs relate to. To sum up this fragment of considerations, it should be noted that classification of costs into those that are dependent on or independent of the manger of a cost centre is correct and necessary. However, for each cost identified on the basis of this classification, it needs to be determined what tasks should be performed by specific individuals in compliance with the suggested rules.

Conclusions

The identification of the scopes of responsibility for costs is today one of the key tasks of management accounting. The main purpose of it is to support the highly important process of the optimisation of the incurred costs. The requirement is drawn from an assumption that the optimisation measures should be taken by the individuals who are responsible for given areas and thus also for the costs related to them. The measures should be applied on continuous basis and in a systematic way, both from the operational and strategic perspective. To be able to use them effectively, it is extremely important that the costs be systemised appropriately and that the tasks that are to be performed by specific employees be clearly defined. The financial accounting system does not allow for identification of costs by scopes of responsibility. The solutions that originate in financial accounting register costs in relation to cost centres and not to responsibility. However, the requirements of today's management accounting demand that such classification be established. Hence, a new dimension of the presentation of cost information, related to cost centres, is needed.

The issues of responsibility for the costs are an important requirement to which modern accounting needs to relate to. The difficulties in determining the responsibility result from the complexity of the tasks performed by many people managing the same costs. The article identifies different types of responsibility for the costs. Moreover, it discusses the tasks that should be performed by particular employees to exercise effective control over the costs, both from operational and strategic perspective.

References

Chalastra M (2012) Subsydiowanie skrośne a koncepcja True and Fair View, Zarządzanie i finanse, Wydział Zarządzania Uniwersytetu Gdańskiego, nr 4 część 3. Sopot

Drury C (1998) Rachunek kosztów. PWN, Warszawa

Gierusz J (2010) Koszty i przychody w świetle nadrzędnych zasad rachunkowości. ODDK, Gdańsk

Janik W, Paździor M (2012) Rachunkowość zarządcza i controlling. Politechnika Lubelska, Lublin

Jaruga A, Nowak W, Szychta A (2001) Rachunkowość zarządcza, Społeczna Wyższa Szkoła Przedsiębiorczości i. Zarządzania, Łódź

Kaplan S (2006) The Demise of Cost and Profit Centers. http://www.hbs.edu/faculty/Publication%20Files/07-030.pdf

Leszczyński Z, Wnuk T (1999) Controlling, Fundacja Rozwoju Rachunkowości w Polsce, Warszawa

Nowak E (2009) Zaawansowana rachunkowość zarządcza. PWE, Warszawa

Nowak E (2011) Rachunkowość zarządcza w przedsiębiorstwie. CeDeWu, Warszawa

Piosik A (2006) Zasady rachunkowości zarządczej. PWN, Warszawa

Sobańska I (2003) Rachunek kosztów i rachunkowość zarządcza. C.H. Beck, Warszawa

Sobańska I (2009) Rachunek kosztów podejście operacyjne i strategiczne. C.H. Beck, Warszawa

Sojak S (2003) Rachunkowość zarządcza. Dom Organizatora, Toruń

Świderska G (2003) Rachunkowość zarządcza i rachunek kosztów. Diffin, Warszawa

Szydełko Ł (2002) Rachunek odpowiedzialności w strategicznych jednostkach biznesowych, Zeszyty Naukowe politechniki Rzeszowskiej, Nr 248, Rzeszów

Walther L (2017) http://www.principlesofaccounting.com/chapter22/chapter22.html

Wilkinson J (2013) Responsibility center. http://strategiccfo.com/wikicfo/responsibility-center/

Wnuk-Pel T (2011) Zastosowanie rachunku kosztów działań w przedsiębiorstwach w Polsce. Wydawnictwo Uniwersytetu Łódzkiego, Łódź

http://www.oxforddictionaries.com/definition/american_english/cost-center

The Use of Management Accounting Information in Non-financial Reporting and Interaction with Stakeholders of Public Companies

Alsu Ahmetshina, Venera Vagizova, and Roza Kaspina

Abstract Sustainability report informs of social, economic, and environmental aspects of a public company. Non-financial report is used as a management accounting tool of rational and prudent corporate strategy. This type of reporting helps businesses to establish effective engagement with stakeholders. Stakeholders are crucial to success of every project. The purpose of the study is to define factors gathered from management accounting information that may affect quality of stakeholder engagement. The article is devoted to several practical aspects of non-financial reporting in public companies. The authors analyze factors affecting quality of stakeholders' engagement and feedback on standards-based GRI; reveal the impact of the company's most important components of sustainable development; and identify internal and external benefits from sustainability report. It is true that non-financial report provides a better understanding of risks and opportunities for both management and stockholders, reducing costs, increasing efficiency, and improving reputation and brand loyalty. That also comes from the latest instructions sent to Russian Parliament by the President to prepare regimentation of non-financial information disclosure for large companies by the end of April 2017. The study results prove that sustainability report allows management to create feedback, improve company's reputation, and increase ratings. However, there are some problems to be solved.

Keywords Stakeholders • Management accounting • Non-financial reporting • Sustainability report

A. Ahmetshina (✉) • V. Vagizova
Kazan Federal University, High School of Business, Podluzhnaya 3a, Kazan, Russia
e-mail: alsoura@yandex.ru; venera.vagizova@mail.ru

R. Kaspina
Kazan Federal University, Institute of Management, Economics and Finance, Butlerova 4, Kazan, Russia
e-mail: rosakaspina@yandex.ru

D. Procházka (ed.), *The Impact of Globalization on International Finance and Accounting*, Springer Proceedings in Business and Economics,
https://doi.org/10.1007/978-3-319-68762-9_47

Introduction

Non-financial information includes important elements such as business model, strategy, sustainable development, human resources policy, and environmental safety. Investors and other stakeholders can recognize the ways of operating with this information (Kaspina 2015).

However, a small number of publications can be found that address the issue of using management accounting information in formation of sustainability report. Russian system of sustainability report has no literature that is dedicated to the problems of non-financial reporting. Nevertheless, there are still some interesting and relevant problems to be addressed.

Sustainability reports can help management of any company to better understand and measure economic, social, environmental, and governance performance. The company's administration can also set goals and manage strategy more efficiently (Kaspina et al. 2014a, b).

Stakeholders are important in the life cycle of any company. They may affect the company's policy and strategy and create the image. Therefore, competent system of interaction with stakeholders is necessary for any business (Kaspina et al. 2014a, b).

Nowadays, a variety of stakeholders uses all available information to be able to adopt different solutions. In order to meet the needs of economic agents, many companies regularly publish non-financial information in addition to the financial information.

The purpose of the study is to investigate the essence of management accounting non-financial information in integrated reporting of economic entities along with the problems and challenges related to interaction with stakeholders. In addition, we determine the feasibility of sustainability reports formation.

Data and Methodology

Building trust in business is the basis of achieving a sustainable development of the world economy. Nowadays various kinds of management decisions have direct impacts on stakeholders, such as financial institutions, labor organizations, civil society, and citizens. These decisions are based on financial and non-financial information. Management assesses risks and opportunities using information on a wide variety of current and future issues (Nurmuhametov et al. 2014).

Non-financial reporting includes information about company's sustainability challenges and impacts on the environment. It encompasses strategies, key performance indicators, results, and future goals. Usually sustainability report is presented by top management in accordance with the principles established at the Global Reporting Initiative (GRI).

This reporting shows the interdependence of social, economic, and environmental factors. Non-financial report also has a moral part – the need to focus on charity and helping the poor, sick, and homeless. With the help of sustainability report, businesses demonstrate their care about the environment, social orientation, and economic policy (Kaspina 2015).

Problems of Sustainability Report

The main problem of this study is the issue of weak discussion practices of non-financial information and perspectives of social responsibility in the community.

Along with this, the most urgent problem is management's desire to create a positive image in spite of business problems. Thus, the company idealizes its activities and system functioning. So information transparency disappears, the accuracy of the data is lost. Disclosure of company's activity fails to be true (Kaspina et al. 2015).

Because management is free to define the indicators of performance measuring, companies face the problem of comparability of information provided.

CEOs are confident that integrated reports serve to achieve great goals. First of all, as it contains information about system of management and social responsibility to employees, sustainability report allows companies to create the image of an attractive employer.

This report is a good management tool for public communication; it provides an opportunity to talk with the company's stakeholders. In addition, integrated report helps management focus on the main activities and purposes.

Results and Discussion

Stakeholders are crucial to any company, and effective management is vital to the business success in their eyes. Efficiency of any project directly depends on the stakeholder's management.

To become a successful participant in the market, companies need to meet the interests of stakeholders and take into account their comments and suggestions. In order to become competitive, management tries to establish a quality system of stakeholder engagement (through personal meetings, video and audio translation of financial statements, publication of information products, presentations, and conferences) (Kaspina and Shneydman 2013).

The list of company's stakeholders can be significant. Therefore, management should structure them according to their influence and interest to control stakeholders by groups (Fig. 1).

Source: authorial view

Fig. 1 Major providers of sustainability reporting guidance (Source: Authorial view)

Fig. 2 The power-interest relationship with stakeholders (Source: Authorial view)

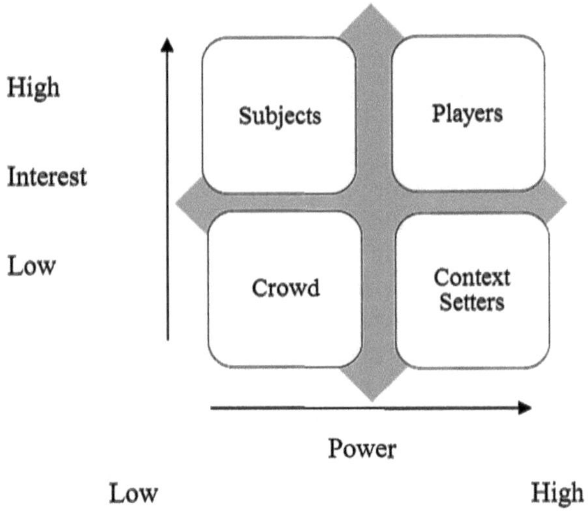

Source: authorial view

In accordance with Fig. 2, the influence is an ability to control or affect the actions, beliefs, and attitudes of other people. Interest is the state of being responsible, affected, involved, concerned, attentive, and curious.

In addition, another classification can be defined by the level of company's project support. Assessment of people's motivation can be based on these categories: allies, supporters, neutral, reluctant, and opponents.

Suppose that the quality of interaction of companies with stakeholders depends on several factors, such as security, quality of website information, and quality non-financial information assessment report.

In order to investigate the impact of these factors on the quality of interaction with stakeholders in details, we used the statistical program "Gretl" and built a

Table 1 The correlation matrix

X1	X2	X3	Y	
1.0000	0.3725	−0.0461	0.6277	X1
	1.0000	0.0269	0.7186	X2
		1.0000	0.3141	X3
			1.0000	Y

Source: author's calculations based on statistical program "Gretl"
Note: 5% critical values (two-sided) = 0.4329 for n = 21

correlation matrix. The study was conducted on the basis of 21 public companies. The correlation matrix is shown in Table 1.

The dependent variable (y) is the quality of interaction between public companies and stakeholders. Factors that influence the result variable are guaranteed security of a public company (x1), quality of the information on a public company website (x2), and quality non-financial information assessment report (x3).

The most important is the correlation coefficient between x1 (guarantee security of a public company) and x2 (quality of information on a public company's website).

With the classical method of least squares, we estimated parameters of the model "Cooperation with stakeholders." The results of the multiple regression are presented in Tables 2 and 3.

Excluding the constant, the largest P-value obtained for x3 (quality non-financial information assessment report). Since the P-value of each factor is less than 0.01, the model is acceptable.

The coefficient of determination equals 0.768596, which is considered to be high.

$$\begin{array}{c} y = -1.59 + 0.387^{*}x1 + 0.562^{*}x2 + 0.407^{*}x3, \\ (0.850)\ \ (0.111)\ \ (0.129)\ \ (0.149) \end{array} \quad (1)$$

where n = 21 and R-square = 0.769. In parentheses, there are the standard errors.

All regression coefficients in the resulting equation are statistically significant.

Checking availability heteroscedasticity in the model, using the test White (White). Null hypothesis: there is no heteroscedasticity.

Test statistics: LM = 21
P-value = P (chi-square (7) > 21) = 0.00377015

The test results show no white heteroscedasticity.

The resulting model of the study is solid as all the regression coefficients are statistically significant, and the coefficient of determination is high. In the model, there is no heteroscedasticity.

According to the results of the study, the hypothesis was confirmed. The quality of the interaction of companies with stakeholders depends on several factors, such as the guarantee of the security of the company, quality of the company's website and information, and quality non-financial information assessment report.

Table 2 The results of multiple regression

Variable	Coefficient	The statistical error	t-statistic	P-value	
Const	−1.59119	0.850371	−1.871	0.0786	*
X1	0.386784	0.110993	3.485	0.0028	***
X2	0.562115	0.129458	4.342	0.0004	***
X3	0.407048	0.148926	2.733	0.0142	**

Source: author's calculations based on statistical program "Gretl"

Table 3 The parameters of multiple regression

The model parameters	Value	The model parameters	Value
The average value of dependent variable	4.047619	The statistical deviation of dependent variable	0.589592
The sum of square residues	1.608811	The statistical error model	0.307630
R-squared	0.768596	Revised R-squared	0.727760
F(3, 17)	18.82150	P-value(F)	0.000012
Log-likelihood	−2.822922	Akaike criterion	13.64584
Schwartz criterion	17.82393	Henna-Quinn criterion	14.55260

Source: author's calculations based on statistical program "Gretl"

Conclusion

Summing up the results, sustainable development of the company integrates economic, social, and environmental management factors, lowers business risks, strengthens competitiveness, and improves the efficiency of staff and customer loyalty as well as company's reputation. Sustainability reports make a positive contribution to business community, economic, and social development of regions.

However, studies on this issue are still ongoing. It is obvious, that the level of practical experience exchange and expertise in this area is not sufficiently developed. Therefore, there are several problems yet to be solved. As mentioned earlier, the issue of comparability of data is one of the majors. It can be solved by comparing provided management information with the GRI standards. Increased attention in media, as well as creating additional opportunities to learn best practices, methodologies and international experience can greatly improve the quality of social reporting.

From the results of our research, it is possible to conclude that management, missing sustainability report, leads their companies to negative consequences. The activities of such companies are less transparent than their competitors; they may gain lagging reputation, even if it's not true.

In our future research, we intend to concentrate on practical aspects of sustainability report formation. Future work will involve the analysis of the domestic and foreign companies' sustainability reports.

References

Kaspina R (2015) Continuing professional development of accounting and auditing: Russian experience and challenges. Procedia - social and behavioral sciences, pp 550–553. ERPA International Congress on Education, ERPA Congress 2015, Istanbul

Kaspina R, Molotov L (2016) Corporate integrated reporting: an efficient tool of economic security management. Acad Strateg Manag J 15(Is.SpecialIssue1):225–232

Kaspina R, Shneydman L (2013) New approach to the oil companies' corporate reporting. Neftyanoe Khozyaistvo. Oil Industry. No. 9, pp 14-17

Kaspina R, Khapugina L, Zakirov E (2014a) Interrelation of Company's business model structure and information disclosed in management reporting. Life Sci J 11(12):778–780

Kaspina R, Molotov L, Kaspin L (2014b) Fuzzy forecasting of the cash flow statement based on accounting data. Mediterr J Soc Sci 5(24):237–241

Kaspina R, Molotov L, Kaspin L (2015) Cash flow forecasting as an element of integrated reporting: an empirical study. Asian Soc Sci 11(11):89–94

Nurmuhametov I, Kaspina R, Davletshina N (2014) Revising the application of the ABC system in the packaging industry companies. Mediterr J Soc Sci 5(24):231–236

The First and the Second Generation of Statistical Methods in Management Accounting Research

Ladislav Šiška

Abstract Calls for more frequent application of the second-generation statistical methods such as structural equation modeling (SEM) have emerged in the field of management accounting recently. The aim of this article is to compare these statistical methods to the first-generation methods using the real-life example. Specifically, the relationship between the organizational capabilities and perceived nonfinancial performance is investigated. Firstly, the sequential combination of principal component analysis and regression analysis is deployed to the outlined case example. Secondly, partial least squares structural equation modeling (PLS-SEM) is applied to the case example. The comparison of both approaches proves SEM to be more vigilant statistical method for capturing the strength of relationship between latent constructs.

Keywords Management accounting • Nonfinancial performance • Factor analysis • Regression analysis • Structural equation modeling

Introduction

According to Fornell (1982), there are two generations of statistical methods. The first generation covers methods such as multiple regression, logistic regression, and analysis of variance but also techniques focusing on exploration and dimension reduction such as exploratory factor analysis, cluster analysis, or multidimensional scaling. The second generation of statistical methods has been developed in the 1980s, and a typical example of these methods is structural equation modeling (SEM). In addition to the first-generation statistical methods, the second-generation methods account for measurement errors when measuring some abstract concepts (hereinafter "latent constructs" or just "constructs"), e.g., the overall performance. Measurement errors are those parts of the observed variables (hereinafter

L. Šiška (✉)
Masaryk university, Faculty of Economics and Administration, Department of Corporate Economy, Lipová 41A, 602 00 Brno, Czech Republic
e-mail: ladislav.siska@econ.muni.cz

D. Procházka (ed.), *The Impact of Globalization on International Finance and Accounting*, Springer Proceedings in Business and Economics,
https://doi.org/10.1007/978-3-319-68762-9_48

"indicators") that are measuring something other than what the latent constructs are hypothesized to measure. Measurement errors arise due to a choice of inappropriate set of indicators, errors in data entry, inconsistent interpretation of questions by researcher and by respondent, etc. Therefore, SEM analysis consists of two stages: Firstly, the reliability and validity of the measurement model must be assessed to exclude the risk of excessive measurement errors. After that, the second stage continues with structural model estimation.

Calls for more frequent application of the second-generation statistical methods have emerged in the field of management accounting research recently. One of the first examples of these calls was the influential article by Chenhall (2003) followed by Smith and Langfield-Smith (2004) and Lee et al. (2011). The number of articles has risen from then. Figure 1 documents the increase in counts of studies published in top management accounting studies and using PLS-SEM, the variance-based branch of the SEM approaches.

The objective of this article is to compare the first- and second-generation statistical methods. Instead of the theoretical demonstration, the real-life data from our own survey are used for comparison so that researches contemplating the use of statistics can see the differences. Specifically, the relationship between the organizational capabilities and perceived nonfinancial performance is investigated. Firstly, the sequential combination of principal component analysis and regression analysis is deployed to the outlined real-life data. Secondly, PLS-SEM is applied to the case example. After that, the findings of both approaches are compared.

Data and Methodology

The goal of our research study, which we have selected for this comparison of statistical methods, was to predict the perceived nonfinancial performance (hereinafter *NonFin Performance*) from the level of stakeholder organizational capabilities (hereinafter *Stakeholder Capabilities*). In order to achieve the goal, the study deployed a web-based survey. The outlined relationship was part of the larger network of hypothesized relationships connecting the use of management accounting tools to the consequences in capabilities and performance. That was why, respondents were asked many questions, but just subset of two batteries of questions will be presented here for the purpose of the comparison. The data stem from companies with more than ten employees. The respondents were from companies domiciled in the Czechia (the majority of 77%) and Slovakia. A total of 101 answers was gathered during the period from December 2015 to February 2016. The count of top managers or owners amounted to 45 and middle managers to 45, and 11 respondents were without managerial rank. The number of standalone companies was 53, and the remainder reported to be part of a group of companies.

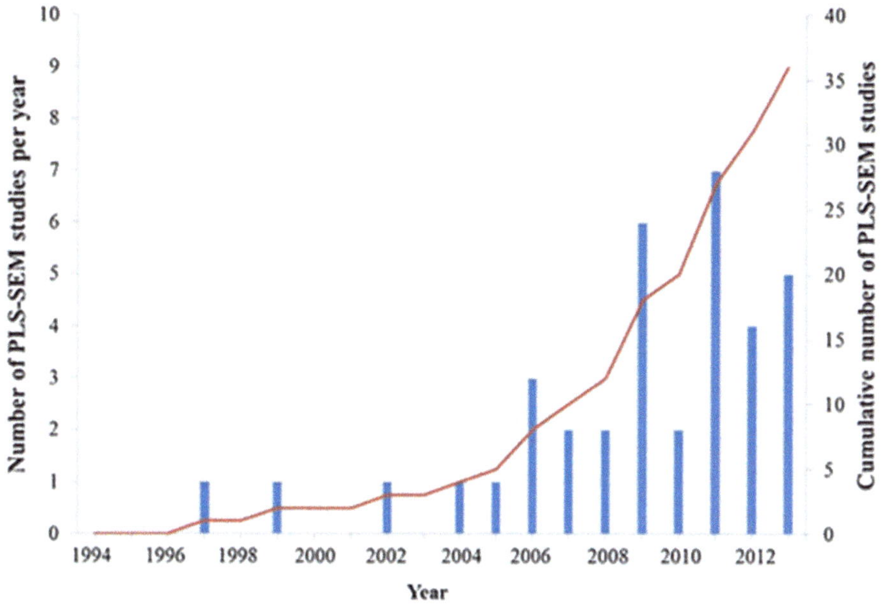

Source: Nitzl (2016, p. 22)

Fig. 1 PLS-SEM studies in management accounting research (Source: Nitzl 2016, p. 22)

Measurement of Constructs

The construct of *Stakeholder Capabilities* is not measurable directly because it is too abstract, each respondent imagines such broad concept differently, and the answers would result in inconsistent outcomes. That was why the whole battery of questions had to be asked. Our battery was inspired by Koufteros et al. (2014). The respondents were asked to rate on the scale "0 = not at all ...10 = totally" whether the management accounting tools deployed by their company:

- (q28f) "Improve the overall company's leadership in the market."
- (q28h) "Improve relationship with customers/clients."
- (q28i) "Increase motivation and commitment of our employees."

Similarly, the *NonFin Performance* construct was measured by question developed by Cadez and Guilding (2008) who asked "Indicate your company's performance relative to its competitors in the following criteria." The respondents were offered the scale ranging from "0=our company totally lacks behind its competitors" to "10=our company is the best of all its competitors" to evaluate:

- (q30j) "Customer satisfaction"
- (q30l) "Quality of products/services"
- (q30n) "Employee satisfaction"

The First-Generation Statistical Procedures Applied

A linear regression analysis suits the goal to predict performance through capabilities levels. Before regressing *NonFin Performance* on *Stakeholder Capabilities*, both constructs had to be extracted from the batteries of questions, which is the task for factor analysis. In other words, the factor analysis was applied first to derive the constructs and then the extracted constructs entered a linear regression model. The listwise deletion was the applied handling of missing values. The statistical package IBM SPSS Statistics version 23 was used for data processing.

"In factor analysis, the variates [constructs] are formed to maximize their explanation of the entire variable set, not to predict a dependent variable(s). The goal of data summarization is achieved by defining a small number of factors that adequately represent the original set of variables." (Hair 2014, p. 96) In our case just the first factor was used to represent each construct. The principal component analysis (PCA) was the method applied for extraction. The Kaiser-Meyer-Olkin measure reported 0.703 which means that sample was adequate or middling according to Hutcheson and Sofroniou (1999). Table 1 presents the rotated factor loadings for both constructs after varimax rotation method. In bold, there are loadings of the questions on their construct. The cross loadings (without emphasizing) on the other construct were lower than commonly accepted threshold 0.3 indicating that each question belongs to just one construct.

Both factors (constructs) explained 71% of the total variance in underlying answers to the questions.

After the outlined verification that the question form only their appropriate construct and not the other, the final constructs for regression analysis were extracted from separate PCAs as the first component. That is why the factor loadings in Tables 1 and 2 differ. The construct of *Stakeholder Capabilities* explained 74.38% of variance of the underlying questions, and *NonFin Performance* explained 65.82% of variance. The factor scores for each construct were derived by regression method.

The next step was the parameter estimation of the following regression model

$$NonFin\ Performance_i = a + b \times Stakeholder\ Capabilities_i + e_i \qquad (1)$$

where $NonFin\ Performance_i$ represents the factor scores for the named construct, a and b are the estimated parameters by ordinary least square (OLS) method, $Stakeholder\ Capabilities_i$ denote the factor scores for the named construct, and e_i means residuals.

Table 1 Factor loadings in rotated component matrix

Question	Stakeholder Capabilities	NonFin Performance
(q28f)	.844	.106
(q28h)	.901	.013
(q28i)	.802	.204
(q30j)	.106	.837
(q30l)	.263	.833
(q30n)	-.017	.701

Source: Author's computation in SPSS based on own survey data

Table 2 Final factor loadings of the constructs

Question	Stakeholder capabilities	NonFin performance
(q28f)	0.842	
(q28h)	0.894	
(q28i)	0.851	
(q30j)		0.865
(q30l)		0.880
(q30n)		0.673

Source: Author's computation in SPSS based on own survey data

The Second-Generation Statistical Procedures Applied

PLS-SEM was realized in SmartPLS ver. 3.2.6 (Ringle et al. 2015). To be comparable with the first-generation procedure, the listwise deletion was applied. The resulting model is presented and commented in the next section.

Before the model interpretation, the measurement reliability and validity were assessed. Composite reliability 0.835 and 0.896 for constructs *Stakeholder Capabilities* and *NonFin Performance*, respectively, correspondents to the recommendations by Hair (2017), "values between 0.70 and 0.90 can be regarded as satisfactory" (p. 102). The main indicators for convergent validity were the outer loadings greater than 0.7 (Lee et al. 2011) and average variance explained (AVE) values greater than 0.50 indicating that the construct explains more than half of the variance of the underlying questions. These assumptions were met with the only exception of indicator (q30n) as documented in Fig. 2. Because this indicator was found statistically significant and theoretically important, I did not exclude it. The Fornell-Larcker criterion and the indicators' loadings on the construct greater than all its cross loadings with other constructs both confirmed the discrimination validity of the constructs used in this study.

Coefficients[a]

Model		Unstandardized Coefficients B	Unstandardized Coefficients Std. Error	Standardized Coefficients Beta	t	Sig.
1	(Constant)	-,011	,097		-,115	,909
	Capabilities_PCA	,266	,097	,275	2,732	,008

a. Dependent Variable: NonFin_PCA

Source: Author's computation in SPSS based on own survey data.
Note: Dependent variable was NonFin Performance construct.

Fig. 2 Coefficients of the resulting regression model. Note: Dependent variable was NonFin Performance construct (Source: Author's computation in SPSS based on own survey data)

Results and Discussion

The results are presented in separate two subsections. The third subsection provides discussion.

Factor and Regression Analyses (The First-Generation Methods)

The first step consisting of constructs derivation resulted in factor loadings presented in Table 2. The comparison with Table 1 reveals that the final separate principle component analysis resulted in more balanced representation of the questions and that the second separate PCA derived question (q30l) to be slightly more dominant than (q30j).

The parameters of the subsequent regression model using the factor scores of the constructs are presented in Fig. 2. The resulting model explained (R^2) 7.6% of variance in dependent variable *NonFin Performance*. This finding corresponds to the square of standardized coefficient beta in Fig. 2. The same figure also reveals that the constant was found statistically insignificant, but the regression coefficient was statistically significant. Due to non-normality, this was verified by bootstrapping, and BCa 95% confidence interval ranging from 0.068 to 0.457 did not contain zero.

PLS-SEM Findings (The Second-Generation Method)

The PLS-SEM algorithm applied in SmartPLS software produced parameter estimates shown in Fig. 3. The constructs are represented by circles and the observed questions in rectangles. The number in gray circle of the construct *NonFin*

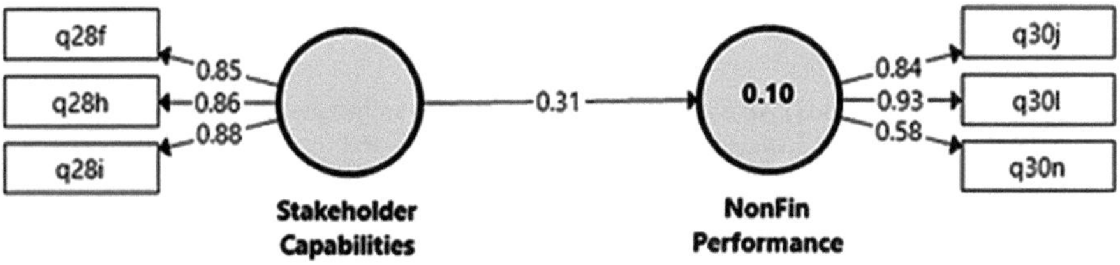

Source: Author's computation in SmartPLS based on own survey data

Fig. 3 Resulting PLS-SEM model (Source: Author's computation in SmartPLS based on own survey data)

Performance is R^2. Numbers overlapping arrows are factor loadings and standardized regression coefficient in case of the arrow between constructs.

Discussion

The comparison of R^2 (coefficient of determination) in the final regression models indicates that the PLS-SEM was slightly more successful in explaining variance of the construct *NonFin Performance* than the two-step application of the traditional methods from the first generation of statistical methods.

Higher R^2 is the consequence of the more favorable construction (the factor loadings) of the constructs in PLS-SEM approach, which in many iterations adjusts the initial factor loadings to get the best estimates as possible.

Conclusion

The aim of this article was to compare the first- and the second-generation methods. Their application on real-life example of regression between stakeholder capabilities and nonfinancial performance shows that both generations of statistical methods provide comparable results when modeling the same reality. The more detailed view of results proves the second-generation PLS-SEM to be more vigilant statistical method for capturing the strength of relationship between latent constructs. The attractive, almost self-explaining depiction of the model is another advantage in favor of the PLS-SEM.

Acknowledgments This paper has been prepared within the research project no. MUNI/A/1001/2016 and the subsidy for development of institutional research of Masaryk University.

References

Cadez S, Guilding C (2008) An exploratory investigation of an integrated contingency model of strategic management accounting. Acc Organ Soc 33:836–863. https://doi.org/10.1016/j.aos.2008.01.003

Chenhall RH (2003) Management control systems design within its organizational context: findings from contingency-based research and directions for the future. Acc Organ Soc 28:127–168. https://doi.org/10.1016/S0361-3682(01)00027-7

Fornell C (ed) (1982) A second generation of multivariate analysis, volume 1: methods. Praeger, New York

Hair JF (ed) (2017) A primer on partial least squares structural equation modeling (PLS-SEM), 2nd edn. Sage, Los Angeles

Hair JF (ed) (2014) Multivariate data analysis, 7th edn, Pearson new internat. ed. Pearson custom library. Pearson, Harlow

Hutcheson G, Sofroniou N (1999) The multivariate social scientist: introductory statistics using generalized linear models. Sage, Thousand Oaks

Koufteros, X., Verghese, A. (John), Lucianetti, L., 2014. The effect of performance measurement systems on firm performance: a cross-sectional and a longitudinal study. J Oper Manag 32, 313–336. doi:https://doi.org/10.1016/j.jom.2014.06.003

Lee L, Petter S, Fayard D, Robinson S (2011) On the use of partial least squares path modeling in accounting research. Int J Account Inf Syst 12:305–328. https://doi.org/10.1016/j.accinf.2011.05.002

Nitzl C (2016) The use of partial least squares structural equation modelling (PLS-SEM) in management accounting research: directions for future theory development. J Account Lit 37:19–35. https://doi.org/10.1016/j.acclit.2016.09.003

Ringle CM, Wende S, Becker J-M (2015) SmartPLS 3. SmartPLS GmbH

Smith D, Langfield-Smith K (2004) Structural equation modeling in management accounting research: critical analysis and opportunities. J Account Lit 23:49

Estimation of Housing Demand with Adaptive Neuro-Fuzzy Inference Systems (ANFIS)

Olgun Aydin and Elvan Aktürk Hayat

Abstract It has always been important to anticipate the demand for a product. To determine the demand for any product, the parameters such as the economic situation and the demands of the rival products are used generally. Especially in the housing sector, which is the locomotive sector for emerging countries, it is critical to anticipate housing demand and its relationship with economic variables. Because of that, economists, real estate developers, banks, development and economy ministers, and land registry cadastral directorates of the countries have focused on explaining housing demand with economic variables. Therefore, the existence of effective model for prediction is very crucial for policy makers in the sector. For these reasons, the aim of this study is estimating housing demand based on relationship between housing sales transactions and important financial indicators using adaptive neuro-fuzzy inference system (ANFIS).

Keywords Housing demand • ANFIS • Demand estimation • Real estates

Introduction

There are many factors affecting the demand of a product, mainly the type of product. Factors affecting the demand for a product in general terms can be listed as product price, other product prices (related products), consumer income level, consumer wealth, and consumer pleasure and preferences (Case et al. 1999).

Housing demand is a concept with demographic, sociopsychological content. The demand for housing is affected by the incomes of individuals, prices, additions, pleasures, and preferences, as well as the prices of complementary and substitute goods as well as the demands of other goods and services.

O. Aydin (✉)
Mimar Sinan University, Institute of Science, Istanbul, Turkey
e-mail: olgun.aydin@ogr.msgsu.edu.tr

E.A. Hayat
Adnan Menderes University, Faculty of Economics, Aydın, Turkey
e-mail: elvanakturk@gmail.com

D. Procházka (ed.), *The Impact of Globalization on International Finance and Accounting*, Springer Proceedings in Business and Economics,
https://doi.org/10.1007/978-3-319-68762-9_49

Housing market is important for the economy and plays a crucial role in the business cycle dynamics and generally follows different patterns in different regions. Recently, Leamer (2007) strongly argued that housing is the business cycle, indicating "any attempt to control the business cycle needs to focus especially on residential investment." (Balcılar 2012). Therefore, models that forecast house price movements can provide policy makers with valuable information on future movements in economic activity and help them better policy design and control.

However, there are many factors that can affect housing demand due to nonlinear structure of macroeconomic variables, which makes it difficult to predict. In recent years, more advanced nonlinear modeling techniques such as ANN and fuzzy inference systems (FIS) have emerged as effective techniques to overcome for these difficulties. Furthermore, a neuro-fuzzy system is defined as a combination of ANN and FIS in such a way that neural network learning algorithm is used to determine the parameters of FIS. Adaptive neuro-fuzzy inference system (ANFIS) is a system that belongs to neuro-fuzzy category (Jang 1993).

This paper contains some empirical contributions that ANFIS model developed by Jang (1993) was used to estimate housing demand. ANFIS has been implemented in many scientific fields such as energy, stock market, robotic applications, and many others. This is the first time that this methodology is used to measure relationship between housing demand and macroeconomic variables. ANFIS approach has many advantages. It doesn't depend on assumptions about the data, it has good predictability capabilities, and more effective estimate can be made by including linguistic terms.

The paper is organized as follows. We review the theoretical and empirical literature relevant for our study in the next section. Section "Data and Methodology" describes the data and method. Section "Results" presents application results, and the final section gives concluding remark.

Literature Review

The strong relationship between housing markets and economic activity has been provided in studies of different researchers so far (e.g., Green 1997; Iacoviello 2005; Case et al. 2005; Leamer 2007; Christensen et al. 2009; Pavlidis et al. 2009; Iacoviello and Neri 2010). Iacoviello (2005) and Iacoviello and Neri (2010) found a strong linkage between economic activity and the residential market in the USA through dynamic stochastic general equilibrium models (DSGE) to study this relationship. Christensen et al. (2009) estimate the model to determine or quantify the links between consumption and house prices in Canada with Canadian data using Bayesian methods. Brooks and Tsolacos (2001) find that unexpected inflation and the interest rate term spread have explanatory powers for the UK property market by using a VAR model on filtered real estate returns, property returns series, and a range of economic and financial factors. Most of housing prices forecasting models use multiple regression analysis (MRA) methodologies. However, it is difficult to map multi-attribute nonlinear relationships using regression analysis. In literature, there are many models based on NN that successfully captures the nonlinearities. More recently, the NN models and hedonic pricing models have also been used to identify the real estate price and housing properties. Tay and Ho (1992) employed and compared the neural networks technique and regression analysis using sample of data from residential apartment properties in Singapore. They reported an error mean of 3.9% compared to 7.5% for the regression method. Do and Grudnitski (1992) note that NN model resulted in having almost twice the number of predicted values within 5% of the actual sales price than their regression model had predicted (40% vs. 20%) on a test sample of 105 houses. They concluded that the neural network model performs better than a multiple regression model for estimating the value of US residential property. Limsombunchai et al. (2004) empirically compare the predictive power of the hedonic model with an ANN model on house price prediction using a sample of 200 houses in Christchurch, New Zealand. Their study shows that ANN model can overcome some of the problems related to the data patterns and better prediction result when compared with the hedonic model.

A few of studies have been carried out to predict real estate prices using fuzzy logic and ANFIS. Gonzalez M. et al. (2006) compared fuzzy logic and MRA models and revealed that fuzzy logic can handle the uncertainty in the real estate market and give better estimates than conventional methods. Guan et al. (2008) explore the use of ANFIS to assess real estate property values and the sales of houses in the Midwest region of the USA and also compare the results of ANFIS and regression models. They showed that ANFIS can yield results that are comparable to those obtained using the traditional regression approach and hence can be considered as a viable approach in real estate value assessment.

Data and Methodology

In this study, total daily housing sales in Dubai are used as a dependent variable. The Dubai Federal Market Overview Index (DFMGI), crude oil price based on US dollar, and gold price per troy ounce based on AED are used as independent variables. Daily total sales of housing are obtained from the Dubai Statistics Center. DFMGI, crude oil price, gold price data are obtained from Investing.com website. The data set used includes observations from time interval October 7, 2013, to October 5, 2015. To estimate housing demand, relationship between DFMGI, crude oil price based on US dollar, gold price per troy ounce based on AED, and total daily housing sales in Dubai is modeled by using ANFIS.

Adaptive neuro-fuzzy inference system (ANFIS) utilizes a hybrid learning algorithm which includes a combination of the least-squares and backpropagation gradient descent methods. ANFIS is a multilayer neural network-based fuzzy including layers where the training and forecasted values exposed through the input and output nodes operating as membership functions (MFs) and rules are presented in the hidden layers. The base of the ANFIS method is the Takagi-Sugeno-Kang fuzzy inference system (FIS). Jang (1993) developed the ANFIS method and used it in modeling nonlinear functions, determining nonlinear components in the control system, and predicting chaotic time series.

The ANFIS model is built based on Sugeno-type fuzzy inference system, in which every rule adopts the following form:

$$\begin{aligned}&IF\ x_1\ is\ A_{1j}\ AND\ x_2\ is\ A_{2j}\ldots AND\ x_n\ is\ A_{nj}\\&THEN\ y = c_0 + c_1x_1 + c_2x_2 + \ldots + c_nx_n\end{aligned} \tag{1}$$

where A_{ij} is the fuzzy set corresponding to the jth linguistic term of the ith variable, n is the number of input variables, y is the predicted value of the dependent variable, and c_i denotes the consequent parameters whose values are derived from the training process. Figure 1 shows the basic structure of the ANFIS model.

In the first layer in Fig. 1, the values of A_i and B_i represent linguistic variables. The values of A_i and B_i are determined by means of a membership function, taking their grades. In the second layer, the inputs are multiplied from the knot. The ignition power values in the third layer are total ignition normalized by proportioning to power values. After the fourth layer, Takagi-Sugeno-Kang model is operated. In Takagi-Sugeno-Kang (TSK) inference method, the output variable is a fixed number, or variable bound polynomial function is defined. The output value in the TSK model is calculated by the average weight model (Babuska 2001) as shown in Eq. 2.

$$x_0 = \frac{\sum a_i x_i}{\sum a_i} \tag{2}$$

ANFIS uses backpropagation learning algorithm to determine the input membership function parameters and the least mean square method to determine the consequents parameters. Each step of the iterative learning algorithm has two parts. In the first part, the input patterns are propagated, and the parameters of the consequents are calculated using the iterative minimum squared method algorithm, while the parameters of the premises are considered fixed. In the second part, the input patterns are propagated again, and in each iteration, the learning algorithm backpropagation is used to modify the parameters of the premises, while the consequents remain fixed.

Results

Before proceeding with ANFIS model, the outliers detected and moved out from the data set. After that, the independent variables, which are the Dubai Federal Market Overview Index (DFMGI), crude oil price based on US dollar, and gold

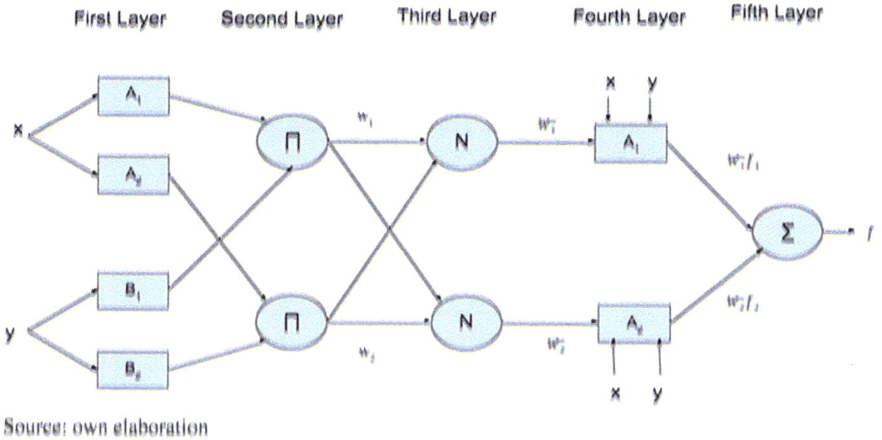

Fig. 1 Basic structure of the ANFIS (Source: Own elaboration)

price per troy ounce based on AED, are normalized and moved to the same range. The summary statistics of the final dataset which is used in this study is shown in Table 1.

In ANFIS modeling, to start the ANFIS model, linguistic terms have to be defined. Three linguistic terms as "high," "medium," and "low" are used for this study. According to five layered fundamental Takagi-Sugeno-Kang inference method, ANFIS structure is built. All of the calculation have been made by the aid of very well-organized R package "fuzzy rule-based systems for classification and regression tasks" called "frbs(v3.1–0)," which was created by Riza et al. (2015).

In this study, data set is divided randomly into two parts as train set and test set. Seventy percent of the data set is used as train set, and the remaining parts of the data set are used as test set. Maximum iteration is defined as 10, and step size is defined as 0.005. Triangle, trapezoid, Gaussian, sigmoid, and bell membership functions are used for five different ANFIS models and compared rooted mean square errors (RMSE) of the models to define the most efficient one.

According to Table 2, it could be said that the ANFIS model with trapezoidal fuzzy membership function is the most efficient model among the other ones.

Predicted values and observed (real) values could be clearly analyzed with Fig. 2. The results in Fig. 2 also support the results shown in Table 1.

Conclusion

The housing sector is more affected by macroeconomic variables relative to developed countries in emerging countries. For this reason, many institutions have carefully followed macroeconomic variables to estimate housing sales, and

Table 1 Summary statistics

Statistics	FMGI close	Gold price UAE	Oil price USD	Dubai housing sales
Min	2993	3970	40.47	3
1st quarter	3812	4344	54.86	34
Median	4106	4488	77.11	45
3rd quarter	4610	4734	99.48	58
Max	5374	5080	107.26	118

Table 2 RMSE of the models using different types of membership functions

Membership function used in models	RMSE
Triangle	0.02144813
Trapezoid	0.01873034
Gaussian	0.02126808
Sigmoid	0.02226681
Bell	0.0256319

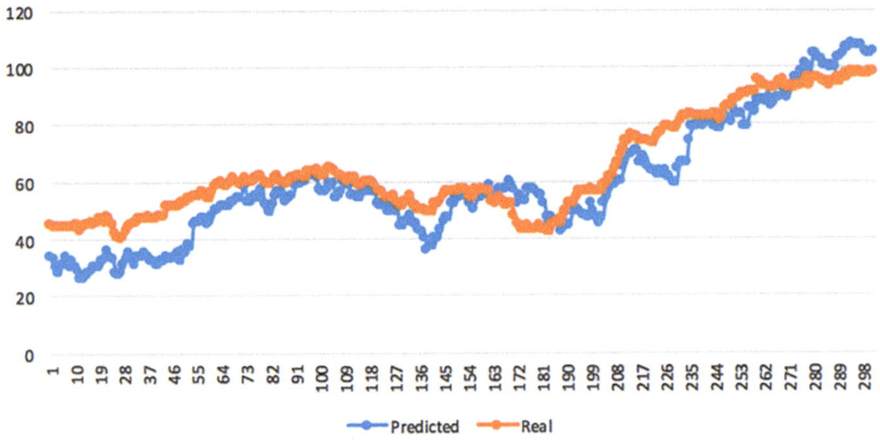

Fig. 2 Predicted and real values

their strategies determine accordingly. An accurate prediction of real property price is important to prospective owners, developers, investors, appraisers, tax assessors, and other real estate market stakeholders. For example, banks are planning mortgage strategies by analyzing economic developments. Housing constructing companies are closely monitoring the market to determine if there is a right time for new housing projects and to determine possible campaign strategies for stocks in their hands. Models developed by traditional methods for predicting housing demand with economic variables and may not include all variables due to some assumptions. In addition, these methods are inadequate to capture the underlying nonlinear relationships between the variables. More advanced nonlinear modeling techniques such as ANFIS provide an accurate and qualitative prediction.

This study showed that the ANFIS method could be used in estimating the housing demand with macroeconomic variables. According to the result of the study, while FMGI decreased by 0.01%, while gold prices increased by 0.09%, and while oil price decreased by 2.5%, it could be said that there will be a decrease of 2.94% in housing demand.

References

Babuska R (2001) Fuzzy and neural control (lecture notes). Delft University of Technology, Delft ftp://ftp.unicauca.edu.co/Facultades/FIET/

Balcılar M, Gupta R, Miller SM (2012) The out-of-sample forecasting performance of non-linear models of regional housing prices in the US. University of Pretoria Department of Economics WP Series No:26

Brooks C, Tsolacos S (2001) International evidence on the predictability of prices of securitised real estate assets: econometric models versus neural networks, ISMA Centre Discussion Papers in Finance 2001–08

Case KE, Fair RC (1999) Principles of microeconomics, 5th edn. Prentice Hall, Upper Saddle River

Case K, Shiller R, Quigley J (2005) Comparing wealth effects: the stock market versus the housing market. Adv Macroecon 5(1):32. https://doi.org/10.2202/1534-6013.1235

Christensen I, Corrigan P, Mendicino C, Nishiyama S-I (2009) Consumption, housing collateral, and the canadian business cycle. Bank of Canada, Ottawa. WP 2009–26

Do AQ, Grudnitski G (1992) A neural network approach to residential property appraisal. The Real Estate Appraiser 58(3):38–45

Green RK (1997) Follow the leader: how changes in residential and non-residential investment predict changes in GDP. Real Estate Econ 25:253–270. https://doi.org/10.1111/1540-6229.00714

Gonzalez MAS, Formoso CT (2006) Mass appraisal with genetic fuzzy rule-based systems. Prop Manag 24(1):20–30. https://doi.org/10.1108/02637470610643092

Guan J, Zurada J, Levitan AS (2008) An adaptive neuro-fuzzy inference system based approach to real estate property assessment. JRER 30(4):395–421

Iacoviello M (2005) House prices, borrowing constraints, and monetary policy in the business cycle. Am Econ Rev 95(3):739–764. https://doi.org/10.1257/0002828054201477

Iacoviello M, Neri S (2010) Housing market spillovers: evidence from an estimated DSGE model. Am Econ J Macroecon 2(2):125–164. https://doi.org/10.1257/mac.2.2.125

Jang J-SR (1993) ANFIS: adaptive-network-based fuzzy inference system. IEEE Trans Syst Man Cybern 23(3):665–685. https://doi.org/10.1109/21.256541

Leamer EE (2007) Housing is the business cycle. Proceedings – economic policy symposium – Jackson Hole, Federal Reserve Bank of Kansas City, p. 149–233. doi:https://doi.org/10.3386/w13428

Limsombunchai V, Gan C, Lee M (2004) House price prediction: hedonic price model vs. artificial neural network. Am J Appl Sci 1(3):193–201. https://doi.org/10.3844/ajassp.2004.193.201

Pavlidis E, Paya I, Peel D, Spiru A (2009) Bubbles in house prices and their impact on consumption: evidence for the US. Lancaster University Department of Economics working paper 2009/025

Riza LS, Bergmeir C, Herrera F, Benitez JM (2015) Frbs: fuzzy rule-based systems for classification and regression in R. J Stat Softw 65(6):1–30. 10.18637/jss.v065.i06

Tay DPH, Ho DKH (1992) Artificial intelligence and the mass appraisal of residential apartments. J Prop Valuat Invest 10(2):525–540. https://doi.org/10.1108/14635789210031181

Corporate Tax as an Instrument of Tax Competition Among the EU Countries

Robert Matusiak

Abstract Recent public debate concerns about tax competition in the European Union. There is a widespread belief that reducing the rate of corporation tax will increase foreign investments (small economy) or reduce capital outflow (large economy). This paper examines changes to the corporate income tax as a tool of tax competition among countries of the European Union, especially against the background of the prevailing tendency to harmonize the tax systems of the EU Member States. It cannot be a straightforward way to assess tax competition only through the prism of tax rates as a phenomenon of positive or negative. Also, the analysis tends to the conclusion that for entrepreneurs it is important not only to the level of tax rates.

Keywords Tax competition • Foreign direct investment • Corporate tax

Introduction

Recent changes in the rhythm of European integration and of globalization have dramatically reduced the scope for independent fiscal policies. The diversity of tax systems in the EU raises tax competition, which generally involves presenting better and more convenient solutions for foreign investors. Domestic companies may also consider transferring firm location to another country that offers better conditions for doing business, for instance, through reduced tax burden or tax preferences (Bénassy-Quéré et al. 2007). As a result, achieving full economic integration is not possible even though the concept of the single currency area and economic development is based on the free movement of goods, capital, and people under the existence of a single currency. In the future European Union will certainly have to include additives in the conditions of deepening European integration processes for two reasons:

R. Matusiak (✉)
Nicolaus Copernicus University in Toruń, Faculty of Economic Sciences and Management, Torun, Poland
e-mail: matusiakk.robert@gmail.com

D. Procházka (ed.), *The Impact of Globalization on International Finance and Accounting*, Springer Proceedings in Business and Economics,
https://doi.org/10.1007/978-3-319-68762-9_50

- The primary source of state income is taxes.
- National tax system is significantly different.

In this paper, I focus to present corporate income tax as a tool of tax competition among countries of the European Union, especially against the background of the prevailing tendency to harmonize the tax systems of the EU Member States. Development is also an attempt to answer the question to what extent the competition through the reduction of CIT rates causes interest of foreign investors.

Corporate Tax as an Element of Tax Competition in the EU Member States

In the economic literature on the phenomenon of international tax competition, there are several possible resolutions regarding tax competition. According to the position represented by Ch. M. Tiebout, tax competition is a phenomenon entirely positive, which can be compared with perfect competition between enterprises, and its effect is to optimize the relationship between the amount received by the taxpayer of public goods and the level of taxation (Tiebout 1956). According to this concept, the mobile factors of production move from countries with a higher level of taxation to countries with a lower level, unless the high tax burden is compensated in the country's adequate level of supply of public goods. One prominent puzzle was presented by G. Zodrow and P. Mieszkowski, according to which tax competition is a process far undesirable because it leads to a decrease in tax rates below the optimum level, which results from the governmental organization delivery of insufficient public goods (Zodrow and Mieszkowski 1986). Mobile factors are able to escape through migration from too high levels of taxation; therefore, tax competition between countries takes the form of a race to the bottom, which in extreme cases can result in a reduction in the tax rate to zero. H. W. Sinn proposes to prevent such a phenomenon by increasing the degree of harmonization of tax systems, relying on the convergence rates of individual taxes on mobile factors of production. Unification rates and tax rules eliminate the need for tax competition and can provide more public goods (Sinn 1994).

Branch of the literature on international tax competition and mass media is under debate about whether international tax competition is positive or negative and whether it should be limited or supported. Recent direct taxes in the EU have not been included in the process of harmonization and remain within the competence of the EU Member States, so they can establish their own rules for corporate taxation, which results in the creation of tax competition (Junevičius and Šniukštaitė 2009).

The subject of this part of the paper is a comparative analysis of rates of corporate income tax in the EU. Table 1 shows how nominal tax rates have developed over the last 11 years in the EU countries. In the case of corporate income tax rate, in 2015, it ranged from 10% (Bulgaria) to 38% (France). In 2005 the average rate of the tax was then 25.3%, but in subsequent years there have been

Table 1 The rate of corporate income tax in the EU in the years 2005–2015

Country	2005	2006	2007	2008	2009	2010
Hungary	17.5	17.5	21.3	21.3	21.3	20.6
France	35.0	34.4	34.4	34.4	34.4	34.4
Slovakia	19.0	19.0	19.0	19.0	19.0	19.0
Cyprus	10.0	10.0	10.0	10.0	10.0	10.0
Portugal	27.5	27.5	26.5	26.5	26.5	29.0
Belgium	34.0	34.0	34.0	34.0	34.0	34.0
Ireland	12.5	12.5	12.5	12.5	12.5	12.5
Croatia	20.0	20.0	20.0	20.0	20.0	20.0
Latvia	15.0	15.0	15.0	15.0	15.0	15.0
Lithuania	15.0	19.0	18.0	15.0	20.0	15.0
Malta	35.0	35.0	35.0	35.0	35.0	35.0
Austria	25.0	25.0	25.0	25.0	25.0	25.0
Poland	19.0	19.0	19.0	19.0	19.0	19.0
Romania	16.0	16.0	16.0	16.0	16.0	16.0
Luxembourg	30.4	29.6	29.6	29.6	28.6	28.6
Greece	32.0	29.0	25.0	35.0	35.0	24.0
Estonia	24.0	23.0	22.0	21.0	21.0	21.0
Denmark	28.0	28.0	25.0	25.0	25.0	25.0
Bulgaria	15.0	15.0	10.0	10.0	10.0	10.0
Italy	37.3	37.3	37.3	31.4	31.4	31.4
Finland	26.0	26.0	26.0	26.0	26.0	26.0
Sweden	28.0	28.0	28.0	28.0	26.3	26.3
Netherlands	31.5	29.6	25.5	25.5	25.5	25.5
Czech Republic	26.0	24.0	24.0	21.0	20.0	19.0
Spain	35.0	35.0	32.5	30.0	30.0	30.0
Slovenia	25.0	25.0	23.0	22.0	21.0	20.0
Germany	38.7	38.7	38.7	30.2	30.2	30.2
United Kingdom	30.0	30.0	30.0	28.0	28.0	28.0
UE	25.3	25.1	24.4	23.8	23.8	23.2
UE-15	30.1	29.6	28.7	28.1	27.9	27.3
UE-13*	19.7	19.8	19.4	18.8	19.0	18.4
Country	2011	2012	2013	2014	2015	Difference 2005–2015
Hungary	20.6	20.6	20.6	20.6	20.6	3.1
France	36.1	36.1	38.0	38.0	38.0	3.1
Slovakia	19.0	19.0	23.0	22.0	22.0	3.0
Cyprus	10.0	10.0	12.5	12.5	12.5	2.5
Portugal	29.0	31.5	31.5	31.5	29.5	2.0
Belgium	34.0	34.0	34.0	34.0	34.0	0.0
Ireland	12.5	12.5	12.5	12.5	12.5	0.0
Croatia	20.0	20.0	20.0	20.0	20.0	0.0
Latvia	15.0	15.0	15.0	15.0	15.0	0.0

(continued)

Table 1 (continued)

Country	2011	2012	2013	2014	2015	Difference 2005–2015
Lithuania	15.0	15.0	15.0	15.0	15.0	0.0
Malta	35.0	35.0	35.0	35.0	35.0	0.0
Austria	25.0	25.0	25.0	25.0	25.0	0.0
Poland	19.0	19.0	19.0	19.0	19.0	0.0
Romania	16.0	16.0	16.0	16.0	16.0	0.0
Luxembourg	28.8	28.8	29.2	29.2	29.2	−1.2
Greece	20.0	20.0	26.0	26.0	29.0	−3.0
Estonia	21.0	21.0	21.0	21.0	20.0	−4.0
Denmark	25.0	25.0	25.0	24.5	23.5	−4.5
Bulgaria	10.0	10.0	10.0	10.0	10.0	−5.0
Italy	31.4	31.4	31.4	31.4	31.4	−5.9
Finland	26.0	24.5	24.5	20.0	20.0	−6.0
Sweden	26.3	26.3	22.0	22.0	22.0	−6.0
Netherlands	25.0	25.0	25.0	25.0	25.0	−6.5
Czech Republic	19.0	19.0	19.0	19.0	19.0	−7.0
Spain	30.0	30.0	30.0	30.0	28.0	−7.0
Slovenia	20.0	18.0	17.0	17.0	17.0	−8.0
Germany	30.2	30.2	30.2	30.2	30.2	−8.5
United Kingdom	26.0	24.0	23.0	21.0	20.0	−10.0
UE	23.0	22.9	23.2	22.9	22.8	−2.5
UE-15	27.0	27.0	27.2	26.7	26.5	−3.6
UE-13*	18.4	18.3	18.7	18.6	18.5	−1.2

Source: Taxation trends in the European Union, Eurostat, Statistical Book, 2016 edition, http://ec.europa.eu/taxation_customs/business/economic-analysis-taxation/data-taxation_en
Note: *countries admitted to the European Union after 2004: Bulgaria, Croatia, Cyprus, Czech Republic, Estonia, Latvia, Lithuania, Malta, Poland, Romania, Slovakia, Slovenia, Hungary

constant reductions, which has resulted in a rate of slightly more than 22.5% in 2016. Great Britain and Germany have introduced the largest reductions, lowering their CIT rates by up to 20.0 and 30.2 percentage points in 2015. Particularly favorable tax rates for corporate income tax are found in Bulgaria, Cyprus, Ireland, Latvia, Lithuania, Romania, and Slovenia. Based on the data presented in Table 1, it can also be observed that lower corporate tax rates are found primarily in the countries that joined the EU in 2005 or in subsequent years.

Presented in Table 1, a drop in the rates of income tax from legal entities reflects the growing tax competition, which results from increasing competition states to attract new foreign investments. The nominal tax rate in 2015 increased compared to the year 2005 only in countries such as Hungary, Slovakia, Cyprus, and Portugal. Tax rates remained unchanged in countries such as Belgium, Ireland, Croatia, Latvia, Lithuania, Malta, and Poland. In other countries, the nominal tax rates were reduced, suggesting aggressive tax policies of these countries oriented to attract foreign investment. Although the observed process can be described as race to the bottom, you certainly cannot tell the direction aimed at reducing tax

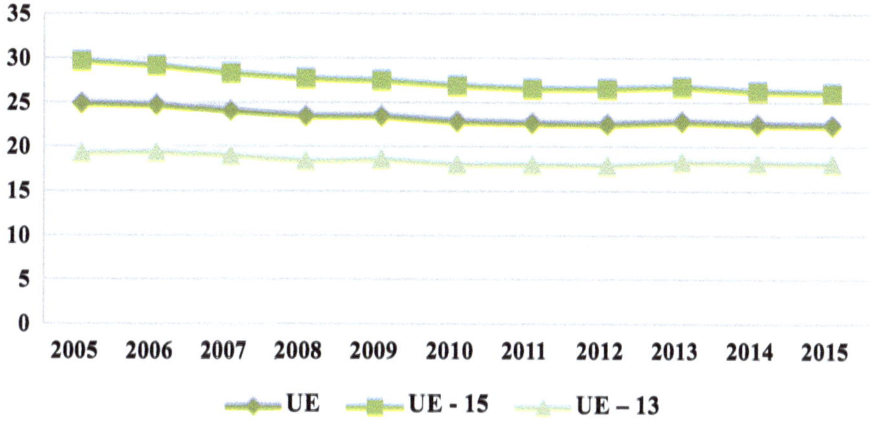

Source: Taxation trends in the European Union, Eurostat, Statistical Book, 2016 edition, http://ec.europa.eu/taxation_customs/business/economic-analysis-taxation/data-taxation_en

Fig. 1 Changes in CIT rates in UE, UE-15, and UE-13 (Source: Taxation trends in the European Union, Eurostat, Statistical Book, 2016 edition, http://ec.europa.eu/taxation_customs/business/economic-analysis-taxation/data-taxation_en)

rates to zero. The downward trend in CIT rates in the European Union also provides Fig. 1.

However, a comparative analysis of the basic tax rates does not fully reflect the actual corporate tax, because often there is an additional burden on the company, or vice versa – an entrepreneur can benefit from tax incentives, which vary in the different Member States of the EU-28. Only by comparing the effective level of corporate taxation can you use such an indicator, effective average tax rate (EATR) (Table 2), calculated as the ratio of tax to the achievement of the gross profit.

Table 2 shows a very diverse development. Effective rates ranged from about 9% in Bulgaria to about 38.3% in France. The average level of EU approached about 23%. For 16 member countries, the effective tax rate remained at a lower level than for the whole of the EU, and in the other at a higher level. Comparison of the amount of nominal and effective rates implies that for all 28 countries, there are discrepancies between the amount of nominal rates and the level of effective average rates. Most often effective rates are lower than nominal. The differences between the nominal and effective tax rate are determined by taking into account such elements of the tax liability, as tax-free, tax credits, and tax exemptions. In only five Member States (France, Spain, United Kingdom, Ireland, and Cyprus), EATR was higher than the nominal rate.

Table 2 Nominal rate (CIT) and the effective average tax rate (EATR) in 2015 (%)

Country	CIT	Ranking*	EATR	Ranking*	Difference CIT to EATR
France	38	1	38.3	1	- 0.3
Malta	35	2	32.2	3	2.8
Belgium	34	3	27.8	5	6.2
Italy	31.4	4	23.8	9	7.6
Germany	30.2	5	28.2	4	2
Portugal	29.5	6	26.6	7	2.9
Luxembourg	29.2	7	25.5	8	3.7
Greece	29	8	27.1	6	1.9
Spain	28	9	32.9	2	- 4.9
Netherlands	25	10	22.5	11	2.5
Austria	25	10	23	10	2
Dennmark	23.5	12	21.3	13	2.2
Slovakia	22	13	19.6	14	2.4
Sweden	22	13	19.4	15	2.6
Hungary	20.6	15	19.3	16	1.3
Estonia	20	16	15.7	21	4.3
Croatia	20	16	16.5	20	3.5
Finland	20	16	18.6	17	1.4
United Kingdom	20	16	21.5	12	-1.5
Czech Republic	19	20	16.7	19	2.3
Poland	19	20	17.5	18	1.5
Slovenia	17	22	15.5	22	1.5
Romania	16	23	14.8	24	1.2
Latvia	15	24	14.3	25	0.7
Lithuania	15	24	13.6	27	1.4
Ireland	12.5	26	14.1	26	- 1.6
Cyprus	12.5	26	15.2	23	- 2.7
Bulgaria	10	28	9	28	1
UE	22.8		21.1		1.7
UE - 15	26.5		24.7		1.7
UE – 13*	19.3		17.6		1.8

Source: Taxation trends in the European Union, Eurostat, Statistical Book, 2016 edition, http://ec.europa.eu/taxation_customs/business/economic-analysis-taxation/data-taxation_en
Note: * numbers indicate the number of ranking countries in terms of level of taxation, the countries with the same rate awarded the same place in the ranking

The Impact of Corporate Income Tax on Foreign Direct Investment

Tax harmonization represents the process of tax system convergence based on common set of rules. Nowadays, direct taxes in the EU have not been included in the process of harmonization and remain within the competence of the Member States. They can establish their own rules for corporate taxation, which means that the individual country has different regulations on CIT. As a result, conditions for business in the EU are not identical. As a form of corporate income tax, corporate tax affects the propensity to invest. The low tax rate encourages investment; the consequence is economic growth (Gale and Samwick 2014). But at high weights, corporate tax entities have a strong motivation to invent loopholes in the tax system, and this is the intensification of the process of tax evasion.

Comparative analysis of the corporate income tax rates in the EU countries shows that, despite the progressive reduction of the rates of these taxes in the EU, the phenomenon of tax competition is still very strong. Against the background of the above considerations, the problem of competition from the tax system for attracting foreign direct investment should be addressed, because the amount of the tax burden should play a key role in business decisions about the allocation of profits. Table 3 and Fig. 2 show a tendency that the inflow of foreign direct investment is relatively higher in countries with a lower tax rate CIT, like the outflow of these investments is lower in countries with lower taxation of companies and higher in countries with higher tax burden.

The investment attractiveness of a country also depends on factors outside the tax, such as economic growth, access to skilled labor or productivity, and labor costs, as well as the importance of the complexity of tax law. For example, it is clear that among the countries that joined the EU after 2004, Poland is a country with the largest amount of resources of foreign direct investment (Fig. 3).

The presented data relating to CIT rates and FDI shows that some countries, especially the part of the countries that joined the EU in 2004, can be accused of dumping taxation and tax competition, hence the determination of countries with higher CIT rates to reduce this – negative in their opinion – phenomenon. In the years 2005–2015, for the countries that joined the EU after 2004, the largest capital foreign direct investment flowed into Poland and Cyprus while the least in Latvia and Slovenia. In the case of Polish tax, rates have not changed, but in the case of Cyprus, it has even increased. Formal restrictions for abused CIT to favor businesses and disrupt the functioning of the market mechanism result from the EU and national legislation on state aid. The effectiveness of these restrictions confirms the slight differences between the nominal and effective tax rates.

The data contained in Table 4 may be from a more objective basis for evaluating changes in taxes. It turns out that in the end period of the observed period, tax burden GDP is almost identical but that the tax burden within the whole group is very diverse: from 50.2% GDP in Denmark to 16.6% GDP in Lithuania. A surprise is that despite substantial reductions in CIT, revenues from this tax to GDP ratio increased slightly, while their height in relation to GDP is much lower than the revenues from indirect taxes. It is impossible to observe some regularity when it comes to relations between corporate tax income and FDI, because tax systems shape the positive investment climate through productivity and labor costs, the stability of legal changes, and better functioning of public administration, not only by tax rates.

Farthest reaching solution would be the use of uniform tax rates in all countries. The problem is that the tax rates in the respective countries have incomplete information about the real loads of income from business activity. This is due to significant differences between countries regarding the rules for calculating the tax base used preferences. This results in a substantial difference between the nominal and effective tax rates. In such circumstances, the harmonization of tax rates does

Table 3 Resources of foreign direct investment (inflow, the top row, and outflow, the bottom row) countries of the European Union in the period 2005–2015 (US $ million)

Country	2005	2006	2007	2008	2009	2010
Bulgaria	13,869	23,483	37,936	44,059	49,225	47,231
	124	453	813	1444	1399	2583
Croatia	13,332	24,377	41,497	27,846	32,829	31,510
	1966	2339	3730	5120	6466	4472
Cyprus	8483	13,754	18,191	180,043	186,227	212,576
	3587	6834	9253	167,272	171,525	197,433
Czech Republic	60,662	79,841	112,408	113,174	125,827	128,504
	3610	5017	8557	12,531	14,805	14,923
Estonia	11,192	12,119	15,671	15,449	15,841	15,551
	1892	3459	5948	6445	6262	5545
Lithuania	8211	10,996	15,062	12,949	13,216	13,271
	721	1041	1570	1990	2300	2086
Latvia	4906	7509	10,991	11,309	11,629	10,935
	281	477	939	1033	893	895
Malta	38,716	61,690	111,756	117,077	125,192	129,770
	22,373	33,015	57,183	66,997	65,071	60,596
Poland	86,345	115,792	164,370	148,417	167,399	187,602
	1776	4402	7279	8205	11,504	16,407
Romania	25,383	44,516	61,610	64,759	69,883	68,093
	213	879	1240	1466	1397	1511
Slovakia	29,595	38,567	47,713	50,416	52,537	50,328
	747	1520	2081	2940	3152	3457
Slovenia	7056	8856	10,939	11,966	11,277	10,667
	3276	4518	7492	8469	8850	8147
Hungary	61,110	80,153	95,469	88,054	98,876	90,845
	8637	13,662	19,290	19,913	21,624	22,314
Austria	82,551	109,050	159,553	145,796	169,124	160,615
	71,807	105,072	150,298	148,192	170,037	181,639
Belgium	378,156	481,356	810,944	854,425	967,601	873,315
	478,170	618,532	648,656	814,049	940,869	950,885
Denmark	74,651	92,097	111,284	103,957	103,196	96,984
	88,076	105,928	127,263	141,119	153,870	165,375
Finland	54,802	70,569	91,703	83,534	85,163	86,698
	81,861	96,208	116,531	114,139	130,230	137,663
France	379,385	493,763	623,625	563,005	648,012	630,710
	633,523	823,515	1,010,034	934,221	1,120,482	1,172,994
Greece	29,189	41,288	53,221	38,119	42,097	35,026
	13,602	22,418	31,650	37,232	39,454	42,623
Spain	384,538	461,528	585,857	588,901	632,246	628,341
	305,427	436,068	582,056	590,694	625,799	653,236
Netherlands	479,420	552,748	767,456	647,414	646,292	588,078
	637,131	803,915	945,453	898,514	965,145	968,142

(continued)

Table 3 (continued)

Country	2005	2006	2007	2008	2009	2010
Ireland	163,530	156,491	203,683	188,290	250,103	285,575
	104,152	120,728	150,060	168,926	295,335	340,114
Luxembourg	64,729	84,845	137,380	125,128	172,217	172,257
	60,796	68,578	116,252	162,952	176,840	187,027
Germany	640,058	799,247	952,220	789,256	963,511	955,881
	794,198	986,324	1,247,080	1,189,785	1,323,030	1,364,565
Portugal	66,697	89,596	119,682	105,511	118,299	114,994
	40,927	52,063	67,726	62,769	66,988	62,286
Sweden	171,902	227,178	293,942	278,802	332,150	347,163
	207,836	262,358	331,607	322,972	353,421	374,399
United Kingdom	851,013	1,133,315	1,113,240	901,515	1,015,805	1,057,188
	1,215,513	1,439,100	1,748,803	1,523,366	1,526,143	1,574,707
Italy	237,474	312,464	376,513	327,911	364,427	328,058
	244,551	313,206	417,875	442,395	487,906	491,208
Country	2011	2012	2013	2014	2015	
Bulgaria	47,381	49,400	51,195	48,179	42,106	
	2875	3216	3516	3394	3083	
Croatia	28,179	29,633	29,855	29,660	26,375	
	4714	4593	4480	5436	5448	
Cyprus	182,687	185,190	177,461	149,440	138,263	
	169,283	170,737	164,337	139,277	133,134	
Czech Republic	120,569	136,493	134,085	121,512	113,057	
	13,214	17,368	20,627	18,235	18,481	
Estonia	16,350	18,936	21,202	19,712	18,914	
	4805	6065	6787	6114	6063	
Lithuania	14,266	15,966	17,542	15,619	14,440	
	2079	2577	3271	2829	2235	
Latvia	12,111	13,534	15,956	14,668	14,549	
	864	1114	1600	1339	1230	
Malta	146,146	165,530	184,584	173,838	163,522	
	67,664	72,887	80,087	73,689	67,930	
Poland	164,424	198,953	229,167	205,581	213,071	
	18,928	26,102	27,725	24,938	27,838	
Romania	69,512	76,329	82,688	73,086	69,112	
	1358	1298	851	321	589	
Slovakia	51,980	55,124	58,021	52,488	48,163	
	4022	4765	4830	2998	2562	
Slovenia	11,490	12,203	12,269	12,299	11,847	
	7827	7534	7142	6453	5473	
Hungary	85,331	104,017	108,517	98,885	92,132	
	26,357	37,720	38,452	39,060	38,503	
Austria	152,768	164,714	178,825	176,607	164,784	
	193,144	209,555	231,836	216,568	208,263	

(continued)

Table 3 (continued)

Country	2011	2012	2013	2014	2015
Belgium	942,817	512,712	571,776	476,405	468,710
	1,002,896	419,490	503,149	459,974	458,794
Denmark	98,406	98,302	94,481	97,216	100,858
	176,065	183,987	190,663	177,394	190,608
Finland	89,232	96,641	88,762	93,901	92,340
	133,781	151,389	145,331	117,314	94,852
France	698,871	717,328	796,488	729,147	772,030
	1,247,959	1,307,743	1,360,287	1,279,089	1,314,158
Greece	29,060	24,765	25,850	22,534	17,688
	48,044	44,965	36,299	30,493	26,487
Spain	628,950	644,677	638,982	591,709	533,306
	656,504	636,731	540,289	528,329	472,116
Netherlands	610,677	628,187	770,976	715,706	707,043
	996,068	1,001,522	1,144,218	1,040,092	1,074,289
Ireland	290,495	364,607	392,915	378,202	435,490
	330,812	412,054	538,746	634,761	793,418
Luxembourg	225,725	167,222	91,396	180,434	205,029
	167,675	272,225	101,281	130,199	169,570
Germany	997,727	1,077,019	1,088,690	1,089,569	1,121,288
	1,434,829	1,571,548	1,611,910	1,718,157	1,812,469
Portugal	103,760	114,573	124,623	118,918	114,220
	61,454	56,927	60,049	60,767	63,565
Sweden	349,058	373,444	386,105	311,786	281,876
	379,286	389,229	422,263	374,496	345,907
United Kingdom	1,145,720	1,428,059	1,489,940	1,744,230	1,457,408
	1,625,994	1,593,785	1,579,829	1,513,222	1,538,133
Italy	355,126	375,029	364,959	346,824	335,335
	521,357	528,815	536,031	487,523	466,594

Source: United Nations Conference on Trade and Development – UNCTAD

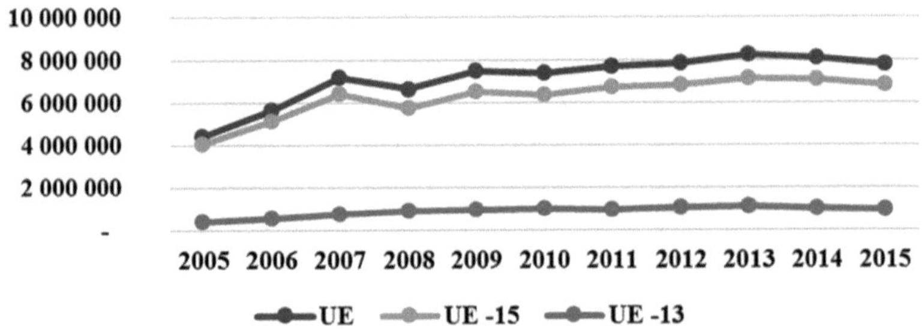

Source: United Nations Conference on Trade and Development – UNCTAD

Fig. 2 Inflow of foreign direct investment in the UE, UE-15, and EU-13 in the period 2005–2015 (US $ million) (Source: United Nations Conference on Trade and Development – UNCTAD)

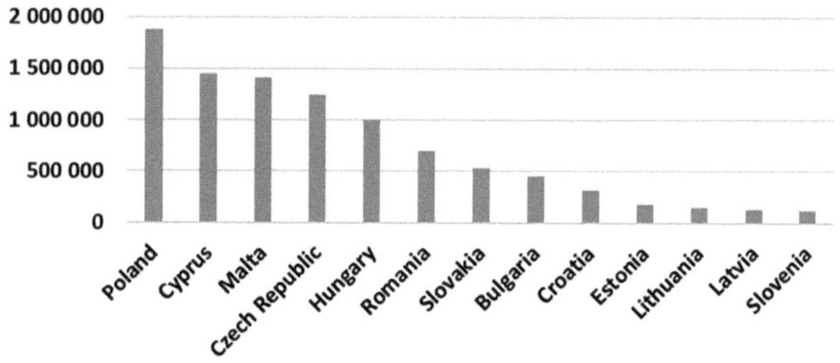

Source: United Nations Conference on Trade and Development – UNCTAD

Fig. 3 The value of acquired assets of foreign direct investment by the EU-13 in the period 2005–2015 (US $ million) (Source: United Nations Conference on Trade and Development – UNCTAD)

Table 4 Tax revenues in relation to GDP in 2005 and 2014

Country	Total taxes (excluding social contributions) as % of GDP		Difference	Corporate income tax as % of GDP		Difference
	2005	2014	2014–2005	2005	2014	2014–2005
Belgium	30.2	31.0	0.8	3.1	3.2	0.0
Bulgaria	20.9	20.1	−0.8	1.8	2.0	0.2
Czech Republic	19.4	19.4	0.0	4.1	3.4	−0.8
Denmark	48.0	50.2	2.2	3.4	2.7	−0.8
Germany	21.2	23.0	1.8	2.3	2.4	0.1
Estonia	19.8	21.3	1.5	1.4	1.7	0.3
Ireland	25.9	24.7	−1.2	3.4	2.5	−0.9
Greece	21.2	25.5	4.4	3.3	1.9	−1.4
Spain	23.7	22.3	−1.4	3.8	2.0	−1.8
France	27.0	29.0	2.1	2.4	2.7	0.3
Croatia	24.7	25.0	0.3	2.3	1.8	−0.5
Italy	27.0	30.3	3.3	2.3	2.2	−0.1
Cyprus	24.0	25.2	1.2	4.2	6.4	2.2
Latvia	19.9	20.5	0.5	1.9	1.5	−0.4
Lithuania	20.4	16.6	−3.8	2.1	1.4	−0.7
Luxembourg	27.6	27.1	−0.5	5.9	4.4	−1.5
Hungary	24.4	25.3	0.9	2.1	1.4	−0.7
Malta	25.6	28.1	2.5	3.7	6.3	2.6
Netherlands	23.2	22.6	−0.5	3.4	2.6	−0.9
Austria	27.1	28.3	1.2	2.3	2.2	−0.1
Poland	20.9	19.9	−1.1	2.1	1.7	−0.4
Portugal	22.6	25.2	2.6	2.6	2.8	0.2
Romania	18.1	19.1	1.0	2.7	2.2	−0.5

(continued)

Table 4 (continued)

Country	Total taxes (excluding social contributions) as % of GDP 2005	2014	Difference 2014–2005	Corporate income tax as % of GDP 2005	2014	Difference 2014–2005
Slovenia	24.1	22.3	−1.7	2.7	1.4	−1.3
Slovakia	18.9	17.6	−1.3	2.7	3.2	0.5
Finland	30.6	31.2	0.5	3.2	1.9	−1.3
Sweden	43.6	40.0	−3.7	3.4	2.7	−0.8
United Kingdom	27.9	26.8	−1.2	3.2	2.4	−0.7

Source: Taxation trends in the European Union, Eurostat, Statistical Book, 2016 edition, http://ec.europa.eu/taxation_customs/business/economic-analysis-taxation/data-taxation_en

not mean the alignment of other factors that actually determine the business environment, which for countries with poorer investment conditions may mean deepening inequality.

Conclusion

Tax harmonization in general is a difficult project because there are a number of arguments against such a concept, as well as many arguments for taking such effort. The harmonization of direct taxes is inevitable, but it will be a lengthy process. The abovementioned research shows that too hasty harmonization can bring negative effects of FDI. A questionable solution, however, is primitive dumping tax. The object of harmonization in the first place should be income taxes on economic activities. Also, the analysis tends to the conclusion that for entrepreneurs it is important not only to the level of tax rates. It cannot be a simple way to assess tax competition only through the prism of tax rates as a phenomenon of positive or negative. The growing problem of standardization of rates of income tax from legal persons in the European Union has attracted considerable controversy and opposition from countries that apply lower tax rates, since their fiscal policy is an incentive for the inflow of foreign direct investment. From this point of view, in the future it would be advisable to increase the degree of harmonization of tax systems capable in relying on standardizing rates, and tax rules eliminate the need for tax competition. The chances of harmonizing CIT are strictly dependent on the discretion of national authorities in the sphere of other taxes. In particular, a question of personal income tax (PIT), which can and should be an essential tool in the implementation of state tax policy of a particular social (Sørensen 2004). This means that the condition of standardized taxation rules and unification of CIT rates are the existence of a diversified income tax due to tax rates (scales) used by the preferences of individual countries. Only such an approach will allow progress in the harmonization of the corporate tax, leaving considerable fiscal autonomy to individual countries. At the end, based on the analysis of the data, it is possible to reduce the tax rate that is capable of limited help to broaden the tax base.

References

Bénassy-Quéré A, Gobalraja N, Trannoy A (2007) Tax and public input competition. http://www.oecd.org/tax/public-finance/36899431.pdf

Gale WG, Samwick AA (2014) Effects of Income Tax Changes on Economic Growth (September 9, 2014). Available at SSRN: https://ssrn.com/abstract=2494468 or https://doi.org/10.2139/ssrn.2494468

Junevičius A, Šniukštaitė B (2009) Tax harmonization and tax competition in european union in the: european integration studies, No 3

Sinn HW (1994) How much Europe? subsidiarity, centralization and fiscal competition. Scott J Public Econ 41(1):85–107

Sørensen PB (2004) Company tax reform in the european union. Int Tax Public Financ 11:91–115

Tiebout Ch. M (1956) A pure theory of local expenditures. J Polit Econ 64:416–424

Zodrow G, Mieszkowski P (1986) Pigou, tiebout,property taxation, and the underprovision of local public goods. J Urban Econ 19:356–370

Index

D. Procházka (ed.), *The Impact of Globalization on International Finance and Accounting*, Springer Proceedings in Business and Economics,
https://doi.org/10.1007/978-3-319-68762-9

Q

MIX
Papier aus verantwortungsvollen Quellen
Paper from responsible sources
FSC® C105338

If you have any concerns about our products,
you can contact us on
ProductSafety@springernature.com

In case Publisher is established outside the EU,
the EU authorized representative is:
Springer Nature Customer Service Center GmbH
Europaplatz 3, 69115 Heidelberg, Germany

Printed by Libri Plureos GmbH
in Hamburg, Germany